THE OXFORD HAND

GLOBAL JUSTICE

THE OXFORD HANDBOOK OF

GLOBAL

JUSTICE

Edited by
THOM BROOKS

OXFORD
UNIVERSITY PRESS

OXFORD
UNIVERSITY PRESS

Great Clarendon Street, Oxford, OX2 6DP,
United Kingdom

Oxford University Press is a department of the University of Oxford.
It furthers the University's objective of excellence in research, scholarship,
and education by publishing worldwide. Oxford is a registered trade mark of
Oxford University Press in the UK and in certain other countries

© Oxford University Press 2020

The moral rights of the authors have been asserted

First published 2020
First published in paperback 2023

All rights reserved. No part of this publication may be reproduced, stored in
a retrieval system, or transmitted, in any form or by any means, without the
prior permission in writing of Oxford University Press, or as expressly permitted
by law, by licence or under terms agreed with the appropriate reprographics
rights organization. Enquiries concerning reproduction outside the scope of the
above should be sent to the Rights Department, Oxford University Press, at the
address above

You must not circulate this work in any other form
and you must impose this same condition on any acquirer

Published in the United States of America by Oxford University Press
198 Madison Avenue, New York, NY 10016, United States of America

British Library Cataloguing in Publication Data
Data available

Library of Congress Cataloging in Publication Data
Data available

ISBN 978-0-19-871435-4 (Hbk.)
ISBN 978-0-19-889081-2 (Pbk.)

Links to third party websites are provided by Oxford in good faith and
for information only. Oxford disclaims any responsibility for the materials
contained in any third party website referenced in this work.

Contents

PART VI BORDERS AND TERRITORIAL RIGHTS

PART VII GLOBAL INJUSTICE

ACKNOWLEDGMENTS

Every book is a collection of words made possible because of the contributions of many people and institutions over time. First and foremost, I am hugely grateful to the contributors for their warm support from the start, the quality of their chapters, and their patience in seeing such a large volume move from proposal to production line. It has been a pleasure to work with each and every scholar involved in this handbook, and its success is a product of the contributions. I owe longstanding debts to Peter Jones, Jeff McMahan, David Miller, Martha Nussbaum, Onora O'Neill, Bhikhu Parekh, Philip Pettit, and Leif Wenar for opening my eyes to the global justice debates, shaping my thoughts, and deep inspiration. If not for them, my interest would not have kindled as brightly and for so long. My thanks to Thomas Pogge for his advice in developing this handbook. Dominic Byatt and Olivia Wells at Oxford University Press deserve medals for their support and patience in equal measure. My work on this handbook was made possible thanks to my terrifically supportive colleagues at Durham Law School, including a period of leave spent at Yale Law School and visiting Harvard Law School. Finally, my thanks to Claire and Eve Brooks for their constant encouragement and support throughout.

Durham, UK

List of Figures and Table

....

Figures

Table

List of Contributors

Christian Barry is Professor of Philosophy in the School of Philosophy at Australian National University.

Samantha Besson is Holder of the Chair *Droit international des institutions* at the Collège de France, Paris, and Professor of Public International Law and European Law at the University of Fribourg (Switzerland).

Gillian Brock is Professor of Philosophy in the Department of Philosophy at the University of Auckland.

Thom Brooks is the Dean of Durham Law School and Professor of Law and Government at Durham University, with associate membership in the Department of Philosophy and the School of Government and International Affairs and Fellow of University College, Durham.

Luis Cabrera is Associate Professor in the Griffith Business School at Griffith University.

Simon Caney is Professor of Political Theory in the Department of Politics and International Studies at the University of Warwick.

Arthur Chin is an Assistant Lecturer in the School of Humanities at the University of Hong Kong.

Jiwei Ci is Professor of Philosophy in the School of Humanities at the University of Hong Kong.

Rainer Forst is Professor of Political Theory and Philosophy at Johann Wolfgang Goethe University in Frankfurt.

Pablo Gilabert is Professor of Philosophy in the Department of Philosophy at Concordia University.

Carol C. Gould is Distinguished Professor in the Department of Philosophy at Hunter College and in the Programs in Philosophy and Political Science at the Graduate Center of the City University of New York.

Nicole Hassoun is Professor of Philosophy in the Department of Philosophy at Binghamton University.

Alison M. Jaggar is College Professor of Distinction in the Departments of Philosophy and Gender Studies at the University of Colorado, Boulder, and Distinguished Research Professor in the Philosophy Department at the University of Birmingham.

János Kis is University Professor, Professor of Philosophy and Political Science at Central European University.

David Miller is Professor of Political Theory at the University of Oxford and Fellow of Nuffield College, Oxford.

Steven R. Ratner is the Bruno Simma Collegiate Professor of Law at the University of Michigan Law School.

Miriam Ronzoni is Reader in Political Theory in the Department of Government at the University of Manchester.

Henry Shue is Senior Research Fellow at the Centre for International Studies of the Department of Politics and International Relations, Professor Emeritus of Politics and International Relations at the University of Oxford, and Senior Research Fellow Emeritus at Merton College, Oxford.

Anna Stilz is Laurence S. Rockefeller Professor of Politics and the University Center for Human Values in the Department of Politics at Princeton University.

Kok-Chor Tan is Professor of Philosophy in the Department of Philosophy at the University of Pennsylvania.

John Tasioulas is Chair of Politics, Philosophy, and Law in the Dickson Poon School of Law and Director of the Yeoh Tiong Lay Centre for Politics, Philosophy, and Law at King's College London.

Jesse Tomalty is Associate Professor of Philosophy in the Department of Philosophy at the University of Bergen.

Laura Valentini is Associate Professor of Political Science in the Department of Government at the London School of Economics.

Effy Vayena is Professor of Health Policy in the Department of Public Health at the University of Zurich.

Krushil Watene is Senior Lecturer in Philosophy in the Department of Philosophy at Massey University.

Christopher Heath Wellman is Professor of Philosophy in the Department of Philosophy at Washington University, St. Louis.

David Wiens is Associate Professor of Political Science in the Department of Political Science at the University of California, San Diego.

INTRODUCTION

THOM BROOKS

GLOBAL justice is an exciting area of refreshing, innovative new ideas. Not only does work in this area challenge how we think about ethics and political philosophy more generally, but its insights contain seeds of hope for addressing some of the greatest challenges facing humanity today. This handbook has been selective in bringing together some of the most pressing topics and issues in global justice as understood by the leading voices, both established and rising stars.[1] This Introduction will provide a general overview of the field and the twenty-five chapters.

1 WHAT IS GLOBAL JUSTICE?

Justice has traditionally been considered within states. Global justice is about justice across and between states. Most interest in the area has focused on issues of distributive justice from the affluent to others in severe poverty. One popular position is to claim that there are positive duties to act for those that we can because we can. It does not matter that we did not cause another to be in need, only that they have needs that we can remedy.

This view is defended powerfully by Peter (Singer 1972: 231), who claims that "if it is in our power to prevent something bad from happening, without thereby sacrificing anything of comparable moral importance, we ought, morally, to do it." We weigh the moral costs to us and those in need of our acting against our inaction to decide which course of action is morally justified. What matters is not the distance between me and another in need, but my ability to provide relief.

This is illustrated in a famous example of a drowning child. Singer says:

> If I am walking past a shallow pond and see a child drowning in it, I ought to wade in and pull the child out. This will mean getting my clothes muddy, but this is insignificant, while the death of the child would presumably be a very bad thing.
>
> (Singer 1972: 231)

Where I am able to act, the moral weight of choosing to act is trumped by the moral weight of refusing to act. The moral cost to me in saving the child is negligible, but the moral cost to the child if I refuse to save him or her is huge. The balance of moral costs weighs in favor of action, and that is enough. It does not matter how the child fell into the pond. This is a positive duty to others.

An alternative position is to claim that there are negative duties that compel us to act, because our activities bring harm to others requiring compensation. This is a more stringent understanding of duties concerned with responding to harms we have caused or contributed to rather than promoting the good. The most prominent exponent of negative duties for global justice is Thomas Pogge. He argues that our duties to those in severe poverty are grounded in our responsibility for their continuing condition.[2]

Pogge claims we have a global institutional order that does not merely allow severe poverty, but engenders it. For example, bodies like the World Trade Organization enforce agreements that favor affluent states over developing countries. Protectionist exemptions prevent less wealthy countries from trading on equal terms benefiting affluent states. Such measures knowingly, foreseeably, and avoidably perpetuate a global order in which severe poverty is found and fostered—and so those affluent states that support such an order are under a negative duty to compensate those in severe poverty because of how this order can trap them in such dire circumstances.

And he goes further. The "we" who are responsible are individuals in affluent democracies. We have a say in the leaders we elect and the system we uphold. We might not vote for whoever wins an elected contest, but share responsibility for its outcome—and those elected represent us or choose others to do so on bodies that maintain the institutional order we have. So it is not merely true that our state is responsible for severe poverty elsewhere; we are individually responsible as well for electing representatives who maintain it on our behalf. Pogge (2002: 109)says: "We, the affluent countries and their citizens, continue to impose a global economic order under which millions avoidably die each year from poverty-related causes... We must regard our imposition of the present global order as a grave injustice." We have a negative duty to stop contributing to this harm and to provide relief to those harmed already.[3]

So, we have two options for thinking about our potential duties to the global poor. We can reflect on what positive duties we have in virtue of our being able to assist alone. Or we can consider what negative duties we have because of some contribution to the situation of the global poor that should be compensated. But we might also think our choice is neither one nor the other, but some possible combination.

A third position is to claim we have remedial responsibilities to act, bringing together positive and negative duties. This is a view of remedial responsibilities: we focus on centering our attention on the distribution of responsibilities to remedy severe poverty elsewhere. This view is championed by David Miller. He says: "it is morally unacceptable for people to be left in that deprived or needy condition, and there is no overriding justification... All that matters is that we find it morally unacceptable if the deprived person is simply left to suffer" (Miller (2007)[4] Our goal is to identify who should help those in need.

Miller offers a connection theory for assessing what remedial responsibilities we have as a political group to assist others in need. Our responsibilities are greater in proportion to the relative weight of the relevant connections to those in need. He argues for six connections, including causal responsibility, moral responsibility, capacity, community, outcome responsibility, and benefit.[5] We consider each group in relation to these six connections and assign responsibilities, and in proportion, to the relative weight of their connections, without giving any special weight to one or more connections. More than one group may have remedial responsibilities, and some more than others. Importantly, this approach brings together positive duty connections (like capacity) and negative duty connections (like causal responsibility) into a unified, coherent framework.

Each view of our duties provides powerful reasons for the duties held by individuals and their states to redistribute wealth to the global poor. This brief survey is far from exhaustive, but the focus of understanding the nature of global inequality and injustice, the kinds of duties we may be under to act, the urgent need to eradicate severe poverty, and our responsibilities as citizens of a state and beyond all come into sharp focus across the chapters to follow.

2 Global Egalitarianism—and its Critics

This handbook begins exploring global egalitarianism and its critics with a critical survey of global justice and the role of the state by Miriam Ronzoni and Laura Valentini. They begin with contrasting accounts of the state. The first is an institutional account viewing the state as a complex set of rules and practices. Such a perspective can be found in John Rawls's work, but also that of others like Bhikhu Parekh.[6] In short, the state is a structure. This is contrasted with a second view, which is the agential account of the state recognizing its group agency as a collective, popularized by Christian List and Philip Pettit.[7]

Ronzoni and Valentini note that theorists might be further divided between cosmopolitans who see the state as largely irrelevant to questions of global justice versus statists who see the state as playing a central role. Despite these differences, they identify a shared commitment to the justificatory relevance of the state and discuss in detail how this might be understood. While the state matters, it is not everything, and there are other sites of egalitarian justice, nor is the state by itself sufficient.

Chapter 2 considers how a morally arbitrary fact about where we are born can play an enormous role in determining our future prospects. Gillian Brock asks how equality of opportunity might be applied to the global context. Building on Rawls's idea of fair equality of opportunity, Brock develops and defends a compelling ideal of global equality of opportunity. This is developed through careful exploration of our intuitions about the ways in which equality matters, pointing to an ideal beyond mere equal opportunities towards a higher bar of sufficiency.

In Chapter 3, Luis Cabrera examines the idea of global citizenship. How can it be possible to act as though we were global citizens in meaningful ways within the current global system? Cabrera argues that the boundaries of citizenship should be more fluid, and potentially more extensive, than at present. Moreover, there is certainly a tradition since Diogenes the Cynic proclaimed himself a citizen of the world of similar cosmopolitan views of the individual of having global citizenship. Cabrera identifies key features for how such a view of self can be understood and promote reforming the present system so it is more morally defensible.

The final chapter in this first part offers a two-level account of distributive egalitarianism. János Kis considers this variant of egalitarianism to hold that distributive inequalities of a certain kind are unjust, irrespective of whether they were produced by an unjust action. He claims the principle of equal shares derives from the principle of equal moral status and is non-relational at its basic level. But at the next level, we must determine what distributions are to count as equal, and here standards of relational equality come into play.

Global justice is often fundamentally about international distributive justice. These chapters help us better understand the role, if any, that states should play in this process, the possibility of an idea of global equality of opportunity and of global citizenship, and what kind of distributive arrangement would be most compelling.

3 HUMAN RIGHTS

The handbook's second part examines different understandings of human rights in this wider context. Chapter 5 by Samantha Besson critically reflects on the main boundary disputes pertaining to the holders of human rights. Identifying human rights holders is an essential part of recognizing the existence of these rights. She forensically explains why human rights are equal rights, developing a connection from moral status through political equality to human rights, and discusses speciesism, children's rights, elders' rights, group rights, and more in a fascinating analysis bridging theories of human rights with international human rights law and practice.

Chapter 6 by Carol C. Gould considers the relation of empathetic politics and responsibility with the problem of motivating solidarity with distant others that global justice presents us with. She argues that solidarity can consist of a kind of fellow feeling shared with others, but yet also go beyond empathy to involve concrete actions to realize shared interests. This sense of connection is more difficult to forge with distant others far away. This problem has relevance for how we motivate fulfilling human rights or basic needs. Gould argues for overlapping transnational solidarities building onf Iris Marion Young's work on social connections, but going much further and deeper in a compelling account.[8]

Chapter 7 by John Tasioulas and Effy Vayena examines just global health, asking what are the demands of justice that apply to global health policy. They contest the all too common perspective of viewing human rights and common goods as necessarily in conflict or incompatible. Instead, they argue that securing human rights is an integral part of some global common goods. To create an artificial divide between them would mean to deny their realization. Human rights are critically important, but not the only relevant ethical consideration. Bringing human rights and common goods together helps us formulate a more compelling approach to just global health.

In Chapter 8, Krushil Watene draws our attention to the absence of indigenous philosophies in global justice theorizing. These highly valuable ideas and wisdom deserve a place within mainstream justice and with appropriate articulation. Without this, she notes intercultural and global justice conversations will be one-sided serving to either regulate or, worse, oppress indigenous philosophies and indigenous communities. In short, Watene demands that global justice must become more "global" and in so doing more "just." This is beautifully and richly illustrated from Watene's examination of her own Māori philosophical insights.

Human rights are central to most discussions of global justice. Such analysis draws on ethical, political, and legal resources, all touched on throughout these chapters with examples of how this might be applied, such as in health care. Finally, it is worth reflecting on how "global" or universal our understanding of these rights is—and whether there are traditions, like indigenous philosophies, left out that should be brought in.

4 Severe Poverty

The third part considers the problem of severe poverty. This is a major concern for many global justice advocates, not least because the numbers in severe poverty worldwide are so high, with as many as a billion people unable to meet basic needs. In Chapter 9, Jesse Tomalty considers whether we have a human right to subsistence, having the means to live a life free from severe poverty. She argues that while the importance of having some means of subsistence is uncontroversial, its inclusion as a kind of human right is not. This is typically bracketed as a social goal or aspiration rather than a genuine right. Tomalty forensically examines what kind of right a right to subsistence is and why.

Chapter 10 by Thom Brooks looks at the use of the capabilities approach for better understanding the kind of problem that severe poverty is. Focusing specifically on Martha Nussbaum's capabilities list, Brooks shows how capabilities provide a more robust understanding of what severe poverty is beyond mere physical deprivation. However, capabilities carve out a space for choice: on this view, the crucial difference between famine and fasting is the latter is freely chosen, and so permissible. Brooks challenges the claim of capabilities that their exercise must be available but they need not be acted upon. He argues that capabilities accounts should not be concerned solely with their possibility, but also with their probability, and this has implications for how it can be applied to thinking about severe poverty.

The final chapter in this part is by Nicole Hassoun. She considers our aiding the global poor in the present and its effect on future generations. Hassoun argues that, in light of issues like climate change, if geoengineering prevents deaths or mass migration, it will affect how those in severe poverty in current and future generations will fare—and even how many will be in severe poverty in future. She develops a model for helping us think about intergenerational ethical issues, to assist dealing with tradeoffs between present and future generations.

Severe poverty affects a great many people today. These chapters help us think more sharply about what kind of right, if any, is a right to subsistence, what kind of deprivation severe poverty is, and what role capabilities might play in developing our understanding of it and how we might grapple better with the present and future consequences of our actions on different generations.

5 CLIMATE CHANGE JUSTICE

The fourth part examines climate change justice. In Chapter 12, Thom Brooks critically examines two approaches championed by most political philosophers for tackling climate change. The first is conservation, or mitigation, and the second is adaptation. Brooks argues that neither of these models offers a compelling response because of serious flaws. But they face a more fundamental problem in misunderstanding the kind of problem they claim to solve. Brooks criticizes their promotion of "end-state" solutions that aspire to either bring climate change to an end or its harmful effects. Brooks argues we must look beyond end-state solutions and reflect on sustainability in the shadow of possible inevitable catastrophe for a tragic world where the normative horizons should shift in recognizing that the challenges before us are greater than many theorists have appreciated.

In Chapter 13, Henry Shue considers the relation between climate, development, and disaster within the context of global justice. What responsibility do we in affluent countries have to distant others in the developing world with regard to climate change? He makes a compelling case for why we should want to leave a planet for others where life is not nasty, brutish, and short with those future generations coming after us having the ability to value and preserve much of what we value and try to preserve. We have a reason to act, and most energetically.

Climate change is already happening. It is a fact. But how should we respond? These chapters force us to think more carefully about what we might hope to achieve and why we should endeavor to achieve it for ourselves and distant others.

6 JUST GLOBAL INSTITUTIONS

Part V looks at just global institutions. In Chapter 14, Pablo Gilabert examines the question of whether there is a human right to democracy and how achieving such rights contribute to the pursuit of global justice. It might be thought that recognizing a human right to democracy would be to tie human rights too specifically to a particular institutional arrangement, curtailing self-determination and demonstrating some degree of cultural intolerance. On the contrary, Gilabert makes a well-crafted case for why the fulfillment of the human right to democratic political empowerment is critically important for the pursuit of global justice.

Chapter 15 considers Thomas Pogge's conception of the global institutional order as the object of justice assessments. Arthur Chin undertakes both a defense of Pogge's position from a range of critics, but also provides a more unified reading of his institutional approach. Chin critically reconstructs this approach from across Pogge's many contributions to show how apparent gaps or inconsistencies can be better understood—and so improve our engagement with an influential account of global justice.

In Chapter 16, Christian Barry and David Wiens explore the options available to egalitarians when faced with potential trade-offs between domestic and global equality. While no conflict need arise when addressing these different kinds of equality, it might arise that feasible mechanisms for reducing the one risk aggravate the other. They examine these trade-offs in the realm of second-best, non-ideal scenarios because they claim political ideals are too indeterminate and they are unable to help us with considering how we should make trade-offs across a range of contexts where desirable policy instruments might not be available. These second-best scenarios are deemed crucial to assisting political philosophers to undertake reflective equilibrium, showing the importance of practices for theories.

Chapter 17 by Alison M. Jaggar provides a critical overview of issues and themes arising in global gender justice—and how gender concerns are integral to many, if not all, aspects of global justice. She rightly highlights how, when social structures are unjust, these can enable systematically imbalanced sets of life options for members of different social groups. Gender is one area where such systematic injustice often occurs. After considering the issue of what gender is, Jaggar presents a compelling account of what global gender justice is and how it contributes to a powerful perspective that should receive much greater prominence.

The final chapter in this part by Steven R. Ratner looks at the system of norms and processes for resolving conflicting claims represented in international law. Ratner argues for the indispensability of international law for global justice as intrinsic to the normative universe of practices, institutions, and expectations that inform our conceptions about global justice more generally. Moral reflection on global justice is improved with reference not merely to practices, but especially to law. Ratner sets out to challenge the suspicion global justice scholars have of how international law and philosophical ethics relate. Our accounts of global justice would improve if we took closer notice of international law.

Just global institutions are important for most accounts of global justice. This part has explored the centrality of a human right to democratic political participation, a reappraisal of Pogge's famous institutional approach, the importance of practice for developing our theories, the rich source of contributions for global justice arising from global gender justice, and how global justice connects with international law.

7 BORDERS AND TERRITORIAL RIGHTS

The sixth part examines the topic of borders and territorial rights. In Chapter 19, David Miller examines immigration—one of the most contested political issues today. He focuses on the justice that migration raises between states. Miller critically examines cosmopolitan arguments for open borders and more communitarian defenders of the state's right to close its border, finding a surprising degree of convergence, but raising serious challenges any just theory of immigration should satisfy.

Chapter 20 by Christopher Heath Wellman considers promising accounts of political legitimacy that have recently come under fire for their inability to account for territorial rights. He challenges this view by arguing that functional theorists are in a better position to account for territorial rights than is often assumed, although unable to vindicate resource rights. Wellman denies this means we should jettison functional accounts of political legitimacy, and his vindication of these accounts will force their critics to rethink their positions.

In Chapter 21, Anna Stilz examines what some have argued is a right to global free movement on moral grounds. She does not reject this, but seeks to define a "colonial" qualification to it grounded in the importance of protecting native inhabitants' ability to permanently engage in their valued ways of life. Stilz argues for the impermissibility of migrants seeking to occupy new territory with a colonizing project. She claims we have a right to move freely so long as we come with good intentions and our entry does not threaten significant harm to current residents.

Justice between and across borders is a crucial site of important work within global justice. These chapters critically explore the justifications for open borders, imposing restrictions and regulation of immigration more broadly. They challenge the view that functional accounts of political legitimacy are undermined by failing to account for territorial rights—and the many implications that arise.

8 GLOBAL INJUSTICE

The book concludes considering not global justice, but global *injustice* through four revealing chapters in its final part. It begins with Rainer Forst, who develops a critical theory of transnational (in-)justice. He argues we can and should combine abstract moral reflection with sociological empirical realism in a unified account—and that this can help assist our understanding of transnational justice by sharpening our grasp of transnational injustice. Forst argues for a persuasive new approach to considering issues of global justice that both raises new questions and generates new answers.

In Chapter 23, Kok-Chor Tan examines personal responsibility and global injustice. He considers the institutional approach to global justice where individuals may pursue nationalistic or other personal and associational goods so long as these pursuits are within the rule of just global institutions. But this requires that just global institutions are in place. Where this is lacking, what personal responsibilities do individuals have in a context of global injustice?

Tan argues that our concern, in this case, is primarily to create just global arrangements. This project does need to entail dropping associational and personal projects while justice is not yet realized. He claims global justice has regulative primacy over nationalist pursuits. The institutional view helps us realize that the legitimacy of our personal and national lives is in doubt if we do not do our part to bring about a more just global order.

Chapter 24 by Jiwei Ci scrutinizes John Rawls's views on global justice from a new and exciting perspective. He highlights the lack of relevance, and clarity, reflected in the inability of Rawls's theory of global justice to connect with the real world it is meant to understand and shape. Ci views this inability as rooted in democracy's relation to capitalism. He argues that Rawls's political liberalism denies that its capitalist economy has a powerful impact on the prospect of achieving political liberalism's global political agenda, which signifies an implicit assumption of the independence of the political from the economic. Such a split is, in Ci's convincing account, a significant oversight with profound negative implications for Rawls's position.

This handbook's final chapter is by Simon Caney, who defends a right to resist global injustice. He notes how in most accounts of global justice the world is characterized by great injustice, and these often ascribe responsibility to the rich and powerful. But what is missing is those who have been treated unfairly and lack what they are entitled to. While most focus only on what we who contribute to harms have a negative duty to do to those in severe poverty, there is no such focus on what duties or rights those in severe poverty have to resist the injustice they endure. Caney defends both direct action and activities that transform the underlying social, economic, and political structures that perpetuate injustice to create greater justice in future.

Global justice is about not only the good and just, but the bad and unjust. The chapters in the book sharpen our understanding of this dark side of global justice that too often evades scrutiny. They help us think more clearly about our personal responsibilities within a context of global injustice, the falsely assumed benign nature of capitalism and its implications, and, finally, the question of whether those harmed by global injustice have a right to resist and, if so, what forms this might take.

9 FURTHER TOPICS

These twenty-five chapters cover a wide range of the most important topics in global justice. No collection can cover them all. The criminalization of international crimes and their punishment raise fascinating issues about how we might understand how crimes cross borders, but more specifically how we might conceive notions of retribution, deterrence, or rehabilitation beyond the state at the global level.[9] What activities should be international crimes and what is different about them from "domestic" crimes? How can we understand desert or adequately employ deterrence on a global scale? These and other such questions have real importance in debates in international law and justice.

An emerging topic is the development of "global philosophy."[10] This recognizes the parochial nature of most theorizing within a bounded tradition whether East or West. The idea is that a more globalized world that is increasingly unbounded, with people of different traditions coming into contact more frequently together, opens up a possibility of unlocking the bounded nature of how we philosophize by making our thinking about global justice more "global" in terms of covering not so much a wider geographical terrain as a wider philosophical terrain. Some inroads have been made over many years by excellent work in comparative philosophy.[11] Of course, different traditions may be largely bounded, but they have not operated in a vacuum-sealed silo.[12] But there is a frontier to be explored with significant benefits for global justice theorizing generally if there was closer engagement with alternative traditions uncovering new conceptual tools or frameworks that could cross-pollinate, enriching all sides. I strongly suspect such work will become an increasing part of our not too distant future.

Another topic is just war theory. Current debates have challenged the orthodox view attributed to Michael Walzer that holds that any soldier in combat has a right of self-defense.[13] Alternatively, philosophers like Jeff McMahan have argued that only soldiers on the side of a just cause have any right to use potentially deadly force—soldiers on an unjust side do not.[14] Moreover, there has been much disagreement about, if non-combatant should be immune from attack by any side, who so counts and under what circumstances non-combatants become liable to attack.[15]

A personal favorite is an argument made decades ago by Albert Camus (1986). In his pamphlet *Neither Victims nor Executioners*, he argues that innocent non-combatants are killed at random in virtually every military conflict. This means that when we as citizens support our country entering into combat with another state, our support will lead necessarily to randomly selected innocent, non-combatants being killed on the other side. We are their executioners.

Camus's challenge is to consider whether we are willing to be victims. If our support for combat means innocent people being killed randomly on the other side, Camus claims we lack integrity—and are hypocrites—if in choosing to be their executioners we are unwilling to be their victims, selected randomly to be killed by military action from the enemy side.

This hypothetical forces us to rethink whether we might still hold fast to our beliefs if we knew they were not cost-free and potentially grave. Given how high the stakes are for innocent people on the other side, should we support combat, Camus correspondingly raises the bar for our level of conviction for or against supporting war. As someone opposed to much of how the so-called "just war" tradition conceives of the justification and overall permissibility of armed conflict for the entirety of my adult life, Camus's insights have been useful in thinking through issues today.[16] Even if he does not reach the most compelling conclusions, he is asking some important questions that need asking today. Perhaps the most that we might hope for from any serious philosopher.

10 CONCLUSION

While not encyclopedic, this handbook covers many of the most pressing issues by their leading scholars selected from around the world in a truly *global* set of chapters about global justice. It is hoped they will stimulate thinking and encourage readers to engage with its ideas. Global justice is a project that includes us all and benefits from all of our contributions.

NOTES

1. For an anthology of classic and modern essays, see Brooks (2008), or of new voices, see Brooks (2014a).
2. See Pogge (2002). See also Jaggar (2010).
3. See Brooks (2007: 519–32).
4. See Brooks (2002: 92–7), (2011: 195–202), and (2014b: 156–66).
5. See Miller (2007: 100–4).
6. See Parekh (2000) and Rawls (1999).
7. See List and Pettit (2011).
8. See Young (2011).
9. See Archibugi and Pease (2018). On the philosophy of punishment more generally, see Brooks (2012).
10. See Brooks (2013: 254–66).
11. See Babb (2018) and Scharfstein (1998).
12. See Raghuramaraju (2006).
13. See Walzer (1977).
14. See McMahan (2011).
15. See Fabre (2009: 36–63) and Brooks (2010: 189–95).
16. See Brooks (n.d.).

BIBLIOGRAPHY

Archibugi, Daniele and Alice Pease (2018) *Crime and Global Justice: The Dynamics of International Punishment*. Cambridge: Polity.

Babb, James (2018) *A World History of Political Thought*. Cheltenham: Edward Elgar.

Brooks, Thom (2002) "Cosmopolitanism and Distributing Responsibilities," *Critical Review of International Social and Political Philosophy* 5: 92–7.

Brooks, Thom (2007) "Punishing States That Cause Global Poverty," *William Mitchell Law Review* 33: 519–32.

Brooks, Thom (ed.) (2008) *The Global Justice Reader*. Oxford: Blackwell.

Brooks, Thom (2010) "Justifying Terrorism," *Public Affairs Quarterly* 24: 189–95.

Brooks, Thom (2011) "Rethinking Remedial Responsibilities," *Ethics and Global Politics* 4: 195–202.

Brooks, Thom (2012) *Punishment*. London: Routledge.

Brooks, Thom (2013) "Philosophy Unbound: The Idea of Global Philosophy," *Metaphilosophy* 44: 254–66.

Brooks, Thom (ed.) (2014a) *New Waves in Global Justice*. Basingstoke: Palgrave Macmillan.

Brooks, Thom (2014a) "Remedial Responsibilities beyond Nations," *Journal of Global Ethics* 10: 156–66.

Brooks, Thom (n.d.) "Against Unjust War," unpublished MS.

Camus, Albert (1986) *Neither Victims nor Executioners*, trans. Dwight Macdonald. Philadelphia, PA: New Society Publishers.

Fabre, Cecile (2009) "Guns, Food and Liability to Attack in War," *Ethics* 120: 36–63.

Jaggar, Alison M. (ed.) (2010) *Thomas Pogge and His Critics*. Cambridge: Polity.

List, Christian and Philip Pettit (2011) *Group Agency: The Possibility, Design, and Status of Corporate Agents*. Oxford: Oxford University Press.

McMahan, Jeff (2011) *Killing in War*. Oxford: Oxford University Press.

Miller, David (2007) *National Responsibility and Global Justice*. Oxford: Oxford University Press.

Parekh, Bhikhu (2000) *Rethinking Multiculturalism: Cultural Diversity and Political Theory*, 2nd edn. Basingstoke: Palgrave Macmillan.

Pogge, Thomas (2002) *World Poverty and Human Rights*. Cambridge: Polity.

Raghuramaraju, A. (2006) *Debates in Indian Philosophy: Classical, Colonial, and Contemporary*. New Delhi: Oxford University Press.

Rawls, John (1999) *A Theory of Justice*, rev. edn. Oxford: Oxford University Press.

Scharfstein, Ben-Ami (1998) *A Comparative History of World Philosophy: From the Upanishads to Kant*. Albany, NY: SUNY Press.

Singer, Peter (1972) "Famine, Affluence, and Morality," *Philosophy and Public Affairs* 1: 229–43.

Walzer, Michael (1977) *Just and Unjust Wars: A Moral Argument with Historical Illustrations*. New York: Basic Books.

Young, Iris Marion (2011) *Responsibility for Justice*. Oxford: Oxford University Press.

Further Reading

Beitz, Charles (1999) *Political Theory and International Relations*. Princeton, NJ: Princeton University Press, 2nd edition.

Brock, Gillian (2009) *Global Justice: A Cosmopolitan Account*. Oxford: Oxford University Press.

Brock, Gillian (2015) "Global Justice," *Stanford Encyclopedia of Philosophy*, https://plato.stanford.edu/entries/justice-global/, accessed August 8, 2019.

Lazar, Seth and Helen Frowe (2020) *The Oxford Handbook of the Ethics of War*. Oxford: Oxford University Press.

Miller, David (1995) *On Nationality*. Oxford: Oxford University Press.

PART I

GLOBAL EGALITARIANISM AND ITS CRITICS

CHAPTER 1

···

GLOBAL JUSTICE AND THE ROLE OF THE STATE
A Critical Survey

···

MIRIAM RONZONI AND LAURA VALENTINI

1 INTRODUCTION

THE role of the state in our globalized age of deep political, economic, and cultural interdependence is heavily debated in political science. While some see globalization as marking the decline of the state as a form of political organization, others see the state as the engine of globalization and its main beneficiary (see, e.g., Evans 1997; Hirst and Thompson 1995; Gritsch 2005; Weiss 1998, 2003).

Similarly debated is the role of the state in normative political theory, and particularly in the context of disputes about the scope of justice, namely about its proper domain of application. Some theorists see the state as the key domain within which demanding principles of justice apply, and an important vehicle for their fulfillment. Other scholars instead insist that the scope of justice is global, and consider the state (at least partly) inimical to its realization. But what exactly do normative theorists have in mind when they invoke the state? And do their appeals to it genuinely serve the purposes for which they are intended?

Our aim in this chapter is to offer both a systematic account and a critical appraisal of appeals to the state in the global-justice literature.[1] Our contribution is threefold. First, we provide a survey of the different roles played by the state in contemporary debates about global justice. Second, we identify two particularly relevant conceptualizations of the state underpinning those different roles. Finally, we critically assess whether the state, in these different conceptualizations, can justifiably play the explanatory or justificatory roles contemporary theorists of global justice have assigned to it.

The chapter is structured as follows. In Section 2, we distinguish between two conceptualizations of the state: institutional and agential. In Section 3, we turn to the global justice debate, and differentiate between two levels of argument at which the state is often invoked: the first concerns the *justification* of principles of justice (i.e. their scope and their content), the second their *realization*. In Section 4, we critically examine the roles played by the state at the *justificatory* level of argument, specifically as (i) a ground of justice, (ii) an agent of justice, and (iii) a recipient of justice. In so doing, we also illustrate some of the implications of understanding the state in institutional or agential terms, respectively. Section 5 offers a very brief discussion of the role of the state in the *realization* of global justice.

We reach the following conclusions. From a *justificatory* perspective, even if we grant that appeals to the state play some role in determining the scope and/or content of principles of justice, such appeals do not succeed in limiting their reach to the domestic realm. Compelling reasons for applying some fairly demanding standards of justice beyond borders—though perhaps not identical to those that hold within them—survive critical scrutiny. From the perspective of *realization*, our verdict is equally balanced. We suggest that, if we want to realize justice, the state—whilst remaining a major actor on the global plane—is in need of reform and supplementation regardless which view of the scope of justice one holds.

Overall, then, our analysis points in the direction of what are sometimes called "intermediate" approaches to global justice—namely approaches that, whilst acknowledging the importance of the state, advocate (i) fairly demanding principles of justice beyond borders, though weaker than those that apply at the state level, and (ii) the establishment of supranational institutional agents—coexisting with states—capable of acting on those principles.

2 The State and How It Can Matter

Conceptualizations of the state vary widely. Some follow Max Weber (1994 [1919]: 310–11) and see it as an entity successfully claiming monopoly over the legitimate use of coercive force. Others conceive of the state as a particular set of institutions, including an executive, a legislature, a judiciary, and a permanent military. Others still think of the state as a "node" within a broader international system (for overviews, see Jessop 2008; Morris 2011).

Offering a defense of a particular account of the state is a task that goes beyond the scope of this chapter. Here, we limit ourselves to distinguishing two *families* of accounts, particularly prominent in contemporary political theory, which we call "institutional" and "agential." Institutional and agential accounts, we should emphasize, are not mutually exclusive.

2.1 The Institutional Account

In the words of March and Olsen (2008: 3): "An institution is a relatively enduring collection of rules and organized practices, embedded in structures of meaning and resources." On the institutional account, the state is a complex set of such rules and practices clustered around different functions. They include legislatures, executives, judiciary organs, armies, and bureaucracies. Each of these institutions is constituted by a set of rules, and distributes particular roles to individuals.

This institutional perspective is rather prominent in contemporary political theory. Its popularity originates in John Rawls's famous claim that the subject of justice is the basic structure of society. Rawls defines the basic structure as "the way in which the major social institutions distribute fundamental rights and duties and determine the division of advantages from social cooperation" (Rawls 1999a: 6). He specifies that those institutions include society's political constitution and its main socioeconomic arrangements, and are appropriately regarded as the subject of justice because their "effects are so profound and present from the start" (Rawls 1999a: 7).

When the state is conceptualized as a set of institutions—as in the above-quoted passages from Rawls—it is a *structure* rather than an *agent*. This structure might matter to individual agents either *in its own right* or *instrumentally* (or both). In the former case, the state matters in so far as it structures and crystallizes a complex set of relationships between its inhabitants, in the same way in which the institutions of friendship and the family are often thought to matter because they constitute valuable relationships. In the latter case, the state matters as a means to one or multiple ends. The institutions constituting it are created to achieve certain goals that could not be realized in their absence, such as the delivery of justice, the preservation of security, or the provision of public goods.

2.2 The Agential Account

From a different, perhaps more "holistic" perspective, the state may also be conceptualized as an *agent*. This suggestion is both unsurprising and puzzling. It is unsurprising because we often talk about the state as if it was a unitary agent, such as when we say: "The U.S. has signed a treaty" or "Russia has annexed Crimea." It is puzzling because it is hard to see how a complex collective entity like the state can be an agent in the familiar sense, i.e. have *its own* will, identity, and intentions. Without an answer to this question, references to the state as an agent are no more than metaphors.

List and Pettit (2011) have recently provided one such answer. An agent, on their account, is a system that can be best interpreted as having beliefs and desires, and as acting on those beliefs in order to satisfy its desires. So characterized, an agent must possess (i) an internal deliberative structure, capable of producing beliefs, desires, and making decisions to act on their basis and (ii) the ability to translate such deliberations into "external" actions (e.g. through bodily movements). When an entity's deliberative capacities are complex enough that it can understand and act on moral reasons, it counts not merely as an agent, but as a *moral* agent. Competent individual human beings clearly meet the conditions for both agency *simpliciter* and moral agency. Theorists of group agency claim, somewhat controversially, that so do some collectives: from universities to firms, from multinational corporations to newspapers (List and Pettit 2011; see also Tuomela 2013; Gilbert 1989; French 1984; Collins and Lawford-Smith 2016).

Crucially, for our purposes, many existing states meet the aforementioned conditions for agency *simpliciter* as well as moral agency.[2] First, many states possess complex decision-making structures, responsible for the formation of collective beliefs and desires. Those decision-making structures are typically sophisticated enough to be responsive to moral reasons. Second, many states possess the ability to translate their deliberations and decisions into external actions, either through the authoritativeness of their directives or through coercion. In other words, the *nature* of the institutions constitutive of (many existing) states allows us to take an agential perspective towards them, to regard them as (collective) moral agents in their own right.

It is important to point out that not all institutional systems possess the qualities necessary to make the agential perspective available. For example, the market is an institution. It is constituted by relatively stable "rules and organized practices." Yet the *nature* of the rules constituting it does not allow us to conceptualize the market as an agent in its own right. The market, after all, does not possess centralized decision-making and implementation mechanisms. Taking an agential perspective towards the market is thus not theoretically warranted.

When the state is conceptualized as an agent in its own right, it may be deemed to be valuable for its own sake, as a means to some other end, or both. The same reflections advanced on the value of the state as a set of institutions, therefore, also apply here. Interestingly, however, when the state is conceptualized as a collective agent, it can in principle acquire additional morally relevant features, which are unavailable in the case of non-agential structures. It can, for instance, qualify as a duty-bearer or a right-holder.

Having laid out two perspectives on the state, let us now turn to the debate on global justice, and the roles that the state, in either of these conceptualizations, plays in it.

3 THE STATE AND THE (GLOBAL) JUSTICE DEBATE

Justice is perhaps the most-discussed notion in contemporary political theory. In Sections 3.1 and 3.2, we first clarify what we mean by *justice*, and then turn to mapping out the different roles the state plays within the debate on *global justice* more specifically.

3.1 Justice: Domestic and Global

For present purposes, we understand justice as designating a special type of moral concern, one that gives rise to what Wesley Hohfeld (1917) called "claim rights," correlative to obligations. Duties of justice, that is, are "directed duties," *owed* to their recipients.[3]

This formal characterization of justice is still too broad for our purposes. Here we are specifically concerned with a subset of rights, namely those that have to be secured for a *sociopolitical system* to qualify as just.[4] Sociopolitical justice, in turn, comprises two categories of rights: substantive and procedural. Substantive rights guarantee access to relevant goods, including individual freedoms as well as socioeconomic resources. Procedural rights provide entitlements to decision-making, to participating in defining the system of substantive rights one is subjected to.

It is important to emphasize that, by defining justice in these terms, we not only exercise some restrictions—e.g. we exclude "justice in the private realm"—but also operate some inclusions. Sociopolitical justice, as we understand it, encompasses, for instance, classic concerns of both "socioeconomic" justice (e.g. What socioeconomic inequalities, if any, are justified?) and "political" justice (e.g. What is a just distribution of political power?).

Civil, political, and socioeconomic rights are widely acknowledged as crucial to the justice of *domestic* political systems: of states. A just state, many contemporary theorists hold, is one that grants its members *equal* individual freedoms, equal access to socioeconomic opportunities, and *equal* rights to political participation.[5]

Over the past four decades it has become increasingly evident that the global realm is also a complex rule-governed system, and arguably one that is susceptible to justice-based assessments. Recognition of this fact is behind the burgeoning debate on global justice. The bulk of this debate revolves around two questions. The first asks whether we may evaluate the global realm by reference to the same standards that we routinely employ at the domestic level, or whether some, if not all, principles of justice are scope-restricted. The second asks how justice can best be realized. In other words, the debate includes two levels of argument: one concerns the *justification* of principles of justice (i.e. their scope and content), the other their *realization*.

3.2 Global Justice and the State

At the *justificatory level*, different theories of global justice offer different substantive principles requiring the fulfillment of specific sets of rights beyond the state. The principles in question share the following structure:

Right-holder (R) is entitled to certain objects (O) against duty-bearer (D) on grounds (G).

While sharing a commitment to normative individualism—that is, to the role of individuals as *ultimate* units of moral concern, entitled to the social conditions to lead autonomous lives—theorists of global justice are divided between those who believe that the state plays no role at this justificatory level and those who believe that it does. The former are so-called "cosmopolitans," who, for a variety of reasons, see the state as irrelevant to the determination of the scope and content of principles of justice.[6] For them, none of the parameters in our four-place relation may be specified by reference to the state (see, e.g., Caney 2005; Beitz 1983; Goodin 1988; Pogge 1989).

The latter are an internally diverse group, ranging from so-called "statists" to "internationalists" to "transnationalists" and others (see, e.g., Nagel 2005; Blake 2001; Sangiovanni 2007; Risse 2006; Ronzoni 2009; Forst 2001; Valentini 2011). For them, the state constitutes an appropriate specification of one or more of the parameters characterizing our four-place relation: a right-holder (recipient of justice/R), a duty-bearer (agent of justice/D), a ground of justice in general (G), and/or a ground of specific principles of justice with particularly demanding, egalitarian content (i.e. principles with a distinctive object O).[7]

It is important to emphasize that theorists belonging to the latter group diverge widely with respect to both (i) the specific justificatory role they attribute to the state and (ii) whether they regard the state as the *only* factor determining the scope and content of justice. For instance, some believe that states are themselves right-holders and/or duty-bearers; others do not. Some, most prominently Thomas Nagel (2005), ostensibly hold that obligations of justice arise *only* within the state. Others insist that there are additional grounds of justice—e.g. common humanity, common ownership of the earth, the global trade system, the international human rights regime, etc.—giving rise to rights-correlative obligations beyond the state, though less demanding than those existing within it (e.g. Blake 2001; Risse 2012; Sangiovanni 2007). Others still claim that the justice-relevant features exhibited by the state—e.g. coercion and domination—are also present, to a lesser degree and/or in different forms, beyond borders, and that this generates demands of "transnational" as well as "global" justice (Forst 2001; Valentini 2011). What matters for present purposes is that, despite holding substantively different views, these theorists share a commitment to the justificatory relevance of the state, in opposition to cosmopolitans' denial of such relevance. Our claim in Section 4 will be that the correct position to hold lies somewhere within this camp, but fairly close to its most demanding end.

At the *realization level* of argument, theorists of global justice set forth institutional proposals which, in their views, would facilitate the fulfillment of their preferred principles of (global) justice. Interestingly, a denial of the relevance of the state at the justificatory level need not be accompanied by a denial of its instrumental relevance, and vice versa. Here, too, the literature exhibits some interesting divisions.[8] Some—both cosmopolitans and anti-cosmopolitans—see the state as an indispensable vehicle for the realization of justice, on grounds of its capacity to apportion and enforce rights and responsibilities, and to mobilize individuals' sense of justice (see, e.g., Ypi 2012; Meckled-Garcia 2008; Goodin 1988; Stilz 2009). Others, by contrast, perceive the state as we know it as an obstacle to the realization of global justice, and recommend its radical reform or replacement with vertical and horizontal systems of dispersals of sovereignty, or with global democratic decision-making structures (see, e.g., Pogge 1992; Kuper 2000; Macdonald 2008; Bohman 2007; Archibugi 2008; Cabrera 2004).

This brief sketch has hopefully provided readers with a flavor of the complexity of the debate on global justice, and the roles the state plays in it. But what conceptualizations of the state underpin those various roles? And which appeals to the state are successful in achieving their justificatory or explanatory aims, and which ones are not? The remainder of this chapter answers these questions, focusing first on the roles the state plays at the justificatory level (Section 4), and then at the level of realization (Section 5).

4 JUSTIFICATION, GLOBAL JUSTICE, AND THE STATE

As we have already mentioned, from a justificatory perspective, the state has been invoked by theorists of global justice—mostly of an anti-cosmopolitan disposition—in the following roles or capacities:

  i. as a ground of justice (G)—in general, or in relation to egalitarian principles (i.e. principles with a particular object O)
 ii. as an agent/bearer of duties of justice (D)
iii. as a recipient of justice/right-holder (R)

We discuss each in turn.

4.1 The State and the Grounds of Justice

By the "grounds of justice" we mean "the reasons why claims of justice apply to a particular population" (Risse 2012: 2). In recent years, participants in the global justice debate have appealed to state membership as a relevant ground for the application of *egalitarian* principles of justice in particular (see, e.g., Nagel 2005; Blake 2001; Sangiovanni 2007; Risse 2006). While sharing the conclusion that egalitarian justice only applies domestically, these theorists have reached it through different lines of argument. Two are particularly prominent in the literature, and articulated in their best-known forms by Michael Blake (2001) and Andrea Sangiovanni (2007).[9]

According to Blake, there are two fundamental grounds of justice. One is *humanity*: everybody is entitled to the necessary means to lead an autonomous life simply in virtue of being a person. Since this only requires having *enough* to formulate and pursue a life-plan, humanity generates principles that are global in scope, yet only *sufficientarian* in content. Blake's second ground of justice is *state coercion*. He observes that some of the resources necessary for individuals to be able to lead autonomous lives—such as the rule of law, food security, basic healthcare, and education—can only be delivered through the coercive apparatus of the state (Blake 2001: 280). Yet state coercion triggers additional justificatory requirements, because it is prima facie problematic from the viewpoint of autonomy: it appears to "bend the will" of its targets, thereby preventing them from being genuinely self-determining and autonomous. For Blake, state coercion can be made fully compatible with autonomy only if it is exercised in line with *egalitarian* standards of justice (Blake 2001: 293). Specifically, to qualify as just, coercive institutions must (i) grant all subjects equal access to basic freedoms and socioeconomic goods, thereby equally protecting everyone's material conditions for autonomy; and (ii) be under all subjects' equal control, thereby ensuring that subjects "coerce themselves." Since the *function* of egalitarian justice is to render state coercion fully compatible with autonomy, there is no reason for *egalitarian* justice to apply when such coercion is absent. In Blake's words, "material inequality [within the state] is ... more like a denial of suffrage than most liberal theorists have previously thought" (Blake 2001: 295).

Like Blake, Sangiovanni (2007) holds that the state is the key site of application of egalitarian justice, but not due to its coercive nature. As he illustrates, if a functioning state were temporarily to lose its coercive capacity, we would not think egalitarian obligations among its members would thereby automatically vanish (Sangiovanni 2007: 10–11). In order to understand why it is that members of the same state have egalitarian obligations towards one another, he argues, we must concentrate on *what the state does*, rather than on *how* it does it (i.e. the coercion it exercises along the way). The point of the state, in Sangiovanni's view, is to enable the kind of *social cooperation* crucial to produce the collective goods necessary for—what Blake would call—an autonomous life. Sangiovanni then goes on to argue that, for such social cooperation to embody genuine reciprocity, rather than be exploitative, its benefits and burdens must be distributed along egalitarian lines (Sangiovanni 2007: 26).

Blake and Sangiovanni give us different—though arguably compatible, and mutually reinforcing (cf. Risse 2006)—reasons for regarding the state as a privileged site of egalitarian justice. But what conceptualizations of the state do they employ? Since their discussions are opaque in this respect, our observations are somewhat conjectural. To the extent that, as it is often assumed, only *agents* have the ability to coerce—i.e. to issue commands backed by the threat of sanctions—Blake's view appears to (implicitly) presuppose an agential perspective on the state. Sangiovanni's, by contrast, seems to conceptualize the state as both a set of institutions embodying particular patterns of cooperation and an agent with distinctive "extractive, regulative, and distributive capacities" (Sangiovanni 2007: 20).

If these observations are correct, those aspects of Blake's and Sangiovanni's arguments that presuppose an agential perspective on the state are susceptible to criticism on the part of those who reject the idea of collective agency. For present purposes, we shall not challenge the notion of group agency, or the role it might play in Blake's and Sangiovanni's views; instead, we only emphasize the need for theorists who regard the state as justificatorily significant to be more explicit about their conceptualizations of it, and what follows from them.

More importantly, does treating the state as justificatorily significant—independently of how it is conceptualized—succeed in restricting the scope of egalitarian justice to the domestic arena? There already exists a rich literature on this issue. Several authors have pointed out that more work needs to be done to demonstrate that state coercion and domestic cooperation are necessary—or even sufficient—to ground egalitarian justice, let alone to limit its reach to the domestic arena (see, e.g., Abizadeh 2007; Caney 2008; C. Barry and Valentini 2009; Cavallero 2010). Our aim in what follows is not to review this literature, but to suggest that Blake's and Sangiovanni's premises, which we grant for argument's sake, do not vindicate statist conclusions, i.e. they do not vindicate confining egalitarian justice to the state. Rather, those premises, coupled with plausible empirical observations, push us towards a more nuanced picture of justice beyond borders, one situated somewhere between statism and cosmopolitanism. What we offer, then, is a modest internal critique of the statist conclusions allegedly following from Blake's and Sangiovanni's views.[10]

Our internal critique begins with the simple—and frequently made—observation that coercion and cooperation have fuzzy contours in a globalized world. Crucially, this applies not only to coercion and social cooperation *simpliciter*, but specifically to those forms of autonomy-enabling coercion and cooperation that Blake and Sangiovanni regard as grounds of egalitarian justice. States still constitute crucial areas of *concentration* of these phenomena, but the scopes of both Blake's coercion and Sangiovanni's social cooperation do not perfectly coincide with their borders.

Let us start with Blake's coercion-based statism. Blake argues that exercising coercion over people and yet affecting them unequally, or not enabling them to have equal control over the forms of coercion that are exercised upon them, are equivalent to disenfranchising them. Recall that, on this view, state coercion is (i) required to secure the means that are necessary for autonomy, and (ii) justified only if its exercise satisfies demanding egalitarian standards. This, however, seems to presuppose, rather than establish, that the *kind* of coercion that matters (namely the one that is will-bending, yet necessary for autonomy) only happens within state borders. We shall, however, provide a couple of examples to show that, in the world as it is today, (i) the state is *not* the only "provider" of the relevant autonomy-enabling coercion and (ii) many states *do not* have the capacity— hence the duty—to coerce their populations in line with egalitarian standards. In other words, we can be both enfranchised or disenfranchised, in Blake's specific sense, by coercion other than state coercion.

Regarding (i), consider the following three cases. For members of the Council of Europe, ultimate protection against human rights violations is granted by the European Court of Human Rights. For EU market actors, a system of reliable expectations and non-discrimination in the market is ultimately guaranteed by the enforcement of EU competition and non-discrimination law. Similar remarks, finally, can be made about the common currency in the Eurozone. In sum, three different kinds of (a) supranational, yet not fully global institutions exercise coercive power to guarantee certain goods that are necessary for autonomy, yet (b) each of them in certain limited (and different) areas only. What seems to follow, for the coercion view, is neither statism nor cosmopolitanism, but a more complex stance. The necessary means for autonomy seem to come from different sources, rather than from the state only, depending on the different institutional web in which we are involved (Council of Europe, EU, Eurozone). What would seem to follow from Blake's account is that the individual citizens of member states of these three different institutions are entitled to egalitarian standards, not across the board, but in those areas where they are subject to the same forms of coercion.

Greeks, for instance, would be entitled, not to the same overall *standards of living* as Germans, but (a) to an equal share of the burdens and benefits of having a common currency, and (b) to equal control over the conditions of the Euro governance itself.

Regarding (ii), it is not clear that states have the *ability* to secure demanding egalitarian standards of socioeconomic and political justice for their citizenry. Take, again, the case of the Euro governance. If the regime of austerity continues, several member states will have little capacity to implement those redistributive policies that are necessary to realize domestic equality. In these cases, state coercion does not meet the standards set by Blake for domestic justice; yet the reasons why this is the case are not themselves entirely domestic. Again, it seems that *part* of what justice requires in those cases is an adjustment *at the Eurozone level* so as to give member states the power to comply with their obligations of domestic justice.[11] Since "ought implies can," individual states, qua collective agents, cannot be under an *obligation* to secure full-blown equality—as Blake would have it—if they do not have the capacity to do so.[12]

Structurally similar remarks can be made in relation to Sangiovanni's cooperation-based view. Sangiovanni argues that egalitarian demands stem from social cooperation in the production of goods necessary for autonomy, including the rule of law, safety, security, and a reliable system of expectations. Yet, for reasons similar to those we have mentioned with respect to coercion, it is clear neither that, today, (i) *all* of these goods are *always* provided via state-based cooperation, nor that (ii) states have full capacity to produce these goods. With respect to (i), Sangiovanni himself has acknowledged this point, by developing, for instance, an account of the intermediate obligations of social justice which hold within the EU (Sangiovanni 2013). With respect to (ii), several transnational dynamics—such as global financialization, the global nature of production chains, or international tax competition—arguably constrain the capacity of states and their members to secure an egalitarian distribution of the benefits and burdens of social cooperation (Dietsch and Rixen 2014). Once again, if "ought implies can," states cannot plausibly be under an *obligation* to secure egalitarian justice; not until their capacity to fulfill egalitarian demands has been restored. In Sangiovanni's own words, equality as a demand of justice only applies to institutions with "autonomous distributive, extractive, and regulative capacities" (Sangiovanni 2007: 22). Our point is that, today, many states have those capacities eroded "from the outside."

If our analysis is correct, the two most prominent appeals to the state as a ground of egalitarian justice provide reasons to assign a special, but not exclusive role to states at the justificatory level of argument. In particular, such appeals fail to vindicate "statist" conclusions—according to which egalitarian justice applies *only* domestically—pointing instead towards more nuanced approaches.

4.2 The State as a Bearer of Duties of Justice

Some theorists explicitly appeal to the state as a uniquely capable *bearer* of demanding duties of egalitarian justice to rebut cosmopolitan—i.e. "global egalitarian"—conclusions.

These theorists point out that principles of justice prescribe securing complex patterns of entitlements within given populations. They further note that only particular kinds of agents or entities have the *capacity* to act on those principles. These must be agents epistemically and socially powerful enough to foresee, and correct for, the cumulative effects of many people's actions. Yet only large-scale, authoritative institutional agents have this ability, since "authoritative institutions can preserve patterns of distribution and individuals cannot. They are able to do this because they can assign duties and responsibilities that are not assignable in the absence of an authority" (Meckled-Garcia 2008: 255; cf. Nagel 2005). Rawls (2013: 266) himself is fully aware of the fact that the cumulative consequences of the actions and transactions of a large number of agents "are often so far in the future, or so indirect, that the attempt to forestall them by restrictive rules that apply to individuals would be an excessive if not an impossible burden." These consequences can only be regulated, and certain patterns of entitlements maintained—what Rawls calls "background justice"—by complex institutional agents.

Crucially for our purposes, while agents with the relevant capacities exist at the domestic level, in the form of states, they do not exist at the global level. And since "ought implies can," the absence of agents capable of acting on the demands of egalitarian justice beyond the state means that those demands do not apply at the global level. As Meckled-Garcia puts it:

> [P]utative, properly cosmopolitan principles, demanding background adjustment in line with a domestic conception of justice, are *incomplete* due to our inability to identify a relevant agency.   (Meckled-Garcia 2008: 267 emphasis added)

The incompleteness can be easily illustrated by reference to our four-place relation:

> Right-holder (R) is entitled to certain objects (O) against duty-bearer (D) on grounds (G).

Cosmopolitan egalitarians argue that all human beings (R) are entitled to equal access to socioeconomic goods (O) on a variety of grounds (G). But Meckled-Garcia and others object that there is no agent who can plausibly occupy the position of a duty-bearer (D), because no agent (or set of agents) has the ability to secure equal access to socioeconomic goods worldwide. Cosmopolitan principles of justice are thus incomplete because one of the relevant parameters in our four-place relation remains empty.

Proponents of this argument acknowledge that *some* principles of justice apply beyond the state, but these are only either (i) interactional principles which each and every state, conceived as an agent, can abide by (e.g. mutual respect and assistance) or (ii) institutional principles which existing supranational institutions have the power to comply with (such as fair rules of trade with respect to the WTO). For both the above demands of justice, putative duty-bearers can be identified, but not for the fulfillment of demanding egalitarian standards between all individuals across the globe.

What to say about this line of argument? First of all, it is worth pointing out that it relies on an agential, as opposed to institutional, conceptualization of the state. This, in turn, means that those who find the somewhat controversial idea of group agency problematic will not be persuaded by it. As anticipated, here we are not challenging the idea of group agency. So, granted collective agency, does the role of the state as uniquely capable of securing the demands of egalitarian socioeconomic justice genuinely under-mine cosmopolitan principles? In what follows, we suggest that it does so *only to a limited extent*—thereby reinforcing the conclusion reached in Section 4.1. In particular, we rely on two arguments.

The first concedes the premise that domestic states are uniquely capable of securing demanding egalitarian justice for their citizens, and that no equivalent agent exists at the global level. This concession does indeed lead to the conclusion that cosmopolitan prin-ciples of global justice, in the world as it is today, do not have *immediate normative* force. That is, they do not set forth immediately action-guiding prescriptions, since there is no agent capable of acting on those prescriptions. From this it follows that, strictly speak-ing, nobody has the *rights* set out by cosmopolitan principles because rights consist of duties *owed* to particular others, and the relevant duty bearers do not exist. However, granting that cosmopolitan principles of justice do not have direct *normative* force does not invalidate their *evaluative* role (on this distinction see Gheaus 2013; Gilabert 2011).[13]

Instead of prescribing what agents ought to do, cosmopolitan theories enable us to evaluate states of affairs. Of course, evaluating states of affairs as regrettable is not enough to condemn them as "unjust," if injustice is defined—as Nagel and Meckled-Garcia do, and as our own definition suggests—as the violation of rights. Yet, despite not being directly action-guiding, evaluative statements are still informative. For instance, in the case of cosmopolitanism, they tell us that the absence of an agent capable of real-izing global egalitarian justice is morally regrettable.

What is more—and this brings us to our second argument—the "no duty-bearer, no injustice" view must be qualified in non-trivial ways to remain plausible. We have already alluded to how it is not at all clear that the state, in an increasingly globalized world, is genuinely capable of performing its justice tasks for its own citizens. What we might call *global* background injustice erodes state sovereignty and renders states increasingly unable to secure some of their citizens' most important rights (Ronzoni 2009). The global financial crisis of 2008 is clear evidence of this, and so are globally harmful phenomena such as tax competition (Dietsch and Rixen 2014), financial vola-tility (Wollner 2014), and the transnational, fragmented character of global production chains. States are increasingly challenged in their capacity to maintain just socioeco-nomic patterns at the domestic level, and these challenges have global causes over which individual states, by themselves, have little if no control. This is a standard case of back-ground socioeconomic injustice.

Similar observations can be made about the procedural ("political") side of justice—which is somewhat less emphasized in the mainstream "global justice" literature. Specifically, as a result of these global dynamics, states are pressurized into being more responsive to global financial markets, rating agencies, multinationals, and international organizations championing austerity-based reforms, and less to their own citizens through mechanisms of accountability and legitimation (democratic or otherwise). Under these circumstances, the same argument that renders egalitarian principles of justice *not* fully normative at the global level erodes their normativity—albeit to a lesser extent—at the domestic level too. States are, as Peter Mair (2013) puts it, "hollowed out" in their agency and capacity (see also Mair 2009; Ronzoni 2012; Laborde and Ronzoni 2016). Therefore, if the "no duty-bearer, no injustice" view is accepted all the way down, one unpalatable conclusion follows: *few* sociopolitical injustices "proper," whether domestic or global, occur in such a scenario, for no capable agents can be identified as the bearers of duties we routinely regard as a matter of justice. This would imply that justice can do little work where it is most needed. The critical capacity of the notion of justice would be seriously undermined.

There is, however, a possible compromise that might allow us both to use the language of justice in cases where no fully capable agents exist and to retain a not merely evaluative understanding of this notion. Interestingly, the possibility of such compromise is forestalled by the examples we have just offered. If the brief analysis sketched above is correct, global institutions are needed to address global dynamics like harmful tax competition, the volatility of global financial markets, the fragmentation of global production chains and global industrial relations, and so forth. This being so, we can say that we have obligations to do what is in our power to bring about these new institutional frameworks.[14] Such obligations might not have perfect contours, but they certainly constrain the set of actions we may permissibly perform in a number of ways (cf. Abizadeh 2007; C. Barry and Valentini 2009: 497–8; Valentini 2011: 103–4, Gilabert 2012).[15]

We can thus again conclude that an emphasis on the state, this time as an agent of justice, is less effective than statists believe in limiting the reach of (egalitarian) socioeconomic and political justice to the domestic realm. The claim that demanding principles of justice can only apply within state borders because only states are capable of acting on those principles relies on an unduly idealized account of state agency. What is more, these observations should induce us to take the link between justice and capable agency with a modicum of caution. Whereas it is true that justice, to remain distinctive, cannot be a merely aspirational value, the stipulation of a fully capable agent as a necessary condition for principles of justice to apply may lead to the somewhat unpalatable conclusion that in our world (and in many other past and possible worlds) very few injustices proper occur.

4.3 The State as a Recipient of Justice/Right-Holder

To conclude our critical survey of the role of state from a justificatory point of view, it is worth addressing one final position, according to which the state, if internally constituted in normatively appropriate ways, is itself the holder of rights at the international level. The argument resonates with traditional claims to sovereignty and non-interference on the part of states.

The strongest philosophical formulation of these claims has been offered by Immanuel Kant (1999 [1797]) and, more recently, by contemporary Kant-inspired authors (Rawls 1999b; Stilz 2009; Flikschuh 2010).[16] For our purposes, one right is particularly relevant: the state's right not to be subjected to coercion and compulsion (Flikschuh 2010). If states cannot be compelled, global institutions realizing putative demands of justice beyond borders can only be voluntary and state-driven, without exercising any direct, ultimate authority. On this view, forcing a state to join a supranational institution on grounds of justice would be a contradiction in terms, since compelling an appropriately constituted state is *ipso facto* unjust.

What to say about this final position? To begin with, it must be stressed that this position too conceptualizes states as (moral) agents, and is, therefore, susceptible to objections on the part of those who find the notion of collective agency problematic. This is not going to be our line of criticism, however, since we are not questioning group agency here. An assumption we are instead making—following the bulk of the literature—is normative individualism, according to which only individuals are ulti-mate units of moral concern. The rights of states qua corporate agents must, therefore, be both (i) ultimately *grounded* in the rights of individuals and (ii) *consistent* with those rights. Note that this is a point about group agency in general. To illustrate, the status of some voluntary collectives (e.g. private associations) as moral agents and patients is *grounded* in their being expressions of some individual, autonomy-based rights (such as the right to freely associate). This standing, though, is also conditional on their existence and operation being *consistent with* the rights of both members and non-members.

Unlike membership in private associations, state membership is typically *non-voluntary*. Consequently, the moral standing of states cannot be grounded in their being an ostensive *expression* of individual autonomy. Instead, as Blake and Sangiovanni help-fully illustrate, their moral status stems from their being *necessary means* for the protec-tion of individual autonomy (cf. also Stilz 2009). States acquire rights as corporate agents in so far as (and to the extent that) they are uniquely positioned to secure the essentials of individual autonomy. We might say, therefore, that states need to be right-holders in order to fulfill their role as duty-bearers towards individuals, and that their enjoyment of rights is conditional on that. Moreover, like voluntary collectives, their existence and operation must be compatible with the rights *of all*. Their enjoyment of rights is conse-quently *qualified* in two crucial ways.

First, internally, they must secure those individual rights the protection of which *grounds* their status as right-holders, e.g. access to the rule of law, security, political participation, and socioeconomic resources. If states fail to secure those rights, their status as right-holders becomes questionable. Externally, states must respect certain constraints towards outsiders: they must act consistently with their rights. Again, when a state can fulfill its duties towards its own citizens only at the cost of, for instance, oppressing outsiders, its status as right-holder may be questioned.

Second, we have established that the state deserves the status of right-holder only to the extent that it fulfills its duties. But in order to fulfill those duties—indeed, in order to bear those duties in the first place—it must be a *capable* moral agent. That is, it must possess (i) an internally sophisticated decision-making structure, and (ii) the ability to translate its decisions into "external" actions. In particular, it must be an effective agent relative to those areas for which it being an agent is necessary for the protection of individual rights. As we have seen in Sections 4.1 and 4.2, however, it is by no means obvious that many (if not all) states currently meet this capacity-condition. But if the capacity of states to secure just socioeconomic standards and just political relations is undermined—i.e. if they lack *the capacity* to stand in the right kind of relationship with their own individual members—it is not clear that their compulsion ought to remain unqualifiedly impermissible.

Once again, we seem to be pushed towards a more nuanced position. On the one hand, states can be right-holders, but only conditionally on meeting certain standards, not, therefore, in every possible world. On the other, with respect to their right not to be compelled in particular, the empirical conditions to waive it, or at least to qualify it significantly, do obtain in our world. Since states currently lack some of the capacities that justify their status as right-holders, we need to supplement them with global institutions, which will limit their sovereignty and therefore exercise *some* compulsion upon them.

Our discussion of the justificatory role of the state in limiting the scope of justice has hereby come to a close. Our provisional conclusion is that a focus on the state, whether as a ground, agent, or recipient of justice, fails to justify uncompromising statism, and instead points in the direction of what we have called "intermediate" positions. What is, however, the role of the state in *realizing*, rather than justifying, principles of justice?

5 THE STATE: A MEANS, OR AN IMPEDIMENT, TO THE REALIZATION OF GLOBAL JUSTICE?

The role of the state in realizing principles of justice is as debated as its justificatory relevance, yet along different lines. Unsurprisingly, most statists see the state as the crucial vehicle through which domestic egalitarian principles of justice can be realized (Nagel 2005; Meckled-Garcia 2008). Cosmopolitans do not constitute an equally united camp. Whereas some think that the model of the fully sovereign state should be overcome and replaced by multilevel forms of governance or even by a world state (Pogge 1992; Kuper 2000; Archibugi 2008; Macdonald 2008; Cabrera 2004), others see the state as indispensable to sustain cosmopolitan allegiances and motivations (Ypi 2012) or as a way of distributing universal obligations (Goodin 1988).

Our assessment of the role of the state when it comes to the realization of justice will be brief, and largely build upon the observations sketched in Section 4. Recall that what leads Blake and Sangiovanni to identify coercion and social cooperation as *grounds* of justice is, at least in part, their *instrumental* role in securing, or realizing, the necessary means for autonomy—that is, their *capacity* to deliver autonomy-enabling goods.

We have rejected the association between either coercion or social cooperation and uncompromising statism on the grounds that (i) states are not the only loci of coercion and social cooperation of the relevant kind and (ii) the capacity of states to exercise these kinds of coercion and social cooperation is severely constrained in many crucial areas under conditions of poorly managed globalization. That is to say, we have challenged the justifications used for confining the scope of egalitarian justice to the state partly on the basis that such justifications both exaggerate and fetishize state *capacity* in the real world. This has clear implications for our views on the role the state can plausibly play in *realizing* justice.

On the one hand, we already live in a world where institutions other than states are necessary to secure certain rights. On the other, the capacity of states to secure justice, in both socioeconomic and political terms, is severely constrained, due to transnational socioeconomic dynamics that affect states internally and are beyond their control. As already noted, it is, therefore, plausible to presume that further global institution-building will be necessary to address such dynamics, and that these new institutions will further constrain the role of states, at least in some respects.

This means that, *even* from a statist justificatory perspective, the realization of justice requires *at least* some of those already existing global institutions, and probably further ones. This is equally, if not more, true for cosmopolitans. Cosmopolitans who wish to rely on states as instruments for the realization of global justice—e.g. on account of states' motivational and organizational capacities—must also recognise that some of these capacities are severely challenged, if not gone for good, and that the state therefore requires, at a minimum, external institutional support. In fact, many of them do.

Whether this implies that we should move towards a radical restructuring of the world order, along the lines suggested by advocates of multilevel systems (Pogge 1992) or a world state (Cabrera 2004), or whether more modest and incrementalist projects can be sufficient is an issue that we cannot address here. The answer to this question will ultimately depend on which view one takes on the *positive* role of the state for the realization of justice. It could very well be that, even if the state system is imperfect, states remain valuable instruments to realize justice for the motivation- and coordination-based reasons Ypi (2012) and Goodin (1988) mention. Moreover, it is fairly plausible to assume that states remain, on balance, more likely to be accountable to their own citizens than more complex systems of global governance. Finally, the very quality of democratic processes, and ultimately political justice, might be better secured within states given, for instance, the presence of a more cohesive demos (see, e.g., Dahl 1999; Miller 2010). All these factors might, on balance, give us reasons to preserve states as important loci of decision-making. If what we have argued is true, however, these are grounds to favor fairly modest agendas of global institutional design over fully transformative models—not reasons for defending a system of fully sovereign states.

6 Conclusion

In this chapter, we have surveyed the different roles played by the state in debates about both the justification of principles of (global) justice and their realization. Even though the main purpose of this chapter has been analytical and expository, our discussion points in the direction of a family of substantive conclusions about global justice, conclusions that lie in between "pure statism" and "pure cosmopolitanism." At the levels of both justification and realization, we have suggested, the state may well matter to justice, but not in an all-or-nothing manner. While it is, plausibly, a key site of egalitarian justice, it is not the only such site: some egalitarian principles of justice also apply beyond borders. And while the state is an important means to the realization of justice, it is not sufficient: it needs to be partly reformed and supplemented to secure the demands of justice in a globalized world. Whether such "intermediate conclusions" are fully defensible, especially against cosmopolitan objections, is a question for another day.

Notes

1. By "global justice literature," here, we mean the literature debating the scope, content, grounds, and application of principles of justice in particular. We do not discuss the role of the state in other important areas of international normative theory, e.g. debates about territorial rights, self-determination, humanitarian intervention, and just war.
2. We say "many," as opposed to "all," in so far as some states—e.g. weak or failed states—may partially or fully fail to meet the relevant conditions. Whether all functioning states meet these conditions is an issue on which we shall remain silent here.
3. Justice so construed is often contrasted with charity or beneficence. See, e.g., B. Barry (1991) and Buchanan (1987).
4. In other words, we ignore other categories of rights, such as those generated by friendship, promising, and personal or professional relationships more generally.
5. Of course, there are exceptions to this general statement, but at least liberal-egalitarian theorists (despite their differences) all appear to be accurately characterized by it.
6. Cosmopolitans may, of course, consider the state relevant to the application of those principles—or, in G. A. Cohen's (2003) words, to the design of "rules of regulation."
7. In the literature we address, these are usually liberal-egalitarian principles of socioeconomic justice and democratic accountability.
8. These differences are, however, less stark than those we encounter at the justificatory level. Very few would hold that the state has absolutely no role to play when it comes to the realization of justice.
9. Nagel's (2005) work is of course also much-debated, but somewhat less transparent in its underlying normative rationale (which includes reference to coercion, authority, and co-authorship). We thus do not directly address it in our discussion. For a critical analysis of Nagel, see, e.g., Julius (2006).

10. For an external critique, which denies that coercion and/or cooperation are either necessary or merely sufficient grounds of egalitarian justice, see Caney (2008).
11. For a coercion-based account of justice beyond borders explicitly sensitive to these nuances, and which controversially regards non-agential systems of rules as also coercive, see Valentini (2011).
12. Blake notably argues that coercion exercised by international institutions is indirect and less comprehensive, and therefore less problematic (Blake 2001: 280). If our picture is correct, however, we live in a world in which different forms of justice-relevant coercion are exercised by different sources, making the state a particularly significant node of concentration, but not qualitatively unique.
13. Incidentally, the evaluative understanding of "justice" seems to be what G. A. Cohen (2003: 243) has in mind when he asserts the importance of political philosophy even when this makes "no practical difference."
14. Cf. the notion of a "meta-right" (Sen 1984), and the natural duty of justice to "further just arrangements not yet established" (Rawls 1999a: 99).
15. Whether these obligations are sufficiently specific to be obligations of justice proper (i.e. correlative to claimable rights) is an issue we cannot solve here. We think, however, that such obligations would be more than merely aspirational. For further discussion see Valentini (forthcoming).
16. Similar views may also be found among nationalists (e.g. Miller 1995, 2007), to the extent that states articulate the rights to self-determination of national communities.

References

Abizadeh, Arash (2007) "Cooperation, Pervasive Impact, and Coercion: On the Scope (not Site) of Distributive Justice," *Philosophy & Public Affairs* 35(4): 318–58.

Archibugi, Daniele (2008) *The Global Commonwealth of Citizens: Toward Cosmopolitan Democracy*. Princeton, NJ: Princeton University Press.

Barry, Brian (1991) "Humanity and Justice in Global Perspective." In *Liberty and Justice: Essays in Political Theory 2*. Oxford: Clarendon Press, 182–210.

Barry, Christian, and Laura Valentini (2009) "Egalitarian Challenges to Global Egalitarianism: A Critique," *Review of International Studies* 35(3): 485–512.

Beitz, Charles R. (1983) "Cosmopolitan Ideals and National Sentiment," *The Journal of Philosophy* 80(10): 591–600.

Blake, Michael (2001) "Distributive Justice, State Coercion, and Autonomy," *Philosophy & Public Affairs* 30(3): 257–96.

Bohman, James (2007) *Democracy across Borders*. Cambridge, MA: MIT Press.

Buchanan, Allen (1987) "Justice and Charity," *Ethics* 97(3): 558–75.

Cabrera, Luis (2004) *Political Theory of Global Justice: A Cosmopolitan Case for the World State*, new edn. London: Routledge.

Caney, Simon (2005) *Justice beyond Borders*. Oxford: Oxford University Press.

Caney, Simon (2008) "Global Distributive Justice and the State," *Political Studies* 56(3): 487–518.

Cavallero, Eric (2010) "Coercion, Inequality and the International Property Regime," *Journal of Political Philosophy* 18(1): 16–31.

Cohen, G. A. (2003) "Facts and Principles," *Philosophy & Public Affairs* 31(3): 211–45.

Collins, Stephanie, and Holly Lawford-Smith (2016) "The Transfer of Duties: From Individuals to States and Back Again." In Michael Brady and Miranda Fricker (eds.), *The Epistemic Life of Groups*. New York: Oxford University Press, 150–72.

Dahl, Robert A. (1999) "Can International Organizations Be Democratic? A Skeptic's View." In Ian Shapiro and Casiano Hacker-Cordón (eds.), *Democracy's Edges*. Contemporary Political Theory. Cambridge: Cambridge University Press, 19–36.

Dietsch, Peter, and Thomas Rixen (2014) "Tax Competition and Global Background Justice," *Journal of Political Philosophy* 22(2): 150–77.

Evans, Peter (1997) "The Eclipse of the State? Reflections on Stateness in an Era of Globalization," *World Politics* 50(1): 62–87.

Flikschuh, Katrin (2010) "Kant's Sovereignty Dilemma: A Contemporary Analysis," *Journal of Political Philosophy* 16(1): 48–71.

Forst, Rainer (2001) "Towards a Critical Theory of Transnational Justice," *Metaphilosophy* 32(1–2): 160–79.

French, Peter A. (1984) *Collective and Corporate Responsibility*. New York: Columbia University Press.

Gheaus, Anca (2013) "The Feasibility Constraint on The Concept of Justice." *The Philosophical Quarterly* 63(252): 445–64.

Gilabert, Pablo (2011) "Feasibility and Socialism," *Journal of Political Philosophy* 19(1): 52–63.

Gilabert, Pablo (2012) *From Global Poverty to Global Equality*, Oxford: Oxford University Press.

Gilbert, Margaret (1989) *On Social Facts*. Princeton, NJ: Princeton University Press.

Goodin, Robert E. (1988) "What Is So Special about Our Fellow Countrymen?" *Ethics* 98(4): 663–86.

Gritsch, Maria (2005) "The Nation-State and Economic Globalization: Soft Geo-Politics and Increased State Autonomy?" *Review of International Political Economy* 12(1): 1–25.

Hirst, Paul, and Grahame Thompson (1995) "Globalization and the Future of the Nation State," *Economy and Society* 24(3): 408–42.

Hohfeld, Wesley Newcomb (1917) "Fundamental Legal Conceptions as Applied in Judicial Reasoning," *The Yale Law Journal* 26(8): 710–70.

Jessop, Bob (2008) "State and State-Building." In Sarah A. Binder, R. A. W. Rhodes, and Bert A. Rockman (eds.), *The Oxford Handbook of Political Institutions*. Oxford: Oxford University Press, 111–30.

Julius, A. J. (2006) "Nagel's Atlas," *Philosophy & Public Affairs* 34(2): 176–92.

Kant, Immanuel (1999 [1797]) *Metaphysical Elements of Justice: Part I of The Metaphysics of Morals*, tr. John Ladd. Indianapolis: Hackett Publishing.

Kuper, Andrew (2000) "Rawlsian Global Justice: Beyond the Law of Peoples to a Cosmopolitan Law of Persons," *Political Theory* 28(5): 640–74.

Laborde, Cécile, and Miriam Ronzoni (2016) "What Is a Free State? Republican Internationalism and Globalisation," *Political Studies* 64(2): 279–96.

List, Christian, and Philip Pettit (2011) *Group Agency: The Possibility, Design, and Status of Corporate Agents*. Oxford: Oxford University Press.

Macdonald, Terry (2008) *Global Stakeholder Democracy : Power and Representation beyond Liberal States: Power and Representation beyond Liberal States*. Oxford: Oxford University Press.

Mair, Peter (2009) *Representative versus Responsible Government*. Working Paper, http://cadmus.eui.eu/handle/1814/12533, accessed August 9, 2019.

Mair, Peter (2013) *Ruling the Void: The Hollowing of Western Democracy*. London: Verso.

March, James G., and Johan P. Olsen (2008) "Elaborating the 'New Institutionalism.'" In Sarah A. Binder, R. A. W. Rhodes, and Bert A. Rockman (eds.), *The Oxford Handbook of Political Institutions*. Oxford: Oxford Univ Press, 3–22.

Meckled-Garcia, Saladin (2008) "On the Very Idea of Cosmopolitan Justice: Constructivism and International Agency," *Journal of Political Philosophy* 16(3): 245–71.

Miller, David (1995) *On Nationality*. Oxford: Oxford University Press.

Miller, David (2007) *National Responsibility and Global Justice*. Oxford: Oxford University Press.

Miller, David (2010) "Against Global Democracy." In Kaith Breen and Shane O'Neill (eds.), *After the Nation: Critical Reflections on Post-Nationalism*. Basingstoke: Palgrave Macmillan, 141–60.

Morris, Christopher W. (2011) "The State." In George Klosko (ed.), *The Oxford Handbook of the History of Political Philosophy*. Oxford: Oxford University Press, 544–60.

Nagel, Thomas (2005) "The Problem of Global Justice," *Philosophy & Public Affairs* 33(2): 113–47.

Pogge, Thomas (1989) *Realizing Rawls*. Ithaca, NY: Cornell University Press.

Pogge, Thomas (1992) "Cosmopolitanism and Sovereignty,." *Ethics* 103(1): 48–75.

Rawls, John (1999a) *A Theory of Justice*. Oxford: Oxford University Press.

Rawls, John (1999b) *The Law of Peoples: With* "The Idea of Public Reason Revisited." Cambridge, MA: Harvard University Press.

Rawls, John (2013) *Political Liberalism*, expanded edn. New York: Columbia University Press.

Risse, Mathias (2006) "What to Say about the State." *Social Theory and Practice* 32(4): 671–98.

Risse, Mathias (2012) *On Global Justice*. Princeton, NJ: Princeton University Press.

Ronzoni, Miriam (2009) "The Global Order: A Case of Background Injustice? A Practice-Dependent Account," *Philosophy & Public Affairs* 37(3): 229–56.

Ronzoni, Miriam (2012) "Two Conceptions of State Sovereignty and Their Implications for Global Institutional Design," *Critical Review of International Social and Political Philosophy* 15(5): 573–91.

Sangiovanni, Andrea (2007) "Global Justice, Reciprocity, and the State," *Philosophy & Public Affairs* 35(1): 3–39.

Sangiovanni, Andrea (2013) "Solidarity in the European Union," *Oxford Journal of Legal Studies* 33(2): 213–41.

Sen, Amartya K. (1984) "The Right Not to Be Hungry." In P. Alston and K. Tomasevski (eds.), *The Right to Food*. Dordrecht: Martinus Nijhoff Publishers, 69–81.

Stilz, Anna (2009) *Liberal Loyalty: Freedom, Obligation, and the State*. Princeton, NJ: Princeton University Press.

Tuomela, Raimo (2013) *Social Ontology: Collective Intentionality and Group Agents*. Oxford: Oxford University Press.

Valentini, Laura (2011) *Justice in a Globalized World: A Normative Framework*. Oxford: Oxford University Press.

Valentini, Laura (forthcoming) "The Natural Duty of Justice in Nonideal Circumstances: On the Moral Demands of Institution Building and Reform," *European Journal of Political Theory*, https://journals.sagepub.com/doi/10.1177/1474885117742094, accessed August 9, 2019.

Weber, Max (1994 [1919]) "The Profession and Vocation of Politics." In Peter Lassman and Ronald Speirs (eds.), *Weber: Political Writings*. Cambridge: Cambridge University Press, 309–69.

Weiss, Linda (1998) *The Myth of the Powerless State*. Ithaca, NY: Cornell University Press.

Weiss, Linda (2003) *States in the Global Economy: Bringing Domestic Institutions Back In*. Cambridge: Cambridge University Press.

Wollner, Gabriel (2014) "Justice in Finance: The Normative Case for an International Financial Transaction Tax," *Journal of Political Philosophy* 22(4): 458–85.

Ypi, Lea (2012) *Global Justice and Avant-Garde Political Agency*. Oxford: Oxford University Press.

FURTHER READING

Abizadeh, Arash (2007) "Cooperation, Pervasive Impact, and Coercion: On the Scope (not Site) of Distributive Justice," *Philosophy & Public Affairs* 35(4): 318–58.

Barry, Christian, and Laura Valentini (2009) "Egalitarian Challenges to Global Egalitarianism: A Critique," *Review of International Studies* 35(3): 485–512.

Caney, Simon (2005) *Justice beyond Borders*. Oxford: Oxford University Press.

Laborde, Cécile, and Miriam Ronzoni (2016) "What Is a Free State? Republican Internationalism and Globalisation," *Political Studies* 64(2): 279–96.

Miller, David (2007) *National Responsibility and Global Justice*. Oxford: Oxford University Press.

....

CHAPTER 2

EQUALITY OF OPPORTUNITY AND GLOBAL JUSTICE

....

GILLIAN BROCK

1 INTRODUCTION

....

CONSIDER some facts about inequality in our contemporary world. The average annual income for a citizen of Malawi is US$320, whereas Japanese citizens enjoy annual incomes of approximately US$48,000.[1] A person born in Sierra Leone can expect to live about forty years whereas one born in Australia can expect to live for eighty years. Malaria has been almost entirely eradicated in high-income countries, but it still kills about a million people in developing countries every year (Brock 2012). Between 1975 and 1979 the average American completed more than fourteen years of schooling, whereas for the same period in Mali this was just two years.[2] A woman in the Niger has a 1 in 7 chance of dying in childbirth, whereas this is 1 in 11,000 for women in Canada (Benatar and Brock 2011).

On reviewing such facts it appears that a morally arbitrary fact about our birth is playing an enormous role in determining our prospects for good lives. Should we be troubled by this realization and, if so, should we embrace an ideal of global equality of opportunity? There is, after all, a deep conviction within liberal and social democracies that individual fellow citizens should enjoy equality of opportunity and so it might appear that the global extension would be required by consistency with this commitment. Before we are in a position to evaluate arguments for global equality of opportunity, two preliminaries are in order.

First, when applying the equality of opportunity ideal to the global context, should we aim to equalize opportunities among individual human beings or among societies? Taking the ideal to apply to societies, one might interpret it as requiring that all states ought to have something like (i) equal chances to benefit from international cooperation

(Loriaux 2008), (ii) equal opportunities for equal levels of economic growth or sustainable development (Kapstein 2006) or (iii) equal opportunities to be self-determining (Rawls 1999). By contrast, when the global ideal of equality of opportunity applies to individuals, it has largely been interpreted as one of providing equal opportunities to hold favored social positions and not being denied such options because of brute luck (such as the luck involved in being born into one society rather than another). By far the most attention in the literature on global equality of opportunity has been on how the ideal applies to individuals, so we focus on this version here, given its dominance and space constraints. Interestingly, as we come to see, the focus on individuals leads us to significant concern about reducing inequalities among societies as well.

Second, a distinction is often drawn between formal and fair equality of opportunity. Formal equality of opportunity is a fairly weak notion. It merely requires that competition for positions should be open to all applicants, but this might entail that certain groups are significantly disadvantaged in any such competition because of background conditions (such as the way poverty limits opportunities for advancement in life). By contrast, fair equality of opportunity requires much more to be done to rectify those background conditions so that a fair competition can ensue. Rawls's famous account of fair equality of opportunity aims to arrange background conditions such that each citizen who is equally talented and willing to make necessary efforts should have the same chance of being able to attain favored social positions (Rawls 1971). This more demanding conception has important implications for the distribution of resources and the structure of institutions within societies.

The ideal of fair equality of opportunity is widely endorsed as a central commitment within liberal democracies. The notion of fair equality of opportunity would seem to give good expression (at least partially) to fundamental orienting democratic ideas, such as respecting our freedom and equality. Given its domestic importance, the attempt to extend the ideal to the global sphere seems like an obvious move to make for those committed to our equal moral standing. After all, if ethnicity or religion would be an arbitrary factor in limiting people's life chances, surely the same applies to nationality? No one chooses where they are born; country of origin is just as arbitrary a fact about human beings as other facts about us over which we have no control. Surely if one is committed to domestic equality of opportunity, one should similarly embrace the global equality of opportunity ideal?

The extension to the global sphere faces many important challenges. As we see in this chapter, critics argue that equality of opportunity is more readily achievable at the domestic level because we have a reasonably reliable sense of which opportunities are the important ones to try to equalize. But once we apply the ideal globally, we note that there can be very different conceptions of valuable lives and favored social positions in different parts of the world. While the ideal might be a worthy one, there is some difficulty assessing whether equality between fairly different lives has been achieved and whether we are even equalizing for the correct categories of opportunities. The difficulties are particularly pronounced when we try to equalize for favored social positions, as the Rawlsian ideal recommends.

In Section 2 we discuss two important challenges for the ideal of global equality of opportunity which both arise in the context of considerable global cultural diversity. In Section 3 we discuss prominent attempts to defend global equality of opportunity. Simon Caney, for instance, argues that instead of trying to equalize for access to the same favored social positions we should rather aim to ensure that people have equal opportunities to attain social positions that enable equally valuable lives. We see that the resultant conception of equality of opportunity is weak on several fronts, despite attempts to introduce a transcultural assessment framework. In Section 4 we examine whether an account of global equality of opportunity sets provides a more robust approach. We examine David Miller's skeptical concerns about how the cross-cultural comparisons play out, in light of problems related to different cultural rankings and constructions of goods. According to Miller, in assessing whether opportunities are equal, our cultural understandings about *which* are the important opportunities plays a crucial role within societies. These shared understandings are unavailable at the global level, according to Miller.

While Miller offers some important skeptical concerns that deserve careful analysis, I also offer some important ways in which we can circumvent their main argumentative force and progress the debate. In Section 5 we discuss one noteworthy attempt to capture a comprehensive set of core ingredients for good lives which aims to be cross-culturally robust. In Section 6 I show that underlying our convictions about equality of opportunity lies a tangle of related intuitions that often get confused. We have a number of intuitions about when concern for inequality is important and why that is the case. We need to separate out some of these threads, in order to weave them back into a coherent account. When we do this, we note that our ideals and concerns related to global equality of opportunity are actually multifaceted. Addressing what concerns us will therefore require reforms in a number of important domains.

2 Two Obstacles Facing Accounts of Global Equality of Opportunity

On the Rawlsian account of equality of opportunity, each citizen should have the same chance of attaining a favored social position, given the same talents and willingness to try. There are at least two important challenges for this ideal, both pressed by Bernard Boxill (1987), which a robust ideal will need to confront and the leading accounts attempt to address. Both are explained next.

2.1 Which Favored Social Position?

Boxill argues that so long as different cultures exist, the principle of fair equality of opportunity can be, at best, only approximately realized. In some societies the most favored social positions will be occupied by people in business, such as finance, investment, and management. But:

> this is by no means always the case; in Hindu society it was occupied by the priest, in old China, by the learned man, and in other societies, by the soldier. For which of these standards are opportunities to be equalized? To choose one over the other seems invidious and presumptuous.   (Boxill 1987: 148)

2.2 The Ethos Problem

In response to the problem just noted, Boxill describes difficulties with taking some obvious paths. He says:

> Nor is it possible to get very far trying to make children of similar talent and drive in these different societies have similar prospects of reaching the standards of success in each society. First, there are the conceptual problems of devising criteria for the equality of prospects that are for radically different ends. And if these can be overcome, there are the practical problems. The bright girl in New York is inevitably going to have better prospects of becoming a businesswoman in New York than the equally bright boy in Hindu society; and he will have better prospects than she of becoming a priest in his society. This is only partly because the education needed to be a success in business in New York is different from, and probably incompatible with, the education needed to be a priest in Hindu society. Even if schools offering both educations existed in both societies, the ethos of each society would ensure that the inequality remained.   (Boxill 1987: 148–9)

Do Boxill's concerns present powerful objections? Leading proponents of equality of opportunity take them as important challenges and aim to address them. We examine how successful these attempts are in Section 3.

3 Two Prominent Attempts to Defend Global Equality of Opportunity

In articulating an account of equality of opportunity, we might use the following schema:

A has equal opportunity with B for C when D

where *A* and *B* are individual human beings, *C* is the target opportunity, and *D* is the account preferred by different theorists. The most prominent contemporary proponents of the global equality of opportunity ideal, Simon Caney and Darrel Moellendorf initially suggested that we should aim to equalize for favored social positions, so for much of this debate, *C* is taken to be "favorable social positions." On this Rawlsian view, regardless of country of origin, all human beings should have the same chance of attaining a favored social position, given the same talents and willingness to try. Various theorists offer different accounts of when *D* is satisfied. So, for instance, Simon Caney's position is that "global equality of opportunity requires that persons (of equal ability and motivation) have equal opportunities to attain an equal number of positions of a commensurate standard of living" (Caney 2001: 120).

In *Cosmopolitan Justice* Darrel Moellendorf argued that a principle of equality of opportunity should apply globally and on this account, as he famously expressed these ideas, "a child born in rural Mozambique would be statistically as likely to become an investment banker as the child of a Swiss banker" (Moellendorf 2002: 79). Moellendorf's initial account runs into at least the first of Boxill's concerns. Why think we should equalize for the positions favored in one society rather than another, so in this case, why think we should equalize for the social position of investment banking? It is too culturally specific and fails to appreciate a range of desirable favorable positions in different cultures.[3]

Does Simon Caney's account of global equality of opportunity fare any better in avoiding Boxill's first problem? Caney defends a global principle of equality of opportunity according to which it is unfair if some have worse opportunities than others because of their national or civic identity. Caney analyzes what equality of opportunity is in the domestic case and then, drawing on the prominent Rawlsian account already introduced, Caney argues for the global analog, which is that "persons should have the same opportunity to achieve a position, independently of what nation or state or class or religion or ethnic group they belong to" (Caney 2001: 114).

The positive argument for this view has much intuitive appeal. The same reasons that make equality of opportunity a normatively compelling ideal at the domestic level apply globally. So, if we object to people having worse opportunities than others because of their ethnic or religious affiliation, we should similarly object if people have worse opportunities than others because of their nationality or citizenship status. "The point can be expressed negatively: people should not be penalized because of the vagaries of happenstance, and their fortunes should not be set by factors like nationality or citizenship. Or, it can be expressed positively: people are entitled to the same opportunities as others" (Caney 2001: 115).

Caney aims to address Boxill's challenges through his particular carefully crafted account of what global equality of opportunity is. For him, "Global equality of opportunity requires that persons (of equal ability and motivation) have equal opportunities to attain an equal number of positions of a commensurate standard of living" (Caney 2001: 120).

Caney believes we can construct a fair metric for evaluating whether standards of living are commensurable via the capabilities approach. According to this approach we can specify important ingredients for a flourishing life by examining what humans are able to do and be. The list of capabilities he offers draws directly from one offered by

Martha Nussbaum (1992) in which capabilities are specified as (1) life, (2) health, (3) the avoidance of pain, (4) use of the five senses, (5) human relationships, (6) the deliberation about the pursuit of personal ideals, (7) relations of care for others, (8) access to the natural environment, (9) experiencing enjoyment, and (10) independence (Caney 2001: 121). Through this strategy Caney believes that it is therefore possible to construct a "transcultural metric by which to judge opportunities" (Caney 2001: 121).

How successful is Caney's attempt? The account Caney offers aims to evaluate whether standards of living are commensurate. However, using this as the fundamental gauge of whether equality of opportunity has been achieved leads to a weak account of equality of opportunity. We might, after all, have commensurate standards of living without opportunities being very equal within a society. In fact, opportunities might be highly structured and constrained by factors that we take to be important hallmarks of barriers to equality of opportunity, and yet Caney's account may not detect this, as I illustrate next.

Consider a particular set of options that Bob has in one society, which we stipulate structures roles along gender lines. He may become a witchdoctor, a storyteller, or a circus performer. Cheryl lives in the same society as Bob, and she may become a witchdoctor's wife, a storyteller's wife, or a circus performer's wife. Cheryl enjoys a commensurate standard of living with her husband, as cashed out by the relevant capabilities: for each of the capabilities, she enjoys the relevant capability to the same extent as her husband. And she has an equal number of positions open to her. Do women have equal opportunities to men in this example? I would argue they do not. In fact, as jobs are structured along gender lines, this would typically be taken as a classic indicator of inequality of opportunity. Similarly and by the same reasoning, Caney's account would be unable to detect inequality of opportunity in societies which assign jobs on racial or ethnic lines, or any other job-irrelevant attribute, as long as the jobs enable equivalent standards of living. So, while Caney may be assessing whether people have commensurate standards of living, his account cannot really successfully claim to be offering us a robust account of equality of opportunity, as we see with these examples. Opportunities that are structured along gender (or race, ethnicity, and so forth) lines would often be standard examples of inequality of opportunity. Yet these go undetected on Caney's account, so long as they result in commensurate standards of living.[4]

Recall the schema introduced earlier: *A* has equal opportunities with *B* for *C* when *D*, and in the cases we have been discussing, *C* is "favorable social positions." Trying to equalize for favorable social positions has a number of difficulties. As I explain first, it seems both too strong in some respects and too weak in others. Second, I summarize some epistemological and implementation difficulties with the ideal.

On the one hand aiming to equalize for favorable social positions seems very ambitious: what we are trying to achieve is to ensure that everyone of equal talent and motivation has the same chance of becoming, say, a CEO of an international financial corporation, an astronaut, or head of the World Health Organization, no matter whether they grow up in the slums of Kolkata, the Sahara Desert, or downtown Manhattan. On the other, it seems too weak: why just aim to equalize job opportunities rather than whole life packages (as it were)? Jobs are, after all, only one aspect of good human lives, even if, for many people, they are important parts of those lives.

Another concern with using opportunities for favored social positions as the goal arises over difficulties with assessing whether x and y have equal opportunities where there is fairly radical cross-cultural comparison to be made. Furthermore, positioning someone to be equally competitive for jobs requires training in a variety of areas, including so-called soft skills. (So the "ethos problem" that Boxill articulates becomes salient.) Immersion in various cultural environments inevitably advantages some in adequately honing skills necessary for certain jobs. But that same cultural immersion often precludes equal honing of other skills necessary for other positions valued in other societies. Compare, for instance, the soft skills needed to become a Hindu priest in India with those needed to be a good trader on Wall Street.

Both Caney and Moellendorf have refined their views since the pieces that are the focus of discussion in this section (and the revisions have been along the lines of the views discussed in Section 4), but since it was these early views that were so influential, tracing their strengths and weaknesses is important for a comprehensive understanding of the issues.[5] In this chapter one of my aims is to give the reader a sense of the relevant influential moves that have been made in this debate, roughly following the chronology of when they were made, so that we can usefully also build on these ideas in advancing discussion on global equality of opportunity. In the development of these ideas, David Miller's account was arguably the one that took the critical discussion forward after Moellendorf and Caney argued for their initial positions, and so we examine Miller's views in Section 4 below.

4 Equalizing for Opportunity Sets

Is a robust account of global equality of opportunity available if we aim to equalize for "opportunity sets" instead of "favorable social positions"? David Miller offers this promising option for us to consider, though he himself is quite skeptical about its prospects. According to Miller, a principle of global equality of opportunity would seem to require that people of similar talents and motivation should have equivalent life chances or opportunity sets irrespective of the society to which they happen to belong. When we try to apply this principle to the global level, Miller argues that we face several problems because (1) there is no common cultural understanding of what metric is to be used when trying to make cross-national comparisons of opportunity sets; and (2) different cultures value and rank opportunities differently. We can only make confident judgments in extreme cases, but in those cases we notice that it is actually concerns about absolute poverty or deprivation that are in play, rather than concern for equality as such.

Why are the cross-cultural comparisons so problematic, according to Miller? A worry arises about how "fine-grained" or "broad-grained" (to use Miller's terms) our comparisons should be. He introduces several cases to illustrate the problem. Consider the first one: "Suppose we have two relatively isolated villages, broadly similar in size and general composition. Suppose that village A has a football pitch but no tennis court, and village B has a tennis court and no football pitch. Do members of the two communities have equal opportunities or not?" (Miller 2005: 61). Most people would think that, in the relevant sense, they do have equal opportunities. If the category we are considering is "sporting facilities," then football pitches and tennis courts are different kinds of facilities that are instances of the broader category. The two communities are more or less equally endowed with respect to access to sporting opportunities.

Now consider the following case. Suppose that village C possesses a school but no church, and village D possesses a church but no school. Do people in these two villages enjoy equal opportunities? Miller reports:

> I think almost all of us would say that they do not. We think that the opportunities provided by a school and a church are just different, that if someone were to suggest a metric such as "access to enlightenment" in terms of which the two villages should be judged as equally endowed, this would just be a piece of sophistry.
>
> (Miller 2005: 61)

How are we able to judge that in the football pitch/tennis court case there is no significant inequality between A and B, whereas in the school/church case there is significant inequality? For Miller the answer is that we rely on cultural understandings about what sorts of opportunities are similar and naturally substitutable. Our cultural understandings suggest that a broader-grained metric such as "access to sporting facilities" is a better way of comparing opportunities when football pitches and tennis courts are at issue. And similarly, these culturally informed understandings suggest that we cannot use the same strategy when comparing access to schools and churches.

How do we figure out what equality of opportunity entails in the domestic case? According to Miller, we single out specific opportunities as significant such as personal security, education, healthcare, or mobility and regard these as non-substitutable. Our mobility opportunities might mean buses for some, trains for others, and these substitutions would be perfectly acceptable. We would, however, resist if it were suggested that poor healthcare facilities could be compensated by better educational opportunities, because, Miller argues, in our public culture education and health are considered to be different kinds of goods, and it is important for citizens to have equal opportunities for both. There are difficulties with a similar strategy at the global level, according to Miller, as we can no longer assume a common set of cultural understandings. There are at least two problems. There is the problem of comparing, when provision for a key opportunity takes different forms, how we judge whether these opportunities are better, worse, or the same. And, second, we have the problem of deciding whether it is appropriate to merge specific metrics into more general ones—whether we can aggregate opportunities to give an "all things considered" summary of opportunity sets. To illustrate, suppose, people in Iceland have better educational opportunities than people in Portugal, but that people in Portugal have better leisure opportunities than people in Iceland. Is it legitimate to say "that people in one of these places are better off (in a global sense) than people in the other" (Miller 2005: 63), or can we only say that, with respect to education Icelanders are better off, while with respect to leisure, the Portuguese are better off, and we can make no aggregative judgments? According to Miller, the problems are ones about what equality of opportunity means:

> in a culturally plural world in which different societies will construct goods in different ways and also rank them in different ways. The metric problem arises not just because it is hard to determine how much educational opportunity an average child has in society A, but because the meaning of education, and the way in which it relates to, or contrasts with, other goods will vary from place to place.
>
> (Miller 2005: 64)

Let us pause to consider the strength of Miller's challenges. What should we make of the central problem Miller raises about knowing when opportunities are equal, given difficulties associated with different cultural understandings about how broad-grained or fine-grained the categories should be? While all of Miller's observations are important and technically he is correct to observe that it is difficult to know in practice exactly when two opportunities are equal, one might argue that the importance of the problems he identifies is somewhat exaggerated, or at least there are ways to circumvent the concerns he raises. One workable way forward which preserves a large part of the original motivation for finding the ideal attractive might be to consider a list of goods or opportunities that all human beings can reasonably be expected to value. Perhaps coming up with a list that has transcultural authority is not as difficult as we might imagine if we adopt such an approach. Furthermore, while it is true that there are sometimes difficulties in assessing whether opportunities are equivalent in different societies, perhaps when people are still fairly far off some basic adequacy standard, scope for debate narrows radically, and the standard still constitutes something of a worthy aspiration which can inform policy. In Section 5 we explore these possibilities before returning to the more general issues of the normative desirability of an ideal of global equality of opportunity.

The aggregation issue that Miller raises also seems tractable. There is no need to assume that aggregation must occur. We could decide that the relevant C (from the schema introduced in Section 3) is not "opportunity sets" but rather each individual opportunity (for health, education, and so on), which should be taken by itself and compared with similar opportunities in other places. So we could reject aggregation as a goal and decide that what is important is to specify a number of goals that define significant aspects of human lives, and we should aim to equalize for those individually. On this strategy we could compile a list which consists of goals we can all be expected to have good reasons to value, and we compare opportunities by each category. We explore these and related issues further in Sections 5 and 6.

5 ONE POSSIBLE TRANSCULTURAL METRIC

Much like the Rawlsian notion of primary goods, which are versatile means no matter what one's ends, we can compile a list of goods people in all societies have reasons to value. Often it is thought such projects are problematically infected by liberal ideas. Can we find any transcultural standards that can be applied to all societies for evaluation purposes? There are a number of major institutions that aim to do just this, collecting comprehensive relevant data for various purposes, including assessing equality of opportunity. For instance, the United Nations Development Program has massive resources to collect relevant data to track progress on important goals and opportunities. But there are other interesting projects that deserve more visibility. Here I discuss the "Ibrahim Index of African Governance."[6] It has several noteworthy features. It enjoys widespread acceptance by citizens of African countries, which also comprise some of the most diverse and "burdened" peoples[7] in the world. The chief purpose of collecting this data is so that civil society in African countries can hold their own governments to account.[8] The comprehensive data collection exercise aims to help citizens gauge their government's progress (or lack thereof) in key areas that should be important to them on plausible accounts of what is needed to secure a decent life. Also, the project's data is actually being used, so it has the advantage of already being implemented. Fifty-seven criteria are grouped into four overarching categories: (1) Safety and the Rule of Law, (2) Participation and Human Rights, (3) Sustainable Economic Opportunity, and (4) Human Development. Though I do not have space to discuss all fifty-seven of these categories, I give a sketch of some relevant features from each of the four groups next, selecting only a sample for discussion. These goods conveniently already have well-developed metrics associated with measurement, so we see in practice how some of the concerns Miller raises can be treated. Here are some of the central categories:

  (i) Poverty and health: seven indicators measure factors such as child mortality, levels of immunization, and incidence of HIV and tuberculosis. Other indicators measure how supportive the welfare system is, how pro-poor policies are, and levels of social exclusion.
  (ii) Education: five indicators measure the general quality of education, for instance through looking at the ratio of pupils to teachers in primary schools, and the proportions of pupils completing primary school, progressing to secondary school, and entering higher education.
 (iii) Personal safety: includes levels of violent crime and social unrest, human trafficking, and domestic political persecution.
 (iv) Rights: includes eight indicators which measure respect for human rights in general, civil liberties, political and collective rights, freedom of expression and association, freedom of the press, and how well international human rights conventions are implemented.

(v) Gender: includes five indicators measuring gender equality, such as the ratio of girls to boys in primary and secondary education, the girls' rate of primary school completion, the proportion of women who are economically active, and the proportion of parliamentary seats that women hold.

(vi) Infrastructure: includes five indicators measuring aspects such as the reliability of the electricity supply, the number of computers, and the number of mobile telephones.

(vii) Economic management includes nine indicators, such as those aimed at evaluating quality of public administration and budget management, management of public debt, the inflation rate, the ratio of budget deficit or surplus to Gross Domestic Product, and the ratio of external debt service to exports.

(viii) Rule of law: includes evaluation of the strength of measures such as the judicial process and independence of the judiciary, time taken to settle contractual disputes, and the orderly transfer of power following changes in government.

(ix) Accountability and corruption: includes six indicators measuring transparency and the accountability of public officials; corruption among government and public officials; accountability, transparency, and corruption in rural areas; and the prosecution of abuse of office.

(x) Participation: there are five indicators used to measure political participation including ones that evaluate the strength of democracy, the level of electoral self-determination, and how free and fair elections are.

(xi) National security: includes seven indicators which measure domestic armed conflict; numbers of internally displaced persons and refugees from the country; levels of government involvement in armed conflict; death (whether military or civilian) that results from war; deaths due to targeted attacks on civilians; and levels of international tensions.

There are many worthwhile features of this index and how it is derived. The index itself has been produced in association with African academics and research organizations. There is much scope for feedback and further development of the index in light of critiques, puzzling data, further developments, theoretical refinements, and the like. Even if the index is not yet perfect, it certainly has in its favor comprehensiveness, significant input from people who hail from some of the poorest developing countries, and much local uptake. While there is certainly plenty more to say about the project of what should go into our transcultural metric for assessing whether individuals have the relevant opportunities for good lives, have them to the requisite degree, what the adequacy benchmarks for each criterion might be, and an abundance of philosophers' puzzles that can be generated about whether different situations are equivalent, this is one area where policy has shown that whatever the theoretical problems, we can find a way forward in working out how to implement reasonably reliable standards for measuring certain kinds of valuable opportunities in practice, at least if we want to capture data on a variety of measures strongly correlated with enjoying prospects for a decent life.

Using this Ibrahim Index as background, we can now reflect on an important question. Should we compare how particular countries perform relative to the list and a set of adequacy benchmarks or should we compare how countries perform relative to each other? There are important lessons to be learned from both kinds of comparisons and we see why in Section 6 below.

6 REFLECTIONS ON GLOBAL EQUALITY OF OPPORTUNITY: WHAT DO WE REALLY WANT?

Ideas about equality of opportunity have a powerful hold on us because they rely on a compelling intuition that it is unfair if some are significantly disadvantaged in life because of morally arbitrary features, so it is unfair if some have much worse prospects in life than others because of their race, ethnicity, class, and so on. If this would be unfair, what does fairness demand? It is commonly taken to involve a commitment to equality of opportunity. I argue that there are actually several driving intuitions and, putting them together, they recommend a more complex set of interconnected but distinct normative goals which I discuss in this section.

In fact, when philosophers and ordinary folk talk about equality of opportunity, they often have in mind very different ideals. Consider the following four claims as examples of some of the views that people are drawn to when they discuss matters of global equality of opportunity:

1) All human beings should have opportunities to live decent lives.
2) All human beings should have opportunities to live equally good lives.
3) All human beings deserve equal consideration of their interests and needs.
4) In competitions, equally endowed and motivated competitors should have equal chances of success.

Strictly speaking, in the first claim the concern is one of (bare) sufficiency—that people have enough for a decent life. In the second, the concern is to produce equally good lives, but this might mean very unequal opportunities, as some might need much more opportunities, resources, and attention than others to produce those equally good lives. In the third claim, the concern is not really with opportunities at all, but rather with equally considering people's interests, which might have implications for fair rather than strictly equal opportunities. And in the fourth claim the concern is with fair competition for scarce and valuable opportunities.

Let us review some of the intuitions that underlie our concern with equality of opportunity. We are often struck by radical inequality in a context where some have rich opportunities and others must suffer severe hardship (Frankfurt 1987). It is frequently the case that we misidentify our reasons for concern in such situations as involving a general concern with inequality. However, in such cases it is often really the importance of having enough and insufficiency that is doing much of the normative work. What troubles us is that some fall well short of a threshold of adequacy, while others are greatly beyond it. While some inequality should rightly command our normative attention, not all inequality should. We need not be troubled by inequalities between millionaires and billionaires, and the fact that they are both well beyond some threshold of having enough for a decent life operates as one important consideration explaining why attention to that inequality is unnecessary.

Furthermore, we need not be concerned with inequalities between millionaires and billionaires when fair procedures govern their abilities to pursue wealth. This leads us to a second important reason for concern with inequalities: they can frequently be traced to unfair processes that generate radically unequal outcomes. Another grounding intuition that does much work in getting us to see what is wrong with radical inequality of opportunity concerns the "rules of engagement," as we see when notions such as "level playing fields" and getting "a fair go" are frequently invoked. We have strong intuitions about fairness and have robust beliefs that people should enjoy fair terms when they engage in various social pursuits such as cooperation. Concern for fair terms of cooperation can constitute further grounds for appropriate attention to inequality and disadvantage.

So, to summarize the discussion so far, these two observations point in the direction of focusing on adequacy standards (in the first case) and procedures or rules governing human beings' prospects (in the second). But our exploration of the driving intuitions underlying concern with equality of opportunity is not yet complete, so let us proceed further with this inquiry. Consider the question: what value should we place on equality? Equality is not always some free-standing value which demands our allegiance come what may. Equality is not, all things considered, *always* intrinsically valuable, as the "levelling down" objection makes clear. Note that we can level down so that all have equal but very poor opportunities. That, I maintain, is not as desirable as a situation in which there is some inequality in opportunities but all have genuine opportunities for good lives and are well above (say) the average opportunity levels in high-income countries. So what is our concern with equality exactly? Underlying our concern here is a powerful and robust intuition, namely that equal respect for persons requires equal consideration of their interests. This matters especially in the design and operation of institutions, rules, practices, and procedures that shape significant interests and life prospects.

So a third intuition points in the direction of endorsing the following view: institutions should be arranged so that they realize equally the interests of all those living under them. I believe this is an important reason to be concerned with equality and one that underlies much of our driving egalitarian intuitions in this domain. On this view, the focus is largely on structures and institutions that can reliably underwrite opportunities, such as well-ordered institutions within societies and international institutions that are robustly committed to equal consideration of people's interests.

What would a robust commitment to equal consideration of interests require? First, it requires substantial concern with the initial and ongoing circumstances in which people find themselves. In considering these circumstances, we should aim to ensure that, in so far as this is under our control, we secure access to those ingredients that promote prospects for a good life. We might use the list approach introduced in Section 5 as a guide, and the idea might be that we compare, in the first instance, how each person in each society rates as measured *against the list*, with the aim being to try to secure a high threshold amount of each good. So our primary task here is to compare life prospects against a list of desirable goods, and then we could endeavor to secure for each person in each society a decent amount of the good listed (again, in so far as this is under our control).

However, the simple comparison with the list approach is too quick, because there is also an important role for looking at inequalities in how people fare with respect to items on the list both within and across societies. Attending to inequalities can be important for a number of reasons. First, looking at inequality can be important, as it gets us to consider whether improvements are possible and, if so, which. So, for instance, if some populations have life expectancy of eighty and others only enjoy average life spans of forty years, this suggests that there is some room for improving the situation of those with life expectancy of forty, or at least this view deserves further investigation. Recall that the intuition motivating the ideal is that it is unfair if some have much worse opportunities in life than others because of arbitrary factors. In the background of this intuition is also a conjunction of considerations: that the factors are socially controllable and that we ought to control them if we consider what all people are reasonably entitled to expect from others. A second important reason why we should be concerned with inequalities is that these can enable further advantages, especially competitive advantages. Large inequalities can result in the advantaged having more opportunities to entrench their advantage at others' expense. So inequalities, and how these can convert into further opportunities for advantage, are relevant to ongoing circumstances and whether they continue to sustain good lives.

Let us collect up some of the intuitions we have assembled so far. As noted, discussions about global equality of opportunity often start with examples of gross inequality such as those given in Section 1. What often strikes people as a grave injustice in this area is the observation of gross inequality—some enjoy so much, while others must make do with so little. Stark inequality can be especially morally troubling when we have the means to correct the situation of those who have so little and must suffer needlessly, it would seem. In the context of discussions about global equality of opportunity, it is frequently concern for gross insufficiency that does much work. More generally, if we add some of the other sets of concerns canvassed—inequality of circumstances and unfairness in cooperative terms which yields further inequalities—we have powerful reasons in play. Putting these further elements together, a plausible interpretation of the ideal that captures many of these intuitions is that each person should be able to live in a society that can provide resources, institutions, and opportunities central to the development and exercise of core capacities that are characteristic of a good human life, and that the institutional rules governing securing access to these elements should be fair ones. This more complex set of ideals requires several focal points for normative concern. Attention to those elements characteristically needed to secure good human lives is significant. Attending to inequality both within and across societies is also important first, because of the ways in which inequality can translate into deprivation for the disadvantaged, and second, because attention to inequality helps indicate what more is possible. Structures and institutions that can reliably underwrite key opportunities, such as well-ordered institutions within societies and international institutions that are robustly committed to equal consideration of people's interests, are also of normative import. This collection of thoughts suggests the following summary collates our concerns:

It is unfair if some do much worse than others in their life chances *at least* when all of the following four conditions are satisfied:[9]

   (i)   there are radical inequalities in people's starting positions
  (ii)   unfair procedures, institutional rules (and the like) govern their prospects
 (iii)   when we have ways to remedy these inequalities described in (i) or unfairnesses described in (ii)
 (iv)   and we have responsibilities to remedy (i) and/or (ii).

We do have responsibilities to attend to gross inequalities in people's starting positions and to ensure the rules governing institutions are fair, and I suggested these flow from various normative concerns, including the normative requirement that people's interests deserve equal consideration.[10]

So, summarizing and systematizing the interconnected views we have surrounding equality of opportunity, we see our intuitions point in the direction of a cluster of concerns, which also show how equality does and does not matter to the valuable ideal of promoting each individual human being's having good prospects for good lives. People should have good prospects in life irrespective of race, ethnicity, and so forth. This requires attention to people's initial and ongoing circumstances and "fair rules of the game." It is notable that on this view the opposite is not really achieved when opportunities are (merely) equal. The concern with equality is largely instrumental to achieving other, in some ways, more valuable goals, though examining inequality has a very important role to play both as an indicator of what is possible and as a measure of success. Inequality is also of concern because of the ways in which it creates obstacles for achieving good lives. What we want is really something more accurately described as high sufficiency, with fair procedures and institutions that give equal consideration to our interests.

Notes

1. Data from 2012 World Bank survey, http://data.worldbank.org/country.
2. World Bank Development Report (2006: 56), http://documents.worldbank.org/curated/en/435331468127174418/pdf/322040WorldoDevelopmentoReporto2006.pdf, accessed August 9, 2019.
3. It is important to note that Moellendorf has revised his account since this early version. According to Moellendorf's more recent work:

    Equality of opportunity in the global economic association, then, is directed toward ensuring that differences in initial condition [particularly socioeconomic condition] do not affect the opportunities of persons (of the morally relevant equal endowments) across a range of goods, including income, wealth, meaningful productive activity, leisure time, health, security, housing, education and basic liberties.   (2009: 307)

However, since it is the early account that is still much-cited and has considerable influence, the critiques are still apropos.

4. I present more detailed versions of these arguments in Brock (2009: ch. 4).
5. I do refer to some of that newer work in Brock (2009: 62–3, esp. n. 52). Importantly, in revising their accounts as they have, they are no longer aiming to equalize opportunities for desirable social positions, such as jobs. The newer goal seems more accurately described as focusing on opportunities for decent lives, including a plurality of goods— so the modified goal is an improvement and is the sort of project explored further in this chapter.
6. For more on this project, see their website, http://www.moibrahimfoundation.org/interact/, accessed August 9, 2019.
7. This is Rawls's terminology. See, for instance, Rawls (1999).
8. It is designed to reflect the nature of African governance, though I believe the criteria also have broad applicability to other regions of the world, and could usefully serve as a universal standard.
9. Though we do not need to take a stand on this, the unfairness also holds when either of (i) or (ii) and both of (iii) and (iv) obtain as well.
10. For further defense, see Brock (2009).

REFERENCES

Benatar, Solomon and Gillian Brock (2011) *Global Health and Global Health Ethics*. Cambridge: Cambridge University Press.

Boxill, Bernard (1987) "Global Equality of Opportunity," *Social Philosophy and Policy* 5: 143–68.

Brock, Gillian (2009) *Global Justice: A Cosmopolitan Account*. Oxford: Oxford University Press.

Brock, Gillian (2012) "Health Inequalities and Global Justice." In Patti Lenard and Christine Straehle (eds.), *Health Inequalities and Global Justice*. Edinburgh: Edinburgh University Press, 102–18.

Caney, Simon (2001) "Cosmopolitan Justice and Equalizing Opportunities," *Metaphilosophy* 32: 113–34.

Frankfurt, Harry (1987) "Equality as a Moral Ideal," *Ethics* 98: 21–43.

Kapstein, Ethan B. (2006) *Economic Justice: Toward a Level Playing Field in an Unfair World*. Princeton, NJ: Princeton University Press.

Loriaux, Sylvie (2008) "Global Equality of Opportunity: A Proposal," *Journal of International Relations and Development* 11: 1–28.

Miller, David (2005) "Against Global Egalitarianism," *Journal of Ethics* 9: 55–79.

Moellendorf, Darrel (2002) *Cosmopolitan Justice*. Boulder, CO: Westview Press.

Moellendorf, Darrel (2009) *Global Inequality Matters*. Houndsmills: Palgrave Macmillan.

Nussbaum, Martha C. (1992) "Human Functioning and Social Justice: In Defense of Aristotelian Essentialism," *Political Theory* 20: 202–46.

Rawls, John (1971) *A Theory of Justice*. Cambridge, MA: Harvard University Press.

Rawls, John (1999) *The Law of Peoples*. Cambridge, MA: Harvard University Press.

Further Reading

Brock, Gillian (2005) "Ideals, Egalitarianism and Cosmopolitan Justice," *Philosophical Forum* 36: 1–30.

Brock, Gillian (2009) "Concerns about Global Justice," *Journal of Global Ethics* 5(3): 269–80.

Caney, Simon (2007) "Justice, Borders and the Cosmopolitan Ideal: A Reply to Two Critics," *Journal of Global Ethics* 3: 267–74.

Loriaux, Sylvie (2012) "Fairness in International Economic Cooperation: Moving beyond Rawls's Duty of Assistance," *Critical Review of International Social and Political Philosophy* 15(1): 19–39.

Moellendorf, Darrel (2006) "Equality of Opportunity Globalized?" *The Canadian Journal of Law and Jurisprudence* 19 (2): 301–18.

CHAPTER 3

GLOBAL JUSTICE AND GLOBAL CITIZENSHIP

LUIS CABRERA

1 INTRODUCTION

ONE way in which the concept of global citizenship can be understood is as a means of giving clarity to individual duties in a framework of global justice or universal human rights. Citizenship, with its typically highly elaborated "legal dimension" of rights and duties, and its understanding of individuals as joined in community, sharing some collective aims and working toward their realization, offers a useful way to conceptualize the possible roles of individuals within current states in advancing justice beyond the state.

Critics, however, have long held that the idea of global citizenship is incoherent when there are no global political institutions within which it could actually be practiced. Citizenship, they say, is appropriately tied to existing states.[1] This chapter engages with these and related criticisms, arguing that the coherence of citizenship beyond the state depends in large part on the view adopted of citizenship's substance and corresponding theory of the state, or political institutions more broadly. It details an approach which views the primary purpose of political institutions as protecting individual rights and securing the discharge of corresponding duties. While such institutions remain mostly absent above the state in the current system, individuals may still assume citizen-like duties, or enact key aspects of a global citizenship, by working to help protect the rights of others who do not share their state citizenship. They also can support the development of institutions above the state capable of playing rights-protective and reinforcing roles, and do so in a frame of equal partnership in the global human community.

Such a developmental approach, while it cannot claim to identify ways in which individuals can formally "be" global citizens in the current global system, offers insight into how it is possible to enact meaningful practices of global citizenship.[2] This approach is assessed against some leading critiques. These include ones claiming that global citizenship cannot embody the reciprocity between individual citizens, or equal membership among them, that is at the core of the concept of citizenship. Both critiques, or more specifically the approaches to citizenship which lie behind them, are shown to have important developmental features. Domestic citizenship is defined in part according to practices that are acknowledged to be in need of further development. Such features, it is argued, weaken claims that global citizenship is incoherent, especially in the case of an institutionally developmental global citizenship.[3]

2 CITIZENSHIP

The focus here, consistent with that of the critiques, will be on democratic political citizenship. A theory or conception of democratic political citizenship will be taken to consist of at minimum the following elements:

1. The first element is an understanding of the **nature of the agents** acting as citizens. This includes whether they are individual citizens of a political system, nation states acting as "international citizens,"[4] etc. Also considered is the psychological nature of actors, e.g. in terms of the sorts of duties they can be expected to routinely assume.

2. The second element is the understanding of community, or **what binds citizens together** in political community. This could be a presumption of common political culture, national or ethnic culture, shared normative commitments, shared territory or governing institutions, or simply shared humanity or capacities for sentience.

3. The third element is the understanding of **rights** held by the citizen agents. These are typically presumed to include a range of civil, political, and social rights, or institutionally backed entitlements to protections, democratic participation, services, and opportunities. Specific rights guarantees may vary widely according to the understanding of the substance of citizenship in play.

4. The fourth element is the understanding of **duties** corresponding to those rights, and the emphases to be placed on duties relative to rights. It also includes an understanding of where lines are generally to be drawn between minimal enforceable duties, standard but non-enforceable duties of citizenship, and more demanding acts of "good citizenship."

5. The fifth element is the **substance of citizenship,** or the overarching good that citizenship practice is to realize, and toward which rights and duties are oriented. This could be some form of minimal rights provision, more comprehensive and robust rights guarantees, or some ideal of equality, reciprocity, enabling human flourishing, etc.

6. The final element is comprised of the **status and institutions** of citizenship. These are formal markers of standing to claim citizen rights which are backed and regulated by political institutions. They include birth certificates, passports and related trappings, or evidence of citizen membership and standing.

Significantly, separate elements often can be found at different stages of development within the same system or set of political institutions. For example, individuals may possess many of the trappings of citizenship without element three, citizen rights, actually being guaranteed. This could occur in a state that is highly fractious in its democratic practice, or especially in one which is under strain from endemic internal conflict, possibly approaching state failure.[5] Likewise, the trappings can be in one's possession even if one contributes very little in element four, duties of citizenship, towards realizing element five, the presumed substance of citizenship.

Most accounts of domestic citizenship go beyond the bare trappings to specify non-enforceable but standard duties oriented to realizing the substance of citizenship. These could be, for example, duties to observe reciprocity toward co-citizens.[6] Beyond those are non-obligatory "good citizen" acts, which may be more demanding or expose the agent to risk, but which may also be necessary to promote the realization of the substance.[7] That substance again will inform understandings of the role or moral purpose of the state, or other political institutions within which citizenship is practiced. For example, liberal conceptions of citizenship, as well as those not focused narrowly on liberty rights but on securing a more comprehensive set, will tend to work from a protective conception of the state. The coercion exercised by shared political institutions will be seen as justified primarily by their instrumental value as protectors and enablers of individual rights or justice: the presumed substance of citizenship.[8] Republican approaches have been typically more concerned with the state as enabler of human flourishing within a community of highly participatory citizens,[9] or enabler of individual freedom through political participation.[10]

Finally, we can note that element two, the understanding of community, will be crucial in determining whether a specific conception of citizenship might extend beyond the state. This element is concerned with what it is that ties co-citizens together, makes it possible for the substance of citizenship to be realized among them—and justifies excluding non-citizens from membership. If the answer to such questions is that only ties of nationality or shared national political culture can do the job,[11] then full citizenship must be confined to the nation. If it is existing ties of territory or political and communal practice, then citizenship is properly bounded by existing states. If the ties are, or plausibly could be, ones of shared normative commitments—to certain individual rights, democratic institutions, etc.—then the boundaries of citizenship should be more fluid and potentially much more extensive.

3 GLOBAL CITIZENSHIP

3.1 Ethical and Institutional Accounts

How, then, has citizenship of global extent been conceived? Diogenes the Cynic, the fourth-century BCE philosopher, is typically cited as the first to declare himself a citizen of the world and seek to challenge local mores from that vantage point.[12] The idea of individuals belonging to a global community, envisioning themselves as filling a role within it and taking some ethical guidance from it, is then traced through such Stoic thinkers as Cicero (106–43 BCE) and especially the Roman emperor-philosopher Marcus Aurelius (121–80 CE).[13] Later thinkers touched on some of the same themes, but arguably it is not until Immanuel Kant's political works of the 1780s and 1790s that we see a clear conception of global citizenship re-emerging. For Kant, individuals were to imagine themselves as co-legislators in a "kingdom of ends," subscribing to moral laws that all in the world should see as incumbent to follow.[14] He is not, however, typically understood to support the creation of some world state or similar institutional framework.[15]

From Kant, the thread can be followed perhaps most clearly, and in more institutionally ambitious form, through the various mid-twentieth-century authors who advocated forms of global citizenship under global government, especially in the aftermath of the nuclear bombing of Hiroshima and Nagasaki, Japan, by the United States in 1945.[16] More recently, the literature falls into two broad camps: those similarly focused on global institutional development, and those focused on identifying or promoting some modern ethic of global citizenship. The latter tend to give emphasis to the transformation of individual attitudes, and the former to transforming and creating the salient global institutions: ones in which the legal dimension of global citizenship would be specified and backed by relatively strongly empowered and democratic global institutions.[17]

Many global ethic accounts offer some form of rooted global citizenship. These hold that individuals should view themselves as citizens of states first, generally observing strong priority to compatriots in distributions of resources and opportunities. Duties to non-compatriots are seen as important but secondary, comprising mainly ones to pressure our own states to give due consideration to outsiders' interests in foreign policy actions. These conceptions are strongly influenced by theorists' understanding of the connective ties of citizen community, generally ones oriented to shared national sentiment. From such understandings flows a conception of state purpose, in particular for Parekh (2003) and Walzer (1983), focused on enabling forms of self-determination and self-expression for domestic (national) citizen communities.[18]

Other global ethic accounts would give far less emphasis to domestic belonging and more to actual or potential ties across borders between activists and other non-state actors. They seek, especially in Richard Falk's (2008) account, to identify ways in which such actors can join together across borders to counter some negative effects of global economic integration and promote more just outcomes generally.[19] Falk also has advocated the creation of a limited world parliamentary body to facilitate such efforts, though not a more fully integrated and strongly empowered set of global institutions in the near term.[20]

Those offering more fundamentally institutional accounts tend to be skeptical that the substance of global citizenship can be realized in the absence of strongly empowered global political institutions. The primary aim would be to make possible a concrete practice of global citizenship within suitably transformed or newly created trans-state and ultimately global institutions.[21] Other institutional accounts are not focused on extending citizenship per se, but on the possible importance of extending democratic participation beyond the nation state in a comprehensively integrated and strongly empowered set of global institutions.[22] Such an extension, however would have the effect also of extending a formalized practice of democratic citizenship, or in David Held's (2004 : 115) words, create an institutional context in which "the elusive and puzzling meaning of global citizenship becomes a little clearer."

I would also include here, contra Mason (2012: 205, n. 12), some recent accounts which focus on global justice rather than global citizenship per se, specifically those which recommend the creation of comprehensive sets of global institutions. They call for extensive global integration to secure more just outcomes globally.[23] Democratic institutions and practices would be features of such accounts, and thus a practice of world citizenship would be formally constituted.

3.2 A Rights-Protective Institutional Account of Global Citizenship

In this account of global citizenship, the presumed connective tie (element two), is a set of normative commitments to recognizing individual rights and corresponding duties. In detailing it, I have previously drawn on a primarily interest-based approach to identifying specific rights, where they are viewed as closely connected to the protection of vital human interests.[24] A rights-protective account could be compatible with a range of other rights foundations, however. Its rights emphasis arguably would go beyond a narrow focus on individual liberty that again many would put at the heart of liberal citizenship[25] to a much more comprehensive conception. This would likely include some robust equal opportunity rights, and some rights against unjust discrimination,[26] which in the global citizenship frame could be constituted as mobility rights across borders similar to those possessed by European Union citizens,[27] as well through South America's Mercosur and other organizations. Whatever the specific conception or comprehensive package of rights, however, the substance of global citizenship—the ultimate aim of the practice—would be reliable guarantees of rights protections for all persons. That substance again deeply informs an understanding of the overarching moral purpose of political institutions, and by extension the likely need for global ones to reliably secure even a moderately comprehensive set of rights for all persons.

It can be noted that, unlike in some accounts in the liberal citizenship tradition, including Locke's (1980), political community is not viewed here as a fully discretionary association. In Locke's account, individuals choose to join in political union and become co-citizens in order to themselves escape the potentially deadly inconveniences of the state of nature.[28] The rights-protective account would see the process as conditionally non-discretionary. It is non-discretionary because all are viewed as having a duty to contribute to rights protections, though it is a duty mediated by institutions. It is conditional because it is only if there is good reason to think that political institutions will advance rights protections, etc. that we have a duty to support their development.

Various "good reasons" to pursue global integration and institutional creation have been proposed. These have focused, for example, on the way a system of competitive sovereign states naturally throws up barriers to the comprehensive realization of rights,[29] or contributes to avoidable harms to the rights of especially the global poor.[30] I have given additional emphasis to ways in which a states system reinforces tendencies to give strong priority to domestic co-citizen insiders in provision, and to strongly discount the rights and interests of those perceived as outsiders.[31] Thus, if the ultimate aim is reliable rights coverage for all persons, full global political integration should be pursued.

Such an approach is presented here as an account of global citizenship, rather than one more narrowly focused on identifying individual duties of justice in a global frame,[32] in part because of the indispensability to it of element two: community. It would, for example, reject stringent "fair share" claims that an individual's duties to help protect the rights of others could be fully discharged in isolation from community by directly aiding some requisite number of persons.[33] Such uncoordinated, personalized protection may at times be the chief available option, as in situations where institutional authority has broken down. As a standard solution, however it would be highly likely to leave the rights of most persons precariously protected at best.[34] Thus, the underlying imperative to achieve and sustain comprehensive rights protection for all persons would be unmet. Ultimately, the creation of an actual democratic political community—and with it a concrete practice of global citizenship—is seen as crucial to realizing this presumed substance of a rights-protective account. Individual global citizens would be equal partners within such a community. They would have actionable rights to make claims on co-citizens and their shared institutions, and clear responsibilities toward co-citizens to make their own contributions. They also would have mechanisms of challenge and various concrete avenues of participation.

Yet such integration is far from being achieved. Some commentators, notably Robert Goodin (2013: 149–65), argue that an early-stage world government is emerging. He sees the current global system as having weakly developed but growing powers of political authority, military and revenue-raising capacity, analogous to a state such as the United States in its very early development. Such a process, however, must at least be many generations away from producing the sorts of global institutions discussed here, which would be able to reliably ensure rights coverage and duties compliance globally. How, then, can we speak of "global" citizenship in their absence? The answer I would offer is that, while it is not possible to *be* a global citizen in such a system—to claim the status and entitlements of citizenship within a concrete legal dimension—it is possible to enact important aspects of global citizenship by assuming some duties oriented toward realizing its substance. These include duties related to immediate rights protections, and also more developmental ones related to institutional transformation and creation.

The more fully elaborated claim is those seeking to enact key aspects of global citizenship will:

(a) reach across international boundaries, or internal boundaries of differential citizenship;
(b) to help secure those fundamental rights that would be protected if there were an appropriately rights-protective system of global institutions in place;
(c) and (in a more institutionally oriented vein) work to help put such a system in place.[35]

I will now consider a central critique of global citizenship, that it is an incoherent concept in the absence of some world state, before offering further details on the institutional approach and defending its coherence.

4 Critiques of Global Citizenship

I will begin by noting a critique separate from incoherence, that global citizenship is little more than repackaged Western, neocolonial normative imperialism, especially in its institutional variants.[36] Briefly, it can be noted in response that in the current global system, powerful, mostly Western states already exercise enormous influence in international relations, within intergovernmental organizations such as the World Trade Organization, International Monetary Fund, and United Nations Security Council, and elsewhere. The development of practices of global citizenship with more accountable and ultimately more democratic supra-state institutions can be seen as a potentially significant check on the power of such agents.[37] Further, there is nothing inherent to the concept of global citizenship per se which means it must be construed as focused on global "haves" reaching out to "have nots." Persons of relatively limited means in less-affluent countries can be seen to engage in myriad practices of global citizenship, including rendering aid to migrants, reaching out for international support to protect the rights of their own co-citizens, and in other ways.[38] I have discussed related issues around diversity and global or cosmopolitan citizenship in some detail elsewhere.[39]

Here I will focus on the most formidable recent incoherence critiques, in particular those offered by David Miller (2013a) and Andrew Mason (2012). Both develop potentially important challenges around the ultimate coherence of global citizenship, and by extension challenge the utility of global citizenship approaches for advancing understandings of individual duties in a global justice frame. Miller, for example, argues that the necessary conditions for concrete political citizenship, as opposed to the purely ethical or "philosophical" conceptions he identifies with global citizenship, include a shared acceptance of the legitimacy of rule and a practice of reciprocity among co-citizens. Legitimacy, or a willingness to accept binding decisions, is said to be the primary condition for a genuinely *political* relationship and citizenship. It is a circumstance in which individuals, "even if in other respects they are fierce rivals or competitors...should be willing, in general, to accept the decisions made by the authority as having normative force" (Miller 2013a: 232).

Reciprocity involves a further willingness by co-citizens to accept decisions that may go against their immediate interests, but with the background expectation that later decisions will be to their benefit.[40] In addition, observing reciprocity means that they should not press for outcomes that they know cannot be acceptable to other citizens. An understanding of such acceptability is said to involve forms of shared knowledge, where co-citizens must know enough about each other to know in advance which outcomes could not be accepted. It also is said to involve a form of trust, where co-citizens can expect one another "to act as citizens, that is to say be motivated to achieve whatever form of political agreement is appropriate to the particular relationship in question" (Miller 2013a: 233).

I discuss below Miller's further claim about necessary expectations about mutual advantage that obtain domestically but not globally. Here, it can be noted that he is offering *developmental ideals* of legitimacy and reciprocity. Consider that the legitimacy claim is presented as a conditional: co-citizens "should" be willing to accept binding collective decisions as authoritative. It is not claimed that they invariably accept such decisions, nor could it be.[41] Yet such acceptance is presented as a core definitional component of domestic citizenship. In terms of reciprocity, Miller has in fact acknowledged that much of the time it is in need of extensive development or inculcation by political institutions, which must take steps to "instill the ethos of citizenship in everyone who is formally admitted to...[citizen] status" (Miller 2000: 89). He cites France as an exemplar of such efforts, and a model preferable to ones which seek to allocate separate citizen status to diverse groups and would be unable to generate reciprocity and a genuinely shared public culture among them.

Thus, in Miller's account, some of the core definitional components of the concept of citizenship at the domestic level are framed as developmental even in some of the most consolidated democracies. Further, in states where democracy is only incompletely consolidated, as well as those situated toward the "failed states" end of the continuum, any such legitimacy and reciprocity claims must be far more tentative. The elements and institutions of citizenship are in need of extensive development. Miller also has highlighted elsewhere (2013b: 66–7) the extension of full citizen status to women in most societies, which itself can be understood as the development of relations of reciprocity with them by enfranchised men.

The overall implication is that Miller cannot so easily reject the coherence of global citizenship. He cannot categorically claim that a citizenship practice which is still under development cannot count as citizenship, given that he also defines domestic citizenship as a set of practices in development. The example of women gaining citizen status (element five) over time also has important implications for other possible extensions of citizenship. That is, men would have had to develop understandings of what would be acceptable (legitimate) outcomes to their new female co-citizens, and be willing to be constrained by the set of such outcomes. Such a requirement would entail significant efforts to *establish* relations of reciprocity among a broader set of persons through extending membership status to them, just as many global citizenship theorists aim to do beyond the state.[42]

Miller's second central claim is that a set of citizens is properly understood as those who are joined in a cooperative enterprise—one which is to their mutual advantage. This fact of shared enterprise is said to give aid rendered to co-citizens a public-spirited character, rather than simply a charitable one, as he says is the case with overseas aid (Miller 2013a: 233–4). Yet even if we presume that such a circumstance of mutual advantage for all co-citizens does obtain in current sets—a dubious claim when shirkers or other non-cooperators are considered—we are actually left with little justification for the present boundaries around those sets. Given that the boundaries of mutual advantage are simply presumed to coincide with the boundaries of current domestic citizen sets, we are effectively told that citizenship cannot be extended beyond the nation state because citizens are to be defined as those who share the same state. Such an argument cannot establish that it is not possible for mutual advantage boundaries to be so extended, or that the initial setting of boundaries was itself justifiable. Miller thus appears inadvertently to arrive at the position for which he critiques Hannah Arendt (1968): a plain stipulation that "A citizen is by definition a citizen among citizens in a country among countries" (Miller 2013a: 228).

Further, if we presume, as is implied in Miller's critique of global citizenship, that robust citizenship practice requires some strongly shared national identity,[43] then the limits of citizenship would be the limits of the *nation* state. Any strong such claim, however, would seem to face immediate challenges in the contexts of many multinational states; for example, India, whose constitution recognizes more than twenty official languages and where hundreds of millions of co-citizens do not share a common language with one another. More crucially perhaps, significant difficulties would arise in determining who "genuinely" belongs to a national community, and with determining who should determine genuine belonging, and determining the determiners of the determiners, and so on.[44] Thus, bounding a citizen community according to shared national sentiment or like criteria could be a non-starter.

In Mason's account, the presumed substance of citizenship is the good of equal membership, defined as "equal opportunity to participate on equal terms and treat each other as equals" (Mason 2012: 36). Mason (2012: 44) critiques Miller's (2000: 83) account as being in one sense too developmental: confusing what it means to be a citizen with what it means to take more demanding "good citizen" action. Those who are politically inactive might be described as bad citizens, he says; "yet they are surely citizens nonetheless" (Mason 2012: 43–4). Mason here is asserting that citizen status, and the definition of the concept of citizenship, is closely tied to its trappings. Yet his presentation of the equal membership conception of citizenship is also strongly developmental.

We can note, for example, that elements three and four, citizen rights and duties, are said in Mason's account to arise from the necessary conditions for securing equal membership, the presumed substance of citizenship. "To act as a citizen is to act in a way that is oriented towards this good. This includes acting in order to express or promote it…and acting to secure the conditions necessary for its realization" (Mason 2012: 36).

Definitionally then, the citizen is one who helps to develop the substance. Mason then adds that in *non-ideal circumstances*, meaning those where not all individuals comply with their duties, individuals can be good citizens "by striving to bring the good of equal membership fully into existence" (Mason 2012: 36). Both citizen actions and good-citizen actions thus involve duties to promote equal membership. In normal, non-ideal circumstances, and given the relatively demanding conception of political equality Mason sees as arising from the good of equal membership, it is likely that any particular society will require large numbers of those with citizen status to take on fairly stringent developmental duties. These would entail rejecting bad citizenship, developing in themselves capacities to fully recognize the equal membership of others, and helping to develop the same among their co-citizens. Mason thus also offers a developmental account of domestic citizenship. Any objection that global citizenship does not "count" because it is also developmental in some elements loses some force.

Mason offers two separate objections to extending citizenship comprehensively beyond state boundaries, and both deserve engagement. The first is based in the nature of citizenship itself, as analogous to the good of friendship. He notes that part of what it must mean to be a friend is to have special duties to another person. Part of what it means to be a citizen is also to have special duties to co-citizens—the duties are partially constitutive of the concept of citizenship. This analogy, however, will be of little help in showing that citizen sets must be confined to their existing state configurations. That is because individuals will be quite limited in the total number of those to whom they can discharge the presumed special duties of friendship. The limits of citizenship appear far more malleable. Existing citizen sets, after all, range in size from those of the micro-states of the South Pacific or Europe to behemoths such as those in India and China, each of which has more than 1.2 billion citizens. Three other countries have more than 200 million citizens, and a further seven more than 100 million. China, of course, remains a hierarchical, one-party state, and so does not fully fit the democratic citizenship frame—though its citizens do observe enforceable distributional and many other duties toward one another. India, with 1.2 billion citizens and counting, is a long-standing democracy with vigorously contested elections and a highly politically active citizenry, though it also has faced challenges specific to lower- and middle-income democracies. The narrow point here is that there does not seem to be an obvious numeric limit on the special duties that are partly constitutive of citizenship, in the same way as there would be on individual friendship.

At most, then, if we accept a claim that citizens by definition owe special duties to one another, all the friendship analogy can show is that, whoever your co-citizens happen to be, you owe them some special duties. It gives no reason by itself to think that co-citizen sets could not extend across multiple countries, for example, the more than two-dozen member states of the European Union, where formal regional citizenship was implemented with the Maastricht Treaty in 1993. EU citizens have rights of free movement across national boundaries, can vote in local elections in their host country, have regional ombuds rights, and portable non-discrimination rights in a range of subject areas.[45] Nor does it necessarily show that "special duties" in a conception of global citizenship could not be interpreted to include all humans, as distinct from duties to different species of animals; or indeed special duties owed to current humans, as possibly distinct from ones to future generations.

The second claim for limiting citizen membership is based in the nature of political coercion. Mason argues for bounding citizen sets, or the set of those who should have full citizen participation rights in democratic decisions, according to an "all actually subjected" principle. Such a principle would limit membership to those subjected to a common system of law, meaning that "most of the laws that comprise it are directed at her (or apply to her) and they are enforceable" (Mason 2012: 73). This principle, he argues, also appropriately defines the set of those who should have the opportunity to become citizens, while leaving due space to include in decision processes some who reside in other countries, if a domestically produced law would clearly apply to them.

Typically at the root of such all-subjected or "all-affected"[46] accounts for setting the bounds of democratic participation is some intrinsic good which whose realization is seen as limited by the coercion that political institutions can exercise in securing compliance with law. Often the good cited is autonomy: individuals are said to deserve a democratic say as a means of appropriately respecting and enabling their autonomy.[47] Mason's account would give greater emphasis to the intrinsic good of equality. Equal democratic input would be required to ensure appropriate respect for the equality of those subject to a system of shared law. In either case, the problem with offering such an approach as the answer to who should be included, or be given the opportunity to later be included, is again that it begs the question by answering "those who are included," or who already are subjected to law produced within a state.

Mason goes one step beyond Miller's "including of the already included" by extending participation to those from other states who clearly would be made subject to specific laws. But those extensions will themselves be deeply conditioned by existing inclusions—the agendas that will arise from them, the decisions that will be made.[48] As with Miller's account, this approach cannot show why those included in the first place *should* have been included. That is, it cannot provide an independent, non-circular justification for accepting historically contingent boundaries as appropriately demarcating citizen and future-citizen insiders from outsiders. Further, the underlying claims around limitations of freedom or equality by which such accounts ultimately justify the exclusion of outsiders are themselves suspect. In a rich, stable democracy, for example, subjection to politically authoritative coercion may not be so much a limitation on individuals as an enabling condition for enjoying the relative wealth and stability provided to them.

5 ENACTING PRACTICES OF GLOBAL CITIZENSHIP

Where does that leave us then, in terms of developing a fully coherent conception of global citizenship? I will reinforce first that the strength of an incoherence critique depends in part on the understanding of the substance of citizenship in play. If we were to adopt a stringently Aristotelian-republican understanding, for example, it would indeed seem incoherent to claim to be realizing the overarching good of citizenship by "ruling and being ruled" in a democratic global public sphere that does not yet exist. If the presumed substance of citizenship is securing reliable rights protections, however, then it is coherent to speak of working toward the realization of that substance in the current system, including by supporting the development of the salient political institutions.

It is the case that the rights-protective global citizenship account is more fundamentally developmental than the domestic conceptions of citizenship offered by Miller or Mason, because both the substance and institutions of global citizenship remain mostly to be realized. There is, of course, a nascent legal dimension of citizenship embodied in international law, in particular the major United Nations human rights covenants, but few individual entitlements are formalized at the global level.[49] Nor are there strongly empowered political institutions whose governance is informed by the presumed substance of citizenship. In the current system, there are primarily individual agents who can act to promote the realization of the substance of citizenship, and also act to avoid impeding it.

The situation of these agents, I will suggest, is importantly analogous to that of citizens of a fragile state, one again that can assert only incomplete coercive authority over portions of its territory—because of an insurgency, local warlords or criminal organizations exerting their own control.[50] In unstable regions of such states, the trappings of domestic citizenship may confer few claimable entitlements, and the state may have little capacity to ensure rights coverage or compliance with duties. In a meaningful sense, then, it is not possible to fully "be" a democratic citizen in such circumstances. Citizen duties would be institutionally developmental, aimed first at filling the gaps in rights coverage by helping to provide protections to others as and where possible. Standard duties in such a situation also could entail institutionally developmental ones to contribute to the construction or reconstruction of crucial political institutions. Those formerly able to act as co-citizens would seek to reconstitute the conditions under which domestic citizenship could actually be practiced, and through which its substance could be most effectively promoted.

An even closer analogy can be drawn between the duties and actions of those seeking to develop a concrete global citizenship and those who hold formal citizenship in nondemocratic states, or states in a process of transition to more democratic rule. Here also, it is not possible to "be" a democratic citizen. This is not because of the collapse of political institutions but because of the absence of key elements of democratic citizenship, including full participation rights and adequately protected civil rights. In such a situation, both the trappings and substance of democratic political citizenship are in need of development, and individuals seeking to become actual citizens must assume a range of developmental duties, including ones to transform existing institutions or create new democratic political institutions. In much the same vein, those enacting key aspects of global citizenship will contribute to rights protections for others, and to institutional creation and transformation, toward developing a global system in which a robust and concrete practice of global citizenship could be constituted.

In such a frame, three general categories of individual "global citizen" duties can be identified. These are interactive contributory duties, accommodation duties, and duties of institutional advocacy. Contributory duties include direct contributions of time, energy, and expertise to provide protections to others, generally those who do not share one's citizenship; as well as aid rendered across borders for disaster relief, development efforts, and rights promotion.[51] They also may include efforts to generate international support for domestic rights struggles. Accommodation duties, involving a willingness to accept the dislocations that would arise from more expansive distributive and immigration regimes in an institutionally integrating global system, are a cousin to toleration. They are distinct, however, in that they will be discharged with the understanding that all persons are coequal partners in the global human community, with equal standing to make claims.

Institutional advocacy duties can take several forms, including interstate advocacy duties, involving pressure on one's own state to promote global rights protections and support integrative transformation. These are structurally similar to the "rooted global citizenship" duties noted above, but would likely be more stringent and aimed at transforming states and the states system, rather than solely pressing states to engage in more ethical foreign policy behavior. Institutional duties also include ones of supra-state institutional advocacy, more directly focused on the transformation and deeper integration of global institutions, and the creation of new global political institutions as needed to promote a concrete practice of global citizenship.

Further, individuals may enact aspects of global citizenship through acts of global principled resistance, as when unauthorized migrants act as though they have a form of global-citizen mobility rights, crossing borders in search of economic and other opportunities. In doing so, they both violate and serve to challenge entry laws and the restrictive global immigration regime.[52] Others could be said to have negative duties not to impede such disobedience or evasion, and rather to support focusing attention on root causes of mass migration. There also could be more general duties not to impede existing projects of regional integration and global institutional development, and lend them critical support as appropriate.

Taken together, these duties, arising from a rights-protective conception of global citizenship, give some guidance for element four, the kinds of duties that those seeking to act as if they were global citizens could assume. The conception also offers specific understandings of connective ties in a global human community, of the overarching substance of a global citizenship practice, and the presumed moral purpose of political institutions that follows. Thus, it should represent a coherent approach to conceiving of global citizenship. It offers a vision of how we can put into practice some meaningful elements of this form of citizenship in the current system. It also gives guidance on developing a more formalized practice which could significantly advance comprehensive rights protections and global justice.

NOTES

1. Arendt (1968); Neff (1998: 105–19); Walzer (2002: 125–7); Bowden (2003: 352; Mason (2012: ch. 8); Miller (2013: 227–43); see also Brown (2000: 7–26).
2. I have previously presented the distinction as one between "being" a global citizen and "acting as" one: Cabrera (2010: 73). Mason (2012: 1–2) has objected that to act as a global citizen would be to actually assume a role that does not exist. I believe it was clear from the context that the sense implied was acting as if one were a global citizen in some important respects, but to avoid any such confusion I will not use the "act as" construction here.
3. Related critiques around the coherence of duties of global justice are engaged in Cabrera (2020: ch.6).
4. States are the presumed citizen agents in theories of good international citizenship. For a wide-ranging dialogue on states' possible ethical or moral duties, see Beardsworth, Brown, and Shapcott (2019).
5. See the Fragile States Index for rankings of states on a dozen indicators related to political, social, and economic stability: Fund for Peace (2019). Of the 178 countries assessed, 9 were ranked as severely unstable, in the Alert category, and 61 others in the Warning category. Another 53 were ranked Stable, and 28 as most stable, or Sustainable.
6. Miller (2013a).
7. Mason (2012: 36).
8. Locke (1980); see Buchanan (2004: chs. 2–3).
9. Aristotle (1984: esp. Book III).
10. Miller (2000); see Leydet (2019). For discussion, see Mason (2012: 42–7).
11. See Walzer (1983); Miller (2000).
12. Nussbaum (2002: 2–17); see Brown (2000).
13. Heater (1996: ch.1).
14. Kant (1999 [1785]: 41–6); see Nussbaum (2002: 8); see also Linklater (1998: 205–6); Kleingeld (1998: 72–90).
15. For an instructive discussion of how far Kant's work may support such extensive forms of global political integration, Pogge (2009: 196–208).
16. Baratta (2004).
17. See Dower (2002: 30–40); Cabrera (2010: ch.1); see also Oxley and Morris (2013: 301–25). They identify eight global citizenship approaches, including institutional or "political" global citizenship.
18. Appiah (2007: 2375–91); see also Walzer (1983: ch. 2); and see Parekh (2003: 3–17); Turner (2006: ch.1).
19. Falk (2008: ch.14); pace Brown (2000).
20. Falk and Strauss (2011); see also Archibugi (2008).
21. Linklater (1999: 35–59); Van den Anker (2002: 158–68); Cabrera (2010).
22. Held (2004); Marchetti (2008).
23. Caney (2005: ch.5); Pogge (2008); Ypi (2013: 75–91); Lu (2018: 232–52).
24. Cabrera (2010: ch. 2); Buchanan (2004); Caney (2005).
25. Schuck (2003: 131–44).
26. See Buchanan (2010: 679–710).
27. Cabrera (2010: ch.7).
28. Locke (1980: 65–7 (Sections 123–8)); see Buchanan (2004: 99).
29. Caney (2006: 725–56).

30. Pogge (2008).
31. Cabrera (2010: chs. 2–3; see also Cabrera (2020: ch.6) for a discussion of ways in which a sovereign states system is conducive to political arrogance and related collective vices which also contribute to rights underfulfillment.
32. See Stemplowska (2009: 466–87).
33. Simmons (2005: 187).
34. Caney (2005: 120–1); see Tan (2016: 19–31).
35. Cabrera (2010: 73–4).
36. See Bowden (2003: 355, 360); Parekh (2003); see also Jefferess (2008: 27–36.)
37. Held (2004); Archibugi (2008).
38. For some exemplar practices, see Cabrera (2010: chs. 5–6).
39. Cabrera (2020: esp. chs. 6, 8).
40. Cf. Brooks (2012: 21–35).
41. For insights on varying citizen perceptions of legitimacy and some determinants across eighty countries, see Magalhães (2014: 77–97).
42. See Cabrera (2020: ch.6) for further engagement with such disanalogy claims.
43. See especially Miller (2000: ch.2); for critical engagement, see Brock (2002: 211–24).
44. See Abizadeh (2012: 867–82).
45. See Carter (2001: ch. 6); Follesdal (2002: 71–83); Cabrera (2010: ch.7). Mason (2012: 194) briefly notes the European Union as a possible exception to his claim that there has as yet emerged no substantive practice of transnational citizenship. On the 2016 referendum vote by Britons to end their EU membership, see Cabrera (2020: ch.9).
46. Held (2004: ch.6); see Pogge (2008: 190–2).
47. See Abizadeh (2008: 121–30).
48. Goodin (2007: 40–68).
49. Though see Hernández-Truyol and Hawk (2004–5: 97–118). The authors offer an innovative proposal, based in emerging practices of dual citizenship, for a formal, treaty-based global citizenship designed to help individuals better claim the rights enshrined in international human rights treaties.
50. Fund for Peace (2019).
51. See Cabrera (2010: ch.4); see also Schattle (2008). Schattle offers numerous examples of others putting global citizenship principles into practice.
52. See Cabrera (2010: ch. 5); Ogunye (2015: 1–23); for more general discussions of institutionally oriented duties, see Cabrera (2020: ch.6).

References

Abizadeh, Arash (2008) "Democratic Legitimacy and State Coercion: A Reply to David Miller," *Political Theory* 38: 121–30.

Abizadeh, Arash (2012) "On the Demos and its Kin: Nationalism, Democracy, and the Boundary Problem," *American Political Science Review* 106: 867–82.

Appiah, Kwame Anthony (2007) "Global Citizenship," *Fordham Law Review* 75: 2375–91.

Archibugi, Daniele (2008) *The Global Commonwealth of Citizens: Toward Cosmopolitan Democracy.* Princeton, NJ: Princeton University Press.

Arendt, Hannah (1968) *Men in Dark Times.* New York: Harcourt Brace Jovanovich.

Aristotle (1984) *The Politics*, tr. Carnes Lord. Chicago: University of Chicago Press.

Baratta, Joseph P. (2004) *The Politics of World Federation,* Vol. 1: *The United Nations, U.N. Reform, Atomic Control.* Westport, CT: Praeger.

Beardsworth, Richard, Garrett Wallace Brown, and Richard Shapcott, (eds.) (2019) *The State and Cosmopolitan Responsibilities.* Oxford: Oxford University Press.

Bowden, Brett (2003) "The Perils of Global Citizenship," *Citizenship Studies,* 7: 349–62.

Brock, Gillian (2002) "World Citizenship: David Miller versus the New Cosmopolitans," *International Journal of Politics and Ethics* 2: 211–24.

Brooks, Thom (2012) "Reciprocity as Mutual Recognition," *The Good Society* 21: 21–35.

Brown, Chris (2000) "Cosmopolitanism, World Citizenship and Global Civil Society," *Critical Review of International Social and Political Philosophy* 3: 7–26.

Buchanan, Allen (2004) *Justice, Legitimacy, and Self-Determination: Moral Foundations for International Law.* Oxford: Oxford University Press.

Buchanan, Allen (2010) "The Egalitarianism of Human Rights," *Ethics* 120: 679–710.

Cabrera, Luis (2010) *The Practice of Global Citizenship.* Cambridge: Cambridge University Press.

Cabrera, Luis (2020) *The Humble Cosmopolitan: Rights, Diversity and Trans-State Democracy.* New York: Oxford University Press.

Caney, Simon (2005) *Justice Beyond Borders: A Global Political Theory.* Oxford: Oxford University Press.

Caney, Simon (2006) "Cosmopolitan Justice and Institutional Design: An Egalitarian Liberal Conception of Global Governance," *Social Theory and Practice* 32: 725–56.

Carter, April (2001) *The Political Theory of Global Citizenship.* London: Routledge.

Dower, Nigel (2002) "Global Citizenship: Yes or No?" In Nigel Dower and John Williams (eds.), *Global Citizenship: A Critical Introduction.* New York: Routledge, 30–40.

Falk, Richard (2008) *Achieving Human Rights.* New York: Routledge.

Falk Richard and Andrew Strauss (2011) *A Global Parliament: Essays and Articles.* Berlin: Committee for a Democratic UN.

Follesdal, Andreas (2002) "Citizenship: European and Global." In Nigel Dower and John Williams (eds.), *Global Citizenship: A Critical Reader.* Edinburgh: Edinburgh University Press, 2002, 71–83.

Fund for Peace (2019) "Fragile States Index", https://fragilestatesindex.org/, accessed August 10, 2019.

Goodin, Robert E. (2007) "Enfranchising All Affected Interests, and its Alternatives," *Philosophy & Public Affairs* 35: 40–68.

Goodin, Robert E. (2013) "World Government Is Here!" In Sigal R. Ben-Porath and Rogers M. Smith (eds.), *Varieties of Sovereignty and Citizenship.* Philadelphia, PA: University of Pennsylvania Press, 149–65.

Heater, Derek (1996) *World Citizenship and World Government: Cosmopolitan Ideas in the History of Western Political Thought.* New York: St. Martin's.

Held, David (2004) *Global Covenant: The Social Democratic Alternative to the Washington Consensus.* Cambridge: Polity Press.

Hernández-Truyol, Berta Esperanza and Matthew Hawk (2004–5) "Traveling the Boundaries of Statelessness: Global Passports and Citizenship," *Cleveland State Law Review* 52: 97–118.

Jefferess, David (2008) "Global Citizenship and the Cultural Politics of Benevolence," *Critical Literacy: Theories and Practices* 2(1): 27–36.

Kant, Immanuel (1999 [1785]) *Groundwork of the Metaphysics of Moral,* tr. Mary Gregor. Cambridge: Cambridge University Press.

Kleingeld, Pauline (1998) "Kant's Cosmopolitan Law: World Citizenship for a Global Order," *Kantian Review* 2: 72–90.

Leydet, Dominique (2011) "Citizenship." In *Stanford Encyclopedia of Philosophy*, ed. Edward N. Zalta, http://plato.stanford.edu/archives/spr2014/entries/citizenship/, accessed May 1, 2019.

Linklater, Andrew (1998) *The Transformation of Political Community*. Cambridge: Cambridge University Press.

Linklater, Andrew (1999)"Cosmopolitan Citizenship." In Kimberly Hutchings and Roland Dannreuther (eds.), *Cosmopolitan Citizenship*. Houndmills: Macmillan, 35–59.

Locke, John (1980) *Second Treatise of Government*, ed. C.B. Macpherson. Indianapolis, IN: Hackett.

Lu, Catherine (2018) "Cosmopolitan Justice, Democracy, and the World State." In Luis Cabrera (ed.), *Institutional Cosmopolitanism*. New York: Oxford University Press, 232–52.

Magalhães, Pedro C. (2014) "Government Effectiveness and Support for Democracy," *European Journal of Political Research* 53(1): 77–97.

Marchetti, Raffaele (2008) *Global Democracy, For and Against: Ethical Theory, Institutional Design, and Social Struggles*. London: Routledge.

Mason, Andrew (2012) *Living Together as Equals: The Demands of Citizenship*. Oxford: Oxford University Press.

Miller, David (2000) *Citizenship and National Identity*. Cambridge: Polity Press.

Miller, David (2013a) "The Idea of Global Citizenship." In Sigal R. Ben-Porath and Rogers M. Smith (eds.), *Varieties of Sovereignty and Citizenship*. Philadelphia, PA: University of Pennsylvania Press, 227–43.

Miller, David (2013b) *Justice for Earthlings: Essays in Political Philosophy*. Cambridge: Cambridge University Press.

Neff, Stephen C. (1998) "International Law and the Critique of Cosmopolitan Citizenship." In Kimberly Hutchings and Roland Dannreuther (eds.), *Cosmopolitan Citizenship*. London: Macmillan, 105–19.

Nussbaum, Martha (2002) "Patriotism and Cosmopolitanism." In Joshua Cohen (ed.), *For Love of Country: Debating the Limits of Patriotism*. Boston, MA: Beacon Press.

Ogunye, Temi (2015) "Global Justice and Transnational Civil Disobedience," *Ethics & Global Politics* 8(1): 1–23.

Oxley, Laura and Paul Morris (2013) "Global Citizenship: A Typology for Distinguishing its Multiple Conceptions," *British Journal of Education Studies* 61: 301–25.

Parekh, Bhikhu (2003) "Cosmopolitanism and Global Citizenship," *Review of International Studies* 29: 3–17.

Pogge, Thomas (2008) *World Poverty and Human Rights: Cosmopolitan Responsibilities and Reforms*, 2nd edn. Cambridge: Polity Press.

Pogge, Thomas (2009) "Kant's Vision of a Just World Order." In Thomas Hill (ed.), *The Blackwell Guide to Kant's Ethics*. Oxford: Blackwell, 196–208.

Schattle, Hans (2008) *The Practices of Global Citizenship*. Lanham, MD: Rowman & Littlefield.

Schuck, Peter H. (2003) "Liberal Citizenship." In Engin F. Isin and Bryan S. Turner (eds.), *Handbook of Citizenship Studies*. Thousand Oaks, CA: Sage, 131–44.

Simmons, A. John (2005) "The Duty to Obey and Our Natural Moral Duties." In Christopher Heath Wellman and A. John Simmons, *Is There a Duty to Obey the Law?* Cambridge: Cambridge University Press, 93–196.

Stemplowska, Zofia (2009) "On the Real World Duties Imposed on Us by Human Rights," *Journal of Social Philosophy* 40: 466–87.

Tan, Kok-Chor (2016) "Does Global Justice Require More Than Just Global Institutions?" *De Ethica. A Journal of Philosophical, Theological and Applied Ethics* 3(1): 19–31.

Turner, Bryan (2006) *Vulnerability and Human Rights*. State College, PA: Penn State University Press.

Van den Anker, Christien (2002) "Global Justice, Global Institutions, and Global Citizenship." In Nigel Dower and John Williams (eds.), *Global Citizenship: A Critical Introduction*. New York: Routledge, 158–68.

Walzer, Michael (1983) *Spheres of Justice: A Defense of Pluralism and Equality*. New York: Basic Books.

Walzer, Michael (2002) "Spheres of Affection." In Joshua Cohen (ed.), *For Love of Country: Debating the Limits of Patriotism*. Boston, MA: Beacon Press, 125–7.

Ypi, Lea (2013) "Cosmopolitanism without If and without But." In Gillian Brock (ed.), *Cosmopolitanism versus Non-Cosmopolitanism: Critiques, Defenses, Reconceptualizations*. Oxford: Oxford University Press, 75–91.

FURTHER READING

Bashir, Hassan, and Phillip W. Gray (eds.) (2015) *Deconstructing Global Citizenship: Political, Cultural, and Ethical Perspectives*. Lanham, MD: Lexington.

Bauböck, Rainer (ed.) (2019) *Debating European Citizenship*. Dordrecht: Springer.

Benhabib, Seyla (2004) *The Rights of Others: Aliens, Residents, and Citizens*. Cambridge: Cambridge University Press.

Isin, Engin F. (2012) *Citizens without Frontiers*. New York: Bloomsbury.

O'Byrne, Darren J. (2003) *The Dimensions of Global Citizenship: Political Identity beyond the Nation-State*. London: Frank Cass.

Sharma, Namrata (2018) *Value-Creating Global Citizenship Education: Engaging Gandhi, Makiguchi, and Ikeda as Examples*. Basingstoke: Palgrave Pivot.

Tully, James (2014) "On Global Citizenship: Reply to Interlocutors," in *On Global Citizenship: James Tully in Dialogue*. London: Bloomsbury, 269–328.

CHAPTER 4

ON THE CORE OF DISTRIBUTIVE EGALITARIANISM

Towards a Two-Level Account

JÁNOS KIS

1 INTRODUCTION

THIS chapter addresses two questions and the way they are connected. First, egalitarians on distributive justice believe that the foundational moral idea of equal moral status of persons has distributive implications: but how do those implications derive from it? Is the core of distributive egalitarianism derivable from equal moral status directly, without reference to social and economic relations mediated by institutions, or does the inference not hold unless the relevant institutional assumptions obtain? The second question translates the first into one regarding the scope of the core of distributive egalitarianism: Is it limited to individuals who stand in special relations with one another? Or does it rather cut across institutional boundaries to apply to any two persons wherever they should live and whether or not they are related to one another by special institutional ties?

For a start, let me clarify what I mean by distributive egalitarianism and its core. Distributive egalitarianism is a member of a family of theories that take distributions to have independent moral significance: it holds that distributive inequalities of a certain kind are unjust whether or not they are produced by unjust action; by the same token, they are unjust whether or not they result in unjust social relations.

The claim that distributions have independent moral significance does not logically entail the further claim that justice requires equal distribution. One can hold, without getting involved in a contradiction, that distributive justice matters, and that the egalitarian conception of distributive justice is mistaken. Some philosophers argue, for example, that a distribution is just if and only if it leaves no one without the means of a minimally decent human life. To be sure, transfers to the needy reduce inequality. But the reduction of inequality is a mere side effect of the action, not its aim. Justice in the sense of everyone having the means of a minimally decent human life permits redistribution to stop once everyone's position is raised to the threshold of an adequate minimum. For egalitarians, on the other hand, inequality itself is morally suspect. It is unjust not to try to correct distributions disallowed by the requirement of equal shares on some conception of it, even if the worse-off have access to an adequate minimum.

"Equal shares" is an abstract concept. Egalitarians disagree on the thing of which persons should have an equal share: is it equal division of the fruits of social production or rather equality of opportunity; if the latter, should equality of opportunity mean equal life prospects for the equally talented or equal life prospects for all; is the proper standard of equal shares welfare, access to advantage, capabilities, social primary goods, or resources, and so on. These questions are to be decided when it comes to specifying the content of equal shares. At its basic level, the theory proposed in this chapter is neutral towards the competing egalitarian conceptions.

The demands of distributive egalitarianism are not exhausted by the requirement that a baseline of equal shares is met. People are involved in social cooperation, and egalitarianism has its word on the distributive aspects of the cooperative practices. But justice requires that the baseline of equal shares is met before it comes to assessing the outcomes and/or the procedures of cooperation. By the core of distributive egalitarianism, I understand the theory of that baseline.[1]

Distributive egalitarianism is a controversial view in need of justification. Its advocates agree that it traces back to the idea that human persons have an equal moral status. But how does it derive from that idea? On this question, egalitarians are divided between two broad conceptions.

The first insists that the principle of equal shares does not bind individuals generally but only if they are related to one another via a certain type of institution. The advocates of this view need not deny the obvious fact that many of the goods individuals pursue lend themselves to a definition independent of institution-based relations and that the principle of equal shares assesses the distribution of such institution-independent goods. But they argue that the principle in question does not come into play unless the relevant institution-mediated relations obtain: people have a claim against one another that they have equal shares in the divisible institution-independent goods if and only if they are tied by such relations to one another. According to their view, the principle of equal shares follows from equal moral status indirectly, as a requirement triggered by the way people are related to each other in society. I will call this the *institutional account* of distributive egalitarianism.[2]

Other egalitarians take a radically different position. They insist that a principle of equal shares derives from the principle of equal moral status without the mediation of institutional relations. On this view, certain distributive requirements belong to the general moral duties individuals owe to one another whether or not they are connected by any special relations. The core of distributive egalitarianism is, for them, a direct implication of the preinstitutional foundations of human morality. It will be fitting to call this type of theory *non-institutional*.[3]

The contrast between the institutional and non-institutional accounts comes with a corollary, and this brings us to the second question of this chapter. The two accounts define the scope of the principle of equal shares differently. For the institutional account, it is determined by the extension of the relevant social relations: two persons owe each other duties defined by the principle of equal shares if and only if they are related in the appropriate way. Advocates of the non-institutional account for their part seem to think that the duties defined by the principle of equal shares hold between any two beings who bear the moral status of persons (see Richards 1982; Caney 2005; Valentini 2011). This chapter will argue for the second view—with a slight qualification. For the principle of equal shares to hold between two individuals, their interests must compete for the same scarce resources, and this condition does not obtain just in virtue of them possessing equal moral status (think of Parfit's Divided World, where there is no movement of people or goods between two continents: Parfit 2000: 87). Even with this qualification, however, the non-institutional account defines the scope of the principle of equal shares in a way markedly different from the definition provided by its institutional rival, and the difference has consequences for how they draw the boundaries within which the principle holds.

Rawls, for example, famously held that the basic structure is coextensive with the jurisdiction of a nation state (Rawls 1999a: 331–2, 1999b: 30–4). He has not made it fully clear why this should be so, but some of his followers, Dworkin and Nagel in particular, offered a detailed explanation. Whatever else it should contain, the basic structure certainly contains the institution of a legal system backed by the power of a coercive organization. True, states are not alone in making valid law; resolutions of the Security Council are global law; decisions of the European Court of Human Rights are law (of sorts) for the member states of the Council of Europe. But as the destiny of many such resolutions and decisions make us painfully aware, only territorial states have coercive power to enforce the law, whether domestic or international. If so, and if the coercive nature of the basic structure is essential for the triggering of the core requirement of equal shares, then it seems obvious that the boundaries of territorial states determine the scope of distributive egalitarianism. Call this version of the institutional account, following Nagel, the *political conception*.[4]

As to the non-institutional account, it is clearly hospitable to the idea that at least some basic egalitarian principles apply across state boundaries and have global force. This account is a natural home for cosmopolitanism on distributive egalitarianism.

To be sure, the institutional account is not barred from accommodating the cosmopolitan idea. Some Rawlsians argue against Rawls that the rise of a global economy led to the emergence of a global basic structure, and so the scope of the principles of justice is now global as well. The coercive powers that maintain the institutions of global economy remain fragmented, to be sure. But the idea of a unified basic structure backed by a plurality of coercive powers, each effectively claiming monopoly over its territory, is not an impossible idea, nor does it rest on a confusion (see Beitz 1979, 1999; Pogge 1989, 1994; Buchanan 2000, 2004).

However, the global basic structure claim is deeply contentious among Rawlsians, and the conceptual tools necessary for settling the disagreement seem to be deficient. Rawls deliberately kept the concept of the basic structure underspecified, and this makes it virtually impossible to find evidence compelling for all to decide whether what can be called the global basic structure is sufficiently close to the domestic basic structure in order to be subjected to the same principles of justice.

The global basic structure conception has a further weakness that it shares with the domestic versions of the institutional conception. As this chapter will try to show, the institutionalist account cannot deliver any principle of egalitarian justice if it does not rely on some such principle (abstract as it may be) as part of its preinstitutional moral foundations. If domestic basic structures cannot generate a principle of egalitarian justice for domestic societies, then neither can the putative global basic structure for the global society. A liberal egalitarian theory of global justice cannot do without a distinctly moral, preinstitutional principle of equal shares.

The non-institutional account is not plagued by difficulties of this type. It argues straightforwardly and without ambiguities for the global scope claim (under the now realistic assumption of a Non-Divided World). For cosmopolitans, this should count in favor of the non-institutional account. So much is not sufficient to accept that account, however. It must prove to be an accurate account of how the conception of equal shares follows from the idea of equal moral status of humans. This chapter will argue that it is not fully accurate.

The core conception of distributive egalitarianism must deliver two things. Clearly, it must establish a principle of equal shares. But this is not enough. In order to gain determinate content, the idea of equal shares must be complemented by an account of what should be divided into equal shares, and what is the proper standard for the equality of shares of that thing. Implicit in both views is the claim that they have sufficient resources to solve the two tasks by themselves alone. In this sense, they are *simple views*. This chapter will argue that no simple view can resolve the two tasks simultaneously. The institutional approach does not have sufficient resources to deal with the first task (Section 2). The non-institutional account is capable of solving the first task (Section 3), but it cannot properly handle the second (Section 4). So my argument will be gesturing towards a *complex view*. More specifically, the account I want to defend is not just complex because its two parts are not on the same level. It is non-institutional at the basic level, where the principle of equal shares is introduced and defended. It mobilizes the conceptual tools of an institutional theory at the next level, where the thing to be divided into equal shares and the standard of the equality of shares will be identified.

The two-level view might strike the reader as seeking a middle way between its simple rivals with respect to the question of the scope of the basic principle of equal shares. I will try to show that this impression is misleading: the two-level view defines the scope of that principle at the basic level, where a merely non-institutional argument is located (Section 5). So if it has better chances of succeeding as a theory of distributive egalitarianism, then it gives additional support to the cosmopolitan position.

2 Purely Institutional?

There is a variety of institutional conceptions of distributive egalitarianism. In this section, I will focus on the outlines of the most sophisticated one, proposed by Thomas Nagel (2005). If the most sophisticated conception fails, it does not follow that, a fortiori, all the other conceptions fail as well. But I will try to show, towards the end of this section, that the objections to Nagel's version are not specific to it: they affect the general structure of the institutional view.

Nagel's paper takes part in two debates. Against non-institutional accounts it argues that "[s]ocioeconomic justice…is fully associative" (Nagel 2005: 127). Against the claims of global justice it argues that the scope of distributive egalitarianism is state-bound. The two arguments are two facets of one and the same argument: Nagel's main claim on both fronts is that the principles of distributive egalitarianism are generated by the way states engage their subjects to cooperate in enforcing their law. Here, I will focus on the first of Nagel's claims; Section 5 will briefly address the second.

As a *liberal* egalitarian, Nagel believes that not all inequalities ought to be eliminated or reduced. Some kinds of inequalities are morally justified. Others lack any moral ground. Inequalities of the latter kind are, as Rawls puts it, "arbitrary from a moral point of view" (Rawls 1999a: 63). For Rawls and his followers, the paradigm of a morally arbitrary inequality is when two individuals have unequal life prospects "just because of a difference between the two of them…over which neither of them had any control" (Nagel 2005: 128). Sheer luck is not a morally acceptable justification for having unequal life prospects.

For some liberal egalitarians, the fact that an inequality originates with morally arbitrary sources is a sufficient reason for trying to eliminate or reduce it. Nagel agrees that moral arbitrariness is a condition for an inequality to call for a change. But he does not think it is a sufficient condition. Like Rawls, he believes that, in itself, a morally arbitrary inequality is neither just nor unjust. The absence of justification does not make it *ipso facto* morally objectionable: it does not entail the positive claim that it is unjust. If an inequality is justified, that is a reason *against* eliminating or reducing it. If it is not justified, that is not a reason *for* eliminating or reducing it. What the appeal to moral arbitrariness of an unequal distribution does is merely to draw attention to the fact that there are no moral reasons *against* changing it. Some further consideration must provide the reason for changing it (Freeman 2007: 120–1).

The missing necessary condition obtains, Nagel argues, when the better-off and the worse-off stand in a relationship to which the principle of *equal concern* applies. Some egalitarians agree but they believe that "we owe [equal concern] in principle to all our fellow human beings" (Nagel 2005: 119) in virtue of "the universal moral relation in which we stand to all persons" (Nagel 2005: 131), whether or not we are connected to them by shared social institutions. According to Nagel, however, equal concern is a principle specific to the relationship between individuals so connected. He agrees with Rawls that "the objection to arbitrary inequalities gets a foothold only because of the societal context" (Nagel 2005: 128).

In his view, the "minimal human morality" is exhausted by the duties from basic human morality" is exhausted by the duties from basic human rights and a duty of humanitarian assistance (Nagel 2005: 131). In our world, where so many "fellow human beings [are] threatened with starvation or malnutrition and early death from easily preventable diseases," humanitarian assistance is the really "urgent issue," and Nagel concedes that the problem of egalitarian justice is "morally less urgent" (Nagel 2005: 118). At the same time, the latter is "philosophically more difficult," at least for those liberal egalitarians who think that there is "no universal pressure towards equal concern" (Nagel 2005: 125).

What kinds of institutional relations are capable of generating principles of egalitarian justice? According to Rawls, morally arbitrary inequalities are changed from merely lacking justification into being positively unjust when they enter as inputs in the workings of an institutional system (a basic structure) that distributes advantages and disadvantages among the participants. Cooperation under such a system is subject to the principle of fairness, and to the extent that the system permits the initial arbitrary inequalities to improperly influence the resulting inequalities, the latter count as unfair and so morally arbitrary of the objectionable kind. In Nagel's succinct summary, "To the extent that such factors, through the operation of a particular social system, generate differences in people's expectations, at birth, of better or worse lives, they present a problem for the justification of that system" (Nagel 2005: 127).

Up to this point, Nagel agrees with Rawls. But he seems to think that even this much is not sufficient to generate principles of egalitarian justice. For he continues the argument by focusing on a property of the requisite social institutions that is mentioned by Rawls without attributing to it special significance for his argument. "What is objectionable," he says, "is that we should be fellow participants in a collective enterprise of coercively imposed legal and political institutions that generates such arbitrary inequalities" (Nagel 2005: 128).

The further necessary condition "comes," Nagel insists, "from a special involvement of agency or the will" (Nagel 2005: 128). The appeal to the "involvement of the will" strikes many as murky, but I think the reconstruction of Nagel's argument can clarify it.

The state claims monopoly of force within its territory. So the individuals whose interactions are regulated by the basic structure of their society are subject to a system of coercive institutions. Their subjection is involuntary: they are not asked for their consent (Nagel 2005: 128). But a state that wants to be legitimate does not stop at de facto using force against people who have not chosen to submit to its rule. It claims a *right* to enforce the law. And it cannot be truly legitimate unless this claim is correct. But if it is correct, then its subjects are *morally required* to accept the use of force against them (as long, of course, as it is exercised in accordance with and within the limits of the principles of justice). Furthermore, a state that wants to be legitimate claims a right that its laws are obeyed as a matter of *obligation*. And it cannot be truly legitimate unless this claim too is correct. But if it is correct, then its subjects have a reason to comply with the law, a reason that is different from the one supplied by the threat of force, and consists in a moral obligation. Finally, a state that wants to be legitimate claims a right to make law in the name of the same people whom it subjects to coercive threats.[5] And it cannot be truly legitimate unless this claim is correct as well. But, again, if that claim is correct, then its subjects are morally required to accept part-authorship of the law that is imposed on them. As Nagel puts it, the people living on the territory of a state "are both putative joint authors of the coercively imposed system, and subject to its norms" (Nagel 2005: 128).

Thus, a state is either not legitimate, or if it is, then the "agency or the will" of its subjects gets "involved": they are made responsible for its acts, even though they are subjected to its rule involuntarily. By obeying the law out of a sense of obligation, they incur responsibility for its enforcement. By accepting part-authorship of the law, they incur responsibility for its content. In this way, they become co-responsible for the arbitrary inequalities reproduced by the institutions of their society, and they "therefore have standing to ask why [they] should accept" those inequalities (Nagel 2005: 129).

Nagel does not makes explicit why he believes these further steps must be added to the Rawlsian argument, but I think the reason must be that, in his view, the participants in the social processes regulated by the basic structure are not subject to a duty of fairness (the central duty of Rawls's theory) unless they owe a duty of equal concern to each other, and, according to him, it is precisely "the involvement of agency or the will" that generates a duty of equal concern for them. This is why he insists that the principle of equal concern is a distinctly *political* principle and calls his version of the conception of egalitarian justice *political conception*. By obeying the duty to cooperate with their state (if it is legitimate) in the imposition of its legal system, citizens incur responsibility *towards each other* for the reproduction of morally arbitrary inequalities. Any two randomly selected citizens are mutually accountable for their willing participation in the process. They have a standing to ask for justification *from each other*—and at the same time they bear a duty to give justification to each other—for their part in the process and in its outcomes. Since what they are required to justify to each other is their willing cooperation with their state's making and enforcing the legal framework of their society, their conduct is not justifiable unless the law and the way it shapes the distribution of advantages and disadvantages are justifiable too. What this implies for the justification that the state owes to its subjects is that it must enable them to justify their compliance to each other. In other words, the state and its law cannot be justifiable unless they admit a justification that makes the compliant conduct of the subjects mutually justifiable.

Since the citizens are in a symmetrical position, each of them being entitled to hold the other accountable and at the same time being accountable to the other, and since they cannot justify their conduct but on the basis of the same justification that confers legitimacy on their common state and its law, that justification must make sure that they are treated by the state and the law with equal concern. And, to the extent that their actions carry out their obligations as part-authors and part-enforcers of the law (rather than consisting in the pursuit of their private aims within the bounds of those obligations), they incur a duty of equal concern to one another.

The state and the law, however, do not treat an individual with equal concern if they regulate the processes of social interaction so that her initial morally arbitrary disadvantage is translated into an outcome of unmitigated disadvantage in her life prospects.

Hence the requirements of egalitarian (distributive) justice. The inequalities from morally arbitrary factors are to be eliminated or reduced if and only if they are generated though the intervention of a state and its legal system and the "involvement of agency and the will" of their subjects.

The argument as reconstructed here raises many questions, but the crucial question is the one raised by this last step: the one from equal concern to egalitarian justice. Is it really the case that the principle of equal concern implies a requirement of eliminating or reducing the morally arbitrary inequalities for which social interactions regulated by political institutions are responsible?

There seem to be good reasons to doubt this. Ronald Dworkin, in a passage quoted by Nagel at length, describes equal concern as "an objective, impartial *attitude*" that a political community owes to all its members (Dworkin 2000: 6). Attitudes, however, are not about distributions. They are about the way agents are disposed to treat one another. Whether the outcome will conform to an egalitarian distributive pattern is a separate and independent question.

To be sure, the principle of equal concern does not amount to a descriptive statement on the psychological attitudes persons hold towards other persons; it is a normative statement on what kind of attitudes they ought to hold towards them. Equal concern as a normative principle includes a variety of standards. Some of these are obviously internal to the requisite attitudes. It is a requirement of equal concern, for example, that the agent manifests equal care in considering the claims, needs, desires, and aspirations of the persons whom he is supposed to treat with equal concern, or that he takes reasonable efforts to confront and overcome his spontaneous biases and socially acquired prejudices against them. Other standards of equal concern, however, are not internal to the attitudes of the agent but external to them: they specify objective features of the treatment owed the persons who are within the scope of the agent's deliberations and decisions.

Suppose, for example, that the treatment owed to those persons is subject to a duty that the state respects their freedom of conscience. Suppose two citizens claim a right to object to military service under this freedom, one giving religious grounds for his objections, the other giving secular moral reasons. And suppose the first citizen's claim is granted, while the claim of the second is rejected. Whether the second has a justified complaint of equal concern will depend on what is the correct theory of freedom of conscience as applied to refusal of military service. If the theory on the basis of which the exemption given to the religious objector and denied to the non-religious one is correct, the complaint is not justified. It is justified, however, if that theory is mistaken. But the correct theory is not one about the attitudes of the decision-makers. It cannot be deduced from the principle of equal concern: it sets independent standards for the decision, and the content of equal concern is not fully specified in this particular context without a reference to that theory. No matter how much care the decision-maker should manifest in deliberating on the issue, if his theory is mistaken, he will not treat the non-religious person's claim of conscientious objection with equal concern.

A similar conclusion holds for the issue of distributive egalitarianism. Suppose the correct theory regarding the distributive claims of citizens is libertarian. Libertarianism is a member of the family of egalitarian conceptions of human moral status. It insists that persons are bearers of equal (negative) rights, and any distribution is just if it arises from another just distribution by just steps, any step being just if it does not violate some-body's rights (Nozick 1973: 171). If the libertarian theory is true, then equal concern does not require that the state treat its subjects in accordance with principles of distributive—let alone egalitarian distributive—justice.

Suppose now that the correct theory entails, besides the libertarian rights, a positive right to the means necessary to satisfy one's basic needs. Then, the justice of socially pro-duced distributions will not exclusively depend on the justice of the steps through which it was achieved but also on whether each person's basic needs are satisfied. This is an independent distributive concern: each person must have enough for fully satisfying their basic needs, and the costs of raising the needy to this level must be absorbed by those better off. Like the libertarian concern for equal negative rights, the concern for the basic needs of all is motivated by an egalitarian view of what persons are owed simply in virtue of their moral status. But, as a distributive concern, it is not egalitarian. Egalitarianism condemns distributions as unjust in virtue of the fact that someone whose moral status is equal to that of someone else is worse off *than* her equal, regardless of whether she is below the basic needs threshold.[6]

Egalitarian principles are comparative: they assess the relative positions of different individuals (the liberal egalitarian principle assesses their relative positions with respect to morally arbitrary advantages). The basic needs principle is not comparative. Whether a person has enough does not depend on whether she has less or more than another. Furthermore, the basic needs principle admits of a threshold (Frankfurt 1987).[7] Once a person meets the threshold (once she has enough), further improvements in her posi-tion are beyond the concern of the basic needs principle. Egalitarian principles are not affected by the basic needs threshold. They hold both below and above it (Casal 2007).

If the correct theory is informed by a basic needs principle and no other distributive principle, then states are not required by equal concern to satisfy any egalitarian principle of distributive justice.

The upshot is that equal concern is either combined with independent standards of egalitarian justice, in which case individuals who end up disadvantaged in ways those standards condemn as unjust have a justified complaint of equal concern against their state and the law upheld by it or, in the absence of egalitarian standards, the complaint is not justified. Equal concern takes for granted the standards of egalitarian justice (provided they are part of the correct theory)—it cannot generate them.

If equal concern fails as a source of a principle disqualifying socially reproduced arbi-trary inequalities, we may have a try with the original Rawlsian theory, in the hope that Rawls's fairness principle proves more successful. After all, when individuals cooperate with each other, the standards of fairness do not apply exclusively to the way they carry out their transactions: they apply, too, directly to the resulting distributions.

This hope seems unfounded. The principle of fairness is as incomplete as the principle of equal concern. By itself alone, it does not specify the standards against which particu-lar distributions should be assessed for their fairness. Depending on what independent theory of distributive justice is the correct one, different distributive outcomes will prove to be fair, and the same distributive outcome may be judged fair under one theory and unfair under another. If the libertarian theory is true, then all distributive outcomes produced by acts, none of which violated anybody's negative rights, are fair, and none is fair that is produced by rights violations committed down the road.[8] If the correct theory is that of basic needs, then any distributive outcome where each person has enough to fully satisfy their basic needs is fair, irrespective of the inequalities above that level, and no distributive outcome is fair where at least one person is left incapable of satisfying her basic needs (provided that the costs for others are not prohibitively high). Only if the correct theory is egalitarian will the principle of fairness require some kind of an equal distribution.

Some interpreters of Rawls focus, in their attempt at justifying distributive egalitarianism, on his conception of reciprocity instead of his conception of fairness (see, for example, Sangiovanni 2007). But the reciprocity-based accounts (or any other institutional account, for that matter) are doomed to fail no less than the accounts based on equal concern or fairness, and for the same reason. The above argument does not hinge on any particular features of the principle of equal concern or that of fairness. It is based on a general feature of the theoretical venture under discussion. Liberal egalitarians committed to the institutional account believe that the preinstitutional human morality does not include any principles of egalitarian justice, and yet they want to uphold egalitarian distributive claims against libertarians and conservatives when it comes to assessing contemporary societies. This puts them in front of a dilemma. They either try to deduce new normative principles from mere statements of fact (on human coexistence under the rule of a state), a logically impossible venture, running against Hume's law, or they try to deduce those principles from a combination of the relevant statements of fact and distributively non-egalitarian prepolitical moral principles, another impossible venture. No matter how complex the account of the institutions and practices egalitarian liberals should provide, no single egalitarian distributive principle will be squeezed out from the distributively non-egalitarian background principles. Liberal egalitarianism is in need of some preinstitutional moral principle of distributive equality. Perhaps a very basic and very vague principle might suffice, but some such principle is absolutely needed.

3 NON-INSTITUTIONAL FOUNDATIONS

The aim of this section is to show that, in fact, there is a basic principle of equal shares and that it derives from a principle of equal moral status without the intervention of any institutional considerations.[9]

What does it mean for a being to have a moral status? As agents, we have a variety of reasons to give attention to the interests of others when we decide what to do. Prudence might recommend us to take a sacrifice for the sake of benefiting someone else if we can expect the recipient to reciprocate, and if the expected indirect gain from reciprocation equals or exceeds the direct loss. Or the recipient might be someone—for example, our child—whose good is part of our own good, in which case giving up some self-regarding advantage is not really a sacrifice.

But suppose no such self-regarding benefits, direct or indirect, justify the sacrifice taken for the sake of another being. Even then, we might be required to give some weight to that being's interests. One reason why its interests might matter for our decision is that it has a moral status. For a being to have a moral status means for it to have a claim that its interests are given consideration in the absence of any non-moral reasons that would count in their favor.

Human persons are not the only beings having a moral status. For example, we are not the only sentient beings, and all sentient beings have interests worthy of moral attention. But humans have higher-order interests. They have a capacity to step back from their perceptions and desires, and to examine whether they provide true reasons for action. They have a capacity to look at their life as a whole, and to assess it in terms of the reasons they find genuine. They have the capacity to lead their life according to their own lights; a capacity to integrate their short-term plans into plans for the long run, to pursue their life plan and to revise it at critical junctures of their career, and so on. This capacity is a ground for a special interest: an interest in making something of their life, something they can identify with as their own achievement. They have an interest in leading their life in accordance with their own conception of what makes their life good for them. The distinctive moral status of humans insists that this higher-order interest is of great importance. The claim of moral importance entails that each individual has special and non-delegable authority over what they should believe and how they should lead their lives: an authority that others must respect. But it entails more. To the extent that persons are the authors of their life, how well that life is going is a matter of their own responsibility. But persons are only part-authors of their life. It is desirable that their part in determining the shape of their life is as large as possible. But it cannot be complete. We have not chosen to be born to become choosers. Our conscious lives start out from unchosen circumstances, and they are affected, down the road, by many contingent events we cannot choose to avoid. Our life chances are, to some extent, determined by factors for which we are not in a position to assume responsibility. These are the factors that Rawls called morally arbitrary. They determine the range of options available to an individual before she has done anything yet, and they interfere with the shaping of her options in the course of her conscious life.

Any two individuals' claim to ultimate authority and to a rich option set is of equal moral importance. To put it in a different way, the interests related to the capacity of persons to make something of their life matter morally. And in so far as they matter just in virtue of their moral status as persons, they matter equally.

Now, equal moral status is not a distributive principle. It does not divide the distinctive moral status of human persons into equal shares, each person's share becoming smaller and smaller with the increase in the number of persons possessing it. My having a full human moral status does not depend on the number of persons with a similar claim to full moral status. And yet the distinctive moral status of human persons is intricately connected to distributive considerations.

I have written above that it matters for each person that they have a rich array of options to choose from. The option set available to an individual depends, however, on the resources at her disposal: on her "personal resources," i.e. her inborn talents, and the resources external to her—economic assets, social networks, cultural goods, educational opportunities, etc. Call this the *resource-dependence assumption*.

Add the resource-dependence assumption to the principle of equal moral status. If it matters morally that human persons have adequate opportunities to set and achieve meaningful short-term and long-term aims, and if they cannot achieve meaningful aims without an adequate stock of resources, then it matters morally that they have access to an adequate stock of resources. And if it matters equally that they have adequate opportunities to set and achieve meaningful aims, then it matters equally that they have access to those resources. The principle of equal moral status and the resource-dependence assumption together imply a principle of *equal moral claims to resources*.

This principle takes us one step closer to a conception of distributive egalitarianism, but it stops short of getting at that conception. Having an *equal claim* to resources is not logically equivalent to having *a claim to an equal share* in the available resources. To see why not, imagine a world where each individual has unlimited access to the resources necessary for fully achieving their aims, simultaneously with everybody else having unlimited access to the means needed to fully achieve theirs. On such an assumption, there are no trade-offs between one individual achieving her aims and another individual achieving his. One person's claims need not be balanced against another's. The question of distributive justice is not raised. The egalitarian claim is meaningless.

In our world, however, many resources are scarce: they are exhausted before all the concerned individuals would achieve all their aims. When a resource is scarce, and an individual gets hold of some amount of it, he thereby reduces the amount remaining for others to use. Trade-offs and balancing between conflicting claims become unavoidable. These are the situations to which principles of distributive justice apply. Those principles set the standards against which the conflicts should be adjudicated. Since we are dealing with access to resources to the extent that it is morally arbitrary, none has any special claim to the available resources. Yet even under such conditions, each person has, in virtue of their moral status, a justified claim to a part of them. Each person's life matters and, since each person's life depends on resources, it matters that each person has access to resources. Each person's life matters equally, and so it matters equally that each person has a share in the total stock of resources. Scarcity raises the problem of distributive justice and transforms the equal claim to a share into a claim to an equal share. Equal moral status, via the principle of equal moral claim to resources and combined with the *scarcity assumption* yields a principle of *equal shares* as a basic principle of distributive justice.[10]

Suppose a distribution is morally arbitrary. Moral arbitrariness does not make it *ipso facto* unjust. It is not a reason for changing it. But it registers the absence of any reason against changing it (Scheffler 2006). So let a morally arbitrary distribution be unequal.

Then, the principle of equal shares provides a reason for eliminating the inequality, and that reason does not meet any resistance from a countervailing reason. Now let a distribution due to brute luck, a morally arbitrary factor, be equal. Although it is produced by morally arbitrary factors, it is not morally arbitrary all things considered. The principle of equal shares provides it with moral justification.[11]

The above inference rests on a tacit assumption. To make that assumption explicit, consider Derek Parfit's Divided World scenario, mentioned in Section 1 (Parfit 2000). Parfit asks us to imagine the two halves of the world population to be separated by an ocean that has not yet been crossed, the two subpopulations being unaware of each other's existence. His aim is to test the intuition that inequality is *bad* in itself. If it is bad in itself, then it is bad if it holds between the two subpopulations in Divided World, even as the worse-off are unaware of the existence of the better-off. Our question here is not whether inequality is bad. We rather ask whether it is *unjust* to leave it as it is.[12] So we can drop the assumption that the two subpopulations are unaware of one another's existence. For our aims, it is sufficient that given the distance between the two continents and the technical means of maritime communication, neither people nor goods can travel from one part of the world to the other. Call the modified case Two Continents. Inasmuch as the inhabitants of the poorer continent can learn that their circumstances reflect bad luck rather than the general necessities of nature, they have a reason for deploring their misfortune, and this makes the intercontinental inequality bad. Does it also make it unjust? The principle of equal shares insists that the better-off have a collective duty to eliminate or reduce the unjust inequality. But taking the "ought implies can" principle for granted, the claim of a duty presupposes that the duty-bearer can act as required. By assumption, there is no way in Two Continents to reduce the inequalities across the ocean. So even if the combined resources of the two continents were to run out before each human person had achieved all their aims, the principle of equal shares would still not apply across populations separated by the ocean. For it to apply, a further assumption must obtain: that of the transferability of resources. The assumption of scarcity transforms the equal claims principle into a principle of equal shares provided that the *transferability assumption* holds too.[13]

Scarce goods that are also transferable within a given population are objects of competing claims within that population. My having some piece of scarce resource under my exclusive control is a benefit to me and a cost (an opportunity cost) to others to whom it is possible to transfer it, and so I am morally answerable to them for having it under my exclusive control. And if the argument presented above is correct, then— to the extent that my holding a piece of scarce resource originates with morally arbitrary factors—my having it cannot be justified unless it is endorsed by the principle of equal shares.

The principle of equal shares is a pure moral principle. Scarcity is a relation between the total stock of the available resources and the totality of individual aims. It generates competition between the interests of different individuals, but that competition does not consist in an institutional social relation. It belongs to the background circumstances under which institution-building and the formation of social relations proceed.

The principle of equal shares derives from the principle of equal moral status without the intervention of any institutional premise that would restrict its hold over individuals united by social relations of a certain kind. At the basic level where the principle of equal shares is established, the non-institutional account is vindicated.

For an illustration, consider Two Valleys. Two parts of a population inhabit two valleys separated by a steeply rising mountain that completely blocks the movement of persons and physical goods. No economic cooperation—division of labor, specialization, and exchange—is possible across the mountain. So far, Two Valleys is like Two Continents in all the relevant respects. However, below the mountain a water pool stretches from one valley to the other, and it is the only source of water on which the two subpopulations can draw. Although there is no cooperation across the mountain, and the water pool does not allow contact, the two subpopulations are, let us suppose, aware of each other's existence as well as of their dependence on the shared water pool. They know that there is a maximum daily amount of water that they can together remove without provoking an irreversible depletion of the supply.

Even in the absence of cross-mountain cooperation and of social relations generated by it, the use of the shared water pool is subject to an assessment in terms of the principle of equal shares, an assessment that applies to the total population of the two valleys, not to the two subpopulations taken separately. For let each inhabitant of Valley One remove more than $1/n$ (1 standing for the maximum total daily amount the members of the total population can jointly remove without provoking an irreversible depletion of the water supply and n for the number of the individuals making up the total population). Then, the inhabitants of Valley Two have to settle on less than their fair share, lest they induce a process of irreversible depletion. Clearly, this is a problem of just distribution, raised by the fact that the water supply is not sufficient to cover all the needs of all the inhabitants of the two valleys simultaneously. Once the problem of distribution is there, the remaining moral work is done by the principle of equal moral status and the resource-dependence assumption.

If so, then the principle of equal shares applies to the total population, even as the two societies are not engaged in any cooperation whatsoever with each other. Two Valleys gives intuitive support to the general principle that resources that are scarce and transferable within a population and to which none has any prior entitlement are to be distributed equally among members of the relevant population, whether or not the population in question is united by networks of special relations.

There is a question we have still to address before concluding this section. In Two Continents, no resources are transferable across the ocean. In Two Valleys, one resource type is transferable; others are not. In the real world, many types of resources are transferable, while some are not. Some non-transferable resources have fairly high predictive force with respect to human life prospects. Genetic talents and handicaps are an important example. Liberal egalitarians interpret genetic endowments as internal resources, and they argue that equality of life prospects obtains if and only if everyone has, in some sense, equal combinations of external *and* internal resources under their control.[14] The conceptual apparatus suggested in this section seems to rule out the liberal egalitarian view as a matter of definition. Advantageous genetic traits cannot be transplanted from one individual into another. And even if they could, such transfers would be still morally impermissible: the authority of each person over their own body would prohibit them. Furthermore, parents do not pick the genetic material of their future children from a total stock equally accessible to all. Nor is there any causal relationship between a child inheriting a gene set of a particular quality and the quality of another child's inherited gene set. But if genetic talents are non-transferable, then they cannot be objects of competition. And yet they have value as factors affecting the opportunities of the person whose talents they are, even though they seem not to have *competitive value*, i.e. value for which different individuals would compete. We interpreted the principle of equal shares as essentially related to competition for valuable things. Shall we conclude that the liberal egalitarian view is a non-starter under the general conception suggested in this chapter?

Here is a tentative answer. In a world where there are both transferable and non-transferable resources, the latter can be ranked into two distinct categories. Those in the first category are complementary to certain transferable resources; those in the second are not. By complementariness of different resources I mean that they are separately necessary and jointly sufficient to produce some benefit. Complementary resources have an impact on each another's value. If one of them is not available, the others are of a reduced value (sometimes, their value is reduced to zero). If the quality of one is improved, the value of having the others increases. So if a non-transferable resource is complementary to transferable resources, its availability and its quality improvements affect the value of the latter. Such a non-transferable resource, although lacking direct competitive value, has indirect competitive value in virtue of the impact of its possession on the value of other resources that are objects of competition.

The same set of transferable resources does not have the same value for different people unequally endowed with complementary non-transferable resources. In order for them to possess sets of transferable resources of an equal value, some transferable resources must be redistributed from those better endowed with the complementary non-transferable resources (for example, genetic talents) to those less well endowed. Thus, inequalities in non-transferable resources may call for compensatory redistribution of transferable resources. Under this interpretation, then, distributive egalitarianism can accommodate the presumptive claim that everyone should start with not just equal shares of the total stock of transferable resources but rather of all resources of competitive value, transferable and non-transferable.[15]

4 Purely Non-Institutional?

If the argument of Section 3 succeeds, the principle of equal shares is established without the intervention of institutional premises. But that principle is insufficiently informative on what things should be distributed equally, and on the precise standard of equal distribution against which different endowments by those things should be assessed. This question requires further theorizing, and Section 4 aims to show that at this stage of the argument, the non-institutional approach runs out of the conceptual tools necessary for tracking the answer. To begin with, securing equal shares in a stock of scarce resources necessitates collective action. Clearly, each individual bears a duty not to use more than his equal share. But an individual's share depends on many variables, such as the total number of individuals, the total amount of the available resources, the rate at which the loss of resources is naturally replaced, and so on. The interaction of these variables demands collective regulation of the distribution of the resources. In Two Valleys, collective regulation across the ridge is unlikely to be feasible. But suppose it is. Then, even if the two subpopulations fail to cooperate for other aims, they do cooperate for securing equal shares in the available water. They organize themselves into a collective agency structured by institutions (rules, procedures, conventions, practices).

There is a variety of ways in which they can achieve coordination. And since what one participant in a cooperative venture is required by distributive egalitarianism to do depends on what other participants are expected to be doing, a particular individual's duties within that venture remain indeterminate until a unique scheme of cooperation emerges such that it is common knowledge that (almost) everyone follows it (rather than following some alternative scheme or not accepting guidance from any scheme at all). It is the job of social institutions to specify which particular members of the group should do precisely what in order for the group as a whole to maintain or restore equality as the principle requires, and to make sure that (almost) everyone acts as required (Miklósi 2008).

This is correct, but I do not think it is damaging to the non-institutional account. The defenders of that account can concede that for a population to be able to meet the standards of distributive equality, it must be suitably organized by a set of institutions. They can agree too that the institutions in question are subject to principles that assess their intrinsic properties. None of this shows that institutions play any constitutive role in defining the content of equal shares. What this argument does show is that institutions are instrumentally necessary for a population to be able to satisfy the independent principle of equal shares.[16]

So if we want to see whether equality of shares can be specified without reference to institutions, their procedures, and the social relations shaped by them, and the principles of procedural and relational justice involved, we have directly to confront the question of what equality of shares is.

For a start, let me put the principle of equal shares in a form slightly different from the way it was spelled out in Section 3. There it was argued that the principle of equal claims to a share in the available resources is changed into a distributive principle of claims to equal shares by the additional assumption of competition for the same stock of scarce resources. Scarcity, as we have seen, involves trade-offs between the interests of different people. If a person has some good under his exclusive control, that is a cost to others who are barred from using it (without his consent). Those costs must figure in the calculus of equal shares. How do they?

One way for them to do it would be this. Suppose, as a first step, people form their life plans prior to and independently of the share they can expect under an equal distribution. Resources are, then, allocated to them in the second step so as to bring everyone to the same level of satisfaction. Here, costs enter the story in the second step, when the limited stock of resources is distributed. This model restricts the satisfaction of each so as to make it equal to the satisfaction of everybody else, and so it is sensitive to the responsibility of individuals for their choices and acts. But it is not sufficiently sensitive: as Dworkin has pointed out, it allows some individuals to form expensive preferences at the cost of others with more modest ambitions (Dworkin 2000: 36–8). A better model brings everyone into a position of equality not after but before they make their significant choices (Rawls 1999c: 369).[17]

Can such a model be constructed without relying on institutional assumptions? Consider Two Valleys modified in the following manner. The subterranean reservoir stretching from one valley to the other does not contain water but some all-purpose liquid capable of being transformed into any distinct resource type, in the absence of cooperation or exchange, and the costs are the same whatever people should decide to create from the liquid at their disposal. Like water, that liquid is homogeneous and infinitely divisible. No other source of useful things and materials is accessible in either of the two valleys.

Under these conditions, one has no difficulty in determining what an equal share is. If the all-purpose liquid is divided into equal units, the number of units being the same as the number of the individuals living in the two valleys, then everyone starts his life with an equal share of the total stock of resources. If everyone has an equal amount of the same all-purpose thing, then the costs of having their part rather than that of someone else are the same for everyone.

Of course, at the end of the day each individual will have transformed his lot into a specific bundle of resources, likely to be qualitatively different from what many others have. But not having someone else's bundle does not come with a cost to anyone. Had they wanted to have that bundle rather than theirs, they could have transformed their lot of all-purpose liquid into it rather than what they have in fact produced for themselves.

This story is wildly unrealistic but that is not necessarily an objection to telling it. Wildly implausible assumptions may be worth making if they facilitate the examination of a difficult problem under simplified conditions, free of the intervention of irrelevant complexities. This is not such a case, however. The simplifying assumption eliminates the problem rather than helping to address its causes directly. This is because the source of the problem is the very diversity of resources. How can the envy test be extended to it?

Dworkin famously proposed an idealized model of a hypothetical auction to show how this is possible (Dworkin 2000: 66–71). This model is based on unrealistic assumptions, too, but these are really helpful. To put that model in the context of the present section, I suggest that we start out from a comparison between it and Rawls's hypothetical model of the original position. Rawls wants the agreement achieved in the original position to yield principles of justice against which, in a second step, individuals can assess alternative institutional systems for their moral acceptability. The principles are for institutions, and they are supposed to regulate institutional procedures. It seems plausible that the choice of principles must precede the institutions that do not come into the picture before the first step is fully completed. In fact, the argument from the original position does not include procedures for reaching an agreement. The informational constraints built into a very thick veil of ignorance making sure that the *ex ante* interests of all are exactly the same, the parties need not engage in negotiations: a randomly selected rational individual can make the choice for all. In the second step, Rawls points out that certain forms of a market economy can satisfy his two principles of justice, but the market plays no role in the specification of the principles.

Dworkin's model is different in more than one way. Most importantly, its aim is different. Rawls's principle for distribution, the difference principle, is not supposed to determine what equal shares are. Its aim is to identify the conditions when a departure from the fallback position of equal shares is permitted by justice. *Theory* leaves entirely open the question of when a distribution counts as egalitarian.

It is precisely this question that is addressed by Dworkin's hypothetical auction model. This model is after the "metric" of equality, but it does not aim to deliver that "metric" with the help of a veil of ignorance. It rather proposes a procedure that makes the informed choices of each participant sensitive in the appropriate manner to the costs to others of their taking a particular bundle of resources under their exclusive control. We do not need, for our present aim, to engage with the details of Dworkin's model. It is sufficient to register that it represents an idealized market, satisfying all the requirements of the economists' standard model of perfect competition, but different from that model in making one further idealizing assumption. It stipulates that, at the start, the participants are endowed with equal amounts of token money. Money possesses "liquidity" of sorts: it can buy anything. Like the liquid in our previous story, it is a homogeneous, sufficiently divisible, and all-purpose resource. But unlike that liquid, it is not a means of production and consumption. It has no use value for either consumers or producers. The only value it possesses is that of a means of exchange (and of savings). Dworkin's hypothetical auction model leaves in place the diversity of goods and measures the value of the qualitatively and quantitatively different bundles by allowing people to engage in a process of market transactions. The procedures being closely adjusted to the normative premises of the theory of equality of resources, it identifies the different bundles as equal in the required sense with the position when the competitive process reaches an equilibrium: when all the markets are simultaneously cleared (Dworkin 2000: 66).

The recourse to an idealized market model is motivated by the moral idea that people committed to the principle of equal shares must take responsibility for not starting with a greater than equal share themselves. And the way to establish whether a share an individual possesses at the start is equal to the share of others is to measure its importance for the individual in question against the importance others attribute to it. Allowing everyone to bid for the resources up for distribution with equal amounts of token money is the proper way to make this measurement, for it determines the value of each item by what equally positioned participants are ready to give up in order to have them.

But the intervention of the idealized market model comes with an important consequence. As I noted earlier, Rawls's original position does not need procedures for making sure that the parties reach an agreement. Dworkin's auction and, more generally, his idealized market are dependent on institutionalized procedures. These procedures are subject to principles of justice that evaluate their internal properties independently of any non-procedural standards that apply directly to the outcomes. If the market process satisfies those principles of procedural equality, the outcome will count as an equal distribution of resources, whatever that should be. The principle of equal shares applies to the outcome indirectly, through its role in stipulating the idealized conditions for the market structure.[18]

Let me take stock. The idea of equal shares is complex, and it is hierarchically organized. At a basic level, it demands that to the extent that the distribution of the relevant goods is determined by morally arbitrary factors, everyone has equal shares. At this level, the argument is not in need of institutional premises. At the next level, where it is determined what distributions count as equal, standards of procedural and relational equality come into play.

A theory of the core of distributive egalitarianism is not complete until the second step is made. A complete theory, therefore, cannot do without factoring principles of institutional procedures and social relations into the definition of what an equal distribution is. But the second step does not supersede the first one. While not directly answering the question what distributions are egalitarian, the abstract principle of equal shares continues to operate in the background by providing guidance to the stipulation of the institutional model that yields the answer to that question. Properly understood, the theory of distributive egalitarianism is neither purely non-institutional nor purely institutional. It is a two-level theory progressing from a basic, non-institutional level to a secondary, institutional level.

As I stated in Section 1, the theory proposed in this chapter is neutral, at its basic level, towards the competing conceptions of egalitarian justice.[19] It is not fully neutral at this second level. It does not accommodate non-liberal conceptions of distributive equality (full-outcome egalitarianism, for example). Of the conceptions that claim to be liberal, it sits more comfortably with those taking seriously that individuals are responsible for the costs, for others, of their having a share in the total stock of resources (for example, equality of resources), than it does with those that are not taking this claim seriously enough (for example, equality of welfare).

So the two-level theory suggested in this chapter is not fully general. But it is fairly general and, perhaps, this is enough for a start.

5 Conclusions: The Problem of Global Justice

This chapter has been written with the aim of supporting four claims. First, institutional conceptions of justice are incapable of constructing *ex nihilo* any principle of egalitarian justice. Unless some such principle can be shown to be part of preinstitutional morality, egalitarian liberalism as a "political conception" cannot get off the ground. Either distributive egalitarianism is delivered by a "comprehensive" liberal theory or liberalism must part company with it.

Second, a "comprehensive" liberal theory can accommodate a principle of egalitarian justice—a principle of equal shares—within its account of the moral foundations of the principles of politics. In fact, the principle of equal shares is but the principle of equal moral status applied to the circumstances of scarcity of (transferable) resources.

Third, the principle of equal shares is highly abstract. It leaves open the question of what counts as an equal share. The specification that best suits the basic idea of liberal egalitarianism (the idea that disadvantages from circumstances beyond the control of the individual are morally arbitrary and the basic principle of moral equality calls for their elimination or reduction, but disadvantages for which the individual can be held responsible admit of a justification compatible with moral equality) is in need of a model of an idealized hypothetical market. But, then, the purely procedural and relational principles assessing the market processes and relations enter in the very definition of what equality of shares is. Any distributive outcome achieved by procedurally egalitarian market processes will count as realizing equality of resources, the principle of equal shares applying to it only indirectly, through determining the normative conditions the market should satisfy.

This leads to a two-level theory, purely moral at the basic level and partly institutional at the next level.

The fourth claim, according to which the two-level theory is favorable to the global justice thesis, has not been addressed so far. Let me say a couple of words on it in this concluding section.

Since the two-level theory combines non-institutional with institutional consider-ations, it might seem plausible to think that it takes a middle ground between the global scope and the state-bound scope theses. I do not think this is the case. Within the two-level theory outlined in this chapter, the problem of the scope of egalitarian justice is decided at the basic level. The second-level, institutional part of the theory has no implications for this problem. It entails a hypothetical model, the scope of which is indeterminate.

The principle of equal shares applies to any resources that are scarce and transferable, and so its scope includes everyone who depends on scarce resources in the pursuit of their aims and to whom the scarce resources can be transferred from where those resources are to be found at present. Whether the existing interstate boundaries coin-cide with the limits of interpersonal transferability is a contingent matter; the likelihood of a general congruence is next to zero. In any event, two persons between whom scarce resources are transferable find themselves within the scope of distributive egalitarianism with respect to those resources, whether they are fellow citizens or not, or whether they are or are not related in some other way. Suppose the citizenries of particular states are less inclusive than the population to which the principle of equal shares applies. Then, on the one hand, each particular state bears primary responsibility for upholding distri-butive egalitarianism within its boundaries. On the other hand, the responsibility of states is not exhausted by the duties they severally owe to their own citizens. They share responsibilities for upholding distributive equality across their boundaries. Distributive egalitarianism across boundaries is a primary responsibility not of particular states one by one but of the community of the states within its scope. It assesses the international system in terms of its capacity to discharge this responsibility, and to the extent that a more efficient coordination of transnational cooperation for promoting justice requires delegating state authority to supra-state institutions, it exerts moral pressure in that direction.

If the scope of the principle of equal shares is not state-bound, is it therefore global? Not necessarily. For it to be global, it must be the case that humans in general depend on scarce resources and that the scarce resources are transferable between any two locations occupied by humans. Whether this is in fact the case is a contingent matter, subject to historical developments. On the one hand, small-scale hunting and gathering societies have been described by anthropologists as not experiencing the problem of scarcity (Sahlins 1972). On the other hand, transferability was not met, for the most part of human history, on the global level (Wallerstein 1974). Nevertheless, as far as the contemporary world is concerned, it seems to be a solid fact about it that small-scale "societies of abundance" are isolated pockets in a technically integrated world of scarcity. In our times, the principle of equal shares has a global scope; its demands are incumbent on us towards virtually every human individual wherever they should live on the Earth. So to the extent that the pure non-institutional account is favorable for the cosmopolitan view, the two-level account is favorable to it too.

NOTES

1. For an illustration, consider the two parts of Rawls's second principle of justice: the first part (the principle of equality of fair opportunity) belongs to the core, since it assesses life prospects at birth, while the second part (the difference principle) regulates the division of the social product and so it is not part of the core. (Rawls 1999a: 53).

2. For the institutional account, see Rawls (1999a); Dworkin (2000: 6); Nagel (2005). In their reading, the institutional account is the view that social institutions and the practices regulated by them are not morally acceptable unless some requirement of equal shares obtains. The family of institutionalist conceptions includes a more radical account that calls itself *relational egalitarianism*. Relational egalitarians reject outright the aim of identifying any independent principles of distributive equality. According to them, egalitarian justice entails no independent distributive requirements at all. If the social relations maintained by an institutional system are egalitarian—if they are free of domination, subjection, marginalization, exclusion, and other forms of morally objectionable status asymmetries—then the distributions produced by that system are just, whatever their structure. See Scheffler (2005). A society based on egalitarian relations is likely to yield more equal distributions than non-egalitarian (Scheffler 2015). Egalitarian social and political relations may not be sustainable unless economic inequalities are kept in check, but, in such cases, economic equality is valued indirectly, as a means or a consequence of maintaining social and political equality. See Anderson (1999). So understood, the institutional view is an alternative to

distributive egalitarianism, not a version of it. In what follows, the term "institutional" will stand for a type of theory *within* distributive egalitarianism; the rejection of the claim that egalitarianism has a separate distributive aspect will be set aside.

3. For the non-institutional account, see Barry (1999). For a helpful discussion of the contrast between the two approaches, see Blake and Risse (2008) and Risse (2012).

4. See Nagel (2005: 120).; Dworkin (2000: 3–6). For critiques of Nagel (2005), see Cohen and Sabel (2006); Julius (2006). Gerald Cohen questioned, famously, the claim that there is a necessary link between the basic structure and coercive power; see Cohen (1997). For a criticism of Cohen's view, see Scheffler (2006).

5. To a question raised by Robert Post, whether the last condition is sufficiently general—more specifically, whether it can apply to societies that are not self-governing societies, Nagel gives a tentative positive answer. See Nagel (2005: 129, n 14.)

6. For a similar contrast, see Scanlon (2018: 15–16).

7. Frankfurt defends a principle of sufficiency but not in its specifically basic needs version. For a basic needs version of the principle, see Shue (1980).

8. Nozick rejects the principle of fairness, but that is here beside the point. See Nozick (1973: 90–5).

9. The commitment to the principle of equal moral status is foundational for liberalism. It cannot be abandoned without giving up on its entire theoretical venture. But this does not mean it can be assumed as a fallback position, without critical examination. It raises difficulties that need to be confronted and resolved. For the controversy about the principle, see Steinhoff (2015). For its most comprehensive (so far) defense, see Waldron (2017). For the aims of this chapter, I have taken the principle for granted.

10. Rawls lists scarcity among the "circumstances of justice" with a qualifier as "moderate scarcity." But by "circumstances of justice" he understands conditions under which the principles of justice not only apply but can also be routinely complied with. See Rawls (1999a: 110). This restriction seems to be related to the fact that he reserves the term "distributive justice" for cooperative ventures regulated by institutions. See Rawls (1999a: 7). He recognizes that the division of goods among individuals, none of whom has taken part in their production, raises distributive problems but he sets aside this case as falling under the category of "allocative justice" (Rawls: 1999a: 77). However, if we recognize the significance of what Rawls calls "allocative justice" for any egalitarian theory of just distributions, then we find it helpful to disentangle the two desiderata from each other and to give separate consideration to the conditions of application. In this case, the qualifier appears unnecessarily restrictive.

11. According to Susan Hurley, luck is neutral between equality and inequality and, therefore, it does not provide any moral ground for equalization. See Hurley (2003: 155–9). But the moral ground for equalization does not reside in luck. It resides in the principle of equal shares. Luck is simply a factor that fails to justify the resistance to equalization. Furthermore, it is true that from the point of view of luck, the positions of equality and inequality are symmetrical. But this does not make their position symmetrical, all things considered. The principle of equal shares explains why equality is the default.

12. Luck egalitarians sometimes speak as if badness and injustice were synonyms or two inseparable aspects of the same thing. Larry Temkin says, for example, that "the ultimate intuition underlying egalitarianism is that it is bad (unfair or unjust) for some to be worse off than others through no fault of their own." See Temkin (1993: 200). I think conflating badness with injustice is a mistake.

13. Here I defined transferability as a binary property, a thing being either transferable or not transferable. But the transfer, when it is technically feasible, has costs: a unit reallocated to the worse-off comes at a price of more than a unit, and the costs may increase along a scale until they reach the level of the benefit from transfer. Even before that point, however, they may become prohibitively high. Thus, the cost factor makes transferability a scalar property. This fact has interesting implications that are, however, beyond the scope of this chapter.

14. See Dworkin (2000: 79). Libertarians, both right and left, strongly object to this view: according to them, persons have full self-ownership over their bodies and minds, including their talents. Some left libertarians take, however, a position closer to that of liberal egalitarians: Hillel Steiner argues, for example, that unchosen germ-like genetic information is a natural resource and should be treated alongside the external resources. See Steiner (1994).

15. Notice that this does not show that the general conception of distributive egalitarianism outlined here depends on the liberal view of equal distribution (which I think is basically correct). It only shows that the latter, if true, can be accommodated by it.

16. For the instrumental view of institutions, see Murphy (2010).

17. Under such a model, "people decide what sorts of lives to pursue against a background of information about the actual cost their choices impose on other people" Dworkin (2000: 69).

18. The auction model's idealizations are guided by a prior conception of equality of resources, an interpretation of the principle of equal shares. Interestingly, Dworkin failed to draw the conclusions from this property of his model for the theory of egalitarian justice: he remained committed to the political conception. This has left its footprint on his view on the scope of egalitarian justice. Although, towards the end of his life, he admitted that international law is subject to a moral pressure towards sharing sovereign authority with supra-state institutions, he located the source of this pressure in the international standing of human rights alone, without even mentioning the problem of cross-border egalitarian justice. See his posthumous article, Dworkin (2013).

19. The resource-dependence thesis and the principle of equal shares in the total stock of resources may seem to contradict this claim, but they do not. The theory of distributive equality called "equality of resources" is a theory about the standards against which the value of the means of consumption and production is assessed. It asks what the morally right construal is of the value in terms of which different bundles of goods should count as equal or unequal. This chapter uses the term "resources" without regard to that question of value.

References

Anderson, Elisabeth (1999) "What is the Point of Equality?" *Ethics* 109: 287–337.

Barry, Brian (1999) "Statism and Nationalism: A Cosmopolitan Critique." In Ian Shapiro and Lea Brilmayer (eds.), *Global Justice*. New York and London: New York University Press, 12–66.

Beitz, Charles R. (1979) *Political Theory and International Relations*. Princeton, NJ: Princeton University Press.

Beitz, Charles R. (1999) 'Social and Cosmopolitan Liberalism,' *International Affairs* 75: 15–529.

Blake, Michael and Matthias Risse (2008) "Two Models of Equality and Responsibility," *Canadian Journal of Philosophy* 38: 165–99.

Buchanan, Allen (2000) "Rawls's Law of Peoples: Rules for a Vanishing Westphalian World," *Ethics* 110: 697–721.

Buchanan, Allen (2004) *Justice, Legitimacy, and Self-Determination. Moral Foundations for International Law.* New York and Oxford: Oxford University Press.

Caney, Simon (2005) *Justice beyond Borders.* New York and Oxford: Oxford University Press.

Casal, Paula (2007) "Why Sufficiency Is Not Enough," *Ethics* 117: 296–326.

Cohen, Gerald A. (1997) "Where the Action is: On the Site of Distributive Justice," *Philosophy and Public Affairs* 26: 3–30.

Cohen, Joshua and Charles Sabel (2006) "Extra Republicam Nulla Justitia?" *Philosophy and Public Affairs* 34: 147–75.

Dworkin, Ronald (2000) *Sovereign Virtue.* Cambridge, MA: Harvard University Press.

Dworkin, Ronald (2013) "A New Philosophy for International Law," *Philosophy and Public Affairs* 41: 2–30.

Frankfurt, Harry S. (1987) "Equality as a Moral Ideal," *Ethics* 98: 21–43.

Freeman, Samuel (2007) *Justice and the Social Contract.* Oxford: Oxford University Press.

Hurley, Susan L. (2003) *Justice, Luck, and Knowledge.* Cambridge, MA: Harvard University Press.

Julius, A. J. (2006) "Nagel's Atlas," *Philosophy and Public Affairs* 34: 176–92.

Miklósi, Zoltán (2008) "Compliance with Just Institutions," *Social Theory and Practice* 34: 183–207.

Murphy, Liam B. (2010) "International Responsibility." In John Tasioulas and Samantha Besson (eds.), *The Philosophy of International Law.* New York and Oxford: Oxford University Press, 299–315.

Nagel, Thomas (2005) "The Problem of Global Justice," *Philosophy and Public Affairs* 33: 113–47.

Nozick, Robert (1973) *Anarchy, State, and Utopia,* Oxford: Blackwell.

Parfit, Derek (2000) "Equality or Priority?" In Matthew Clayton and Andrew Williams (eds.), *The Ideal of Equality.* London: Palgrave, 81–125.

Pogge, Thomas W. (1989) *Realizing Rawls.* Ithaca, NY: Cornell University Press.

Pogge, Thomas W. (1994) "An Egalitarian Law of Peoples," *Philosophy and Public Affairs* 23: 195–224.

Rawls, John (1999a) *A Theory of Justice,* rev. edn., Cambridge, MA: Belknap.

Rawls, John (1999b) *The Law of Peoples.* Cambridge, MA: Harvard University Press.

Rawls, John (1999c) "Social Unity and Primary Goods." In *Collected Papers.* Cambridge, MA: Harvard University Press.

Richards, David A. J. (1982) "International Distributive Justice." In J. Roland Pennock and John W. Chapman (eds.), *Ethics, Economics, and the Law.* New York and London: New York University Press, 275–99.

Risse, Mathias (2012) *On Global Justice.* Princeton, NJ: Princeton University Press.

Sahlins, Marshall D. (1972) "The Original Affluent Society." In *Stone Age Economics.* Chicago: Aldine, 1–39.

Sangiovanni, Andrea (2007) "Global Justice, Reciprocity, and the State," *Philosophy of Public Affairs* 35: 3–39.

Scanlon, Thomas M. (2018) *Why Does Inequality Matter?* New York and Oxford: Oxford University Press.

Scheffler, Samuel (2005) "Choice, Circumstance, and the Value of Equality," *Politics, Philosophy and Economics* 4(1): 5–28.

Scheffler, Samuel (2006) "Is the Basic Structure Basic?" In Christine Sypnowich (ed.), *The Egalitarian Conscience: Essays in Honour of G. A. Cohen*. New York and Oxford: Oxford University Press.

Scheffler, Samuel (2015) "The Practice of Equality." In Carina Fourie, Fabian Schuppert and Ivo Wallimann-Helmer (eds.), *Social Equality: On What It Means to be Equals*. New York and Oxford: Oxford University Press, 102–30.

Shue, Henry (1980) *Basic Rights*. Princeton, NJ: Princeton University Press.

Steiner, Hillel (1994) *An Essay on Rights*. Oxford: Blackwell.

Steinhoff, Uwe, ed. (2015) *Do All Persons Have Equal Moral Worth?* New York and Oxford: Oxford University Press.

Temkin, Larry (1993) *Inequality*. Oxford: Oxford University Press.

Valentini, Laura (2011) *Justice in a Globalized World, A Normative Framework*. New York and Oxford: Oxford University Press.

Waldron, Jeremy (2017) *One Another's Equals*. Cambridge, MA: Belknap.

Wallerstein, Immanuel: *The Modern World System*, Vol. 1. New York: Academic Press 1974.

FURTHER READING

Beitz, Charles R. and Robert E. Goodin (eds.) (2009) *Global Basic Rights*. New York and Oxford: Oxford University Press.

Brock, Gillian (2009) *Global Justice: A Cosmopolitan Account*. Oxford: Oxford University Press.

Pogge, Thomas W. (ed.) (2001) *Global Justice*. Oxford: Blackwell.

Sangiovanni, Andrea (2012) "The Irrelevance of Coercion, Imposition, and Framing to Distributive Justice," *Philosophy of Public Affairs* 40: 79–110.

Scheffler, Samuel (2001) *Boundaries and Allegiances*. New York and Oxford: Oxford University Press.

Ypi, Lea (2011) *Global Justice and Avant-Garde Political Agency*. Oxford: Oxford University Press.

PART II

HUMAN RIGHTS

....

CHAPTER 5

THE HOLDERS
OF HUMAN RIGHTS

The Bright Side of Human Rights?

....

SAMANTHA BESSON

1 INTRODUCTION

....

IN her essay "The Dark Side of Human Rights," Onora O'Neill (2005) criticizes the duty-side or supply-side of human rights and some of its inherent limitations. By contrast, therefore, one may expect the right-side or benefit-side of human rights to amount to their bright side.

As a matter of fact, human rights are usually referred to by human rights theorists as the most obvious of rights: the rights that human beings have merely by virtue of being humans.[1] This is how they are said to differ fundamentally from other moral and legal rights that are status-dependent.[2] This apparently obvious statement seems in turn to warrant an unbounded and general account of the personal scope of human rights.[3] The generality of human rights is actually also echoed in contemporary international human rights law and practice. To quote Article 1 of the Universal Declaration of Human Rights (UDHR), for instance, human rights are the rights of "all human beings," who are described as being "born free and equal" in those rights.[4] This makes the question of the identity of human rights-holders redundant on the identity of human beings themselves.

So if human rights are simply the rights of human beings, why should human rights theorists be concerned about the holders of human rights? The first thing to say is that philosophers are and should be wary about deriving an "ought" from an "is" and about the idea that our *being* human implies our *having* human *rights*. Interestingly, human rights are one of the few entities in morality, and in international law, that are referred to in terms that relate directly to our identity as a species or a natural kind. This may cause confusions akin to the naturalistic fallacy, but also lead to other types of moral entanglements with biology.

More importantly, secondly, parts of the international human rights law and practice do not seem to sit easily with the generality of human rights. It is both more generous to some when it grants special protection to them through special rights, on the one hand, and more limitative to others when it excludes them from the scope of general human rights, on the other. I will refer to those boundaries in the general scope of human rights-holders as, respectively, their internal and external boundaries.

First of all, the so-called "international bill of rights"[5] includes general human rights, of course, i.e. rights that belong to all, such as those included in the two International Covenants on Economic, Social, and Cultural Rights (CESCR) and on Civil and Political Rights (CCPR), the Genocide Convention, the Convention against Torture, or the Convention on the Protection of All Persons from Enforced Disappearance. However, in some cases, they also grant special protection that not only reinforces the protection of general rights of individuals belonging to vulnerable groups (e.g. children for the Convention on the Rights of the Child (CRC), people with disability for the Convention on the Rights of Persons with Disabilities (CRPD)) or individuals under special threats due to their activity (e.g. migrants for the Convention on the Protection of the Rights of All Migrant Workers (CRMW)), but also grant them special rights (e.g. non-discrimination rights on racial or sexual grounds for the Conventions on the Elimination of Racial Discrimination (CERD) and on the Elimination of All Forms of Discrimination against Women (CEDAW) or non-discrimination rights of children on all usual grounds in the CRC[6]).[7]

Besides special protection and its prima facie non-egalitarian flavor within the scope of human rights-holders, secondly, there are also at least three exclusions from the scope of rights-holders in the international human rights practice that call for theoretical attention. First of all, what should one make of the exclusion or, at least, the limitation of the human rights of infants and of those who are elderly or have dementia, but also of those whose mental capacities are impaired? The fact that some human rights require a certain level of rational competence to be recognized and protected seems to belie the claim to guarantee the same rights to all human beings qua human beings. Secondly, how about the rights of vulnerable groups whose members' individual human rights do not suffice for protecting? Human rights' individual focus seems to artificially exclude the human rights of groups and hence the many benefits of collective belonging in human life. Finally, how should we justify the exclusion of non-human animals whose competences are equal and sometimes superior to those of some human beings? Human rights seem to be inegalitarian in their rejection of the (equal) moral status of the members of other species.

Human rights theorists have reacted differently to this ambivalence regarding the scope of rights-holders in the law and practice of human rights. So-called "ethical" theories of human rights that approach human rights as moral rights independent from their political and legal practice need not be too concerned by contradictions in the practice. Whenever the practice does not fit their moral blueprint, they may simply suggest it should be reformed. Still, authors in this group differ with respect to the scope of human rights-holders –albeit for reasons distinct from the variations in international human rights law[8]: some approach human rights as "birthrights" at the risk of proposing a list of human rights that is too broad,[9] while others stipulate a threshold of normative agency and cap the range of human rights on that basis.[10] By contrast, so-called "political" theories of human rights that refer to human rights as political only cannot but be overconstrained by the practice.[11] Curiously, however, they do not really seem to be concerned by the latter's contradictions with respect to the scope of human rights-holders.[12]

In a legal theory of human rights like the one propounded here, i.e. one that starts from the practice of human rights, takes human rights as both, and at once, legal and moral rights as its object and aims at interpreting them in their best light, fidelity to the practice is key.[13] Nevertheless, disowning it, even partly if it is contradictory, and interpreting it in its best but also most coherent light are also an option just as justifications and critiques of the practice are inherent to human rights law qua normative practice. Of course, critical interpretations require a serious justification in each case. And this is what I will endeavor to provide in this chapter.

The aim of this chapter is to discuss the main boundary disputes pertaining to the holders of human rights. After a few remarks about what being a moral right-holder implies (Section 2), I will explain why being a human rights-holder means holding them equally (Section 3). The next section will be devoted to justifying the external boundaries of human rights against the corresponding critiques, starting from the most external boundary in three concentric circles (Section 4): the "species" boundaries, and the speciesism critique (Section 4.1); the "capacity" boundaries, and the rationalism critique (Section 4.2); and the "individuality" boundaries, and the individualism critique (Section 4.3). Finally, I will turn to the internal boundaries in the scope of human rights-holders, and in particular to the boundary between general and special human rights-holders. I will argue that the proposed egalitarian reading of human rights fits and justifies the core of the practice and accounts for the existence of some special human rights, but not all of them (Section 5).

A caveat is in order before starting. This chapter's discussion of the scope of human rights-holders is conditioned by other arguments made elsewhere,[14] and in particular arguments about the object of human rights, their justification, and their duty-bearers. Because human rights-holders are identified at the same time as their rights, they are tied to the latter's object of protection and to their specific and general justifications, but also, in the proposed relational account of human rights, to their duty-bearers. It should not come as a surprise, therefore, that in an account of human rights that approaches them as protective of interests and justified by reference to the equal political status they are constitutive of, it is the egalitarian dimension of human rights that also drives much of the argument for the identification of their holders.

2 HOLDING RIGHTS

Human rights are "rights," i.e. normative relationships between a right-holder and a duty-bearer.[15] As such, human rights duties are directed: they are owed to someone, i.e. the right-holder.[16] Because most human rights are or may be reconstructed as claim-rights,[17] the right-holder also has a claim to that duty.

Two main features of human rights-holding flow from this. First of all, identifying a right implies identifying its right-holders, even though not necessarily all its concrete duty-bearers.[18] Human rights arise together with their holders becoming human rights-holders. This makes the identification of human rights-holders an essential part of the recognition of the existence of human rights and a primary concern in that context. Secondly, human rights qua normative relationships correspond to relationships of jurisdiction between a given State (or international institution) and a given person.[19] Without jurisdiction over certain people, whether territorial or extraterritorial, those people do not have human rights against that entity and that entity has no human rights duties towards those people.

What this means for the active or benefit-side of human rights is that human rights-holders are identified at the same time as their rights, on the one hand, and arise as a normative relationship together with a general jurisdictional relationship between the right-holder whose rights are identified and the duty-bearer, on the other.

Those structural features of the benefit-side of human rights may be derived from an analysis of the legal practice of human rights. First of all, international and European human rights law treats human rights as "claim-rights." Of course, some international and European human rights instruments include other normative entities than rights, such as imperfect duties, goals[20] to be realized progressively, and non-directly invocable principles. Their catalogue of rights *stricto sensu*, however, lists "rights" that are claimed by their holders against public institutions that owe them duties. Secondly, even though the legal practice of human rights focuses mostly on the supply-side or passive side of human rights, and hence on the identification and specification of human rights duties, their allocation and the justifications for their restrictions, one also finds, albeit more rarely, references in human rights-reasoning to structural features of the right-side or active side of human rights. The latter is not usually questioned, however, for its identity is taken to flow from the rights themselves and their recognition in the first place. Finally, jurisdiction is mostly considered as the trigger or condition for the application of human rights (e.g. Article 1 of the European Convention on Human Rights (ECHR)). It is understood as a relationship of effective and overall normative control or authority[21] between a State or international institution of jurisdiction over a person that gives rise to human rights between that person and the entity of jurisdiction.

3 HOLDING RIGHTS EQUALLY

Human rights are "equal" rights. This is because human rights qua relationships are equal relationships, but also relationships of equality to the extent that they are constitutive of our equal moral status in political circumstances. Their egalitarian dimension is what explains why they are held by all and are considered as general rights.

The first task in the elucidation of the relationship between human rights and equality, and hence of how they are independent of any other status, is clarifying the concept of equality that is at stake in the human rights context. This requires an analysis of the most basic notion of equality: that of equal moral status (Section 3.1). In a second step, the discussion moves to a more robust notion of equality: that of political equality (Section 3.2). A final step in the argument turns to human rights as constitutive of our equal moral status in political circumstances (Section 3.3).

3.1 From Equal Moral Status...

Basic moral equality is usually referred to as equal moral status or basic equal status. It is useful to distinguish between the concept of equal moral status and its justification.

The concept of equal moral status, first of all, is best explained by dissociating the notion of moral status from that of equal moral status. In a nutshell, *moral status* pertains to the way in which a being is subject to moral evaluation, how it ought to be treated, whether it has rights, and what kind of rights it has.[22] Moral status goes further, therefore, than mere moral considerability: the latter is a standing that may be shared with many other sentient animals and even with things, whereas moral status only belongs to human beings.[23] When it is *equal*, moral status refers to the idea that "all people are of equal worth and that there are some claims people are entitled to make on one another simply by virtue of their status as persons" (Scheffler (2003: 22)).

There are two core ideas in this understanding of equal moral status: (i) the idea that all persons should be regarded as having the same moral worth and (ii) the idea that this equal moral status is relational and the basis for mutual moral claims. Those two aspects of equal moral status are non-dissociable.

First of all, the idea of equal moral worth of all persons pertains to the intrinsic and non-instrumental value of personhood. According to that idea, no person may be deemed inferior morally to another: all those who have the characteristics that are sufficient for being a person and hence the capacity for rational and moral agency have the same moral status.[24] This capacity threshold is a datum of moral experience and an inherent feature of equality. Equal moral status is, of course, compatible with important inequalities on other counts such as health, beauty, luck, etc. It is important to stress that what matters here is personhood and not human nature. The former captures what ought to be protected morally in human beings qua moral agents, and it escapes the naturalistic fallacy and many other misconceptions that come with the notion of human nature, as we will see.[25]

The second core idea in equal moral status pertains to its inherently relational nature.[26] One is at once a person valuable in oneself and a person equal to others, i.e. a person whose status and moral worth is defined by one's moral relations to others. The relational or, as Elizabeth Anderson (1999: 288–9) calls it, the social nature of equal moral status explains why the latter amounts to more than mere autonomy or rational capacity that is covered by the first core idea. The denial of equal status amounts to a judgment of exclusion and inferiority *to others* where this kind of judgment is "thought to disqualify one from participation as an equal in important social practices or roles."[27]

As a result, equal moral status does more than simply entitle persons to mutual claims. It can actually be defined by reference to those mutual claims. This is why it is often deemed as consisting in those mutual moral entitlements themselves.[28] Those mutual entitlements inherent in equal moral status are usually described as mutual basic moral rights.[29] Those basic moral rights are equal rights, as a result.[30] Since the equal moral status is universal, they may also be referred to as universal moral rights. As we will see, human rights are among those basic moral rights that constitute one's equal moral status in political circumstances, although they do not exhaust those basic moral rights even in political circumstances. Those mutual moral entitlements include other basic moral rights than human rights: rights that may bind other individuals and not institutions like human rights, on the one hand, and rights that do not need to be institutionalized and legalized unlike human rights, on the other.

The second question is the justification of a persons' equal moral status. Curiously, given its pivotal role in morality, but maybe because of that pivotal or even liminal role, the concept of equal moral status remains a largely unquestioned notion in much of contemporary moral theory.[31] So, the problem with the justification of equal moral status is not so much that moral philosophers are divided but that they rarely provide a justification of the equal moral status of persons.[32] Some authors, like Jeremy Waldron (2002a), actually see this lack of justification as a shortcoming of current moral theory on basic moral equality. Others, like Bernard Williams (2005), see that absence of justification as a virtue of the idea of equality.

Schematically, one may distinguish between two kinds of justification of basic moral equality: a Christian one that refers to God (and the idea of *imago dei*) and that is mostly based on Locke[33] and a non-religious one that refers to shared rational nature and that is mostly based on Kant.[34] The difficulty with the former is its religious and hence non-inclusive and teleological nature.[35] But the latter also suffers from important shortcomings. One of them is its metaphysical, and non-naturalistic or empirical inclination.[36] A way of rebutting this objection may actually be found in the second core idea to equal moral status, however: its relational and hence social nature. The social nature of basic moral equality enables one to make a certain number of empirical assumptions about people and their relationship in society.[37] More generally, there is no reason why the search for justification should be one for ultimate foundations and why a failure to identify those ultimate foundations should be a problem. The regress in the search for justifications has to halt at some stage. One may be satisfied with pausing at equality without further justification. This may be, for instance, because those moral values and principles are so widely accepted as part of people's moralities that one does not have to argue for them before using them to argue for human rights.[38]

3.2 Through Political Equality...

Equal moral status holds an intermediary ground between moral considerability, on the one hand, and more specific or robust notions of equality, like political equality, on the other. Political equality is the kind of robust equality that matters in a legal order and, accordingly, in the context of human rights law. Before discussing political equality itself, it is important to explain how one can get to political equality from basic moral equality and elaborate on the relationship between the two.

First of all, the circumstances of political equality. The relational or social nature of equal moral status alluded to before implies that, to borrow Allen Buchanan's words, "the proper acknowledgement of a person's moral status requires some sort of fundamental public recognition of equality (Buchanan 2009: 379)"[39] Equality is inherently public or political as result.[40] In a nutshell, public or political equality implies that people can see that they are being treated as equals by others and this takes the form of its recognition by the law and institutions.[41]

Of course, there are prepolitical circumstances in which individuals merely benefit from a social form of equal moral status. This means that not all individuals may claim political equality in a given political community on grounds of their equal moral status; their claim to political equality will follow their full membership in the community, i.e. their being subjected to the community's decisions and law, and their sharing interdependent and roughly equal stakes with others. Their equal moral status is intact, however, and they have the universal moral rights that constitute that status. They actually have a universal moral right to have human rights in a future or actual political community qua universal moral right to political membership, but that universal moral right is not yet a human right.[42]

Secondly, the vindication of political equality. Once the political conditions are such that political equality may be required on the grounds of equal moral status, the next question to arise is how political equality can be vindicated. The political dimension of equal moral status together with its rights-based nature lead to a further process: the struggle for equal participation rights is based on the public vindication of equal moral status.[43] This in turn implies struggling for the establishment of a democratic regime that includes all those subjected to a decision in the decision-making process. Democracy is indeed the way "of publicly realizing equality when persons who have diverse interests need to establish rules and institutions for the common world in which they live" (Christiano 2010: 121–2) and this in spite of persistent and widespread reasonable disagreement.[44]

3.3 To Human Rights...

The passage and relationship between equal moral status and equal political status are reflected in the recognition of universal moral rights as human rights (moral and legal), and the passage from one to the other.

As I explained elsewhere,[45] human rights amount to a subset of universal moral rights that are also legal rights, that protect fundamental objective interests against standard threats (urgency), and that belong to all human beings (generality) merely on the basis of their humanity (universality). Four structural elements qualify a human right on that account, among which the first and the second deserve most attention for our purpose in this chapter. To become a human right, the objective interest protected has to be sufficiently fundamental to give rise to a universal and general right, first, and to be threatened generally and universally, second. Furthermore, the burden placed by the duties on the duty-bearer(s) has to be fair, third, and feasible, finally.

Corresponding to a general and universal interest is not enough for a human right to arise: there has to be a threshold of importance at which a given general and universal interest is regarded as sufficiently important to give rise to duties, and hence to a general and universal human right. What makes it the case that a given individual interest is regarded as sufficiently important to generate a human right duty and hence a human right may be found, I claim, in the normative status of each individual qua equal member of the moral-political community, i.e. their political equality or equal political status.[46] Only those interests that are recognized as socio-comparatively important by members of the community can be recognized as sufficiently fundamental to give rise to duties and hence as human rights. The recognition of human rights is done mutually and not simply vertically and top-down, and as a result human rights are not externally promulgated but mutually granted by members of a given political community.[47] This is particularly important for the generality of human rights, as it allows for the mutual assessment not only of the generality of the interests protected but also of the standard or general threats bearing on those interests, on the one hand, and of the general burdens and costs of the recognition of the corresponding rights and duties, on the other.

Evidence of the egalitarian threshold of human rights may be found in the relational and socio-comparative nature of human rights in practice. One may think of their systematic nature, for instance.[48] Human rights belong to everyone not only equally, but mutually, so qua rights not only of all but also against all. Another confirmation may be found in the non-inherently individualistic nature of human rights that protect basic individual interests that are also sufficiently general and hence deemed comparatively important within the political community. Actually, some human rights also protect individual interests in collective goods, like cultural rights, or individual interests whose social importance is part of the reason to protect them as rights, like the right to free speech.[49] Finally, the democratic dimension of human rights that is a regime-requirement of international human rights law post-1945[50] also confirms the egalitarianism of human rights.

Two objections may come to mind at this stage. The first pertains to the general or "generic"[51] dimension of human rights qua equal or general rights. If human rights are equal in the way I have argued they are, it is difficult to see how they could also be individual rights that protect each person specifically. It is key here to draw a distinction between an abstract human right that is general and the concrete human right and human right duties that correspond to that abstract human right in a specific individual case. Each abstract right has to be specified in an individual case and in the specific context of that individual to protect an individuated version of the generalized or generic interest protected by the human right.[52]

The second objection pertains to the parochialism of the proposed account of the equality of human rights and its democratic requirements. If human rights and political equality are tied in this way, one needs to explain how human rights may still be sufficiently universal.[53] As I discussed elsewhere,[54] international human rights law has consolidated progressively from transnational domestic practice and consensus over time, and this is how, once it is entrenched within the international legal order, it may legitimately constrain domestic politics in return. Moreover, once entrenched in international human rights law, the egalitarian and hence democratic dimension of human rights remains minimal. It can and should then be specified further in the domestic context.[55]

4 HOLDING RIGHTS EQUALLY, ALBEIT EXCLUSIVELY

Because they are equal along the lines explained so far, the holders of human rights are, I will argue in this section, born human beings who have reached (if they are adults) or have the ability to reach (if they are children) a threshold or minimal level of rational capacity.[56] This is also the way in which human rights-holders are approached in most of the contemporary international human rights practice and law.

There are three inherent limitations to the scope of right-holders in the proposed egalitarian reading of the practice, and three corresponding critiques, starting from the broadest set of boundaries: the "species" boundaries, and the speciesism critique (Section 4.1); the "capacity" boundaries, and the rationalism critique (Section 4.2); and the "individuality" boundaries, and the individualism critique (Section 4.3).

Before turning to a discussion of those three boundaries, two remarks are in order. First of all, there is another boundary underlying the scope of human rights-holders, and that is birth, on the one hand, and death, on the other. I am considering rights as post-birth rights, on the one hand, and as pre-death rights of the living and not the dead, on the other. The reason for this focus pertains to the individuality of human rights and to the circumstances of politics and their relationship to equal political status here and now. Those two structural features of human rights cannot be reconciled with pre-birth and post-death rights.[57] Again, there may be other moral considerations applicable to the fetus and to the dead, such as dignity[58] and various other duties of respect, but not human rights that constitute our equal political status as living individuals. Secondly, and for the same reasons, the idea of human rights as rights of the living excludes the protection of the interests of future generations qua human rights. Their interests may be protected through other moral considerations, but not as human rights here and now.[59] Qua rights, human rights are directed and hence require the identifiability of their right-holders as existing and not merely as potential right-holders (unlike their duty-bearers, who may only be potential[60]).[61]

4.1 Species-Related Boundaries and the Speciesism Critique

Human rights are rights that belong to human beings. Belonging to the human species seems, therefore, to constitute the most external boundary to the personal scope of human rights. To quote Article 1 UDHR, for instance, human rights are the rights of "all human beings" who are described as being "*born* free and equal" in those rights.

Human rights amount to the sole area of morality that seems to bear a direct reference to our identity as a species. Speciesism about human rights, i.e. the idea that human rights only belong to human beings and not to the members of other species, may be justified by reference to such biological qualities, but it need not.[62] It may also be grounded on moral qualities that happen to be held equally by human beings only.[63] Of course, this second brand of human rights' speciesism may be defeated by reference to other moral arguments.[64] Such critiques of moral speciesism are a version of a more general critique made against the "human prejudice" of morality.[65]

The problem with this critique of speciesism in the human rights context is that, first of all, human rights do not exhaust morality and the moral duties we have to other human beings and animals.[66] Secondly, the moral rights of members of other species are not excluded by the proposed account either. As a matter of fact, members of other species may share the same interests as human beings (e.g. health, security), and those interests may be protected by moral rights in some cases—although I am not making this argument here. We may even happen to have rights that have the same content (e.g. a moral right not to be tortured). However, their rights are not equal to ours. They cannot, therefore, be described as equal or shared rights and cannot amount to "human rights." Importantly, this does not amount to a human "nature" or human "species" privilege, but it is merely a matter of what makes us equal. What matters, indeed, is that, as things stand, we can only share them with those who we are in a public relation with, i.e. other human beings.

If human rights were called "persons' rights," along the lines of a suggestion made by Buchanan (2011: 214), things would look clearer with respect to both the naturalistic fallacy and the speciesist critique. Not only would the critique of speciesism be defeated as I have just argued it should and can, but it would no longer bite as a critique of a claim that looks speciesist in the first place, but merely as a critique of an egalitarian claim about human rights. As any egalitarian claim, it is bounded by reference to the group of those to whom we are equal. However, it is independent from our "nature."[67] This would also avoid the danger of normative essentialism.

To conclude, one cannot exclude that some non-human sentient animals may become equal to us one day, just as one may not exclude that intelligent machines may eventually.[68] On this view, human rights are not birthrights that only human beings have, or may acquire under further conditions, by the mere fact of their being born as human beings. In short, the claim is merely that humanity qua personality is currently a condition for having these rights, not that it is a necessary condition or even a sufficient one.[69] The question then becomes: what are the characteristics that give rise to our equal moral and political status and to the corresponding human rights? This is the question I will turn to now in the context of a second boundary to the scope of human rights-holders: their rational capacity.

4.2 Capacity-Related Boundaries and the Rationalism Critique

I claimed before that human rights belong to human beings who have reached (if they are adults) or have the potential to attain (if they are children) a threshold level of rational capacity. Rational capacity, therefore, amounts to a second boundary to the personal scope of human rights. The proposed reading corresponds to international human rights law and practice, where, although the exclusion is not explicit, incapable individuals are not regarded as right-holders.

Rational capacity as a practical capacity for rationality amounts in short to the capacity to reason and deliberate with others.[70] It goes beyond normative agency,[71] as a result. It is what makes us equal, and hence gives rise to our equal political status and the corresponding human rights. First of all, equality qua relational status implies sharing some common traits. The more basic and inclusive the equality, the more basic and widespread the traits. However minimal, some form of threshold for equality is a datum of moral experience. Secondly, in the political circumstances of human life, the capacity to reason and deliberate is an implication of politics and hence of equal political status.

Rational capacity works as a minimal threshold, and is not scalar. Whatever variations there are above that threshold do not matter for reasons of equality: what matters is who falls above or below the threshold, and hence who is to be treated equally and who is not.[72] The level at which the minimal threshold of rational capacity is set should reflect an average that has consolidated over time. The fact that it is indeterminate should not worry us given how indeterminate morality is. Nor should it be a concern that setting it is a matter of stipulation,[73] and hence largely contingent on law and democratic politics, and especially on international human rights law (e.g. Article 18 CRC and the age of 18 as trigger for (adult) human rights).

On the proposed egalitarian reading, human rights are not birthrights that all human beings have by the mere fact of their being born as human beings. Being born a human being is a condition under current circumstances, but not a sufficient one.[74] It is only if or once individuals have achieved a certain degree of rational capacity that they may be said to be human rights-holders. True, some human rights may require less or more rational capacity depending on their object, i.e. the interest protected, but they all require some minimal level thereof to amount to human rights. Human rights may not only be acquired above that level, but also be lost or never be acquired below. Importantly, human rights do not protect rational capacity itself. The latter is a threshold for one's equal moral and political status, but not something that is protected by that status and the human rights that constitute it.

Reacting to the consequences of the equality threshold and the requirement of rational capacity, some authors have tried to distinguish between paradigmatic and non-paradigmatic right-holders depending on whether the right-holder is situated above or below that threshold.[75] The problem with this compromise is that it is not tenable. Individuals situated below the threshold cannot be holders of a claim-right in a meaningful sense, as I argued before. Nor is it sufficient to defer to the supply-side of human rights and to understand the duties corresponding to the rights of those non-paradigmatic right-holders as being conditional upon their attaining the right level of rational capacity. Human rights duties cannot be conditional or progressive, but have to be unconditional and immediate. Since "ought implies can," the lack of feasibility of any of the corresponding duties at any given time prevents the human right from arising.[76]

The critique of setting rational capacity as a threshold for human rights is that it excludes certain human beings from the scope of human rights-holders and that this is prima facie contrary to the idea of the generality or equality of human rights. More precisely, it excludes those with impaired mental abilities: some, because they are still developing, like children, and others, because they never had them, like mentally disabled people, or have lost them, like elderly people. I will take those three groups of individuals in turn, and defend their complete or partial exclusion from the personal scope of human rights by showing how one should approach their "rights" when they have not yet acquired or have lost their rational competences. Note that excluding certain individuals from the scope of human rights-holders does not exclude them from the scope of morality.[77] Their interests should be protected and various imperfect duties may arise towards them without being owed to them as right-holders.[78] Moreover, as we will see, children and elderly people have special rights that protect their acquiring and loss of rational capacity and hence of human rights just before and after that acquisition and loss.

First of all, children's rights. Children's incomplete rational development leads to lesser or no human rights in some cases to the extent that human rights require a minimal level of rational competence. Infants and, to a lesser extent, children falling below that threshold have no human rights.

Interestingly, before the 1989 CRC, children were not regarded as holders of human rights, even general ones, under general international human rights instruments. As a matter of fact, children's interests were protected only indirectly and not as subjects of human rights by those instruments (e.g. Articles 25-6 UDHR; Articles 14 and 24 CCPR; Articles 10, 12, and 13 CESCR).[79] Nowadays, children's rights are recognized expressly and are either reinforced general rights or special rights that protect children only. Still, they do not belong to all children at once from their birth and very infancy onwards.[80] On the contrary, they are acquired by the child gradually, together with their acquisition of rational competences. This corresponds to the idea of "rights in stages."[81] Following Feinberg (1982), one may consider the rights of children whose relevant rational competences have not arisen yet to be "in trust" with their parents and/or the State (e.g. Article 5 CRC).[82]

Interestingly, the age limit of 18 (Article 1 CRC) as the cutoff date at which children's rights become adult rights, i.e. full general rights, confirms the rational competence threshold for the acquisition of human rights. Age is used as a shorthand for intellectual development and competence. Even if it remains largely imperfect, it is sufficiently general to capture the different stages in the rational development of human beings and sufficiently determinate. Hence the distinction between infants who have no human rights, children who acquire them in stages and whose rights are in trust until then, and adults who are deemed rational (unless proven otherwise, as we will see) and who have all human rights.

Secondly, elderly people's rights. This is the other end of the spectrum of development of rational capacities, as it were, and a very sensitive issue. To date, there is no international regime of human rights specific to elderly people's rights.[83]

There are difficulties applying the "rights in stage" approach to elderly people, as their rights are not being acquired, but lost, on the one hand, and age cannot be used as a shorthand for loss of rational capacity by contrast to its development, on the other. Of course, the "rights in trust" construction may apply, and actually echoes much of the domestic civil law for the protection of the person. The problem remains as to when this should apply. We are left with a case-by-case assessment of that loss of rational capacity. This may explain why this task has been left to domestic administrative and judicial authorities in practice so far, and why there has been no international human rights law on the issue yet.

Finally, mentally impaired people's rights. The rights of mentally impaired people are non-existent in international human rights law and practice. For instance, the CRPD does not mention the issue of rational competences. The only exception is that of the developing child with disability (e.g. Article 7 CRPD), but this is for reasons pertaining to child development precisely.[84] This is no surprise given that it is the hardest case of all. Mentally impaired people only benefit from general human rights to the extent they reach the minimal threshold of rational capacity needed for the rights to arise. If they do not, there is no possibility of applying the "rights in stage" and "rights in trust," for their rights will simply not arise. They either never did or have ceased to for lack of rational capacity.

I will come back to two of those three groups of right-holders in the context of special rights and the internal boundary within human rights between general and special rights.

4.3 Individuality-Related Boundaries and the Individualism Critique

My argument so far has been that human rights belong to human beings who have reached (if they are adults) or have the potential to attain (if they are children) a threshold level of rational capacity. Individuality therefore, amounts to a third boundary to the personal scope of human rights: groups are excluded from the scope of human rights-holders. The proposed egalitarian reading of human rights-holders fits the core of international human rights law and practice where most human rights are rights of individuals.

Before discussing the reasons for restricting the personal scope of human rights to individuals, it is important to clarify what is meant by collective rights. Given their egalitarian dimension, the collective dimension of human rights is particularly central and does not necessarily turn them into group rights.[85] Thus, many individual human rights may be rights that pertain to interests that have a social or collective dimension or are constitutive of a social or political "role."[86] Such "collective" rights are not regarded as group rights *stricto sensu* on the proposed account.

There are three understandings of collective rights one may encounter depending on the criterion used to qualify them as collective.[87] The first understanding of collective rights understands group rights by reference to the *exercise* of the right. The interest and the right are individual, but the right is exercised collectively, such as the right to self-government. The second understanding of collective rights refers to the *kind of interest* protected by the right. The interest and the right are individual, but the interest protected is an interest in a collective good.[88] One may mention the right to be elected, the right to due process, or "minority rights,"[89] such as the rights that belong to women, children, or ethnic or religious groups. The right to self-determination is an example of a right falling into the first and second categories. Finally, a third understanding of group rights is based on the *right-holder*, when both the interest and the right are collective.[90] As examples, one may mention certain participatory cultural rights or the right to security.

Of all three, it is the third kind of group rights that is most commonly referred to qua group rights *stricto sensu*. It is also the only one whose exclusion is required by the proposed egalitarian reading of the personal scope of human rights. Among the difficulties raised by group rights *stricto sensu*, one should, first of all, mention their qualification as rights. While many authors regard group rights as moral rights, some argue against them for ontological reasons pertaining to the moral agency of groups.[91]

Secondly, among authors who favor the existence of moral group rights, very few accept that group rights qualify as human rights.[92] First of all, under the interest-based approach to human rights followed in this chapter, for a moral right to qualify as a human right, it has to protect a fundamental and general interest. Unlike their members, however, groups do not have fundamental interests. Even if they did, those interests are not general enough: they are group-relative. Even in a world of groups, the generality of groups could not be sufficiently transitive with that of individuals to warrant the egalitarian dimension of human rights. A second difficulty with the qualification of group rights as human rights has to do with the high-priority mandatory nature of human rights in morality. Group rights do not have the relational and systematic features of human rights qua moral entitlements.[93] Finally, groups cannot be equal to individuals politically, and cannot be said to participate in a meaningful way in politics (with individuals or among themselves).[94] There is only one relevant group on this understanding of political equality, and that is the relevant polity or group of citizens.

Of course, this interpretation of international human rights law leaves a small fraction of the practice unaccounted for— and, for instance, the alleged human rights of business corporations or religious groups under the ECHR. Even under the proposed reading, however, collective rights in the third category could be salvaged by being interpreted as individual rights. An alternative may be to refer to collective rights in the third category as rights of peoples (e.g. Articles 1(1) CCPR and CESCR) or as "group rights" *stricto sensu*, and not as human rights.[95]

5 Holding Rights Equally, albeit Specially

If human rights are equal rights that belong to all, the special protection granted by international human rights instruments to some people still needs to be explained and accounted for within the proposed egalitarian reading of human rights. This is the second kind of boundaries to the personal scope of human rights mentioned in Section 1: their internal boundaries.

The special protection granted to some human rights-holders in international human rights law occurs through different mechanisms. It may take place through a reinforced protection of general rights (e.g. religious freedom of the child in Article 14 CRC) or through special rights (e.g. the right to registration of the child under Article 7 CRC). In the latter case, special rights may be granted expressly or merely derived from the general ones through judicial interpretation (e.g. the right to security of vulnerable people derived from the prohibition of torture and degrading treatment in Article 3 ECHR[96]).

The reasons most commonly advanced for special rights pertain to the special vulnerability of right-holders, whether as such (e.g. children, elderly people, or people with disability) or due to the circumstances in which they are situated (e.g. migrant workers).[97] There are many difficulties with the concept of vulnerability in this context. Standard vulnerability to standard threats is indeed a key element in the structure of human rights.[98] Only those generalized or generic individual interests threatened by general or standard threats may be protected as human rights, for only those rights may be equal rights. Special vulnerability to special threats, as a result, cannot give rise to general or equal human rights.[99] Of course, within the category of general human rights-holders, some may be more vulnerable than others to standard threats. While this kind of special vulnerability may be protected while saving the egalitarian dimension of human rights, the former cannot. Special rights in that sense are not, at least prima facie, compatible with the equality of human rights. For instance, reinforcing positive duties of protection of the right to privacy of HIV patients or pregnant women is compatible with the equality of human rights, while granting a special right to migrants by mere virtue of their special vulnerability is not.

The way out of this dilemma may be to distinguish between special rights that are inegalitarian, and should be rejected on the proposed reading of the generality of human rights, and two subsets of special rights that may be justified on egalitarian grounds: non-discrimination rights (Section 5.1) and development rights (Section 5.2).

5.1 Non-Discrimination Rights and the Equality of Human Rights

Non-discrimination rights are individual rights, but the interests protected are individual interests in collective goods. Indeed, the inequalities at stake affect individuals with heightened vulnerability to the standard threats protected by human rights due to their belonging to a structurally disadvantaged group. Those individual rights are needed to protect the equal moral status of each individual within the larger group when his or her belonging to a subgroup is a source of social inequalities.[100] The key difference from other human rights, however, is that the absence of unequal treatment constitutes the actual objective interest protected by non-discrimination rights. Equal moral status does not merely play a role as a threshold of recognition of the importance of the protected interests, but actually becomes the interest to protect as well.

Of course, the prima facie inegalitarian nature of those group-specific or group-differentiated non-discrimination rights has been criticized.[101] Recognizing unequal rights to correct social inequalities seems, indeed, to fly in the face of the principle of equal moral status qua threshold of importance of all protected interests and human rights. It is difficult, however, to see how the egalitarian dimension of other human rights could be respected were those social inequalities to subsist. In that respect, non-discrimination rights reinforce the protection of the equal moral status of every person by other individual human rights. This echoes James Nickel's (2007: 163) idea that only those group-differentiated rights that can be derived from general human rights for their own protection may be justified.

5.2 Development Rights and the Equality of Human Rights

There is another group of prima facie special rights that may be justified on egalitarian grounds, and those are "development rights." They arguably may be justified on egalitarian grounds to the extent that they protect a person's rational capacity when it is developing (or waning[102]), the very capacity that can make its subject a human rights-holder and hence an equal member of the political community.

A case in point is children's rights.[103] The main feature of children's rights qua special rights is their concern for children's incomplete rational development. Special rights of the child that protect the specific interests of the child in acquiring rational competences are likely to have lower requirements of rational competence, albeit still situated above the minimal threshold of rational competence. Thus, one distinguishes between "liberty rights" (e.g. Articles 12–16 CRC) that only arise once the child is well above the rational threshold and is a quasi-adult, as it were, on the one hand, and "welfare rights" (e.g. Article 24 CRC) or "development rights" of the child (e.g. Article 28 CRC) that accompany the acquisition of rational capacity by the child, on the other.

6 Conclusion

International human rights law and practice reveal an ambivalent approach to the personal scope of human rights: human rights are often less equal or general than they claim and are claimed to be. The inequalities of human right are of two kinds: some vulnerable individuals are also protected by special rights, thus drawing an internal boundary within the scope of human rights-holders, while others have limited or no human rights at all, thus delineating an external boundary around the scope of human rights-holders.

In this chapter, I have presented an argument that fits and justifies the core of the practice of international human rights law regarding the scope of human rights-holders, while criticizing it at the same time for some of its contradictions. More specifically, I have argued for an egalitarian reading of human rights, before accounting on that basis for the humanity-based, capacity-related, and individualistic boundaries of human rights, on the one hand, and defending it against the tendency to expand the scope of special rights beyond what I have referred to as justified "non-discriminatory rights" and "developing rights," on the other.

Acknowledgments

Thanks to Detlef von Daniels and the DFG Graduierten Kolleg Grakov *Verfassung jenseits des Staates* for the invitation to present an earlier version of this chapter at the Humboldt University in Berlin on June 24, 2014, and to the participants for their comments and critiques. Thanks to Odile Ammann, my research assistant, for her help with the formal editing of the chapter.

Notes

1. e.g. Tasioulas (2012a: 17); Griffin (2008: 83). See also Nickel (2007: 37); Gérard (2007: 21).
2. The generality of human rights should be distinguished from their universality: the former pertains to the personal inclusion of every single individual in every polity ("rights of all human beings qua *human beings*"), whereas the latter pertains to the territorial inclusion of all polities and hence of all individuals in those polities ("rights *of all human beings...*"). Of course, the generality of human rights implies their universality, but I will focus only on the former in this chapter.
3. I am not considering the rights of States under international human rights law in this chapter. See Besson (2012).
4. See Morsink (2009: 29).
5. See http://www2.ohchr.org/english/law/ and http://www.ohchr.org/EN/ProfessionalInterest/Pages/CoreInstruments.aspx, accessed July 8, 2014.
6. See also Besson (2013a).
7. See Mégret (2008), (2011).
8. Contra: Griffin (2008: 93); and Tasioulas (2012a).

9. See Tasioulas (2012a), based on Wolterstorff (2008: 327–9).
10. See Griffin (2008: 50, 92).
11. See, e.g., Beitz (2009); Raz (2010a), (2010b).
12. See, e.g., Nickel (2007: 37).
13. See Besson (2013d), (2015a).
14. See, e.g., Besson (2013c), (2014a), (2015a).
15. See Besson (2014a).
16. On the directedness of rights, see, e.g., Sreenisavan (2009); Wenar (2013: 207–8); Cruft (2013).
17. On "molecular" rights, see Wenar (2005).
18. See Nickel (2007: 23).
19. See Besson (2015a).
20. See Nickel (2013).
21. See Besson (2011), based on ECtHR, *Al-Skeini and others v. the United Kingdom* (appl. no. 55721/07), Judgment (Grand Chamber), 7 July 2011, Reports 2011; [2011] 53 EHRR 589.
22. See Buchanan (2009).
23. On the threshold of equal moral status, see, e.g., Buchanan (2009: 358–71) See also Section 4.1 of this chapter, "Species-Related Boundaries and the Speciesism Critique."
24. Buchanan (2009: 347).
25. See Buchanan (2009: 348–9).
26. See Anderson (1999: 289 and 313).
27. See Buchanan (2010: 708–10, at 708).
28. See Buchanan (2009: 378–9); Buchanan (2011: 233).
29. See Buchanan (2011: 233).
30. This is compatible with people having other moral rights that are different and non-general as long as they are neither basic moral rights nor human rights. See Buchanan (2009: 378–9).
31. See, e.g., Tasioulas (2013).
32. See Tasioulas (2013).
33. See, e.g., Waldron (2002: ch. 3). See also Wolterstorff (2008: 352–61).
34. See, e.g., Habermas (2010).
35. See Buchanan (2009).
36. See Tasioulas (2013); Williams (2005: 102).
37. See, e.g., Buchanan (2005: 77–8).
38. See Nickel (2007: 61).
39. See also Anderson (1999: 288–9); Habermas (2010: 472).
40. See Anderson (1999: 288–9).
41. See Christiano (2010: 121).
42. See Besson (2013b), (2015a).
43. See Buchanan (2009: 380) with reference to Waldron (2002: ch. 3). See also Anderson (1999: 317–18).
44. See also Anderson (1999: 289).
45. See Besson (2014a).
46. See Forst (2010), (1999: 48); Christiano (2008: 138, 156).
47. See Cohen (2004: 197–8; Forst (2010); Baynes (2009: 382).
48. See, e.g., Waldron (2002).
49. See Raz (1986: 180); Wenar (2013: 206, 218).

50. See, e.g., ECtHR, *Zdanoka v. Latvia* (appl. no. 58278/00), Judgment (Grand Chamber), 16 March 2006, Reports 2006-IV; [2007] 45 EHRR 17, par. 98.
51. I owe this term to Rowan Cruft.
52. See Besson (2014a).
53. See Besson (2013c).
54. See Besson (2015b).
55. See, e.g., Buchanan (2005: 78–80), (2008). See also Besson (2015b).
56. See also Tasioulas (2012a).
57. See also Griffin (2008: 83).
58. On (equal) dignity as a redundant justification of human rights, see Besson (2013c).
59. For a defense of the human rights of future generations, see Feinberg (1980); Caney (2008).
60. See Besson (2014a). Contra: O'Neill (2005).
61. For a rebuttal of the potentiality argument, see also Griffin (2008: 84).
62. Note that these biological arguments themselves are far from uncontroversial. For instance, the definition and boundaries of the human species (e.g. *homo sapiens*) are still evolving. This makes biology-based moral arguments like those of Tasioulas (2012a) or Wolterstorff (2008: 313) difficult to maintain.
63. See, e.g., Liao (2012), although he may object to the qualification of his argument as a type of "moral speciesism."
64. See, e.g., Singer (2009).
65. See Williams (2006: 150).
66. e.g. Griffin (2008: 95).
67. Buchanan (2011: 122).
68. See Buchanan (2011: 209–41.). See also Liao (2012).
69. Buchanan (2011: 213–4).
70. Buchanan (2011: 121).
71. See, e.g., Griffin (2008: 93).
72. See Buchanan (2011: 215).
73. See Griffin (2008: 88 and 91–4) (on the criteria for a justified stipulation).
74. See also Griffin (2008: 50).
75. See, e.g., Tasioulas (2012b).
76. See Besson (2014a).
77. For a similar exclusion, see Kant (1996: nos. 15–21).
78. See O'Neill (1988); Griffin (2008: 91, 95).
79. See, e.g., Inter-American Court of Human Rights, *Legal Status and Human Rights of the Child* (OC-17/2002), Advisory Opinion, 28 August 2002, par. 137.
80. See Locke (1988: ch. 6, no. 55): "Children, I confess are not born in this full state of Equality, though they are born to it."
81. See Archard (2006); Griffin (2008: 94–5).
82. Of course, those entrusted "rights" are neither the parents' nor the children's, for the latter have no human rights yet.
83. See Mégret (2011).
84. See Mégret (2008).
85. See Raz (1986: 179, 247–8).
86. See Raz (1986: 180). See also Wenar (2013: 206, 218).
87. Buchanan (2004: 409–13).
88. See, e.g., Raz (1986: 247–55); Réaume (1988: 10).

89. See Nickel (2007: 155); Gérard (2007: 188 ff.).
90. See, e.g., Waldron (2002).
91. See Waldron (2002); Tamir (1999).
92. See, for a discussion, e.g. Waldron (2002); Tamir (1999).
93. See Waldron (2002); Tamir (1999).
94. See also Gérard (2007: 201).
95. See also Gérard (2007: 59–66).
96. See ECtHR, *L. v. Lithuania* (appl. no. 27527/03), Judgment, 11 September 2007, Reports 2007-IV; [2008] 46 EHRR 22, par. 46. See the critique by Judge Sajo in ECtHR, *MSS v Belgium and Greece* (appl. no. 30696/09), Judgment (Grand Chamber), 21 January 2011, Reports 2011; [2011] 53 EHRR 2.
97. See Besson (2014b).
98. See Besson (2013c). On standard or general threats in general, see Shue (1996: 13–34).
99. Nor does vulnerability in itself justify rights in the first place: see also Griffin (2008: 85 and 90–1).
100. See Altman (2011). See also Nickel (2007: 155).
101. e.g. Waldron (2002); Nickel (2007: 161–3).
102. Even though, strictly speaking, aging is not a form of development in biological terms (mostly for reproductive reasons), I will refer to those special human rights as development rights.
103. See O'Neill (1988); Archard (2004).

References

Altman, Andrew (2011) "Discrimination." In Edward. N. Zalta (ed.), *Stanford Encyclopedia of Philosophy*, https://plato.stanford.edu/entries/discrimination/, accessed August 11, 2019.

Anderson, Elizabeth S. (1999) "What Is the Point of Equality?," *Ethics* 109(2): 287–337.

Archard, David (2004) *Children's Rights and Childhood*, 2nd edn. London: Routledge.

Archard, David (2006) "Children's Rights." In Edward. N. Zalta (ed.), *Stanford Encyclopedia of Philosophy*, https://plato.stanford.edu/entries/rights-children/, accessed August 11, 2019.

Baynes, Kenneth (2009) "Toward a Political Conception of Human Rights," *Philosophy and Social Criticism* 35(4): 371–90.

Beitz, Charles R. (2009) *The Idea of Human Rights*. Oxford: Oxford University Press.

Besson, Samantha (2011) "The Extra-Territoriality of the European Convention on Human Rights—Why Human Rights Depend on Jurisdiction and What Jurisdiction Amounts to," *Leiden Journal of International Law* 25(4): 857–84.

Besson, Samantha (2012) "The Right to Have Rights—From Human Rights to Citizens' Rights and Back." In M. Goldoni and C. McCorkindale (eds.), *Hannah Arendt and the Law*. Oxford: Hart Publishing, 335–55.

Besson, Samantha (2013a) "The Egalitarian Dimension of Human Rights," *Archiv für Sozial- und Rechtsphilosophie Beiheft* 136: 19–52.

Besson, Samantha (2013b) "International Human Rights and Political Equality—Implications for Global Democracy." In E. Erman and S. Näsström (eds.), *Political Equality in Transnational Democracy*. London: Palgrave, 89–123.

Besson, Samantha (2013c) "Justifications of Human Rights." In D. Moeckli and S. Shah (eds.), *International Human Rights Law*, 2d edn. Oxford: Oxford University Press, 34–52.

Besson, Samantha (2013d) "The Law in Human Rights Theory," *Zeitschrift für Menschenrechte—Journal for Human Rights* 7(1): 120–50.

Besson, Samantha (2014a) "La structure et la nature des droits de l'homme." In M. Hottelier and M. Hertig (eds.), *Introduction aux droits de l'homme*. Schulthess: Zurich, 19–38.

Besson, Samantha (2014b) "La vulnérabilité et la structure des droits de l'homme—L'exemple de la jurisprudence de la Cour européenne des droits de l'homme." In L. Burgorgue-Larsen (ed.), *La Vulnérabilité saisie par les juges en Europe*. Brussels: Bruylant, 59–85.

Besson, Samantha (2015a) "The Bearers of Human Rights Duties and Responsibilities for Human Rights—A Quiet (R)Evolution," *Social Philosophy & Policy* 32(1): 244–68.

Besson, Samantha (2015b) "Human Rights and Constitutional Law." In Rowan Cruft, S. Matthew Liao, and Massimo Renzo (eds.), *Philosophical Foundations of Human Rights*. Oxford: Oxford University Press, 279–99.

Buchanan, Allen (2004) *Justice, Legitimacy, and Self-Determination: Moral Foundations for International Law*. Oxford: Oxford University Press.

Buchanan, Allen (2005) "Equality and Human Rights," *Politics, Philosophy & Economics* 4: 69–90.

Buchanan, Allen (2008) "Human Rights and the Legitimacy of the International Order," *Legal Theory* 14(1): 39–70.

Buchanan, Allen (2009) "Moral Status and Human Enhancement," *Philosophy and Public Affairs* 37(4): 346–81.

Buchanan, Allen (2010) "The Egalitarianism of Human Rights," *Ethics* 120(4): 679–710.

Buchanan, Allen (2011) *Beyond Humanity?*. Oxford: Oxford University Press.

Caney, Simon (2008) "Human Rights, Climate Change, and Discounting," *Environmental Politics* 17(4): 536–55.

Christiano, Thomas (2008) *The Constitution of Equality: Democratic Authority and its Limits*. Oxford: Oxford University Press.

Christiano, Thomas (2010) "Democratic Legitimacy and International Institutions." In Samantha Besson and John Tasioulas (eds.), *The Philosophy of International Law*. Oxford: Oxford University Press, 119–37.

Cohen, Joshua (2004) "Minimalism About Human Rights: The Most We Can Hope For?," *The Journal of Political Philosophy* 12(2): 190–213.

Cruft, Rowan (2013) "Why Is It Disrespectful to Violate Rights?," *Proceedings of the Aristotelian Society* 113(2): 201–24.

Feinberg, Joel (1980) "The Rights of Animals and Unborn Generations." In *Rights, Justice and the Bounds of Liberty: Essays in Social Philosophy*. Princeton, NJ: Princeton University Press, 159–84.

Feinberg, Joel (1982) "A Child's Right to an Open Future." In W. Aiken and H. LaFollette (eds.), *Whose Child? Parental Rights, Parental Authority and State Power*, edited by. Totowa, NJ: Littlefield, Adams and Co, 124–53.

Forst, Rainer (1999) "The Basic Right to Justification: Toward a Constructivist Conception of Human Rights," *Constellations* 6(1): 35–60

Forst, Rainer (2010) "The Justification of Human Rights and the Basic Right to Justification—A Reflexive Approach," *Ethics* 120: 711–40.

Gérard, Philippe (2007) *L'Esprit des droits—Philosophie des droits de l'homme*. Brussels: Publication des Facultés universitaires Saint-Louis.

Griffin, James (2008) *On Human Rights*. Oxford: Oxford University Press.

Habermas, Jürgen (2010) "The Concept of Human Dignity and the Realistic Utopia of Human Rights," *Metaphilosophy* 41(4): 464–80.

Kant, Immanuel (1996) *The Metaphysics of Morals*, tr. and ed. by Mary Gregor. Cambridge: Cambridge University Press.

Liao, S. Matthew (2012) "The Genetic Account of Moral Status: A Defense," *Journal of Moral Philosophy* 9(2): 265–77.

Locke, John (1988) *Two Treatises of Government*, ed. by Peter Laslett. Cambridge: Cambridge University Press.

Mégret, Frédéric (2008) "The Disabilities Convention: Towards a Holistic Concept of Rights," *The International Journal of Human Rights* 12(2): 261–78.

Mégret, Frédéric (2011) "The Human Rights of Older Persons: A Growing Challenge," *Human Rights Law Review* 11(1): 37–66.

Morsink, Johannes (2009) *Inherent Human Rights—Philosophical Roots of the Universal Declaration*. Philadelphia, PA: University of Pennsylvania Press.

Nickel, James W. (2007) *Making Sense of Human Rights*, 2d edn. Oxford: Blackwell.

Nickel, James W. (2013) "Goals and Rights—Working Together?." In M. Langford, A. Sumner and A. E. Yamin (eds.), *The Millennium Development Goals and Human Rights: Past, Present and Future*. Cambridge: Cambridge University Press, 37–48.

O'Neill, Onora (1988) "Children's Rights and Children's Lives," *Ethics* 98(3): 445–63.

O'Neill, Onora (2005) "The Dark Side of Human Rights," *International Affairs* 81(2): 427–39.

Raz, Joseph (1986) *The Morality of Freedom*. Oxford: Clarendon Press.

Raz, Joseph (2010a) "Human Rights in the emerging World Order," *Transnational Legal Theory* 1(1): 31–47.

Raz, Joseph (2010b) "Human Rights without Foundations." In Samantha Besson and John Tasioulas (eds.), *The Philosophy of International Law*. Oxford: Oxford University Press, 321–37.

Réaume, Denise (1988) "Individuals, Groups and Rights to Public Goods," *University of Toronto Law Journal* 38(1): 1–27.

Scheffler, Samuel (2003) "What Is Egalitarianism?," *Philosophy and Public Affairs* 31(1): 5–39.

Shue, Henry (1996) *Basic Rights: Subsistence, Affluence and US Foreign Policy*, 2d edn. Princeton, NJ: Princeton University Press.

Singer, Peter (2009) "Speciesism and Moral Status," *Metaphilosophy* 40(3–4): 567–81.

Sreenisavan, Gopal (2009) "Duties and Their Direction," *Ethics* 120: 465–94.

Tamir, Yael (1999) "Against Collective Rights." In C. Joppke and S. Lukes (eds.), *Multicultural Questions*. Oxford: Oxford University Press, 158–81.

Tasioulas, John (2012a) "On the Nature of Human Rights." In G. Ernst and J. C. Heilinger (eds.), *The Philosophy of Human Rights: Contemporary Controversies*. Berlin: Walter de Gruyter, 17–59.

Tasioulas, John (2012b) "Towards a Philosophy of Human Rights," *Current Legal Problems* 65(1): 1–30.

Tasioulas, John (2013) "Justice, Equality, and Rights." In R. Crisp (ed.), *The Oxford Handbook of the History of Ethics*. Oxford: Oxford University Press, 768–92.

Waldron, Jeremy (2002a) *God, Locke, and Equality: Christian Foundations in Locke's Political Thought*. Cambridge: Cambridge University Press.

Waldron, Jeremy (2002b) "Taking Group Rights Carefully," in G. Huscroft and P. Rishworth (eds.), *Litigating Rights: Perspectives from Domestic and International Law*. Oxford: Hart Publishing, 203–20.

Wenar, Leif (2005) "The Nature of Rights," *Philosophy and Public Affairs* 33(3): 223–52.

Wenar, Leif (2013) "The Nature of Claim-Rights," *Ethics* 123(2): 202–29.

Williams, Bernard (2005) *In the Beginning Was the Deed: Realism and Moralism in Political Argument*, ed. G. Hawthorn. Princeton, NJ: Princeton University Press.

Williams, Bernard (2006) "Human Prejudice," in *Philosophy as a Humanistic Discipline*. Princeton, NJ: Princeton University Press, 135–52.

Wolterstorff, Nicholas (2008) *Justice: Rights and Wrongs*. Princeton, NJ: Princeton University Press.

FURTHER READING

Cruft, Rowan, S. Matthew Liao, and Massimo Renzo (2015) "The Philosophical Foundations of Human Rights: An Overview." In *Philosophical Foundations of Human Rights*. Oxford: Oxford University Press, 1–41.

Waldron, Jeremy (2017) *One Another's Equals. The Basis of Human Equality*. Cambridge, MA: Harvard University Press.

CHAPTER 6

....

MOTIVATING SOLIDARITY WITH DISTANT OTHERS

Empathic Politics, Responsibility, and the Problem of Global Justice

....

CAROL C. GOULD

1 INTRODUCTION

....

IF distributive justice requires solidarity or forms of mutual identification and support as a condition within nation-states, so the conditions for achieving global justice would seem to presuppose a measure of solidarity stretching between people across borders. Even if the requirements for realizing global justice are grounded in economic and social human rights or are interpreted in other normative terms, they would need to draw on feelings of solidarity and actions to aid distant others who are impoverished or oppressed, inasmuch as meeting those rights or requirements takes the provision of resources and other conditions beyond what particular nation-states can provide for their own poor or disadvantaged people. Indeed, with the intensification of transnational economic integration, new forms of regional and global democracy would likewise demand new solidarities within these emerging cross-border communities. As I have discussed in previous work such as Gould (2014), transnational labor, social, and political movements, as well as a variety of civil society organizations, already incorporate certain modalities of solidarity, in the interest of achieving justice or providing aid. I have conceptualized the transnational solidarities emerging from social movements or associations of groups in civil society (online or offline) in terms of the notion of a network, understood as distinct from but still consistent with the more unitary solidarities that may exist within national communities.

In those works, I proposed that solidarity in this normative sense consists of fellow feeling and action on the part of individuals or groups in which they stand with others with the aim of overcoming oppression or alleviating suffering. Ideally, their relations are characterized by a sharing of resources and the readiness to provide mutual aid. A requirement is that those standing in solidarity exhibit *deference* to those they are trying to help in their efforts, who are to take the lead in these processes, and solidaristic actions are based on some degree of empathy with them. Yet solidarity goes beyond empathy or fellow feeling to involve concrete actions to realize both the shared interests and the fundamental rights of others. Some fully developed solidarity groups which involve this sort of readiness to offer mutual aid are characterized by a tendency to reciprocity, though in practice we often see better-off groups aiding those less well off (Gould 2007, 2014).

Examples of solidarity groups can be found in traditional labor union solidarity—involving picketing, along with sharing of information and resources; the anti-sweatshop movement, e.g. as discussed by Iris Marion Young (2006); and the solidaristic social movements that arose in opposition to dictatorships in Latin America. But we can also include the transnational networks of civil society organizations that spring into action following various natural disasters, e.g. hurricanes or tsunamis, where the disasters are often exacerbated by deeply inegalitarian social conditions.

People may share economic interests with those with whom they join in solidarity, but in other cases their common interests are less obvious, particularly when solidarity actions are between the better off and those less well off, or oppressed, or else suffering great hardship. I have proposed that these various cases tend to exemplify a new network form of solidarity, extending across borders, and they require theorizing in ways that go beyond classic accounts of solidarity within a single community or nation. Unlike the more unified forms of solidarity that bind people within national or small group contexts, the newer and looser network modes involve overlapping relations of cooperation where people or groups link up to work on specific projects, and, indeed, often make use of communications or social networks to organize and coordinate their action (Gould 2014). Needless to say, such transnational solidarities are only a part of what is needed to realize justice—clearly institutional innovation is required as well, but I will put aside that important topic here.

The specific problem I want to address in this chapter is the motivation that people have or might come to have to stand in solidarity with distant others. We can see such a problem of motivation arising in regard to the variety of norms that theorists have argued apply to the domain of transnational politics. Thus, they have variously focused on global justice and the obligation to alleviate extreme poverty and have urged consideration of the differential impacts of climate change on people around the world; they have explored the possibilities for new forms of democracy extending across borders; and they have argued for the importance of helping to fulfill the human rights not only of co-nationals but of people across the globe. Yet in practice, these well-founded normative requirements, as with the requirement for transnational solidarity itself, come up against the following major difficulty: while people often concern themselves with the well-being of family, friends, and others close to them, perhaps extending to their own national group, they may not show much concern for the situation of distant others who have salient needs and important rights that demand realization. I suggest that this raises the insufficiently explored question of the motivation for fulfilling human rights or basic needs (and also for working towards transformative change in institutions). Indeed, reflecting on this issue may lead us to question the very possibility of solidaristic feeling and action toward distant others so as to promote justice.

Where this issue of motivation has been considered in ethics or political philosophy to date, the emphasis has most often been placed on the importance of rationally reflecting on people's equality worldwide and the correlative significance of respecting their human rights. Needless to say, a variety of causes—whether pressing personal needs or the call of nationalism—can overwhelm these dictates of reason. Yet even where such causes are absent, we find that a simple recognition of people's equality, as a moral status, though clearly of great importance, may be insufficient to motivate the requisite feelings of solidarity and concern. Even more difficult to motivate is the solidaristic action required to address the urgent needs of these distant people or to deal with the deeply insecure situation of those who are, or will be, disproportionately affected by climate change. In the first part of this chapter, I want to focus constructively on what I take to be one missing element in the existing analyses, namely the role that can be played by empathy, in its relation to reasoning, in motivating people to take seriously the situation of the people who are impacted by contemporary transnational politics, and the ways that empathy can help generate action in solidarity with them. In fact, other sorts of emotions also play a crucial role, for example outrage and indignation, but I will not be able to develop those here.

My general thesis is that a more empathic politics, together with the wide cultivation of a disposition to empathy, would have significant impact on cross-border social movements oriented to the achievement of global justice, and on deliberations concerning ecological governance. To understand how this is the case, we would need to closely examine the relation of reason and empathy, and how they interrelate in the recognition of people's equality and in people's readiness to support initiatives aimed at global and ecological justice, but I will only be able to sketch the outlines of this project here. We should perhaps mention at the outset that we find a lack of concern with the situation of others not only in transnational contexts but even among co-nationals within the boundaries of a given nation-state when we move beyond feelings for people one is close to, especially family and friends. This lack of concern can manifest itself in intolerance, as well as in the reluctance to include others within the nation-state itself, or to support them through governmental policies, e.g. regarding redistribution through taxation. I would suggest that empathy has a place in extending people's concern in those national contexts as well.

But I have another—related—interest in this chapter, which I will address in Section 3. I believe that the proposed approach to solidarity with distant others and the motivation for taking part in solidaristic social movements has implications for the current issue of how to conceive of responsibility for global justice. There has been considerable discussion of the viability of a new social connections model of responsibility, proposed especially by Iris Young. In that model, a forward-looking sense of political responsibility is said to follow from our actual social connections, in our webs of interrelations with others as consumers, producers, etc., within an increasingly global political economy, with the employment of sweatshop labor being a case in point. In her posthumously published book, *Responsibility for Justice*, Young (2011) briefly mentions solidarity as an aspect of this model, but that dimension is not much theorized there. I believe that much of what Young says about the social connections that are relevant for forward-looking responsibility are best cashed out in terms of a notion of transnational solidarity such as the one I have theorized (Gould 2007, 2014).

Clearly, Young was strongly influenced by notions of social critique, and takes seriously the range of social movements oriented to social justice. However, the social connections model can be subjected to some criticisms (see, for example, Gould 2009), and I believe a closer look at solidarity and the motivation for it will enable us to give a somewhat different account of what I would call *social* (rather than only political) *responsibility* in these transnational or global contexts. Indeed, a focus on empathy and its relation to solidarity can yield a distinctive approach to social change, one that ties in not only with social critique, but takes our specific social connections in the context of a more universalistic and inclusive conception of human rights and of who is responsible for fulfilling them.

2 EMPATHETIC CONCERN, RATIONAL RECOGNITION, AND SOCIAL CRITIQUE

We can turn now to the analysis of empathy and then in Section 3 consider solidarity itself as a model for responsible action oriented to global justice. Of course, empathy (or the related notion of sympathy) is not a new focus in political thought. Indeed, the broader issue of the relation of reason to the passions or to sentiment has been a significant theme for political philosophy for millennia. But it has only recently come to prominence in democratic theory in regard to deliberative processes where reasoning is held to be ineffective without the presence of empathy or concern for one's interlocutor (e.g. Morrell 2010). Similarly, John Rawls's account of public reason within political liberalism (Rawls 1993) and even his earlier treatment of reasoning to principles of justice in an original position (Rawls 1971) have been analyzed as requiring empathy for others (Okin 1989, 1994). Social movement theorists have emphasized the way movements engage feelings of shame, anger, and moral outrage, and depend on care and concern for those they are designed to benefit (Dunn 2004; Goodwin, Jasper, and Polletta 2011; Jasper 2011). And philosophers as well as social psychologists have analyzed the relationships between the notions of sympathy, empathy, and care (Darwall 2010 ; Slote 2007; Hoffman 2000). Yet there has been little attention within political philosophy to the interrelations of reason and empathy within the new forms of transnational politics.

What, then, are the motivational and epistemic functions of empathy and what capacity does it have to transform reasoning in transnational (and national) political contexts? I want to suggest that empathy, in a distinctive social interpretation, is required for the full recognition of others and their distinctive needs, thereby potentially rendering cross-cultural dialogue and deliberation more effective. So, whereas theorists have articulated the importance of rational respect for each person's dignity, as in Gewirth (1998) or Griffin (2008) on human rights; or deliberation aimed at "the force of the better argument" (Habermas 1984: 25); or public reasoning about matters of justice (Rawls 1997) as a means of achieving normative agreement within ongoing systems of cooperation under conditions of "reasonable pluralism," yet what is missing from these accounts, I suggest, is the understanding of the perspective of the other and some degree of "feeling with" them that is connoted by the notion of empathy (Bartky 2002; Gould 2007).

Along these lines, feminist ethics has prioritized empathy and sympathy, and has extended care to politics, as in the work of Joan Tronto (1993, 2013) and Virginia Held (2006). The import of caring dispositions and care work for the international and transnational domain have been examined, e.g. by Fiona Robinson (2011). Would empathizing with distant others transform the instrumental types of reasoning prevalent there? Thus far, the tie between reason and the sentiments has had a national focus, as in Martha Nussbaum's (2013) study of political emotions, in which love for one's nation is taken as paradigmatic. Yet the transnational domain raises special problems: Despite the intensification of cross-border communications enabled by the Internet and economic globalization, ongoing cooperative arrangements comparable to nation-states are lacking, there is little public deliberation in the institutions of global governance, and global justice movements remain limited. Moreover, the potential dangers with empathy also need to be held in view, e.g. a too easy identification with the other, with an attendant reinforcement of privilege, and the insufficiency of empathy without the correction of reasoning, and without awareness of differential power positions.

The contemporary literature that bears on these issues includes work on practical reason and the emotions in politics (e.g. Marcus 2002; Deigh 2008), the feminist critique of the gendered emphasis on reason (e.g. Lloyd 1984), and care ethics (Gilligan 1982; Held 2006). Although not intended for political contexts, I think we can make use of Stephen Darwall's (2010) helpful meta-ethical analysis of empathy and sympathetic concern in his discussion of "rational care." Beyond the basic phenomena of motor mimicry and emotional contagion, which Darwall calls "primitive forms of empathy," he goes on to analyze *projective empathy*, in which we "place ourselves in the other's situation and work out what *to* feel, as though we were they" (Darwall 2010: 60). Darwall notes that here "feelings present themselves as warranted by that person's situation to which they apparently respond," and if someone believes that another's feeling are not warranted by her situation, it will be more difficult to share them through empathy (Darwall 2010: 61). This suggests the importance of some awareness and understanding of the other's context, with interesting implications for the case of global justice, as we will see. Darwall goes on to observe about projective empathy:

> When we projectively mirror others' feelings, we not only show them how they feel, we also indicate to them that we agree about how to feel. We show we understand their feelings and signal our willingness to participate with them in a common emotional life. This makes projective empathy central to the formation of normative communities—like-minded groups who can agree on norms of feeling.
>
> (Darwall 2010: 62)

Of course, a question will arise about how extensive such like-minded groups or shared feelings can be, or even whether this is a useful model for social or political solidarity movements, and I will return to this question later.

Darwall goes on to consider what he calls *proto-sympathetic empathy*, in which we "simulate, not just a person with the relevant feelings, but someone conscious of their feelings and their relevance for that person's life." This form of empathy "brings the other's relation to his situation into view in a way that can engage sympathy on his behalf" (Darwall 2010: 63). This form of empathy places emphasis on awareness of, and sharing, the person's feelings in their situation, rather than just projecting oneself into the situation of the other. Darwall is concerned to distinguish empathy from sympathy, but this developed form of empathy certainly includes concern for the other, if not sympathy per se, so that his sharp distinction is not entirely convincing.

In any case, it is evident that empathy and sympathy are sometimes used interchangeably in the literature (as well as in ordinary language), and there is far from an agreed conception of empathy. It is widely seen to involve a cognitive understanding of the perspective of another, but some (like Darwall 2010: 51) believe that it need not entail sympathy, such that a sadist can manifest empathy. But I will not follow Darwall in that interpretation. In my view, drawing more on work in the continental and aesthetics tradition, the notion of empathy, from *Einfühlung* (as "feeling into"), retains its ties with concern, as "feeling with" the other (or *Mitgefühl*), combined with cognitively sharing the other's perspective. But as we have already observed, understanding something of the concrete context of the other is helpful in this process. In this connection, empathy towards others across borders poses special challenges. For one thing, while global media episodically generate sympathy and empathy, they highlight only a few victimized others, and provide little background on their concrete social conditions. Moreover, empathy with distant others tends to lack the immediacy of more primitive forms of empathy, and must often rely on what Darwall calls projective empathy, where one imagines what life must be like for them.

The complexities involved in sharing another's perspective have been regarded by some—like Jesse Prinz—as making empathy too cognitively burdensome to be useful for morality. Indeed, Prinz argues that it plays little role in motivating action to benefit others, which he thinks emerges more from an emotion of outrage at human suffering (Prinz 2011). However, I am not clear where our sense of the outrageousness of human suffering comes from, if it does not involve some element of empathy with the suffering of others. Prinz further argues that experimental psychology does not support a central role for empathy. Martin Hoffman (2011), in contrast, cites numerous experiments to support just this centrality of empathy for morality and the law, and he specifically argues for its importance for judges and jurors. Our focus, though, is less on either of these dimensions, that is, the moral or the legal per se, and instead is primarily on social solidarity movements, as well as on the motivation ordinary people feel for the sufferings and oppression of others as a basis for solidaristic action toward them. The feeling in question here, then, is that of solidarity with these others, based on some degree of empathy with them.

For purposes of a social and political analysis (rather than ethics or meta-ethics or the law), I think we can operate with a more ordinary sense of empathy. As Heather Battaly characterizes it:

> Pre-theoretically, we think that empathy involves caring about, or sharing the emotions of, or knowing another person. To see this, we need only consider paradigm cases of empathy; for example, the empathy of a close friend, or therapist. Empathic friends and therapists care about the subject, share in her emotional highs and lows, and reliably predict her thoughts, feelings, and behavior.   (Battaly 2011: 277)

I should note that Battaly ends up rather dismissive of this "folk" concept and suggests that it may not be any sort of a virtue. Fortunately, at least many aestheticians tend to be more appreciative of empathy's importance in this sense (e.g. Lopes 2011).

Where distant others are involved, it seems clear that empathy requires linguistic (or pictorial) mediation, through which these others are represented to oneself or by which one represents them to oneself. This suggests a significant role for imagining, in conjuring both the perspective and the feelings of the other. Thus, such forms of empathy necessarily go beyond emotional contagion or mimicry, although they can be prompted by depictions of the tribulations of these others.

Yet, while empathy may help us address global injustice by enhancing our concern with others, as I have suggested, it is also subject to what has been called *empathic bias*. That is, people often display a bias toward their kin, friends, or ethnic group, which Hoffman (2011: 251) calls *in group* or *familiarity bias*. It is also highly sensitive to the salience and intensity of distress cues, as he puts it (Hoffman 2011: 250), and people tend to empathize more easily with those who are present rather than absent or distant, which Hoffman calls *here and now* or *salience bias*. He proposes that what is needed is to correct empathy with principles, especially that of fairness, and also to educate people in processes of extending empathy. Hoffman even proposes using some tricks, like imagining a family member or friend to be among the absent potential victims in need of empathy (Hoffman 2011: 254). Yet another problem (noted by Goldie 2011: 303) is when the perspective taking involved in empathy takes the form of usurping the agency of the other or failing to recognize their distinctiveness.

Although these problems suggest that empathy alone cannot be relied on to generate sensitivity to the needs of others, they should not lead us to dismiss empathy's role. Rather, they support the need to couple empathy with reasoning, as well as with social critique. It can be recognized that empathy itself engages some of the basic forms of reciprocity ingredient in ordinary experience, especially in its core aspects of taking the perspective of the other, and feeling with them. But it is clear that, to be effective for social and political understanding or for transnational solidarity with distant others, empathy needs to be coupled with the more reflective reciprocities involved in the application of notions of fairness and equality. It is here that reasoning and an appeal to principles play an essential role, in correcting for bias, and positively affirming a fundamental equality among people as possessors of human rights.

We can observe that in a context of reciprocal recognition of others, empathy interestingly can work at one and the same time to enhance commonalities and to highlight relevant differences. The commonalities come in with the sharing of perspectives (as well as the perception of shared needs), and the differences with attention to the person's unique situation to which those perspectives are responsive. This double function of empathy emerged clearly in Darwall's analysis as described earlier. I propose that from a normative standpoint we can discern four factors that need to come together: (1) a feelingful identification with the situation of others, as empathetic concern; (2) the sharing of perspectives, as the cognitive and recognitive side of empathy; (3) the extension of empathetic concern by means of rational notions of equality and fairness, such that empathy becomes less exclusivist and open to being extended to others who are similarly situated to those to whom one is attending; inevitably, some application of imagination will also be needed here; and (4) the noting and appreciation of relevant differences (involved in empathizing with others in the particularities of their situation).

This last dimension—the role of differences—can effectively address the worry that empathy inevitably leads to disregard of the specific agency of others. It need not do so, especially if it is coupled with deference to the other's own self-interpretation of needs and their context for action. I have already suggested that this element of deference is essential in regard to standing in solidarity with others Moreover, we can see that the requirement to take one's lead from the others interestingly ties empathy and solidarity in social and political contexts to the requirement of democracy, in giving rise to a desideratum to actually hear from these others concerning their interpretation of their interests. We can observe, then, that although imagination is important to empathically understanding the perspective and situation of the other, in transnational politics more than imagination is needed. Forms of democratic input need to be devised to hear from affected others what their needs are and the optimal forms that solidarity and aid can take (Gould 2014: part 3).

We can call the form of recognition of others that is involved here an empathetic or generous one rather than a bare or rigorous recognition, where the latter involves only a moral recognition of them as humans, without attention to the specificities of their needs and their situation (Gould 2014). Nonetheless, we can see that the application of reasoning and principle is essential to correct for empathic bias. Thus, full recognition of others cannot be expected to result from empathy alone. Yet, as feminist authors have observed, reasoning itself should not be understood here in a narrow sense in which it would simply be a matter of, for example, equating one thing to another. Rather, reason can be supple and nuanced in discerning both relevant similarities that support the extension of principles in inclusive ways, as well as relevant differences that are involved in casuistic application of principles to diverse cases.

If we also take seriously the appreciation of context and its variability that is involved in appropriate extensions of empathy to others, particularly to groups of people, we need to make a place for social critique, which itself has empirical as well as normative dimensions. That is, the perception of the situation of others would need to engage an understanding of its oppressive, dominating, or immiserating dimensions. This critical understanding is especially important for effective solidaristic action in support of others, keeping in mind the requirement of considerable deference to their agency.

From this perspective of the need for a more empathic politics, we can briefly raise the question of the full adequacy of a Rawlsian conception of public reason, unless it is taken to require that even shared reasons have to be developed in an empathic context. Recall that for Rawls, citizens in a political society, understood as an ongoing cooperative scheme, are to offer each other fair terms based on reciprocal respect, and political power is to be exercised in ways that "all citizens can publicly endorse in the light of their own reason" (Rawls 2001: 26), at least where "constitutional essentials and matters of basic justice" (Rawls 2001: 62) are at stake (though the scope of public reason is in dispute, e.g. Quong 2004). Leaving aside the viability of Rawls's political-metaphysical distinction, we can ask whether his political approach can work to bridge cultures within a democratic state if it does not also recognize the distinctive perspectives and needs of others with different backgrounds.

Moreover, moving to the transnational domain, which lacks a single cooperative framework or the coercive law characteristic of a political society, a Rawlsian notion of public reason may need to give way to other forms of dialogue. Some models of deliberative democracy, such as that proposed by John Dryzek (2002), extend transnationally, and there is a growing recognition of the importance of emotion and rhetoric within such deliberations, e.g. in Mansbridge (1999); Young (2002); O'Neill (2002); and Dryzek (2010). In such contexts, where cross-border deliberations are needed, I have elsewhere proposed the need for a new model of inclusive dialogue—online and off—which would include criticism (and self-criticism) in regard to one-sided perspectives, along with empathy for participants and for those affected by its results (Gould 2014, This may suggest a role for imagination, as in Hannah Arendt's concept of an "enlarged understanding," despite her critique of the concept of empathy (Arendt 1989).

3 EMPATHIC POLITICS, SOLIDARITY, AND RESPONSIBILITY FOR GLOBAL JUSTICE

I would now like to briefly sketch the implications of the above account for a conception of responsibility for global justice, taking as a point of comparison the social connections model that Iris Young promulgated in some articles and the book *Responsibility for*

Justice (Young 2004, 2006, 2011). A critical examination of her view and a consideration of an alternative, though related theory will enable us to get clearer on the function of empathy and of solidarity in fulfilling the requirements of global justice.

In *Interactive Democracy* (Gould 2014), I argue for a human rights approach to global justice, giving major weight to the realization of economic and social rights. I see this as a way of more fully actualizing a principle of equal positive freedom, understood as prima facie equal rights of access to the conditions of self-transformative activity, individual and collective. Transnational solidarities aiming at justice, and consisting in overlapping networks of people and groups working to counter oppression and eliminate suffering, can take the lead in fulfilling these rights, especially when coupled with the development of new forms of transnational democracy in both economic and political institutional contexts. As in Young's approach, social movements and a socially critical perspective play a major role in my own theory. However, unlike her, I suggest that human rights, as specifying the basic conditions for people to be able to act and develop over time (whether as individuals or groups), constitute an indispensable guide for these social and political processes. There is, accordingly, a role for such general or universalistic norms (with the proviso that there may be varying interpretations of them). However, in my account, particularistic social relations, for example those of social solidarity movements, can help to construct these universals on the ground, or in practice.

In "Varieties of Global Responsibility: Social Connection, Human Rights, and Transnational Solidarity" (Gould 2009), I analyzed Young's claim that in virtue of our social connections we have forward-looking political responsibility rather than backward-looking liability for structural injustice. Young writes:

> The social connection model of responsibility says that individuals bear responsibility for structural injustice because they contribute by their actions to the processes that produce unjust outcomes. Our responsibility derives from belonging together with others in a system of interdependent processes of cooperation and competition through which we seek benefits and aim to realize projects.   (Young 2011: 105)

Generally eschewing the notion of guilt and blame for such cases, Young, nonetheless, holds that, as participants in these processes, we are responsible for structural injustice. She writes:

> Most of us contribute to a greater or lesser degree to the production and reproduction of structural injustice precisely because we follow the accepted and expected rules and conventions of the communities and institutions in which we act...If we contribute by such actions to the processes that produce structural injustice, we are responsible in relation to that injustice.   (Young 2011: 107)

Indeed, in the original article on this theme, Young writes that "On the social connection model, workers share responsibility for combating sweatshop conditions and ought to be organized in order to do so" (Young 2006: 124).

In my earlier article (Gould 2009), I objected to the idea that the workers share responsibility for the situation, since they are subject to exploitation in a system not of their choosing. Indeed, they participate in it only in an equivocal sense, since their own choice to work in the conditions they do is constrained by the requirement for work itself. Although workers do not have to work for a given capitalist firm, they generally have to work for one or another capitalist firm. And I believe that workers would choose to avoid exploitative conditions if they could, and also would generally (though probably not in every case) prefer to have more control over the work process, certainly if they thought that was achievable. Thus, despite the present emphasis in the feminist and global justice literature on the responsibility of victims for their own situation, I am wary of any suggestion that would amount to "blaming the victim."

It is clear that Young would characterize this sense of responsibility and blame in terms of liability as opposed to the forward-looking political responsibility she emphasizes, but I am not sure that the responsibility of capitalist corporations for exploitation of workers is best understood simply in terms of a legal notion of liability in any case, though that could well be part of the matter. Moreover, the causality that Young restricts to the liability model would seem to remain indispensable to a full account even of our political and social responsibility (Nussbaum 2009). In the presentation of her views incorporated in the book *Responsibility for Justice*, Young gives more weight than in the initial articles to the applicability of the liability model, as far as top executives and managers are concerned (Young 2011: 131), and that is justified. To my mind, exploitation is indeed blameworthy. But it is also structural, with complex implications for how to understand the responsibility involved and how to distribute it to owners and managers within corporations.

Inasmuch as exploitation is not caused by the workers themselves, it seems to me at best misleading to say that they share responsibility for remedying the situation, even from a forward-looking perspective. What I find troublesome is to regard the difference between capitalists and workers in regard to responsibility as only a matter of degree. After all, the structural injustice would be largely remedied if the capitalists simply stopped exploiting. Getting them to do so is both a practical matter of interest, as well as a matter of justice. Although the workers too have a responsibility to achieve justice, as everyone does, I suggest below that this general responsibility does not arise primarily from their specific social connection to capitalists. Granted, some aspects of their responsibility for justice will concern their specific situation—in particular, workers should properly take the lead in achieving their freedom, in the sense that they are the ones best situated to know what is needed and what will be effective. It is in this sense that the relevant relation we can take to them is one of standing in solidarity with them.

Indeed, we could hope that workers would not only lead the effort to overcome any exploitative features of their situation in their own interest and for the sake of justice, but would willingly take on subsequent responsibilities to co-determine their own conditions of production and participate in directing the production process, in forms of workplace democracy. But explicating that latter sort of responsibility, which would arise from their reciprocal obligations to each other as workers as well as their participation in common activities with others within firms, would take us somewhat far afield from the present theme. It can be noted that the notion of common activities also designates a sort of social connection, but a different sort from the type Young theorizes and in my view it gives rise to rights of democratic participation within the firm or in political contexts. What this shows, I think, is that the idea of social connections is too broad, taken as such, and needs to be specified and differentiated, where different sorts of social connections give rise to different arenas and types of social and political responsibility, as well as to different senses of solidarity.

We can see, then, that an additional problem with the claim that everyone who participates in a particular set of social connections or political economic processes is responsible for remedying the structural injustice is its vagueness. What is the scope of these processes, who exactly are the participants, and how should degrees of responsibility be determined (Gould, 2009; Neuhäuser 2014)? It almost seems as if Young's view leads to precisely what she is determined to avoid—namely, "if everyone is responsible, then no one is."

There is certainly one very general sense in which participating in social and political processes leads to forward-looking responsibility. This would refer to the fact that social systems are created and therefore changeable phenomena, although only through collective action. But I do not think that Young has this extremely abstract point in mind, and that general claim is not easily specified to particular social connections in any case. Specific social contexts for action are not always easily demarcated, and everyone participates one way or another in the global political economy, particularly in terms of its impacts on climate change. It does make sense to say that to the degree that one participates and reproduces particular oppressive or exploitative features of the economic order, one has special responsibilities to remedy those, and that is probably the root insight in Young's model. But I think that is only one of the responsibilities that one has and not always the most salient. Often, the dire situation of people with whom one is not directly connected in social, political, or economic contexts may be more urgent than those with whom one is connected. Further, the responsibilities that emerge from these social connections are best seen as having both backward-looking and forward-looking dimensions, where these types of responsibilities are intertwined. (Nussbaum 2009). And I have also suggested that the aspects that concern one's complicity in those unjust processes are not adequately summed up with the term liability, with its reference exclusively to the legal dimension. It can, indeed, involve moral responsibility as well as guilt.

In my view, there is a somewhat different and very general respect in which everyone is responsible, but one that differs from Young's account, although it shares the premise that the social order is a human creation in some deep sense and is open to change. This wide application of the notion of responsibility importantly supplements conventional understandings of both liability and political responsibility. Without working out the argument for this in depth here, we could say that this general responsibility arises from the fundamental features of interdependence and neediness that mark the human condition—that we all require others to meet our needs and to establish economic and social contexts for our development. Given that there is no clear bound to these processes, which extend in any case beyond families and even nation-states, we are all ultimately responsible for meeting each other's human rights and for realizing justice. Needless to say, this does not mean that everyone must meet everyone else's needs and rights. But it would require efforts to support (or, where relevant, help to create) institutions that would serve to fulfill or realize them. As Robert Goodin has effectively argued, this responsibility must of necessity be fulfilled in a more practical and delimited fashion short of a fully universal one, so that our general responsibility is devolved to political communities or other smaller units (Goodin, 1988). If those units cannot fulfill this responsibility, however, others must step in to help. This latter process often calls for action in solidarity with others, as well as action by the existing political communities themselves. (Indeed there may eventually be useful regional or global modalities that can be employed as well, e.g. new and more democratic institutions or global governance, or forms of global taxation or redistribution.) Moreover, this general responsibility would seem to imply the requirement, stressed by Pogge, not to prevent others from fulfilling their basic human rights (Pogge, 2002). The latter might apply especially in regard to the specific social connections in which one participates in the global political economy, with the requirement to work to eliminate the structural injustice they may entail, as emphasized by Young.

We can discern a crucial twofold role for transnational solidarity networks within this framework: (1) where existing political communities or societies are unable to adequately meet human rights and the demands of justice, there is a need for solidaristic action by outsiders; and (2) where solidarity is a way of meeting our social and political responsibility to help eliminate unjust economic processes of exploitation or domination, in the first place with regard to those with whom we are closely connected and secondarily those at more remove from our own situation. Interestingly, Young does include a brief discussion of solidarity in the final version of the social connections model, introducing it by way of Derrida's notion of political friendship (Young 2011). But I think that solidarity plays a more central role than she envisions there. Indeed, much of what Young says about the social connections that can help realize our forward-looking social or political responsibility to work for justice is in my view better framed as concerning the solidarity relations and actions that we should pursue within the transnational domain. As in Young's account, I understand people's participation in any given solidarity network as largely voluntary (Gould, 2007). And I believe such solidarity networks provide one of the key ways in which global justice can be realized across borders.

The version of solidarity that I espouse grows out of a quasi-Marxist notion of labor movement solidarity, but I see it as extending beyond the sphere of laborers to interrelations between civil society organizations, as well as between individuals and social movement groups operating on and offline. It is goal-oriented—to the achievement of justice and the elimination of oppression and suffering. Yet, importantly, solidarity also retains a role for interest, understood as both self-interest and collective interests around which people may organize themselves. Thus, this view does not interpret solidarity in the first place as general human solidarity, although that remains a horizon of possibility. Instead, solidarity binds people together who share interests, both narrower economic ones and those that follow from their joint commitment to justice. And it most often retains its antagonistic sense in opposing those who oppress or exploit others. In this respect, it differs from Young's version of social connections.

Despite this tie with interest, however, solidarity can move to become a more inclusive movement in the interest of justice, understood as an effort not only to meet people's basic needs and rights, but also to enable more democratic forms of decision-making about production and distribution processes. In this view, solidarity is the middle term, as it were, which explains how ordinary people and groups can plausibly seek to establish the connections that enable human rights fulfillment. In this reading, the responsibility for justice flows from our fundamental interdependencies, although the responsibilities are normally devolved to political communities and pertain to our specific economic connections as well, whether localized within firms or extending more broadly.

Within this perspective, the global norms of justice and human rights can be seen to gain purchase in practice through the solidaristic construction of new social connections in the interest of justice and human rights fulfillment. That is, people rightly take on these responsibilities, in the first place to particular individuals and groups who are oppressed, and often beginning with those to whom they are more closely connected. In such contexts, solidarity retains its ties to individual and collective interests. Yet there needs to be some scope for the choice of the objects of solidaristic affiliation and mutual aid. It does not have to be limited to those with whom one has a previously established direct social connection. And all the particularistic forms of solidarity actions and networks ought to remain open to including other participants who want to act in the interest of justice.

We can turn in conclusion to some observations about the role of empathy in such solidarity processes, as well as in the recognition of others as deserving of fulfillment of their human rights. Empathy, in connection with reason, plays a somewhat different role in the recognition of human rights than it does in concrete solidaristic acts that work to fulfill those rights, though these solidaristic acts are ultimately undertaken for the sake of human rights realization and justice more generally. The abstract or general recognition of the rights of others requires empathy as a ready *disposition*, and to be successful needs to take the form of empathic or generous recognition of others, with attention to their needs, wants, and differentiated context of existence. It requires a readiness to feel empathy with others, although it does not require actually feeling empathy with all others, which would be impossible. And despite its abstract character, this form of recognition and the empathic disposition could be expected to have some beneficial effects in our everyday moral dealings, and not only in politics.

The empathy involved in solidarity is necessarily more particularistic, and is addressed in the first place to understanding those who are oppressed or suffering, with the aim of aiding and ameliorating their situation. Such solidarity too needs to involve elements of a generous or empathic recognition of the specificity of others and their situation. But these particularistic solidaristic actions, most often on the part of social movements, can be undertaken with a universalistic intent, understood both in terms of the goals of realizing justice and human rights and in terms of the methods or modes of operation, which need to be as inclusive as possible. Through such overlapping transnational solidarities, I would suggest, new connections can be established and essential networks of mutual aid brought into being.

REFERENCES

Arendt, Hannah (1989) *The Life of the Mind*. New York: Harcourt.

Bartky, Sandra Lee (2002) *Sympathy and Solidarity*. Lanham, MD: Rowman & Littlefield.

Battaly, Heather (2011) "Is Empathy a Virtue? " In Amy Coplan and Peter Goldie (eds.), *Empathy: Philosophical and Psychological Perspectives*. Oxford: Oxford University Press, 277–301.

Darwall, Stephen (2010) *Welfare and Rational Care*. Princeton, NJ: Princeton University Press.

Deigh, John (2008) *Emotions, Values, and the Law*. Oxford: Oxford University Press.

Dryzek, John (2002) *Deliberative Democracy and Beyond: Liberals, Critics, Contestations*. Oxford: Oxford University Press.

Dryzek, John (2010) "Rhetoric in Democracy: A Systemic Appreciation," *Political Theory* 38(3): 319–39.

Dunn, Jennifer L. (2004) "The Politics of Empathy" *Sociological Focus* 37(3): 235–50.

Gewirth, Alan (1998) *The Community of Rights*. Chicago: University of Chicago Press.

Gilligan, Carol (1982) *In a Different Voice*. Cambridge, MA: Harvard University Press.

Goldie, Peter (2011) "Anti-Empathy." In Amy Coplan and Peter Goldie (eds.), *Empathy: Philosophical and Psychological Perspectives*. Oxford: Oxford University Press, 302–17.

Goodin, Robert (1988) "What is So Special about our Fellow Countrymen?," *Ethics* 98(4): 663–86.

Goodwin, Jeff, James M. Jasper, and Francesca Polletta (eds.) (2011) *Passionate Politics: Emotions and Social Movements*. Chicago: University of Chicago Press.

Gould, Carol C. (2004) *Globalizing Democracy and Human Rights*. Cambridge: Cambridge University Press.

Gould, Carol C. (2007) "Transnational Solidarities," Special Issue on Solidarity, ed. Carol Gould and Sally Scholz, *Journal of Social Philosophy* 38(1): 146–62.

Gould, Carol C. (2009) "Varieties of Global Responsibility: Social Connection, Human Rights, and Transnational Solidarity." In Ann Ferguson and Mechthild Nagel (eds.), *Dancing with Iris: The Philosophy of Iris Marion Young*. Oxford: Oxford University Press, 199–211.

Gould, Carol C. (2014) *Interactive Democracy: The Social Roots of Global Justice*. Cambridge University Press.

Griffin, James (2008) *On Human Rights*. Oxford: Oxford University Press.

Habermas, Jürgen (1984) *The Theory of Communicative Action*, Vol. 1, tr. Thomas McCarthy. Boston, MA: Beacon Press.

Held, Virginia (2006) *The Ethics of Care: Personal, Political, and Global*. Oxford: Oxford University Press.

Hoffman, Martin L. (2000) *Empathy and Moral Development* .Cambridge: Cambridge University Press.

Hoffman, Martin L. (2011) "Empathy, Justice, and the Law." In Amy Coplan and Peter Goldie (eds.), *Empathy: Philosophical and Psychological Perspectives*. Oxford: Oxford University Press, 230–54.

Jasper, James M. (2011) "Emotions and Social Movements," *Annual Review of Sociology* 37: 285–303.

Lloyd, Genevieve (1984) *The Man of Reason*. Minneapolis, MN: University of Minnesota Press.

Lopes, Dominic McIver (2011) "An Empathic Eye." In Amy Coplan and Peter Goldie (eds.), *Empathy: Philosophical and Psychological Perspectives*. Oxford: Oxford University Press, 118–33.

Mansbridge, Jane (1999) "Everyday Talk in the Deliberative System." In Stephen Macedo (ed.), *Deliberative Politics*. New York: Oxford University Press, 211–39.

Marcus, George E. (2002) *The Sentimental Citizen: Emotion in Democratic Politics*. University Park, PA: Pennsylvania State University Press.

Morrell, Michael (2010) *Empathy and Democracy: Feeling, Thinking, and Deliberation*. University Park, PA: Pennsylvania State University Press.

Neuhäuser, Christian (2014) "Structural Injustice and the Distribution of Forward-Looking Responsibility," *Midwest Studies in Philosophy* 38: 232–51.

Nussbaum, Martha (2009) "Iris Young's Last Thoughts on Responsibility for Global Justice." In Ann Ferguson and Mechthild Nagel (eds.), *Dancing with Iris: The Philosophy of Iris Marion Young*. Oxford: Oxford University Press, 133–46.

Nussbaum, Martha (2013) *Political Emotions: Why Love Matters for Justice*. Cambridge, MA: Harvard University Press).

Okin, Susan Moller (1989) "Reason and Feeling in Thinking about Justice," *Ethics* 99(2): 229–49.

Okin, Susan Moller (1994) "Political Liberalism, Justice, and Gender," *Ethics* 105(1): 23–43.

O'Neill, John (2002) "The Rhetoric of Deliberation," *Res Publica* 8: 249–68.

Pogge, Thomas (2002) *World Poverty and Human Rights*. Cambridge: Polity Press.

Prinz, Jesse (2011) "Is Empathy necessary for Morality." In Amy Coplan and Peter Goldie (eds.), *Empathy: Philosophical and Psychological Perspectives*. Oxford: Oxford University Press, 211–29.

Quong, Jonathan (2004) "The Scope of Public Reason," *Political Studies* 52: 233–50.

Rawls, John (1971) *A Theory of Justice*. Cambridge, MA: Harvard University Press.

Rawls, John (1993) *Political Liberalism*. New York: Columbia University Press.

Rawls, John (2001) *Justice as Fairness: A Restatement*, ed. Erin Kelly. Cambridge, MA: Harvard University Press).

Robinson, Fiona (2011) *The Ethics of Care: A Feminist Approach to Human Security*. Philadelphia, PA: Temple University Press.

Slote, Michael (2007) *The Ethics of Care and Empathy*. New York: Routledge.

Tronto, Joan (1993) *Moral Boundaries: A Political Argument for an Ethic of Care*. London: Routledge.

Tronto, Joan (2013) *Caring Democracy*. New York: New York University Press.

Young, Iris Marion (2002) *Inclusion and Democracy*. Oxford: Oxford University Press.

Young, Iris Marion (2004) "Responsibility and Global Labor Justice," Journal of Political Philosophy 12(4): 365–88.

Young, Iris Marion (2006) "Responsibility and Global Justice: A Social Connection Model," Social Philosophy and Policy 23(1): 102–30.

Young, Iris Marion (2011) *Responsibility for Justice*. Oxford: Oxford University Press.

FURTHER READING

Ackerly, Brooke (2018) *Just Responsibility: A Human Rights Theory of Global Justice*. New York: Oxford University Press.

Aragon Corwin, and Alison Jaggar (2018) "Agency, Complicity, and the Responsibility to Resist Structural Injustice," *Journal of Social Philosophy* 49(3): 439–60.

Bayertz, Kurt (ed.) (1999) *Solidarity*. London: Springer.

Brunkhorst, Hauke (2005) *Solidarity: From Civic Friendship to a Global Legal Community*. Cambridge, MA: MIT Press.

Ferguson, Ann (2009) "Iris Young, Global Responsibility, and Solidarity." In Ann Ferguson and Mechthild Nagel (eds.), *Dancing with Iris: The Philosophy of Iris Marion Young*. Oxford: Oxford University Press, 185–97.

Gould, Carol C. (1993) "Feminism and Democratic Community Revisited." In J. Chapman and I. Shapiro (eds.), *Democratic Community: NOMOS XXXV*. New York: New York University Press, 396–413.

Gould, Carol C. (2006) "Recognition, Care, and Solidarity." In Georg W. Bertram, Robin Celikates, Christophe Laudou, and David Lauer (eds.), *Socialité et reconnaissance. Grammaires de l'humain*. Paris: Éditions L'Harmattan, 243–56.

Gould, Carol C. (forthcoming) "Solidarity between the National and the Transnational: What Do We Owe to 'Outsiders'?" In Helle Krunke, Hanne Petersen, and Ian Manners (eds.), *Transnational Solidarity: Concept, Challenges and Opportunities*. Cambridge: Cambridge University Press.

Hall, Cheryl (2007) "Recognizing the Passion in Deliberation," *Hypatia* 22(4): 81–95

Held, Virginia (2018) "Taking Responsibility for Global Poverty," *Journal of Social Philosophy* 49(3): 393–414.

Kolers, Avery (2016) *A Moral Theory of Solidarity*. Oxford: Oxford University Press.

McKeown, Maeve (2018) "Iris Marion Young's 'Social Connection Model' of Responsibility: Clarifying the Meaning of Connection," *Journal of Social Philosophy* 49(3): 484–502.

Marcus, George E., W. Russell Neuman, and Michael MacKuen (2000) *Affective Intelligence and Political Judgment*. Chicago: University of Chicago Press.

May, Larry (2007) "The International Community, Solidarity and the Duty to Aid," *Journal of Social Philosophy* 38(1): 185–203.

Meyers, Diana Tietjens (1994) *Subjection & Subjectivity*. New York: Routledge.

Quong, Jonathan (2011) *Liberalism without Perfection*. Oxford: Oxford University Press).

Rawls, John (1999) *The Law of Peoples*. Cambridge, MA: Harvard University Press.

Roughley Neil, and Thomas Schramme, (eds.) (2018) *Forms of Fellow Feeling: Empathy, Sympathy, Concern and Moral Agency*. Cambridge: Cambridge University Press.

Sangiovanni, Andrea (2015) "Solidarity as Joint Action," *Journal of Applied Philosophy* 32(4): 340–59.

Sangiovanni, Andrea (2018) "Structural Injustice and Individual Responsibility," *Journal of Social Philosophy* 49(3): 461–83.

Satz, Debra (2005) "What Do We Owe the Global Poor?" *Ethics & International Affairs* 19(1): 47–54.

Scholz, Sally (2008) *Political Solidarity*. University Park, PA: Pennsylvania State University Press.

Schwarzenbach, Sibyl (2009) *On Civic Friendship*. New York: Columbia University Press.

Shelby, Tommie (2009) *We Who Are Dark: The Philosophical Foundations of Black Solidarity*. Cambridge, MA: Harvard University Press.

CHAPTER 7

....

JUST GLOBAL HEALTH

*Integrating Human Rights
and Common Goods*

....

JOHN TASIOULAS AND EFFY VAYENA

WHAT are the demands of justice that apply to global health policy? By global health policy we mean those practical measures, whether adopted and implemented by international organizations, states, corporations, or agents of some other kind, that have as their ultimate goal, in the words of the World Health Organization's evocative motto, "health for all." They are legal and other measures aimed at protecting and promoting the interest in health of every human being around the globe. In keeping with a long philosophical tradition, we deploy two distinct senses of the idea of justice. According to the first, justice concerns moral duties that are owed to and claimable by others as a matter of *individual rights*. In another, broader sense, justice concerns moral *duties* governing our conduct towards others, especially in so far as they fall within the proper remit of public decision-making.[1] The second sense of justice, the domain of other-regarding moral duties, includes the first sense, the domain of justice as rights, as a component. But the second sense of justice also encompasses other moral duties, notably duties to preserve and promote the *common good*, which are not linked to rights.

Transposed to the global context, justice to a significant degree consists in the morality of individual human rights and global common goods. To this extent, a justice perspective on global health policy must be bifocal in character. However, we contend that it is a profound error, if nonetheless a common one, to construe the two strands of justice as being in an inherently dichotomous and generally antagonistic relationship. Not only do we need to draw on both human rights and common goods, but the "individualism" of human rights is not to be starkly juxtaposed with the "collectivism" of the common good. On the contrary, the securing of human rights is an integral component of some global common goods. This chapter seeks to make a start on elaborating the meaning and implications of such an integrated, bifocal perspective in relation to global health policy.[2]

We begin by outlining the distinctive character of human rights: they are moral rights possessed by all human beings simply in virtue of their humanity (Section 1). In light of its prominent role in global health policy debates, the next two sections focus on the human right to health. One important question is how that right is to be individuated within the overall set of human rights. Contrary to a popular, radically "inclusive" interpretation, we suggest characterizing the human right to health's scope of concern primarily by reference to obligations regarding healthcare services and public health measures. This way of understanding the human right to health makes it clear that it is only one among a number of human rights that serve our interest in health and to which global health policy needs to be responsive (Section 2). We then offer an account of how to specify the content of the human right to health, i.e. the content of the duties regarding healthcare services and public health measures associated with the right. The process of content-specification, we argue, involves the application of a threshold criterion that incorporates considerations of possibility and burden. In addition, we question the utility of three ideas that have been widely thought to provide essential guidance in specifying the content of human rights: that human rights secure "minimum conditions" of a decent life, that they protect their holders against "standard threats," and that they are specified through decisions made in conformity with fair or democratic procedures (Section 3). In the Section 4, we explain why human rights cannot do all the work in shaping a just global health policy, giving special attention to the crucial role of health-related global common goods. We also respond to the converse hypothesis that global health policy must be overwhelmingly concerned with common goods *as opposed to* human rights. This response turns on showing how common goods may include, as a component, arrangements that secure human rights.

1   INTRODUCING HUMAN RIGHTS

Global health policy advocates have repeatedly called for a post-2015 development agenda that gives a prominent place to policy objectives couched in the language of human rights. These calls echo the chorus of agreement among a wide variety of international actors—including the United Nations, NGOs, governments, and ordinary citizens—on the vital importance of a human rights basis for the new development goals more generally.[3] Charitably interpreted, as more than just a rhetorical ploy intended to convey a sense of urgent commitment, this emphasis on human rights embodies a vital insight. The adoption of goals simply concerned with the promotion of human welfare—such as our interests in health, prosperity, education, etc.—is not enough. Human rights inject a distinctive moral dimension into policy objectives, one that is especially responsive to the plight of victims of injustice throughout the globe.

The distinctive character of human rights consists in the fact that they are universal moral rights: moral rights possessed by all human beings simply in virtue of their humanity.[4] They mark the threshold at which each individual human being's interests generate *duties* or *obligations* on the part of others to respect, protect, and promote those interests in various ways. The violation of an obligation is a moral wrong; by contrast, no wrong is committed simply by thwarting another's interests or leaving those interests unpromoted. For example, neither beating a rival for a coveted job nor failing to donate your spare healthy kidney for a transplant need be wrongful. Human rights are a distinctive moral register of critical assessment, beyond assessments tracking rises and falls in individual or collective welfare. The foregoing does not mean that well-being as such, or elements of it such as the global burden of disease, lacks normative significance. It is just to say that it cannot displace the distinctive kind of moral assessment introduced by human rights: the idea of moral duties owed to each and every human being, the violation of which specifically victimizes the right-holder. Indeed, the discourse of human rights is at the core of a "global justice" approach to health: justice, on one historically influential interpretation, consists in the rights-involving part of morality, and the subcategory of human rights is those moral rights that are held globally because they are possessed by people simply in virtue of their humanity.

So far, we have spoken of human rights as a certain kind of moral norm. Of course, there is now a firmly established doctrine of international human rights law in which various health-related human rights form an integral part.[5] Moreover, in excess of two-thirds of national constitutions explicitly include health rights, often by incorporating provisions in international human rights treaties.[6] But the morality of human rights is independent of its recognition by domestic or international law. A right does not need to be actually legally enshrined, let alone enforceable, to exist as a human right. On the contrary, human rights law is best understood as deriving its distinct identity from the attempt to give legal effect to background human rights morality, in so far as it is appropriate to do so through the medium of universally held individual legal rights. It is the background morality of human rights that is the main focus of this chapter. Three further preliminary observations are worth making in this connection.

First, the duties associated with human rights include positive duties to engage in certain forms of conduct, such as the provision of healthcare services, as well as negative duties to refrain from certain conduct, such as administering medical treatment without consent. Moreover, the positive duties associated with a right may be primary duties. In other words, they are duties that are not parasitic on other duties associated with the right, such as positive duties to compensate or make reparation triggered by a violation of some prior duty. Instead, human rights also impose primary positive duties to make certain goods and services available to their holders. Of course, there are special problems in the allocation of positive primary duties to duty-bearers, and in the specification of their content, which do not arise in the case of negative primary duties.[7] But these differences between the two kinds of rights, which are largely matters of degree, rather than kind, do not warrant the wholesale expulsion of so-called "socioeconomic rights," with positive primary duties, from the category of bona fide human rights.[8]

Second, there is no compelling a priori reason why the duties associated with human rights should be thought to fall exclusively on states, at least as primary duty-bearers. This idea is a distortion that a misplaced focus on legal instruments—constitutions and treaties—has introduced into thinking about human rights. Instead, we should maintain an open-minded and flexible attitude to the question of who the relevant duty-bearers are in any given time and place.[9] Multinational corporations, international organizations, and even individuals can be directly subject to human rights-related duties. Pharmaceutical companies, for example, may be directly subject to human rights obligations to make antiretrovirals and other drugs available to developing countries at a significantly lower cost than market price.[10] In an environment of accelerating globalization, with a concomitant decline of state power relative to various other global actors, the importance of not conceptually restricting human rights obligations to states is all the more pronounced. Indeed, precisely this insight is at the heart of the innovative Guiding Principles on Business and Human Rights that were approved by the United Nations in 2011. The Principles seek to provide an authoritative specification of the human rights responsibilities that directly bind corporations irrespective of their legal obligations in the jurisdictions in which they operate.[11]

Finally, another a priori commitment we should resist is the idea that a pro tanto case always exists for enshrining human rights as legal entitlements, let alone for taking the further step of making them enforceable legal entitlements.[12] Law is a vitally important mechanism of implementation, but it remains one mechanism alongside others, including social conventions, public opinion, and the inculcation of a rights-respecting ethos through fostering the internalization of human rights norms by individual and collective agents. Whether, and to what extent, individual human rights should be enshrined in counterpart legal rights is a matter of what is inherently appropriate and works in all the circumstances, which is subject to considerable variation in time and place. Evidence exists that making human rights legally claimable is sometimes counterproductive. For example, in Brazil the constitutionalization of the right to health appears to have facilitated a transfer of health resources to the better-off who can afford the cost of litigation.[13] The overall health budget remained fixed, but the better-off engaged in litigation against the government to siphon off a larger share of it for themselves, often in order to treat less serious ailments.[14] To take another example, the economist Jeffrey Sachs (2012) one of the chief architects of the Millennium Development Goals (MDGs), has ascribed the success in meeting those goals partly to the fact that they were not legally binding on states. This lowered the cost of states publicly signing up to the goals in the first place, thereby enhancing the likelihood that they would do so. In short, the difficult and multifaceted question of legalization is one that deserves extensive consideration on a case-by-case basis. No presumptive answer to it is already inscribed in the very nature of human rights.

2 INDIVIDUATION AND INCLUSIVITY

Human rights arise when universal human interests generate obligations on others to respect, protect, and promote those interests in various ways. Interests are here understood as the elements of well-being, the realization of which in a person's life make it a better life for them. We favor an objectivist and pluralistic account of the interests that ground human rights.[15] They are interests we have independently of whether we actually desire their realization, and they are not limited to one kind of interest—the interest in autonomy, for example—or to one category of interests, such as those interests that qualify as basic needs.[16] Instead, they comprise any of the genuinely universal human interests that are capable of generating duties on the part of others in the case of all human beings, simply in virtue of their humanity. Moreover, essential to the rights-generative role of human interests is that they belong to distinct individuals with equal moral status in virtue of their humanity: the status of human dignity. This is central to explaining the resistance of human rights to trade-offs both against other rights and against non-rights based considerations.[17]

In contrast to some human rights advocates in global health policy,[18] we resist characterizing the normative foundations of human rights exclusively in terms of capabilities rather than the more capacious notion of universal human interests. Capabilities, understood as the capacities to choose to realize various forms of valuable functioning in one's life—such as to be educated, have friends, enjoy good health— seem an unduly restrictive basis for human rights in at least two ways. First, in relation to the *scope* of human rights: human beings who lack a capacity for choice, whether through immaturity, congenital defect, or illness, would become problematic as subjects of human rights. Yet a program of involuntary euthanasia targeted at those in an advanced stage of senile dementia arguably constitutes a paradigmatic human rights violation. Second, in relation to the *content* of human rights: many duties imposed by human rights are not concerned simply with the protection of a sphere of individual choice as to whether to realize a functioning or not, but with the protection of interests independently of choice. And this is so with respect not only to those whose agency is non-existent or impaired but even to fully mature agents. This is how we would normally understand the rights not to be enslaved, tortured, or murdered, which partly explains why we do not treat these rights as waivable at the discretion of their holders. So, in the case of the right to health, sometimes what is at issue is respecting people's choices: enabling them to realize the functioning of good health by giving them the choice whether or not to undergo medical treatment, for example. On other occasions, such as the right to protection from an infectious disease, what may be called for is a program of vaccination that leaves little or no room for individual choice as to whether to realize the valuable functioning of immunity from the disease. This example illustrates a wider point: that some rights involve access to common goods, such as clean air or herd immunity, which, by their very nature, heavily constrain the possibility of individual opt-outs (see Section 4 below). In short, capabilities theory is undoubtedly a marked improvement on previous measures of social welfare, such as aggregate GNP. And capabilities will certainly figure prominently in articulating the moral significance of the interests recognized by a more pluralistic approach of the kind that we favor. But there is no compelling reason to limit from the very outset the human rights-generative considerations to capabilities.

The pluralistic theory of human rights claims not only that a plurality of interests are relevant to the justification of human rights generally, but also that typically any given individual human right is grounded in a plurality of interests, such as autonomy, health, knowledge, friendship, accomplishment, play, etc.[19] The right not to be tortured, for example, is grounded not only in our interest in autonomy, but also in our interest in being free from pain and in being able to form intimate and trusting relationships. This is also true of the human right to health: it serves not only our interest in health, but also various other interests which enjoying good health can enable us to realize, such as making and sustaining friendships, acquiring understanding of the world around us, or accomplishing something with our lives. Indeed, the right to health may even include entitlements to medical services, such as non-therapeutic abortions or cosmetic surgery, that are not primarily intended to serve the health interests of the right-holder. Hence, a diversity of interests helps to justify the existence of a human right to health and to shape the content of its associated obligations.

One way of falling into the trap of assuming that the human right to health is grounded exclusively in our interest in health is by adopting an unduly expansive interpretation of health. This is precisely what the WHO did in the preamble to its constitution, which notoriously states that "health is a state of complete physical, mental and social well-being and not merely the absence of disease and infirmity."[20] But, as has been repeatedly shown, this definition is far too broad. Health, on any remotely useful understanding, is one element of well-being among others, not the whole of it. And this remains the case even though health bears pervasive constitutive and instrumental relations to the other elements of well-being. For the purposes of this chapter, we can take health to be centrally concerned with the effective functioning of standard human physical and mental capacities.[21] A person can enjoy such functioning even when they are deficient in other elements of well-being, such as accomplishment and enjoyment. Moreover, they may even intelligibly put their health at risk in order better to achieve some other aspect of well-being, such as accomplishment or friendship.

There is a further crucial point worth making about the individuation of the human right to health. Although many familiar human rights serve our interest in health in all sorts of important ways, this does not automatically render these rights emanations of the general human right to health. Yet such an overly inclusive interpretation of the right to health has been propagated by the Committee on Economic, Social and Cultural Rights (2000), in its influential General Comment 14, as well as by other United Nations organs and leading global health scholars.[22] So, for example, Lawrence Gostin (2014: 257) notes that General Comment 14 treats as "integral components of the right to health" entitlements to food, housing, life, education, privacy and access to information. Indeed, Gostin goes on to suggest that this specification is probably too "constrained" and should be widened to include "gender equality, employment, and social inclusion." This inclusive approach is echoed, and perhaps taken even further, in a "Fact Sheet" on the Right to Health produced by the Office of the United Nations High Commissioner for Human Rights and the World Health Organization (2008: 3).

According to this document, the human right to health incorporates a slew of other rights, including gender equality and freedom from torture and other cruel, inhuman, or degrading treatment or punishment. By a process parallel to the WHO's inflation of the notion of health to embrace all of human well-being, such interpretations appear to absorb within the human right to health every right that bears positively on our interest in health. Indeed, on this radically "inclusive" approach, it is an open question, whether there is any right in the Universal Declaration of Human Rights, or in any of the two leading Conventions on Human Rights, which cannot be subsumed within the right to health, at least in so far as they involve duties that serve the right-holder's interest in health. After all, a colorable story can be told of how denial of the rights to citizenship, political participation, a fair trial, freedom of speech, religion, movement, and association, among others, can have a seriously detrimental impact on individuals' health.

Now, something has clearly gone awry if we are lumbered with such a bloated interpretation of the human right to health.[23] The mistake is to individuate the scope of the right simply by reference to whether a putative rights-based duty is justified in part by its service to our interest in health. Many—if not most—human rights serve our interest in health, and this is because they serve a multiplicity of interests, among which is health. Consider, for example, the fact that improvements in adult women's education accounted for 40 percent of the reduction in mortality between 1960 and 1990, although the steps taken to enhance educational provision are not obviously "healthcare" measures.[24] However, a human right is not picked out straightforwardly by the profile of interests it serves, we claim, but by reference to the subject matter of the obligations associated with it.

More specifically, our contention is that the right to health should be construed as principally ranging over obligations concerned with the provision of healthcare services by medical professionals and public health measures, such as sanitation, potable water, clean air, alcohol and tobacco control, and so on. On this view, there is a moderate sense in which the human right to health is an "inclusive" right. It "includes," as justified implications, various more specific rights to healthcare or public health measures, such as a right to health insurance or measles vaccination. By contrast, however, many so-called "social determinants of health," which are crucial in promoting the health of individuals, do not come under the right to health. Instead, determinants such as education, housing, employment, and a social environment free of gender and racial discrimination, in so far as there is a right to them, more plausibly fall under other rights. The rationale for excluding these social determinants is partly a holistic one, turning on the need to avoid excessive overlaps with other rights we feel compelled to recognize. But there is also a deeper rationale, which brings back the role of the interests served by the right in a more sophisticated manner. The question is whether or not the object to which one has a right serves the interest in health as its primary and direct objective, as in the case of clean air and water, or whether it does so indirectly, via the serving of other interests which are its primary goal, as in the case of education and employment. Healthcare services and public health measures satisfy this criterion, but the social determinants of health typically do not.

We cannot, therefore, infer that the right not to be tortured or the right against degrading treatment are incorporated in the right to health, since these rights are not properly understood as having some specific connection with the provision of healthcare or public health measures.[25] However, it is not always an uncomplicated matter to draw clear lines between different human rights. Sometimes the boundaries will be fuzzy, and there will occasionally be overlaps in the scopes of a given pair of rights. For example, the provision of training in first aid, or of health education more generally, might plausibly come under both the rights to health and to education. In consequence, it may sometimes be that the identical course of conduct constitutes a violation, or a fulfillment, of more than one human right. Often, we will need law to draw sharper lines between human rights that avoid overlaps where this would be beneficial in some way. We offer no general prescription for resolving these difficulties of line-drawing in a principled way, beyond the remarks about holism and primary and direct goals. What we have suggested, instead, is that the starting point in delineating the human right to health is very different from that adopted by the radical "inclusive" view. We need to individuate that right by reference to the subject matter of the obligations associated with it.

It might be objected that the rejection of the radical inclusivity thesis expresses little more than a preference for tidy normative housekeeping. But this is not so: it also makes sense of the idea that there are a number of fairly specific and irreducibly distinct human rights, so that enumerating a list of rights such as that in the Universal Declaration is a meaningful endeavor. It further caters to the idea that separating out distinct human rights is the best way of highlighting distinct normative concerns that might otherwise be obscured through conflation or subsumption. It is worth underlining a significant practical pay-off of the approach we advocate. If we follow the radically "inclusive" account to the right to health, we will face a needlessly Herculean task when assessing the extent to which the right to health is being fulfilled globally. This is because it will be necessary to keep track of the extent to which all health-enhancing rights are fulfilled. Progress towards such a massively sprawling goal is hard to monitor, and extremely difficult to achieve. This inevitably breeds uncertainty, frustration, and despair. In order to set ourselves a more determinate and manageable but still demanding target, we should adopt the more constrained interpretation of the right to health.

It is clear, on the view we have developed above, that global health policy cannot be exclusively responsive to the right to health. This is so even if we limit ourselves to human rights that serve our interest in health, as opposed to merely placing constraints on how we may serve it. Other human rights are also extremely relevant, such as the rights to life, physical security, religious freedom, privacy, education, work, and so on. Indeed, as noted earlier, if our main concern is with the promotion of health overall, securing a right such as that the right to education may be more important in some contexts than other healthcare related rights, such as the right to a minimum level of health insurance. Adopting a radically "inclusive" interpretation of the right to health threatens to obscure the vital independent role these other rights must play in shaping global health policy.

3 CONTENT SPECIFICATION

The preceding discussion of the fallacy of radical inclusivity concerned mainly the individuation of the human right to health at an abstract level: the question of how it was to be distinguished from other human rights. But a deeper problem concerns the speci-fication of its normative content, i.e. the content of the obligations associated with that right, even after we have identified their general subject matter. This is a difficult and many-sided topic, and here it is only possible to offer a few comments. Recall that a human right exists when, in the case of each human being, universal human interests generate obligations on others to respect, protect, and promote those interests in various ways. Obligations, or duties, are categorical and exclusionary reasons for action, non-compliance with which is a pro tanto basis for assigning blame (on the part of others) and experiencing guilt or self-blame (on the part of the duty violator).

It is a challenging task to articulate, in a general way, the conditions that need to be satisfied for the threshold from interests to duties to be crossed. However, at least two dimensions of this threshold are worth highlighting: *possibility* and *burden*. Both go some way towards unpacking the familiar maxim "ought implies can."[26] On the one hand, an obligation will only arise when it is possible to comply with the counterpart duty in relation to all of the supposed right-holders. The impossibility that prevents a duty arising may be of different sorts, ranging from logical impossibility to practical impossibility given fixed conditions of contemporary life. Taking an illustration of the latter kind, there may be inadequate resources now or in the foreseeable future to fulfill a proposed right for each individual human being. This would rule out, on any literal reading, a human right to health that imposed a duty to secure for all "the highest attain-able standard of physical and mental health."[27] Understood as an absolute standard, it is impossible to bring all human beings to this very high level of good health, irrespective of the vagaries of their personal history and genetic constitution. But this supposed right is also ruled out by a more complex reason, even if we relativize what is "attainable" to the personal history and genetic makeup of any given individual right-holder. This is the fact that the state of a right-holder's health depends not only on what others do, but on decisions made by the right-holder themselves. It would seem that the relativized right would require unacceptable interventions in the right-holder's life, interfering with and potentially overriding their own health-affecting choices on such matters as diet, exer-cise, leisure activities, occupational choice, and so on. This would thwart the autonomy interests of the right-holder in ways that would preclude such a duty from arising. The content of the right might then be further weakened, so that it creates, for example, a duty to afford access primarily to the highest attainable standard of physical and mental *healthcare*, rather than health itself. This may leave it largely to the discretion of the right-holder to decide whether or not to avail themselves of such care.

But even if a pro tanto case for such a demanding right to health could be made out, it will very likely be defeated once we factor in the second dimension of the threshold. This is the dimension of burdensomeness, which registers the costs of affirming the right in relation to the interests of duty-bearers, the fulfillment of other human rights, as well as other values, such as respect for non-human nature, to which we also properly subscribe. The right to health that arises from this process will, in all likelihood, be far less demanding than a right to the highest attainable standard of physical and mental healthcare, which is manifestly too costly. It is important to keep in mind, however, that "cost" here is not a simple function of the real-world market price of various medical services and public health measures. So, for example, we cannot simply take as given the market price that pharmaceutical companies, exploiting their market position and the rights afforded to them by existing regimes of intellectual property law, actually charge for their products. Equally, the cost cannot simply be a matter of the emotional strain and its consequences that compliance with the putative duty would entail, irrespective of the origin and nature of that strain. So, for example, the racist sentiments that make it "burdensome," in some sense, for racists to conform with the rights of members of groups they despise do not bear on the question of whether members of those groups genuinely possess these rights. To take them into account would be to infect our thinking about which human rights exist with their deeply flawed beliefs about the relative moral standing of human beings. However, costs of both sorts might figure in deciding whether and how, all things considered, we should insist on compliance with the rights in question. This is especially so in virtue of the fact that we need not regard (all) human rights as absolute demands that are never overridden by competing considerations.

In navigating the perilous crossing from interests to rights we have made no reference to three ideas that have been widely invested with great importance in determining the content of human rights. The first is the idea that human rights in general secure certain "minimum conditions of a decent life."[28] The second is that human rights protect us against certain "standard threats" to our basic interests.[29] The third is the central role of fair (and democratic) decision-making procedures in specifying the content of human rights obligations.[30] We believe that the claims pressed on behalf of these ideas are generally exaggerated or misleading, where they are not straightforwardly false.

The main challenge that arises for the first idea is that of identifying the threshold of decent minimalism. At this juncture, a dilemma looms. Talk of a "decent minimum" may simply be a shorthand way of referring to the point at which the interests of each individual generate an obligation on the part of others. But this effectively recapitulates the threshold account we have previously sketched without adding anything substantively new. Alternatively, it may be that an independent standard for identifying the decent minimum is proposed, e.g. by reference to a notion such as basic needs. This generates a problem, even assuming a non-arbitrary independent standard has been elaborated. The problem arises in those cases where the basic interests satisfy the threshold but not this further minimalist condition. This leads to a potential dualism of universal moral rights, leaving the question why it is that only rights that satisfy the latter minimalist condition count as human rights proper. The question is simply accentuated if that condition presupposes, but goes beyond, the fulfillment of the threshold criterion introduced by the interest-based approach to human rights. On balance, it would seem preferable to grasp the first horn of this dilemma.

As for the common idea that human rights protect us against standard threats, skepticism centers on whether either term is a necessary condition for the existence of a human right. First, must there be a *threat*, in the sense of some possible event which, if it occurs, is likely to be significantly detrimental to the right-holder's level of well-being? Certainly, some obligations corresponding to the human right to health protect us from threats so construed, e.g. the human right to vaccination against measles. But why should we exclude the possibility that human rights also impose obligations to provide us with opportunities to improve our level of well-being? For example, assuming costs are not excessive, there may be a human right to certain means of extending one's life or enhancing the quality of one's physical or mental functioning. If the response is that "threats" include the non-provision of something that could potentially benefit us, and perhaps which there is a duty to provide, then that locution is a misleading gloss on the threshold account. All this is compatible with the idea of "threat" playing an important role downstream from the issue of content specification, for example in establishing priorities among the demands of human rights. Thus, it may be that, other things being equal, duties to address threats to health generally take priority over duties to enhance it.

Now, leaving aside these qualms about "threat," the reference to "standard" in the "standard threat" formulation has rather more going for it. However, it would be a mistake to construe it as a brutely statistical notion. Why should the fact that inhabitants in many parts of the world are highly unlikely to be at risk of contracting malaria prevent protection from malaria from figuring in the content of the human right to health? A preferable understanding of "standard" is that it refers to situations that are in some sense genuinely accessible for right-holders in the context of modern-day life, quite apart from the question of their statistical incidence. Exclusion of men from high-paying jobs simply on the grounds of their sex may be a highly non-standard occurrence, statistically; yet it satisfies the second, generic sense of "standard."

This generic sense of "standard" leads us to the vexed question of how much "relativity" we should permit in the specification of the content of human rights standards across different cultures and societies. One kind of relativity, call it "parametric relativity," is rather anodyne: it holds the level of protection of interests secured by a given human right constant across all right-holders, but allows that the specific means adopted to secure that invariant level of protection may vary from one society to another. The human right to adequate clothing may be satisfied in the tropics by means of access to shorts and T-shirts, whereas much warmer clothing, including a winter coat, would be required to meet the same standard of protection in Northern Europe. But some theorists have gone further, appealing to differences in resources, cultural standards, and the prevalence of health-related problems across cultures, in order to argue that the substantive level of protection afforded by human rights may vary depending on the social context inhabited by the right-holder.[31] On this view, inhabitants of impoverished developing countries may have a human right to little more than rudimentary healthcare services, whilst those in the rich parts of the world would have a human right to very costly high-tech interventions.

This attempt to register the significance of inter-societal variation is understandable, but it has worrisome implications. On the basis of this view, for example, the level of protection afforded by the human right not to be killed or raped will presumably vary from one society to another, given differences in available resources for societal mechanisms and institutions concerned with deterring, apprehending, prosecuting, and punishing murderers and rapists. If we find this hard to countenance in the case of the human rights not to be killed or raped, why should the right to health be any different? Moreover, there is the fact that the differences in available resources across societies are not simply matters of brute fact, but are often the product of human decisions—to establish borders, to engage in colonial practices, to spend resources in one way rather than another, to adopt certain intellectual property regimes, to set the prices of drugs at certain levels, etc.—that should not be taken as simply given in determining what the content of human rights is, but instead must themselves be interrogated in the light of applicable moral standards.

These concerns suggest that we should construe the content of the right to health, so far as the level of protection it affords, invariantly across existing societies (but not necessarily invariantly across time).[32] In doing so, however, we should keep in mind the following three points. First, local shortage of resources may sometimes justify the infringement of the human rights duty by the primary duty-bearers, which, let us assume, typically include the state. Of course, the state will come under consequent secondary obligations to take measures to rectify this situation in the longer term. Second, when a situation of this kind obtains, a third-party secondary duty may arise to help the state fulfill its primary duty or take other remedial action, a duty that may fall on other states, corporations, or international agents who possess the relevant capabilities. Finally, it is important to remember that not all the moral rights possessed by individuals are human rights. Some rights are possessed not in virtue of our humanity, but in virtue of our membership (e.g. citizenship or long-term residence) in a particular society. Hence, it may well be that people in wealthy countries have rights-based entitlements to levels of healthcare that greatly exceed those afforded by their human right to health. Acknowledging plural rights-based grounds for health-related entitlements makes it easier to accept an invariant reading of the content of the human right to health.

The specification of the content of the human right to health is evidently a formidably complex matter. In this domain, as in others, a fully adequate specification through pure moral reasoning is typically unavailable; instead, a workable standard must to a significant degree be the product of social decision-making, whether conventional or legal. This is especially so when we address difficult questions of priority-setting in the use of limited resources. Of course, any such specification through fiat must operate within tolerably determinate parameters set by moral reasoning.[33] As an illustration of the potential "value added" that law and political practice can bring, consider the related notions of "progressive realization" and "minimum core obligations." Both ideas are addressed to the time frame for complying with socioeconomic human rights. Unlike the civil and political human rights, those set out in the International Covenant on Economic, Social and Cultural Rights are subject to a doctrine of "progressive realization." Given resource constraints, they need not all be fully complied with immediately; instead, according to Article 2(1), each state party is obligated "to take steps, individually and through international assistance and co-operation, especially economic and technical, to the maximum of its available resources, with a view to achieving progressively the full realization of the rights" in the Covenant (General Assembly of the United Nations 1966). The idea of "progressive realization" is meant to accommodate constraints on available resources, broadly construed, that prevent the immediate fulfillment of socioeconomic rights, such as the human right to health, by some states. However, in the practice of the UN's Committee on Economic, Social and Cultural Rights an associated doctrine of "minimum core obligations" has arisen according to which certain components of the obligations associated with such rights must be complied with immediately.[34] The "minimum core" is that part of a socioeconomic human right's normative content that is not subject to the doctrine of "progressive realization" and so regarding which full compliance must be immediate, not deferred to the future. General Comment No.3 identifies "essential primary health care" as belonging to the minimum core of the human right to health.[35] This distinction between obligations of immediate effect, on the one hand, and those that, although no less real, may be fulfilled over an extended period of time, has a long pedigree.[36] Standards established through law and political practice can help us specify in a more determinate way the appropriate time frame for compliance with a human rights obligation. In this way, a doctrine such as that of "minimum core" obligations enables us to rebut the accusation made by some critics of human rights that, given the multiplicity of obligations imposed by human rights, it is always possible for a state plausibly to claim to be trading off the fulfillment of some human rights obligations against other such obligations.[37]

So far, we have spoken of *supplementing* pure moral reasoning through legal and political determinations operating within boundaries that it sets. However, some theorists go considerably further, responding to the problem of indeterminacy of content by appealing to a procedural-institutional criterion. On this view, the content of the human right to health will be largely fixed through institutions that conform to fair processes of (in particular, democratic) decision-making.[38] Of course, the question of what counts as a fair or democratic procedure is itself a contested matter. Bracketing that important concern, it is still worth distinguishing at least two general roles that procedure may be being invoked to perform here.

The first is that of a reliable epistemic guide to the actual content of the human right to health. But, if so, we need independent reasons for believing that procedures of the relevant sort are more likely to lead to correct specifications of that right than other procedures, such as judicial review or executive directives. Perhaps some of these reasons will be found in general epistemic virtues typically possessed by democratic institutions, such as their inclusiveness regarding the range of interests and perspectives taken into account in law-making. However, it is doubtful that we can have confidence in a given decision-making process to specify the content of the right to health unless we have some prior, albeit incomplete grip on the content of that right, and on pain of circularity this grip cannot merely consist in the fact that the putative content was the outcome of that kind of process. In short, even granting its main premises, the epistemic appeal to procedure is by no means a comprehensive solution to the problem of content specification.

The second role decision-making procedures might perform is that of conferring legitimacy on any given legal specification of the right to health that it generates. Even if the content specified by law is not (obviously) correct as a matter of moral logic, that law may, nonetheless, be binding on its purported subjects in virtue, say, of its democratic pedigree. The first point to be made here is that the connection between procedure, including democratic procedures, and political legitimacy is not quite as straightforward as is often assumed. Contrary to a common view, it can be doubted whether democracy is generally either a necessary or a sufficient condition of legitimacy.[39] But the second—and more salient—point for present purposes is that the appeal to legitimacy effectively changes the subject. We are no longer addressing the original question—what is the content of the human right to health?—but instead the different question: when is a law purporting to enact that right binding on its subjects? The latter question is certainly important, and it is also true that some of the indeterminacy surrounding the first question may be, as a practical matter, dispelled at the level of the second question. Nevertheless, in moving to the second question the focus has shifted from the requirements of justice to the legitimacy of law.

4 JUSTICE AS THE COMMON GOOD

Imagine a world in which the human rights of all people were fully met. Could there yet be grave health deficits in this world? The answer, it seems, is clearly yes. It follows, at least presumptively, from this that global health policy must attend to more than securing people's human rights.[40] One potential health deficit in a human rights utopia is a high prevalence of obesity arising from the readily avoidable failure of people to maintain a healthy diet and exercise regimen. This could lead to severe health problems, but it would be strained to suppose they are also necessarily human rights problems. Human rights are about how we treat others, not how we treat ourselves. In avoidably neglecting my health, I do not violate my own rights. On the contrary, I may be exercising my rights when I freely engage in unhealthy behavior, such as smoking, overeating, and avoiding exercise, being fully informed about the risks and having viable alternatives at my disposal. So, global health policy must be concerned with the reasons people have to promote their own health, including their duties to do so, and not just with human rights.

Another way health deficits might creep into a human rights utopia is if it is too demanding or intrusive for certain kinds of health-enhancing behavior to be claimable as a matter of individual right. Consider someone in dire need of a kidney transplant. Although being given a matching kidney would dramatically promote this person's health interests, it is very doubtful that she has a right to another's healthy kidney. This is because her interest in a kidney transplant is insufficient, by itself, to impose an obligation upon another to provide the organ for this purpose. Indeed, the right to bodily security stands in the way of others having a right to one's kidney. Or consider participation in clinical trials. There are familiar difficulties in recruiting a sufficient number of trial participants in wealthier countries, something that in turn hampers the pursuit of valuable medical research. Yet we should not normally suppose that anyone's human right is being violated when people refrain from participating in clinical trials; instead, it seems more natural to suppose that there is a human right of non-participation.

To clarify, our contention is not the manifestly false one that obesity, organ donation, and research participation are utterly devoid of any human rights dimension. Certainly, people have a human right to such things as access to a healthy diet and treatment for obesity. But the incidence of obesity does not necessarily betoken a rights-violation, something signaled by the fact that in the developing world it is a condition more prevalent among those of a higher socioeconomic status.[41] Presumably, also, there are human rights-based obligations to facilitate organ donation and research participation and to offer or conduct them without discrimination, exploitation, or undue cost. But even when we have fully complied with these demands, problems of obesity, lack of organs for transplant, and low research participation may, nonetheless, persist. Consequently, more than just human rights will be required to guide health policy in formulating and addressing these problems.

Global health policy must, therefore, promote compliance with various health-related norms, including duties to oneself and duties of charity, that are not claimable as a matter of human rights. Now, in the remainder of this chapter, we wish to outline a further type of ethical consideration—common goods, in particular, global common goods—that should also have an important place in global health policy. By "common good" we do not mean aggregate social utility—the utilitarian notion of maximizing the aggregate welfare in society by means of a process of trading-off some people's interests against those of others. Instead, according to a broadly Aristotelian interpretation, something qualifies as a common good if it serves the interests of all in a given community [universality], serves those interests in a uniform way for each person [uniformity], and does so in a non-rivalrous manner, i.e. the serving of anyone's interests is not at the expense of serving any other's [non-rivalrousness].[42] A shared language in a given society, such as English, is a common good so understood. It serves the interests of all in that society in communication, it does so by furnishing all with a common means of communicating, and one person's use of English in no way detracts from anyone else's capacity to draw on that language. In the health context, we can recognize the common good of a social ethos that both helps maintain an adequate supply of organs for transplant and ensures sufficient participation in valuable health-related research. Cultivating such a culture of compassion and participation goes beyond anything demanded by human rights; yet it is of great significance for the promotion of the health of all. The second sense of justice, distinguished at the outset, prominently includes duties to promote common goods. Such goods must also be key concerns of global health policy.

The thrust of our argument so far has been that global health policy has to maintain a bifocal perspective in so far as justice is concerned: it has to be responsive both to human rights, including but not exclusively the right to health, and to global common goods that bear on health. Now, Gopal Sreenivasan (2012) has recently expressed skepticism about the global health policy significance of the human right to health. His claim is that, once we have common or public health goods in our sights, we will find that most of the requirements ordinarily thought to derive from the human right to health cannot be so understood. Instead, they belong to the category of public (or common) goods. The argument proceeds on the basis that rights and common goods are mutually exclusive so that "no individual can have a moral claim-right to any pure public good" (Sreenivasan (2012: 256). Let us accept the assertion that much that is claimed under the heading of human rights involves securing a common good. What justifies Sreenivasan's contention that such claims therefore fail? In effect, his thesis is that the relevant threshold from interest to duty is not satisfied. In particular, an individual's interest in a public good, taken in isolation from others' interests in that good, never suffices to impose a duty on others to deliver it. To take his example: securing the common good of herd immunity to diphtheria through a program of vaccination involves the imposition of various burdens, not only the materials costs of the program, but also the "moral" costs of compelling people to submit to it. In Sreenivasan's judgment, it is "very doubtful that a single individual's health has the moral significance to underwrite either cost, let alone both" (Sreenivasan (2012: 257).[43]

Sreenivasan's novel argument merits attention for at least two reasons. The first is that it forces us to clarify the interest-based approach to human rights in order to explain more fully how interests generate duties and how the ensuing rights are related to the common good. Second, and just as importantly, Sreenivasan's argument highlights an ambivalence within contemporary global health policy, one starkly illustrated by Lawrence Gostin's (2014) treatise on *Global Health Law*. Gostin is a prominent advocate of a human rights approach to global health, having taken the lead in calling for a global health framework convention grounded in the human right to health (Gostin (2014: 437–9). On the other hand, he also places great weight on public health measures and the social determinants of health, in contrast to medical services, partly on the grounds of their relatively superior preventive value (Gostin (2014: 419–28). But these considerations look like common goods, which may explain Gostin's startling assertion, introduced without elaboration only fourteen pages shy of the conclusion of his treatise, that the right to health is not best seen as an individual right. Instead, he contends it is principally a "collective right" that requires the implementation of broader public health and societal measures that are preconditions for securing more specific, individual rights.[44] The radical idea that the right to health is a group right seems to presuppose something like Sreenivasan's thesis that there can be no individual right to a common good. But this takes us far away from the ordinary understanding of the human right to health, which is precisely that it is a right of individuals.

So, does Sreenivasan's skepticism hold up? If his interpretation of when an individual's interests suffice to generate a duty is correct, then his conclusion seems assured. After all, how could the health benefits of herd immunity for one individual, taken by themselves alone, justify the massive costs involved in instituting policies aimed at securing and maintaining herd immunity, such as compulsory vaccination? But our first indication that something is amiss here is that this pattern of argument generalizes alarmingly even to paradigmatic rights, such the right not to be tortured. How could the benefits to any given individual of the criminal justice apparatus aimed at the prevention, detection, and punishment of torture, taken by themselves alone, justify the massive costs of such a system? Indeed, it evidently follows that, on Sreenivasan's approach, the morality of rights, including human rights, will justify *far fewer* entitlements than we ordinarily suppose that it does. This is a conclusion drawn with alacrity by Allen Buchanan (2013) in a book that deploys Sreenivasan's insight across a broad range of standardly acknowledged human rights.[45]

Rather than take Sreenivasan's argument to reveal the severe limitations of rights morality, however, we do better to treat it as resting on a questionable interpretation of the threshold criterion for the emergence of human rights. For, surely, no proponent of the interest-based view ever contemplated that the benefits to any single individual alone sufficed to impose a duty to create and maintain vastly expensive public goods, such as a criminal justice system. Now, one response to this problem is to find ways in which the interests of others than those of the right-holder can be made to do work in justifying the right to health, e.g. by pointing out that their interests are served *through* serving the interests of the right-holder. This is an avenue that has been explored by Joseph Raz (1997), a leading proponent of the interest-based approach to individual rights. However, we believe that although service to others' interests may bear on the *weight* to be accorded to individual rights in practical deliberation, making them determinants of the very *existence* of those rights threatens to efface the distinction between the rights-based and non-rights-based parts of morality. Therefore, maneuvers of this kind should not be our first line of response.

Instead, we should simply reject the idea that on the interest-based account the individual right-holder's interest must suffice to justify a duty to bear the *whole* costs of the relevant public-good securing system. This fails adequately to acknowledge the fact that the right-holder is just one among many enjoying the benefits of the system. Just as the right-holder does not enjoy all of the benefits of a public good system, so too the justification of his right does not entail that his notional portion of the benefits justify the entirety of the cost. Instead, our contention is that what needs to be justified is the right-holder's share of the costs among other right-holders who also benefit from the system. Given that we are dealing with human rights, and a standardized profile of interests that abstracts from certain variations among individuals, this share will be notionally the same for all. This notional equality applies a fortiori with respect to public health measures, which are typically not targeted on individuals and produce highly dispersed benefits. So, the real question posed by the threshold criterion is: does the benefit to any given right-holder of herd immunity justify a proportionate share of the costs involved in a vaccination program aimed at securing it? The answer is much more plausibly in the affirmative than the answer to Sreenivasan's question.

An immediate consequence of this view is that the relationship between human rights and common goods is not mutually exclusive. So, it is misleading for Sreenivasan to claim that individuals cannot have a moral claim-right to any pure public good. On the contrary, some *aspects* of the common good are rights-based, in the sense that they include elements to which we have a right; and what these rights confer is a right to benefit from the common good in question.[46] Compare two common goods in an academic department: a culture in which plagiarism is scrupulously avoided and, on the very few occasions on which it occurs, it is justly condemned and punished, and a culture in which academics adopt a friendly, highly collegial attitude towards each other. Both kinds of culture are common goods, meeting the requirements of universality, uniformity, and non-rivalrousness. But arguably only the former is a common good that involves the securing of an individual right as part of its content. This is because the benefits to each individual of their participation in a culture of anti-plagiarism have the significance needed to ground in others duties to bear the proportionate share of the costs entailed in generating those benefits. Now, something similar can be said about two health related common goods: the common good of herd immunity from diphtheria and the common good of a vibrant leisure culture. Both facilitate the health of members of the relevant community, but it is really only in the first case that the benefits to the individual of participation plausibly ground a duty on others to undertake the proportionate share of the costs of sustaining the relevant common good.

5   CONCLUSION

Human rights have a vital role to play in global health policy. But more than human rights matter in the formulation of such policy, and in so far as human rights matter, more than just the human right to health matters. We should resist a normative monism in global health policy that operates only with human rights, or only with the human right to health in so far as it engages with human rights. Instead, it is also important to factor in other ethical considerations, such as health-related duties to oneself and duties to foster health-related common goods, as well as human rights other than the human right to health. Moreover, we need to plot the complex relations between human rights as they bear on global health policy, and between them and other aspects of the ethics of global health, resisting in particular the dogma that human rights and common goods are mutually exclusive and fundamentally antagonistic. By understanding human rights in this way, we can rescue them from the distortion that they are liable to undergo at the hands of some of their most fervent and influential advocates in global health. Still, we have only embarked on the early stages of a rescue mission. It is worth highlighting two of the many other topics that need to be addressed. The first is the ubiquitous problem of priority-setting in contexts of scarce health resources, a problem on which human rights have been thought to shed meager light.[47] The second concerns the best means of giving embodiment and effect, through institutions, laws, and practices, to a just global health policy.[48] The value of the approach outlined here will partly depend on whether it helps us to make progress with question such as these.

Notes

1. For these two senses of justice, see Finnis (2011: 161–4).
2. An important thrust of the human rights campaign in relation to the AIDS pandemic pioneered by Jonathan Mann was to reject "the prevailing view…that individual-centered human rights conflicted with community-oriented public health," quoted in Gostin (2014: 245). This chapter aims to contribute to this attractive integrationist view by deepening its philosophical basis.
3. For example, Secretary General's High-Level Panel of Eminent Persons on the Post-2015 Development Agenda (2013); United Nations High Commissioner for Human Rights (2013); and Amnesty International (2013).
4. For a general account of the nature of human rights relied on here, see Tasioulas (2012: 17–59). This paper offers a critique of rival "political" interpretations of the concept of a human right offered by Rawls (1999); Beitz (2009); and Raz (2010: 321–37).
5. For a fine study of the latter right, see Tobin (2012).
6. Gostin (2014: 263).
7. O'Neill (2000: chs. 6–8).
8. Tasioulas (2007: 75–101).
9. O'Neill (2001: 180–95); Tasioulas (2012).
10. Griffin (2008: ch. 5).
11. United Nations, Office of the High Commissioner for Human Rights (2011).
12. Sen (2006: 2913–27); Tasioulas (2012).
13. Ferraz (2009: 33–4).
14. This need not be an inevitable consequence of legalization; cf. the South African Constitutional Court's decision in Soobramoney v. Minister of Health (Kwazulu-Natal) (1997), where it was held that provision of dialysis for a patient with chronic renal failure was not required by the constitutional right to health, partly because this would prejudice the satisfaction of other health needs that have to be met out of the state's budget.
15. See Tasioulas (2015).
16. For agency and needs-based accounts of human rights, see Griffin (2008) and Miller (2007: ch. 7).
17. See Tasioulas (2013: 293–314).
18. e.g. Ruger (2010: ch. 5), following in the footsteps of the pioneering work on capabilities theory by Amartya Sen and Martha Nussbaum.
19. Tasioulas (2015).
20. World Health Organization (1948), preamble, https://www.who.int/governance/eb/who_constitution_en.pdf (accessed October 4, 2019).
21. Daniels (2008: 36–46).
22. Committee on Economic, Social and Cultural Rights (2000).
23. The upshot is so peculiar, one might wonder why radical inclusivism is so popular. Mindy Roseman has suggested (p.c.) that it is sometimes viewed as a way of upholding the credentials of the human right to health against those who are skeptical of "socioeconomic" human rights, by showing that it incorporates traditional civil and political rights. Whatever its efficacy at the level of rhetoric, however, this strategy offers no real defense of the positive primary duties associated with the right to health.
24. Wolff (2012b: 94).

25. For a similar interpretation of "the human right to health care," see Buchanan and Hessler (2009: 205–6). However, the authors erroneously suppose that the human right to health exclusively reflects our interest in health (p. 206).

26. For a fuller account of the threshold, Tasioulas (2015).

27. General Assembly of the United Nations (1966: Art 12(1)), affirming "the right of everyone to the enjoyment of the highest attainable standard of physical and mental health."

28. Nickel (2006: 36): "Human rights block common threats to a decent or minimally good life for human beings." See also Miller (2007) and Buchanan (2014: 28–31) (the latter, however, articulates this as a notion that applies to those rights that ought to be enshrined in international human rights law, rather than to universal moral rights).

29. Shue (1996: 5): "a [moral] right involves a rationally justified demand for social guarantees against standard threats." For an extension of this idea to human rights generally, see Beitz (2009: 109) and to the human right to health in particular, see Wolff (2012a: 222).

30. Gruskin and Daniels (2008: 1573–7) and Buchanan and Hessler (2009).

31. Dworkin (2011: 338); Buchanan and Hessler (2009).

32. For this synchronic, not diachronic, interpretation of universality, see Tasioulas (2012).

33. On the process of *determinatio* through which law gives specific content to objective moral requirements, see Finnis (2011: 284–9).

34. Committee on Economic, Social and Cultural Rights (1990: para.10).

35. In conformity with its generally maximalist approach to the right to health, General Comment 14, para 43(a)-(f) identifies a much more demanding minimum core, one that is not even satisfied by contemporary Western liberal democracies and, moreover, treats this demanding minimum core as non-derogable (Committee on Economic, Social and Cultural Rights 2000). We leave aside the question of the correct specification of the minimum core of the human right to health, save to express our sympathy with John Tobin's assessment of General Comment No,14:

    the vision of the minimum core obligations of states under the right to health, as advanced by the ESC Committee, is disassociated from the capacity of states to realize this vision. It simply does not offer a principled, practical, or coherent rationale which is sufficiently sensitive to the context in which the right to health must be operationalized.   (Tobin 2012: 240)

36. For example, Immanuel Kant draws a very similar distinction between those of his "Articles of a Perpetual Peace between States" that are "leges strictae," requiring that "the abuses they prohibit should be abolished *immediately*" and those that are "leges latae," which:

    need not necessarily be executed at once, so long as their ultimate purpose…is not lost sight of. But their execution may not be *put off* to a non-existent date…for any delay is permitted only as a means of avoiding a premature implementation which might frustrate the whole purpose of the article.   (Kant 1991: 97)

37. "The dilemma for human rights enforcers is that they cannot demand that states comply with all rights perfectly, but if they do not, then they have no basis for criticizing a country's decision to allocate more resources to satisfy one rather than another" Posner (2014: 92). Posner discusses the doctrine of "minimum core" (p. 88), but in our view dismisses its significance too quickly.

38. Norman Daniels (2011: 134), for example, has characterized the human right to health as "implying entitlements that individuals have to a socially relative array of services (in the case of healthcare) that is the outcome of a process of fair deliberation under reasonable resource constraints." The point is developed with regard to priority setting in Gruskin

and Daniels (2008: 1573–7). For the claim that democratic states should be largely exempted from the authority of international human rights institutions when it comes to specifying the content of the human right to health, at least with respect to their own citizens, see Buchanan and Hessler (2009).

39. Raz (2006: 1003–44).
40. The idea that global health policy should be exclusively grounded in human rights (and in the human right to health in particular), animates the proposal for a framework convention on global health advanced by Gostin et al. (2013: 790–3); Gostin and Friedman (2013: 1–75).
41. Dinsa, Goryakin, Fumagalli, and Suhrcke (2012: 1067–79).
42. Raz (1997: 127–42). Economists go further and add a condition of non-excludability, i.e. it is impossible to exclude others (cheaply) from enjoying public goods if they are provided at all; see the helpful discussion in O'Neill (2013). Although non-excludability is particularly relevant in addressing issues of self-interested incentives to contribute to the maintenance of a common good, we take as our focus the wider notion. As O'Neill shows, an emphasis on non-excludability makes it especially difficult to establish the existence of *global* common or public goods. Hence her suggestion that it is preferable to focus on goods with dispersed benefits, the weaker definition of public goods adopted in UNDP-sponsored Kaul, Grunberg, and Stern (1999).
43. This is Sreenivasan's critique on the variant of the argument for a right to a public good that invokes an interest-based account of rights. He also has an argument against the possibility of a right to a public good on a will-based account of rights (see Sreenivasan 2012: 257–8). We find the latter persuasive, given the inconsistency of many public goods, e.g. herd immunity, with the comprehensive individual opt-outs (waivers of rights) that a will-based theory would require (see Sreenivasan 2012: 256–7).
44. See Gostin (2014: 426):

> The right to health must be conceived primarily as a collective right, imposing obligations on governments, and in turn implicating all of society. There remains an important role for safeguarding individual rights and the rights of vulnerable groups, but the implementation of broader public health measures is a precondition for securing these more targeted rights.

45. Buchanan (2013: ch.2). The pay-off for Buchanan is that international human rights law, which contains these ambitious requirements, is not best understood as "mirroring" a background morality of human rights. For criticism, see Tasioulas (2017).
46. Finnis (2011: 210–18).
47. Arras and Fenton (2009: 27–38); and Weale (2012: 473–93).
48. Tobin (2012); Gostin (2014).

REFERENCES

Amnesty International (2013) "Human Rights and the Post-2015 Development Agenda: Time to Deliver," September 19, 2013, https://www.amnesty.org/download/Documents/8000/act350212013en.pdf, accessed November 18, 2013.

Arras, John D. and Fenton, Elizabeth M. (2009) "Bioethics and Human Rights: Access to Health-Related Goods, " *Hastings Center Report* 39: 27–38.

Beitz, Charles (2009) *The Idea of Human Rights.* Oxford: Oxford University Press.

Buchanan, Allen (2013) *The Heart of Human Rights.* Oxford: Oxford University Press.

Buchanan, Allen, and Kirsten Hessler (2009) "Specifying the Content of the Human Right to Health Care." In Allen Buchanan (ed.), *Justice and Health Care: Selected Essays*. Oxford: Oxford University Press, 203–18.

Committee on Economic, Social and Cultural Rights (1990) General Comment No. 3, "The Nature of States Parties' Obligations." U.N. Document E/1991/23, https://www.refworld.org/pdfid/4538838e10.pdf, accessed October 4, 2019.

Committee on Economic, Social and Cultural Rights (2000) General Comment No. 14, "The Right to the Highest Attainable Standard of Health." U.N. Document E/C.12/2000/4, http://www.ohchr.org/Documents/Issues/Women/WRGS/Health/GC14.pdf, accessed July 19, 2016.

Daniels, Norman (2008) *Just Health: Meeting Health Needs Fairly*. Cambridge: Cambridge University Press.

Daniels, Norman (2011) "Health Justice, Equality and Fairness: Perspectives from Health Policy and Human Rights Law," *The Equal Rights Review* 6: 127–38.

Dinsa, G. D., Y. Goryakin, E. Fumagalli, and M. Suhrcke (2012) "Obesity and Socioeconomic Status in Developing Countries: A Systematic Review," *Obesity Review* 13: 1067–79.

Dworkin, Ronald M. (2011) *Justice for Hedgehogs*. Cambridge, MA: Harvard University Press.

Ferraz, Octavio (2009) "The Right to Health in the Courts of Brazil: Worsening Health Inequities?," *Health and Human Rights* 11: 33.

Finnis, John (2011) *Natural Law and Natural Rights*, 2nd edn. Oxford: Oxford University Press.

General Assembly of the United Nations (1966) "International Covenant on Economic, Social And Cultural Rights." Resolution 2200A (XXI) of December 16,1966, http://www.ohchr.org/EN/ProfessionalInterest/Pages/CESCR.aspx, accessed July 19, 2016.

Griffin, James (2008) *On Human Rights*. Oxford: Oxford University Press.

Gruskin, Sofia, and Norman Daniels (2008) "Justice and Human Rights: Priority Setting and Fair Deliberative Processes," *Government, Politics, & Law* 98: 1573–7.

Gostin, Lawrence (2014) *Global Health Law*. Cambridge, MA: Harvard University Press.

Gostin, Lawrence, and Eric Friedman (2013) "Towards A Framework Convention on Global Health: A Transformative Agenda for Global Health Justice," *Yale Journal of Health Policy, Law, Ethics* 13: 1–75.

Gostin, Lawrence, Eric Friedman, Kent Buse, et al. (2013) "Towards a Framework Convention on Global Health," *Bulletin of the World Health Organization* 91: 790–3.

Kant, Immanuel (1991) *Kant's Political Writings*. Cambridge: Cambridge University Press.

Kaul, Inge, Isabelle Grunberg, and Marc A. Stern (eds.) (1999) *Global Public Goods: International Cooperation in the 21st Century*. New York: Oxford University Press.

Miller, David (2007) *Global Justice and National Responsibility*. Oxford: Oxford University Press.

Office of the United Nations High Commissioner for Human Rights and the World Health Organization (2008) "The Right to Health: Fact Sheet No. 31," http://www.who.int/hhr/activities/Right_to_Health_factsheet31.pdf?ua=1, accessed July 19, 2016.

O'Neill, Onora (2000) *Bounds of Justice*. Cambridge: Cambridge University Press.

O'Neill, Onora (2001) "Agents of Justice," *Metaphilosophy* 32: 180–95.

O'Neill, Onora (2013) "Broadening Bioethics: Clinical Ethics, Public Health and Global Health," http://nuffieldbioethics.org/wp- content/uploads/Broadening_bioethics_clinical_ethics_public_health_global_health.pdf, accessed November 18, 2013.

O'Neill, Onora (2016) *Justice across Boundaries: Whose Obligations?*. Cambridge: Cambridge University Press.

Posner, Eric (2014) *The Twilight of Human Rights Law*. Oxford: Oxford University Press.

Rawls, John (1999) *The Law of Peoples*. Cambridge, MA: Harvard University Press.

Raz, Joseph (1997) "Rights and Individual Well-Being," *Ratio Juris* 5: 127–42.

Raz, Joseph (2006) "The Problem of Authority: Revisiting the Service Conception,"*Minnesota Law Review* 90: 1003–44.

Raz, Joseph (2010) "Human Rights without Foundations." In Samantha Besson and John Tasioulas (eds.), *The Philosophy of International Law*. Oxford: Oxford University Press, 321–38.

Ruger, Jennifer Prah (2010) *Health and Social Justice*. Oxford: Oxford University Press.

Sachs, Jeffrey (2012) "From Millennium Development Goals to Sustainable Development Goals," *The Lancet* 379: 2206–11.

Secretary General's High-Level Panel of Eminent Persons on the Post-2015 Development Agenda (2013) *A New Global Partnership: Eradicate Poverty and Transform Economies through Sustainable Development*. New York: United Nations Publications, https://sustainabledevelopment.un.org/content/documents/8932013-05%20-%20HLP%20Report%20-%20A%20New%20Global%20Partnership.pdf, accessed October 4, 2019.

Sen, Amartya (2006) "Human Rights and the Limits of Law," *Cardozo Law Review* 2: 913–27.

Shue, Henry (1996) *Basic Rights: Substistence, Affluence, and U.S. Foreign Policy*, 2nd edn. Princeton, NJ: Princeton University Press.

Soobramoney v. Minister of Health, Kwazulu-Natal (1997) (1) SA 765 (CC); 1997 (12) BCLR 1696 (CC), http://www.saflii.org/za/cases/ZACC/1997/17.html, accessed July 19, 2016.

Sreenivasan, Gopal (2012) "A Human Right to Health? Some Inconclusive Scepticism," *Aristotelian Society Supplementary* Volume 86: 239–65.

Tasioulas, John (2007) "The Moral Reality of Human Rights." In Thomas Pogge (ed.), *Freedom from Poverty as a Human Right: Who Owes What to the Very Poor?*. Oxford: Oxford University Press, 75–101.

Tasioulas, John (2012) "On the Nature of Human Rights." In Gerhard Ernst and Jan-Christoph Heilinger (eds.), *The Philosophy of Human Rights: Contemporary Controversies*. Berlin: de Gruyter, 17–59.

Tasioulas, John (2013) "Human Dignity and the Foundations of Human Rights." In Christopher McCrudden (ed.), *Understanding Human Dignity*. Oxford: Oxford University Press, 293–314.

Tasioulas, John (2015) "On the Foundations of Human Rights." In Rowan Cruft, Matthew Liao, and Massimo Renzo (eds.), *Philosophical Foundations of Human Rights*. Oxford: Oxford University Press, 45–70.

Tasioulas, John (2017) "Exiting the Hall of Mirrors: Morality and Law in Human Rights." In Tom Campbell and Kylie Bourne (eds.), *Political and Legal Approaches to Human Rights*. London: Routledge, 73–89.

Tasioulas, John, and Effy Vayena (2015) "Getting Human Rights Right in Global Health Policy," *The Lancet* 385: 42–4.

Tobin, John (2012) *The Right to Health in International Law*. Oxford: Oxford University Press.

United Nations High Commissioner for Human Rights (2013) "Open letter to member states," June 6, 2013, http://www.ohchr.org/Documents/Issues/MDGs/OpenLetterMS_Post2015.pdf, accessed November 18, 2013.

United Nations, Office of the High Commissioner for Human Rights (2011) "Guiding principles on business and human rights: Implementing the United Nations 'protect, respect, and remedy' framework," http://www.ohchr.org/Documents/Publications/GuidingPrinciplesBusinessHR_EN.pdf, accessed November 18, 2013.

Weale, Albert (2012) "The Right to Health versus Good Medical Care?," *Critical Review of International Social and Political Philosophy* 15: 473–93.

Wolff, Jonathan (2012a) "The Demands of the Human Right to Health," *Proceedings of the Aristotelian Society* 86: 217–37.

Wolff, Jonathan (2012b) *The Human Right to Health*. New York: Norton.

World Health Organization (1948) Constitution of the World Health Organization, https://www.who.int/governance/eb/who_constitution_en.pdf, accessed October 4, 2019.

FURTHER READING

Brownlee, Kimberley (2015) "Do We Have a Human Right to the Political Determinants of Health?" In Rowan Cruft, S. Matthew Liao, and Massimo Renzo (eds.), *Philosophical Foundations of Human Rights*. Oxford: Oxford University Press, 502–14.

Brudney, David (ed.) (2016) "Special Issue on the Right to Health," *Theoretical Medicine and Bioethics* 37.

De Campos, Thana Cristina (2017) *The Global Health Crisis: Ethical Responsibilities*. Cambridge: Cambridge University Press.

Mason Meier, Benjamin, and Lawrence O. Gostin (eds.) (2018) *Human Rights in Global Health: Rights-Based Governance for a Globalizing World*. Oxford: Oxford University Press.

Ruger, Jennifer Prah (2018) *Global Health Justice and Governance*. Oxford: Oxford University Press.

Tasioulas, John (2017) The Minimum Core of the Human Right to Health. Washington DC: World Bank, https://openknowledge.worldbank.org/handle/10986/29143, accessed August 14, 2019.

Tobin, John (2018) "Still Getting to Know You: Global Health Law and the Right to Health." In Gian Luca Burci and Brigit Toebes (eds.), *Research Handbook on Global Health Law*. London: Edward Elgar Press, 56–81.

Venkatapuram, Sridhar (2011) *Health Justice: An Argument from the Capabilities Approach*. Cambridge: Polity Press.

Wolff, Jonathan (2015) "The Content of the Human Right to Health." In Rowan Cruft, S. Matthew Liao, and Massimo Renzo (eds.), *Philosophical Foundations of Human Rights*. Oxford: Oxford University Press, 491–501.

CHAPTER 8

TRANSFORMING GLOBAL JUSTICE THEORIZING

Indigenous Philosophies

KRUSHIL WATENE

1 INTRODUCTION

AT least two interrelated projects are required to remedy the absence of indigenous philosophies in global justice theorizing. First, space within mainstream justice must be made for the articulation of indigenous philosophies. That is, space in which indigenous ways of being, knowing, and doing can flourish. Second, and more importantly, indigenous philosophies need to be appropriately articulated. That is, articulated by people and in ways that are appropriate according to indigenous communities. Without either of these things, intercultural and global justice conversations will be one-sided, serving to either regulate or oppress indigenous philosophies and indigenous communities.

Following a discussion of indigenous self-determination, and of the significance of indigenous philosophies today, this chapter explores the extent to which mainstream justice theorizing can accommodate indigenous philosophies. We focus on the capability approach to justice, as a mainstream approach most open to diverse philosophical views, and as a framework suited to opening up space within mainstream justice theorizing for indigenous philosophies. The chapter provides a brief overview of the recent scholarship concerned with bringing the capability approach into conversation with indigenous communities, and highlights the components of the capability approach that commit it to the inclusion of diverse perspectives. Our conclusion is that the capability approach, despite having the potential to make significant contributions to diversifying philosophy, falls short. In such a way, this section provides a way to outline—and serves to illustrate—both the opportunities and challenges for creating space for indigenous philosophies in justice theorizing.

The chapter then explores what it means to include indigenous philosophies on their own terms. That is, on terms consistent with the practice of indigenous concepts and values in philosophical research. In so doing, the chapter explores the importance of indigenous methodologies—and Kaupapa Māori theory in particular—for articulating Māori concepts and ideas. The chapter first provides a brief overview of Kaupapa Māori theory, explaining how that theory informs research practice in Aotearoa New Zealand. The chapter then explores how Kaupapa Māori research is able to inform philosophical research—particularly with Māori philosophies. The aim is to think seriously about what is required within philosophy for indigenous philosophies to be appropriately articulated, and thus, what is required to engage indigenous philosophies in justice theorizing.

2 INDIGENOUS PHILOSOPHIES AND GLOBAL JUSTICE

The United Nations Declaration on the Rights of Indigenous Peoples (UNDRIP) remains the most important statement of indigenous rights to date (UNPFII 2007, 2008; Anaya 2004; Waitangi Tribunal 2011a, 2011b). Outlining minimum standards "for the survival, dignity and well-being of the indigenous peoples of the world" (UNPFII, 2007), the declaration recognizes the need for protections from such things as assimilation (Article 8), discrimination (Article 9), and from forced removals from traditionally owned lands (Article 26). The declaration includes the right to self-government (Article 4), the right to participate in, and consent to, any decisions which affect them (Articles 19 and 32), and the right to control (and have returned) traditionally owned lands and natural resources (Article 26). Most relevant for our present purposes, the declaration recognizes that "indigenous peoples have the right to revitalize, use, develop and transmit to future generations their histories, languages, oral traditions, philosophies, writing systems and literatures" (Article 13). Together these rights enable indigenous peoples to be self-determining—that is, to "freely determine their political status and freely pursue their economic, social and cultural development" (Article 3).

The place of self-determination within the UNDRIP is most evident in the way the UN approached the question of how (and whether) indigenous peoples should be "defined." The UN took the view that a fixed definition of indigenous peoples would be inconsistent with a commitment to self-determination, and that it would pay no attention to the diversity within and between indigenous groups. As a result, the UN decided against offering a definition of indigenous peoples, with the view that the aim would be for indigenous peoples to define themselves (Anaya 2004). By doing so, the UN reinforces that the point of the declaration is to articulate rights that enable indigenous peoples to decide who they are and who they want to be. The aim is to create the conditions in which indigenous peoples (as individuals and collectives) are truly capable of pursuing the lives and futures that they value (UNPFII 2007; Anaya 2004; Acuna 2016; Whyte 2016a, 2016b, 2016c; Napoleon 2005).

This way of thinking is appropriate. Indigenous peoples have intimate knowledge of how assumptions and imposed ideas about who they are and who they ought to be has impacted on their lives. In Aotearoa New Zealand, the process of colonization systematically undermined the centrality of concepts and values—such as "whānau" (community, relationships)—that lay at the heart of the Māori world (Taskforce 2010; Watene 2016a, 2016b; Smith 1999; Waitangi Tribunal 2011a, 2011b). Western land tenure systems altered the physical relationships Māori were able to have with ancestral lands, and opened the way for widespread land dispossession (Kawharu 1989, 1997; Williams 2007; Mutu 2012). The physical disconnection from lands and natural resources impacted on the life and capabilities of Māori kin-communities. The imposition of the English language and of policies preventing the Māori language from being spoken in schools exacerbated cultural disconnection (see Hohepa 2014). Many Māori were forced to move away from ancestral "marae" (kin) communities in search of the stability and opportunities available in urban centres (see Tapsell 2014). Today, less than 6 percent of New Zealand's total land area remains under collective ownership (see Kingi 2008). The majority of tribal descendants live outside of their tribal areas (Statistics New Zealand 2014). Around 20 percent of Māori speak the Māori language (Statistics New Zealand 2014).

In short, the ideas inherent in colonization silenced, oppressed, and marginalized indigenous ways of knowing, being, and doing (Smith 1999; Jackson 1992; Whyte 2016b, 2016c, 2017; Lefevre 2015). Continuing struggles for recognition, rectification, and self-determination by indigenous communities around the world serve to illustrate the extent of this continuing oppression and domination. Unsurprisingly, indigenous activists and scholars have written widely on the structures of colonial oppression—including the extent of colonizing processes even within systems designed to mitigate them today (for example, Walker 2004; Smith 1999, 2006; Coulthard 2014; Alfred 2005; Mutu 2013; Poata-Smith 2004; Napoleon 2005). Central to this scholarship and activism are projects concerned with transforming (social, political, economic) institutions in ways that nourish and privilege indigenous philosophies (Matike Mai Aotearoa 2016; Smith 1999; Taskforce 2010; Durie 2003; Deer 2009; Zion and Yazzie 1997). The pursuit and realization of indigenous peoples' self-determination is, thus, intimately bound up with the revitalization of indigenous philosophies. The capabilities of indigenous peoples to be able to define who they are and to pursue and realize lives they value relies on the extent to which indigenous communities are able to articulate and appropriately apply and reapply their concepts and values to their lives and futures.

Indigenous philosophies are diverse bodies of knowledge within which indigenous worlds were framed prior to European colonization, and which have come to also include deep knowledge of the (ongoing) experiences of colonization (Smith et al. 2016; Turner 2006; Marsden 2003; Whyte 2016b, 2017; Mead 2003). These philosophies chart ideas about time and space, reality, being, knowledge, beauty, well-being, right and wrong, and justice (among many other things) (Smith et al. 2016; Marsden and

Henare 1992; Marsden 2003). The philosophies have travelled across geographical spaces, and are woven through multiple generations of lived experiences within diverse (social, political, cultural, economic, and natural) environments (Smith et al. 2016; Whyte 2013). Indigenous philosophies find expression in oral histories, narratives, ceremonies, social and political organizations, the natural environment, astronomy, and in art forms such as weaving, carving, architecture, music, and dance (Smith et al. 2016; Marsden 2003; Royal 2002, 2009, 2014; Waitangi Tribunal 2011a, 2011b; Sadler 2007; Walker 1978).

Despite moves to globalize justice theorizing from within mainstream political philosophy itself, very few attempts to open up justice theorizing to a wider range of philosophical perspectives have been made (Brooks 2014; Graness 2015; Oruka 1990a, 1990b; Metz 2007; Watene 2016a, 2016b; Whyte 2010, 2013; Whyte and Cuomo 2016). The "global" in global justice has primarily concerned extending the scope within which existing ideas about justice apply, rather than with widening the scope of perspectives from which ideas and principles of justice can be drawn (see, for example, Brock 2009; Nussbaum 2006; Moellendorf 2002; Rawls 1999; Beitz 1999; Singer 2002, 1972). As such, indigenous philosophies—indeed, a whole host of perspectives relevant for our ideas about justice—remain largely absent from justice theorizing. The result is that indigenous peoples occupy a silent space in mainstream justice theorizing. Not only is this is a space in which indigenous peoples remain unable to define who they are and want to be, but it is also a space in which indigenous peoples are denied an active role in our (social, political, economic, cultural, and environmental) conceptual landscapes.

A commitment to conceptions and principles of social and global justice must resonate with the concepts and values of the communities that make up our social and global landscapes. What is more, we know that many of our challenges are global, and that we need global conversations and solutions to move forward. A commitment to including indigenous peoples in global justice requires a commitment to the philosophies of indigenous peoples so fundamental to the pursuit and realization of self-determination. A commitment to global justice requires that we create space for what indigenous peoples (indeed all local communities) themselves have to say about justice. The pursuit and realization of justice in our world today require (at the very least) global conversations—of which indigenous peoples must be part. Can mainstream global justice theorizing open itself up to indigenous philosophies? To additional forms of knowing, being, and doing? Can global justice theorizing acknowledge its own present limitations? Moving forward requires that we recognize the importance of these questions and that we are committed to creating space to begin to rethink global justice theorizing in light of them.

Most worryingly, the lack of indigenous philosophies in global justice theorizing is disproportionate to the growing use of indigenous concepts and values in policy and law. Indigenous philosophies have already transformed law and policy in ways that reimagine our relationships with each other, and with the natural environment (Taskforce 2010; Ruru 2014; Deer 2009, Yazzie 1994; Borrows 2002; Napoleon 2007; Whyte 2013, 2016a, 2016b; Whyte and Cuomo 2016; Meissner and Whyte 2018; McGregor 2009; Kawharu 2000; Yazzie 1994). Environment and conservation law in

Aotearoa New Zealand is, for instance, ushering in what Jacinta Ruru calls "a new dawn"—that is, an approach to environment law grounded in new ways of thinking about ownership over the natural environment and ultimately our relationships with lands and natural resources. Writing about Te Urewera Act 2014, Ruru remarks that:

> A new dawn for conservation management in Aotearoa New Zealand has arrived with the enactment of Te Urewera Act 2014. Te Urewera, named a national park in 1954 and most recently managed as Crown land by the Department of Conservation became Te Urewera on 27 July 2014: "a legal entity" with "all the rights, powers, duties, and liabilities of a legal person" (section 11(1)). Te Urewera Act is undoubtedly legally revolutionary here in Aotearoa New Zealand and on a world scale.
>
> (Ruru 2014)

The Act recognizes the deep connection that Ngai Tuhoe (the people of Tuhoe) have with Te Urewera, describing Te Urewera as: "ancient and enduring, a fortress of nature, alive with history; its scenery... abundant with mystery, adventure, and remote beauty" and as having "an identity in and of itself, inspiring people to commit to its care" (quoted in Ruru 2014). The inclusion of indigenous philosophies in the transformation of environment law raises more significant questions for global justice theorizing and for philosophy generally. Can global justice theorizing capture these developments? Is justice theorizing still relevant for our changing world? So far, these (and many other) questions—as they pertain to the places and uses of indigenous philosophies in our world—remain unexplored.

What is needed to move forward from here? At least two interrelated projects are required to remedy this shortcoming. First, we must create space within mainstream justice theorizing for indigenous philosophies to flourish. Second, and ultimately, indigenous philosophies need to be appropriately articulated. That is, articulated by people and in ways that are appropriate according to indigenous communities. Only then can the contributions of indigenous philosophies be understood and appreciated. Only then can intercultural conceptual conversations take place on just terms (Acuna 2016). This chapter, in what follows, aims to make contributions to both of these projects.

3 MAINSTREAM JUSTICE THEORIZING: THE CAPABILITY APPROACH

The usefulness and relevance of global justice theories stand and fall on whether they resonate with the values of the communities that make up—and thus the contemporary challenges that define—our global landscapes. Given this contention, and despite the exclusion of indigenous philosophies from global justice theorizing, indigenous communities have always had a role to play in determining the usefulness and relevance of global justice theories. From activism within indigenous communities themselves to the collective voices of indigenous peoples globally, these voices continue to transform our global landscapes, and the issues that shape global justice. The aim of this section is, then, to better understand why mainstream justice theorizing continues to fall short of creating space to fully include indigenous philosophies. The further aim is to show why—unless this is remedied—indigenous philosophies will remain on the margins and global justice theorizing will remain irrelevant. We do this by focusing on the capability approach to justice as articulated by Amartya Sen.

We focus on the capability approach because of its commitment to including the voices of local communities both in how justice is conceptualized and in what the pursuit of justice requires. Briefly, the capability approach tells us that the extent to which people are able to live the kinds of lives they value and have reason to value ought to be the focus of such things as well-being and justice (Sen 1999). What matters for justice are the kinds of lives that people *actually live* (our functionings), the kinds of lives that people are *able to live* (our capabilities), and whether people are truly able to live lives *they value* (our freedom) (Alkire 2002; Robeyns 2016; Nussbaum 2006; Qizilbash 2012). This commitment to people's lives shapes Sen's writings on poverty, well-being, and justice. In the context of justice, for Sen—alongside earlier writers such as Charles Mills—the pursuit of the ideal just society (what Sen terms the "transcendental approach") seems fruitless and unnecessary. Instead, we ought to be concerned with justice in a "comparative" sense. That is, we should engage with and work to mitigate injustices as they exist on the ground. What we want from a theory of justice is not an answer to the question of what the ideal just society is, but guidance for which actions and policies are better from the perspective of where we are currently situated (Sen 2009; Mills 1997, 2005, 2009).

Given these commitments, the capability approach provides a useful way to outline—and serves as one way to illustrate—both the opportunities and challenges for creating space for indigenous philosophies in global justice theorizing (Drydyk 2011). Two points, however, must be made. First, it is beyond the scope of this chapter to engage in debates about lists, the listing of capabilities, and related debates about whether we should focus on dignity (as Nussbaum contends) or agency (as Sen contends) to ground a capability theory (Sen 2005a, 2005b; Nussbaum 2000, 2006; Watene 2016b). Similarly, it is beyond the scope of this chapter to engage in debates about how individuals and communities should be positioned within the approach. By referring to the capability approach in its broadest sense—as an approach that orients our concern to focus on peoples' capabilities to live lives they have reason to value—I take the view that what matters is that people (as individuals and communities) can be self-determining. No substantive capability theory is required to make this general claim, or indeed for the purposes of this chapter.

This is important because, secondly, I have argued elsewhere that—despite opening up space for Māori concepts—the capability approach is unable to fully cover the ground required for their expression (Watene 2016b). Within an indigenous worldview, relationships and community are central. Understanding the role and the importance of relationships for well-being and development is vital. To be sure, work on the idea of collective capabilities is useful for bringing ideas about community to bear on capability-based discussions of justice. For instance, Rao and Walton's (2004: 361) contention that collectives can "create an enabling environment to provide members with the tools and the voice to navigate their way out of poverty" provides pathways toward conversations about indigenous conceptions of well-being and the potential of the capability approach to support them. So far, however, this literature remains under-developed. More significantly for indigenous peoples, and more problematically for the capability approach, the foundation of "community" is intimately connected to place. Lands and natural resources provide the context for indigenous peoples' values, and are crucial for revitalizing, reproducing, and maintaining indigenous ways of being, know-ing, and doing. Such a holistic view requires a move beyond the ways in which the capa-bility approach is currently grounded (Sen 2004b; Nussbaum 2006). Thus, by thinking about the capability approach in its broadest form, I not only explore the use of the approach in what I take to be the most charitable way, but in a way most open to including indigenous philosophies (see Watene 2016b).

The work of capability scholars and practitioners has almost always traversed issues of relevance to indigenous communities. Only recently, however, have we seen scholars begin to engage specifically with issues as they affect indigenous communities on their own terms. In other words, only recently have capability scholars and practitioners begun to attempt to give voice to indigenous peoples' needs and aspirations framed within or supplemented by the capability approach in some way (see Bockstael and Watene 2016; Binder and Binder 2016; Acuna 2016; Watene 2016b; Yap and Yu 2016; Klein 2016). The growth and transformation of indigenous communities within capability scholarship can be linked to a number of things, not least the emphasis that the approach places on peoples' actual lives. The capability approach is critical of approaches to well-being and justice that ignore the full range of activities and diversities that shape our experiences. The capability approach acknowledges that there are a range of valuable functionings and capabilities that shape and can ground a theory of global justice. Any concern with well-being and justice must not only include a variety of "goods," but must also be able to capture the different ways in which these goods can be significant for our lives (Binder and Binder 2016).

By committing to the lives that people live and the diversity that can be found within the human experience, the capability approach recognizes that many things impact on our ability to live lives we value. Our ability to convert goods into valuable capabilities is shaped by a range of (social, political, environmental, cultural, individual, and collective) diversities. Most importantly, the capability approach recognizes that culture is a consti-tutive part of well-being and a constructive factor in how life is valued (Nussbaum 2000; Rao and Walton 2004; Sen 1999, 2004a, 2006; UNDP 2004). Any concern with well-being and justice must have a way of recognizing not only the challenges that cultures may pose to well-being and justice, but also the opportunities inherent in cultures and our cultural histories for realizing well-being and justice. As Sen puts it, the issue is not *whether* culture matters, but rather *how* (Sen 2004a). Discussions of justice need to take account of not just the "cultural exclusions" (cultural limitations on freedom), but also the "cultural liberties" (the freedom "to live and be what we choose") so pervasive in our lives (UNDP 2004).

On this reading of the capability approach, the needs, aspirations, and values of indigenous peoples (indeed all local communities) are central for the pursuit and realization of global justice. In line with the declaration on the rights of indigenous peoples, the capability approach takes freedom (i.e. peoples' abilities and real opportunities to live lives they value) to be of central importance. We should pay attention to the kinds of lives indigenous peoples live, and to their capabilities to live lives they value for themselves and their descendants. In addition, we should expand the capabilities of indigenous communities to live the lives they value. In so doing, the capability approach not only reinforces the central importance of indigenous aspirations for self-determination, but also what realizing indigenous self-determination requires. As I have argued elsewhere, justice for indigenous peoples is about (among other things) healing. Understanding what this means requires that we face the extent to which colonial oppression continues to shape the lives and communities of indigenous peoples (Watene 2016a). The capability approach is not merely equipped to provide support for these sentiments, but is in fact committed to supporting them.

Of central importance for the capability approach is that our concepts and ideas are able to affect change in the world. In the spirit of this aim, the approach seeks to empower people to be agents of change, and seeks to include people and situations often ignored in discussions of well-being and justice. Additionally, by focusing on and by recognizing the need for multidimensional, intercultural, and interdisciplinary engagement to enact real-world change, the approach is committed to supporting ideas that may be marginalized. We see this in the way that the capability approach resonates with the Māori potential approach which grounds innovations and transformations in Māori health policy (the Whānau Ora policy) in Aotearoa New Zealand (Barcham 2012; Taskforce 2010; Durie 2003). We also see this in the contention that well-being and justice must be conceptualized from the ground up—that is, through the voices and lived experiences of real people (Yap and Yu 2016). The capability approach is thus committed to the perspectives of indigenous peoples themselves and to their active involvement in the development of just policies and institutional arrangements. That is, the approach is itself committed to the creation of space for indigenous peoples to voice their concerns and aspirations for their own lives, and to undertake those activities required to realize them.

These commitments result in the capability approach being open-ended and incomplete. The approach is open to the inclusion of different values, and committed to being led by the voices and concerns of real people. One of the key strengths of the capability approach, then, lies not so much in what it purports to be able to do, but in what it is open enough to admit that it is unable to do on its own. The strength lies in its commitment to admitting its own limitations; in its commitment to requiring engagement with the perspectives of communities that lie on the margins; and in its multidisciplinary and pluralistic framework, and in the way that it sets out from the diversity within human experiences from the very start. By focusing on real-world challenges and change, the approach is unwilling to ignore oppression and domination as it exists in the world. More importantly, the approach is willing to listen to, learn from, and be transformed by the perspectives and experiences of local communities. These are qualities that create space for engagement, and qualities that create space for fruitful conversations. There is, then, a great deal that mainstream global justice could learn from the capabilities approach.

So why, then, does the capability approach still fall short? For the capability approach to truly create this space, a deeper range of questions must be raised. That is, what is needed for indigenous philosophies to be appropriately articulated? On whose terms should intercultural conversations take place? What barriers prevent these questions from being answered? Any mainstream approach to justice theorizing that is serious about opening up space to engage with indigenous philosophies must be open to these questions. Discussions must center not merely on what indigenous peoples value (and how those values shape the content of justice theorizing), but how those values shape our philosophical interactions and our philosophical inquiry. Although very little discussion has taken place about how indigenous philosophies ought to be included, such a discussion is something which the capability approach is (despite its silence on it) committed to. Without these discussions, intercultural conversations run the risk of misinterpreting and hijacking indigenous concepts. Without space for the appropriate articulation of indigenous philosophies, conversations will be unable to be undertaken in equal partnership.

At least two points should be taken away from this discussion. First, if we take the commitment to including local communities, so central to the capability approach, to its full conclusion, then a commitment to a plurality of values must be matched by a commitment to a plurality of methodologies. Such a move opens the capability approach up in the truest sense, and meets the aims of interdisciplinary research so prized by it. Second, the capability approach—as a mainstream approach to justice itself—is able to enrich global justice theorizing by creating space for indigenous philosophies to flourish. The capability approach is, therefore, able to play a central role in the continued transformation of global justice theorizing toward the realization of global justice. To achieve this, however, the capability approach (and mainstream justice theorizing generally) must engage with indigenous methodologies.

4 KAUPAPA MĀORI JUSTICE THEORIZING

What does it mean to include indigenous philosophies in global justice theorizing on its own terms? This section explores the importance of indigenous methodologies—and Kaupapa Māori theory in particular—for articulating Māori concepts and ideas. As such, the chapter provides an overview of Kaupapa Māori theory and explains how the theory is able to inform philosophical research—particularly Māori philosophical research. The aim is to think seriously about what is required within philosophy for indigenous philosophies to be appropriately articulated, and thus, the opportunities and challenges to truly engaging indigenous philosophies in justice theorizing. This section does this by asking what role does Kaupapa Māori theory have for articulating Māori philosophies? What insights can be gained from thinking about global justice theorizing within the space of Kaupapa Māori? This section provides one starting point for a more comprehensive discussion.

"Kaupapa Māori theory" is a theoretical "space" pioneered by Māori scholars and practitioners for the articulation, pursuit, and realization of the transformation and liberation of Māori (Smith 1999; Pihama 2001; Smith 1997). Within the context of research, it is both a challenge to dominant Western frameworks and forms of knowledge, as well as a platform from which culturally legitimate research "by Māori and for Māori" can be undertaken. At the heart of Kaupapa Māori theory are commitments to such things as (1) the self-determination of Māori, (2) the legitimacy of Māori ways of knowing, being, and doing, and (3) the improvement of the individual and collective lives of Māori communities (see Smith and Reid 2000). Kaupapa Māori has been the driving force at the heart of the development and success of Māori language schools (Kura Kaupapa Māori) in Aotearoa New Zealand, and has been applied to a range of areas of research and practice by scholars and practitioners in Aotearoa and elsewhere.

Linda Tuhiwai Smith's (1999) seminal *Decolonizing Methodologies: Research and Indigenous Peoples* provides the most comprehensive account of Kaupapa Māori theory, and continues to inspire generations of scholars and practitioners around the world— indigenous and non-indigenous alike. At the heart of this important work is the claim that research has privileged Western ways of knowing and being. As such, research and researchers have played important roles in oppressing, dominating, and excluding indigenous communities:

> "research" is probably one of the dirtiest words in the indigenous world's vocabulary... It galls us that Western researchers and intellectuals can assume to know all that it is possible to know of us, on the basis of their brief encounters with some of us. It appals us that the West can desire, extract and claim ownership of our ways of knowing, our imagery, the things we create and produce, and then simultaneously reject the people who created and developed those ideas and seek to deny them further opportunities to be creators of their own culture and nations.
>
> (Smith 1999: 1)

Kaupapa Māori theory is a response to the conditions described by Smith in the passage above. These conditions make assumptions about indigenous communities, and take ownership over indigenous philosophies. These conditions limit the extent of indigenous knowledges, and diminish the relationships between indigenous peoples, ancestral lands, and the knowledges embedded within them. They limit what indigenous peoples are able to do and be. These conditions are built on oppressive research systems and structures, and they frame research relationships in which indigenous peoples are mere objects. As such, Kaupapa Māori research creates space where research can be redefined, reimagined, and reclaimed. The centrality of the Māori language and the significance of Māori concepts become important for a legitimate research undertaking, and the legitimate creation of knowledge. Indigenous communities are centered as having legitimate forms of knowledge and as being knowers in their own right (Smith 1999; Dotson 2011). Privileging Māori philosophies lies at the heart of Kaupapa Māori theory.

What does this mean in practice? Linda Smith provides seven general practices to guide kaupapa Māori research:

1. aroha ki te tangata (a respect for people)
2. kanohi kitea (the seen face; that is, present yourself to people face to face)
3. titiro, whakarongo...korero (look, listen...speak)
4. manaaki ki te tangata (share and host people, be generous)
5. kia tupato (be cautious)
6. kaua e takahia te mana o te tangata (do not trample over the mana of the people)
7. kaua e mahaki (do not flaunt your knowledge).

(Smith 1999: 120)

Together, the practices provide guidelines to chart a way of thinking about, designing, and undertaking research within Māori communities. That is, in ways that respect and empower Māori communities, and which build, and are themselves built on, mutually beneficial relationships. Most significantly, the guidelines chart a way of thinking about, designing, and doing research that privileges the needs, aspirations, and values of the community itself. The guidelines set out a way of being (humility, generosity, patience, attention, presence), and frame the role and practice of research within the community.

Why are these guidelines important for philosophy? An exploration of Māori philosophy requires consideration of the concepts and values as they are situated within the Māori world, and as they are bound up with the lived experiences of those communities today. Māori philosophical perspectives are attached to people and to places. Māori philosophies are embedded in the landscapes and stories of "marae" communities, and they are woven through the lived experiences of ancestors, present generations, and in the aspirations of those yet to be born. On such a view, the inclusion of Māori philosophy within research is, at the same time, the inclusion of the lives of Māori communities, of their landscapes, waterways, art forms, histories, and futures. Kaupapa Māori theory helps us to see that research about Maori philosophy—that is, thinking about Māori concepts removed from their places and communities of origin—will be inadequate. Research must be undertaken with communities, and in ways consistent with the application and practice of Māori values in philosophical research.

The inclusion of indigenous philosophies in justice theorizing is one thing. The inclusion of indigenous philosophies in justice theorizing *on their own terms* is quite another. Kaupapa Māori justice theorizing is able to open up space for new ways of theorizing justice. Yet this requires a new way of thinking about philosophy generally. It requires acknowledging the expertise within these communities themselves. It requires a willingness—on the part of these communities—to share this knowledge, and to enter into (intercultural) conversations on equal terms. It requires a willingness—on the part of scholars, if welcomed to do so—to co-create knowledge with and within a community. It requires that we create space for indigenous voices to speak their own stories, their own theories, and their own principles (Napoleon and Friedland 2016; Kawharu 2008; Debassige 2010; Gross 2002; Matiu and Mutu 2003; Williams 2001). It requires enabling interdisciplinary conversations. It requires that we open up space for the inclusion of indigenous philosophers committed to articulating indigenous philosophies in partnership with indigenous communities. Most fundamentally, it requires that we confront questions about the nature of our research processes and questions. Who will benefit from this research? What are my responsibilities to the community? Who should decide which questions, concepts, and ideas are important? What are the limits of my knowledge? Am I the right person to be writing about and articulating these concepts? How can I create space for (more of) the right people to do so?

Global justice theorizing will be at its strongest when it includes the voices of all of the communities that make up our global landscapes. This level of inclusion requires that justice theorizing is able to make room for indigenous philosophies to be articulated in ways appropriate to those communities. The continued relevance of global justice theorizing depends on the extent to which justice theorizing is willing to acknowledge our diverse philosophical landscapes, and celebrate the role that they play in shaping our world.

5 CONCLUSION

Understanding indigenous philosophies is vital for the pursuit and realization of justice globally. We need to find ways of acknowledging, nurturing, and then somehow navigating our diverse conceptual landscapes and currents. To do this, global justice theorists need to build a platform for the articulation of indigenous philosophies, and for just intercultural conversations. More specifically, as this chapter has argued, justice theorizing must create space to recognize the self-determination of indigenous peoples so intimately bound up with indigenous philosophies. As this chapter has highlighted in light of Māori philosophies and Kaupapa Māori theory, doing this may not seem like an easy task. Engagement with communities, open-mindedness, and the willingness to acknowledge our own limitations is required. Yet doing this opens up new pathways forward, and new forms of inquiry that can transform the way that justice theorizing can take place. In particular, these pathways could create opportunities for innovation and opportunities to theorize justice in a much more open way—that is, with the voices and perspectives of peoples that remain on the margins. Creating space in which to collectively navigate these landscapes presents both an opportunity and challenge that contemporary philosophy—and justice theorizing—must face.

Indigenous methodologies, and Kaupapa Maori theory in particular, provide us with a starting point for conversations that can enrich global justice. Kaupapa Māori provides us with a way for justice theorizing to look back on itself, to reassess its commitments, and to reimagine what justice theorizing might look like if it was open to including the voices of communities on their own terms. As such, indigenous philosophies and Kaupapa Māori provide us with a way to begin a conversation that has the potential to transform the way justice theorizing takes place, by rethinking the very terms by which these conceptual conversations take place. This has the potential to provide us with ways to rethink global justice, to rethink our places in the world, and to resolve our shared global challenges. It has the potential to provide us with the diverse tools needed to navigate our rich, multifaceted, and enduring conceptual landscapes toward a more just future.

ACKNOWLEDGMENTS

I am grateful to Kyle Whyte for comments on an earlier draft of this chapter.

REFERENCES

Acuna, Roger Merino (2016) "An Alternative to "Alternative Development"?: Buen vivir and Human Development in Andean Countries," *Oxford Development Studies* 44(3): 271–86.

Alfred, Taiaiake (2005) *Wasáse: Indigenous Pathways of Action and Freedom*, Peterborough: Broadview Press.

Alkire, S. (2002) *Valuing Freedoms: Sen's Capability Approach and Poverty Reduction*. Oxford: Oxford University Press.

Anaya, James (2004) *Indigenous Peoples and International Law*. Oxford: Oxford University Press.

Beitz, Charles (1999) *Political Theory and International Relations*. Princeton, NJ: Princeton University Press.

Binder, Christina, and Constanze Binder (2016) "A Capability Perspective on Indigenous Autonomy," *Oxford Development Studies* 44(3): 297–314, DOI: 10.1080/13600818.2016.1167178.

Bockstael, Erika, and Krushil Watene (2016) "Indigenous Peoples and the Capability Approach: Taking Stock," *Oxford Development Studies* 44(3): 265–70.

Borrows, John (2002) *Recovering Canada: The Resurgence of Indigenous Law*. Toronto: University of Toronto Press.

Brock, Gillian (2009) *Global Justice: A Cosmopolitan Account*. Oxford: Oxford University Press.

Brooks, Thom (2014) "How Global is Global Justice? Towards a Global Philosophy." In Thom Brooks (ed.), *New Waves in Global Justice*. New York: Palgrave Macmillan, 229–457.

Coulthard, Glen (2014) *Red Skin, White Masks: Rejecting the Colonial Politics of Recognition*. Minneapolis, MN: University of Minnesota Press.

Debassige, Brent (2010) "Re-Conceptualizing Anishinaabe mino-bimaadiziwin (the GOOD LIFE) as Research Methodology: A Spirit-Centered Way in Anishinaabe Research," *Canadian Journal of Native Education* 33(1): 11–28.

Deer, Sarah (2009) "Decolonizing Rape Law: A Native Feminist Synthesis of Safety and Sovereignty," *Native Feminism* 24(2): 149–67.

Dotson, K (2011) "Tracking Epistemic Violence, Tracking Practices of Silencing," *Hypatia* 26: 236–57.

Durie, M. (2003) *Nga Kahui Pou: Launching Maori Futures.* Wellington: Huia Publishers.

Drydyk, Jay (2011) "Responsible Pluralism, Capabilities, and Human Rights," *Journal of Human Development* (Special Issue on Human Rights) 12(1): 39–61.

Graness, Anke (2015) "Is the Debate on Global Justice a Global One? Some Considerations in View of Modern Philosophy in Africa," *Journal of Global Ethics* 1(1): 126–40.

Gross, Lawrence W. (2002) "Bimaadiziwin, or the Good Life, as a Unifying Concept of Anishinaabe Religion,"*American Indian Culture and Research Journal* 26(1): 15–32.

Hohepa, Margie (2014) "Te Reo Māori and Schooling." In Merata Kawharu (ed.), *Maranga Mai! Te Reo and Marae in Crisis?.* Auckland: Auckland University Press, 103–27.

Jackson, Moana (1992) "The Colonisation of Māori Philosophy." In Graham Oddie and Roy Perrett (eds.), *Justice, Ethics, and New Zealand Society.* Auckland: Oxford University Press, 1–10.

Kawharu, Ian Hugh (1989) "Mana and the Crown: a marae at Orakei." In I. H. Kawharu (ed.), *Waitangi: Maori and Pakeha Perspectives of the Treaty of Waitangi.* Auckland: Oxford University Press, 211–33.

Kawharu, Ian Hugh (1997) *Maori Land Tenure: Studies of a Changing Institution.* Oxford: Clarendon Press.

Kawharu, Merata (2000) "Kaitiakitanga: A Maori anthropological perspective of the Maori socioenvironmental ethic of resource management," *Journal of the Polynesian Society* 110(4): 349–70.

Kawharu, Merata (2008) *Tahuhu Korero: The Sayings of Taitokerau.* Auckland: Auckland University Press.

Kingi, Tanira (2008) "Maori Landownership and Land Management in New Zealand." In AusAID (ed.), *Making Land Work. Volume Two: Case Studies on Customary Land and Development in the Pacific.* Canberra: AusAID, 129–52.

Klein, Elise (2016) "The Curious Case of Using the Capability Approach in Australian Indigenous Policy," *Journal of Human Development and Capabilities* 17(2): 245–59.

LeFevre, Tate. A. (2015) "Settler Colonialism." In John L. Jackson, Jr. (ed.), *Oxford Bibliographies in Anthropology.* New York: Oxford University Press, doi: https://dx.doi.org/10.1093/obo/9780199766567.016.0125.

Matiu, McCully , and Margaret Mutu (2003) *Te Whānau Moana: Ngā Kaupapa me ngā Tikanga: Customs and Protocols.* Auckland: Reed.

McGregor, Deborah (2009) "Honouring Our Relations: An Anishnaabe Perspective." In Julian Agyeman, Peter Cole, Randolph Haluza-DeLay, and Pat O'Riley (eds.), *Speaking for Ourselves: Environmental Justice in Canada.* Vancouver and Toronto: UBC Press, 27–41.

Marcham, Manuhuia (2012) "Thinking about Maori Development in Terms of the Capability Approach: The Shift towards the Adoption of the Maori Potential Approach." In Francesca Panzironi and Katharine Gelber (eds.), *The Capability Approach: Development Practice and Public Policy in the Asia-Pacific Region.* New York: Routledge, 55–67.

Marsden, Rev. Māori (2003) *The Woven Universe: Selected Writings of Rev. Māori Marsden.* Otaki: Estate of Rev. Māori Marsden.

Marsden, Rev. Māori, and Te Aroha Henare (1992) "Kaitiakitanga: A Definitive Introduction to the Holistic Worldview of the Maori." MS.

Matike Mai Aotearoa (2016) "He Whakaaro Here Whakaumu Mō Aotearoa: The Report of Matike Mai Aotearoa—The Independent Working Group on Constitutional Transformation," http://www.converge.org.nz/pma/MatikeMaiAotearoaReport.pdf, accessed August 16, 2019.

Mead, Hirini M. (2003) *Tikanga Maori: Living by Maori Values*. Wellington: Huia.

Meissner, Shelbi Nahwilet, and Kyle Whyte (2018) "Theorizing Indigeneity, Gender, and Settler Colonialism." In L. Alcoff, L. Anderson, and P. Taylor (eds.), *Routledge Companion to the Philosophy of Race*. New York and Abingdon: Routledge, 152–67.

Metz, Thaddeus (2007) "Towards an African Moral Theory," *Journal of Political Philosophy* 15(3): 321–41.

Mills, Charles W. (1997) *The Racial Contract*. Ithaca, NY: Cornell University Press.

Mills, Charles W. (2005) "Ideal Theory" as Ideology," *Hypatia: A Journal of Feminist Philosophy* 20(3): 165–84.

Mills, Charles W. (2009) "Rawls on Race/Race in Rawl," *The Southern Journal of Philosophy* 47: 161–84.

Moellendorf, Darrell (2002) *Cosmopolitan Justice*. Boulder, CO: Westview Press.

Mutu, Margaret (2012) "Custom Law and the Advent of New Pākehā Settlers: Tuku Whenua Allocation of Resource Use Rights." In Danny Keenan (ed.), *Huia Histories of Māori: Ngā Tāhuhu Kōrero*. Wellington: Huia Publishers, 93–108.

Mutu, Margaret (2013) "Te Tiriti o Waitangi in a Future Constitution: Removing the Shackles of Colonisation, 2013 Robson Lecture, 22 April 2013," http://www.converge.org.nz/pma/shackles-of-colonisation.pdf, accessed August 16, 2019.

Napoleon, Val (2005) "Aboriginal Self Determination: Individual Self and Collective Selves," *Atlantis* 29(2): 31–46.

Napoleon, Val (2007) "Thinking about Indigenous Legal Orders and Law, the National Centre for First Nations Governance," http://www.fngovernance.org/ncfng_research/val_napoleon.pdf, accessed August 16, 2019.

Napoleon, Val, and Hadley Friedland (2016) "An Inside Job: Engaging with Indigenous Legal Traditions through Stories," *McGill Law Journal* 61(4): 725–54.

Nussbaum, Martha (2000) *Women and Human Development: The Capabilities Approach*. Cambridge: Cambridge University Press.

Nussbaum, Martha (2006) *Frontiers of Justice: Disability, Nationality, Species Membership*. Cambridge, MA: Belknap Press.

Oruka, H. (1990a) *Sage Philosophy: Indigenous Thinkers and Modern Debate on African Philosophy*. Leiden: E.J. Brill.

Oruka, H. (1990b) "Four Trends in Current African Philosophy." In H. Oruka, *Trends in Contemporary African Philosophy*. Nairobi: Shirikon Publishers, 13–22.

Pihama, L. (2001) "Tihei mauri ora Honouring Our Voices: Mana wahine as Kaupapa Maori Theoretical Framework." Ph.D. thesis. Auckland: University of Auckland.

Poata-Smith, E. (2004) "Ka tika a muri, ka tika a mua? Maori Protest Politics and the Treaty of Waitangi Settlement Process." In Paul Spoonley, Cluny Macpherson, and David Pearson (eds.), *Tangata Tangata: The Changing Ethnic Contours of New Zealand*. Southbank, Victoria: Thomson/Dunmore Press.

Qizilbash, M. (2012) "The Capability Approach: Its Interpretation and Limitations." In F. Panzironi and K. Gelber (eds.), *The Capability Approach: Practice and Public Policy in the Asia-Pacific Region*. New York: Routledge, 9–22.

Rao, V., and M. Walton (2004) *Culture and Public Action*. Stanford, CA: Stanford University Press.

Rawls, John (1999) *The Law of Peoples (with "The Idea of Public Reason Revisited")*. Cambridge, MA: Harvard University Press.

Robeyns, Ingrid (2016) "Capabilitarianism," *Journal of Human Development and Capabilities* 17(3): 397–414.

Royal, Te Ahukaramu Charles (2002) "Indigenous Worldviews: A Comparative Study," (Report for Ngāti Kikopiri, Te Wānanga o Raukawa, Te Puni Kōkiri, Fulbright New Zealand and the Winston Churchill Memorial Trust), http://static1.squarespace.com/static/5369700de4b045a4e0c24bbc/t/53fe8f49e4b06d5988936162/1409191765620/Indigenous+Worldviews, accessed August 16, 2019.

Royal, Te Ahukaramu Charles (2009) "Mātauranga Māori: Perspectives, monograph five of Te Kaimānga: Towards a new Vision for Mātauranga Māori," https://charles-royal.myshopify.com/products/matauranga-maori-perspectives, accessed August 16, 2019 .

Royal, Te Ahukaramu Charles (2014) "Indigenous Ways of Knowing,"*Argos Aotearoa* 1. Special Issue "The University Beside Itself".

Ruru, Jacinta (2014) "Tūhoe-Crown Settlement—Te Urewera Act 2014," *Māori Law Review*, http://maorilawreview.co.nz/2014/10/tuhoe-crown-settlement-te-urewera-act-2014/, accessed August 16, 2019.

Sadler, Hone (2007) "Mātauranga Māori (Māori Epistemology)," *The International Journal of the Humanities* 4(10): 1–16.

Sen, Amartya (1999) *Development as Freedom*, 1st edn. New York: Oxford University Press.

Sen, Amartya (2004a) "How Does Culture Matter?" In V. Rao and M. Walton (eds.), *Culture and Public Action*. Stanford, CA: Stanford University Press, 37–58.

Sen, Amartya (2004b) "Why We Should Preserve the Spotted Owl: Sustainability," *London Review of Books* 26(3): 10–11.

Sen, Amartya (2005a) "Amartya Sen Talks with Bina Agarwal, Jane Humphries and Ingrid Robeyns. " In B. Agarwal, J. Humphries, and I. Robeyns (eds.), *Amartya Sen's Work and Ideas: A Gender Perspective*. New York: Routledge, 321–34.

Sen, Amartya (2005b) "Capabilities, Lists, and Public Reason: Continuing the Conversation." In B. Agarwal, J. Humphries, and I. Robeyns (eds.), *Amartya Sen's Work and Ideas: A Gender Perspective*. New York: Routledge, 335–9.

Sen, Amartya (2006) *Identity and Violence: The Illusion of Destiny*. New York: W. W. Norton.

Sen, Amartya (2009) *The Idea of Justice*. London: Penguin.

Singer, Peter (1972) "Famine, Affluence, and Morality," *Philosophy and Public Affairs* 1: 229–43.

Singer, Peter (2002) *One World: The Ethics of Globalisation*. Melbourne: Text Publishing.

Smith, G. H. (1997) "The Development of Kaupapa Maori: Theory and Praxis. Ph.D. thesis. Auckland: University of Auckland.

Smith, L., T. K. K. Maxwell, H. Puke, and P. Temara (2016) "Indigenous Knowledge, Methodology and Mayhem: What Is the Role of Methodology in Producing Indigenous Insights? A Discussion from Mātauranga Māori," *Knowledge Cultures* 4(3): 131–56.

Smith, Linda T. (1999) *Decolonizing Methodologies: Research and Indigenous Peoples*. London: Zed Books.

Smith, Linda T. (2006) "Colonizing Knowledges." In R. Maaka and C. Andersen (eds.), *The Indigenous Experience: Global Perspectives*. Toronto: Canadian Scholars' Press Inc.

Smith, Linda T., and Papaarangi Reid (2000) "Māori Research Development: Kaupapa Māori Principles and Practices, A Literature Review." (Report prepared for Te Puni Kokiri), http://www.rangahau.co.nz/assets//SmithL/Maori_research.pdf, accessed August 16, 2019.

Statistics New Zealand (2014) "Te Kupenga 2013 (English)—Corrected," http://archive.stats. govt.nz/browse_for_stats/people_and_communities/maori/TeKupenga_HOTP13/ Corrections.aspx, accessed August 16, 2019.

Tapsell, Paul (2014) "Tribal Marae: Crisis? What Crisis? ." In Merata Kawharu (ed.), *Maranga Mai! Te Reo and Marae in Crisis?*. Auckland: Auckland University Press, 35–64.

Taskforce on Whānau Centred Initiatives (Taskforce) 2010. *Whānau Ora: Report of the Taskforce on Whānau-Centred Initiatives.* (Report produced for Hon Tariana Turia, Minister for the Community and Voluntary Sector.) Wellington: Ministry of Social Development.

Turner, Dale (2006) *This is Not a Peace Pipe: Towards a Critical Indigenous Philosophy.* Toronto: University of Toronto Press, Scholarly Publishing Division.

United National Development Programme (UNDP) (2004) *Human Development Report 2004.* New York: Oxford University Press.

United Nations Permanent Forum for Indigenous Issues (UNPFII) 2007. "United Nations Declaration on the Rights of Indigenous Peoples," http://www.un.org/esa/socdev/unpfii/en/drip.html

United Nations Permanent Forum for Indigenous Issues (UNPFII) 2008. "United Nations Development Group Guidelines on Indigenous Peoples Issues," https://www.ohchr.org/EN/Issues/IPeoples/Pages/UNDGGuidelines.aspx, accessed August 16, 2019.

Waitangi Tribunal. 2011a. *Ko Aotearoa Tenei: Te Taumata Tuatahi (Wai 262).* Wellington: Legislation Direct.

Waitangi Tribunal. 2011b. *Ko Aotearoa Tenei: Te Taumata Tuarua (Wai 262).* Wellington: Legislation Direct.

Walker R. (2004) *Ka Mau Tonu te Whawhai: The Struggle Continues from Ka Whawhai Tonu Matou: Struggle without End.* Auckland: Penguin.

Walker, Ranginui (1978) "The Relevance of Maori Myth and Tradition." In Michael King (ed.) *Tihe Mauri Ora: Aspects of Maoritanga.* Wellington: Methuen, 19–32.

Watene, Krushil (2016a) "Indigenous Peoples and Justice." In Krushil Watene and Jay Drydyk, *Theorizing Justice: Critical Insights and Future Directions.* New York: Rowman and Littlefield International, 133–51.

Watene, Krushil (2016b) "Valuing Nature: Māori Philosophy and the Capability Approach," *Oxford Development Studies* (Special issue: Indigenous Peoples and Human Development), https://www.tandfonline.com/doi/abs/10.1080/13600818.2015.1124077, accessed October 20, 2019.

Whyte, K. P. (2010) "An Environmental Justice Framework for Indigenous Tourism," *Journal of Environmental Philosophy* 7: 75–92.

Whyte, K. P. (2013) "Justice Forward: Tribes, Climate Adaptation and Responsibility," *Climatic Change.* 120: 517–30.

Whyte, Kyle (2016a) "Indigenous Environmental Movements and the Function of Governance Institutions." In John M. Meyer, Teena Gabrielson, Cheryl Hall, and David Schlosberg (eds.), *The Oxford Handbook of Environmental Political Theory.* Oxford: Oxford University Press, 563–79.

Whyte, Kyle (2016b) "Indigenous Experience, Environmental Justice and Settler Colonialism." In Bryan E. Bannon (ed.), *Nature and Experience: Phenomenology and the Environment.* London: Rowman & Littlefield, 157–74.

Whyte, Kyle (2016c) " Indigeneity and U.S. Settler Colonialism." In Naomi. Zack (ed.), *The Oxford Handbook of Philosophy and Race.* Oxford: Oxford University Press, 91–101.

Whyte, Kyle (2017) "Our Ancestors' Dystopia Now: Indigenous Conservation and the Anthropocene." In Ursula K. Heise, Jon Christensen, and Michelle Niemann (eds.), *The Routledge Companion to the Environmental Humanities*. New York: Routledge, 206–15.

Whyte, Kyle Powys, and Chris J. Cuomo (2016) "Ethics of Caring in Environmental Ethics: Indigenous and Feminist Philosophies." In Stephen M. Gardiner and Allen Thompson (eds.), *The Oxford Handbook of Environmental Ethics*. Oxford: Oxford University Press, 234–47.

Williams, D. V. (2007) "Māori Social Identification and Colonial Extinguishments of Customary Rights in New Zealand," *Social Identities: Journal for the Study of Race, Nation and Culture* 13(6): 735–49.

Williams, David (2001) *Mātauranga Māori and taonga: The Nature and Extent Of Treaty Rights Held by iwi and hapū in Indigenous Flora and Fauna, Cultural Heritage Objects, Valued Traditional Knowledge*. Wellington: Waitangi Tribunal.

Yap, Mandy, and Eunice Yu (2000) "Community Wellbeing from the Ground Up: A Yawuru Example." (Bankwest Curtin Economics Centre Research Report 3/16), https://caepr.cass.anu.edu.au/sites/default/files/docs/bcec-community-wellbeing-from-the-ground-up-a-yawuru-example-1_2.pdf, accessed October 20, 2019.

Yazzie, Robert (1994) "Life Comes from It: Navajo Justice Concepts," *New Mexico Law Review* 24(2), https://digitalrepository.unm.edu/nmlr/vol24/iss2/3, accessed October 20, 2019.

Zion, James W., and Robert Yazzie (1997) "Indigenous Law in North America in the Wake of Conquest," *Boston College International and Comparative Law Review* 20(1): 55–84.

PART III

SEVERE POVERTY

CHAPTER 9

THE LINK BETWEEN SUBSISTENCE AND HUMAN RIGHTS

JESSE TOMALTY

1 INTRODUCTION

IT is by now a familiar fact that a huge number of people worldwide suffer from chronic and severe poverty. Exactly how many is difficult to ascertain; but even conservative estimates suggest that one in ten people worldwide has difficulty consistently meeting their most basic human needs.[1] This widespread poverty is mirrored by vast wealth owned by the global rich.[2] This suggests that eradicating global poverty is feasible, at least in the sense that there are sufficient resources to do so at relatively little cost.[3] The persistence of extensive poverty in the face of the feasibility of its eradication strikes many as a serious injustice. According to one prevalent view, this is because it constitutes a violation of universal human rights, and in particular of the human right to subsistence (e.g. Ashford 2007; Caney 2005; Gilabert 2006; Miller 2007).[4]

The human right to subsistence is a right to the means necessary to live a life free from severe poverty. These means include at least food adequate to avoid malnutrition, clean water adequate to avoid dehydration, and clothing and shelter adequate to avoid exposure to the elements. The human right to subsistence is generally argued for on the basis of the importance for all humans of the interest in having secure access to these means (e.g. Caney 2005; Griffin 2008; Tasioulas 2007). Lacking the means for subsistence is unquestionably among the worst situations that can befall any human. Malnutrition, dehydration, and exposure cause physical pain, illness, developmental problems, and premature death, not to mention the profound psychological distress associated with these. Furthermore, when a person cannot meet her most basic needs, she will struggle to lead an autonomous life in that she will be unable to pursue her desired projects. Lacking the means for subsistence also tends to perpetuate social and political marginalization. The very poor often lack any power to shape the institutions to which they are subject. In short, lacking the means for subsistence undermines physical and mental well-being as well as autonomy, and therefore constitutes a serious harm.

While it is uncontroversial that having the means for subsistence is of paramount importance for all humans, the inclusion of a right to subsistence among human rights is not. It is widely accepted that there are human rights to a variety of civil and political goods such as freedom from torture and freedom of speech, association, and religion; but the human right to subsistence and other socioeconomic human rights are often regarded as social goals or aspirations rather than genuine rights. Powerful challenges to the inclusion of a right to subsistence among human rights come from those who argue that we cannot move directly from interests to rights, regardless of how strong the interests may be. I will advocate one version of this view in Section 3. According to this view, the justification of rights can include considerations about interests; but the move from interests to rights must be mediated by other conditions, which ultimately preclude the human right to subsistence, while allowing for at least some civil and political human rights.

It is unclear, however, that the denial of a human right to subsistence is compatible with the affirmation of other human rights. It has been forcefully argued that there is an important link between civil and political human rights on the one hand and subsistence on the other, such that a commitment to the former entails a commitment to the inclusion of a right to subsistence among human rights. This kind of "linkage argument" has notably been advanced by Henry Shue (1996), and has more recently been developed by Elizabeth Ashford (2009). This line of argument will be our focus in what follows. In Section 4 and Section 5, I critically discuss both Shue's and Ashford's versions of the linkage argument. The innovation of the linkage argument is that it eschews the standard move from the interest in subsistence to a human right to subsistence, and in this way promises to circumvent challenges that rest on a rejection of this move. While I ultimately argue that the success of the linkage argument in vindicating the human right to subsistence is limited, it nevertheless contains important insights, some of whose implications I explore in Section 6.

2 HUMAN RIGHTS DISAMBIGUATION

We are primarily interested here in a debate over the *content* of human rights, but it will be helpful to begin by saying a little about the *concept* of human rights, since what human rights *are* is likely to affect what human rights *there are*. One of the central debates in the recent philosophical literature on human rights is between *naturalist* and *political* accounts. According to naturalist accounts, human rights are the fundamental moral rights held universally by all humans simply in virtue of being human (e.g. Gewirth 1978; Griffin 2008). Naturalist accounts differ from each other with respect to what it is about our humanity that gives rise to these rights, but they all agree that human rights are grounded in characteristics shared by all humans and that they are, therefore, held necessarily by all humans.

Naturalist accounts have been challenged on the grounds that they overlook the essentially political nature of human rights. According to political accounts, the nature and content of human rights must be gleaned from facts about the international legal and political practices in which human rights figure prominently as norms (e.g. Sangiovanni 2008; Beitz 2009; Buchanan 2013). Looking at international human rights doctrine which centrally includes the 1948 Universal Declaration of Human Rights and the two International Covenants of 1966, and at the political and legal apparatus surrounding them, we can identify at least two senses in which human rights are political. First, they are held primarily against political institutions—states in particular—by their members. Second, they are characterized and distinguished from other norms by the function(s) they have in international political and legal practice.

I argue that the debate between naturalist and political accounts of human rights presents a false dichotomy. We need not see either naturalist or political accounts as offering the exclusively correct account of the concept of human rights. Rather, we can see them each as identifying a distinct concept. This is supported by the fact that the term "human rights" is widely used to pick out *both* the rights held by all humans simply in virtue of being human *and* the rights articulated in international human rights doctrine and belonging to international political practice. The former are essentially moral rights, and the latter are essentially legal rights that form part of a broader international political practice. Rather than determining which of these constitutes the *correct* use of the term "human rights," I propose that theorizing about human rights should be focused on developing a better understanding of moral human rights (MHRs) and legal human rights (LHRs) independently, and, importantly, on determining what kind of relationship holds between them.[5]

As to the relationship between MHRs and LHRs, three positions are available: One is that LHRs are context-sensitive manifestations or applications of MHRs, and so the justification of a given LHR necessitates the justification of a corresponding MHR (e.g. Gewirth 1978; Griffin 2008). This is what Buchanan (2013) refers to as the "mirroring view," since it requires that the justification of any LHR be mirrored by a corresponding MHR. The second available position is that LHRs are completely independent of MHRs, and so the justification of MHRs plays no part in the justification of LHRs (e.g. Beitz 2009). And the third position is that there are some connections between LHRs and MHRs, but that the justification of a given MHR is neither necessary nor sufficient for the justification of a corresponding LHR (e.g. Wellman 2011; Buchanan 2013).

My purpose here is not to settle the question of the relationship between MHRs and LHRs. Rather, I wish only to point out (a) that MHRs and LHRs are two distinct concepts of human rights, and (b) that there is an open question of how they relate to each other. This is important because in discussing the debate over the inclusion of a right to subsistence among human rights, it must be clear whether we are talking about MHRs, LHRs, or both. The central debate I will discuss in Sections 3–5 concerns the inclusion of a right to subsistence among *moral* human rights. In Section 6 I consider the implications of this discussion for the inclusion of a right to subsistence among *legal* human rights. As we shall see, these will depend on which of the above views on the relationship between MHRs and LHRs turns out to be most apt.

3 The Claimability Objection

There are a number of objections to the moral human right to subsistence that challenge the inference from the interest of all humans in subsistence to a moral human right. In what follows, I will discuss only the one that I find most persuasive, namely the *claimability objection*.[6] This objection has been most notably advanced by Onora O'Neill (1996, 2000, 2005), who argues that a right to subsistence cannot be included among moral human rights because such a right is not claimable, and is, therefore, not a genuine right. In the absence of claimability, O'Neill argues, the universal interest in having the means for subsistence is not sufficient for the justification of a human right to subsistence.

The claimability objection hinges on the distinction between positive and negative rights. Negative rights are distinguished from positive rights on the basis of their correlative duties: Positive rights correlate with positive duties, and negative rights correlate with negative duties.[7] The distinction between positive and negative duties reflects the distinction between actions and omissions: A negative duty is a duty that can be fulfilled by omission alone. While it is widely acknowledged that the human right to subsistence entails negative duties on the part of others to abstain from action that deprives right-holders of the means for subsistence, it also characteristically correlates with positive duties to assist those who are unable to obtain access to the means for subsistence on their own. It is, therefore, a positive right.

According to the claimability objection, the problem with the moral human right to subsistence is that moral human rights cannot be positive. Moral human rights, as we have seen, are the rights held by all humans simply in virtue of being human. Moral human rights are, therefore, *general* rights. Rights are either special or general. Special rights are held in virtue of special relationships in which some people stand to others, such as institutional membership, kinship ties, and contractual agreements. By contrast, general rights are held regardless of such special relationships, and are, therefore, held by each right-holder against all moral agents (Hart 1955: 183–8). Since moral human rights are held by all humans *simply in virtue of being human*, they must be general rights, since they are, by definition, not contingent on any special relationships in which right-holders stand to others. Moral human rights are, then, held by each and against all.

According to O'Neill's objection, there cannot be a right to subsistence among moral human rights because (a) the right to subsistence is positive, (b) moral human rights are general, and (c) rights cannot be both positive and general. This is because positive general rights would have to have as their correlates positive general duties; but positive general duties are imperfect, and therefore cannot be the correlates of any right. Duties that are imperfect in the sense relevant to this objection are not owed to anyone in particular, although their fulfillment will typically benefit some.[8] Perfect duties, by contrast, are owed either to all others or to some specified others on the basis of special relationships. The general duties of assistance and protection associated with the moral human right to subsistence are imperfect because, for any given duty-bearer, it is impossible to provide assistance and protection to all those in need. Therefore, in the absence of institutional mechanisms that serve to allocate specific duties to specific duty-bearers, these duties are not owed to anyone in particular. Although this does not detract from their stringency, it is left to the discretion of duty-bearers to decide whom to assist and protect.

As O'Neill argues, imperfect duties cannot be the correlates of rights because they are not claimable. On this view, to have a right is just to have a claim to the performance of some duty by some particular duty-bearer. But where duties are imperfect, they are not owed to anyone in particular, and so no one can have a claim to their fulfillment. According to the claimability objection, for any given person suffering from severe poverty, it is indeterminate who, if anyone, is required to assist and protect them. This indeterminacy makes it "systematically obscure" who has neglected or violated their (moral) human right to subsistence, or whether there is any perpetrator at all (O'Neill 2000: 105). This in turn calls into question the normative value of affirming such a right.

Although a full-fledged defence of the claimability condition is beyond the scope of this chapter, I will mention two reasons that suggest that we should take it very seriously.[9] First of all, it is difficult to see how a right could be fully justified unless it is determinate against whom it is held. All rights involve both claims *to* some particular object(s) and claims *against* some particular duty bearer(s) (Feinberg 1966). The claimability condition requires that both the claim-to and claim-against dimensions of a right be justified in order for the right itself to be justified. In the case of the human right to subsistence, it is the claim-against dimension that is not justified. This is because, for any given right-holder, it is indeterminate against whom they have a claim. A reason for thinking that both dimensions of a right must be justified is that the justification of either dimension depends on the content of the other dimension. The justification of what a right is a claim *to* always depends in part on who it is a claim *against*.[10] For example, my claim to a suitable workspace is justified as a claim against my employer, but not as a claim against my neighbour. (Unless, of course, my neighbour also happens to be my employer. But even then, my right would be held against my neighbour in her capacity as my employer, and not simply as my neighbour.) Even claims that are held against all moral agents and grounded in very important interests nevertheless presuppose that it is reasonable to require all moral agents to fulfill the relevant duty. For example, the justification of my general claim not to be tortured assumes that it is reasonable to require all moral agents to abstain from torturing me. In order to know whether the object of a claim is justified, we must, therefore, also know against whom the claim is held. Otherwise, what we have is not really a claim, but merely a consideration in support of a claim.

Second, even if it were possible to justify the claim-to dimensions of rights independently of their claim-against dimensions, such partially justified rights would lack many of the distinctive characteristics of rights as they are normally understood. For example, rights are widely thought to have important implications in case they are violated. In particular, where a right is violated, the victim or her agents can demand *compensation* or *restitution* from the perpetrator. Rights are also widely thought to have implications prior to their violation. In particular, the affirmation of a right implies at least pro tanto grounds for its *coercive enforcement* by or on behalf of the right-holder. It is difficult to see, however, how an affirmed right could have these implications where it is indeterminate against whom it is held. Compensation and restitution can only be demanded of the perpetrator of a rights violation if it is known against whom the claim is held, which in turn requires that the duty-bearers are determinate. Furthermore, to say that the duties correlative to a right are justifiably enforceable prior to knowing who the relevant bearers are contributes nothing to normative reasoning, since no action can be justified on its basis.

These reasons suggest that the claimability condition applies, and that the claimability objection thus provides a powerful challenge to the inclusion of a (positive) right to subsistence among (general) moral human rights.[11] Any persuasive argument in support of the moral human right to subsistence should, therefore, have a convincing answer to it. Simply insisting that the importance of the interest of all humans in having the means for subsistence can all on its own give rise to a right will not do. This is precisely what the claimability objection denies in its affirmation of the claimability condition, which imposes a constraint on the inference from interests (even highly important ones) to rights. In what follows, I aim to ascertain whether the linkage argument might succeed in vindicating the moral human right to subsistence in the face of the claimability objection.

4 The Linkage Argument

On the face of it, the linkage argument looks like a promising way of defending the moral human right to subsistence, since it does not rely on drawing the inference from the importance of the interest of all humans in having the means for subsistence to the existence of a moral human right to subsistence. The linkage argument aims, instead, to show that a commitment to any human rights at all, including civil and political human rights, entails a commitment to the inclusion of a right to subsistence among them. In what follows, I argue that as a defence of the moral human right to subsistence against the claimability objection outlined above, the linkage argument misses the mark.

4.1 Shue's Linkage Argument

Building on the widespread commitment to civil and political human rights, the original articulation of the linkage argument by Shue emphasizes an important connection between these rights on the one hand and subsistence on the other. The relevant connection, according to Shue, is that the enjoyment of subsistence is necessary for the enjoyment of all other rights, including civil and political moral human rights. This, he argues, is because the lack of secure enjoyment of the means for subsistence poses a standard threat to the enjoyment of any other right (Shue 1996: 22–9).

For Shue, the enjoyment of a right involves not merely having the object of the right contingently, but rather having it guaranteed (pp. 15–16). For example, on Shue's account, an individual who is highly susceptible to being physically assaulted but who has not so far endured physical assault does not enjoy his right against physical assault. Of course, nothing can be guaranteed against any and all threats. Shue's view is that a right is enjoyed by the right-holder in so far as its object is reasonably guaranteed against standard threats. Standard threats are threats that are "common, or ordinary, and serious but remediable" (p. 23). The enjoyment of a right thus requires not just that others refrain from violating it, but also that social mechanisms are in place to protect the right-holder against violations.

Shue's linkage argument employs a "transitivity principle" for rights: "If everyone has a right to y, and the enjoyment of x is necessary for the enjoyment of y, then everyone also has a right to x" (p. 23). To say that "everyone has a right to y" can be read as expressing a moral human right to y. The transitivity principle can then alternatively be put as follows: If there is a moral human right to y, and the enjoyment of x is necessary to the enjoyment of y, then there is a moral human right to x. Shue argues that not only is the enjoyment of subsistence necessary for the enjoyment of the objects of *some* other rights, but that it is necessary for the enjoyment of the objects of *all* other rights.[12] His claim, then, is that, in so far as there are any moral human rights at all, the right to subsistence must be among them. Of course, this leaves open the possibility that there are no moral human rights at all, and so by extension no moral human right to subsistence. Shue's argument, therefore, relies on a commitment to the existence of at least some moral human rights. This is not unreasonable, given that even opponents of the moral human right to subsistence tend to endorse other moral human rights, notably at least some civil and political rights.

Shue's linkage argument can helpfully be summarized as follows:

1. If there is a moral human right to y, and the enjoyment of x is necessary to the enjoyment of y, then there is a moral human right to x (the transitivity principle).
2. There are some moral human rights (for example, against torture and to freedom of speech, assembly, and religion).
3. The enjoyment of subsistence is necessary for the enjoyment of the object of any moral human right.

Therefore,

4. There is a moral human right to subsistence.

The bulk of Shue's effort goes to defending premise (3). He argues that lacking subsistence constitutes a standard threat to the enjoyment of all other rights. One reason that Shue provides for thinking this is that lacking the means for subsistence has the effect of physically weakening individuals to the point at which they are incapable of exercising their rights (pp. 24–5). For example, freedom of assembly cannot actually be enjoyed by those who are too sickly to assemble. As Caney (2005 : 119–20) points out, whether this is true for all rights is not clear. Some rights, it seems, can be enjoyed even by those who are too weak to act. Enjoyment of the right against physical assault or of equality before the law, for example, does not seem to require persons to be strong enough to act. The second reason Shue offers is stronger. He argues that where people's subsistence needs are not met, their vulnerability to coercion constitutes a standard threat to the enjoyment of other rights (pp. 185–7, n. 13). This, he contends, is true for any right.

Shue offers the following example in support of the latter claim: The widely accepted moral human right against torture, he argues, cannot be fully enjoyed by those who cannot meet their subsistence needs because they will always be vulnerable to offers of subsistence goods in exchange for submitting to a limited amount of non-fatal torture (ibid.). The central claim is that subsistence is so fundamentally important to all human beings that, without it, we cannot enjoy any other right because the susceptibility to this sort of trade-off constitutes a standard threat to the enjoyment of other rights. As such, Shue holds that in so far as we are committed to the enjoyment of any moral human rights at all, we must affirm a moral human right to subsistence because there is a necessary connection between this right and the enjoyment of any other right, including all moral human rights.

Shue's claim is that the enjoyment of subsistence rights is "inherently necessary" for the enjoyment of all other rights (p. 27). What he means by "inherent necessity," however, is somewhat vague. A plausible way of interpreting the claim that *A* is inherently necessary for *B* in light of what Shue says is that there is a conceptual connection between *A* and *B*. Shue is explicit that "an 'inherent necessity' needs to be distinguished carefully from a mere means to an end" (p. 27). His suggestion is not merely that subsistence is a means to the enjoyment of other rights; rather, his claim is that part of what it means to enjoy any other right is that one has access to the means for subsistence.

But the idea that there is a conceptual connection between the secure enjoyment of all rights and having the means for subsistence falls prey to the following powerful objection: It is in fact possible to securely enjoy other rights while suffering severe shortfalls in subsistence goods.[13] It is possible, according to the critic, to enjoy freedom from torture despite being severely malnourished. It may be the case, as Shue suggests, that those who do not have secure access to the means for subsistence are liable to agree to compromise their other rights in exchange for subsistence goods; but then these sorts of contracts could simply be outlawed. Recall that the enjoyment of a right for Shue means that its object is socially guaranteed against standard threats. If the rules against torture are strictly enforced, as are rules against such torture contracts as have been described, then it seems that people do in fact enjoy their right against torture even if they fall below the threshold for subsistence. Therefore, the objection goes, enjoying the right to subsistence is not necessary in order to enjoy freedom from torture, among other rights.

The claim that there is a conceptual connection between the enjoyment of all moral human rights and the enjoyment of the moral human right to subsistence is, then, surely misguided, since there is nothing conceptually incoherent about the possibility of enjoying, say, one's moral human right against torture despite suffering severe malnourishment, so long as effective enforcement mechanisms are in place to guarantee that people do not engage in torture as well as to guarantee that people do not enter into torture contracts.

4.2 Ashford's Variation of the Linkage Argument

Ashford (2009) offers a more plausible variation of Shue's original linkage argument. According to her variation, the connection between subsistence and the enjoyment of other rights is not conceptual, but rather substantive. Although it is conceptually possible to enjoy one's right against torture while lacking the means for subsistence, this would require the banning of torture contracts. Banning torture contracts, Ashford rightly notes, would, however, be against the interests of people who lack the means for subsistence. The reason that a person would be willing to enter into a torture contract in the first place is that the interest in subsistence is so important as to outweigh the interest in not being tortured. That is to say that lacking access to the means for subsistence while enjoying freedom from torture is worse for a person than gaining access to the means for subsistence by submitting to (a limited amount of non-fatal) torture. As such, denying someone who lacks access to the means for subsistence the option of the torture contract would make her worse off than she would be if such contracts were available to her; if they were not, there would be insufficient motivation for her to enter into the contract in the first place, and so such contracts would not constitute standard threats.

The point is somewhat easier to illustrate with outlandish cases like the torture contract, but Ashford points out that there are real cases in which guaranteeing one right through enforcement actually results in people being worse off in terms of subsistence than they would have otherwise been. She appeals in particular to child labour (pp. 106–12). While it is widely accepted that children have a right not to be forced to work, securing this right by banning child labour will in many cases result in families being unable to obtain the material means for subsistence. Although the children may then be said to enjoy their right not to be forced to work, they are subsequently made to suffer malnourishment and poverty-related illness, among other harms.

Ashford goes on to argue that if we hold the plausible view that, at the very least, the secure enjoyment of a right should not thwart the very fundamental interests of the right-holder, banning the torture contract in order to protect the right against torture, or banning child labour practices in order to protect the right against child labour would fail to be appropriate measures. The only way to ensure that torture contracts and other perverse trade-offs do not constitute a threat to the enjoyment of rights is, therefore, to annihilate the incentive for entering into them in the first place. This entails, inter alia, guaranteeing access to the means for subsistence. So while we can perhaps conceive of the enjoyment of the right against torture and the right against child labour, among other rights, independent of guaranteed access to the means for subsistence, this kind of situation is morally inconsistent in light of the needs that human beings actually have and the social circumstances in which they actually exist. Ashford concludes that having guaranteed access to the means for subsistence is thus a substantively necessary condition for the enjoyment of any other right; and so the moral human right to subsistence can be derived from the existence of any other moral human right. Therefore, in so far as we think that there are any moral human rights at all, the right to subsistence must be among them. Or so the linkage argument goes.

5 THE LIMITS OF LINKAGE ARGUMENTS

Ashford's argument for the substantive necessity of subsistence for the enjoyment of other moral human rights provides a forceful defense of premise (3) of Shue's original linkage argument, as stated in Section 4.1 above. In what follows, however, I offer a novel challenge to the linkage argument which targets the transitivity principle expressed in premise (1). In particular, I argue that the transitivity principle is incompatible with the conception of rights that underpins the claimability objection. The linkage argument thus begs the question against the claimability objection rather than providing an answer to it.

Recall that according to the transitivity principle, if there is a moral human right to y, and the enjoyment of x is necessary for the enjoyment of y, then there is a moral human right to x. An initial problem with the transitivity principle is that it conflates the right to y and the enjoyment of y. On Shue's account, all rights are rights to the enjoyment of some object. A right, according to Shue, "provides (1) the rational basis for a justified demand that (2) the actual enjoyment of a substance be (3) socially guaranteed against standard threats" (Shue 1996: 13). Thus, the right against physical assault, for example, implies a right that freedom from physical assault be socially guaranteed against standard threats.

By contrast, opponents of the moral human right to subsistence tend to draw a sharp distinction between the enjoyment of rights on the one hand and their non-violation on the other. On this sort of account, rights correlate directly with obligations of non-violation, and indirectly with obligations of protection (e.g. Pogge 2009). The right against physical assault is one thing; the right to the enjoyment of freedom from physical assault another. The former correlates with obligations not to physically assault the right-holder; the latter correlates with obligations to protect the right-holder against threats of physical assault. And because the latter is a positive duty, according to the claimability objection, it is either special and therefore perfect or it does not correlate with any right. To the extent that there are rights to be protected against physical assault, they must therefore be special rights, and cannot therefore be moral human rights.

Shue argues that we should resist dissecting rights in this way, since, even if there is a meaningful line to be drawn between the non-violation of a right and its enjoyment, the former is of little interest to persons living in the sorts of social conditions in which they actually live in the absence of the latter (p. 38). Shue is certainly right in thinking that the enjoyment of rights is of greater interest to right-holders than merely not having them violated as a matter of contingency. But this does not give us reason to think that there is no morally relevant distinction to be drawn between the two. At the very least, the violation of a right can aptly be regarded as morally worse than the failure to prevent the violation of that right.

Shue and Ashford argue that in so far as we take rights seriously, we should not downplay the importance of protecting right-holders against standard threats to the enjoyment of the substance of their rights, and that this in turn requires that right-holders enjoy access to the means for subsistence. I think this is a point of crucial importance in thinking about the implementation of rights, as Shue himself rightly notes (p. 38). I doubt, however, that it provides support for the existence of a moral human right to subsistence, as the linkage argument suggests.

The transitivity principle infers a moral human right to x on the basis of a moral human right to y, and the necessity of the enjoyment of x for the enjoyment of y. This principle thus assumes that the existence of a moral human right to y entails a moral human right to the enjoyment of y—otherwise, it is unclear why we should infer a moral human right to x. But the claimability objection suggests that we should reject this move. This is because of the constraints on rights that hold on this account. Recall that the claimability objection denies that there can be general positive rights because they are not claimable. If the objection holds—which I have argued it does—we should thus reject the move from the existence of a moral human right to y to the existence of a moral human right to the *enjoyment* of y. And without this step, we cannot draw the inference to the existence of a moral human right to x on the basis that the enjoyment of x is necessary for the enjoyment of y.

In order to engage with the claimability objection to the moral human right to subsistence, defenders of this right must explain why the claimability condition need not apply. The linkage argument fails in this respect by simply assuming that it does not. The linkage argument builds on the highly plausible point that secure access to the means for subsistence is necessary for the enjoyment of civil and political moral human rights; but this is something that can be accepted without endorsing a moral human right to subsistence. A moral human right to subsistence only follows if we presuppose that other moral human rights are in fact claims to the enjoyment of some object rather than simply claims to non-violation. But those who reject the moral human right to subsistence on the grounds that it is positive will reject this presupposition for the same reason. As we have seen, in order for any right to be enjoyed it must be socially guaranteed against standard threats; and social guarantees against standard threats involve considerably more than mere forbearance on the part of duty-bearers.

6 Subsistence as a Legal Human Right

I have so far argued that the linkage argument does not avoid the claimability objection to the inclusion of a right to subsistence among moral human rights. This is because it must assume that each moral human right comes with a built-in claim to its own enjoyment, which, I have argued, is to beg the question against the claimability objection. But while I think that the claimability objection is ultimately successful in undermining positive moral human rights, including the moral human right to subsistence, it does not preclude positive *special* rights including the right to be provided with reasonable guarantees against the violation of one's moral human rights. And where such special rights exist, the linkage argument supports the (substantive) necessity of special rights to subsistence. This, I argue, has important implications for the justification of a *legal* human right to subsistence.

The rejection of a right to subsistence among *legal* human rights only follows from the rejection of a right to subsistence among *moral* human rights on the mirroring view, mentioned in Section 2, above according to which, for each LHR, there must be a corresponding MRH. This view has recently been subject to damaging criticism on the grounds that it fails to provide a plausible interpretation of LHRs, given their content, nature, and function within the context of international legal and political practice (Beitz 2009; Wellman 2011; Buchanan 2013). Critics of the mirroring view tend to point in particular to the extensive lists of LHRs included in international doctrine, which they argue could not plausibly be derived solely from the relatively meagre set of MHRs.

It might, of course, be that LHRs actually manifest a conception of MHRs that is flawed in its failure to give due regard to the claimability condition or other constraints on the justification of rights, and that their content should therefore be curtailed accordingly. On a more charitable interpretation of international legal and political practice, however, LHRs simply do not manifest MHRs in any straightforward sense, but rather function (at least partly) so as to protect and promote their enjoyment. This would account for their more extensive content, since, as we have seen, the enjoyment of a right requires more than its mere non-violation. Furthermore, it is consonant with the fact that, in international practice, LHRs are systematically held in the first place against states by their members, and only secondarily impose duties of concern on the international community at large. LHRs are, in this regard, special rather than general rights. As such, they can be positive without facing the claimability objection.

There is an extensive discussion to be had about the relative merits of the mirroring view and its alternatives, which will be largely set aside here, as it would take us beyond the scope of our present concern. What I want to point out in what remains is that it is on the above-mentioned conception of LHRs as institutionalized special rights whose function is at least partly to promote the enjoyment of MHRs that the linkage argument really comes into its own.

Recall that the transitivity principle on which the linkage argument is premised is articulated above as follows:

> If there is a moral human right to y, and the enjoyment of x is necessary to the enjoyment of y, then there is a moral human right to x.

I have argued that this principle must be rejected on account of the claimability condition. But if LHRs are institutionalized special rights whose function is at least partly to promote the enjoyment of MHRs, then a modified version of the transitivity principle is available:

> If there is a moral human right to y and the enjoyment of x is necessary for the enjoyment of y, then there ought to be a *legal* human right to x.

This principle holds because LHRs on this conception are *by definition* meant to promote the enjoyment of MHRs, and as special rights they fulfill the claimability condition.

The modified transitivity principle provides a premise in a successful linkage argument in support of the inclusion of a right to subsistence among *legal* human rights, since, as Ashford (2009) persuasively argues, the enjoyment of subsistence is substantively necessary for the enjoyment of widely acknowledged *moral* human rights such as the right against torture and the right against child labour. The complete argument can be stated as follows:

1. LHRs are institutionalized special rights whose function is at least partly to promote the enjoyment of MHRs.
2. If there is an MHR to y, and the enjoyment of x is necessary to the enjoyment of y, then there ought to be an LHR to x (the transitivity principle).
3. There are some MHRs.
4. The enjoyment of subsistence is (substantively) necessary for the enjoyment of the object of any MHR.

Therefore:

5. A right to subsistence ought to be included among LHRs.

While the linkage argument as originally stated in Section 4 does not succeed in vindicating the MHR to subsistence, this modified version provides a strong case in support of the inclusion of a right to subsistence among LHRs.

It might be pointed out that this argument in support of an LHR to subsistence is actually superfluous. To see why, consider what kind of justification might be given for thinking that the promotion of the enjoyment of MHRs should be institutionalized in international practice in the form of LHRs and the extensive legal and political apparatus surrounding them. The reason, presumably, would refer to the tremendous importance for all humans of the interest not just in having their MHRs contingently non-violated, but in having reasonable guarantees to their non-violation. But if we think that LHRs to these guarantees can be justified on the basis of interests, then presumably the interest in having the means for subsistence would on its own support the inclusion of a corresponding LHR. As an argument in support of the inclusion of a right to subsistence among LHRs, the linkage argument, then, amounts to preaching to the choir. But preaching to the choir need not be superfluous. We all occasionally need to be reminded of our commitments and to have their implications pointed out. Even where the LHR to subsistence and other socioeconomic LHRs are affirmed, their importance tends to be downplayed in relation to that of civil and political LHRs. The modified version of the linkage argument is a powerful reminder of the inefficiency of efforts to promote the latter without also working to promote the former.

7 Conclusion

I have argued that the versions of the linkage argument advanced by Shue and Ashford fall short of their aim of vindicating a *moral* human right to subsistence. Nevertheless, they are founded on an important insight, namely that the expression of a commitment to the promotion of civil and political human rights rings hollow if not accompanied by a concern for the material conditions necessary to meaningfully enjoy and exercise those rights. This, I have suggested, has important implications with respect to the question of the justification and status of a *legal* human right to subsistence.

Notes

1. For example, according to the United Nations Development Programme (2016), around 10% of the world's population fall below the World Bank's income poverty line of US$1.90 per day.
2. According to Credit Suisse (2018), the wealthiest 10% of the world's population hold around 84% of total wealth, with around 45% of total wealth being held by just the wealthiest 1% of the world's population.
3. Of course, the eradication of global poverty is more complicated than this suggests. It might be argued that there are other constraints on the feasibility of eradicating severe poverty, such as motivational and political obstacles. But even if these sorts of obstacles make it infeasible to eradicate severe poverty *right now*, they might be overcome in the foreseeable future. If overcoming an obstacle to the feasibility of realizing some goal is itself feasible, then we can still judge the realization of that goal to be feasible. For an illuminating discussion of issues surrounding the feasibility of the eradication of severe poverty, see Gilabert (2009).
4. What I am calling the human right to subsistence goes by other names, such as the human right against poverty and the human right to basic necessities.
5. I borrow the terminology and abbreviations from Buchanan (2010, 2013).

6. Other objections include the feasibility objection made, for example, by Cranston (1983, 2001), and the libertarian objection advanced, for example, by Jan Narveson (1988). Powerful replies to these can be found in Gilabert (2006, 2009).

7. Following Shue (1996), the distinction between positive and negative rights now tends to be regarded with skepticism. Shue argues that all rights entail both positive and negative duties, and therefore resist classification as positive or negative. But the various duties entailed by any given right stand in different relations to that right. In particular, only the violation of certain duties entailed by a right constitutes the violation of that right. We can, therefore, distinguish between positive and negative rights on the basis of these duties. See Pogge (2009).

8. There are other ways of understanding what it means for a duty to be imperfect, but this is the one relevant to the discussion at hand, so I set aside the others here. For a helpful discussion of various interpretations of imperfect duties, see Hope (2011, 2014).

9. For an extended discussion of the claimability condition, see Tomalty (2014).

10. Kramer (1998: 48) makes a similar point.

11. There is a further possibility in defense of the moral human right to subsistence against the claimability objection, namely to show that it is in fact claimable (e.g. Ashford 2007; Stemplowska 2009). I will not discuss this possibility here except to say that I am doubtful of its success largely because it tends to involve distorting either the content of the right or what is required for claimability. See Tomalty (2014) for a more extended discussion.

12. One of Shue's central claims is that the right to subsistence is a "basic right." A basic right on Shue's (1996: 18–20) account is one whose enjoyment is necessary for the enjoyment of any other right.

13. Shue (1996: 184, n. 13) attributes this objection to Mark Wicclair. Thomas Pogge (2009: 119–21) makes a similar point.

References

Ashford, Elizabeth (2007) "The Duties Imposed by the Human Right to Basic Necessities." In Thomas Pogge (ed.), *Freedom from Poverty as a Human Right: Who Owes what to the very Poor?*. Oxford: Oxford University Press and UNESCO, 183–218.

Ashford, Elizabeth (2009) "The Alleged Dichotomy Between Positive and Negative Rights and Duties." In Charles R. Beitz and Robert E. Goodin (eds.), *Global Basic Rights*. Oxford: Oxford University Press, 92–112.

Beitz, Charles (2009) *The Idea of Human Rights.*Oxford: Oxford University Press.

Buchanan, Allen (2010) "The Egalitarianism of Human Rights," *Ethics* 120: 679–710.

Buchanan, Allen (2013) *The Heart of Human Rights* (Oxford: Oxford University Press.

Caney, Simon (2005) *Justice Beyond Borders: A Global Political Theory*. Oxford: Oxford University Press.

Cranston, Maurice (1983) "Are There Any Human Rights?" *Daedalus* 112: 1–17.

Cranston, Maurice (2001) "Human Rights, Real and Supposed." In Patrick Hayden (ed.), *The Philosophy of Human Rights*. St. Paul, MN: Paragon House, 163–73.

Credit Suisse Research Institute (2018) *Global Wealth Report 2018*. Zurich: Credit Suisse.

Feinberg, Joel (1966) "Duties, Rights, and Claims," *American Philosophical Quarterly* 3(2): 137–44.

Gewirth, Alan (1978) "The Basis and Content of Human Rights," *Georgia Law Review* 13: 1143–70.

Gilabert, Pablo (2006) "Basic Positive Duties of justice and Narveson's Libertarian Challenge," *The Southern Journal of Philosophy* 40: 193–216.

Gilabert, Pablo (2009) "The Feasibility of Basic Socioeconomic Human Rights: A Conceptual Exploration," *The Philosophical Quarterly*, 59: 659–81.

Griffin, James (2008) *On Human Rights*. Oxford: Oxford University Press.

Hart, H. L. A. (1955) "Are There Any Natural Rights?," *The Philosophical Review* 64: 175–91.

Hope, Simon (2011) "Subsistence Needs, Human Rights, and Imperfect Duties," *Journal of Applied Philosophy* 30: 88–100.

Hope, Simon (2014) "Kantian Imperfect Duties and Modern Debates over Human Rights," *Journal of Political Philosophy* 22: 396–415.

Kramer, Matthew H. (1998) "Rights without Trimmings." In Matthew H. Kramer, N. E. Simmonds, and Hillel Steiner (eds.), *A Debate over Rights*. Oxford: Oxford University Press, 7–111.

Miller, David (2007) *National Responsibility and Global Justice*. Oxford: Oxford University Press.

Narveson, Jan (1988) *The Libertarian Idea*. Peterborough, Ontario: Broadview Press.

O'Neill, Onora (1996) *Towards Justice and Virtue: A Constructive Account of Practical Reasoning*. Cambridge: Cambridge University Press.

O'Neill, Onora (2000) *Bounds of Justice*. Cambridge: Cambridge University Press.

O'Neill, Onora (2005) "The Dark Side of Human Rights," *International Affairs* 81: 427–39.

Pogge, Thomas (2009) "Shue on Rights and Duties." In Charles R. Beitz and Robert E. Goodin (eds.), *Global Basic Rights*. Oxford: Oxford University Press, 113–30.

Sangiovanni, Andrea (2008) "Justice and the Priority of Politics to Morality," *Journal of Political Philosophy* 16(2): 137–647.

Shue, Henry (1996) *Basic Rights: Subsistence, Affluence, and U.S. Foreign Policy*, 2nd edn. Princeton, NJ: Princeton University Press.

Stemplowska, Zofia (2009) "On the Real World Duties Imposed on Us by Human Rights," *Journal of Social Philosophy* 40(4): 466–87.

Tasioulas, John (2007) "The Moral Reality of Human Rights" in Thomas Pogge (ed.), *Freedom from Poverty as a Human Right: Who Owes what to the very Poor?*. Oxford: Oxford University Press and UNESCO, 75–100.

Tomalty, Jesse (2014) "The Force of the Claimability Objection to the Human Right to Subsistence," *Canadian Journal of Philosophy* 44: 1–17.

United Nations Development Programme (2016) *Human Development Report 2016: Human Development for Everyone*. New York: United Nations.

Wellman, Carl (2011) *The Moral Dimensions of Human Rights*. Oxford: Oxford University Press.

FURTHER READING

Jones, Charles (1999) *Global Justice: Defending Cosmopolitanism*. Oxford: Oxford University Press.

Gilabert, Pablo (2012) *From Global Poverty to Global Equality: A Philosophical Explanation*. Oxford: Oxford University Press.

Nickel, James W. (2007) *Making Sense of Human Rights*, 2nd edn. Malden, MA: Blackwell Publishing.

CHAPTER 10

CAPABILITIES, FREEDOM, AND SEVERE POVERTY

THOM BROOKS

1 INTRODUCTION

SEVERE poverty is a key challenge for theorists of global justice. Most theorists have approached this issue primarily by developing accounts for understanding which kinds of duties have relevance and how responsibilities for tackling severe poverty might be assigned to agents, whether individuals, nations, or states. All such views share a commitment to ending severe poverty as a wrongful deprivation with profoundly negative impact on affected individuals.

While much attention has prioritized identifying reasons for others to provide relief, this chapter will examine the nature of the wrongful deprivation that characterizes severe poverty. One influential view is championed by Martha Nussbaum in her distinctive capabilities approach.[1] An individual might be considered to experience severe poverty where she is unable to enjoy the use of the capabilities which should be available to her. But this position raises several questions. Take the fact that about 1 billion people are unable to meet their basic needs today. Would the capabilities approach claim the number is much higher given its wider grasp of human flourishing beyond mere material subsistence—and what implications would flow from this? Or would the capabilities approach claim only a portion of those unable to meet their basic needs are in a wrongful state because their circumstances are a result of free choice—and what would this mean? These questions indicate a potential concern about whether the approach is over- or underinclusive and why, with practical, not merely theoretical implications.

This chapter will proceed by first (Section 2) providing a general overview of Nussbaum's capabilities approach, with an indication (Section 3) about how her list of ten capabilities might be reformulated differently. Section 4 applies this approach to severe poverty in a critical discussion of how such poverty is best understood within the capabilities framework. Section 5 considers the importance of freedom and choice that underpins the approach and its implications for how we apply it to severe poverty. The chapter ends with some concluding remarks (Section 6) about the broad limitations for understanding severe poverty as a kind of capabilities deprivation.

2 Nussbaum's Capabilities Approach

Nussbaum's approach builds off from pioneering work by Amartya Sen (1980, 1985, 1999a). He made a crucial distinction between functionings and capabilities.[2] Functionings reflect the achievements made by someone, such as the fact of drinking a glass of water or eating a bowl of rice. Capabilities are different because they capture our freedom to achieve functionings.[3]

Sen claimed this distinction was crucial because it allowed us to normatively assess the difference between a person starving or another fasting. Both persons share the same basic functionings: neither is eating food or receiving nourishment. Their difference is primarily with regard to the presence or absence of capabilities. Only the person fasting has the freedom to achieve being nourished, but he has chosen to not exercise this choice. The other person starving is without food and without choice. So, it is not all important that we do function in any particular way, but it is necessary that we possess the capability to function in particular ways should we choose to do so.[4] Capabilities prioritize opportunities over achievements.

This model is a direct challenge to the orthodox way economists have understood the measurement of development and poverty alleviation. In essence, this is done too crudely by relying on comparisons based on Gross Domestic Product (GDP) and using thresholds like a nominal poverty line—such as $1.90 per day—to consider progress.[5] The problems using a purely resource-driven metric like monetary spending power are it masks inequality of wealth and seems divorced from well-being.

Take GDP. Country *Alpha* has an average GDP that is at the line between general subsistence or severe poverty: any more or less would place it above or below this threshold. In contrast, country *Beta* has an average GDP that places it slightly above this threshold. If we look at average GDP, Beta appears to have achieved greater economic development than Alpha. But then consider the fact that in Alpha the majority of citizens have the same level of wealth. Their place on the threshold line is an accurate indication of where most of their citizens are. However, in Beta there is a fabulously wealthy king whose wealth is half of his country's GDP. Despite the fact that Beta has a higher average GDP and so appears on that measure to be more developed than Alpha, far more of Beta's population are actually living in severe poverty. This shows how one country having a higher average GDP than another is not sufficient evidence that it has more successfully combated severe poverty, as this crude measure masks inequalities among a population.

But a resource-driven metric should also be rejected because it is also divorced from well-being. One country may be far wealthier than another, yet score much worse on indicators like longevity, infant mortality rates, literacy, and access to clean water.

Resources can be critical to delivering improvements in well-being, but they are not a sufficient guarantee that satisfactory well-being has been achieved or that the general well-being of one community will be higher than that of another. Capabilities cast a wider net to assess the well-being of individuals with a sensitivity to variations within communities. In these ways, it has become the dominant alternative to orthodox, resourcist approaches and is attracting increasing support.

Nussbaum (2011: 14) shares with Sen this idea of capabilities, how it is distinguished from functionings, and its importance as an improved way of evaluating human development. Her view has many differences from Sen's approach, including her understanding capabilities as capturing a plurality of qualitative distinct elements. So both understand capabilities as what we are able to do or be, but Nussbaum's key departure from Sen is in fleshing out these capabilities into a list summarized here:

1. **Life**—the ability to live a human life of normal length and worth living
2. **Bodily health**—the ability to be adequately nourished, possess adequate shelter, and maintain good health, including reproductive health
3. **Bodily integrity**—the ability to move freely, being secure against violent assault, having opportunities for sexual satisfaction, and reproductive choice
4. **Senses, imagination, and thought**—the ability to receive an adequate education, possessing freedom of expression and religious exercise, being able to experience literary or musical works or events, and the ability to have pleasurable experiences
5. **Emotions**—the ability to have attachments to things and people outside of ourselves, to love those who love and care for us, and not have our emotional development stunted by fear or anxiety
6. **Practical reason**—the ability to form conceptions of the good and engage in critical reflection in planning one's life
7. **Affiliation**—(A) the ability to live with and toward others, engaging in social interaction; (B) the ability to have the social bases of self-respect and non-humiliation, being treated as a dignified person of equal worth, and non-discrimination on the basis of race, sex, sexual orientation, ethnicity, caste, religion, or national origin
8. **Other species**—the ability to live with concern for and in relation to plant and animal species
9. **Play**—the ability to laugh, play, and enjoy recreational activities
10. **Control over one's environment**—(A) *Political*: the ability to participate effectively in political choices, enjoying protections of free speech and association; (B) *Material*: the ability to have property rights on an equal basis with others, the right to seek employment on equal basis with others, and freedom from unwarranted search and seizure (Nussbaum 2011: 33–4).[6]

Each capability on this list is of central importance and of equal weight. Nussbaum denies that a capability to life is necessarily more valuable than emotions. All capabilities must be available for any individual to exercise with none closed off (Nussbaum 2000b: 74, 81). It is vital that everyone has access to capabilities and the same opportunities to exercise them—and it is assumed that capabilities will not clash. These capabilities mutually support each other in a competitive framework. She rejects making trade-offs between them. A lack in one capability cannot be compensated by a high enjoyment of another (Nussbaum 2000b: 81).

A second key difference between Sen's and Nussbaum's competing conceptions of capabilities is that Nussbaum emphasizes the importance of having opportunities to exercise capabilities above a threshold, or otherwise fail to enjoy a minimally basic conception of justice. She says that all "citizens be placed above an ample (specified) threshold of capability, in all ten of those areas" or they will be denied their requisite human dignity (Nussbaum 2011: 36). Capabilities are intended to capture human well-being and when any one is denied, then individual dignity is not achieved.

The state has a role to play in bringing the capabilities approach to life. Nussbaum says it is "the job of government to secure them, if that government is to be even minimally just" (Nussbaum 2011: 36). This does not necessarily require more than a minimal state. For some capabilities, like affiliation, it might be enough for the state to facilitate individuals exercising capabilities by avoiding interventions. In other areas, perhaps bodily health, the state might play a more active role. Neither is prescribed. What counts is that capabilities can be exercised. Whether or not the state runs a public healthcare system is less important than whether a sufficient threshold of bodily health is secured for all.

3   Time to Revise the Capabilities List?

Nussbaum's list is complex. She recognizes that several overlap or interrelate. While she defends having these ten on her list as each making an individual contribution to our understanding of dignity and well-being, Nussbaum recognizes that capabilities can also help support or develop each other. So while "senses, imagination and thought" and "emotions" are meant to capture different aspects of well-being, it is difficult to see how one capability could be achieved without the other. The inability to enjoy a healthy emotional development seems essential to enjoy the experience of literary or musical works in the way she describes, and vice versa. Likewise, the ability to achieve satisfactory levels of "practical reason" seems to require sufficient education, as again found in "senses, imagination and thought." If there are lines between capabilities, they may appear thinly porous—and might encourage us to revisit the list's formulation.

But aside from similarities in what different capabilities are called, there are also similarities in their use. Each is meant to be understood and assessed within a community.

What it means to meet or exceed a satisfactory threshold of "bodily integrity" or "practical reason" can differ from one community to the next and may change over time. But what counts for a capability and its content is given by Nussbaum's list.

Nussbaum claims her list is not written in stone. It is "a proposal" (Nussbaum 2011: 36). Furthermore, she says: "Nor is the list final: if it turns out to lack something that experience shows to be a crucial element of a life worthy of human dignity, it can always be contested and remade" (Nussbaum 2011: 15). There may be additional capabilities not yet recognized that can and should be added to her list, expanding the number beyond ten. Likewise, it should also hold that if some element on the list were no longer deemed crucial to a life worthy of human dignity, it should be removed. A living list open to revision must continually reassess both current capabilities and prospective capabilities when confirming them at any time.

Some revisions seem warranted to achieve how Nussbaum understands her approach within a broader conception of justice. For example, she says the capabilities approach "aspires to be the object of an Overlapping Consensus" (Nussbaum 2011: 93; see also Nussbaum 2006: chs. 1–3). In John Rawls's formulation, which Nussbaum accepts, his theory of political liberalism "looks for a political conception of justice that we hope can gain the support of an overlapping consensus of reasonable religious, philosophical and moral doctrines" (Rawls 1996: 10). It can do this by avoiding incompatibility with these doctrines, broadly held to constitute all major religious traditions (see Rawls 1996: 157). Nussbaum claims her capabilities approach is compatible with Rawls's political liberalism, and its place within this view of justice is as an overlapping consensus that all major philosophical and religious traditions can connect with (Nussbaum 2006: 6).

The main difficulty for Nussbaum is the content she gives for capabilities on her list (see Brooks 2015). For example, Roman Catholicism officially opposes abortion. Nussbaum's capabilities list includes items like "bodily integrity" that adherents of Catholicism might reasonably accept from within their comprehensive religious doctrine. But Nussbaum gives this capability specific content that would act as a bar. She claims this capability includes "choice in matters of reproduction," which Catholics might reject (see Nussbaum 2011: 33).

Nussbaum may well be justified in giving this capability such content—and, to avoid any doubt, I support this understanding of bodily integrity too. The issue is that bodily integrity cannot be the object of an overlapping consensus: if not every relevant view of the good can, at least in principle, reasonably support the content given, then either not all such views of the good have equal standing or the content of this capability must be redefined—at least if it is to serve as an overlapping consensus in this way. Nor is this an isolated example. Not every major doctrine accepts other views, such as the essential need for "play" and recreational activities. These views might be unjustified and subjected to challenge, but they create obstacles in the way of capabilities being reasonably endorsed by all the different normative perspectives that Rawls claims as reasonable. If capabilities are to serve as the object of a consensus, then their content must be changed even if their number is not.

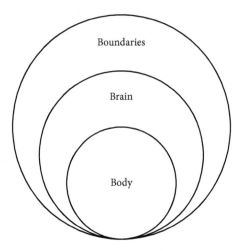

FIGURE 10.1 Nussbaum's Capabilities as Body, Brain, and Boundaries

The recognized overlap and interrelation between capabilities are acknowledged by Nussbaum. She claims that they can be understood in three different groupings: basic capabilities forming "innate faculties," making later development possible, internal capabilities relating to education and affiliation, and combined capabilities regarding "opportunities for choice in specific political, social and economic" circumstances (Nussbaum: 2011: 21–4). Such categorization can help sharpen our understanding of how capabilities overall contribute to a compelling view of well-being and dignity. But she maintains that basic (or innate) capabilities have no greater merit or weighting than sociopolitical capabilities on her list.[7]

This division begins to illuminate three different circles we might categorize roughly as Body, Brain, and Boundaries (see Figure 10.1):

The first group concerns capabilities of the *Body*, of the physical person. Together, they identify the immediate, our bodily well-being. Relevant capabilities might include "life" and "bodily health." The second group concerns capabilities of the *Brain*, of our personality and mental development. These might include "senses, imagination, and thought," "emotions," and "practical reason." The third group concerns capabilities of *Boundaries*, of our external position, our contextual backdrop, and how we relate to our social and material environments. Relevant capabilities might include "bodily integrity," "affiliation," "other species," "play," and "control over one's environment."

The utility of such a grouping is to further accentuate certain features of capabilities. Capabilities of the "body" are those that focus on our bare physiological needs as a living organism to satisfactory levels of food, water, and other essentials that makes possible the pursuit of any other capability grouping. It is clearer that satisfactory bodily health can contribute to our ability to live with concern for and in relation to plant and animal species than vice versa.

This is not to argue that one group can or should be pursued with greater urgency than another, nor is this to say that non-"body" capabilities are inessential for securing a life worth living. But it is to recognize that capabilities of the body can better enable other capability groupings than the other way around. Likewise, capabilities of our boundaries that focus on our engagement going beyond our person are more reliant on the sufficient securement of bodily and mental health than vice versa. Control over one's environment may be critically important, but its achievement is best enabled through possession of sufficient levels of capabilities like "bodily health" and "practical reason"— while seemingly no more reliant on a capability like "affiliation" than "affiliation" is dependent on a capability such as "control over one's environment."

These *groupings* could be used to spell out three new capabilities where their content is given by Nussbaum's list of ten capabilities. For example:

1. **Body**—the ability to achieve (sub)capabilities of life and bodily health
2. **Brain**—the ability to achieve (sub)capabilities of senses, imagination, and thought; emotions and practical reason
3. **Boundaries**—the ability to achieve (sub)capabilities of bodily integrity, affiliation, other species, play, and control over one's environment

Each *capability grouping* here– Body, Brain, and Boundaries—could be understood in the same way that Nussbaum conceives of any capability. While each relates to others in a particular way, none has greater urgency, they remain noncompetitive without trade-offs, and all must be secured above a threshold to secure human dignity and adequate well-being.

The benefits of this shorter list of groupings are that it might be easier to assess our relative ability to secure each capability where they encapsulate a family of (sub)capabilities. This avoids the problems of the porous boundaries between more closely overlapping capabilities on Nussbaum's list. It may be easier to discern our progress on securing a capability of boundaries more generally than between affiliation and control over one's political environment, for example. Capturing the full range of indicators that Nussbaum endorses by channeling them through three capabilities can provide a more elegant and, it would appear, no less comprehensive grasp in making assessments—this is because the content further specifying each of the three main capabilities is the (sub) capabilities she supports.

Furthermore, the content of each of the three capabilities is reduced to key (sub)capability indicators. This leaves more open-textured the specification of each capability, making more likely its being an object for an overlapping consensus. Again, perhaps there are critically important rights we would want to endorse, like reproductive rights. If we wish to see capabilities fit more comfortably within political liberalism, then such content renders capabilities more of a comprehensive doctrine in their own right—as Rawls once claimed—than a consensus among all other reasonable doctrines. The more parsimonious model I offer can more easily achieve this goal.

4 CAPABILITIES AND SEVERE POVERTY

Let us return to Nussbaum's list of ten capabilities and how she sees them helping us better understand the kind of harm that severe poverty is. She says: "the Capabilities Approach, in my version, focuses on the protection of areas of freedom so central that their removal makes a life not worthy of human dignity" (Nussbaum 2011: 31). If any one of her ten capabilities is not satisfied, individuals are harmed. She links capabilities closely with human rights, as both demarcate fundamental features of human dignity requiring universal protection (Nussbaum 2011: 62).

Persons suffering in severe poverty fail to meet one or more sufficient levels of capability satisfaction. This might range from "life," "bodily health," and "practical reason" to encompass all ten on Nussbaum's list. Such a failure could be easily seen as a violation of human rights as well (see Pogge 2007). What matters most is how well we can meet the capability threshold. Nussbaum says: "If people are below the threshold on any one of the capabilities, that is a failure of basic justice, no matter how high up they are on all the others" (Nussbaum 2006: 166–7). Human dignity and well-being are not achieved when any capability on her list is not secured above a threshold. She adds: "In general, the failure of a person to have various basic human capabilities is important in itself, not just because the person minds it or complains about it" (Nussbaum 2000b: 144). Capability failure is not for non-affluent states alone, but many, if not all, countries have a blemished record or worse in securing capabilities for all. Nussbaum claims:

> All nations, then, are developing nations, in that they contain problems of human development and struggles for a fully adequate quality of life and for minimal justice. All are currently failing at the aim of ensuring dignity and opportunity for each person. For all, then, the Capabilities Approach supplies insight.
>
> (Nussbaum 2011: 16)

As noted, crucial to the ability of the capabilities approach to diagnose deprivations is its ability to discern whether or not a threshold has been reached. As already discussed, the range of capabilities goes beyond mere material needs of the body for food, drink, and shelter to our mental health and a healthy engagement with our surroundings. It is more than a crude, material, or resourcist measure. For Nussbaum, capability "specifies a rather ample social minimum. Delivering these ten capabilities to all citizens is a necessary condition of social justice. Justice may well require more" (Nussbaum 2011: 40)

This idea of a social minimum is borrowed from Rawls's work on justice (Rawls 1999: 251–2, 1996: 181).[8] He stipulates for his ideal of justice that all citizens must be above this social minimum: it is not a choice (Rawls 1996: 187). An attraction of Rawls's view is that it provides a sharper dividing line for understanding when individuals fall short of this minimum. But the downside is that it relies on a too limited, perhaps even impoverished view of an individual's well-being that the capabilities approach captures much better.

The issue, then, is whether there is too great a trade-off: in aiming for a more robust understanding of well-being, the capabilities approach might render judgments about threshold achievement unworkable. For example, Flavio Comim claims "the measurement of capabilities is the most pressing challenge ahead for the operationalization of the capability approach" (Comim 2008: 157). So are we better off with a less complete model like Rawls's social minimum that is easier to measure? It is unclear.

While the capabilities approach has been operationalized by the UN and various local and national governments, there remain challenges in measuring capabilities that are widely acknowledged even by proponents of the approach.[9] A particular problem is the available data. As Sabina Alkire observes, "most data reflect achieved functionings rather than capabilities . . . However, functionings data do not necessarily reflect freedom" and so it can be difficult to discern when individuals have secured sufficient capabilities irrespective of whether they have freely chosen to exercise them (Alkire 2016: 631; see also Robeyns 2005). In rejecting average GDP per capita as the gold standard for measuring well-being and development, we might look to capture achievements across a wider spectrum of well-being indicators, such as longevity, infant mortality, literacy levels, and so on. This would expand on the unidimensional utility of average GDP per capita tracking to provide a more robust picture. But it would also seem to be about measuring actual functionings and not capabilities. Is this the best we can do?

Sen acknowledges the problem:

> The assessment of capabilities has to proceed primarily on the basis of observing a person's actual functionings, to be supplemented by other information. There is a *jump* here (from functionings to capabilities), but it need not be a big jump, if only because the valuation of actual functionings is one way of assessing how a person values the options she has.   (Sen 1999a: 131)

Actual functionings can be useful in giving a wider picture than the cruder average GDP per capita approach and so serve as a step in the right direction. But this still falls far short of the kind of assessment that the capabilities approach aspires to deliver.

To be fair, this problem of lacking adequate or sufficient data might be solved by developing better means of appropriate data capture. For example, there is frequent use of questionnaires to measure perceptions people have about the opportunities they possess (see Comim 2008: 177–8). Such information is necessary, but insufficient, for confirming what capabilities individuals genuinely have beyond their actual functionings. Improved data could help us understand how lower actual functionings in one community might be more problematic than in another if in the one community poor functioning is a product of denying citizens opportunities for exercising capabilities, but in the other community poor levels of functioning is a product of choice. We have tools to measure capabilities even if there remains more to be done. No doubt the complexity of capabilities—and disagreement about their content—contributes to this.

5   A FREEDOM TO CHOOSE DEPRIVATION?

Let us suppose we have an acceptable measure of capabilities. We can determine with confidence when and where individuals fall short on any measure—whether on Nussbaum's list of ten capabilities or my more compact list of three. We have seen how the approach can offer a more robust view of well-being (and why we might seek to revise its content). Much has centered so far on the necessity of ensuring all persons have opportunities to exercise their capabilities. Where they cannot, a serious wrong is suffered. If falling beneath a threshold in any capability is so problematic, why, then, are we free to live below this level provided that we choose it? Or put more pithily, if severe poverty is such a significant denial of our dignity and failure to achieve well-being, then why can we choose to put ourselves in severe poverty at all? A freedom to live in deprivation may appear like a contradiction.

Nussbaum's demand is for capabilities to be available, not that they are always exercised. She says: "the use of the list is facilitative rather than tyrannical: if individuals neglect an item on the list, this is just fine from the point of view of the political purposes of the list, so long as they don't impede others who wish to pursue it" (Nussbaum 2000b: 96).[10] But it is not clear why this is satisfactory. Henry Richardson (2000: 317) has argued that whether we *can* enjoy a capability seems less important than whether we *do*. He claims it is better to support libraries that citizens actually use and enjoy, rather than could potentially enjoy if only they visited (Richardson (2000: 316). For Richardson, if capabilities are to matter, they should be exercised. Perhaps not enjoyed by everyone every minute, but fulfillment should be widespread and sufficiently frequent. Otherwise, capabilities seem more like an ideal wish list than a guide to understanding severe poverty and human development.

This raises an important point where we might make a distinction between capabilities *as possible* versus capabilities *as probable*. The former view, which we might attribute to Nussbaum, is satisfied by sufficient opportunities for enjoying capabilities. The second view addresses Richardson's concern about the importance of maintaining some frequency of satisfying capabilities. Suppose there was a community where all individuals *could* satisfy the capabilities threshold, but everyone chose not to do so (see Brooks 2014). Their failure to reach a satisfactory minimum would indicate their human dignity was threatened, but the ability to make this choice appears to exemplify their possession of dignity. So, which is it? Can we maintain that a level of dignity is met if we could exceed a threshold of capabilities satisfaction while choosing to live below this threshold?

One reply might be to say capabilities as possible, not probable, care more for what we *can* achieve than what we *do* achieve. For example, Dale Dorsey (2012: 57) argues: "Because she does not grant moral importance to the *achievement* of human dignity, rather only to the capability for such achievement, the extent to which any given person actually maintains a life of minimal human dignity on Nussbaum's view is up for grabs."

This criticism seems unfair. While Nussbaum does not want to prescribe that every individual must always achieve above the capabilities threshold, it is untrue that achievement is of no moral importance.

Reconsider the example of a community where everyone can, but does not, enjoy use of their capabilities. It might be objected that no such a community would exist. Individuals would want to exercise their capabilities overall. If so, then certainly moving to the view of capabilities as probable captures this better. It would allow individual freedom to choose whether or not to exercise capabilities, but against a context where most people are most of the time.

Consider other examples. Slavery would be prohibited on either view of capabilities.[11] It violates capabilities as probable because none can secure them, and it also violates the view of capabilities as possible too because none will secure them in future (see Nussbaum 2011: 26). Nussbaum says: "human beings who are force-fed, even if well-nourished, aren't using food in a fully human way. This line of reflection, I think, should lead us to the conclusion that capabilities, not actual functionings, are the appropriate political goal" (Nussbaum 2000a: 363–4). My freedom to choose whether I am nourished is more important than my being fed, if done in a not fully human way, even if the state guarantees my nourishment.

But suppose we chose addiction to a narcotic drug.[12] The addict renders himself incapable of likely achieving sufficient capability thresholds across most, if not all capabilities. His addiction may stunt his longevity, permanently damage his health, inhibit his use of practical reason, lead to destructive personal interactions, and undermine his effective participation in political affairs. Supposing his addiction is chosen, it might also be broken. While his use might become long-term, it is not necessarily permanent. A community of such willing addicts, contra force-fed individuals in the example above, might not have sufficient actual functioning, but what little they had would be a product of their choices. If what matters is capabilities as possibilities and such willing addicts need not be permanently addicted, but choose deprivation as an acceptable by-product of their addictions, would Nussbaum find their dignity intact and well-being secured—despite the fact their actual functionings might be little better than someone in severe poverty?

The answer is probably yes if Nussbaum dogmatically insisted on choice always trumping probability. But she does not. Like Sen, she is very critical of "adaptive preferences" (Nussbaum 2000b: 139–48). Nussbaum's support for choice requires such choices be free, uncoerced, and unconditioned. A homeless beggar who decides which shop entrance to sleep in has made a choice, but not from a list of sufficient options on her view. That we choose is important, but so too is what kinds of choices we make. Furthermore, some persons are unable to make choices, whether young children or someone in a vegetative state (see Nussbaum 2011: 24). The fact that the latter is kept alive is not a matter of her dignity being violated, because it might not have been chosen by her. She might be force-fed, but in a fully human way, as the kinds of choices and our abilities to make them matter too.

But the key to unlocking Nussbaum's position on this issue of whether we can be free to choose deprivation, if not slavery, is found in the following passage:

> In a sense, capabilities are important because of the way in which they may lead to functionings. If people never functioned at all, in any way, it would seem odd to say that the society was a good one because it had given them lots of capabilities. The capabilities would be pointless and idle if they were never used and people slept all through life. In that limited way, the notion of functionings gives the notion of capability its end-point. But capabilities have value in and of themselves . . . To promote capabilities is to promote areas of freedom, and this is not the same as asking people function in a certain way.   (Nussbaum 2011: 25)

There is a false dichotomy drawn between saying either actual functionings or capabilities count: it is not either or. Actual functioning and achievement of well-being do matter. Our focus should not be on tracking capabilities without notice of functionings, but to consider them in tandem. Functionings are an indication of well-being that is more robust and useful than average GDP per capita, but likewise can give an incomplete picture of the range of choices available for individuals and how these are determined. Our assessment should consider not only *what we do* but *why we do it*, with a focus on the promotion of free choice.

6 Concluding Remarks

Severe poverty is one of the world's greatest ills that accounts of global justice attempt to address. The capabilities approach developed in different ways by Sen and Nussbaum is a significant contribution to our understanding of what kind of wrong severe poverty is and how we might better promote human development. This chapter has focused on Nussbaum's influential capabilities list and its greater specification of what constitutes human dignity and well-being.

One finding is that there are reasons to recommend her list's reformulation. She does not oppose, in principle, revising her list. One reason to do so is that the content she specifies for some capabilities clashes with some comprehensive doctrines, and so undermines her capabilities approach's ability to serve as an object of an overlapping consensus. If the content was changed so as to render it more compatible with comprehensive doctrines, then this problem might be resolved.

A second reason for reformulating the capabilities list is to better recognize, as Nussbaum acknowledges, that her ten capabilities can be organized into different groupings that sharpen our understanding of how these capabilities contribute overall to a compelling view of well-being and dignity. This leads to a second finding, that her list of ten might be more economically be repackaged into a list of three—Body, Brain, and Boundaries—that splits her list of ten between them. Each figures differently in larger circles that indicate their different relations between each other, but while accepting none has greater urgency than others, they remain noncompetitive without trade-offs between them and all must be secured above a threshold to secure dignity and well-being. Added benefits include their easier use while still capturing all relevant indicators, and their more open texture in terms of content better renders this group of three capabilities an object of an overlapping consensus than Nussbaum's list of ten.

A third finding is that capabilities lack a complete data set for easy comparisons and study. Resourcist approaches give an incomplete and misleading picture of human development, but have a ready data source in using measures like average GDP per capita. The lack of a complete data set is not fatal for capabilities, as the UN and other bodies do use capability measures, although there remain more to develop. However, it appears many of the existing measures rely on data of actual functionings.

This, in turn, leads us to consider whether actual functioning really does matter. A related fourth finding is that there appears a distinction we can draw between capabilities as possibilities (which focus on options but not achievements) and capabilities as probabilities (which require some threshold of general achievement in addition to options). Despite many comments suggestive of the former view, Nussbaum ultimately endorses the latter, recognizing that a world where free options promoting capabilities that are never exercised is not a place where full dignity and well-being are established.

In conclusion, we are led to a final finding that the choice between actual functionings and capabilities is not either or notwithstanding much ink spilled to separate them. Actual functionings without exercising capabilities are as problematic as having capability opportunities without actual functionings. Capabilities force us to consider how to do or be, but we must not neglect that we do—or at least generally much of the time.

Notes

1. See Nussbaum (1997) , (2000b), (2003), (2006), and (2011). Most of my direct quotations come from Nussbaum (2011) mainly because it is her latest major statement. But the core ideas can also be readily found in the other work listed above. For a survey of capability approaches, see Brooks (2013) and Robeyns (2011).
2. Strictly speaking, Sen speaks of capability, not capabilities, for reasons that will be presented later in this section. To simplify the use of terminology I will refer only to capabilities, as my focus will be on Nussbaum's formulation and not Sen's.
3. Sen (1999a: 75). See Nussbaum (1999: 42) and (2011: 20).
4. See Sen (1999b: 234, 237). But see also Sen (1993: 38–9).
5. See World Bank (2016).
6. While I have been faithful to Nussbaum's names for each capability, I have paraphrased her descriptions.
7. This trinity of capabilities relates to more sophisticated models of basic human needs. For example, David Miller (2007: 179-81) claims such needs "are those items or conditions it is necessary for a person to have if she is to avoid being harmed—thus food is an intrinsic need because in its absence people suffer the harms of hunger and malnutrition." At the same time, these needs are not merely physiological. He says: "Human beings are social as

well as biological creatures, and they can be harmed by being denied the conditions of social existence." One interesting contrast between Miller's view and Nussbaum's specifically is on the point of choice. He claims need is not a choice, whereas capabilities hold there is no choice about what is capability but only whether to exercise it. In other words, basic human needs are needed all the time without exception; capabilities must also be available but not always enjoyed.

8. On differences between Rawls and Nussbaum on capabilities and political liberalism, see Brooks (2015).

9. For a helpful overview, see Brighouse and Robeyns (2010).

10. See also Nussbaum (2000: 149): "the list is not totalitarian."

11. Similarly, Nussbaum objects to female genital mutilation, even if someone freely chose to receive it, because it denies any possibility of satisfying the capability for "bodily integrity" (which includes having opportunities "for sexual satisfaction") as the procedure is irreversible. There is no possibility or probability of securing the capability and so both views of capabilities would prohibit female genital mutilation. See Nussbaum (1999: 44, 118–29) and (2000b: 87).

12. This example is inspired by the willing addict hypothetical in Frankfurt (1971).

REFERENCES

Alkire, Sabina (2016) "The Capability Approach and Well-Being Measurement for Public Policy." In Matthew D. Adler and Marc Fleurbaey (eds), *The Oxford Handbook of Well-Being and Public Policy*. Oxford: Oxford University Press, 615–44.

Brighouse, Harry and Ingrid Robeyns (eds) (2010) *Measuring Justice: Primary Goods and Capabilities*. Cambridge: Cambridge University Press.

Brooks, Thom (2013) "Capabilities." In Hugh LaFollette (ed.), *International Encyclopedia of Ethics*. Oxford: Blackwell, 692–8.

Brooks, Thom (2014) "A New Problem with the Capabilities Approach," *Harvard Review of Philosophy* 20: 100–6.

Brooks, Thom (2015) "The Capabilities Approach and Political Liberalism." In Thom Brooks and Martha C. Nussbaum (eds), *Rawls's Political Liberalism*. New York: Columba University Press, 139–73.

Comim, Flavio (2008) "Measuring Capabilities." In Flavio Comim, Mozaffar Qizilbash, and Sabina Alkire (eds), *The Capability Approach: Concepts, Measures and Applications*. Cambridge: Cambridge University Press, 157–200.

Dorsey, Dale (2012) *The Basic Minimum: A Welfarist Approach*. Cambridge: Cambridge University Press.

Frankfurt, Harry (1971) "Freedom of the Will and the Concept of a Person," *Journal of Philosophy* 68: 5–20.

Miller, David (2007) *National Responsibility and Global Justice*. Oxford: Oxford University Press.

Nussbaum, Martha C. (1997) "Capabilities and Human Rights," *Fordham Law Review* 66: 273–300.

Nussbaum, Martha C. (1999) *Sex and Social Justice*. Oxford: Oxford University Press.

Nussbaum, Martha C. (2000a) "Reply," *Quinnipiac Law Review* 19: 349–70.

Nussbaum, Martha C. (2000b) *Women and Human Development: The Capabilities Approach*. Cambridge: Cambridge University Press.

Nussbaum, Martha C. (2003) "Capabilities as Fundamental Entitlements: Sen and Social Justice," *Feminist Economics* 9: 33–59.

Nussbaum, Martha C. (2006) *Frontiers of Justice: Disability, Nationality, Species Membership.* Cambridge, MA: Harvard University Press.

Nussbaum, Martha C. (2011) *Creating Capabilities: The Human Development Approach.* Cambridge, MA: Harvard University Press.

Pogge, Thomas (2007) "Severe Poverty as a Human Rights Violation." In Thomas Pogge (ed.), *Freedom from Poverty as a Human Right: Who Owes What to the Very Poor?* Oxford: Oxford University Press, 11–53.

Rawls, John (1996) *Political Liberalism.* New York: Columbia University Press, 1996.

Rawls, John (1999) *A Theory of Justice,* rev. edn. Oxford: Oxford University Press.

Richardson, Henry S. (2000) "Some Limitations of Nussbaum's Capabilities," *Quinnipiac Law Review* 19: 309–32.

Robeyns, Ingrid (2005) "Assessing Global Poverty and Inequality: Income, Resources, and Capabilities," *Metaphilosophy* 36: 30–49.

Robeyns, Ingrid (2011) "The Capability Approach: A Theoretical Survey," *Journal of Human Development and Capabilities* 6: 93–117.

Sen, Amartya (1980) "Equality of What?." In Sterling M. McMurrin (ed.), *Tanner Lectures on Human Values,* Vol. 1. Cambridge: Cambridge University Press, 195–200.

Sen, Amartya (1985) "Well-being, Agency, and Freedom: The Dewey Lectures 1984," *Journal of Philosophy* 82: 169–221.

Sen, Amartya (1993) "Capability and Well-being." In Martha C. Nussbaum and Amartya Sen (eds.), *The Quality of Life. Oxford:* Oxford University Press, 30–53.

Sen, Amartya (1999a) *Development as Freedom.* Oxford: Oxford University Press.

Sen, Amartya (1999b) *The Idea of Justice.* London: Allen Lane, 1999.

World Bank, (2016) "Principles and Practice in Measuring Global Poverty," http://www.world-bank.org/en/news/feature/2016/01/13/principles-and-practice-in-measuring-global-poverty, accessed August 17, 2019.

FURTHER READING

Adler, Matthew D., and Marc Fleurbaey (eds) (2016) *The Oxford Handbook of Well-Being and Public Policy.* Oxford: Oxford University Press.

Brooks, Thom (ed.) (2008) *The Global Justice Reader.* Oxford: Blackwell.

Comim, Flavio, and Martha C. Nussbaum (eds) (2014) *Capabilities, Gender, Equality: Towards Fundamental Entitlements.* Cambridge: Cambridge University Press.

Comim, Flavio, Mozaffar Qizilbash, and Sabina Alkire (eds) (2008) *The Capability Approach: Concepts, Measures and Applications.* Cambridge: Cambridge University Press.

Robeyns, Ingrid (2011) "The Capability Approach," *Stanford Encyclopedia of Philosophy,* url: https://plato.stanford.edu/entries/capability-approach/.

CHAPTER 11

AIDING THE POOR IN PRESENT AND FUTURE GENERATIONS

Some Reflections on a Simple Model

NICOLE HASSOUN

1 INTRODUCTION

THIS chapter discusses and brings together two lines of research on global justice—one on aiding the poor and another on obligations to those in future generations. There has been a lot of work on obligations to provide aid and institutions and policies for doing so.[1] There is also some work on obligations to future generations and institutions and policies that might impact those in future generations (Caney 2010; Gardner et al. 2010; Hassoun 2015).[2] However, it is essential to bring work on aiding the poor and intergenerational ethics together. Almost any way we try to aid the poor will have a significant impact on poor people in future as well as present generations. Consider, for instance, a policy to implement geoengineering in response to climate change. Even if geoengineering does nothing but prevent some of the deaths and migration that climate change is expected to cause, it will have a significant impact on how poor people in present and future generations fare and even how many poor people there will be in the future. Poor people are the most vulnerable, and least able to adapt, to climate change. If we do nothing, climate change will probably kill hundreds of thousands of poor people (IPPC 2007; Broome 2005). It will likely exacerbate extreme weather events like floods and droughts that kill people directly. Droughts and floods may lead to other problems like famine or disease. If sea levels rise significantly, and many coastal areas are submerged, climate change may lead to mass migration (IPPC 2007; Mayell 2002). If poor people in present or future generations die as a result of climate change, that will change the size of the population in those generations as well as how people fare. If many of those who die would otherwise have reproduced, or climate change leads to migration that changes the number of children poor people have, that may also change the size of future generations. So, if geoengineering prevents deaths or mass migration, it will affect how poor people in present and future generations fare and even how many poor people there will be in the future. Similar observations apply to many other policies.

The literature in political philosophy, population ethics, and related disciplines like economics and political science provides some guidance for thinking about policies for aiding the poor in present and future generations. This chapter provides an introduction to some of this literature and sketches one line of argument for a few principles for aiding the poor. Finally, it presents a highly abstract model for testing and thinking through the consequences of such principles that might be of some use to those interested in different policies for aiding the poor in present and future generations.[3]

Part of this chapter's contribution lies in its implicit suggestion of a new "bottom-up" rather than "top-down" approach to population ethics. It does not attempt to provide a complete axiological theory. Rather it provides some arguments for a few principles for aiding the poor. By remaining modest in this way, it becomes quite reasonable to reject theories with implausible consequences as long as one might accept the principles advocated here without contradiction. Perhaps we can eventually arrive at a plausible relatively complete theory in this way, but I believe the desire for completeness may, in the context of population ethics, lead people to too quickly endorse broad claims that become radically implausible in some contexts.

2 Principles for Aiding the Poor in Present Generations

A lot of work on obligations to aid considers how extensive (any) such obligations can be (Miller 1999; Ashford 2003). Some argue that we have to give up everything we do not need (even to the point of diminishing marginal utility (Singer 1972)). Others complain that this is too demanding and suggest that we only have to do our fair share (Cullity 2006; Murphy 2003).

Many also consider the grounds and scope of obligations to aid (Pogge 2008; Miller 1998; Hassoun 2012, 2013; Nussbaum 2000; Caney 2003; Buchanan 2013). Is the obligation to aid purely a requirement of humanity or are there obligations of justice to provide some aid? Do we have obligations to aid in ways that protect others' basic interests, rights, or autonomy? Must we help people secure resources, capabilities, welfare, or opportunities? Do we only have to help those who are close to us or do we have truly global obligations to aid the poor?

This chapter will try to stay neutral between different answers to questions about the extent, grounds, and scope of obligations to aid. It will just assume that there is some obligation to provide some aid and will not consider what grounds this obligation. It will try to stay neutral between different conceptions of poverty. It will refer to whatever people *need to avoid poverty* as a *good*.[4] Material goods and utility may be *goods* in this sense. Alternately, opportunities might be necessary to alleviate need (Miller 1999).[5] For simplicity, this chapter will also assume full interpersonal comparisons of need.[6] It is important for the arguments that follow, however, that what constitutes a need is something very significant. Those who are in need are in a *very* bad state or lack *essential* resources or opportunities.

This chapter will focus on questions about what principles we should adopt for aiding the poor. A few people have considered this question specifically—though most focus on how we should aid those in present generations (Miller 1999; Brock 2009). There is also a lot of work on principles for distribution in the literature that might be extended to provide answers to the question how should we aid the poor (Casal 2007; Temkin 1993; Frankfurt 1988).

Perhaps the best-known principles that might govern the distribution of aid are consequentialist. Maximizing consequentialists about aiding the poor might suggest that we should just distribute aid in the most efficient way. That is, assuming a single unit of aid alleviates a single unit of need for all people, we should provide as much aid as possible; it does not matter how this aid is distributed. Other principles guiding the distribution of aid are deontological (Kamm 2006).

Interestingly, some debates about principles for distribution may become otiose when we focus our attention on aiding the poor in particular—namely debates about whether it matters if we help those above the poverty line. On some sufficiency theories, it does not matter how we distribute goods above this threshold. Utilitarians and closely related prioritarians—deny this. Prioritarians hold, for instance, that it matters that we help those who are less well-off at all levels of good. Still, there may be reason to focus only on the poorest of the poor, and this focus does not resolve debates about whether we should be utilitarians or prioritarians below the poverty line.

Consider one prioritarian argument against utilitarianism—Thomas Nagel's famous thought experiment. This thought experiment illustrates the prioritarian intuition that it is better to enable less well-off people to secure necessary goods: Barring threshold effects, Nagel suggests that parents should decide to help their sick child over their healthy one, even if the healthy child will benefit more from what his or her parents can do (Nagel 2001). If prioritarianism is correct, it would suggest pursuing those policies that have the best consequences for those who are less well off (even amongst the poor). It might, for instance, suggest doing more scientific research on those genetic diseases that impact the poorest the most (like sickle cell anemia).

Arguments for prioritarianism are most compelling when there are no special entitlements in the cases at hand. Many hold that parents have special obligations to their offspring that, for instance, allow them to neglect some impartial reasons in favor of helping others' sick children first. Similarly, some believe people have stronger obligations to compatriots than outsiders (Brock 2009; Blake 2001). Still, when there are no such special obligations in play and we are just concerned to evaluate policies in so far as they aid the poor, prioritarianism is plausible.[7]

I have argued elsewhere, however, that prioritarianism should be modified so that it also takes into account the fact that it matters how many people we help in present generations (Hassoun 2009). Although I will not repeat these arguments here, the problem with prioritarianism, when it is specified in the usual ways, is roughly this: It suggests it can be acceptable to ignore an arbitrarily large amount of need for an arbitrarily large number of better-off people to help the least well-off. To illustrate why this is unintuitive, suppose the prioritarian adopts some particular weighting schema. Suppose, for instance, that the prioritarian thinks we should allocate in proportion to need and one unit of necessary good alleviates one unit of need. Suppose, further, that the weight given to fulfilling a unit of need for a person equals the number of units the person needs before receiving the unit. So, for instance, giving a person three units below the poverty line three units of necessary good yields a score of six—three points for alleviating the first unit, two points for alleviating the second unit, and one point for alleviating the third unit of need. Now suppose that we must choose how to allocate 100 units of necessary good between 200 people. Finally, suppose that 199 people need only one unit of necessary good but the last person needs 100 units. The problem is that alleviating the first unit of the last person's need is 100 times as good as completely alleviating any other person's need ($100*1 = 100(1*1)$). So, helping the least well-off person secure a single unit would be better than helping 99 other people secure a single unit each.[8] If the prioritarian does not think this is unintuitive, it is possible to create similar cases where this weighting schema suggests neglecting the needs of thousands or millions to help a single (much more) poorly off person just a bit. Simply by multiplying the needs in the example above we can also make the amount that the better-off need in the example arbitrarily large.

It should be easy for the reader to demonstrate that similar problems arise for other seemingly intuitive weighting schemas, so it is plausible that triage is sometimes required even when it does not alleviate the greatest amount of weighted need. Triage requires helping those who have great needs but not those who need the most first (even if the neediest could be helped). One way to justify policies that effectively require triage is by appeal to this principle: We should try to help *as many people as possible* meet their needs.[9] In some situations it is better to help a greater number than to help the least well-off, *even if helping the least well-off is better on a prioritarian weighting schema*. This principle expresses a concern for persons. If persons matter, we should not just care about fulfilling as much (even appropriately weighted) need as possible; we should care about helping each person. The fact that some have greater (even appropriately weighted) needs cannot always trump the fact that there are others in need. People merit respect as separate individuals.[10] Consider the following: it seems plausible that it is not the existence of goods (welfare, capabilities, or whatever) per se that matters. It matters that people have goods (welfare, capabilities, or whatever). Similarly, the idea here is not that helping a greater number of people is better for that reason. Rather, the idea is that each person matters and, since people matter equally, we should try to help as many people as possible.

One might object that prioritarianism already includes a concern for helping a greater number of people. One might argue that, on one way of looking at the prioritarian weighting system, it balances the number of people helped versus the amount of need people have.

This is simply not the case. Prioritarianism just tells us to weight individuals' needs and then minimize the sum of weighted need.[11] The number helped does not enter into this equation. It is clear that numbers do not matter when one reflects on the fact that, holding weighted need constant, it is never better to help a greater number of people on prioritarianism.

If these arguments are correct (for further defense, see Hassoun 2009), there is reason to endorse what is sometimes called:

(1) The Effectiveness Principle: Use resources to reduce weighted need and increase the number helped in present generations.

At least in a single (present) generation (with a constant-size population), there is reason to temper prioritarianism with a concern for helping a greater number of people (Hassoun 2009). I will assume this principle is correct in what follows to illustrate the model that constitutes this chapter's main contribution to the literature.[12]

I believe it is important to be careful, however, even in advancing the arguments above. They are plausible when choosing between policies if we can only do a limited amount of good for needy people. Principles for arbitrating between such policies are not intended to help us decide between all possible policies that impact the poor. They are not supposed to answer questions about potentially impermissible trade-offs such as: Can we sacrifice one poor person to make other poor people rich? Can we allow one poor person to die to stop several others from falling into poverty?[13]

Even questions like "Should we choose a policy that benefits some poor people in present generations or one under which people in the future would do better?" may be otiose when there is enough for all. For poverty is, presumably, a bad thing we should eliminate if we can. Jesus's claim that the poor will always be with us, if true, is very sad.[14] We often assume too quickly that we have to make hard choices that keep some from getting what they need.[15] Still, if there is not enough for all, there is reason to take both weighted need and numbers into account.

3 Choosing Policies for Aiding the Poor in Future Generations

Most of the work on intergenerational ethics focuses on whether or not it makes sense to talk about the interests, or rights, of future people. Perhaps the best-known reason for worrying about talk about the interests, or rights, of future people is called the non-identity problem (Parfit 1984). The basic worry is that if people in future generations cannot be harmed by our actions, it is not clear in what sense they can have interests or rights. It is, moreover, not possible to harm many future people whose very existence depends on the actions of those in present generations. Different people will be born as a result of many of the things those in present generations do, so whoever comes into existence who would not have existed but for their action has not been harmed by it.

There are many ways of responding to this problem. Some say that people are harmed if they are brought into existence in a bad state or below some threshold (Harman 2004: 92–3 and 107, 2009 139; Rivera-López 2009: 337; Shiffrin 1999: 120–35). Some argue that there is impersonal value in ensuring that whoever comes into existence does well (Temkin 1993: 221–7; see also Broome 1992 and Feldman 1995). Some say we can wrong people we have not harmed or point to the importance of acting with due caution or concern (Kavka 1981: 97 and 104–5; Wasserman 2005: 132–52). Yet others point out that the notion of harm at issue may be *de dicto* harm—the idea is that the people who come into existence, whoever they are, can be harmed by present generations' actions (Hare 2007: 512–23).

Some object to the idea that future people can have rights, or interests, based simply on the fact that they will only exist in the future or on the fact that their existence is contingent (de George 1981: 161; see also Macklin 1981: 151–2). These objections are compelling in so far as what is at issue is whether future people have rights now, but when these people come into existence, they will have rights or interests and we should consider all of our policies' impacts on interest and rights (Wasserman 2008: 529–33).

Others object that bringing people into existence in the future is wrong. David Benatar argues, for instance, that if we bring someone into existence, then we are responsible for all of the bad aspects of their life but for none of the good ones. He also thinks most lives are not worth living (Benatar 2006).

Contrast this conclusion with a view that suggests we should not consider the size or composition of future generations in decision-making. At least from an impersonal perspective, it may be neither better nor worse to bring someone into existence. The question of whether this judgment is sound from a "personal point of view" is much more difficult (SEP 2009). Moreover, some accept the (narrow) "person-affecting" principle—that all that matters is how our actions impact people (Temkin 1993; Boonin 2011).[16]

To avoid a few of these difficulties, the rest of this chapter will take an impersonal perspective. It will then illustrate how focusing in on aiding people below some poverty threshold can help us avoid some of the difficulties in dealing with "different number cases," where what we do will influence the number of people as well as the amount of goods people have (Parfit 1984). Finally, it will offer some, speculative, new arguments for how we should think about aiding the poor in present and future generations. Obviously, it is impossible to resolve all the debates about these issues in what follows. So, this chapter will conclude with a model that should be useful for testing different principles, no matter how these debates are resolved.

3.1 The Number in Existence in Future Generations

It should be clear from the preceding discussion that to arrive at well-justified principles for arbitrating between policies that do different amounts of good for people in future (as well as present) generations, we not only need to know how good it is to help people with different levels of need; we also need to know whether the number of people in a population matters. Different policies, from investing in solar research to offering genetic counseling or therapies, may change future population size. So what follows will, first, consider whether the number of people in a population matters. The next section will, then, consider whether it is better to help a greater number of future people and how we should think about meeting their needs.

First, it may be reasonable to treat existing and future people differently (this itself should be a surprising and interesting conclusion). Recall, that poverty is, presumably, a bad thing. This fact has some pretty straightforward implications for how we should think about bringing more poor people into future generations—there is at least one reason not to do so—we are creating more poverty in a population. On the other hand, we cannot affect the birth of existing people (and it is rarely, if ever, possible to reduce the number of existing people in a morally acceptable way). If this reasoning is sound, there is reason to accept:

(1) No Mere Addition of Poor: As long as there will be some people, it can be worse to add some poor people to a population.[17]

This proposition does not imply that poor people's lives are not worth living. Rather, once a poor person exists, their life may be quite valuable.

Nor does No Mere Addition of Poor entail that we should prevent poor people from reproducing, or even prevent people from reproducing who would have poor children. Doing so would, presumably, violate existing individuals' rights (Sen 1999). We might, instead, educate girls as they tend not to reproduce as much when they have better opportunities and ensure that whoever comes into existence avoids poverty (Sen 1999).

Moreover, a stronger claim than that there is at least one reason not to bring more poor people into future generations seems plausible: As long as there will be some people in future generations, it is not always better—it may even be worse—to have a greater number of people in a population (Rolston 2012). Presumably, it would be better to have more people in some situations. Perhaps we will need to increase our population size at some point to maintain a decent standard of living for all. Sometimes, however, it is worse to have more people—people will fare worse if we overpopulate the planet (Hardin 2012). So we might accept this axiom:

(2) No Mere Addition: As long as there will be some people, it can be *worse* to add some (even sufficiently well-off) people to a population.[18]

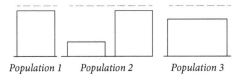

Population 1   Population 2   Population 3

FIGURE 11.1 Parfit's Paradox

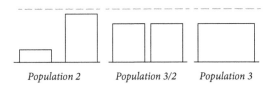

Population 2   Population 3/2   Population 3

FIGURE 11.2 Parfit's Paradox Elaborated

We might also use a version of Parfit's paradox (using goods rather than welfare, in particular) to motivate the No Mere Addition axiom (Parfit 1984). Consider the three populations shown in Figure 11.1.

Here the dotted line is the poverty line, the width of the boxes indicates the size of a segment of the population, and the height indicates the amount of goods that segment of the population has. Population 1 might have to choose between two policies—say Free Trade, in which case Population 2 will result, and Constrained Trade, in which case Population 3 may result. Suppose one rejects No Mere Addition and accepts:

(2) Mere Addition: The mere addition of people with lives worth living is not worse (other things equal), than failing to bring these people into existence.

It follows that population 2 is not worse than population 1. Next, one might suggest that population 3 is better than population 2 and, hence, better than population 1. For population 3 is the same size as population 2 but everyone is equal and has at least the average amount of goods in population 2, maybe more. So, by transitivity, population 3 is better than population 1. If one has trouble seeing why population 3 is better than population 2, compare Figure 11.2.

Population 3/2 is better than population 2 because it has the same number of people in it and they are, on average, better off. But population 3/2 is equal to population 3—the merging of the two subpopulations in moving from 3/2 to 3 makes no difference to our evaluation of these populations. So a situation with a greater number of people but fewer necessary goods can be better than a situation with fewer people who all have more necessary goods. One can follow Parfit in iterating the example to arrive at the repugnant conclusion. Namely, that a situation with many people whose lives are barely worth living is better than a situation with a modest population containing only people with much better lives—or who are, at least, a lot less poor (Parfit 1986). One might take this as reason to reject the innocuous-sounding Mere Addition axiom. One way of avoiding Mere Addition just is to accept No Mere Addition.[19]

Of course, this argument is not definitive (though it is compelling). One could also avoid Parfit's paradox by denying that population 3/2 is equal to 3 or that 3/2 (or 3) is better than population 2 (and one cannot avoid Parfit's paradox if one is a total utilitarian). It is very hard to see how one could reject the claim that population 3/2 is equal to population 3. One might argue that neither population 3/2 nor population 3 is better than population 2, even though people in 3/2 and 3 are, on average, better off than people in 2 (and all of these populations have the same number of people). It is not clear whether this move will work. Perhaps one could refuse to endorse the claim that population 3/2 and population 3 are better than population 2 because it requires one to endorse what may be impermissible trade-offs. This would be quite plausible if 3 and 3/2 came from 2 (by making some better off and others worse off). But this need not be the case.[20] They could be the populations of two completely isolated islands.

One need not accept No Mere Addition in what follows; this chapter will just assume that No Mere Addition of Poor is defensible. To accept No Mere Addition of the Poor, one need not endorse any complete axiological theory—though views some, like critical-level utilitarianism, entail the falsity of No Mere Addition of the Poor (Blackorby et al. 1995: 1303–20). On critical-level utilitarianism, there is a single level (of welfare) at which the addition of a person is neutral, below that level it is worse to add people to the population, and above that level it is better. If poor people are above the threshold for a life worth living, critical-level utilitarianism provides a reason to reject No Mere Addition of Poor. This view is, however, subject to a version of the repugnant conclusion above the critical-level threshold.

One might object to No Mere Addition of Poor by arguing that there *is* something intrinsically better about adding a poor person to a population. To do so, one might adapt Gustaf Arrhenius's argument for the conclusion that is always better to exist (especially if an existing person has some positive amount of goods). Arrhenius's argument proceeds primarily by criticizing the alternatives—that it is worse to exist or that existence and non-existence are equally valuable or incommensurable.

There is an important ambiguity in each of these statements, however. It can be better or worse *if* a person exists (in an impersonal sense) for reasons that may have nothing to do with how that person fares or it can be better or worse *for* that person if they exist (in a personal sense). I do not believe that it is generally worse *for* (even very poor) people to exist in a personal sense—they can have lives worth living.[21] The claim that there is nothing better about (or that there is a reason against) bringing some (poor) people into existence does *not* imply that it is, normally, worse *for* these people to exist; it does not imply that these peoples' welfare, for example, is lower if they exist. So let us grant that it is *not* generally worse *for* (even very poor) people to exist and consider whether Arrhenius's argument can establish that it is better to exist by showing that existence and non-existence are not equally valuable or incommensurable, all things considered.[22]

Granting that it is not generally worse *for* (even very poor) people to exist, if existence and non-existence are not equally valuable or incommensurable, on Arrhenius' view, it is supposed to follow that it is better to exist (irrespective of persons' poverty levels).

Arrhenius says that the view that existence and non-existence are equally valuable or incommensurable yields a few radically implausible conclusions when combined with what he calls the Person Affecting Restriction.

The Person Affecting Restriction says:

(a) If outcome A is better (worse) than B, then A is better (worse) than B for at least one individual.

(b) If outcome A is better (worse) than B for someone but worse (better) for no one, then A is better (worse) than B. (Arrhenius 2011:160)

Arrhenius says the Person Affecting Restriction and the idea that existence and non-existence are incommensurable (or, presumably, equally valuable) yield Strict Comparativism. Strict Comparativism (put here in terms of need rather than welfare) is the idea that only the needs of those who exist in all of the situations we are considering matter. We do not have to consider the needs of those who exist in only some situations (Arrhenius 2011: 164). Arrhenius thinks Strict Comparativism is implausible. To see why, consider Future Bliss and Future Hell (see Figure 11.3; we can suppose everyone is below the needs threshold in this diagram but only the x people exist in both outcomes; the y and z people are potential future people).

Since only the x people exist in both outcomes, Future Bliss is as good as Future Hell on Strict Comparativism (the x people's needs are equal in both situations and Strict Comparativism says only these people's needs count) (Arrhenius 2011: 166). Arrhenius says this is implausible. Strict Comparativism also requires rejecting a principle Arrhenius believes is quite compelling:

> The Egalitarian Weak Dominance Principle: If population A is a perfectly equal population of the same size as population B, and every person in A has at least as high welfare as every person in B, and some people in A have higher welfare than some people in B, then A is better than B, other things being equal.
>
> (Arrhenius 2011: 165)

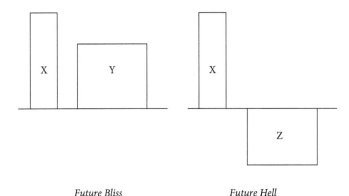

Future Bliss   *Future Hell*

FIGURE 11.3 Future Bliss and Hell

So, Arrhenius says, it is not the case that existence and non-existence are equally valuable or incommensurable. Arrhenius concludes that existence is better than non-existence.

Note, first, that even if Future Bliss and Future Hell are *future* situations, the principles this chapter endorses would suggest choosing Future Bliss over Future Hell if we had to decide between them (assuming all are below the poverty line).[23] There is no immediate tension between this conclusion and the view that it is not better that a greater number of poor people exist. The relevant principles sufficient to support this conclusion might be conditional ones like this: *if* more future people exist, it is better if they have less need rather than more. So there is reason to believe that there is a problem with Arrhenius's argument.[24] This problem may stem from the ambiguity in Arrhenius's claims that it is better or worse to exist or that existence and non-existence are equally valuable or incommensurable. As noted above, the claim that there is nothing better about (or that there a reason against) bringing some (poor) people into existence does *not* imply that it is, normally, *worse for* these people to exist (that is that these peoples' welfare is lower if they exist). Nor does it imply that existence and non-existence are equally valuable or incommensurable *for* these people. Saying that there is nothing better about (or that there a reason against) bringing some (poor) people into existence is compatible with it being better for these people to exist. The necessary claim for this chapter's argument is a *ceteris paribus* claim about what kind of future we should choose, not a claim about how individuals will (or would) fare.

However, to make his case Arrhenius simply assumes the Person pose a challenge to the conclusion that there is nothing better about (or that there is a reason against) bringing some (poor) people into existence. It provides a reason to think bringing more poor people into existence is a good thing—it is better for these people to exist. However, to make his case Arrhenius simply assumes the Person Affecting Restriction.[25] It seems to me that there is no reason to accept this restriction. The Person Affecting Restriction rules out views on which more than humans matter, for instance. It is also incompatible with impersonal values like peace or equality—in so far as those things do not impact how individuals fare.[26] If one rejects the Person Affecting Restriction, then one can avoid the conclusions Arrhenius believes are radically implausible and yet hold that it is not always better that poor people exist. Rather, there is some reason against bringing more poor people into existence, since poverty is bad and there is reason to reduce it.[27]

Similarly, one cannot object that it would be better to bring a person into existence who would be below the poverty line for some short period of time than not to bring that person into existence at all. It is not clear why it would be a good thing to create need even for a short period of time.[28] There is at least one reason against bringing a person into existence who would be below the poverty line for some short period of time—that would increase poverty. This point can be put in different ways. If people have a right against poverty, for instance, then one might say this person's right would be violated for at least some period of time. Perhaps this kind of argument would not be successful if entailed by a complete population axiology that had other implausible consequences. Since, however, this chapter does not attempt to provide such an axiology, this form of argument is entirely reasonable (and the fact that this argument form is a good one is a good reason to accept this chapter's methodological approach).

3.2 The Number Helped in Future Generations

Consider, then, what we should say about helping people in future generations (again, focusing only on those in need). Most surprisingly, in future generations, it seems nothing is gained by helping a greater number of people who are born—or even one person—if it is possible not to bring them into existence at all. For then, that person, or those people, will be in need for some period of time until they are helped. Intuitively, it would better if they did not have to suffer from lack of necessary goods for that amount of time. It would be better if they just came into existence with those goods. Trade-offs may be appropriate, however, if we must choose between preventing a person from coming into existence with some need and alleviating a greater amount of need for a person who will come into existence (when s/he does).

One cannot use the preceding observations to argue against helping a greater number in present generations, though a similar argument suggests a distinction between what we should do for existing people from an *ex ante* and *ex post* perspective. It would be great were there no one we could help in present generations at all because everyone came into existence with whatever we could give them. Nevertheless, we can often help people in present generations (whether that is due to our mistakes in the past or not). So, right now, there is (*ceteris paribus*) reason to help as many people as possible in present generations.

3.3 Summing Up: How to Think about Numbers in Future Generations

To sum up, in so far as we can implement policies that affect whether people come into existence in the future with what we could instead give them once they are around, we should:

> (4) Minimize Prioritarian-Weighted Need In Future: Given that poverty is bad, there is, *ceteris paribus*, reason to just minimize weighted poverty in future generations (rather than, say, embrace the Effectiveness Principle for future generations).

For, if neither numbers in existence nor numbers helped matter and there are no special entitlements, it is intuitive that it is only the amount of weighted need poor individuals have that matters.[29]

4 A Two Generation Model for Testing Principles

Combining (1) with (4), it should be clear that this chapter has provided some prelimi-nary defense for the following principle for choosing between policies that differentially aid (but do not harm) the poor in present and future generations:

> (A) Use resources in order to minimize weighted need in the future and to reduce weighted need and increase the number helped in the present.

That is, in the future, we should have a prioritarian concern for alleviating need and, in the present, we should also consider the number helped. For recall that (1) said we should use resources in order to reduce weighted need and increase the number helped in present generations and (4) said use resources in order to minimize weighted need in the future.

This does not provide a complete account of how we should arbitrate between policies that aid the poor, never mind a complete account of intergenerational justice. In fact this principle is quite vague and potentially contradictory. It does not explain the exact weight we should give to minimizing weighted need in present or future generations. Nor does this principle explain how either suggestion should be weighed against help-ing a greater number of people in present generations. Some other principles for meet-ing need are vague. Prioritarianism, for instance, does not tell us *how much* weight to give to helping people who are less well off. Unlike prioritarianism, however, the differ-ent parts of this chapter's principle might conflict.

Nevertheless, this chapter will not attempt to detail or defend its account of how we should aid the poor further; its contribution is in demonstrating that even such an incomplete account can provide significant guidance in a simple two-person model with non-overlapping generations. It will also explore the model's prospects for testing principles for arbitrating between policies.[30] More precisely, it will argue that (A) pro-vides significant guidance in this model if one accepts the following, almost uncontro-versial, principle:

> (B) When two policies have the same impact on present generations, they should be judged solely on the basis of their impact on future generations. When two policies have the same impact on future generations, they should be judged solely on the basis of their impact on present generations.

Next, this section will suggest that, to get further guidance about what policies to pur-sue, one must answer harder questions about how to deal with trade-offs between aiding those in present and aiding those in future generations.

The model below should, moreover, provide fruitful avenues for further inquiry. Researchers can use it to explore rankings of situations specifying some of the missing parameters in (A) in different ways. They can consider, for instance, how including a discount rate will impact judgments about situations with people who are more or less poor in the present and future and with different numbers of people in the future. Alternately, if researchers provide a fully cashed-out account of how we should arbitrate between policies that impact the poor, the model may also allow them to consider whether the resulting ranking is, ultimately, plausible. One may find that the proposed ranking conflicts with some other plausible principles of global or inter-generational justice.

Consider the model's basic components Figure 11.4. First, the model supposes that each person can have one of three levels of good below the poverty line in the initial, present, and future situations. (The initial situation shows what is the case in the present before we give aid.) The model will use H, M, and L to represent high, medium, and low levels of good and vectors to represent a situation profile with the same two people in the initial and present situations and up to two additional people in the future. The number 0 will be used to represent the lack of a person in the future. So, for instance, the situation profile below would be: (M,L;M,H;H,0).[31]

The model also assumes anonymity—that a person's particular identity does not matter. So it need not consider, for instance, both (L,M;H,L;M,0) and (M,L;L,H;0,M). It supposes our judgments about these two situation profiles will be the same.

Furthermore, let us suppose that when a person has H, they have no need, so we do not need to represent situation profiles where there are no future people or only one future person. That is, suppose the "scores" in the situation profiles where a future person has H will be the same as the scores in the otherwise equivalent situation profiles where the future person does not exist. So (L,L;L,L;H,H) receives the same score as (L,L;L,L;0,0), for instance. Whether this is plausible depends on exactly how one thinks about the significance of adding people who are not poor to a population. This assumes that preventing a poor person from coming into existence is as good as bringing someone who is not poor into existence.[32] However, this assumption just simplifies the representation of possibilities in Table 11.1. (If preventing a poor person from coming into existence is better (or worse) than bringing someone who is not poor into existence, the ranking of possible situations *might* not be *as* extensive, but the ranking of at least one-half of these situations would be the same. So the assumption that preventing a poor person from coming into existence is

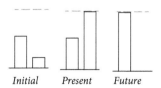

Initial   *Present*   *Future*

FIGURE 11.4 Levels of Goods across Time

Table 11.1 Relevant Possibilities

(L,L;L,L;L,L)	(L,L;L,L;L,M)	(L,L;L,L;L,H)	(L,L;L,L;M,M)	(L,L;L,L;M,H)	(L,L;L,L;H,H)
(L,L;L,M;L,L)	(L,L;L,M;L,M)	(L,L;L,M;L,H)	(L,L;L,M;M,M)	(L,L;L,M;M,H)	(L,L;L,M;H,H)
(L,L;L,H;L,L)	(L,L;L,H;L,M)	(L,L;L,H;L,H)	(L,L;L,H;M,M)	(L,L;L,H;M,H)	(L,L;L,H;H,H)
(L,L;M,M;L,L)	(L,L;M,M;L,M)	(L,L;M,M;L,H)	(L,L;M,M;M,M)	(L,L;M,M;M,H)	(L,L;M,M;H,H)
(L,L;M,H;L,L)	(L,L;M,H;L,M)	(L,L;M,H;L,H)	(L,L;M,H;M,M)	(L,L;M,H;M,H)	(L,L;M,H;H,H)
(L,L;H,H;L,L)	(L,L;H,H;L,M)	(L,L;H,H;L,H)	(L,L;H,H;M,M)	(L,L;H,H;M,H)	(L,L;H,H;H,H)

as good as bringing someone who is not poor into existence does not challenge the conclusion that the principles this chapter relies upon can yield an *extensive* ordering of possible situations).

One way of representing the relevant possibilities where there are (up to) two people in the future is shown in Table 11.1.[33]

The model increments the amount those in future generations have going across each row and increments the amount those in present generations have going down each column (in the same way).

This diagram does not include boxes where the amount in the present is less than the amount in the initial situation.[34] For, recall that the principles defended above do not allow us to judge those.

It is not necessary to consider anything beyond the first six rows in what follows. (Subsequent rows would be added by incrementing the amount in the initial situation in the same way.) The reason why it is not necessary to show all the rows in the model is that the scores the improvements from the initial situation to the present receive in subsequent boxes are the same as the scores improvements from the initial situation to the present receive in some of the cases above. (L,M;M,M;o,o) = (L,L;L,M;o,o), for instance. This is because principles (A) and (B) do not require us to consider how much need there is to begin with. They just require us to look at the amount of need fulfilled in present and future generations and the number helped in present generations (for further explanation, see the Appendix). Of course, one might argue that we should accept additional principles that focus on the amount of need in a situation. It is plausible, for instance, that the world would be better if there were never any need at all.[35] If we take into account the amount of need in the initial situation, we would have to consider the remaining rows beyond the sixth. Recall, however, that we cannot do anything about the need in the initial situation right now—though we might have been able to do something about it in the past—and we are only evaluating policies we might implement now.[36] That said, the principles above should suffice for illustrating the advantages of this chapter's model for arbitrating between a wide range of possible policies.

Let us employ the following representation of rankings between situation profiles: (L,L;L,M;H,o) < (L,L;M,M;H,o) means that (L,L;L,M;H,o) is ranked lower than (L,L;M,M;H,o) on the appropriate principle. Recall that, in the future, we should have a prioritarian concern for alleviating need and, in the present, we should also consider the number helped. Given (B), it follows that (L,L;L,L;L,L) < (L,L;L,L;L,M) < (L,L;L,L;L,H) and (L,L;L,L;L,L) < (L,L;L,M;L,L) < (L,L;M,M;L,L), for instance.

With two exceptions, each box below another or to the right of it in the Table 11.1 is ranked higher than the preceding box. The first exception is this: Sometimes the boxes in the third row are ranked higher than the corresponding boxes in the fourth row and vice versa. That is (L,L;L,H;L,L) may be better than (L,L;M,M:L,L), (L,L;L,H;L,M) may be better than (L,L;M,M;L,M), and so on (or vice versa). Which is ranked higher depends on the relative weighting of needs and numbers helped in present generations.[37] The second exception is this: Sometimes the boxes in the third column are ranked higher than the corresponding boxes in the fourth and vice versa. Which is ranked higher depends on whether bringing one person into existence with H is better than bringing two people into existence with M (though this will be decided once the numerical value of M and H are known—that is, if M>½H then the fourth column is ranked higher than the third, if ½H>M then the third column is ranked higher than the fourth, and if M=½H the scores in the third and fourth columns will be equal).[38]

Since the ranking of rows is determined by what happens in present generations alone, and the ranking of columns is determined by what happens in future generations alone, the overall ranking will not change in other ways. We can know, for instance, that (L,L;M,M;M,H) < (L,L;M,H;H,H). Since (L,L;M,M;M,H) < (L,L;M,H;M,H) by the second part of (A) (or (1)), irrespective of the order of the third and fourth rows, and (L,L:M,H:M,H) < (L,L;M,H;H,H) by the first part of (A) (or (4)), irrespective of the order of the third and fourth columns, (L,L;M,M;M,H) < (L,L;M,H;H,H) by the kind of transitivity specified in (B). That such incomplete and underspecified principles (A) and (B) allow us to arrive at such a complete ranking in this model is remarkable. What is interesting about this is that we did not have to decide how to treat present generations compared with future generations to rank many of the situation profiles in the model above where both present and future situations are different. Nor did we need to decide exactly how much weight to give fulfilling need in present or future generations. Nor did we have to decide how to compare helping a greater number in present generations to either of these things. Of course, we would have to make all of these decisions to get a full ranking over all possible situations. Still, that we can know so much about the ranking of possible situations using such incomplete principles is fantastic.

To see how this model can help us evaluate the impact of many policies, consider three possible responses to climate change—adaptation, mitigation, and geoengineering. Suppose that adaptation brings large gains to present people (it moves them from L to H) and ensures that those in the future have only a moderate amount of poverty— M. Suppose mitigation brings modest gains to present people (it moves them from L to M) and also ensures that those in the future have a moderate amount of poverty— M. Finally, suppose geoengineering has no impact on the present (so they will remain at L) but ensures that those in the future have no need—H. The box in the fourth column of the bottom row demonstrates the effect of adaptation if there are two people in the future (L,L;H,H;M,M). The box in the fourth column of the fourth row demonstrates the effect of mitigation with two people in the future (L,L;M,M;M,M). Geoengineering yields the final column on the right of the top row (L,L;L,L;H,H). So, adaptation is always better than mitigation in this example,[39] but the model does not tell us whether either should be preferred to geoengineering (or vice versa).[40] To answer that question, we would need to know the relative importance of helping present people vs. ensuring that (any) future people have more. The model does suggest, however, that if a policy could achieve (L,L;H,H;H,H), it would be better than all the alternatives (whether the policy ensures that all the people in the future are rich or just refrains from creating poor people in future generations).[41]

5 Conclusion

This chapter has considered how we should choose between some policies that have different impacts on present and/or future generations. It provided a preliminary defense of the following principles: Choose policies that minimize weighted need in the future and reduce weighted need and increase the number helped in the present. If we should judge two policies with the same impact on present (future) generations solely on the basis of their impact on future (present) generations, these principles tell us quite a bit about what we should do in a simple model. To get further guidance, we must answer harder questions about how to deal with trade-offs between present and future generations. The model this chapter laid out should, moreover, provide fruitful avenues for further inquiry. We can use it to explore rankings of situation profiles when the missing parameters in this chapter's proposed principles for choosing between policies that aid (but do not harm) the poor are specified in different ways. We can consider, for instance, how including a discount rate will impact judgments about situation profiles with people who are more or less poor in the present and future and different numbers of people in the future. The model can also be used to test principles for arbitrating between possible policies that impact the poor. We can use it to see if the ranking of situation profiles on these principles is, ultimately, plausible. Moreover, it is possible to see how this chapter's principles (or others) fare in similar, but more complicated, models (e.g. with more than two people in present or future generations). In any case, further research on how we should choose between policies that impact the poor in present and future generations is pressing and important.

Appendix

Consider a more complicated example to illustrate how it is possible to determine the score for boxes in rows beyond the sixth row in the model by considering the scores in one or more boxes in these first six rows. Looking only at initial and present situations it is reasonable to suppose, for instance, that (L,L;L,L) receives the same score as (L,M;L,M), (L,L;L,M) receives the same score as (L,M;M,M), and (L,L;L,H) receives the same score as (L,M;M,H). Further, it seems reasonable to suppose that, just with respect to the amount of need met, (L,L;M,H) should receive the same score as the sum of (L,M;M,M) and (L,M;M,H). In (L,L;M,H) the first person is moved from L to M and the second person is moved from L to H in transitioning from the initial situation to the present. Similarly, in (L,M;M,M) the first person is moved from L to M and in (L,M;M,H) the second person is moved from L to H in transitioning from the initial situation to the present. Finally, with respect to numbers helped (L,M;M,M) and (L,M;M,H) are the same as (L,M;M,H); they all help one person. So aggregating the relevant components of the scores from (L,M;M,M) and (L,M;M,H) it is possible to arrive at the score for (L,L;M,H). I trust that, from these examples, one can work out the other equivalences between the first six and remaining rows for the improvements between the initial situation and the present (for those inclined to generate the complete matrix).

Acknowledgments

The author would like to thank audiences and colleagues at Carnegie Mellon University, the Workshop on Intergenerational Justice for the Chaire Hoover in Louvain-la-Neuve, Belgium, the Franco-Swedish Program in Philosophy and Economics in Paris, France, the Center for Ethics in Society at Stanford University, and the Justitia Amplificata Colloquium at the Free University Berlin, Germany for helpful comments or discussion. She is especially grateful for comments from Efthymios Athanasiou, John Weymark, Julian Culp, Peter Stone, Subbu Subramanian, Lucio Esposito, Hyunseop Kim, and Kevin Zolleman. She apologizes to anyone she has carelessly forgotten to mention.

Notes

1. There is, for instance, some important work on the justification of particular aid institutions and policies—like the WB and USAID's policies for distributing aid to countries in need (Hassoun 2014).
2. See, for instance, the extensive literature on climate justice (Gardiner et al. 2010)
3. For good work on how to value changes in population as well as welfare, see (Arrhenius 2000; Blackorby, Bossert, and Donaldson 2003; Räikkä 2002; Carlson 1998; Broome 2005; Christiano and Braynen 2008; Tungodden and Vallentyne 2006).
4. For discussion that may be relevant to resolving the issue of what constitutes the proper basis for poverty measurement, see (Pogge 2002, 2009; Nussbaum 2000; Sen 1997).
5. Talk about needs and goods does not presuppose that any particular way of distributing goods (in the relevant broad sense) is best. It might, for instance, alleviate just as much need to give ten children a year of schooling as to inoculate a single child against measles.
6. For one way of doing this, see (Hare 1981). Recent work on theory of mind may add to Hare's account by helping to explicate the process by which such comparisons are made. See (Goldman 1993; Gopnik and Wellman 1992).
7. Prioritarianism is a kind of egalitarian concern that should be distinguished from concern for inequality. On inequality, see (Temkin 1993).
8. This does, of course, presume that there is some significance to the threshold for need drawn on resources, welfare, or whatever—that it matters if some cannot secure what they need. The case is not like a choice between giving the least well-off a little bit of food and giving 99 other people a bit of dessert.
9. Again, need is supposed to be significant here; we are not concerned with helping people attain luxuries but with helping them avoid poverty.

10. This is obviously not the end of the debate on this issue. Prioritarians will likely reply that their theory does account for the separateness of persons because each person counts for one and no one for more than one, but note that people do not count at all on the theory. It is only their needs that count. The pure aggregative aspect of prioritarianism—even below the poverty threshold—is only concerned with maximizing the satisfaction of weighted need no matter how it is distributed. Moreover, the account of the separateness of persons at issue is obviously different than an account which gives each individual a veto over alternative distributions. Accepting this kind of justification does not preclude other moral concerns, however (e.g. for groups as well as individuals).

11. On standard construals of prioritarianism, the weighting function must be strictly decreasing and strictly convex in well-being, resources, welfare, or whatever. For a detailed discussion of the prioritarian weighting and value functions, see (Lumer 2005).

12. The two propositions that make up the Effectiveness Principle can conflict. Sometimes we must choose between helping a greater number of people and helping those who are worse off and, on any plausible way of specifying prioritarianism, we also need to specify how much priority we should give to the worse-off. This, however, is not a problem for present purposes. Rather, it is part of the reason this chapter's conclusions are so significant. This chapter suggests that even from such incomplete and underspecified principles (the effectiveness principle and a few others suggested in the literature), we can still arrive at a significant partial ranking of all potential policies in the simple model it lays out below.

13. I prefer not to consider choices about, for example, which people we should kill when we may not have to make such tragic decisions. I prefer to spend my time trying to find ways of avoiding having to make such choices. I believe there is something to Karl Popper's claim that "we should never attempt to balance anybody's misery against somebody else's happiness" (Popper 1986). In any case, this chapter does not focus on how to make such hard trade-offs. There may also be other reasons to constrain or modify this chapter's account of how we should arbitrate between policies that aid (but do not harm) the poor in present generations. One may care, for instance, about every individual's "life trajectory"—how necessary goods are distributed within a person's life. The way one cares, and the arguments for caring, may have an interestingly similar structure to the arguments for prioritarianism. If an individual must choose between having less total poverty over the course of their life and a better distribution of necessary goods within it, it may be reasonable to choose the latter. This chapter will not pursue this line of thought further, however. The only thing this chapter may need to suppose in the intra-personal case is that it is, *ceteris paribus*, better if more of a person's needs are satisfied than if fewer of their needs are satisfied. This may follow directly from the fact that poverty is, presumably, a bad thing.

14. Those who think some poverty is acceptable can limit their attention to desperate, involuntary poverty.

15. There is some evidence in behavioral economics that we fail to search long enough in looking for solutions to all kinds of problems (Bearden et al. 2005).

16. Some also consider whether we should only bring into existence the best people, and there is a large literature on how to respond to historical injustice (Boonin 2011). This chapter will not consider either of these issues.

17. This principle is much weaker than the claim that we should neutral about "making happy people" (Broome 2005: 401), though, I am not convinced by the main arguments against this claim (Broome 2005).

18. Note that population seems to matter in both of these cases just because of how it impacts how people will fare. I doubt this will always be the case—perhaps our population size matters for environmental reasons.

19. Alternately, one can accept a stronger principle like Population Neutrality: As long as there will be some people, the number of people in future generations does not matter intrinsically (non-instrumentally). However, numbers can impact people's welfare, etc., so numbers matter instrumentally. We have reason to care about those who will be around when they are around, but there may be no non-instrumental reason to bring them into existence. This may not allow one to avoid Parfit's paradox, however. See further (Broome 2005).

20. There may be an impartial sense in which 2 is better than 3 and 3/2 without it necessarily being permissible to move from 2 to 3/2 or 3. If one who took this line did endorse Mere Addition, one would say that a repugnant world is better than a world like 2 but would not have to say that we should, therefore, choose a repugnant world over a world like 2 (there may be a better alternative). Since this still seems somewhat implausible, however, there is reason to reject Mere Addition and accept No Mere Addition. Moreover, it is especially hard to see why 2 would be impartially better than 3/2 or 3. Further argument is necessary for No Mere Addition, however, as one could suggest that there is a threshold distinct from the poverty line below which people's lives are very bad but still worth living and it is at that level at which No Mere Addition is true. This debate hangs on the nature of poverty about which this chapter has said little.

21. It is also not clearly worse if poor people exist—the necessary claim is one about actions—it is generally worse to bring poor people into existence without reason.

22. Though I believe Arrhenius is primarily concerned with the latter type of claim in this section of his book, he does consider the *if* claim in examining what he calls asymmetrical views (Arrhenius 2011: 167–8). On these views it is only worse if those with negative welfare exist but neutral whether those with positive welfare exist. I do not believe anything this chapter says commits its proponents to this view. So I will not discuss the issue at length due to space constraints (for some discussion, see note 23). However, even if one believes this chapter's argument commits us to a corresponding kind of (poverty) asymmetry (on which it is normally neutral if the non-poor are brought into existence but bad if poor people are brought into existence), I do not think that the problems Arrhenius raises for asymmetrical views will plague this view.

23. Assume here Z cannot represent negative welfare.

24. Consider Broome's argument against this proposal (Broome 2006). Broome considers a version of the Mere Addition Paradox where most of the individuals in A have 4 units of good and one has 5. He then considers an otherwise identical situation, B, where the individual with 5 has 6 and there is an additional person who has 1 unit of good. Finally, C is the same as B but the person with 6 only has 4 and the person with 1 also has 4. He says that A is just as good as B and C for the last person (who does not exist in A). B is better than A for the second to last person (who has 6 rather than 5) and A is better than C for that person (who has 5 rather than 4). So B is overall better than A, which is better than C. This, however, violates transitivity of betterness. We can represent the situations this way:

$$A = (4,4,\ldots 4,5,^*)$$
$$B = (4,4,\ldots 4,6,1)$$
$$C = (4,4,\ldots 4,4,4)$$

The problem with this argument is that it is not clearly the case that A is just as good as B and C for the last person (who does not exist in A). It is true that A is neither better nor worse for that person than B and A is neither better nor worse for that person than C. But this tells us nothing about how B and C compare to each other. If either B or C will be the case, it is clearly better for the last person to be in C than in B. So C is impersonally better than B in one respect—because the last person will be better off in C than in B. A is incomparable with B and C for the last person. Nevertheless, C is clearly better than B for that person and better impersonally in one respect. That is, C>B for the last person. So even though B>A>C for the second to last person, it is not clearly the case that B>A>C all things considered.

25. Moreover, even setting worries about semantic coherence aside, it does seem odd to say I am better off existing since there is nothing to compare my state to if I do not exist (or, more precisely, if it is not the case that there is an I that exists).

26. Arrhenius (2011) admits this in a note.

27. Incidentally I am not particularly concerned about the provision of only partial and incomplete principles. Arrhenius is trying to find a complete consistent population axiology and I am not sure whether that is possible, but perhaps the piecemeal approach demonstrated in this chapter will get us as close as possible.

28. The concern for separate persons might be used to justify some analogue to concern for numbers here—where each time a person is brought into existence deprived (assuming it could be prevented) that would be a separate mark against a policy. This would seem to provide additional reason against bringing poor people into existence, however. Further, if a policy wrongly brings extra people in need into existence, it would generally be better to help more of those people.

29. This way of putting the point actually goes some way beyond what this chapter has established in favor of the neutrality assumption even with respect to poor people. If, however, it can be worse to add poor people to a population and allowing that trade-offs may make it permissible to do so, the idea that we should be neutral about numbers seems like a reasonable background presumption. Moreover, at least in so far as we are certain of our policies' impact on future generations, it is quite plausible that we should minimize weighted need. For we are making the same kinds of decisions about situations like the following that we would make for present generations if there were no initial situation (and hence, no number who could be helped.)

Suppose Situation A includes two people, one with 2 units of goods and another with 4 units, while Situation B includes two people with 2 units of goods each. Furthermore, suppose the poverty line is set at 6 units. Situation A may be worse than B, though there is less need, because the worse-off are worse off. There may be 6 units of unmet need in A and 8 in B. The prioritarian intuition is reasonable when there are no differences between situations in terms of the number helped and everyone's claims are equal.

30. In variable population situations generations overlap. This chapter, however, only considers what we should say about two generations that do not overlap.

31. It should be easy to see how to extend the model so that it can be used to consider impacts on different future generations. One can also incorporate uncertainty into the model.

32. It would, presumably, be better to bring a person into existence with more rather than fewer goods. So there is a sense in which it is better to bring someone into existence rich (that is, to bring the person into existence at or above the poverty line) than to prevent that person from coming into existence poor. But there is another sense in which this is not clearly

true. It is not clearly better to bring someone into existence with a lot of goods than to prevent that (or a different) person from coming into existence at all because they would be poor if they came into existence.

33. To construct the rows, start from (L,L;L,L;L,L) then increase the amount the people in future generations have along each row as follows: (L,M), (L,H), (M,M), (M,H), (H,H). In each of the first six columns increase the amount in the present and then the initial situation in the same way. For each increment in the initial situation, e.g. when it is (L,M), repeat the process in the present and future situations to generate new rows and fill in columns. That is, this method will yield this diagram if one also takes into account the exceptions discussed later in this section.

34. So, when the initial situation is (L,M), the first row with a present situation has (L,M) as well.

35. Moreover, suppose that changes in situations that we are evaluating are due to our actions.

36. So (L,M;L,M;H,0) would be better rather than worse than (L,L;L,M;H,0), for instance. For there is less total need in (L,M;L,M;H,0) than in (L,L;L,M;H,0), and it would not be better to help a greater number (because the person helped could otherwise have had less total need over the course of their life).

37. Consider a case where the third row is higher than the fourth row. The ranking of rows is determined by what happens in present generations alone. So suppose, for instance, that in present generations moving a person from L to M is worth 2 points in present generations, moving a person from M to H is worth 1 point, and moving a person from L to H is worth 3 points. Further, suppose that in present generations helping each person gets 1 point. In present generations the score for the first row = 0, the second row = 3, the third row = 4, the fourth row = 6, the fifth row = 7, and the sixth row = 8. The score increases along each row. A similar pattern holds (in all cases) for future generations—the score increases within each group of six situation profiles. Suppose, for instance, that in future generations if a person with L is in the population, one receives no credit, if a person with M is in the population, one receives 2 points and if a person with H is in the population, one receives 3 points. So (L,L;L,L;L,L) = 0, (L,L;L,L;L,M) = 2, (L,L;L,L;L,H) = 3, (L,L;L,L;M,M) = 4, (L,L;L,L;M,H) = 5, (L,L;L,L;H,H) = 6. That is, things get better on this chapter's suggested principles as we move to the right across rows and down each column.

38. Consider a case where the fourth row is higher than the third row. Suppose, for instance, that alleviating the first unit of a person's need is worth 10 points in present generations, alleviating the second unit of a person's need is worth 9 points, and alleviating the third unit is worth 8 points. Suppose further that someone with L has no units of necessary good, someone with M has one unit of necessary good, and someone with H has three units of necessary good. So, alleviating the first unit of a person's need moves them from L to M, but one must alleviate the second and third unit of a person's need to move them from M to H. Finally, suppose helping a single person is worth only 1 point. The score in present generations for the first row = 0, the second row = 11, the third row = 28, the fourth row = 22, the fifth row = 39, and the sixth row = 56. The reason the fourth row is higher (has less poverty) than the third row is that more weighted need is alleviated in helping someone move from M to H than in moving two people from L to M. This pushes in the opposite direction to numbers. So, if helping a person was worth 10 points rather than 1, the ranking of the third and fourth rows would be reversed. The score in present generations for the first row would = 0, the second row would = 20, the third row would = 37, the fourth row would = 40, the fifth row would = 57, and the sixth row would = 74.

39. It does not matter what the relative weight of needs and numbers helped in present generations is or whether helping one person move from L is better than helping two people move from L to M.

40. This ranking would not change if there were only one person in the future on adaptation. It does not tell us what to do if there are two people in the future on adaptation and only one person on mitigation.

41. Assume, for simplicity, that some people will exist who are not affected by the policy.

References

Arrhenius, Gustaf (2000) "An Impossibility Theorem for Welfarist Axiologies," *Economics and Philosophy* 16: 247–66.

Arrhenius, Gustaf (2011) *Population Ethics: The Challenge of Future Generations.* March Draft of Manuscript provisionally accepted by Oxford University Press. Chapter 9.

Ashford, Elizabeth (2003) "The Demandingness of Scanlon's Contractualism," *Ethics* 113: 273–302.

Bearden, J. Neil, Ryan O. Murphy, and Amnon Rapoport, (2005) "A Multi-Attribute Extension of the Secretary Problem: Theory and Experiments," *Journal of Mathematical Psychology* 49: 410–25.

Benatar, David (2006) *Better Never to Have Been: The Harm of Coming into Existence.* Oxford: Oxford University Press.

Blackorby, Charles, Walter Bossert, and David Donaldson (1995) "Intertemporal Population Ethics: Critical-Level Utilitarian Principles," *Econometrica* 63: 1303–20.

Blackorby, Charles, Walter Bossert, and David Donaldson, (2003) "The Axiomatic Approach to Population Ethics," *Politics, Philosophy & Economics* 2(3): 342–81.

Blake, Michael (2001) "Distributive Justice, State Coercion, and Autonomy," *Philosophy and Public Affairs* 30(3): 257–96.

Boonin, David (2011) *Should Race Matter?* Cambridge: Cambridge University Press.

Brock, Gillian (2009) *Global Justice: A Cosmopolitan Account.* Oxford: Oxford University Press.

Broome, John (1992) *Counting the Cost of Global Warming.* Cambridge: White Horse Press.

Broome, John (2005). "Should We Value Population?" *The Journal of Political Philosophy* 13(4): 399–413.

Broome, John (2006) *Weighing Lives.* Oxford: Oxford University Press.

Buchanan, Allen (2013) *The Heart of Human Rights.* Oxford: Oxford University Press.

Caney, Simon (2003) "Cosmopolitan Justice and Equalizing Opportunities," *Metaphilosophy* 32(1–2): 113–34

Caney, Simon (2010) "Climate Change, Human Rights and Moral Thresholds." In Stephen M. Gardiner, Simon Caney, Dale Jamieson, Henry Shue, and R. K. Pachauri (eds.), *Climate Change: Essential Readings.* Oxford: Oxford University Press, 163–78.

Carlson, Erik (1998) "Mere Addition and Two Trilemmas of Population Ethics," *Economics and Philosophy* 14: 283–306.

Casal, Paula (2007) "Why Sufficiency is Not Enough," *Ethics* 117: 296–326.

Christiano, Thomas, and Will Braynen (2008) "Inequality, Injustice and Leveling Down," *Ratio.* 21: 392–420.

Cullity, Garrett (2006) *The Moral Demands of Affluence.* Oxford: Oxford University Press.

de George, Richard T. (1981) "The Environment, Rights and Future Generations." In E. Partridge (ed.) Environmental Ethics. New York: Prometheus Books, 157–66.

Feldman, Fred (1997) "Justice, Desert, and the Repugnant Conclusion," *Utilitas* 7: 567–85.

Frankfurt, Harry G. (1988) *The Importance of What We Care About: Philosophical Essays.* Cambridge: Cambridge University Press.

Gardiner, Stephen, Simon Caney, Dale Jamieson, Henry Shue, and R. K. Pachauri (2010) *Climate Ethics: Essential Readings.* Oxford: Oxford University Press.

Goldman, Alvin I. (1993) "The Psychology of Folk Psychology," *Behavioral and Brain Sciences* 16: 15–28.

Gopnik, Alison, and Henry M. Wellman (1997) "Why the Child's Theory of Mind Really is a Theory," *Mind and Language* 7: 145–71.

Hardin, Garrett (2012) "The Tragedy of the Commons." In David Schmidtz and Elizabeth Willott (eds.), *Environmental Ethics: What Really Matters, What Really Works.* New York: Oxford University Press, 403–5.

Hare, Caspar (2007) "Voices from Another World: Must We Respect the Interests of People Who Do Not, and Will Never, Exist?" *Ethics* 117: 498–523.

Hare, R. M. (1981) *Moral Thinking: Its Levels,Method, and Point.* Oxford: Clarendon Press.

Harman, Elizabeth (2004) "Can We Harm and Benefit in Creating?" *Philosophical Perspectives* 18: 89–113.

Harman, Elizabeth (2009) "Harming as Causing Harm." In M. A. Roberts and D. T. Wasserman (eds.), Harming Future Persons. (International Library of Ethics, Law, and the New Medicine, vol. 35). Dordrecht: Springer, 137–54.

Hassoun, Nicole (2009) "Meeting Need," *Utilitas* 21: 250–75.

Hassoun, Nicole (2012) *Globalization and Global Justice: Shrinking Distance, Expanding Obligations.* Cambridge: Cambridge University Press.

Hassoun, Nicole (2013) "World Bank Rules for Aid Allocation: New Institutional Economics or Moral Hazard." In Helen M. Stacy and Win-Chiat Lee (eds.), *Economic Justice: Philosophical and Legal Perspectives.* Dordrecht: Springer, 221–42.

Hassoun, Nicole (2014) "New Institutionalism and Foreign Aid," *Global Justice: Theory, Practice, Rhetoric* 7: 12–27.

Hassoun, Nicole (2015) "Coercion, Legitimacy, and Global Justice," *Journal of Social Philosophy* 46: 178–96.

IPCC (2007) "Summary for policymakers. " In M. L. Parry, O. F. Canziani, J. P. Palutikof, P. J. van der Linden, and C.E. Hanson (eds.), *Climate Change 2007: Impacts, Adaptation And Vulnerability. Contribution of Working Group II to the Fourth Assessment Report of the Intergovernmental Panel on Climate Change,* Cambridge: Cambridge University Press, https://www.eea.europa.eu/data-and-maps/indicators/soil-organic-carbon-1/IRationale Reference1232455014617, accessed August 18, 2019.

Kamm, F. M. (2006) *Intricate Ethics: Rights, Responsibilities, and Permissible Harm.* Oxford: Oxford University Press.

Kavka, Gregory S. (1982) "The Paradox of Future Individuals," *Philosophy & Public Affairs* 11: 93–112.

Lumer, Christoph (2005) "Prioritarian Welfare Functions: An Elaboration and Justification." In Daniel Schoch (ed.), *Democracy and Welfare.* Paderborn: Mentis, 43 S.

Macklin, Ruth (1981) "Can Future Generations Correctly Be Said to Have Rights?" In E. Partridge (ed.) Environmental Ethics. New York: Prometheus Books, 151–6.

Mayell, H. (2002) "Climate Studies Point to More Floods in this Century," National Geographic News. January, 30th.

Miller, David (1999) *Principles of Social Justice.* Cambridge, MA: Harvard University Press.

Miller, Richard W. (1998) "Cosmopolitan Respect and Patriotic Concern," *Philosophy and Public Affairs* 27: 202–24.

Murphy, Liam B. (2003) *Moral Demands in Nonideal Theory.* Oxford: Oxford University Press.

Nagel, Thomas (2001) *Equality and Partiality.* Oxford: Oxford University Press.

Nussbaum, Martha C. (2000) *Women and Human Development: The Capabilities Approach.* Cambridge: Cambridge University Press.

Parfit, Derek (1984) *Reasons and Persons.* Oxford: Clarendon Press.

Pogge, Thomas (2002) "Can the Capability Approach Be Justified?," Philosophical Topics 30(2): 167–228.

Pogge, Thomas (2008) *World Poverty and Human Rights.* Cambridge: Polity Press.

Pogge, Thomas (2009) "Developing Morally Plausible Indices of Poverty and Gender Equity: A Research Program." Paper presented at Carnegie Mellon's Center for the Advancement of Applied Ethics and Political Philosophy, Carnegie Mellon University, Pittsburgh, PA.

Popper, Karl 1986) "Utopia and Violence," *World Affairs* 149(1) 3–9.

Räikkä, Juha (2002). "Problems in Population Theory," *Journal of Social Philosophy* 31(4): 401–12.

Rivera-López, Eduardo (2009) "Individual Procreative Responsibility and the Non-Identity Problem," *Pacific Philosophical Quarterly* 90: 99–118.

Rolston III, Holmes(2012) "Feeding People Versus Saving Nature." In David Schmidtz and Elizabeth Willott (eds.), *Environmental Ethics: What Really Matters, What Really Works.* New York: Oxford University Press: 504–15.

Sen, Amartya (1997) "Poor, Relatively Speaking." In S. Subramanian (ed.), *The Measurement of Inequality and Poverty.* Readers in Economics. Oxford: Oxford University Press.

Sen, Amartya (1999) *Development as Freedom.* Oxford: Oxford University Press.

Shiffrin, Seana Valentine (1999) "Wrongful Life, Procreative Responsibility, and the Significance of Harm," *Legal Theory* 5: 117–48.

Singer, Peter (1972). "Famine, Affluence, and Morality," *Philosophy and Public Affairs* 1(1): 229–43.

Stanford Encyclopedia of Philosophy (SEP). 2009. "The Nonidenitity Problem," http://plato.stanford.edu/entries/nonidentity-problem/, accessed August 18, 2019.

Temkin, Larry S. (1993) *Inequality.* Oxford: Oxford University Press.

Tungodden, Bertil, and Peter Vallentyne (2006) "Person-Affecting Paretian Egalitarianism with Variable Population Size." In John Roemer and Kotaro Suzumura (eds.), *Intergenerational Equity and Sustainability.* New York: Palgrave Publishers, 176–200.

Wasserman, David (2005) "The Nonidentity Problem, Disability, and the Role Morality of Prospective Parents," *Ethics* 116: 132–52.

Wasserman, David (2008) "Hare on De Dicto Betterness and Prospective Parents," *Ethics* 118: 529–33.

PART IV

CLIMATE CHANGE JUSTICE

CHAPTER 12

CLIMATE CHANGE ETHICS AND THE PROBLEM OF END-STATE SOLUTIONS

THOM BROOKS

1 INTRODUCTION

How best to response to climate change is one of the most pressing challenges facing us all.[1] There is no uncertainty about whether it is happening, only the likely negative effects beyond the short term. The need for a compelling analysis of what to do is more than a question of justice, but a matter of human survival. The stakes could not be higher.

Proposed solutions come in one of two approaches.[2] Each takes a different route to addressing the negative effects of climate change. The first is conservationist and seeks to minimize these effects by reducing, if not eliminating them by bringing climate change to a stop. This can take form of advocating the use of an ecological footprint or implementing a polluter pays principle. The second is focused specifically on adaptation mostly through technological advances to help us endure climate change by minimizing its effects on us. Many theorists advocate some use of both approaches in tandem, as climate change is happening, making necessary some form of adaptation and conservationism together.[3] Yet it is also clear that most give greater weight to either conservation or adaptation as the primary mode of securing climate change justice.[4]

The dilemma for these proposed solutions is in their aim of being a solution to the problems that climate change brings. In short, they mistake the kind of challenge that climate change presents us. This is what I call *the problem of "end-state" solutions*.[5] It is where we attempt to bring to an end a circumstance that might be *influenced* positively or otherwise by our activities, but *beyond our full control*. So to claim a so-called "solution" to such an ever-changing problem could make it better or worse without concluding it. If climate change is this kind of problem—and I will claim it is—then end-state "solutions" can be no more than a Band-Aid and the nature of our challenge is different, requiring an alternative future strategy. This chapter will set out how the problem of climate change is understood through attempted solutions that do not succeed. It concludes with some ideas about why this matters and the arising implications for how we should think about climate change justice beyond the false prism of end-state solutions.

2 The Climate is Changing with Harmful Effects

Climate change and its causes are not controversial. A global consensus accepts human activity is responsible for this change and its associated effects.[6] The Intergovernmental Panel on Climate Change has reaffirmed that "scientific evidence for warming of the climate system is unequivocal" (IPCC 2013: 4).[7] The changes include a rise in global temperature, warming oceans, shrinking ice sheets, rising sea levels, extreme weather events, and more.[8] These changes are interrelated. Increased global temperature both melts ice sheets and warms oceans. The melted ice adds to sea levels, as well as to the amount of water in the global weather system. With more unlocked water freed from polar icecaps, this fosters more extreme weather patterns with more moisture in the air that increase risks of damaging storms.

These climate changes bring many harmful effects. Increased global temperature raises risk of drought in more arid areas while significantly impacting on local ecology elsewhere. This can damage crops, leading to food shortages. Rising sea levels threaten coastal communities and can force migration.[9] The changing weather system can help spread tropical diseases to new geographical regions unprepared for combating it.

So climate change is not one thing or a single event. It is a trend that can be observed for over fifty years manifest in rising sea levels, droughts affecting agricultural production, and the spread of tropical diseases to new areas. These observable happenings over decades are caused by human activity, and this is leading to harmful effects for people worldwide, threatening homes, reducing harvests, and increasing risks of catching diseases.

The aim of most—if not all—influential approaches to combating climate change is to minimize these harmful effects by either reducing—if not eliminating—climatic changes so that no such effects are manifest or by reducing—if not eliminating—the harm arising from climatic change effects through adaptation. Or some combination of the two. Both aim at a solution leading to an end-state where, if a proposed solution is closely adhered to, there is no additional climate change-related concern to address in future.

3 CONSERVATION 1: THE ECOLOGICAL FOOTPRINT

Conservationist approaches to solving the problem of climate change are the most prevalent and influential. They seek to halt this change to end contributions to further associated harmful effects. Conservationism is sometimes referred as "mitigation," because its aim is to enable the mitigation of harmful environmental effects on human beings.[10]

One popular form this broader approach can take is *an ecological footprint*.[11] This footprint corresponds to a share of human carrying capacity, understood as the maximum rate of resource consumption that can be sustained indefinitely.[12] If everyone consumes no more than their ecological footprint, then our planet will become permanently hospitable. Climate change can be brought to an end and so too its harmful effects.

Calculating sustainable consumption as a footprint can be through measuring its maximum rate per person. Others consider everyone having an equal share of absorption capacity in our atmosphere's sink.[13] The idea is that the atmosphere belongs to all in common: no individual has a greater claim to a larger share. The atmosphere can only absorb a finite amount of emissions in a sustainable way. It is a zero-sum game where your using more than your share would deprive others of their fair share. This creates a duty for everyone to use no more than their fair share or owe compensation when we fail to perform our duty.[14] Our having equal shares of a sustainable absorption capacity would entail a significant reduction in global consumption. Living within an ecological footprint means consuming much less than at present, whichever method for determining the footprint is preferred.

The problem that the ecological footprint highlights is the imprint too many of us make is much larger than can be sustained long-term. There is much evidence for this.[15] Common estimates show that seventeen of eighteen of the warmest years recorded over 136-years have occurred since 2001, with the exception of 1998.[16] Living within our footprint means a significant reduction in global consumption, including the production of carbon emissions.

An important motivation for reducing consumption levels to within a sustainable ecological footprint is because failing to do so would contribute to climate changes and their associated effects that may give rise to causing harm to others.[17] Environmental change is not always the same as environmental damage. Plant and animal species may change in relation to ecological factors without experiencing harm in any obvious sense. But where such change is detrimental to their flourishing, this presents a case of avoidable harm.[18] Additionally, such harmful effects might impact on future generations, a complex topic with its own literature that I will bracket here.[19]

The ecological footprint faces four key limitations against endorsing it. The first is its problematic anthropocentrism.[20] Footprints are determined to ensure the indefinite sustainability of human beings. We measure the impact of our activities on the environment, but not the impact of plant and animal species as well. Such a perspective may be critically important for setting a measure of *human* sustainability, but a sustainable carrying capacity of humans may not be coextensive with such a capacity of *non-human* sustainability. The flourishing of the former could be secured at a cost to the latter. This might be a price some may find worth paying, but it is at least counterintuitive as a form of *climate change* justice to potentially neglect or harm non-human species to achieve *justice*.

A second limitation concerns inequality. The ecological footprint is thought to derive part of its normative power from its treating every individual equally.[21] We each have the same-sized footprint whoever or wherever we are. This falsely assumes satisfactory nourishment and bodily needs are the same, but they can differ. For example, childbirth and old age may require a need for greater resources. Individuals will also differ in resource needs according to height and body mass. There may be potential gender differences in resource needs pertaining to pregnancy. Plus, people living in different climates will have variable needs to inhabit such contrasting environments.[22] So there is no "one size fits all" ecological footprint we can apply equally to everyone. Nor is there any single fixed footprint for any individual, because resource needs will change during the course of most lives. To treat everyone the same at all times is what the ecological footprint calls us to do to achieve justice for all, but at the same time to do so is to impose an injustice on many.

The ecological footprint can, if adopted, create global injustice in pursuit of climate justice. Consider this third limitation by supposing we imposed an equal footprint for all. Each country would have a footprint equal to the collective footprints of its population— and this would lead to a reduction in global consumption. This equal distribution would have the likely consequence of benefiting wealthy states over the poor. Affluent countries more technologically advanced would be in a much stronger position to adapt and thrive in these conditions than countries affected by severe poverty, which would be far more vulnerable to climatic changes.[23] Securing an equal footprint for all would ossify the global privileges of the wealthy over others.

A similar scenario potentially arises with carbon trading.[24] The idea is each country has an equal share of emissions based on population size. If a country wishes to produce carbon emissions in addition to their share, this is only permissible through purchasing emission credits from others. One benefit is that it makes it easier for countries with higher emissions to bring them down gradually to lower levels. Typically, the more wealthy produce more emissions than less affluent states.[25] Carbon trading has a second benefit in helping redistribute wealth from more wealthy states to the less affluent.

A common complaint by pro-conservation theorists concerns motivations.[26] They are troubled that carbon trading could have a negative effect on motivations to conserve. Carbon trading does not ensure every state is more sustainable, only the system overall. Since sufficiently wealthy countries have the spending power to purchase carbon credits, they could choose to continue with overconsuming lifestyles and luxuries at the expense of the less well-off, which might be left with even less.[27] So even if overall consumption was reduced, it would come at a cost of ensuring the rich stayed rich, while the poor remained poor.[28] Ossifying the status quo might also be seen as a price worth paying, but yet again this approach to climate change justice might increase risk of increasing other systemic injustices.

A fourth limitation is that the ecological footprint requires no possibility of human overpopulation. The footprint is a share of a sustainable ecological space. If there were so many humans that equal shares would become too small for all to be sustained, then no such footprint would be possible. So ecological footprints require the absence of overpopulation and assume sufficient sustainable ecological space for everyone present and future, which may be untrue in the long term. Since the relative size of everyone's footprint would increase if the overall human population were less, this might hypothetically offer unjust regimes a perverse reason to launch military attacks in order to expand the size of their footprints.[29]

The ecological footprint offers itself as a fair and equal way to reduce global consumption to an indefinitely sustainable level. Adopting this approach is potentially likely to be unfair, effect individuals and countries unequally, and create global injustice—but its chance of success in achieving its conservationist aim requires the possibility of achieving such a sustainable end state.

4 Conservation 2: The Polluter Pays Principle

A second popular conservationist approach is *the polluter pays principle*.[30] The principle claims we each have a negative duty to compensate others for the harm we cause them through our carbon emissions. In contributing to exposing people to a risk of harmful effects, we have a (negative) duty to annul however possible the environmental damage caused by our activities.

The polluter pays principle utilizes complex and contested concepts like harm and conservationist compensation. It has already been noted in Section 2 that harm is about detrimental effects: environmental change might not always be an instance of environmental damage. But there is an additional consideration of cause and effect. Overconsumption globally causes climate change's harmful effects, but not every case of extreme weather is caused by such change. Extreme weather existed before human beings, even if human activity increases its frequency. It is difficult to pinpoint any specific individual human activity to any particular weather event.[31]

Compensation for risk of environmental damage is no less unclear. The polluter pays principle can be understood as a compensation principle: the polluter ought to pay because she did some wrong requiring recompense. Paying can compensate for polluting. The idea that polluters should compensate rather than merely pay highlights their polluting activity as a wrong to be put right. This indicates that the polluter pays principle is a kind of fine and not a fee.[32] A fine likewise evokes a wrong, whereas a fee does not.

But this assumes the possibility, and permissibility, of compensation. What compensation should be owed for making a species extinct—and who would be paid? What if an offer of compensation is rejected? The polluter pays principle assumes too much in taking for granted that any potential harmful effect will have a price. Some environmental goods, like a species' existence, may be non-compensatory in their nature, lacking any discernible monetary price. Such effects can be beyond compensation. Nor is it clear why, in principle, we should permit compensation from others to address our being continually subjected to the ongoing harmful effects if polluters are able to pay something to do so.

Suppose compensation was possible. How much should polluters pay? Greenhouse gas emissions have been called "the greatest market failure the world has ever seen," by Nicholas Stern (2009: 11). This is because the prices of many goods do not reflect the full costs of their production and use. The polluter pays principle focuses on consumption, but not on production: it should cover both.[33] If we claim that creating carbon emissions entails having to pay for the pollution caused, then we should recognize that emissions are linked with production too. Both should be reflected in how much polluters should pay.

There are further limitations concerning the problem of identifying relevant polluters. We are all the polluters and victims of pollution. So who pays whom?[34] For example, we might think that states with collective responsibilities are the relevant agents.[35] This would raise issues of whether present generation should compensate for the policies of the past that have contributed to climate change today. James Garvey (2008: 115) argues: "It is a straightforward fact that some countries emitted more greenhouse gases—used up more of the planet's atmospheric sink, caused more climate change—than others. It's a quantifiable fact: we know something about cumulative emissions." So how far back in time should we go to assess past emissions? Our data per country do not conclusively cover the full range of all gases previously emitted and remaining in our atmosphere. We then lack a clear rationale for penalizing some states more than others based on these past emissions.

A more fundamental problem is that the polluter pays principle does not guarantee conservation. Most proposals for implementing the principle take the form of a tax on oil consumption. The idea is that increasing costs will incentivize reduced consumption and secure carbon emissions at an indefinitely sustainable level. While higher costs can help reduce emissions, there is no evidence that these costs will reduce levels sufficiently by themselves.[36]

Moreover, polluters can pollute as much as they can afford to pay.[37] If polluters have sufficient resources, they might not reduce emissions and so conservation will not be secured. For example, Thomas Pogge (2008: 202–21) supports a Global Resources Dividend (GRD). Pogge argues that the consumption of oil products and its corresponding production of carbon emissions, especially by affluent states, present significant threats to states with populations in severe poverty. Affluent states receive benefits of improving economies at the expense of less wealthy states left to bear the costs of the resulting environmental damage to which they are more vulnerable. So affluent states have a negative duty to provide some effective means of compensation. Pogge offers his

GRD—a tax of about $2 per barrel of oil—which is collected by governments and paid to less affluent states as compensation funding mitigation and adaptation strategies.[38] We can tax our way to climate change justice and a sustainable future.[39]

The GRD is an imaginative way for affluent states to recognize negative duties while reducing global inequality. But it assumes too much in guessing that a tax raising the price of oil for consumers only slightly will yield a sustainable path to long-term conservation despite all evidence to the contrary that global consumption would remain at unsustainable levels. Taxes may be inevitable in modern states, but they do not inevitably lead to ending the harmful effects of climate change.

Some advocates of the polluter pays principle are sensitive to these concerns. For example, Simon Caney argues we are all under a duty not to exceed an equal quota of greenhouse gas emissions, in his defense of the principle.[40] Our global emissions must be capped at an indefinitely sustainable level. The emissions produced under this cap— and within this sustainable amount—are subject to a tax. In this way, Caney brings the polluter pays principle to operate within an overall cap providing funding for compensating the harmful effects produced in a sustainable way.

The problem with this framework is that the polluter pays principle loses its motivational and justificatory force. Caney wants to retain the principle because of the view that negative duties are more compelling than positive duties. Polluters pay not out of charity, but because of justice for the harmful effects they contribute towards. But if there is a global emissions cap that secures a sustainable level of emissions that the atmosphere's sink can reasonably absorb, then it appears polluters do not cause any harmful effects under this cap and so do nothing to compensate others. What is doing the conservationist work is the cap, acting like the ecological footprint but without dividing out the equal shares. Instead of operating like a fine, Caney's principle becomes a fee that helps raise resources to support conservation efforts. However, it is not justified as a negative duty, and what does the justificatory work is enforcing the overall cap, but not any need to compensate, because no such harmful effects would arise.

The polluter pays principle is a second popular approach to achieving an indefinitely sustainable future. Most variations assume we can set a tax that will sufficiently incentivize such a sustainable effort, but there is little to no evidence this could be achieved. These models assume we can put a price on compensation where it would seem unlikely, if not impossible, we could do so for any environmental goods at risk of damage. While Caney's framework is more persuasive than its rivals, it does not really utilize a polluter pays principle and, like other versions, assumes a sustainable end state is achievable.

5 THE ADAPTATION ALTERNATIVE

Conservationists do not have a monopoly on popular proposals for responding to the harmful effects of climate change. The main alternative is adaptation. This is widely understood to be a reality and not an option, given that environmental damage is happening already—conservation "will not be enough" on its own.[41] Stephen Gardiner says:

> The first thing to note...is that adaptation measures will clearly need to be part of any sensible climate policy, because we are already committed to some warming due to past emissions, and almost all of the proposed abatement strategies envisage that overall global emissions will continue to rise for at least the next few decades, committing us to even more.   (Gardiner 2004: 573)

While most policymakers would concede any climate change policy should include conservation/mitigation and adaptation strategies together, we find that some believe we should prioritize adaptation aims over conservation (as we saw others claim the opposite in Sections 3 and 4).

Adaptation advocates share several core commitments. The first is skepticism about how much of a reduction in carbon emissions will be necessary to secure indefinite survival. Matthew Kahn (2010: 7, 12) argues: "we will save ourselves by adapting to our ever-changing circumstances" because "At the end of the day, the story will have a happy ending." While such views do not deny climate change is happening, there is greater certainty that such storms can be endured through adaptation to these changing conditions.[42] We can adapt sustainably through greater urbanization of our communities, increasing our reliance on weather-resistant genetically modified foods and using nuclear energy.[43] As the climate changes, we can change with it and immunize ourselves to many harmful effects.

This priority of adaptation over conservation is, for some, about cost-effectiveness. For example, Bjorn Lomborg (1998: 318) claims "it will be far more expensive to cut CO_2 emissions radically than to pay the costs of adaptation to the increased temperatures." Conservation efforts have been estimated to cost approximately 2 % of GDP per annum, or roughly $1 trillion each year.[44] Lomborg (2008: 8, 35) argues that we can spend much less than this amount in adapting ourselves to changing climatic conditions and using our savings on other major social issues like poverty alleviation where this cash could go much further and do more good.[45]

Adaptation can take many forms. Flood defenses or relocation can adapt coastal communities to rising seawater threatening coastlines. Genetically modified crops that can thrive in more arid conditions can permit farming to adapt to less agriculturally productive conditions. Inoculation measures can protect us from the spread of tropical diseases to new geographical areas. Such measures are designed to adapt us to withstand or overcome any otherwise harmful effects of climate change. We reduce the effects of change primarily by adapting to them, rather than through conservation. All such forms are primarily anthropocentric.[46] We are first and foremost adapting ourselves, although some advocate ways of adapting habitats to reduce the impact of climate change on plant and animal species living in those habitats.

There are several key limitations to adaptation. The first is an overconfidence in our ability to adapt successfully. We have uncertainty about the future environment—but must know to which future we must adapt ourselves to. Adaptation is a strategy for enduring a future that we lack sufficient clarity and certainty about to ensure an indefinitely sustainable future.

This uncertainty about the future environment is amplified by uncertainty how successful our adaptation measures will be to overcoming such changes. This is what might be called a "Unknown Unknown" and the least confident position we could have.[47] So even if we could be confident in our models of what future conditions will be like, we cannot safely test proposals in the way a chemist might conduct experiments in a controlled laboratory. The high uncertainty is matched by the very high costs of failure. Many proposed measures of adaptation have never been tried or do not yet exist.[48] For example, one such measure is "carbon capture," where carbon is removed from the atmosphere and pumped into depleted oilfields underwater.[49] The problem is that the future risk to human and marine life is unknown, with potentially deadly consequences for both.[50] Far too much faith is put in our non-existent future technology saving the day from an unknown future environment. Claims that "in a world with billions of educated, ambitious individuals, the best adaptations and innovations will be pretty good" (Kahn 2010: 243) beg the question of how can we be sure that this will be good enough? This may be a risk not worth its potentially catastrophic costs.

Surprisingly, technological advances can produce unforeseen problems too. For example, consider how the creation of energy savings has led to higher overall energy use:

> More power-efficient washing machines or better insulated homes will help the environment; but they also cut our bills, and that immediately means we lose some of the environmental gain by spending that saved money on something else. As cars have become more fuel-efficient we have chosen to drive further. As houses have become better insulated we have raised standards of heating, and as we put in energy-saving light bulbs the chances are that we start to think it doesn't matter so much leaving them on.   (Wilkinson and Pickett 2010: 223)

Technological advances producing much greater energy efficiencies have not led to a reduction in overall energy consumption, but instead increased it. If we are to put most of our eggs in an adaptation basket, we must have confidence that we can correctly guess the future climatic changes, the technology required for adapting to them, and that no such counterproductive (and perhaps counterintuitive) consequences will follow. Otherwise, the adaptation alternative is less compelling than conservation where the uncertainty remains but is less.

Adaptation is an important part of any climate change policy. But it is built more on faith in what the future will yield and a reduced aversion to risks that are at least questionable, if not reckless, as a primary strategy. Like conservation-focused proposals, adaptation promises the possibility of "a happy ending" (Kahn 2010: 12) indefinitely, assuming yet again that climate change does have an end-state solution.

6 BEYOND END-STATE SOLUTIONS

Conservation and adaptation are not incommensurable. Most theorists advocating for how to address climate change emphasize one or the other, but in fact policymakers usually support some combination of both conservationist and adaptation measures. It is not fundamental to my argument that we can only support one side or the other.[51]

But what is critically important is how the wide array of approaches considered understand the challenge of climate change in the same way, notwithstanding their different ways of addressing it. This shared viewpoint is of seeing climate change as a problem that can be solved, bringing about an end state of indefinite sustainability. Others, like Stephen Gardiner (2011: 7), argue that "existing theories are extremely underdeveloped in many of the relevant areas, including intergenerational ethics, international justice, scientific uncertainty, and the human relationship to animals and the rest of nature."

I agree, and my main aim has been to critically highlight the ways in which the main proposals advanced on each side of the climate change debate are unconvincing, but also drawing attention to the problem of their sharing a belief in the myth of end-state solutions for our climate. One side claims "the world now has the technologies and financial resources to stabilize climate" (Brown 2011: 198). The other claims that if only governments had us live within an ecological footprint or launched a polluter pays principle, then the harmful effects of climate change would begin to disappear as changes are brought to an end.

This is not to deny that most commentators taking either approach might accept additional policies may be required beyond what they recommend. It remains the case that if something more than adoption of conservation or adaptation is required, then this too often goes unacknowledged. This is not a question of making clearer the precise combination of conservationist and adaptation approaches within a unified policy. Instead, this is about the failure of most commentators to acknowledge the limits of their favored policies as a kind of end-state view that might do no better than temporarily manage the climate change we experience in the short to medium term.[52]

In short, end-state solutions are no solutions at all for the kind of problem that climate change presents us with; they are not a reliable roadmap of how to save the planet.[53] The problem is there is no guarantee of a happy ending notwithstanding our best efforts. It is as false to believe only human activities can impact on the climate as it is to claim our activities could put the global climatic system in a kind of holding pattern. We cannot stop the climate from changing any more than we can stop the world from turning. The climate changed before there were humans and would almost certainly do so still without us. Likewise, environmental catastrophes have not required human beings to cause them in the past even if our activities make them more likely in our future. Such an event is not something we might prevent forever, but rather postpone or mitigate, at least for the foreseeable future.

If this is correct, our response should not be to surrender. The fact the climate is changing is not a compelling reason to exacerbate conditions likely to increase the risk and severity of harmful effects creating problems more frequently. We should ask new ethical questions: What are the moral implications of a future climatic catastrophe that might only be delayed, but not averted? What practical consequences might these implications yield? We must reflect on sustainability in the shadow of catastrophe for a tragic world—*our* tragic world—where there is no magic wand to cast away these challenges.[54]

The fact of a foreseeable—and perhaps inevitable—climatic catastrophe expands our normative horizons. If such an event is avoidable by adopting a particular policy, our judgment about how best to proceed will focus on the certainty of success. This is how climate change policy looks like from an end-state perspective. But now consider that this catastrophe is not avoidable. There is not one right course of action to take, but a future of many different actions in a future of changing climatic conditions. This changes not only what we might do about climate change; it changes how we might think about the nature of the problem as well.

7 Possible objections

There are several potential objections worth considering. The first is that just because there have been catastrophes in the past does not mean there will more again in future: what is done is gone. It might be replied that we are much better at understanding how to damage or destroy the planet than save it. Climate scientists accept climatic changes happen cyclically, but yet remain divided on what causes them.[55] One scientist explained: "Many aspects of ice-age dynamics remains a mystery" (Marshall 2013: 159–60). We need to understand better such fundamental aspects of climate change before we can begin to imagine how our efforts might control or halt them. Until that time, end-state solutions are beyond our grasp.

A second objection is, if I am correct and a future environmental catastrophe is foreseeable and likely unavoidable, what should we do now that we are not doing already? In other words, what does this change? A response might be that reducing our impact on the climate through conservationism may be one important—if not the most important—means to delay a future environmental catastrophe for as long as possible. This is because the more manageable route to sustainability is to foster conditions that are easier to adapt to—and increased conservationism would better enable adaptation to the circumstances. Reducing our emissions globally might not be achieved by a polluter pays principle or reach a level of indefinite sustainability, as aimed for by the ecological footprint. But having this as our main focus is the best way to prepare ourselves for whatever future conditions are ahead.

A third objection claims my analysis confuses theory and practice. It says that "the value of philosophy rests not on successful policy action, but in the process of moral evaluation" (Lee and Kincaid 2016: 142). Philosophy can continue to guide moral mitigation even in a world where mitigating the climate is no longer possible—and so climate ethics is immune from my critique, not least what is presented in this chapter. In response, it is unclear what guidance philosophy can bring where we cannot act on it, especially when we are grappling with *applied philosophy*, as we are here. If the polluter pays principle purports to provide an end-state solution which it cannot, in fact, secure, then perhaps there is ethical merit in its drawing attention to a negative duty we might have. But our assessment of this principle which claims to bring about a certain state of affairs should not be unconcerned with its efficacy. It is a part of the theory that it is best placed to achieve certain outcomes in particular ways. In applied philosophy, this matters.

A final objection is that my critical strategy, such as my concerns about the ecological footprint, misses the point of it. Affluent states are living beyond their means, and poorer states suffer from the change-related harms their overconsumption creates.[56] An ecological footprint makes possible a sustainable global economy that would help buy time to pursue the adaptation strategy I have advocated.

In reply, my criticism of the footprint strategy took more than one form. I argued its one-size-fits-all footprint does not treat countries equally (some will have greater or smaller resource needs, depending on local climates) or fairly (some individuals over a lifetime will require different-sized footprints). I further observed that locking countries into the same-sized footprints relative to their populations would likely ossify the privileged position of the affluent over less wealthy states, because the former would be best placed to exploit conditions to their advantage. If our reason for supporting the footprint approach is a desire to improve conditions for the global poor, it is unclear that the global order will necessarily become more equal through use of the footprint model alone.

8 CONCLUSION

Climate change is happening. The only question is about how best to respond, not whether to act. This chapter examined conservationist and pro-adaptation approaches aiming to solve this problem. The first can take multiple forms, such as ensuring we all live within an ecological footprint or adopt a polluter pays principle. The second takes various shapes, putting its faith in future technologies. The former seeks to minimize, if not end, climate change and so stop its negative effects, while the latter aspires to mitigate the effects of these changes through adapting to them. In short, both approaches see themselves as enabling an end-state solution to the problem of climate change's harmful effects.

I have raised concerns with both approaches, but they also get wrong their fundamental understanding of the kind of problem that climate change presents us with. It is not like a puncture that only needs the right patch. Nor is it simply a matter of coordinating an enormous global effort across continents, as difficult politically as that is. Even if there was no problem of collective action, the proposed solutions on offer will not achieve their desired aims.[57]

A core issue is viewing climate change as a phenomenon that can be fully controlled; that through conservation and/or adaptation an end state can be achieved. Such a happy ending is beyond our grasp, at least for the foreseeable future. While our actions can influence the speed and intensity of climate change effects, the planet has not required human beings to undergo an ice age in the past. Catastrophe is not something we can simply avert forever if human emissions are cut sufficiently or even if all of us left the planet for a new life on Mars.

This is not a pessimistic perspective, but a sober reflection. Dale Jamieson (2014: 9) claims that we should "not let the perfect be the enemy of the good." This is correct. Likewise, we should not let an imperfect set of circumstances demotivate us, but instead raise the stakes. Achieving global climate justice is a bigger challenge than many assume and one that lacks any ready-made off-the-shelf solution. My critical look at existing proposals is meant not to claim such attempts are destined to be futile, but rather to inspire others to embrace this challenge for the good of all today, and in future generations.

ACKNOWLEDGMENTS

I am indebted to many colleagues for discussions about issues raised in this paper that have greatly improved my considered views beyond earlier versions. Specific thanks are owed to Robin Attfield, Gillian Brock, Alan Carter, James Connolly, Rowan Cruft, Liz Fraser, Fabian Freyenhagen, Clare Heyward, Pauline Kleingeld, Melissa Lane, Jonathan Lowe, David Miller, David Owen, Soran Reader, Esther Shubert, Matthew Noah Smith, Suzanne Sreedhar, Daniel Star, Martin van Hees, Jo Wolff, Hiro Yamazaki, and Lea Ypi.

NOTES

1. See Gore (1992).
2. For an excellent if somewhat dated survey, see Gardiner (2004).
3. For example, see Moellendorf (2009). For alternative views, see Hulme (2009) and Lovelock (2000).
4. See Giddens (2009: 13).
5. The idea of such an "end-state" approach is inspired from Nozick's critique of end-state distributive principles. See Nozick (1974: 167–74).
6. See Doran and Zimmerman (2009).
7. See NASA (2019a). See also IPCC (2014), its most recent and fifth report. There are multiple websites reaffirming these findings. Those selected are chosen for their accessibility as much as their scientific authority.
8. See NASA (2019c).
9. On the phenomenon of environmental refugees, see Nine (2010).
10. See the Society for Ecological Restoration, https://www.ser.org/default.aspx, accessed August 18, 2019.
11. See Wackernagel and Rees (1996) and Vanderleiden (2008).
12. See Rees (1992) and Jamieson (2008: 184).

13. See Singer (2004: 28).
14. The idea of compensation for harming the environment will be discussed in Section 4.
15. See Bleys, Defloor and Ootegem (2018).
16. NASA (2019b).
17. See Singer (2004: 14–50).
18. This is one of many ways to conceptualize such harm. Another is of a damage to our aesthetic experience of nature. See Jamieson (2008: 158–62).
19. One compelling approach is offered by Mazor (2010). See Parfit (1984: 351–80).
20. On anthropocentrism and climate change justice more generally, see Hassoun (2011).
21. See Baer (2002).
22. See Ding and Peng (2018: 765).
23. See Hayward (2005: 198).
24. See Lederer (2017); Caney and Hepburn (2011); and Tietenberg (2006: 25–47, 192–203).
25. There is some evidence of increased resource efficiency weakening the link between economic growth and domestic resource use. See Sadler (2018).
26. See Dobson (2003: 2–3) and Posner and Sunstein (2009). For an alternative view, see Aldred (2012).
27. See Shue (1993).
28. See Vanderheiden (2008: 446–7).
29. I do not seriously think such a regime would care so much for climate change justice that they would resort to war in order to achieve a larger footprint through reducing the total number of human beings. My aim is only to signpost this hypothetical scenario.
30. See Caney (2005); Gaines (1991); Giddens (2009: 92); Neumayer (2000); and Shue (1999).
31. This has relevance for claims that an individual violates the human rights of another by producing emissions and that other person suffers later from some harmful climate-related effect. Such cause and effect on the level of individual human rights is difficult to establish. Those wanting to link emissions to human rights violations are on firmer, but contested ground when viewing responsibility for contributing to a cause enabling demonstrable risks of harm that do befall a group violating the rights of that group. For an overview of these issues, see Moellendorf (2012).
32. See Sandel (2005).
33. Stern, *A Blueprint for a Safer Planet*, 159.
34. See Baer (2006).
35. See Caney (2005: 755). But also see O'Neill (2001).
36. For example, see US Energy Information Administration (2011: 6–7).
37. See Brooks (2012).
38. Pogge (2008: 202–21).
39. See Brooks (2015), esp. p. 423.
40. See Caney (2005: 769).
41. Mastrandrea and Schneider (2010: 13). See Giddens (2009: 161).
42. See Levitt and Dubner (2010: 169).
43. See Brand (2010).
44. See Stern, *A Blueprint for a Safer Planet*, 54.
45. But on problems with such cost-benefit analysis in this area, see Broome (1992).
46. See Lomborg (1998: 11).
47. See Graham (2014).
48. See Pacala and Socolow (2004).

49. See Haszeldine (2009).

50. See Fogarty and McCally (2010).

51. It is fundamental to my argument that the scientific consensus for the existence of climate change and its observable effects are accepted. Those that are skeptical about the pace of change—for whatever reason—can still accept my conclusions even if their expectation of human-caused catastrophe will not be until much further into the future. However, those who reject the existence of climate change not only disbelieve the kind of problem others, in my view, have wrongly characterized but the challenge that does face us and so will not accept my conclusions. But this is a problem for their non-scientific analysis and not mine.

52. For an exception, see Jamieson (2014).

53. See Brooks (2016); Loo (2016); and Brooks (2013).

54. While an ice age might now be much less likely than previously thought, now the concern has shifted to whether short-term catastrophe due to global warming is inevitable. So while the nature of the form of any future catastrophe might take is changing, there is no less a concern about the likelihood of an environmental catastrophe because of climate change and its possible effects.

55. See Abe-Ouchi, Saito, Mawamura, Raymo, Okuno, Takashi, and Blatter (2013).

56. Schwartz (2016).

57. On the problem of collective action, see Hardin (1968) and Knapp (2011).

REFERENCES

Abe-Ouchi, Ayako, Fuyuki Saito, Kenki Mawamura, Maureen E. Raymo, Jun'ichi Okuno, Kunio Takashi, and Heinz Blatter (2013) "Insolation-Driven 100,000-Year Glacial Cycles and Hysteresis of Ice-Sheet Volume," *Nature* 500: 190–3.

Aldred, Jonathan (2012) "The Ethics of Emissions Trading," *New Political Economy* 17: 339–60.

Baer, Paul (2002) "Equity, Greenhouse Gas Emissions, and Global Common Resources." In Stephen H. Schneider, Armin Rosencranz and John O. Niles (eds), *Climate Change Policy: A Survey*. Washington DC: Island Press, 393–408.

Baer, Paul (2006) "Adaptation: Who Pays Whom." In Neil Adger (ed.), *Fairness in Adaptation to Climate Change*. Cambridge: MIT Press, 131–54.

Bleys, Brent, Bart Defloor, and Luc van Ootegem (2018) "The Environmental Impact of Individual Behavior: Self-Assessment versus Ecological Footprint," *Environment and Behavior* 50: 187–212.

Brand, Stewart (2010) *Whole Earth Discipline*. London: Atlantic.

Brooks, Thom (2012) "Climate Change and Negative Duties," *Politics* 32: 1–9.

Brooks, Thom (2013) "The Real Challenge of Climate Change," *PS: Political Science and Politics* 46: 34–6.

Brooks, Thom (2015) "Climate Change Justice through Taxation?" *Climatic Change* 133: 419–26.

Brooks, Thom (2016) "How Not to Save the Planet," *Ethics, Policy and Environment* 19: 119–35.

Broome, John (1994) *Counting the Cost of Global Warming*. Strond, Isle of Harris: White Horse Press.

Brown, Lester R. (2011) *World on Edge: How to Prevent Environmental and Economic Collapse.* New York: W. W. Norton.

Caney, Simon (2005) "Cosmopolitan Justice, Responsibility, and Global Climate Change," *Leiden Journal of International Law* 18: 747–75.

Caney, Simon, and Cameron Hepburn (2011) "Carbon Trading: Unethical, Unjust and Ineffective?" *Philosophy* 69: 201–34.

Ding, Yu, and Jian Peng (2018) "Impacts of Urbanization of Mountainous Areas on Resources and Environment: Based on Ecological Footprint Model," *Sustainability* 10: 765.

Dobson, Andrew (2003) *Citizenship and the Environment.* Oxford: Oxford University Press.

Doran, Peter T., and Maggie Kendall Zimmerman (2009) "Examining the Scientific Consensus on Climate Change," *EOS* 90: 286–300.

Fogarty, John, and Michael McCally (2010) "Health and Safety Risks of Carbon Capture and Storage," *Journal of the American Medical Association* 303: 67–8.

Gaines, S. (1991) "The Polluter-Pays Principle: From Economic Equity to Environmental Ethos," *Texas International Law Journal* 26: 463–95.

Gardiner, Stephen M. (2004) "Ethics and Global Climate Change," *Ethics* 114: 555–600.

Gardiner, Stephen M. (2011) *A Perfect Moral Storm: The Ethical Tragedy of Climate Change.* Oxford: Oxford University Press.

Garvey, James (2008) *The Ethics of Climate Change: Right and Wrong in a Warming World.* London: Continuum.

Giddens, Anthony (2009) *The Politics of Climate Change.* Cambridge: Polity.

Gore, Al (1992) *Earth in the Balance: Ecology and the Human Spirit.* Boston, MA: Houghton Mifflin.

Graham, David A. (2014) "Rumsfeld's Knowns and Unknowns: The Intellectual History of a Quip," The Atlantic, https://www.theatlantic.com/politics/archive/2014/03/rumsfelds-knowns-and-unknowns-the-intellectual-history-of-a-quip/359719/, accessed August 18, 2019.

Hardin, Garrett (1968) "The Tragedy of the Commons," *Science* 162: 1243–8.

Hassoun, Nicole (2011) "The Anthropocentric Advantage? Environmental Ethics and Climate Change Policy," *Critical Review of International Social and Political Philosophy* 14: 235–57.

Haszeldine, R. Stuart (2009) "Carbon Capture and Storage: How Green Can Black Be?" *Science* 325: 1647–52.

Hayward, Tim (2005) *Constitutional Environmental Rights.* Oxford: Oxford University Press.

Hulme, Mike (2009) *Why We Disagree about Climate Change: Understanding Controversy, Inaction and Opportunity.* Cambridge: Cambridge University Press.

IPCC (2013) *Climate Change 2013: The Physical Science Basis.* Cambridge: Cambridge University Press.

IPCC (2014) "AR5 Synthesis Report: Climate Change 2014," http://www.ipcc.ch/report/ar5/syr/, accessed August 18, 2019.

Jamieson, Dale (2008) *Ethics and the Environment.* Cambridge: Cambridge University Press.

Jamieson, Dale (2014) Reason in a Dark Time: Why the Struggle against Climate Change Failed—and What It Means for Our Future. Oxford: Oxford University Press.

Kahn, Matthew E. (2010) *Climatopolis: How Our Cities Will Thrive in the Hotter Future.* New York: Basic Books.

Knapp, Christopher (2011) "Tragedies without Commons," *Public Affairs Quarterly* 25: 81–94.

Lederer, Markus (2017) "Carbon Trading: Who Gets What, When, and How?" *Global Environmental Politics* 17: 134–40.

Lee, Alexander, and Jordan Kincaid (2016) "Two Problems of Climate Ethics: Can We Lose the Planet but Save Ourselves?" *Ethics, Policy & Environment* 19: 141–4.

Levitt, Steven D., and Stephen J. Dubner (2010) *Superfreakonomics*. London: Penguin.

Lomborg, Bjorn (1998) *The Skeptical Environmentalist: Measuring the Real State of the World*. Cambridge: Cambridge University Press.

Lomborg, Bjorn (2008) *Cool It: The Skeptical Environmentalist's Guide to Global Warming*. New York: Vintage.

Loo, Clement (2016) "Environmental Justice as a Foundation for a Process-Based Framework for Adaptation and Mitigation: Commentary on Brooks," *Ethics, Policy and Environment* 19: 145–9.

Lovelock, James (2000) *The Ages of Gaia: A Biography of Our Living Earth*, 2nd edn. Oxford: Oxford University Press.

Marshall, Shawn J. (2013) "Climate Science: Solution Proposed for Ice-Age Mystery," *Nature* 500: 159–60.

Mastrandrea. Michael D., and Stephen H. Schneider (2010) *Preparing for Climate Change*. Cambridge: MIT Press.

Mazor, Joseph (2010) "Liberal Justice, Future People, and Natural Resource Conservation," *Philosophy and Public Affairs* 38: 380–408.

Moellendorf, Darrell (2009) "Treaty Norms and Climate Change Mitigation," *Ethics and International Affairs* 23: 247–65.

Moellendorf, Darrell (2012) "Climate Change and Global Justice," *Climate Change* 3: 131–43.

NASA (2019a) "Scientific Consensus: Earth's Climate Is Warming," https://climate.nasa.gov/scientific-consensus, accessed August 18, 2019.

NASA (2019b) "Global Temperature," https://climate.nasa.gov/vital-signs/global-temperature, accessed August 18, 2019.

NASA (2019c) "Climate Change: How do we know?," https://climate.nasa.gov/evidence, accessed August 18, 2019.

Neumayer, Eric (2000) "In Defence of Historical Accountability for Greenhouse Gas Emissions," *Ecological Economics* 33: 185–92.

Nine, Cara (2010) "Ecological Refugees, States Borders, and the Lockean Proviso," *Journal of Applied Philosophy* 27: 359–75.

Nozick, Robert (1974) *Anarchy, State and Utopia*. New York: Basic Books.

O'Neill, Onora (2001) "Agents of Justice," *Metaphilosophy* 32: 180–95.

Pacala, S. , and R. Socolow (2004) "Stabilizing Wedges: Solving the Climate Problem for the Next 50 years with Current Technologies," *Science* 305: 968–72.

Parfit, Derek (1984) *Reasons and Persons*. Oxford: Oxford University Press.

Pogge, Thomas (2008) *World Poverty and Human Rights*, 2nd edn. Cambridge: Polity.

Posner, Eric, and Cass Sunstein (2009) "Should Greenhouse Gas Permits Be Allocated on a Per Capita Basis?" *California Law Review* 97: 51–93.

Rees, William E. (1992) "Ecological Footprints and Appropriated Carrying Capacity: What Urban Economics Leaves Out," *Environment and Urbanization* 4: 121–30.

Sadler, Konstantin (2018) "Growth in Environmental Footprints and Environmental Impacts Embodied in Trade: Resource Efficiency Indicators from EXIOBASE3," *Journal of Industrial Ecology* 22: 553–64.

Sandel, Michael J. (2005) "Should We Buy the Right to Pollute?" In *Public Philosophy: Essays on Morality in Politics*. Cambridge: Harvard University Press, 93–6.

Schwartz, Jonathan Peter (2016) "On Staying Focused: Response to Thom Brooks' *How Not to Save the Planet*," *Ethics, Policy & Environment* 19: 157–9.

Shue, Henry (1993) "Subsistence Emissions and Luxury Emissions," *Law and Policy* 15: 39–59.

Shue, Henry (1999) "Global Environment and International Inequality," *International Affairs* 75: 533–7.

Singer, Peter (2004) *One World: The Ethics of Globalization*, 2nd edn. New Haven, CT: Yale University Press.

Stern, Nicholas (2009) A Blueprint for a Safer Planet: How to Manage Climate Change and Create a New Era of Progress and Prosperity. London: Bodley Head.

Tietenberg, T. (2006) *Emissions Trading: Principles and Practice*, 2nd edn. Washington DC: Resources for the Future, 2006.

US Energy Information Administration (2011) *International Energy Outlook 2011*. Washington DC: US Energy Information Administration.

Vanderleiden, Steve (2008) "Two Conceptions of Sustainability," *Political Studies* 56: 435–55.

Wackernagel, Mathis, and William E. Rees (1996) *Our Ecological Footprint: Reducing Human Impact on the Earth*. Gabriola Island: New Society Publishers.

Wilkinson, Richard, and Kate Pickett (2010) *The Spirit Level: Why Equality is Better for Everyone*, rev. edn. London: Penguin.

FURTHER READING

Brennan, Andrew, and Yeuk-Sze Lo (2015) "Environmental Ethics," *Stanford Encyclopedia of Philosophy*, https://plato.stanford.edu/entries/ethics-environmental, accessed August 18, 2019.

Brooks, Thom (ed.) (2020) *The Global Justice Reader*, rev. edn. Oxford: Blackwell.

Dobson, Andrew (1990) *Green Political Thought*. London: HarperCollins.

Dryzek, Jay (1997) *The Politics of the Earth: Environmental Discourses*. Oxford: Oxford University Press.

CHAPTER 13

....

DISTANT STRANGERS
AND THE ILLUSION
OF SEPARATION
Climate, Development, and Disaster

....

HENRY SHUE

> Any man's death diminishes me, because I am involved in mankind. And
> therefore never send to know for whom the bell tolls; it tolls for thee.
>
> (Donne 1624: 394–5).

IF India's poor have rights that can be satisfied only through economic development—
only by, for example, electricity for the hundreds of millions of Indians whose "energy
poverty" extends to the extreme of having no access at all to electricity—but massive
burning of the world's dirtiest coal, which is the most plentiful source of energy that
India now has the infrastructure to exploit, makes the air in major Indian cities more
polluted than even the notoriously polluted air of Beijing and in addition greatly reduces
the odds of limiting climate change across the globe to levels that are not dangerous for
billions of people across many generations, what should be done? And how much of
this, if any, is the problem of us who live in a wealthy country? Do we share in the responsibility to find a way out of India's dilemma? If so, why? And how much?

In a probing 1995 exploration, Samuel Scheffler suggested that our inherited conception of responsibility rests in part on what he called "a complex phenomenology of
agency": a set of assumptions about what matters about what we do and do not do
(Scheffler 2001: 39). Specifically, he saw that among the concepts deeply ingrained in our
understanding of the world are the following two assumptions: the near effects of our
acts are more important ethically than the remote effects, and the effects we produce as
individuals are more important ethically than the effects we produce as members of a

group. The first assumption, I think, reflects its origins in somewhat less globalized times, although we should not exaggerate the simplicity of earlier times (Parker 2014). That the near effects of one's actions are more significant than the remote effects made sense in earlier centuries when, in fact, one's most powerful influence—for most people most of the time, one's only influence—was local. In those times if one wanted to have some effect on people elsewhere than where one lived, one needed to go to that other place in order to act there. Now one's greenhouse gas emissions over the course of one's life in Ireland contribute to the rise of the sea level on the coast of Africa, and a tweet from Peru can cause a riot in Moldova.

The second assumption, that the effects one produces acting alone are ethically more significant than the effects one produces as a member of a group, was, I suspect, never entirely true, because, apart from utter hermits, individuals are normally embedded in communities—even collections of the homeless and the stateless affect others. The conventional assumption may be largely explained by individualistic ideological commitments. It is not true that the effects of what one does by oneself are always more important than the effects of one's participation in institutions and practices, like being a life-long customer in a consumer society based on carbon energy, the energy from fossil fuels, which is used in the production of consumer items, the transportation of consumer items, and the use of consumer items (Lichtenberg 2014: 73–96; Ashford 2007: 194–200). Climate change is indeed a giant example of *remote*—indeed, global—effects that are also the *group* effects of individuals participating in an international energy regime that is dependent on coal, oil, and natural gas. And climate change is a powerful reason why we need to try to follow Scheffler's early lead in rethinking our understanding of responsibility, to which I hope this chapter will constitute another, small contribution.

Any normal person whose conception of herself extends beyond personal material comforts and psychological pleasures to include attachments to children and grandchildren and to practices and institutions—be they football or opera—that endure across time and are likely to be enjoyed also by children and grandchildren has broadly self-interested reasons for caring about climate change because of its potential to disrupt ordinary lives and the travel habits of both strikers and sopranos. Except for sociopaths who literally care only about themselves—and even they should worry that they may find their house flooded or their food more expensive—ordinary humans who care about at least some of the people and activities that survive them have good reason to take action to limit climate change in order to preserve what they value.[1] But, as my title indicates, I am inviting us to think about most other people, all the people who are strangers to us—in many cases, distant strangers—for whom we have no reason to feel affection and whose activities and practices we may have no particular reason to care about—the vast majority of other people in the world. Do we here in the wealthy countries have any responsibility toward them with regard to climate change? If so, why? And how much?

1 CONTEMPORARY STRANGERS AND THE AFFORDABILITY OF ALTERNATIVE ENERGY

Most societies are now to some degree engaged in some kind of effort to respond to climate change, even though in the case of my own American society the votes of many Senators and Congresspersons appear to have been bought by campaign contributions from fossil-fuel interests. So we need to reflect on both the climate problem itself and the proposed responses, because, of course, every response to a problem comes with its own problems. We should consider any responsibilities we might have to distant strangers regarding either the climate change itself or our responses to the climate change. Rather than catalogue the increasingly well-understood dangers of climate change itself, I will simply recall two of the notorious general features of climate dangers. First, the distribution of the dangers bears no relation to the distribution of the benefits from the emissions that are causing the dangers. Sea-level rise, for example, will affect those who live near sea level—thus, hundreds of millions in Bangladesh and India who do not even have electricity will suffer from encroachment, flooding, and storm surges partly caused by electricity generation from coal. Second, the death tolls from storms are heavily affected by the wealth of the society that suffers the storm: hurricanes that hit the U.S. kill relatively few people—sometimes no one—because buildings are sturdy, communication of warnings is effective, medical care is excellent, and so on—while cyclones that hit the Philippines regularly have high death tolls. Anyone may be affected by climate change, but, generally speaking, the poor will suffer the most.

The dangers that will come from our response to climate change may be less well known, so it is worth noting them slightly less briefly. By far the most important factor in causing climate change is the accumulation in the planet's atmosphere of carbon dioxide from the burning of fossil fuels. And it turns out that because carbon dioxide remains in the atmosphere for almost unimaginably long times—between roughly 10% and 25% of it stays for several hundred thousand years (Ciais et al. 2014: 472–3)—the crucial factor is the *cumulative* amount of carbon dioxide emitted since 1870 (the conventional baseline, when the Industrial Revolution gathered momentum), the vast bulk of which still remains in the atmosphere. The atmospheric physicists have established—and there is now very wide consensus on this—that there is a fairly specific *cumulative* carbon budget for not exceeding each degree of temperature rise beyond the pre-Industrial Revolution temperature (Frame et al. 2014). The *cumulative* carbon budget for a temperature rise of not more than 2°C would, if current trends in emissions increases continue, be exceeded by the end of 2034 (www.trillionthtonne.org). So if we are serious about the unambitious goal of not exceeding a 2°C rise, it is critical for global emissions to peak and then start down sharply very soon, which is physically and technologically possible.

It simply has to be made politically possible by acts of determination and will. A strong trailing off in emissions would move the date for exceeding the cumulative budget back from 2034—further into the future. By about 2050 carbon dioxide emissions from energy use must completely stop, which means humanity must exit the fossil fuel—or carbon—energy regime entirely and use nothing but alternative energy, that is, non-carbon energy—anything but fossil fuel (Kartha and Baer 2015). This is because, if we keep adding to the cumulative total, the atmospheric concentration must exceed the budget for 2°C.

This should all occur, then, within the lifetime of the current under-50s. Either way the next decades will be an amazing time to live on earth. Today's young will witness—and, I hope, participate in, on the right side—one of history's greatest struggles, which will result in either one of humanity's most glorious triumphs—a successful Energy Revolution eliminating carbon emissions from fossil fuels—or one of humanity's most dismal failures, the coming of dangerous climate change. They will not be bored.

What I want to focus on here is the danger that comes, not with the climate change itself, but with our response to it. Fossil fuels, especially coal, which is by far the worst, need to be made extremely unattractive extremely fast—80% of the known reserves of coal must be left in the ground to avoid overshooting the goal of a rise in temperature of no more than 2°C (McGlade and Ekins 2015; Kartha et al. 2018). Governments could simply regulate and eventually ban them, but no democratic government has so far had the guts to regulate fossil fuel use to save the climate, as was done, for instance, during World War II through rationing to win the war. So all the proposals for reducing fossil-fuel use involve political action to make it more expensive until consumers themselves choose to turn away from it to other energy sources. It can be made more expensive in one of at least two ways: a carbon tax or so-called cap-and-trade. My impression is that a carbon tax would be more straightforward and efficient, but so far no national government has had the courage to impose a carbon tax either. So cap-and-trade may win by default through requiring the least political courage. In any case I have nothing to add to the disputes between cap-and-trade and carbon tax, except the obvious point that political leaders need to get serious about one or the other immediately.

If politicians can be pressured by concerned citizens into acting, fossil fuels will start to become more expensive, which is good in itself. But this is where the danger for developing countries from the necessary response to the dangers of climate change begins. And this danger means that the response to climate change must not have only one dimension. The danger is disrupting development by depriving the poorest of the only energy source that they can currently afford: fossil fuel. Now, there is no good reason why fossil fuels should be the cheapest energy source now—this is the result of two mistaken political policies. First, many poor-country governments heavily subsidize fossil fuels as part of an effort to promote development, but the dangers of climate change make this a deeply misguided policy that needs to end immediately, even if it made sense before we understood climate change—the world total of fossil-fuel subsidies in 2013 was $5 trillion (Carrington 2015; Gupta and Keen 2015). Amazingly, G20 governments heavily subsidize fossil fuels, with both producer subsidies and consumer subsidies, in spite of their rhetoric in support of capping temperature rise at 2°C (Bast et al. 2014).

Second, the price of fossil fuel is as artificially low as it is also because gross lack of political regulation has permitted all its enormous health and environmental costs to be externalized, that is, they are not covered by the price for the purchasers of the energy but are dumped upon society generally—we all pay for the hospital expenses of fellow citizens with lung and heart diseases from breathing the pollution from the burning of coal—and often dumped on beyond fellow citizens to the world's population even more generally. Neither a carbon tax nor cap-and-trade would be necessary if the price of fossil fuel covered the huge health costs of the lung diseases and shortened life spans caused by coal burning and the monumental environmental costs, above all climate change itself, but also the despoliation of land and pollution of water from the extraction of all fossil fuels, including coal mining, especially strip mining, which is about to be greatly increased in India, and fracking, which both wastes and pollutes shared supplies of water (United States, Environmental Protection Agency 2017; Kondash et al. 2018:1).

Much of the environmental damage is hidden from our view in the affluent countries because it is in the oceans or in the developing world, such as the gigantic mess Shell made in Nigeria with horrific oil leaks that it has failed for years to clean up (Vidal 2015; Associated Press 2015), leading to the deaths in protests by the Nigerian people that inspired Nnimmo Bassey's poem, saying in part:

> The heavens are open
> Above our heads
> Toasted dreams
> In a scrambled sky
> A million black holes
> In a burnt out sky
> Their pipes may burst
> But our dreams won't burst.
>
> We thought it was oil
> But it was blood
> We thought it was oil
> But it was blood

(Bassey 2002).

In general, fossil fuels and corporations like Shell, BP, and Exxon have been given by politicians by far the biggest free ride from respect for the environment of any corporations in human history. Plus government tax breaks! Is it possible that leading politicians are in their pockets?

In any case, if we belatedly act against climate change by pricing carbon through either carbon taxes or cap-and-trade, the prices of fossil fuels will finally rise, and what is now the most affordable energy for the poorest will become more expensive, will specifically become unaffordable for many of the poor who can afford it now, and will rise even farther out of reach for those who already cannot afford it. We have no choice but to limit climate change, but if we do it this way, the implications for development are ominous if we do nothing else. Obviously, then, we must not simply price the poorest out of the energy market and leave them as helpless as we would then have made them. Our efforts to limit climate change cannot be pursued in isolation. We must simultaneously pursue complementary policies that avoid undermining development and forcing those who are already humanity's worst off to become even worse off. Which complementary policies?

Fairly obviously it is our responsibility to protect the poorest from the results of our choice of policy instruments—a rise in fossil fuel prices—by encouraging the rapid spread of alternative forms of energy by the most effective means available. This could mean, for example, feed-in tariffs, as used by Germany, or special tax concessions for entrepreneurs and/or early adopters of new technology, or increased research and development funds for universities, or other techniques that a theorist like me would be the last person to know about—perhaps a Grameen Bank focused on non-carbon energy. The crucial goal is that the alternative forms of energy must be made accessible and affordable to the poorest in the developing world soon and instead of electricity generated by burning coal. So the primary focus of the developed world must be strategies designed to put the alternative energy into the hands of the poor in the developing world, not acquisition of alternative energy ourselves, which is also good as a secondary goal. If the state subsidies come off the fossil fuels and are put on alternative energy instead for a transition period, there is no reason why non-carbon energy that does not undermine the climate cannot become competitive in price with damaging and now grossly underpriced fossil fuels. This is happening: the prices of, for example, solar and wind have plummeted in recent years and are already in many places competitive in price with fossil fuels even with the latter's misguided public subsidies (Landberg and Hirtenstein 2018).

Not only will sufficiently affordable alternative energy help to overcome "energy poverty" in the developing world, but it will directly assist in eliminating carbon emissions by making replacements for fossil fuel readily available in the developed world. In the affluent world much of our energy is wasted, and we can by simply reducing waste fairly easily use less carbon energy without replacing it with anything. But where people, including those who do not appreciate the seriousness of the dangers from climate changes, are unwilling or unable to reduce energy usage, they will give up carbon energy only if they have a price-competitive replacement for it. In order to stay within the cumulative carbon budget for the planet as a whole, carbon emissions need to come down sharply in the developed world but not go up very much in the developing world. At both ends of the line, affordable non-carbon energy is crucial. For once at least the same response, alternative energy, serves the desires of the rich and the needs of the poor. But it will require smart targeted initiatives to make it accessible to the poor quickly enough—prompt affordability for the poor is not a challenge that unaided market mechanisms can possibly meet.

I have tried, then, to be reasonably concrete (for a theorist) about what needs to be done, although I have not tried to say which specific forms of alternative energy should be encouraged, since I do not think that needs to be a top-down decision. I should perhaps mention that I would count effective forms of carbon capture and storage, if they are ever developed, as alternative energy: if energy is provided without allowing carbon dioxide to escape into the atmosphere, that counts as alternative energy. Carbon capture and storage so far remain undeveloped because the fossil-fuel companies have refused to invest much of their vast profits in making the products they sell less polluting and harmful. If they became willing to invest seriously in carbon capture and storage, they might be able to rescue the now threatened value of their reserves, which otherwise are liable to become stranded because people cease to be willing to tolerate the damage their technologically avoidable emissions do to the only planet we have (Carbon Tracker Initiative 2013).

But I want to return now to the question of general responsibility. Why do we in the rich countries share in the responsibility for the dissemination of alternative energy within the developing countries? How did this get to be a task that falls to us? I will brush over familiar reasons that have nothing to do with climate change. For example, if every human being is to have a meaningful basic right to subsistence, then there needs to be an international division of moral labor sufficient to see that those who are now unable to provide for their own subsistence are enabled to become capable of providing for themselves, which will involve in many cases the provision from outside of resources not now available locally and therefore will involve the rest of us (Shue 2020: 13–64). But some less familiar, but important and interesting reasons have to do specifically with climate change.

The Indian government ought to give priority to reducing poverty in India. India will cut its own throat, however, if it injects large additional amounts of carbon dioxide into the atmosphere and contributes to humanity's exceeding the cumulative carbon budget for some "non-disastrous" amount of temperature rise, not to mention creating danger-ous amounts of ground-level pollution that will multiply cases of lung and heart disease within Indian cities.

It is vital, however, to recognize that additional Indian carbon emissions will be such a dangerous problem for the planet only because of past emissions from developed nations and more recently from the surge of heavily coal-driven development by China. The cumulative greenhouse gas emissions of the United States, Great Britain, and China each considerably exceed the cumulative emissions of India at this point, although this could unfortunately change rapidly if India throws itself into the arms of coal (Ge et al. 2014; World Resources Institute). India's contribution to the fact that humanity as a whole may soon exceed the global cumulative carbon budget has so far been rela-tively minor—far less than the contribution of the United States or the EU, and per capita, only a fraction. But like China a decade ago, India is on the threshold of rapid, massive increases in energy consumption.

Now as Indian and Chinese leaders argue—and indeed I myself have argued for twenty-five years—it would be wildly unjust for us in the rich countries to say, "Sorry, but our own development and our own continuing enjoyment of affluence have used up most of the cumulative carbon budget so there is no room within the budget for the emissions that your escape from poverty would generate, so you will unfortunately sim-ply have to remain poor" (Shue 2014b). On the other hand, the cumulative carbon budget is not an artifact that can be modified by choice. The cumulative carbon budget is an unrelenting feature of the dynamics of the climate of this planet. If we exceed the cumulative carbon budget for a given temperature rise, the temperature rise will be larger and the concomitant climate change will be more dangerous. There is no overdraft privilege for the planetary carbon budget (Shue 2017). It is conceivable that the scientists have miscalculated it, although the evidence becomes stronger and stronger, but the politicians cannot fudge it (Pierrehumbert 2013; Collins et al. 2014; Frame et al. 2014).

Nevertheless, it would be profoundly unjust if India—and China, and Africa—could not develop because the emissions budget is about to be used up. But development produced at the price of exceeding the emissions budget would simply not be sustainable— it would in fact undercut itself. This is the global dilemma of the twenty-first century. Therefore, development must proceed, but proceed sustainably, which can only mean with sharply declining carbon emissions, not rising carbon emissions. The only good alternative is a rapid scaling up of non-carbon energy within developing countries, plus measures for women like education, jobs, and access to affordable contraception to slow population growth. These are a tremendous challenge politically and technologically, but the responsibility to see that they happen is shared by the developed countries, then, for the following reasons.

First, we have seen that India's looming emissions are dangerous only because our emissions preceded them. The Indian trunk may break the camel's back, but only because the camel is already carrying the American, European, and Chinese trunks (Shue 2015). Secondly, it would be our decision to discourage carbon emissions by raising the price of carbon that risks pricing poor Indians out of the market for what may still for some be their only affordable source of energy, if they have one. Both these actions of ours contribute to India's plight and make us partly causally responsible for resultant harm. Our causal responsibility grounds moral responsibility to assist them in gaining access to alternative energy—responsibility for the creation of an escape route for them from the corner they have been forced into by our emissions, including many unnecessary ones, plus our chosen means of responding to the climate dangers caused by our emissions. These are two reasons we bear moral responsibility, and they appeal, in turn, to a rock-bottom principle: avoid deprivations of necessities that leave people helpless, if humanly possible (Shue 2020: 119–127).

Thirdly, and very closely related, if we allow the world's poorest to bear the brunt of the transition out of carbon energy and into alternative energy, we are, in the common phrase, balancing the energy transition on the backs of the poor. Putting it less informally, we would in effect be producing an upward redistribution of wealth from the poor to the rich by making those who are already among the worst-off members of humanity suffer the costs of the global transition between unsafe and safe energy regimes rather than allocating some of our own wealth to lighten their costs, thus keeping all the benefits for ourselves while dumping the pain of the energy transition on them. We would reduce carbon emissions in India, which in itself is a good thing, but we would do it by depriving poor Indians of any source of energy they could afford, and thereby effectively depriving them of energy. "A life without access to energy is a life of drudgery" (Practical Action 2013). We would be saving the climate by leaving the world's poorest in misery that they had no means to escape (Moellendorf 2014: 22).

We have now seen good reasons why we have three specific responsibilities: we should not use so much inexpensive fossil fuel ourselves that our emissions do not leave enough of the cumulative carbon budget to allow the poorest to rely for a little longer on inexpensive fossil fuel to satisfy their needs, we should not in the course of preventing the cumulative carbon budget from being exceeded price the poorest entirely out of the energy market, and we ought not to pursue a policy that creates benefits for most people but costs for the poorest. And we have seen that an alternative policy is readily available: we can contribute substantially to making alternative energy accessible and affordable for today's poorest. We must keep "the poor of the future in mind, but also today's poor, whose life on this earth is brief and who cannot keep on waiting" (Pope Francis 2015: 120).

2 Future Strangers and the Time-of-Last-Opportunity to Prevent a Disaster

Yet one group is even more vulnerable than the poorest living today: the poorest who will live in future. Our relationship with future generations is totally asymmetrical: we control the world in which they will have to begin to shape their lives, but they have no way to influence our decisions about them—indeed, even which individuals will be born is affected by us. In this context the people of the future, whoever they are, need two things from us. First, they need sustainable development now so that they later can have the resources for better lives than today's poorest. This is another powerful reason why we must urgently get alternative energy into the hands of today's poor rather than allowing them in desperation to use more fossil fuel and undercut their own development by injecting more carbon dioxide into the atmosphere. The best way to improve the lives of tomorrow's poor is to improve the lives of today's poor, who will bring them into the world and provide them with what nutrition and education they will get. Second, they need for us to bring climate change under control and to fix as firm a ceiling as we can on the disruptions that climate change will bring, especially in order to prevent disasters (Shue 2014a: 265; Hartzell-Nichols 2017). The necessity for us to act if they are to be spared extreme climate change is the basis for one crucial but underappreciated responsibility for us that I now want to explore.

The critical time to consider is not the date at which a disastrous event will begin to occur, which may be sometime in the future. The critical time is what we can call the Time-of-Last-Opportunity, that is, the last time at which it is—or was—still possible to prevent the disastrous effect in question, which for some effects may be now, and sadly for some disasters is already past. This is starkly and tragically embodied in the melting of the West Antarctic Ice Sheet [WAIS]. When I began to work on climate change in the early 1990s, the debates had already begun about what should be the target of mitigation efforts, and a rise in average global temperature of not more than 2°C beyond the pre-Industrial Revolution average temperature had not yet been politically anointed as the official goal. So, many activists said roughly, "Whatever the target is exactly, we must at least be sure not to pass any catastrophic thresholds, like the threshold for the melting of the West Antarctic Ice Sheet." But, sure enough, in 2014 two different teams of scientists converged on the conclusion that this melting is now irreversible—this Time-of-Last-Opportunity, the last chance to prevent this effect from becoming irreversible, has receded into history as a tragic lost opportunity (Sumner 2014; Joughin et al. 2014; Rignot et al. 2014). The kilometers-deep WAIS—vast mountains of frozen water—is already melting and will continue to melt, and from this additional water alone ocean levels will ultimately rise around 4 or 5 meters above their current level. The process of melting will most likely take two or three centuries, but we have no good reason to doubt that it will definitely happen (Meredith and Sommerkorn, forthcoming).

This will in itself be catastrophic for tens of millions of people who live in coastal cities and will be forced to abandon their homes. It will be at best deeply burdensome economically for their fellow citizens, who will bear the tax burden from the forced relocations and, in many cases, the influx into their communities of additional people who will need shelter and medical care and whose children will also need education, and the costs of building entire new cities as large as, say, Miami, New Orleans, Kolkata, Mumbai, and Shanghai, all of which will probably be substantially inundated within around 250 years, along with much of Bangladesh and numerous small island nations. Nevertheless, other catastrophic thresholds, known and unknown, certain and uncertain, may loom in the mists of the not very distant future—like various thresholds for the massive release of methane either from permafrost on land—releases are already occurring in Siberia—or from ocean depths, and the threshold for disruption of the Atlantic Meridional Overturning Circulation [AMOC] (Portnov et al. 2013; Caesar et al. 2018; Mooney 2018). The direct effects of the methane would be very brief compared to the effects of carbon dioxide, but even a brief surge of methane could, for instance, drive average global temperature past the thresholds for the melting of major additional bodies of ice, such as, most notably, Greenland's ice sheet (larger than WAIS), which would produce further extremely long-term, but large sea-level rise beyond that caused by the now-inevitable addition to the oceans of the water melted from the West Antarctica ice. Disruption of the AMOC would interrupt the European warming from the Gulf Stream and allow countries in Europe to cool toward the temperature to be expected from their latitude.

One can, I think, view the fact that whether profoundly important events—sometimes disastrous events—will occur centuries into the future will be determined by the choices made by the present set of generations as a fundamental kind of structural feature of the asymmetrical relationship between present generations and generations in the far future. It shows decisively in yet another way why the elements of our phenomenology of agency that Scheffler describes as "the primacy of near effects over remote effects" (Scheffler 2001: 39) and "the primacy of individual effects over group effects" (Scheffler 2001: 39) are profoundly mistaken.

But perhaps it would have been an unreasonable demand upon the set of generations living at one time, even at the Time-of-Last-Opportunity, to have expected them to have prevented even a disaster involving massive human losses, as avoiding the irreversible melting of the WAIS would have done—too much responsibility to be reasonable. A crescendo of reasoning, however, supports the conclusion that it would not have been too much to ask. The first two steps of reasoning are very familiar, so I will quickly hint at them and try to cast a little more tentative light on the third.

First, even when a threatening disaster is in no way one's own causal responsibility, if the disaster can be prevented at relatively modest cost, and the disaster is extreme, one ought to act to prevent it. This is the fundamental reasoning illustrated by the parable of the Good Samaritan. The Samaritan is in no way causally responsible for the man's being in the ditch. But the man cannot get out of the ditch without help, and help is easy for any passerby to give. One need not be committed to any kind of maximizing requirement, like a requirement that one should always perform the best available act in every situation, in order to believe simply that if on a particular occasion someone needs to be rescued from a bad situation, and one can do so with relatively little effort and cost, one ought to do it. Apart from any religious authority, this seems to be an element of common sense, although it is difficult to put one's finger on exactly why it seems so obvious.

I suspect that the common-sense rationale is something like a fundamental sense of proportionality: it seems absurd that one should allow such a great difficulty to persist when it would involve so little trouble to deal with it—it smacks of taking oneself ridiculously seriously to assign so much significance to avoiding so little trouble for oneself rather than relieving so much trouble for another person. But even granted the general principle, the question remains whether what it would have taken to have prevented the melting of WAIS would have constituted too much to ask of the set of generations living at one time.

Second, however, the climate change case is, as we have already seen, in fact not a case like the Good Samaritan in which "a threatening disaster is in no way one's own causal responsibility" if one belongs to a nation with high cumulative carbon emissions that are continuing. This is one point at which the intergenerational argument cannot be entirely separated from the international. One's responsibility to deal with intergenerational climate threats is affected by one's general responsibility for the occurrence of climate change, and such causal or historical responsibility varies across nations, very roughly according to the extent of their industrialization.

The basic reason is that the industrialization that enabled the developed countries to develop included a generally harmful kind of national-level externalization of environmental costs made possible by an extreme interpretation of sovereignty, which allowed industrializing nations to retain the benefits of industrialization—the wealth produced—and to dump the health and environmental costs onto the globe generally (Shue 2015). If one's nation has been contributing substantially to climate change and is at present still contributing, then one's nation's responsibility to contribute to the prevention of a disaster like the melting of the WAIS by reducing emissions is a negative responsibility to cease harming the climate system and to stop creating threats for members of future generations, not a positive responsibility to rescue future generations from a threat not of one's own making analogous to the Good Samaritan's (Chakravarty et al. 2009).

In general, most people think that such negative responsibility deserves high priority, and that where one is actively contributing to damage and harm, one's duty is to stop it, even if stopping it involves considerable costs. One has no right to continue creating threats to the lives and welfare of others, whoever they are. This consideration makes it reasonable that any one set of generations in a nation that has contributed substantially to climate change and is continuing to do so should already bear a considerable burden to stop making matters worse (Shue 2015). "Stopping" would be constituted by sharp reductions in emissions, which seem to have been precisely what would have been needed to prevent the inexorable melting of the WAIS.

The third reason why the burdens are not excessive for a single set of generations would arise when they were the ones with the last chance to avoid the addition of finality to the severity of the loss—when they were those alive at the time-of-last-opportunity to prevent a disaster. We have just seen that in responding to a time-of-last-opportunity the people in a nation with strong obligations to stop exacerbating climate change might be doing no more than, or only a little more than, they ought for other reasons already to have been doing in any case. Now I want to consider whether beyond other such prior grounds for action and beyond the sheer magnitude of the potential catastrophe in, say, numbers of rights thwarted and numbers of lives blighted in future from inaction now, it is additionally significant whether the potential agents are—or may be (Shue 2016)—the ones alive at the time-of-last-opportunity: the last opportunity to avoid sealing the virtual certainty of a disaster. It would be as if the Good Samaritan not only had caused the man to fall into the ditch but also somehow knew that he would be the last to pass that way before nightfall and that the stranger in the ditch could not make it through the night.

If in, say, 1992 leaders had realized that the generations then alive could still prevent the melting of the WAIS but that they were the last ones—that it was "now or never"—they not only should have expended the share of effort and expense that would be the fair share of any similar set of generations, but should have borne a heavier burden precisely because they were the last to have the opportunity (Karnein 2014). In an important battle one should do one's fair share every day, but if one could somehow know that the decisive day had arrived, and the outcome would be decided on this day, any ordinary person would think, I believe, that one should give even more on this day just because it is the last chance to win. But why? Why would its being a last chance matter beyond the magnitude of the disaster that it is the last chance to avoid?

In a way the value of the sacrifices everyone has already made on every other previous day depends on whether the sacrifices one makes on this day are adequate for victory. If they are adequate, all the sacrifices on all the other days will have led to victory; if not, they will have issued in defeat. It is as if at this point in time everything depends on the effort made on this climactic day. The present controls the past's value.

If one is fighting a fifteen-round fight, and has won seven rounds and lost seven, everything depends on who wins the fifteenth round. It seems reasonable to give it all you have got in the fifteenth round. And the generations alive at the time-of-last-opportunity to prevent a disaster seem to me to be analogously bound to make a maximum (non-suicidal) effort. One could think of them as unlucky to be alive at that time and to have to do so much, as the Good Samaritan could have peevishly thought, "Why me?"; or one can think of them as fortunate to live then and to be the ones who have the opportunity to accomplish so much for untold generations—to be the ones who made the difference.

Is there some fallacy or illusion here? This reasoning initially seems disturbingly similar to the reasoning that makes it so difficult to withdraw from a losing war. If one has been fighting a long but unsuccessful war, one has substantial "sunk costs"—substantial sacrifices have already been made. And one may think, if we withdraw now, it will all have been for naught, but if by fighting a little longer, we can turn it around and win, it will all have been worthwhile. And so pointless wars drag on and on. But I think that it could be perfectly valid to reason, if by fighting a little longer we can turn it around and win, it may all have been worthwhile. The usual mistake is automatically to assume that if one fights a little longer, one will win, when one has been losing all along—why is something suddenly going to change? So the fighter who thinks, "I have taken a considerable beating so far, but I have won half the rounds, and if I can win the last round, I will break the tie and win the fight," is not engaged in fallacious reasoning. He simply needs to be as sure as he can that he wins the last round by, if possible, fighting better than he has fought in any other round—maximum effort could indeed pay off. It seems similarly reasonable to expect the generations alive at the time-of-last-opportunity to prevent a disaster to do more than could be expected of other otherwise similar sets of generations, lest all previous efforts come to nothing, provided only that the further effort is not certainly futile.

If one misses the last opportunity to prevent a loss, that regressive change becomes irreversible and what is lost is irretrievable. I am not sure one can give any deeper reason why an irretrievable loss of a disastrous magnitude is vital to avoid, but one can add three brief conjectures, one about hope, one about past generations, and one about continuity in valuing.

First, before a change for the worse becomes irreversible, there is hope that it can be avoided, and hope itself can be precious. Irreversibility is the death of hope. The loss of hope represents, as Jonathan Schell wrote of extinction, a kind of second death: beyond the deaths of all the individuals, the death of the possibility of any more such individuals: "death cuts off life; extinction cuts off birth" (Schell 1982: 117). In the case of the WAIS we have lost a major battle (before we had even begun to fight). We have lost any hope of avoiding a major rise in sea level up every coast onto every continent and into scores of metropolises and countless villages (Oppenheimer and Glavovic, forthcoming). This is discouraging, and one thing that humanity cannot do without in the struggle to limit climate change is hope. We cannot succeed in preventing additional disasters unless we can lick our wounds and then return to the fight with hope and determination to succeed. Rationally, of course, the frustration of one specific hope, even such a major one, is no reason to abandon other specific hopes. And there are many more battles that we can win. But emotionally it is still a blow, for hope in itself is of value and to be preserved unless definitely ill-founded.

Those of us who understood or should have understood have already failed to prevent all climate change. The climate is changing now, and will change more through many tomorrows. These changes will be especially difficult to adapt to for those to come who command the fewest resources. But ahead lie many more important battles that can be won if people do not give up the fight and whose outcomes will determine crucially how much more severe and dangerous climate change becomes. One ought to keep hope alive for those generations of strangers who must make a life in the world we will have shaped and prevent as much irreversible decline in the livability of the planet as possible so that they can enjoy lives of dignity, not drudgery.

Second, one may have some additional responsibility to the people of the past who did what they should have to avoid the disaster, to keep their efforts from having been futile. Perhaps out of human solidarity one bears some responsibility to the people of the past as well as to the people of the future to preserve what reasonable humans—past, present, and future—value and struggle to preserve.

Third, the preceding arguments appeal primarily to the humanity and potential dignity of those to come and infer that one ought to bequeath them, at a very minimum, living conditions in which dignity is practically possible. Samuel Scheffler has more recently made the provocative suggestion that "the world of the future becomes, as it were, more like a party one had to leave early and less like a gathering of strangers" if one appreciates that "many of the things in our own lives that now matter to us would cease to do so or would come to matter less" if one were not confident that one will be succeeded by others who can and will value what we value (Scheffler 2013: 30 and 26). This resonates with Hannah Arendt's reflection on the other of the two greatest threats to humanity besides climate change, nuclear weapons: "man can be courageous only as long as he knows he is survived by those who are like him, that he fulfills a role in something more permanent than himself, 'the enduring chronicle of mankind,' as Faulkner once put it" (Arendt 1994: 421–2).

If either the thesis about the dependence of our valuing upon subsequent valuing by others or the thesis about the dependence of courage on a confidence in survival is correct, it provides an at least partly self-interested additional reason why we would be wise to leave a planet on which human life will not be nasty, brutish, and short, but will be lived in circumstances in which those who arrive at the party after we have departed will have the leisure and capacity to value and preserve much (at least) of what we value and try to preserve. This means at an absolute minimum that we must not allow conditions to become such that the struggle for mere survival becomes all-consuming, and that in turn requires that we stringently limit severe negative changes that would be irreversible. This is a further reason to act and to act even more energetically.

John Donne's thought rings true: we have reasons to believe that solidarity with distant strangers is possible, desirable, and even necessary.

ACKNOWLEDGMENTS

An earlier version was valuably critiqued by Simon Caney and Nicole Hassoun. Originally presented, in part, as a keynote for "Rights to a Green Future," Soesterberg, the Netherlands, sponsored by the European Science Foundation, and, in part, as the 2014 Kapuscinski Development Lecture at Trinity College, Dublin; I appreciate both invitations and comments received at each event.

NOTE

1. For a potentially even deeper connection to self-interest, see the final paragraphs of this chapter.

REFERENCES

Arendt, Hannah (1994 [1954]) "Europe and the Atom Bomb." In Jerome Kohn (ed.), *Essays in Understanding, 1930–1954: Formation, Exile, and Totalitarianism*. New York: Schocken Books, 418–22.

Ashford, Elizabeth (2007) "The Duties Imposed by the Human Right to Basic Necessities." In Thomas Pogge (ed.), *Freedom from Poverty as a Human Right: Who Owes What to the Very Poor?* Oxford University Press, 183–218.

Associated Press (2015) "Nigeria: Shell Agrees to Pay $83.5 Million for Oil Spills," New York Times, January7, https://www.nytimes.com/2015/01/07/world/africa/nigeria-shell-agrees-to-pay-835-million-for-oil-spills.html?rref=science/earth&module=Ribbon&version=context&region=Header&action=click&contentCollection=Environment&pgtype=article, accessed April 6, 2019.

Bassey, Nnimmo (2002) *We Thought It Was Oil, But It Was Blood*, Ibadan: Kraft Books, Ltd.

Bast, Elizabeth, Shakuntala Makhijani, Sam Pickard, and Shelagh Whitley (2014) *The Fossil Fuel Bailout: G20 Subsidies for Oil, Gas and Coal Exploration*, London: Overseas Development Institute and Washington: OilChange International.

Caesar, L., S. Rahmstorf, A. Robinson, et al. (2018) "Observed Fingerprint of a Weakening Atlantic Ocean Overturning Circulation," *Nature* 556: 191–6. doi:10.1038/s41586-018-0006-5.

Carbon Tracker Initiative (2013) *Unburnable Carbon 2013: Wasted Capital and Stranded Assets*, London: Carbon Tracker Initiative, http://www.carbontracker.org/wp-content/uploads/2014/09/Unburnable-Carbon-2-Web-Version.pdf , accessed April 9. 2019.

Carrington, Damian (2015) "Wealthiest Countries' Fossil Fuel Subsidies Equal to $1,000 for Each Citizen, IMF Says," The Guardian, August 4.

Chakravarty, Shoibal, Ananth Chikkatur, Heleen de Coninck, et al. (2009) "Sharing Global CO2 Emission Reductions among One Billion High Emitters." *Proceedings of the National Academy of Sciences* 106(29): 11884–8.

Ciais, Philippe, Christopher Sabine, Govindasamy Bala, et al. (2014) "Carbon and Other Biogeochemical Cycles." In Thomas F. Stocker, Dahe Qin, Gian-Kasper Plattner, et al. (eds.), *Climate Change 2013: The Physical Science Basis. Contribution of Working Group I to the Fifth Assessment Report of the Intergovernmental Panel on Climate Change*. Cambridge: Cambridge University Press, 465–570.

Collins, Matthew, Reto Knutti, Julie Arblaster, et al. (2014) "Long-Term Climate Change: Projections, Commitments and Irreversibility." In Thomas F. Stocker, Dahe Qin, Gian-Kasper

Plattner, et al. (eds.), *Climate Change 2013: The Physical Science Basis. Contribution of Working Group I to the Fifth Assessment Report of the Intergovernmental Panel on Climate Change*. Cambridge: Cambridge University Press, 1029–136.

Donne, John (1624) "Meditations upon our Human Condition." 17. In *Devotions upon Emergent Occasions*, 2nd edn London: Thomas Jones, 389–97.

Frame, David J., Adrian H. Macey, and Myles R. Allen (2014) "Cumulative Emissions and Climate Policy." *Nature Geoscience* 7: 692–3. doi:10.1038/ngeo2254.

Ge, Mengpin, Johannes Friedrich, and Thomas Damassa (2014) "6 Graphs Explain the World's Top 10 Emitters," Climate Insights Blog, 25 November. Washington: World Resources Institute, http://www.wri.org/blog/2014/11/6-graphs-explain-world%E2%80%99s-top-10-emitters, accessed April 6, 2019.

Gupta, Sanjeev, and Michael Keen (2015) "Global Energy Subsidies Are Big—About $5 Trillion Big," IMF Direct: The International Monetary Fund's Global Economy Forum, http://blog-imfdirect.imf.org/2015/05/18/global-energy-subsidies-are-big-about-us5-trillion-big/, accessed April 6, 2019.

Hartzell-Nichols, Lauren (2017) *A Climate of Risk: Precautionary Principles, Catastrophes, and Climate Change*, Abingdon and New York: Routledge.

Joughin, Ian, Benjamin E. Smith, and Brooke Medley (2014) "Marine Ice Sheet Collapse Potentially under Way for the Thwaites Glacier Basin, West Antarctica." *Science* 344: 735–8. doi:10.1126/science.1249055.

Karnein, Anja (2014) "Putting Fairness in its Place: Why There Is a Duty to Take Up the Slack." *Journal of Philosophy* 111: 593–607.

Kartha, Sivan, and Paul Baer (2015) *Zero Carbon Zero Poverty the Climate Justice Way: Achieving an Equitable Phase-Out of Carbon Emissions by 2050 While Protecting Human Rights*, Report 1 2015 V1 Feb. Dublin: Mary Robinson Foundation—Climate Justice, https://www.mrfcj.org/pdf/2015-02-05-Zero-Carbon-Zero-Poverty-the-Climate-Justice-Way.pdf ,accessed April 5, 2019.

Kartha, Sivan, Simon Caney, Navroz K. Dubash, and Greg Muttitt (2018 [corrected 2019]) "Whose Carbon Is Burnable? Equity Considerations in the Allocation of a 'Right to Extract'," *Climatic Change* 150: 117–29. doi:10.1007/s10584-018-2209-z.

Kondash, Andrew J., Nancy E. Lauer, and Avner Vengosh (2018) "The Intensification of the Water Footprint of Hydraulic Fracturing," *Science Advances* 4(8), eaar5982, 1–8. doi:10.1126/sciadv.aar5982.

Landberg, Reed, and Anna Hirtenstein (2018) "Coal Is Being Squeezed Out of Power by Cheap Renewables." Bloomberg, 19 June [corrected 21 June], https://www.bloomberg.com/news/articles/2018-06-19/coal-is-being-squeezed-out-of-power-industry-by-cheap-renewables, accessed April 7, 2019.

Lichtenberg, Judith (2014) *Distant Strangers: Ethics, Psychology, and Global Poverty* Cambridge: Cambridge University Press.

McGlade, Christopher, and Paul Ekins (2015) "The Geographical Distribution of Fossil Fuels Unused When Limiting Global Warming to 2°C," *Nature* 517: 187–90 [+ "Methods"]. doi:10.1038/nature14016.

Meredith, Samuel, and Martin Sommerkorn (forthcoming) "Polar Regions." In H.-O. Pörtner, D. C. Roberts, V. Masson-Delmotte, et al. (eds.), *IPCC Special Report on the Ocean and Cryosphere in a Changing Climate*, Cambridge: Cambridge University Press, ch. 3.

Moellendorf, Darrel (2014) *The Moral Challenge of Dangerous Climate Change: Values, Poverty, and Policy*, Cambridge: Cambridge University Press.

Mooney, Chris (2018) "The Oceans' Circulation Hasn't Been This Sluggish in 1,000 Years. That's Bad News." Washington Post, 11 April. https://www.washingtonpost.com/news/energy-environment/wp/2018/04/11/the-oceans-circulation-hasnt-been-this-sluggish-in-1000-years-thats-bad-news/?utm_term=.3be3b0282343, accessed April 7, 2019.

Oppenheimer, Michael, and Bruce Glavovic (forthcoming) " Sea Level Rise and Implications for Low Lying Islands, Coasts and Communities." In H.-O. Pörtner, D. C. Roberts, V. Masson-Delmotte, et al. (eds.), IPCC Special Report on the Ocean and Cryosphere in a Changing Climate, Cambridge: Cambridge University Press, ch. 4.

Parker, Geoffrey (2014) Global Crisis: War, Climate Change and Catastrophe in the Seventeenth Century. New Haven, CT: Yale University Press.

Pierrehumbert, R.T. (2013) "Cumulative Carbon and Just Allocation of the Global Carbon Commons," Chicago Journal of International Law 13: 527–48.

Pope Francis (2015) Laudato Si': Encyclical Letter of the Holy Father Francis on Care for Our Common Home, para. 162. http://w2.vatican.va/content/francesco/en/encyclicals/documents/papa-francesco_20150524_enciclica-laudato-si.html, accessed April 6, 2019.

Portnov, Alexey, Andrew J. Smith, Jürgen Mienert, et al. (2013) "Offshore Permafrost Decay and Massive Seabed Methane Escape in Water Depths >20m at the South Kara Sea Shelf," Geophysical Research Letters 40: 3962–67. doi:10.1002/grl.50735.

Practical Action (2013) Poor People's Energy Outlook 2013: Energy for Community Services, Rugby: Practical Action Publishing Ltd.

Rignot, E., J. Mouginot, M. Morlighem, H. Seroussi, and B. Scheuchl (2014) "Widespread, Rapid Grounding Line Retreat of Pine Island, Thwaites, Smith, and Kohler Glaciers, West Antarctica, from 1992 to 2011." Geophys. Res. Lett. 41: 3502–9. doi:10.1002/2014GL060140.

Scheffler, Samuel (2001 [1995]) "Individual Responsibility in a Global Age." In Boundaries and Allegiances: Problems of Justice and Responsibility in Liberal Thought, Oxford: Oxford University Press, 32–47.

Scheffler, Samuel (2013) Death & the Afterlife, ed. Niko Kolodny. New York and Oxford: Oxford University Press.

Schell, Jonathan (1982) The Fate of the Earth. New York: Alfred A. Knopf, Part II.

Shue, Henry (2014a [2010]) "Deadly Delays, Saving Opportunities: Creating a More Dangerous World?" In Climate Justice: Vulnerability and Protection. Oxford: Oxford University Press, 263–86.

Shue, Henry (2014b [1992]) "The Unavoidability of Justice." In Climate Justice: Vulnerability and Protection. Oxford: Oxford University Press, 27–46.

Shue, Henry (2015) "Historical Responsibility, Harm Prohibition, and Preservation Requirement: Core Practical Convergence on Climate Change," Moral Philosophy and Politics 2(1): 7–31. doi:10.1515/mop-2013-0009.

Shue, Henry (2016) "Uncertainty as the Reason for Action: Last Opportunity and Future Climate Disaster," Global Justice: Theory Practice Rhetoric, Special Issue on Global Justice and Climate, 8: 86–103, https://www.theglobaljusticenetwork.org/global/index.php/gjn/article/view/89/65, accessed April 6, 2019.

Shue, Henry (2017) "Climate Dreaming: Negative Emissions, Risk Transfer, and Irreversibility," Journal of Human Rights and Environment 8: 203–16. doi:10.4337/jhre.2017.02.02.

Shue, Henry (2020) Basic Rights: Subsistence, Affluence, and U.S. Foreign Policy, 40th anniversary edn. Princeton, NJ: Princeton University Press.

Sumner, Thomas (2014) "No Stopping the Collapse of West Antarctic Ice Sheet," Science 344: 683.

United States, Environmental Protection Agency (2017) *Hydraulic Fracturing for Oil and Gas: Impacts from the Hydraulic Fracturing Water Cycle on Drinking Water Resources in the United States*, EPA-600-R-16-236ES. Washington DC: EPA.

Vidal, John (2015) "Niger Delta Communities to Sue Shell in London for Oil Spill Compensation," The Guardian, 7 January, https://www.theguardian.com/environment/2015/jan/07/niger-delta-communities-to-sue-shell-in-london-for-oil-spill-compensation, accessed April 6, 2019.

WEBSITES

www.trillionthtonne.org, accessed September 29, 2019.

World Resources Institute, CAIT Climate Data Explorer. http://cait2.wri.org/historical/Country%20GHG%20Emissions?indicator[]=Total GHG Emissions Excluding Land-Use Change and Forestry&indicator[]=Total GHG Emissions Including Land-Use Change and Forestry&year[]=2014&sortIdx=NaN&chartType=geo, accessed April 6, 2019.

FURTHER READING

Berners-Lee, Mike (2019) *There Is No Planet B: A Handbook for the Make or Break Years*, Cambridge: University of Cambridge Press.

Bond, Kingsmill (2018) *2020 Vision: Why You Should See Peak Fossil Fuels Coming*, London: Carbon Tracker Initiative, https://www.carbontracker.org/reports/2020-vision-why-you-should-see-the-fossil-fuel-peak-coming/, accessed April 8, 2019.

Caney, Simon (2019) "Justice and Posterity." In Ravi Kanbur and Henry Shue (eds.), *Climate Justice: Integrating Economics and Philosophy*. Oxford: Oxford University Press, 157–74.

Geden, Oliver (2018) "Politically Informed Advice for Climate Action," *Nature Geoscience*, 11: 378–83. doi:10.1038/s415611-018-0143-3.

Ghosh, Amitav (2016) *The Great Derangement: Climate Change and the Unthinkable*. Chicago: University of Chicago Press.

Helm, Dieter (2017) *Burn Out: The Endgame for Fossil Fuels*. New Haven, CT: Yale University Press.

McKinnon, Catriona (2012) *Climate Change and Future Justice: Precaution, Compensation, and Triage*. London: Routledge.

Nolt, John (2019) "Long-Term Climate Justice." In Ravi Kanbur and Henry Shue (eds.), *Climate Justice: Integrating Economics and Philosophy*. Oxford: Oxford University Press, 230–46.

Oreskes, Naomi, and Erik M. Conway (2014) *The Collapse of Western Civilization: A View from the Future*. New York: Columbia University Press.

Pissarskoi, Eugen (2019) "The Controllability Precautionary Principle: Justification of a Climate Policy Goal Under Uncertainty." In Ravi Kanbur and Henry Shue (eds.), *Climate Justice: Integrating Economics and Philosophy*. Oxford: Oxford University Press, 188–208.

Robinson, Mary, with Caitríona Palmer (2018) *Climate Justice: Hope, Resilience and the Fight for a Sustainable Future*, London: Bloomsbury.

Steffen, Will, Johan Rockström, Katherine Richardson, et al. (2018) "Trajectories of the Earth System in the Anthropocene," *Proceedings of the National Academy of Sciences of the United States of America [PNAS]* 115(33): 8252–9. doi:10.1073/pnas.1810141115.

Wallace-Wells, David (2019) *The Uninhabitable Earth: A Story of the Future*. London: Allen Lane.

PART V

JUST GLOBAL INSTITUTIONS

CHAPTER 14

THE HUMAN RIGHT TO DEMOCRACY AND THE PURSUIT OF GLOBAL JUSTICE

PABLO GILABERT

1 INTRODUCTION

THIS chapter addresses two interconnected questions about human rights and the pursuit of global justice: Is there a human right to democracy? How does the achievement of human rights, including the human right to democracy, contribute to the pursuit of global justice? In Section 2, the chapter answers the first question in the affirmative. It identifies three reasons for favoring democracy and explores the significance of those reasons for defending it as a human right. It answers important worries that acknowledging a human right to democracy would lead to intolerance and lack of respect for peoples' self-determination, exaggerate the importance of democracy for securing other rights, generalize institutional arrangements that only work in some contexts, and tie human rights to specific ideas of freedom and equality that do not have the same universal appeal and urgency. In Section 3, the chapter answers the second question. It distinguishes between basic and non-basic global justice and argues that democracy is significant for both. It claims that the fulfillment of human rights constitutes basic global justice, explains how a human right to democracy has significance for the legitimacy of international besides domestic institutions, and shows how forms of global democracy and the exploration of cosmopolitan and humanist commitments underlying human rights may enable and motivate the pursuit of non-basic demands of global justice (such as those concerning socioeconomic equality). The key claim in the chapter is that the fulfillment of the human right to democratic political empowerment is crucial for the pursuit of global justice.

2 THE HUMAN RIGHT TO DEMOCRACY

2.1 General Case for Democracy

A system of political decision-making is democratic when those subject to it have effective and equal opportunities to participate in it and shape its results. There are at least three important reasons for favoring democracy over other ways of organizing decision-making structures that do not involve this idea of effective political equality. That democracy is preferable on these reasons does not mean that no democracy ever fails to honor them. Actual democracies can be better or worse at honoring these concerns; the point is that feasible nondemocratic regimes are likely to do worse. Here are the three reasons, stated as features of democracy:

(a) *Expressive recognition and respect (Intrinsic significance)*: Democracy involves an expressive recognition of and respect for human beings as agents with the capacity for political judgment and self-determination.
(b) *Strong accountability (Instrumental significance 1)*: Democracy involves strong mechanisms of accountability of decision-makers to decision-takers.
(c) *Epistemic enhancement (Instrumental significance 2)*: Democratic rights, institutions, and practices help political agents to identify and justify to themselves and to each other what political principles, agendas, and policies are appropriate.

The first consideration addresses the intrinsic value of a political decision-making procedure, and the other two capture its instrumental value: the former concerns how people treat each other within the practice of decision-making, and the latter concerns the issue whether decision-making tracks the interests or good of those subject to it. An underlying principle is, of course, that the worth and interests of all subjects deserves equal respect and concern within some range.

These three kinds of considerations should be familiar, even if I formulate them in my own words.[1] My concern in this chapter will be to show how they link to the theory and practice of human rights. I think that the three reasons are very important, even though in the context of human rights the focus had tended to be on (b). Democracy's strong accountability certainly is crucial, as it involves a powerful incentive mechanism for decision-makers to cater for the interests of decision-takers (they may be sacked if they do not). But the other features are important as well. The intrinsic dimension in (a) is crucial: an adult person's self-respect may be deeply wounded if they are treated as a second-class citizen, if their public status in their social world is that of someone who cannot or should not participate on equal terms with every other adult in the shaping of the coercive rules that frame that world. The epistemic dimension in (c) is important (inter alia) because we need strong political freedoms to gain understanding of the political process via active experience in it, to deliberate with each other about our political views so as to make up our minds, reach agreements or narrow disagreement, find fair compromises, and develop less crude or biased pictures about what we and others need and are entitled to. Of course, these features interact. For example, political agents with enhanced political knowledge will have more of the information they need to hold decision-makers accountable; and the opportunity to do the latter will be an incentive to seek political information. Agents who recognize each other as able to make political judgments and as worthy of political self-determination will treat each other in certain ways, for example by pursuing forms of accountability and public debate that involve appropriate levels of civility.

2.2 Developing the Case for a Human Right to Democracy

2.2.1 *Is Democracy a Human Right?*

The three reasons for democracy mentioned support the view that a society that is democratic is in some respects more just than a society that is not. But not every right of justice is a human right. In general, a right is a legitimate claim that one person can make against others.[2] A right is justified when the conditions and interests its fulfillment protects or promotes, and more generally the reasons it is based on, are sufficiently important to warrant negative or positive duties on the part of certain duty-bearers. Is the right to democracy also a moral human right? This depends on whether it has the standard features that characterize moral human rights, such as being universal, having high normative priority or great normative weight, being primarily a critical rather than a positive standard, and being often at least in part to be pursued through political action and institutions. I believe that a right to democracy has these features. The last two features are obviously held by a right to democracy: it is a right to be largely articulated institutionally and it can function as a critical standard for appraising different social structures even when those structures do not explicitly recognize it and when people do not currently endorse it. The real difficulty is to show that there is a right to democracy that has the features of universality and high priority. Is democracy a right that holds for everyone in the contemporary world? Is its pursuit a matter of global concern? Does it have the great weight that other, less controversial human rights such as the civil right to religious freedom or the socioeconomic right to subsistence have?[3]

To show that a right to democracy has these features I will proceed dialectically, by addressing the four most important recent challenges to the idea that there is a human right to democracy (hereafter HRD). All of these challenges precisely deny that the right to democracy is both universal and of high priority. Underlying the polemical engagement with these challenges there is a positive argument for a HRD. It is in fact quite simple, and can be stated succinctly. The main idea is that we should accept a HRD because (at least contemporary) social life involves circumstances that make considerations (a)–(c) (stated in Section 2.1) practically relevant in a widespread and urgent way. These common circumstances include the tendencies to (i) exclude groups of people from political power and other social advantages, (ii) be self-serving and biased when wielding decision-making power, (iii) disagree on moral matters, and (iv) have limited knowledge of the needs and views of others. These tendencies impose standard threats: wielders of political power may monopolize control of social regulations, brand some persons as second-class citizens, impose agendas and policies that fail to take account of the basic needs and the normative views of others, and render many of those subject to the resulting social order impotent to evaluate and to change it. The three dimensions of democracy are essential to respond to these threats. When they are in place, political power wielders are more likely to guarantee basic conditions of respect and concern for all persons. To the extent that people are recognized as having irreplaceable political status as equals, they are able to keep decision-makers in check, and they have the capability to join the public debate about what is the just way to arrange their social lives, it is that much harder to block their achievement of a decent life of basic human dignity. Given these threats and the significance of dimensions (a)–(c) to respond to them, when people can be but are not granted democratic political opportunities, they are seriously wronged: they are denied what they are owed to live a decent or basically dignified life. Sections 2.2.2–2.2.5 flesh out this argument.

2.2.2 *Toleration, Peoples' Self-Determination, and Intervention*

The first challenge says that accepting a HRD would lead to supporting problematic forms of international intervention. Since a human right merits global concern and action, pursuing the fulfillment of a HRD would license forceful international intervention in countries that are not democratic, and this would involve intolerance toward other forms of political organization and the violation of peoples' self-determination. If we value international toleration and peoples' self-determination, we should be skeptical about a HRD.

Each key aspect of this challenge is problematic. Although the ideas of toleration and peoples' self-determination are, of course, valuable, they do not support the denial of a HRD, and the pursuit of the latter does not require the obliteration of the former. Regarding toleration, there is the immediate worry that in nondemocratic countries governments do not tolerate a wide range of political actions by their members. Why accept an entitlement to toleration for a regime that does not tolerate its own people?[4] It would not help to focus on the toleration of *peoples* as the fundamental concern. Human rights are primarily held by individual human beings, not by peoples, societies, or states. On the other hand, the ideal of toleration is quite vague. To be made precise it needs a substantive account of the conditions that must be met for the conduct of other agents to be acceptable even if they are different from one's own.[5] I do not deny the importance of the value of toleration and that it could be given a reasonable construal. But clearly any plausible account of what may be tolerated will be constrained by the recognition of the independent and high-priority rights that people have, and this surely includes their human rights. One of the obvious functions of human rights is precisely to set reasonable limits to claims of toleration. So we should be skeptical about limits on an account of the content of human rights that draws on toleration; the direction of limitation is the opposite.

Consider next the idea of peoples' self-determination. First, there is the obvious but important point that there is no necessary conflict between the fulfillment of a people's right to self-determination and the HRD, as a people can determine itself while being democratically ordered. Second, notice also that the problem of taking peoples rather than people as the unit of fundamental concern applies here as well, and this undermines the force of the invocation of collective self-determination in the face of violation of a HRD. If in a certain circumstance the invocations of the two claims collide, we should consider whether catering for individuals' interest in their independence as a group should be qualified, or at least joined by serious attempts to pursue the honoring of their interest in democratic political opportunities. The multiple considerations spelled out in this chapter in favor of a HRD also tell in favor of such combination (which does not automatically ground a permission for foreign intervention—see two paragraphs below). If the members of a people are not themselves self-determining, then the self-determination of the group has less moral standing: there is less self-determination when the members of a group are blocked from shaping its political life than when they are allowed to control the group they constitute. This does not entail that there is no morally relevant way in which a society can be self-determining if it is not democratic. The point is that an invocation of collective self-determination cannot mute the concern with democratic freedom.

There is, then, a serious and internal problem with bypassing the wills of the members, as nondemocratic regimes do, and then proceeding to claim that that group's will (that is, the will of the rulers) expresses them.[6] The rulers of the nondemocratic country may object that their subjects themselves accept the nondemocratic nature of their government. But this maneuver would be problematic on several counts. First, how do we know that the subjects prefer a nondemocratic system if they are not allowed to fully participate in the political process? In the absence of strong accountability, they may be afraid to express their views fully even if they are allowed to speak publicly. Second, without experience in wielding political power, how do they themselves manage to form reflective judgments about political justice? Nondemocratic regimes are epistemically deficient. Third, if the legitimation of the regime appeals to what the people living under it take to be just, then why deprive the people of the kind of regime (i.e. a democracy) whose procedures and outcomes are really powered by what the people think?[7] A view of collective self-determination that crushes the political self-determination of the members of the collective does not take seriously the freedom of human beings.

The worry about forceful international intervention is real, however. Such interventions often fail to achieve their publicly avowed goals, involve serious violations of other rights, and cement relations of arrogant patronage. But these problems do not really show that there is no HRD unless we assume that if something is a human right, then its violation makes international forceful intervention permissible. And this assumption goes against the grain of the legal and political practice of human rights, and it is in any case morally unwarranted. Justifiable intolerance toward human rights violation need not be coupled with international coercion. There are other options.

As many critics have argued in response to Rawls's narrow construal of human rights in terms of the conditions for coercive intervention, there are many ways in which domestic and international action can respond to human rights violations; "human rights serve *many* international roles, some of them unconnected to enforceability" (Nickel (2007: 101).[8] Forceful intervention is just one kind of response, which is likely to be warranted only in extreme cases (such as genocide), and even then only as a result of a delicate balancing of many considerations. Human rights are primarily obligatory goals that should inform various forms of national and international political action. They are not primarily triggers of international coercion.

This is as it should be, as human rights are best achieved from the ground up. Institutional structures that fulfill the HRD are likely to be best generated primarily domestically, as the achievement of a people's members' own political struggle. This, of course, does not mean that international solidarity is not warranted.[9] At a minimum, features of the international institutional order that foreseeably and avoidably create means and incentives for domestic elites to impose nondemocratic regimes on their people should be eliminated.[10] The dilemma between aggressive international interventionism and international passivity is a spurious one.[11] We can understand how belief in something like it may have arisen as a result of the recent history of American military adventurism, which has sometimes been carried out in the name of democracy. But we can reject such aggressive adventurism without letting down fellow human beings in other countries who are fighting for their rights. Human rights indeed ground global concern. In the case of democracy, such concern can be expressed in innumerable ways that stop short of intervention. Several forms are already being explored, from protests and mutual assistance by pro-democracy social movements in different countries to attempts at persuasion in several forums of international civil society, to economic and political incentives such as making membership in advantageous regional organizations conditional upon democratic reforms.[12]

2.2.3 *Instrumental Considerations about the Protection of Other Rights*

One of the strongest defenses of the HRD is that we should accept it because democracy helps prevent unacceptable outcomes in terms of uncontroversial human rights, such as famines and brutally oppressive tyrannies. This instrumental argument relies on aspects (b) and (c) of democracy: where there is a functioning democracy, decision-makers tend to avoid engaging in serious abuses because they anticipate that if they do so, it will be known and discussed, and they will be held accountable. Sen (2009: ch. 16) famously argues that because of incentive mechanisms such as these, there has been no famine in a functioning democracy. So, if we want to avoid the underfulfillment of civil and socio-economic human rights, we should accept a HRD. Democracy inherits the great weight of the rights it protects.

This instrumental argument for a HRD has recently come under fire from Joshua Cohen.[13] Cohen's first challenge says that we can imagine a regime that involves collective self-determination, is not democratic, and protects human rights. Collective self-determination involves three conditions:

1. "[B]inding collective decisions result from, and are accountable to, a political process that represents the diverse interests and opinions of those who are subject to the society's laws and regulations and expected to comply with them."
2. "[R]ights to dissent from, and appeal, those collective decisions are assured for all."
3. "[G]overnment normally provides public explanations for its decisions, and those explanations—intended to show why decisions are justified—are founded on a conception of the common good of the whole society" (Cohen 2010: 357–8).[14]

These conditions can be fulfilled even if there is political inequality (for example, if members of a certain ethnic group are denied access to decision-making positions in government). As long as there are mechanisms of representation of interests, dissent and appeal, and explanations that track fundamental interests such as those protected by basic civil and socioeconomic rights, the human rights of those partially excluded are not violated. They do not have a human right to be treated as political equals.

A concern about this view is whether it is realistic to expect that conditions 1–3 will reliably be satisfied, and lead to the protection of people's fundamental interests, without political equality. It is not enough to wonder whether it is *possible* for this to happen. For example, an enlightened despot certainly *could* exist who satisfies these conditions without democratic accountability. But it would be irresponsible to determine what political rights to recognize on the basis of just this possibility. We must also consider the *relative probability* that different political arrangements will protect fundamental interests. And it seems that the burden of proof is here on the side of those who entertain the avoidance of democracy. Given the overwhelming wealth of historical evidence about the tendency to bias and abuse of political power, it is imprudent for agents not to favor regimes including mechanisms of strong accountability through equal rights to affect the political process of the kind only democracy affords.[15] As historical experience concerning manual workers and women suggests, those who lack equal and effective rights to affect the political process are more likely to be ignored by decision-makers. Their interests are less likely to be duly represented, and they are less likely to be consulted or offered explanations. And to be consulted, allowed to dissent and appeal, and given explanations is not enough. People also have reason to be able to sack decision-makers who do not in fact cater to the fundamental interests they pledge to track. Thus, instrumental considerations regarding the fulfillment of civil and socioeconomic rights in principle tell in favor of accepting strong political rights.

Cohen has a second challenge. He worries that:

it is not clear how strong a case we have for the claim that a society that ensured a relatively rich set of human rights, including conditions of collective self-determination short of democracy, would nevertheless be so clearly unacceptable as to bear so much argumentative weight in the case for a human right to democracy.

(Cohen 2010: 371)

The instrumental argument for democracy discussed here assumes that it is the lack of specifically democratic rights that is crucial when explaining the occurrence of famine, tyranny, etc. But, Cohen notes, when these terrible outcomes ensue, we often find other factors that might be explanatorily relevant, such as weak or absent rule of law, freedom of the press, and collective self-determination.

Does this challenge succeed at overturning the received wisdom that in the absence of democracy the fundamental interests of all are less likely to be reliably protected? We cannot answer this question without looking at the empirical evidence. In a recent paper, Christiano (2011) has argued that, in fact, the empirical evidence available supports the instrumental case for democracy. The empirical debate is set to continue.[16] I would like to add, however, that we should not put endorsement of a HRD aside until the empirical dispute is settled. First, the instrumental argument should not be construed in unduly strong terms. From a practical standpoint, to support democracy instrumentally we do not need to find that famines and other terrible outcomes can only occur when and only because democracy is absent. It is enough if the evidence shows that democracy is an important (even if not the only) relevant contributory factor, so that in its absence the likelihood of such conditions increases significantly. Second, in the face of uncertainty about the precise composition of the explanatory factors leading to severe underfulfillment of human rights, and given that so far research appears to show that democracy is an important factor,[17] it is only prudent to be risk averse and err on the side of keeping the list of rights ample (including democracy besides the rule of law, freedom of the press, and the other important factors). It would be a reckless bet to choose a nondemocratic regime before the empirical evidence develops enough to actually tip the balance away from the received wisdom that those with less political power are less secure in the enjoyment of their rights.

2.2.4 *Institutional Specificity and the Problem of Generalization*

Another challenge to a HRD is that it may lack universal application and high priority because it relies on too specific an account of the institutions of collective self-determination needed to protect other, uncontroversial human rights (such as basic civil, socioeconomic, and other political rights). In some—perhaps most—cases, democratic institutions will likely do best, but in some cases they may not. Beitz (2009: section 26) has recently pressed this charge, arguing that we cannot generalize the instrumental argument discussed in Section 2.2.3 because there may be cases of nondemocratic societies in which either (i) economic conditions are such that the instauration of democracy may not lead to a stable regime or might involve lower protection of uncontroversial rights than some alternative, feasible regime; or (ii) the political culture is one in which the strong political equality that HRD involves is widely rejected, while the less demanding form of collective self-determination discussed by Cohen enjoys wide allegiance. I think that the most serious worry concerns (i). As stated, the second puzzle risks a conventionalist view of the validity of human rights that is incompatible with seeing them as critical standards. The existence of rights does not depend on people believing that they exist. Slavery would involve a violation of rights even if most people (including the slaves) did not think there is a right against it. Such beliefs are relevant for the feasibility of implementing rights in the short term, but that is a different matter.

Let us grant, for the sake of argument, that in the short term the instauration of democracy in a certain country would likely lead to higher costs in terms of other, uncontroversial rights than the instauration of an authoritarian regime that approximates the features of collective self-determination discussed in Section 2.2.3. How could a defender of a HRD respond? The first thing to say is that the high priority of human rights should not be interpreted too narrowly, as meaning that, to have it, a demand should be immediately and fully implementable. Human rights set up a normative agenda for the political future. What is crucial is that we recognize them as setting political goals of great importance, which we can achieve sometime in the future and should pursue to the extent that we reasonably can from now on. When we encounter circumstances in which an obligatory goal cannot be achieved, we should acknowledge *dynamic duties* to progressively change them so that the obligatory goal becomes achievable.[18] Cases like the one we are here granting for the sake of argument can be seen as part of the nonideal theory of human rights. Such nonideal theory would depend on an ideal theory that sets the optimal feasible targets of long-term reform, and it would deal with cases of partial compliance and conditions in which the fulfillment of the ideal demands is not immediately feasible. Given that democratic regimes are feasible in the long-term, and that (as Beitz recognizes) they are more likely than the alternatives to reliably protect the whole set of other urgent rights when stable, we should take them as the target for long-term reform. But since in the case under consideration we face nonideal circumstances, we should adopt a transitional standpoint that explores the process rendering the final target accessible. Such a process need not start with an immediate push for democratic institutions if the likely outcomes are worse on balance.

Second, the long-term view favoring democracy is not idle in the short term. It would have immediate bite in at least two ways. First, it would impose high evidentiary standards for choosing nondemocratic alternatives in the short term. The presumption would be that democracy should be pursued unless compelling evidence is given that an alternative regime would be better overall in the short term. Second, it would demand that among the several feasible nondemocratic regimes that would do better, in the short term, at catering for other rights, we choose the one that is most likely to ease the transition to democracy in the future.[19] Thus, the goal of achieving democracy plays an immediate role in determining whether we should favor a nondemocratic regime in the short term, and which one we should favor if we must indeed favor some.

Third, including democracy in the long-term political agenda of human rights would not only be reasonable, given its likelihood to do better than the alternatives in the instrumental ways discussed so far once a stable form of it is achieved. In addition, democracy has intrinsic significance. An account of collective self-determination that is nondemocratic (accepting, for example, unequal rights to vote or hold public office for people of different ethnic, religious, or other groups) violates the normative individualism and the commitment to some forms of equality and liberty that are constitutive of the human rights perspective. I will explore this point in Section 2.2.5. But if this is correct, a consequence for the present discussion is that even if we construe human rights as making immediate demands of full implementation, the problem discussed in the hypothetical case would not be whether democracy is a right, but what is its relative weight when other rights (such as certain civil and socioeconomic rights that would be better served by a nondemocratic regime) conflict with it in practice.[20] (It would also not need to be an issue whether democracy involves a high right: Democracy could be a member of a package of high priority rights even if in some circumstances its implementation has less priority than that of other rights in the same package.) The loss in terms of the intrinsic value of democracy leaves a reminder when a different regime is chosen that does better in the short term with respect to instrumental considerations concerning other rights. We are here facing a tragic choice rather a mere trade-off, and thus that reminder must be acknowledged. The first and second points mentioned above then reapply, this time regarding the future satisfaction of what has been left out in terms of the intrinsic concern.[21]

Fourth, and finally, there is the issue of institutional specificity. The problem with the hypothetical case discussed here may be less likely to arise if we notice that the HRD can be stated at different levels of institutional abstraction. At the level of principle, HRD can be stated in a relatively vague way that captures the key idea of political equality. The specific institutional form that political equality should take depends on the circumstances of the context in hand.[22] So if one specific institutional form of democracy (say, a certain electoral system, or organization of the relation between the legislative, executive, and judicial branches of government) is not likely to be stable in a certain context, this does not entail that democracy as such has no immediate stable application. Perhaps another specific articulation of political equality will be immediately stable. This *argumentative triangulation* (responding to the immediate unworkability of a certain institutional implementation by moving up one level to the relevant animating principle and then envisaging alternative respecifications of it to see whether one is workable) must be pursued before moving to the concessive, nonideal parts of the exercise discussed above. When we think about the universality of democracy, we should ask whether the key principle has general hold, not whether any of its specific incarnations is generalizable.[23]

2.2.5 *Intrinsic Considerations of Freedom and Equality*

The intrinsic argument for democracy supports democracy because it involves an organization of the ultimate political decision-making structures and practices of society such that through them human persons express the respect and recognition due to human persons given their capacity to form political judgments and determine themselves politically. Beings with these capacities (and most human beings have them to a sufficient degree—although, of course, they differ beyond it) are seriously harmed when they are treated as political puppets or inferiors. This thought involves ideas of political freedom and equality. Democratic institutions aim at giving the adults subject to the political system equal political freedoms, which amount to equal and effective opportunities to participate in shaping the political process and its outcomes. A political system is procedurally unfair if it gives some of its subjects more rights of participation than others: all agents with the capacity of political judgment and self-determination deserve equal rights. Of course, those capacities can and should be developed. And democracies will be in one way better, or deeper, to the extent that they facilitate such development.

The intrinsic argument for a HRD is more controversial than the instrumental one. To see this, we can address another important recent challenge posed by Cohen. The worry is that in invoking ideas of freedom and equality, this defense of a HRD may present an unduly maximalist view of human rights in which the distinction between human rights and justice is simply erased. But intuitively we think such a distinction exists, that human rights are only a proper subset of what justice demands, and that this distinction is important for the role of human rights as especially weighty demands of both domestic and global political action. Ideas of freedom and equality seem better located at the complement of human rights in the wider set of demands of liberal-egalitarian justice, which do not so readily seem to have the kind of global priority that human rights are meant to have. A right to democracy is then best seen not as a human right, but as a wider (less weighty, not so uncontroversially universal) demand of justice.

I discuss the details of Cohen's challenge elsewhere.[24] Here I want to make three positive, but related points. The first is that ideas of freedom and equality are already operative in the founding document of the contemporary human rights political practice, the Universal Declaration, and that it is natural to see them as helping in making the intrinsic argument for a HRD. Cohen (2010: 365) takes political democracy to depend on the following two ideas: (a) "each member is understood as entitled to be treated with equal respect, and therefore as entitled to the same basic rights, regardless of social position"; (b) "the basis of equality lies, in particular, in . . . political capacity: we owe equal respect to those who have sufficient capacity to understand the requirements of mutually beneficial and fair cooperation, grasp their rationale, and follow them in their conduct." Now consider the Preamble and Articles 1 and 2 of the Universal Declaration. The Preamble opens by referring to the "recognition of the inherent dignity and of the equal and inalienable rights of all members of the human family" as being "the foundation of freedom, justice and peace in the world." Article 1 says that "[a]ll human beings are born free and equal in dignity and rights," and "are endowed with reason and conscience and should act toward one another in a spirit of brotherhood," and Article 2 claims that "everyone is entitled to all the rights and freedoms set forth in this Declaration without distinction of any kind, such as race, colour, sex, language, religion, political or other opinion, national or social origin, property, birth or other status." These three framing clauses evidently support an idea of equal respect of the kind envisaged in (a), according to which all should be seen as equal in rights regardless of their social position and background. Article 1's reference to certain cognitive and volitional endowments, if applied to human adults who are not severely mentally impaired (i.e. those in whom the endowments are clearly present), also identifies aspects of the idea of political capacity targeted by (b). If all such human adults are free and equal in dignity and rights, and have reason and conscience, and can (given that they ought to) act toward each other in a spirit of brotherhood, then arguably they have enough political capacity to be responsible citizens in a democratic polity. These points can clearly be used to support the idea that a HRD has intrinsic significance.

Could the ideas mentioned be reasonably accepted, in global public reasoning, by people who disagree in their comprehensive religious, moral, and philosophical outlooks, and who have also disagreements about what justice in the wide sense demands? The second point is that the ideas of freedom and equality just mentioned are relatively thin in two ways that are relevant for making a case for their universality and high priority. The first way concerns the levels of depth of ideas and principles in normative argument. The ideas of freedom and equality mentioned could be intermediate premises by reference to which we can justify the view that political decision-making should be democratic. But such intermediate premises can in turn be defended by appeal to different and often incompatible deeper commitments. A Kantian might say that democratic freedom is derived from the more fundamental idea of autonomy as the source of value and normative validity. Defenders of some forms of religious morality could say that humans are equal in the eyes of God, who designed them with certain powers of autonomous political decision-making that is their duty to respect and use. Agreement on the idea of political freedom and equality does not require agreement at the level of these deeper comprehensive doctrines. The second way in which the ideas of political freedom and equality are relatively thin concerns the relation between political and other social institutions. Some may challenge the view that people should be equally free to determine decision-making in every domain of social action. Some hierarchies may be justifiable in some settings. But this point is not incompatible with political freedom and equality. What has high priority is that equal freedom be recognized at the level of the main political institutions. Why is it crucial that equal freedom exist at that level? Because politics is the master social institution; it sets conditions on every other social institution in a society. This is why agents have very strong reason to be equally free at the political level. At other levels it is less important, and sometimes not even desirable, to live in conditions of equal freedom.

A consequence of the previous point is that although the thin ideas of freedom and equality support a HRD, they do not obliterate the distinction between human rights and maximalist claims of justice. There clearly are more demanding views of freedom and equality as a matter of justice. The third point is that in fact equal political freedom helps frame the discussion about maximal justice in a fair way. Disagreement about justice is an enduring fact of contemporary social life. People disagree on whether, and how, ideas of freedom and equality (and other ideas of justice) are to be elaborated in different spheres of society (including, prominently, the economic one). Human rights are not meant to settle such disagreements. They can, however, enable their fair treatment. They do this by securing a *floor of dignity* on which disagreeing agents can stand. Such a floor of dignity clearly includes basic civil and socioeconomic rights such as bodily integrity and subsistence. But it should also include robust political rights of the kind democracy secures. Without them, the elaboration of disputes about wider justice would not give all a fair chance to contribute to the debate and to decide what proposals in it should be tried out, and later on perhaps repelled or amended, by the coercive decision-making political institutions.

At this point the intrinsic argument for democracy joins forces with the instrumental argument in both its accountability and epistemic dimensions. We should have democratic forms of egalitarian politics to recognize and respect and give full play to the cognitive and volitional capacities of all political agents: democracy enables us to learn from each other, and to negotiate our disagreements in fair and informed ways. More specifically, democracy is important in the following ways. First, the intrinsic value of democracy is evident once we try to explain why of two final outcomes that are equal in every respect in terms of rights protection (other than democracy) the one reached through a decision-making process that involves equal political liberty is better than the other that does not. Being publicly recognized and empowered as an equal in shaping one's social world is something we have reason to care about. Second, equal participation, including public deliberation, is of great importance. It helps identify appropriate (desirable and feasible) specifications of abstract rights for the circumstances we face. It helps us find appropriate balancing acts if the implementation of several rights must conflict in practice. It enables us to reach fair compromises when full agreement is not viable. It provides us with a way to learn about the specific circumstances, beliefs, and needs of others in diverse multicultural settings in which we cannot simply assume that everyone shares our worldview. Finally, democratic institutions and practices help cement a public culture of respect and attention to the interests and voice of each that makes social cooperation more stable. That public culture helps make cooperation more dynamic and productive as well; democratic power does not only help us protect ourselves from threats by others; it also enables us to join with others to design and pursue social projects that improve people's lives in various ways. These points have general significance for the pursuit of global justice, the topic to which I now turn.

3 Human Rights, Democracy, and the Pursuit of Global Justice

3.1 Basic and Non-Basic Global Justice

How does the recognition of a HRD affect the pursuit of global justice? To answer this question, we first need to distinguish between *basic* and *non-basic*, including *maximal*, global justice. Basic global justice targets the most urgent global demands concerning the conditions for a decent life for all, i.e. the fulfillment of human rights, whereas non-basic global justice includes, but goes beyond that. Consider economic justice. The universal fulfillment of the human right to an adequate standard of living including basic levels of nutrition, education, healthcare, and housing (stated in Article 25 of the

Universal Declaration) would be an achievement of basic global justice. Beyond that, we can imagine more demanding claims of global justice. Some say that we should, as a matter of justice, aim for global equality of access or opportunity regarding goods such as advanced education and healthcare, income, wealth, forms of work involving self-realization, etc. These goods go beyond the objects of human rights. If access to them is an entitlement of global justice, it must be one of non-basic global justice. How does democracy fit this distinction? First, if it is a human right, democracy is a matter of basic global justice. As we saw, some critics disagree; they think that it is not weighty or universal enough to be a human right and that it might perhaps, at best, be seen instead as a demand of non-basic global justice. The response to such worries presented in Section 2 amounts to defending a right to democracy as a demand of basic global justice. But we still need to consider what is the significance of democracy for the design of international institutions, if any. How does a HRD affect the reform and creation of international institutions? A second question is: how does a HRD affect the pursuit of non-basic global justice? In what follows I present a brief exploration of these two questions. Answering them is important for completing the defense of a HRD. Given limits of space, my remarks will be short, but I hope they offer illuminating hypotheses for future discussion.

3.2 The Pursuit of Basic Global Justice

How should we think about international institutions if we aim at the global fulfillment of human rights? What is the role of a HRD in this exercise? Consider Article 28 of the Universal Declaration, according to which "Everyone is entitled to a social and international order in which the rights and freedoms set forth in this Declaration can be fully realized." From the discussion in Section 2 we can claim that domestic social orders should be democratic. We can also claim that a just "international order" would be one that promotes democracy in domestic settings. These are not minor results. But should we think of the institutions making up the international order as themselves bound by democratic norms? If so, how and why?[25]

Should international institutions such as the World Trade Organization be democratically organized? In an illuminating recent article considering this question, Thomas Christiano (2010) identifies two kinds of answers and important challenges they face. I will reconstruct Christiano's points and then (in the next paragraph) offer a critical assessment of them. One option is a revision of the common "voluntary association model," which legitimizes international institutions and their actions on the basis of the consent to them given by member states. This model seems relatively feasible, given the importance of states for any stable international institution (it would not last without their cooperation), and desirable, given that states may be quite successful at defending the interests of their subjects. However, this model faces two serious problems. The "representativeness problem" arises when some of the participating states are not democratic. The "asymmetric bargaining problem" arises when states have enormous differences in bargaining power that allow stronger states to dragoon weaker ones into accepting conditions of international association that are unfair. For example, negotiations in the WTO may yield exploitative conditions for poorer countries. This model could be revised into a "fair democratic association" model in which member states are democratic and certain institutional restrictions on unfair bargaining are imposed. However, the accessibility of this model is problematic given the existing global inequalities in economic and political power. Still, Christiano thinks that it is overall better to work toward realizing this model than to pursue another, more ambitious model of "global democracy" calling for the legitimation of the international global order through a global parliament with representatives of constituencies of individuals. This model faces insurmountable problems. The most serious are these. First, democracy is a valid ideal for institutions only if those bound by them have roughly equal stakes in their decisions. This condition is met by modern states but not by international institutions. (For example, some countries are much more involved in international trade than others.) Second, there is not enough in the way of an international civil society (in terms of political parties, interests groups, and media outlets) to establish a sufficiently meaningful communication between global institutions and individuals across the world. Again, the contrast with the domestic case is too deep.

I think that Christiano is right that we should pursue some version of the fair democratic association model (and that we should do it for the reasons he states). But his rejection of global democracy is too quick. First, the condition of equal stakes could be met by a global parliament if its remit is properly circumscribed.[26] Importantly for our discussion, it could be focused on legislating on conditions on any *other* international institution (such as the WTO) so that its activities are consistent with the promotion and protection of *human rights*.[27] Everyone has a strong and equal stake in that. And international institutions directly representing individuals rather than states are appropriate here because it is the former, not the latter, who have human rights.

Second, the problem of weak civil society could be progressively resolved over time. The current process of globalization is already generating many forms of supranational political action, forums, and organizations. This could be accelerated by the creation of a global parliament focused on human rights, whose presence and action would create an incentive for the creation of new arenas of international civil society. That parliament could at first be only deliberative and perform tasks of recommendation, and develop the power to yield binding regulation only later on, when international civil society thickens to a sufficient degree. Interestingly, this progressive pursuit of a circumscribed global parliament might have positive interactions with the pursuit of the conditions for fair bargaining within the interstate association. The former could press for action to remove conditions of extreme vulnerability, and thus bolster the negotiation power of the excluded or exploited.

Two key ideas underlying the position I suggested in the previous paragraphs concern (a) the natural duties based on the cosmopolitanism of human rights and (b) the dynamic and long-term nature of the political practice they ground. Regarding (a): If we owe equal moral concern and respect to every human being at least when it comes to the fulfillment of their human rights, then the idea of an "international order" invoked in Article 28 of the Universal Declaration (United Nations 1948) should be interpreted as demanding not only the reform of existing international institutions, but also the creation of new ones (when this can be done at reasonable cost to those affected) that will *respond* to the preexisting equal stake of every person in (either existing or feasible to create) institutions protecting human dignity. Such institutions should be democratic in order to target that goal—and the three dimensions of democracy discussed in this chapter point in that direction.

Regarding (b): Global institutions focused on human rights, if they include the third, epistemic dimension of democracy, will help us navigate more lucidly the uncertainties concerning what is the most reasonable way to protect human rights in the world. Given the first and the second dimensions, they will also make such protection lose the aura of unilateral imposition that human rights policies sometimes have in contemporary politics. They would constitute a form of global egalitarian empowerment through which the members of the global community of human beings (and there always is such a community from the moral point of view) pursue, in an autonomous way, the fulfillment of the human rights of each.

3.3 The Pursuit of Non-Basic Global Justice

The preceding discussion concerns human rights and basic global justice. But the pursuit of basic global justice affects the pursuit of non-basic global justice in important ways.

First, the generation of institutions and practices of supranational democracy (of the two kinds discussed) provides a *political bridge* between the pursuit of basic and non-basic justice. A world where basic global justice is achieved is one in which people have a floor of dignity to stand on. That floor is also a *floor of power*, as these people are in control of the political shape of their social world, both domestic and international.[28] That power gives them the capability to explore together, on fair terms, the issue whether global justice involves more than human rights, and, if so, what. The three aspects of democratic empowerment are important for this exploration: the exploration can be undertaken by those who will be subject to its results, whoever makes decisions on the implementation of emerging proposals will be accountable to those subjected to them, and everyone will have effective opportunities to improve through political experience and public deliberation everyone's epistemic grasp of the practical alternatives and their likely consequences on agents placed in different circumstances.[29]

The global fulfillment of human rights, including a HRD, constitutes a bridge in the movement from basic to non-basic global justice. But secondly, although human rights are only a proper subset of the demands of global justice, they rely on ideas that can, and arguably should, be developed further at the level of non-basic global justice. I conclude by suggesting the importance of two such ideas: cosmopolitanism and humanism. First, human rights mark the entrance of cosmopolitanism in domestic and international politics.[30] This has an important consequence for the kinds of duties the pursuit of basic justice should involve. Those duties should be not only agent-relative but also agent-neutral: human rights in the cosmopolitan sense should be respected and promoted by everyone toward everyone else. Duty-bearers may have responsibilities to right-holders whether they are intertwined in certain associative ventures or not. There are pro tanto duties to promote human rights with strictly universal scope. This prompts the hypothesis that there are some duties of non-basic global justice that also have a cosmopolitan nature. This point is already part of the practice of global movements focused on introducing and deepening democracy. [31]

Second, and relatedly, the pursuit of non-basic global justice may also inherit the humanism of human rights (i.e. the view that some claims are based in our shared humanity). Consider global economic justice. Some pro tanto demands of global economic equality may be worth considering, in which certain conditions for human flourishing that all human beings as such have reason to value (such as advanced forms of healthcare and education) are pursued, whether their promotion occurs amongst those who already share associative frameworks or not. Once we acknowledge universal socioeconomic humanist rights with a sufficientarian target, why not acknowledge some universal egalitarian entitlements?

Of course, I am not here attempting to show that these two suggestions about how the cosmopolitanism and humanism of human rights might shape the pursuit of non-basic global justice are true. The aim is simply to suggest that these are relevant hypotheses to explore. And the political conditions for such an exploration, as I have argued above, are precisely one of the achievements that the fulfillment of a HRD would deliver for all. The central conclusion is, then, that the fulfillment of the human right to democratic political empowerment is crucial for the pursuit of global justice.[32]

Acknowledgments

For helpful comments or conversations I thank Charles Beitz, Luis Cabrera, Rowan Cruft, Maks Del Mar, Carol Gould, Stephen Macedo, Dean Machin, and audiences in workshops with the International Studies Association and the Princeton University Center for Human Values.

Notes

1. See Beitz (1989); Christiano (2008); Habermas (1996); and Sen (1999).
2. Waldron (2007: 746).
3. In this chapter I assume that the universality of human rights ranges over all persons in the contemporary world. A wider scope could be argued for, but I restrict my argument to the weaker account of universality that most critics of a human right to democracy accept. I also assume that that the high priority of human rights depends on their ranging over the conditions enabling a decent or basically dignified life. The focus is on conditions enabling a minimally good life rather than (as arguably wider demands of justice concern themselves with) a flourishing life. On the last point, see Nickel (2007: 62). The idea of human dignity in its basic and maximal forms is explored in Gilabert (2015a, 2015b).

4. I am not claiming that a nondemocratic regime necessarily is intolerant towards its own people in every important respect. A nondemocratic regime could, for example, tolerate many of its residents' exercise of their civil rights (such as their freedom of religion). But toleration with respect to civil (and other) rights does not entail that intolerance with respect to political participation does not exist. So the nondemocratic regime is still intolerant in an important respect. (Furthermore, one should worry about how secure other rights are when residents do not have effective power to respond to a regime that changes course and decides to violate them.) A possible difficult question is how to respond to practical circumstances in which the two immediately feasible options are (a) a democratic regime under which serious underfulfillment of civil and social rights is likely to occur and (b) a nondemocratic regime under which significantly greater fulfillment of civil and social rights is likely. I tackle this question in Section 2.2.4.

5. Forst (2004).

6. A sentiment of this kind may underlie the struggle of many oppressed groups. Consider, for example, MP Sophia Abdi's reaction after the Kenyan government decided to ban female genital mutilation: "Today is independence day for women. Men got their independence in 1963—but today women have achieved independence from the cruel hands of society." Cited in Boseley (2011: 13).

7. I thank Carol Gould for discussion on this point. There is the conceptual possibility that a people democratically choose to become nondemocratic. Would this be acceptable or should it be as problematic as the case of voluntary slavery? My intuitive answer is that the latter is true, but the issue requires further discussion.

8. For Rawls's view, see Rawls (1999: 78–81). An important function of human rights is that they warrant global concern and action, but the latter can take many forms. See Beitz (2009: 31–42).

9. Democracy most often comes from the streets, not from foreign warships. The recent Arab Spring (e.g. in Tunisia) and the transition to democracy in Latin America and Eastern Europe around the 1980s are possible examples. The achievements of the movements behinds these transitions were supported by various forms of international solidarity, but they were not the outcome of international coercive intervention.

10. These include, for example, the international "resources," "arms," and "borrowing" privileges through which elites in poor countries can sell natural resources, purchase weapons, and contract debt in their people's name, which enables them to cement their despotic rule. See Pogge (2008).

11. I share Benhabib's worry that a "laudable concern for liberal toleration and peaceful coexistence can also lead to liberal indifference, and…to an unjustified toleration for the world's repressive regimes such as many 'decent, hierarchical peoples' (Rawls) may be and often are." Benhabib (2011: 78).

12. Rich (2001: 20–34). An important and hopeful recent development in Latin America is the introduction (in 2010) of the "democratic clause" within the UNASUR (Union de Naciones Suramericanas—Union of South American Nations). It authorizes coordinated responses to threats to the democratic institutions of any member state.

13. What follows draws, with revisions, on my more detailed discussion on Cohen's views in Gilabert (2012b: 10–3, 22–3).

14. See also Rawls (1999: section 9).

15. "The fundamental interests of adults who are denied opportunities to participate in governing will *not* be adequately protected and advanced by those who govern. The historical evidence on this point is overwhelming" Dahl (1998: 77); see further Dahl (1998: 77–8 and 52–3).

16. Christiano's conclusions are not undisputed. A worry (discussed in section 2.2.4) is that the comparison between democratic and nondemocratic regimes in terms of overall human rights fulfillment may be less favorable to democratic regimes in very poor societies than in middle- and upper-income ones.

17. For the strong correlation between democratization and support for international human rights law, see Simmons (2009: 24–7). Simmons does not claim that democracy causes, but she says that it supports, the legalization of international human rights, and she explores some possible mechanisms (such as strong accountability) underpinning this contribution.

18. On the idea of *dynamic duties*, see Gilabert (2009). A worry could be that it is unrealistic to expect that we will know enough about what is likely to happen in the future for considerations about the long term to affect our current choices. I am not sure this is always the case. But when it is, we may still have dynamic duties to expand our level of political knowledge. Second, we must also factor in the undesirability of the status quo. The worse it is, the less strict we need to be about our foresight of the future to choose to make moves away from it. Even if the status quo is desirable, notice, third, that if we are unable to foresee the future, this may include an inability to foresee whether the status quo will continue if we do not choose to change it, or if we choose to keep it. A radical skepticism about foresight would hamper *any* choice.

19. This example assumes that the feasible nondemocratic regimes are roughly equivalent in terms of catering for the other rights.

20. Christiano (2011: 170) also discusses the potential conflict between a HRD and other strong rights, but my conclusion differs from his. Since his paper focuses only on the instrumental argument for a HRD, he concludes that in the circumstances a HRD is defeated rather than merely outweighed (as it would not serve the purpose that determines its value, which is to protect other strong rights).

21. A possible objection is that since Beitz and Cohen accept that democracy is a demand of justice, they would also agree that it gives rise to obligatory goals of reform over the long term. But if the goals are not also seen as responding to human rights (which are a subset of the claims of justice), then their great weight will not be recognized: their pursuit will be seen as having a lower level of priority and will be more easily put aside to attend to other goals.

22. See Dahl's illuminating general framework, which includes a distinction between democratic "principles," "criteria," and "institutions." For discussion of specific institutions that are appropriate in different contexts, see Dahl (1998: chs. 8–11). For a distinction between principles and institutions concerning the HRD, see Buchanan (2004: 145–7). We can also distinguish between minimal and maximal democratic political equality, seeing only the former as the focus of a HRD. Christiano (2011: 146) suggests that the former demands institutions securing effective and equal voting, equal opportunity to engage in consequential forms of political organization and action, and a rule of law supporting independent judicial control over the executive power.

23. The Universal Declaration's Articles 19–21 (which can be interpreted as formulating specific democratic rights) might be too specific.

24. Gilabert (2012b: section 3.2). This paragraph partly draws on p. 19.
25. One way to motivate this question is to say that our globalizing world involves a "democratic deficit," as decision-makers on issues of great importance (such as environmental protection and trade) are not democratically accountable to decision-takers. Beitz (2011) criticizes this approach.
26. Another possible response would rely on a proportional view of democratic rights. According to this view, some may be entitled to more say on a certain issue to be decided upon than others if they have more stakes in it. Global democratic arrangements giving a different say to different people could then be argued for. On this view, some form of global democratic governance would be appropriate because some issues importantly affect everyone in the world, although, since some would have more stakes in some of those issues than others, rights of political participation in decision-making would not be strictly equal with respect to all global issues. On the proportionality view, see Brighouse and Fleurbaey (2010). For a response to Christiano that develops this view, see Valentini (2014: 795).
27. On the human rights focus for global democratic governance, see also Gould (2004: 178), and Habermas (2009: ch. 7).
28. For further discussion on human rights and empowerment, see Gilabert (2018).
29. For another argument that securing human rights and fair global governance provides an appropriate starting point for the pursuit global justice, see Forst (2012: ch. 12). My argument is compatible with Forst's, but it is different because it does not rely on a constructivist approach to justice.
30. Cosmopolitanism is the moral view that all individuals are ultimate units of equal moral concern and respect for everyone. See Pogge (2008: 175).
31. For example, the pursuit of democratic empowerment occurs in countries moving away from nondemocratic rule, as in the recent Arab Spring. It also seeks to deepen democracy in countries that already have democratic institutions but face the domestication of the political process by the rich, as illustrated by the recent Occupy movement in the United States. Furthermore, and interestingly, the Occupy movement campaigned in solidarity with democratic movements in other countries. These movements converge in calling for democratic governance both at the domestic and international level. For example, the manifesto "United for # Global Democracy" said in 2011 that:

> Undemocratic international institutions are our global Mubarak, our global Assad, our global Gaddafi. These include: the IMF, the WTO, global markets, multinational banks, the G8/G20, the European Central Bank and the UN Security Council. Like Mubarak and Assad, these institutions must not be allowed to run people's lives without their consent. We are all born equal, rich or poor, woman or man. Every African and Asian is equal to every European or American. Our global institutions must reflect this, or be overturned.   (Suarez and Zameret 2014)

A further clarification: The cosmopolitan duties (and the humanist ones mentioned in the next paragraph of the text) are pro tanto because they can be limited by considerations of feasibility and reasonable costs, and because they have to be weighted against agent-relative and associative duties, which can sometimes (perhaps often) be stronger. (Notice that agent-relative and associative duties may rely on the generic value of certain special relationships, and be thus significant even from the cosmopolitan and humanist point of view.) For explorations of cosmopolitanism and humanism in relation to human rights and egalitarian distributive justice, see Gilabert (2011, 2012a, 2013).

32. For helpful comments or conversations I thank Charles Beitz, Luis Cabrera, Rowan Cruft, Maks Del Mar, Carol Gould, Stephen Macedo, Dean Machin, and audiences in workshops with the International Studies Association and the Princeton University Center for Human Values.

References

Beitz, Charles (1989) *Political Equality. An Essay in Democratic Theory*. Princeton, NJ: Princeton University Press.

Beitz, Charles (2009) *The Idea of Human Rights*. Oxford: Oxford University Press.

Beitz, Charles (2011) "Global Political Justice and the 'Democratic Deficit.'" In R.Jay Wallace, Rahul Kumar, and Samuel Freeman (eds.), *Reasons and Recognition. Essays on the Philosophy of T. M. Scanlon*. Oxford: Oxford University Press, 231–55.

Benhabib, Seyla (2011) *Dignity in Adversity*. Cambridge: Polity.

Boseley, Sarah (2011) "Kenya Bans Mutilation," The Guardian Weekly, 16 September.

Brighouse, Harry, and Marc Fleurbaey (2010) "Democracy and Proportionality," *Journal of Political Philosophy* 18: 137–55.

Buchanan, Allen (2004) *Justice, Legitimacy and Self-determination*. Oxford: Oxford University Press.

Christiano, Thomas (2008) *The Constitution of Equality*. Oxford: Oxford University Press.

Christiano, Thomas (2010) "Democratic Legitimacy and International Institutions." In Samantha Besson and John Tasioulas (eds.), *The Philosophy of International Law*. Oxford: Oxford University Press, 119–37.

Christiano, Thomas (2011) "An Instrumental Argument for a Human Right to Democracy," *Philosophy and Public Affairs* 39: 142–76.

Cohen, Joshua (2010) *The Arc of the Moral Universe*. Cambridge, MA: Harvard University Press.

Dahl, Robert (1998) *On Democracy*. New Haven, CT: Yale University Press.

Forst, Rainer (2004) "The Limits of Toleration," *Constellations* 11: 312–25.

Forst, Rainer (2012) *The Right to Justification. Elements of a Constructivist Theory of Justice*. New York: Columbia University Press.

Gilabert, Pablo (2009) "The Feasibility of Basic Socioeconomic Human Rights: A Conceptual Exploration," *Philosophical Quarterly* 59: 659–81.

Gilabert, Pablo (2011) "Humanist and Political Perspectives on Human Rights," *Political Theory* 39: 439–67.

Gilabert, Pablo (2012a) *From Global Poverty to Global Equality: A Philosophical Exploration*. Oxford: Oxford University Press.

Gilabert, Pablo (2012b) "Is There a Human Right to Democracy? A Response to Joshua Cohen," *Revista Latinoamericana de Filosofía Política/Latin American Journal of Political Philosohy* 1: 1–37.

Gilabert, Pablo (2013) "The Capability Approach and the Debate between Humanist and Political Perspectives on Human Rights. A Critical Survey," *Human Rights Review* 14: 299–325.

Gilabert, Pablo (2015a) "Human Rights, Human Dignity, and Power." In Rowan Cruft, S. Matthew Liao, and Massimo Renzo (eds.), *Philosophical Foundations of Human Rights*. Oxford: Oxford University Press, 196–213.

Gilabert, Pablo (2015b) "The Socialist Principle 'From Each According to Their Abilities, to Each According to Their Needs," *Journal of Social Philosophy* 46: 197–225.

Gilabert, Pablo (2018) "Reflections on Human Rights and Power," In Adam Etinson (ed.), *Human Rights. Moral or Political?* Oxford: Oxford University Press, 375–99.

Gould, Carol C. (2004) *Globalizing Democracy and Human Rights*. Cambridge: Cambridge University Press.

Habermas, Jürgen (1996) *Between Facts and Norms*. Cambridge, MA: MIT Press.

Habermas, Jürgen (2009) *Europe: The Faltering Project*. Cambridge: Polity.

Nickel, James (2007) *Making Sense of Human Rights*, 2nd. edn. Oxford: Blackwell.

Pogge, Thomas (2008) *World Poverty and Human Rights*, 2nd. edn. Cambridge, Polity.

Rawls, John (1999) *The Law of Peoples*. Cambridge, MA: Harvard University Press.

Rich, Roland (2001) "Bringing Democracy into International Law," *Journal of Democracy* 12: 20–34.

Sen, Amartya (1999) *Development as Freedom*. New York: Anchor Books.

Sen, Amartya (2009) *The Idea of Justice*. Cambridge, MA: Harvard University Press.

Simmons, Beth (2009) *Mobilizing for Human Rights. International Law in Domestic Politics*. Cambridge: Cambridge University Press.

Suarez, Ana Sofia, and Shimri Zameret (2014) "A Manifesto for Regime Change on Behalf of All Humanity," *The Guardian* , accessed August 19, 2019.

United Nations (1948) "Universal Declaration of Human Rights," https://www.un.org/en/universal-declaration-human-rights/, accessed October 22, 2019.

Valentini, Laura (2014) "No Global Demos, No Global Democracy? A Systematization and Critique," *Perspectives on Politics* 12: 789–807.

Waldron, Jeremy (2007) "Rights." In Robert E. Goodin, Philip Pettit, and Thomas Pogge (eds.), *A Companion to Contemporary Political Philosophy*. Oxford: Blackwell, 745–54.

FURTHER READING

Abizadeh, Arash (2012) "On the Demos and its Kin: Nationalism, Democracy, and the Boundary Problem," *American Political Science Review* 106: 867–82.

Buchanan, Allen (2013) *The Heart of Human Rights*. Oxford: Oxford University Press.

Christiano, Thomas (2015) "Self-Determination and the Human Right to Democracy." In Rowan Cruft, S. Matthew Liao, and Massimo Renzo (eds.), *Philosophical Foundations of Human Rights*. Oxford: Oxford University Press, 459–80.

Crocker, David A. (2008) *Ethics of Global Development: Agency, Capability, and Deliberative Democracy*. Cambridge: Cambridge University Press.

Dryzek, John (2016) "Can There Be a Human Right to an Essentially Contested Concept? The Case for Democracy," *Journal of Politics* 78: 357–67.

Forst, Rainer (2010) "The Justification of Human Rights and the Basic Right to Justification: A Reflexive Approach," *Ethics* 120: 711–40.

Gilabert, Pablo (2018) *Human Dignity and Human Rights*. Oxford: Oxford University Press.

Gould, Carol C. (2014) *Interactive Democracy: On the Social Roots of Global Justice*. Cambridge: Cambridge University Press.

Griffin, James (2008) *On Human Rights*. Oxford: Oxford University Press.

Lafont, Cristina (2010) "Democratic Accountability and Global Governance: Challenging the State-Centric Conception of Human Rights," *Ethics & Global Politics* 3: 193–215.

Lafont, Cristina (2019) *Democracy without Shortcuts. A Participatory Conception of Deliberative Democracy*. Oxford: Oxford University Press.

Lister, Matthew (2012) "There Is No Human Right to Democracy, but May We Promote it Anyway?" *Stanford Journal of International Law* 48: 257–76.

Nickel, James (2019) "Human Rights," *The Stanford Encyclopedia of Philosophy*, https://plato.stanford.edu/archives/sum2019/entries/rights-human/, accessed August 19, 2019.

Peters, Fabienne (2015) "A Human Right to Democracy." In Rowan Cruft, S. Matthew Liao, and Massimo Renzo (eds.), *Philosophical Foundations of Human Rights*. Oxford: Oxford University Press, 480–90.

CHAPTER 15

....

THOMAS POGGE'S CONCEPTION OF TAKING THE GLOBAL INSTITUTIONAL ORDER AS THE OBJECT OF JUSTICE ASSESSMENTS

....

ARTHUR CHIN

1 INTRODUCTION

....

DOES the same type of reasoning we employ at the domestic level about what social justice requires of us appropriately apply at the global level? If so, what should our justice assessments in the first instance be concerned with? Should our justice assessments at the global level be guided by the same set of principles of social justice that governs the design of domestic institutions? Or should we expect principles of justice to have a substantially different content and to play a significantly different role at the global level in view of certain normatively significant differences between the domestic and international contexts? These are the questions around which much of the current global justice debate revolves.

One prominent participant in this debate is philosopher Thomas Pogge who, I submit, has provided us with a set of answers that for the most part retain their plausibility despite the barrage of criticism his work has provoked, answers that merit more serious consideration than they have received thus far. While Pogge is especially renowned for, and much of the debate his work has generated is revolving around, the contention that citizens and governments of the affluent societies have been unduly harming the global poor by collaborating in imposing upon them the present global institutional scheme, which is unjust on account of there being a feasible alternative arrangement under which there will foreseeably be a lower global incidence of human rights underfulfillments, this chapter will not be weighing in on this debate. Rather, it seeks to examine a theoretical commitment that occupies a more fundamental role in Pogge's conception of global justice: If we are to take the basic institutional scheme of a domestic society as the primary subject of justice "because its effects are so profound and present from the start" (Rawls 1999b: 7), then, in view of the fact that the living conditions of persons across the world are profoundly and pervasively influenced by an ever deepening network of global institutions, consistency requires us to subject the global institutional scheme to the same type of justice analysis, and to devise a set of reasonable principles of global justice that governs its design.[1] Through clarifying the meaning and implications of this thesis, this chapter hopes to bring out a more lucid and unified reading of Pogge's institutional approach to justice theorizing, one that is both appealing and remains viable even in the absence of a world government, thereby making some contribution towards establishing the overall defensibility of Pogge's conception.

This chapter will be divided into three sections. Section 2 will examine how Pogge stands in relation to the two following questions: Does reasoning about what justice requires of the global institutional order become a relevant moral concern only upon the realization of extensive global economic interdependence? Does the present system of territorial states properly fall within the scope of our justice analysis? With regard to the first question, while some remarks Pogge himself has made suggest otherwise, I will argue that on a more unified reading he should be understood as giving a negative answer, which in turn obliges him to answer the second question with a resounding yes. And I will argue that it is a failure to realize Pogge's commitment to subjecting the global institutional order *in its entirety*—the states system included—to justice analysis that has given rise to certain misleading characterizations of his position by some theorists.

Building on the conclusion reached in Section 2, in Section 3 I will bring in Samuel Freeman's forceful objection to Pogge's idea of global justice, the view that, in the absence of a unified political authority at the global level, the project of applying the same type of justice reasoning to the international realm is misguided.[2] And I will show how Freeman's ideas can reasonably be used to construct an argument for the claim that the present states system, being itself a perquisite for the type of social interactions that provides the occasion for principles of justice to apply in the first place, should be regarded as part of the circumstances of justice and hence cannot properly be subject to justice analysis. In response, I will argue that such a view is unpersuasive on account of its failure to sufficiently appreciate the historical contingency of the current states system.

In Section 4, I will further explicate Pogge's notion of institutional justice analysis by contrasting it with Mathias Risse's defense of the classic states system, and his argument for rejecting Pogge's proposal to reform the present states system through a vertical dispersal of political authority.[3] By identifying the limitation of the approach to institutional assessment exemplified by Risse's treatment of the subject, this section serves to highlight another appealing feature of Pogge's approach, namely, the flexibility with which it endows our justice reasoning by adapting it to the differential distributive effects particular sets of institutional arrangement would have in different empirical circumstances.

Section 5 contains concluding remarks in which I will highlight certain aspects of Pogge's position that call for closer examination and further development.

2 Global Justice, Economic Interdependence, and the States System

In chapter 1 of *Politics as Usual*, Pogge (2010) has eloquently argued for the urgency of not restricting the kind of institutional justice analysis so familiar at the domestic level but extending it to the world at large in light of what he calls the "double transformation of the traditional realm of international relations" (Pogge 2010: 14): In recent decades the world has witnessed not only a proliferation of important actors at the international level, such as the United Nations, the WTO, and multinational corporations, but also a rapidly growing network of treaties and conventions regulating the interactions between these newly emerged actors and the more traditional ones of national governments:

> Those actors and these rules powerfully influence the domestic life of national societies: through their impact on pollution and climate change, invasive diseases, conflict and violence...and (most profoundly) through market forces that condition access to capital and raw materials, export opportunities, domestic tax bases and tax rates, prices, wages, labor standards, and much else.   (Pogge 2010: 14)

This formulation of the rationale for our giving serious thought to global justice might lead one to infer that justice analysis gains relevance at the global level only upon the advent of globalization, that "a criterion of justice for domestic institutions would be sufficient if modern states were...closed schemes. In this case there simply would not be a global basic structure for principles of global justice to apply to" (Pogge 1989: 240)[4]

However, if we are to have a unified understanding of Pogge's position on this, we should be careful, I submit, in distinguishing between two senses of national societies being "closed schemes." Societies are closed schemes in a relatively superficial sense when a plurality of political communities are each self-contained and their members do not engage in any routinized and rule-based economic, political, or social interactions with one another, while they are fully aware of one another's existence and, more importantly, they owe their juridical status as independent political communities to the mutual recognition of, and general compliance with, some public system of rules and norms which assign to each certain rights and duties vis-à-vis one another. We can imagine such a global state as having come about through the world's inhabitants, or their representatives, coming together to agree upon some variant of the Treaty of Westphalia, creating a state-centric system of world organization, followed immediately by each state's adopting an autarkic policy.[5] On a deeper sense of national closedness, not only are the members of various political communities not engaging in any regular rule-based interaction, but they either have no knowledge of one another's existence or do not coexist as independent political communities, the juridical status of which is mutually recognized in accordance with any public system of rules or norms.

It should be clear that, for Pogge, concern with institutional justice at the global level fails to get off the ground when national societies are closed in the deep sense. His position with regard to the relatively superficial sense of national closedness is less clear. On the one hand, there is evidence indicating that he would give the same answer, denying the relevance of the notion of global justice. One piece of evidence comes from Pogge's assessment of Charles Beitz's having come to deny, *pace* his former view in *Political Theory and International Relations*, that the presence of extensive economic interdependence among states is a necessary condition for concerns of global justice to arise. This change is due to Beitz's worries that there would otherwise be a perverse incentive for states to evade the demands of justice simply by withdrawing their participation in the global economy. By saying in response that he fails to see this danger, for "at this stage of world history we cannot realistically avoid international interaction, and so the members of rich societies have no incentive to exploit the fact that the criterion of global justice would not apply if societies were self-contained" (Pogge 1989: 241, n.3), Pogge seems to be sharing the view that withholding participation in the global economy would be sufficient for national societies to become closed schemes in a sense that renders the notion of global justice inapplicable, even if they are not closed schemes in the deep sense mentioned above.

In spite of this, I am of the view that, on a more unified reading of Pogge, he should be seen as affirming the relevance and importance of global justice analysis even where national societies are each closed schemes in the relatively superficial sense. The reason stems partly from his observations that the system of territorial states can be expected to exercise profound and pervasive impact upon our life conditions even in the absence of extensive global economic interactions. Consider the fact that under the states system a state government enjoys the right to unilaterally decide its border regime, and that it is only recently that states have come to recognize a limited human rights-based obligation to grant asylum to foreigners under certain exceptional circumstances. Also integral to that system is the norm that, for the most part, a state government does not bear the onus of justifying to foreign nationals its entry policy, even in cases where entry denial would foreseeably have tremendous impact upon the basic interests of the would-be immigrants. Pogge recognizes how damaging an effect such practice could have on the destitute would-be-immigrants independently of the presence of extensive economic interdependence: "That the effects of flawed domestic institutions are as bad as they are is often due to global institutions—to the institution of the territorial state, for instance, which allows affluent populations to prevent the poor from migrating to where their work could earn a decent living" (Pogge 2002: 73). But if the urgency for reflecting on the moral quality of global institutions in our world of heightened economic interdependence stems from the profundity and inescapability of their effects on persons' living conditions, then for the sake of consistency the defensibility of the practice concerning border control is certainly not something we can take for granted, regardless of whether there exist substantial economic ties between societies. Indeed the recognition of the need to subject such practices to justice evaluation has found expression in much philosophical debate about whether this unilateral state right of border control conflicts with the human right to freedom of movement or whether it is required by the democratic right to self-determination.[6]

Making it clear that, following Pogge's line of reasoning, concerns of global justice legitimately arise even when national societies are mutually isolated in the superficial sense is of importance, for it highlights an important feature of Pogge's institutional approach to justice theorizing: our selection of what global institutions are to fall within the purview of justice analysis must be comprehensive. It is due to a failure to realize this, and a tendency to take for granted the justice credentials of the states system that, I submit, accounts for some theorists' problematic characterizations of Pogge's position.

Consider a hypothetical scenario described by Michael Blake (2002: 289–90) to illustrate the distinction between the cosmopolitan conceptions of global justice held by Pogge and Beitz and those which see global justice as essentially about the reallocation of resources between the economically better-off and worse-off societies in order to redress undeserved inequalities. Blake has us imagine two autarkic nations divided by a high mountain, Borduria and Syldavia, which, despite their having heard of each other's existence, have "no links established between [them] of any sort" (p. 290). Mainly due to the differential natural endowments of these two societies, citizens in Borduria enjoy a much higher living standard. One day, a group of Syldavian explorers cross the mountain into the more affluent Borduria and find out how much inferior their living conditions have been. They come to be filled with a sense of resentment and demand a reallocation of resources, asking: "Why...is it fair that you have more than we do?" (p. 290). Blake acknowledges that Pogge would not regard the Syldavians as having a valid claim of justice against the Bordurians for redistribution in view of their societies' constituting two schemes that are closed in the deep sense. Indeed Blake admits the example above as being "fanciful," that "few have endorsed the idea that simply sharing a world is enough to give rise to egalitarian duties such as a Rawlsian would endorse domestically" (2002: 290). But what he says immediately afterwards is worrying:

> The more relevant case, of course, is what happens once widespread links of trade and diplomacy begin to take place between two nations. Charles Beitz and Thomas Pogge have both argued that a sufficient degree of such links comprises a cooperative scheme for mutual benefit of the sort appropriate for analysis through Rawlsian methods.   (Blake 2002: 290)[7]

This reading of Pogge is problematic, for it suggests that Pogge is committed to the following dichotomy: either there is occasion for justice analysis at the global level, as societies are mutually isolated in the deep sense, or global justice comes to gain relevance *only* upon the establishment of "sufficient" trade and diplomatic ties between them. This is not a dichotomy that Pogge holds, or should hold, because it simply takes the moral quality of the background system of territorial states for granted, ignoring the possibility that the states system can be a proper object of justice assessments in its own right independently of the presence of extensive interdependence among societies, that justice might require that it be substantially reformed on account of its having unjustifiably given rise to much of our world's deprivations and other basic interest-non-fulfillments.[8]

3   Global Justice in a Politically Decentralized World

A number of theorists have cast doubt concerning the viability of extending onto the global plane the type of institutional justice reasoning familiar at the domestic level in our politically decentralized world. Due to space limits in this section I will focus on only some of the relevant challenges forcefully presented by Samuel Freeman, explaining how they might be understood as having the implication that it would be a category mistake to subject the states system to justice analysis, and why, in my view, they do not suffice to defeat the legitimacy of Pogge's project of comprehensive institutional justice analysis at the global level.

An extension presupposes a starting point. At the domestic level, the starting point is a society's basic institutions. Principles of domestic justice are used to govern the specification of those rules that, among others, condition production and distribution: the property institutions that structure production, consumption, use, and exchange of resources, and more generally, our day-to-day economic and social cooperation. But these basic institutions must come from somewhere, as Freeman (2007: 444) points out: "there is no invisible hand that has given rise to these complex basic economic and social background institutions against which transactions among individuals and associations take place." These institutions are themselves political products that exist because of the implementation, interpretation, and enforcement of the various executive, judicial, and legislative agencies. For instance, Rawls's difference principle is meant to govern the decision-making of legislators and other public officials by prohibiting them from implementing policies and regulations that generate inequalities of income and wealth without optimizing the economic position of the least advantaged. But then it is not clear how institutional justice analysis, or principles of justice, can properly be extended beyond domestic context, for "there can be no global basic structure on a par with the basic structure of society. Indeed, there is nothing in the global relations anywhere near to being comparable to a society's basic structure of political, legal, property, and other economic institutions" (Freeman 2006a: 246). In the absence of a world state, there is nothing for a putative principle of global justice to apply to.

How serious a threat does this pose to Pogge's idea that we may legitimately subject the global institutional scheme, in particular its component states system, to the same type of justice analysis we employ at the domestic level?[9] While Freeman has not extensively addressed this question, I submit that his ideas can reasonably be understood as having the implication that a state-centric mode of organizing our global political authority is, at least under modern conditions, part of the circumstances of justice and therefore prior to justice analysis. This reading is suggested by the way in which he responds to one of the criticisms made by Pogge against Rawls's position on international justice. To begin with, let me summarize Pogge's criticism. In *The Law of Peoples*, Rawls (1999a) finds applying principles of justice restricting economic inequalities at the global plane objectionable, for it would require constant transfers of wealth and resources from the self-determining better-off peoples to the worse-off, transfers without "a cut-off point" (1999a: 119). Pogge criticizes this reasoning by arguing that it stems from treating as a pre-theoretical given the defensibility of the current mode of international economic organization under which a state is entitled to full control and ownership of the economic benefits it can derive from marketing the natural resources found within its border, the geographical distribution of which is a matter of pure natural contingency. In taking this feature of our current global order for granted, as a natural or morally neutral baseline, Pogge (1994: 212–14) takes Rawls to have committed the same kind of fallacy as libertarians when they take the laissez-faire distribution of income and wealth as the default or natural baseline from which any plausible reasoning of economic justice must start.

In defense of Rawls, Freeman criticizes Pogge for failing to see that a Rawlsian people's exclusive territorial control is an *existence* condition of a system of social interaction. Freeman says:

> the analogy between a people's independent control of a territory and an individual's rights over property (however extensive) is unfitting. By exercising political jurisdiction over a territory, a people establishes a system of property, which is a complicated system of rules and interdependent expectations. By contrast, individuals do not establish systems of property; rather, they hold and use possessions within property systems... A people's control over a territory is not a kind of property; it is the condition for the *existence* of the social institution of property. More generally, it is a condition for social and political cooperation and the very existence of a political people.   (Freeman 2006b: 58–9; my italics)

This view is echoed in another of Freeman's writings: "[R]ather than a kind of property, a people's control of a territory provides the *necessary* framework for the legal institution of property and other basic social institutions" (Freeman 2006a: 247–8; my italics).

The thrust of Freeman's reply seems to be this: Exclusive territoriality—one of the defining features of the existing states system—is among those conditions, the fulfillment of which gives social justice its relevance in the first place. And this kind of condition is referred to by Rawls as the circumstances of justice, the presence of which is analytically prior to justice analysis. According to Rawls, such circumstances include, among other things, a group of people cohabiting and interacting with one another within a definite territory. What is of particular relevance here is that, for concerns of justice to arise, their interactions must be conducted on the basis of systems of rules that are publicly known and generally complied with, systems which define positions and offices with their rights and duties, powers and immunities, and the like (Rawls 1999b: 47). It is the existence of these systems of rules that provides social justice with its subject matter. In addition, justice is not concerned with just any system of rules. Even though games and rituals are rule-based social practices, they typically fall outside the purview of justice because "they are, at least in modern Western culture, marginal to the ongoing competition over control of conduct and resources" (Pogge 1989: 22). In other words, justice is concerned with the justifiability of the design of a proper subset of social practices: those public ground rules that define and secure our basic rights and liberties, and property rules that govern what can be owned, how items can come to be owned, what rights one has by owning something, and so forth.

What follows is this: If justice analysis becomes relevant only upon the prior existence of a system of social interaction that rests upon some form of property system, then any condition which is a prerequisite for property relations to exist must itself be prior to justice analysis, and, as such, cannot reasonably be judged to be either "just" or "unjust." For Freeman, one such condition is the exclusive territorial control by a polity.

And it is not only territoriality but more generally the statist mode of political organization that enjoys this status, Freeman seems to think:

> The institution of property is presupposed by economic cooperation; property is largely a legal institution and *cannot* exist—except perhaps in primitive form—in the absence of political cooperation according to the terms of a political constitution and a legal system ... What makes possible the incredibly complicated system of legal norms that underlie economic production, exchange and consumption is *a unified* political system that specifies these norms and revises them to meet changing conditions.   (Freeman 2006b: 38–9; my italics)

The state-centric character of Freeman's notion of a "unified" political system can be thrown into sharp relief by contrasting it with Pogge's proposal that the present states system be drastically reformed by a vertical dispersal of political authority rather than have it concentrated at the state level (Pogge 2008: ch.7). It is clear that under such a system, wherein decision powers over different policy areas are held separately by different political units (with none of them having comprehensive authority) and/or the power over a particular policy area is handled by various units (with none of them having supreme authority), whatever economic activities take place within such a system will not be ones under the auspices of a political authority that is in any recognizable sense "unified."

To sum up Freeman's reasoning: Since a people's right to independent control of a territory and. more generally, a state-centric and unified mode of political organization is a precondition for the existence of a property system, such an assignment of territorial right and mode of political organization are, *pace* Pogge, beyond the pale of justice analysis.[10]

Does this show one to be making a category mistake when one deems the present states system, as an integral component of the current global order, just or unjust? The major problem with the reasoning outlined above is that it rests upon a dubious empirical premise: it is highly doubtful that exclusive territoriality or, more generally, a concentration of governmental functions at the single level of territorial states is a necessary condition for property relations and a relatively stable system of rule-based social interactions to exist. A system of property existed in medieval feudal Europe, even though there did not exist any state-like entity enjoying exclusive control over a territorial area with clear boundaries. Peasants were granted the right to use the land on condition that they rendered homage and military services. In case Freeman might disqualify this as a property system for its being too "primitive," we can consider the institutional arrangement of the German city-leagues, which lasted from the twelfth to the seventeenth centuries in response to the increasing opportunities of long-distance trade in the North Sea and Baltic over that period. One prominent example of such city-leagues was the Hanseatic League. The Hanseatic League as a confederated body exhibits an organizational form that is diametrically opposed to the sovereign state model.[11] On the one hand, it did not have clearly demarcated territorial boundaries. On the other, it did not have a recognized locus of final decision-making authority: it lacked a constitution, and the internal authority was fragmented between individual member cities and the league of towns. In spite of these, the city-league had proved quite capable of protecting the property system that underlay the growing commerce in the form of east-west maritime trade both between its member cities and other actors. Admittedly, the commercial activities undertaken during the Late Middle Ages were incomparable to what we have at present in terms of their relative volume and efficiency, and so forth, as Freeman (2006b: 61) has reminded us that "[t]here are an enormous number of laws, regulations, legal precedents, and conventions that structure property and economic systems (literally millions in the US federal system)." In addition, a case might well be constructed for the claim that economic globalization with its present magnitude and extent would not have occurred but for the existence of the modern states system. Granting these claims for argument's sake, it is still not clear how one can credibly argue that the enabling of such complex business activities should be regarded as a *defining* feature of a system of property, the design of which social justice is concerned with.

A number of proposals have been put forward by cosmopolitan scholars on how to reform the existing political international order to make it better align with democratic principles and cosmopolitan aspirations, the implementation of some of which will result in a global distribution of political authority that is no longer recognizably statist. In spite of this, Freeman (2006b: 61) claims that "for a variety of reasons, the existence of a number of different societies, each with their own political institutions, is a *permanent* fact about social life…there is no escaping the fact of independent societies each with their own basic structure." Pending further exposition and defense of that "variety of reasons," the contention that the current system of territorial states cannot properly be included in our global justice analysis on the grounds that a state's exclusive territorial control, or a statist system of world organization, is an existence condition of property institution and should, therefore, be regarded as part of the circumstances of justice remains unconvincing.

4 Assessing the Justice of the Global Order and the States System

Having argued for the significance and legitimacy of examining the justice credentials of the global order in its entirety, in this section I aim to illustrate another important aspect of Pogge's understanding of justice analysis: the justice of an institutional scheme cannot be vindicated by merely showing its superiority over some specific alternative arrangements, each of which enjoys some initial plausibility. I will illustrate this through an examination of the defense of the classic states system put forward by Mathias Risse (2006). Risse recognizes that the existence of a states system does legitimately raise question concerning its moral justifiability. He thinks that one appropriate justificatory standpoint to answer that question is what he calls a "quasi-Rawlsian" global original position. It is called "quasi-Rawlsian" because, rather than constructed for the purpose of choosing a set of principles guiding the formulation of foreign policy by liberal and decent peoples, as Rawls (1999a) has done in *The Law of Peoples*, the parties are now tasked with choosing from the following three alternative arrangements of global political authority:

Proposal 1:   Classical states system, with the stipulation that "what these states can do internally and externally will have to be constrained: their actions towards their citizens must be guided by certain moral standards; they must allow for certain forms of immigration; and they must grants rights of refuge and asylum if other states fail (as some inevitably will)" (Risse 2006: 694).

Proposal 2:   The same as proposal 1, except that the borders are under international control.

Proposal 3:   Pogge's proposal that political authority be dispersed vertically at a number of levels rather than being concentrated on the state level.

Risse first contends that the cases put forward for both proposals 2 and 3 have serious weaknesses. Firstly, with regard to proposal 3, he contends that we have no reasonable basis to decide whether its implementation will indeed bring about the benefits alleged by Pogge:

[Pogge] insists that the existence of states undercuts peace, security, global justice, democracy, the reduction of oppression, and the maintenance of ecology...Yet how can we tell whether problems that Pogge asserts arise because of the sheer existence of a system of self-determining entities or because of its local failures, and its general need for reform (e.g., independence of states to be transformed into independence of peoples)? It is difficult to acquire the relevant knowledge to decide whether the states system needs "reform" or "revolution," since we can observe only this one world.

(Risse 2006: 695)

With regard to proposal 2, Risse, drawing on Freud's idea that human beings have a penchant for certain forms of destructive behavior regardless of the form of society they live in, claims that "one does not need to be overly pessimistic to doubt the stability of such an arrangement, and whether the benefits of such a system make up for the loss of self-determination" (Risse 2006: 695).

While the credentials for proposals 2 and 3 are dubious, Risse suggests that two reasons can be given in favor of proposal 1. The first points to the states' superior efficiency in the provision of public goods, while the second points to the value of self-determination: the desires of persons to live in groups in which members are bound to one another by ties of common sympathies, groups which are the "primary locus of social, economic, and political structures" to which they belong (Risse 2006: 694).

Acknowledging that the considerations adduced so far are insufficient to provide the parties at the original position with a decisive case in favor of Proposal 1, Risse contends that the most promising way to proceed is to take seriously Rawls's advice that moral reasoning about global justice must be realistically utopian; and in our world, a principle of global justice that is realistically utopian would be one that places great emphasis upon the self-determination of peoples:

> Pursuing self-determination of peoples is *utopian* in the sense that, although self-determination is widely desired, many peoples are not self-determining… At the same time, pursuing this ideal is *realistically* utopian in the sense that self-determination is, as an ideal, already embodied in the global order, especially through occupying a central place in the UN documents.   (Risse 2006: 696)

For Risse, this means the quasi-Rawlsian original position should be constructed accordingly, such that the parties will have their deliberations guided by the assumption that the clients they represent have a fundamental interest in belonging to self-determining peoples. Upon such reconstruction, Risse thinks the parties will rule out proposals 2 and 3 for their failure to be realistically utopian and endorse proposal 1. For Risse (2006: 697), "[t]his sort of defense of the state (and hence of Proposal 1 above) is the best we can do".

It is not clear that the case constructed by Risse is the best we can do. Even though through the inclusion of Proposal 3 Risse is thereby distancing himself from an untenable unitary, all-or-nothing conception of state sovereignty, by rigidly limiting the set of candidate institutional arrangements to three and taking that a satisfactory case for the classic states system can be made out of showing its superiority to the other two candidates, Risse has failed to recognize the genuine possibility that the claims, duties, powers, and liabilities currently thought to define statehood can be "unbundled" in many other alternative ways. For instance, establishing Pogge's Global Resource Dividend (GRD), which involves removing a state's full property right to enjoy the benefits derived from exploiting the natural resources found within its territory, would result in a world order that diverges from the classic states system characterized in proposal 1 in an important way. Yet it is also distinct from and is not implied by either proposal 2 or 3.[12]

What accounts for the inadequacy of this approach to institutional justice analysis is its construing such an analysis as consisting essentially in an exercise of comparing and choosing from a list of alternative institutional arrangements that is priorly fixed, rather than, as Pogge sees it, as an open-ended exercise of examining whether there exists *any* alternative to the existing arrangement that both is feasible and tends to produce a better outcome according to some defensible principle of justice. On Pogge's understanding, it would be a non sequitur for one to argue that, since for various reasons an existing institutional arrangement is superior to certain specific candidate alternatives that are seemingly appealing, the existing arrangement is, therefore, just. It is a non sequitur because there is no a priori reason to think that those alternatives exhaust all reform proposals of the status quo, the implementation of which, first, will foreseeably bring about a global distribution of morally significant goods and ills that we have moral reasons to prefer, second, is feasible and, third, is assessable from where we are now without incurring unacceptable transition cost. Another way of articulating the weakness of this approach is as follows. Risse doubts that we can ever gather enough information to determine with confidence whether Pogge's proposal of a vertical dispersal of sovereignty will indeed bring about the promised benefits of better peace, security, global economic justice, and less oppression. But in expressing such doubts, Risse is thereby implicitly accepting that these concerns with the global incidence of world peace, security, and so forth do provide us with some rudimentary principles of global justice on the basis of which we are to access the relative moral quality of alternative global institutional schemes. In light of this, the direction that Risse's reasoning ought to have taken is to actively *explore* whether we can come up with any proposal that tends to generate a distributive pattern superior to that of the status quo by the lights of those rudimentary principles (and perhaps also taking into account peoples' interest in self-determination), rather than confining his best case for the states system to an attempt to demonstrate its moral supremacy within a closed set of alternative arrangements.

Noticing the limitation of such an approach to institutional justice analysis helps bring out another attractive feature of Pogge's approach, namely its flexibility. Taking the cue from Rawls, Pogge reminds us that, since the same set of institutions operating under different empirical circumstances—for instance, the varying cultures and levels of economic and technological development across societies—will probably produce different patterns of interest fulfillment, there is no single set of institutions that is required by justice to be universally put in place. Taking a principle of justice to be rigidly demanding or forbidding a specific set of domestic institutions might then lead us astray, as when we are led from the judgment that, for instance, measures giving preferential treatment to certain ethnic minorities ought to be implemented in a given society in order to redress the historic subordination suffered by members of those minorities to the mistaken judgment that similar measures ought to be implemented in other societies which have been free from such historic injustice. With no good reason standing in the way of generalizing this to the global plane, we must guard against the tendency to treat the problem of global institutional justice as one that can *readily* be reduced to the choice between, for instance, a plurality of sovereign states in their present form, an absolute world sovereign, or some specific reform proposal favored by a certain theorist.

5 Concluding Remarks

Admittedly the considerations adduced above are far from sufficient to establish the overall defensibility of Pogge's conception of global justice. And indeed certain aspects of it do call for closer examination and further development. One aspect concerns Pogge's view on the assignment of moral responsibility for global injustice. While Pogge's work on world poverty is mainly targeted at the affluent adult citizens of Western democratic societies, what about those living in an affluent society with extensive civil liberties whose government is playing a substantial role in the design and upholding of global institutions, except that these citizens are denied the right to meaningful democratic participation? A case in point is that of Hong Kong, which is a part of the sovereign state of China.

Pogge's notion of feasibility also merits closer examination: What is the epistemic threshold that must be crossed for us to reasonably regard the existing global order as unjust on account of there being a *feasible* alternative that generates a morally superior global distributional profile? On the one hand, given the extremely profound and pervasive repercussions any significant modification of the global order might have across the world, a sufficiently rigorous epistemic threshold is called for if we are to avoid gross irresponsibility. On the other hand, raising the bar beyond a certain level would risk depriving the whole exercise of subjecting global institutions to justice assessment of its practical relevance, as, with "no simultaneous alternative worlds to be observed" (Pogge 1988: 230), we are faced with a dearth of comparative statistical data at the global level. Coming up with a principled account of feasibility that is both robust and defensible upon taking adequate account of our epistemic limitation in conducting counterfactual reasoning at the global level without thereby draining Pogge's conception of global justice of its action-guiding power would constitute a significant step towards establishing its overall reasonableness.

Notes

1. Note that this thesis is not equivalent to, or nor does it entail, the claim that domestic and global institutional schemes should be subject to the same set of justice principles. One might consistently hold that the domestic basic structure should fulfill requirements of *egalitarian* justice in view of certain normatively significant features of the relations

between citizens, while there are certain minimal constraints of justice, for instance ones that are couched in terms of human rights, that apply to *any* institutional scheme irrespective of whether those subject to it are bound by ties of common citizenship.

2. Freeman (2006a), (2006b), (2007: chap.10).

3. Risse (2006).

4. For a similar remark by Pogge, see Pogge (2008: 177).

5. In this chapter the states system is taken to consist of a public system of rules that constitutes a mode of world political and economic organization within which the principal bearers of rights and duties are sovereign states. With regard to the idea of state sovereignty, I will follow Simon Caney (2005: ch. 5) in taking its primary features to include supremacy, comprehensiveness, and territoriality.

6. See, for instance, Abizadeh (2008); Carens (1987).

7. Richard Miller makes a similar remark when he characterizes Pogge's view of global justice as appealing to "a characterization of global realities that is one easy step beyond the elementary facts of global wealth and poverty: the obvious *mere* fact of extensive and important global commerce, asserted without commitment to any further feature of interactions across borders" (Miller, 2010: 32; my italics).

8. One might also suspect that Blake's description of the case already carries with it an implicit naturalization of the states system, which helps prevent such a system from coming into view as a proper object of justice assessment. One might wonder, instead of merely demanding that an international panel be set up and transfer payments be made from Borduria to their society, why would the Syldavian explorers not be putting forward the even more fundamental challenge to the Bordurians' claim-right to exclusive control of their territory and the natural resources found within?

9. Freeman has also argued specifically that the various international treaties, despite their having profound transnational effects, are not appropriate vehicles for global distributive justice in view of their having only secondary as opposed to original political authority. His view on this merits a separate treatment which I cannot give here due to space limits.

10. Since Freeman typically talks about a Rawlsian *people's* exclusive control of territory rather than that of a *state*, one might be tempted to think that Freeman's remarks have no bearing on the issue of whether it is legitimate to subject the states system to justice analysis. I think we should resist this temptation, for the reason that Rawls's notion of peoples remains essentially a state-centric one, with peoples' each possessing the defining features of state sovereignty.

11. Spruyt (1994: ch. 6).

12. For Pogge's GRD, see Pogge (2008: ch.8). I am of the view that, upon the introduction of a world order featuring Pogge's GRD as a candidate option, it is not clear that the states system would remain the parties' clear favorite, granting that proposals 2 and 3 are foregone conclusions in view of the parties' concern to protect their interest in self-determination. Given that GRD allows political communities to retain full control rights as to whether they are to extract any of their natural resources, and should they choose to do so, whether they are to be used entirely for domestic consumption or for exports, why would the parties not regard whatever loss incurred by the GRD to their self-determination to be sufficiently compensated for by the benefits in terms of, for instance, a lower global incidence of severe poverty that Pogge contends GRD will bring about? It is anticipated that Risse here would retort by saying that, while we can "draw on the historical, sociological, and other insights…about the one world we know and the one history it has gone through," "such insights will be insufficient to assess confidently how the world's political

system as a whole" would transpire were the GRD to be implemented, that we cannot tell whether, despite all the good intentions, GRD would be counter-productive in poverty reduction (Risse 2006: 695–6). See also Risse (2012: ch. 16). And it is on account of such epistemic considerations that Risse has stated that, even though "there will be other proposals on the agenda, but since the deliberators will be unable to choose between them, it is irrelevant whether their choice problem is more complicated" (Risse 2006: 694). In response, it should be noted that Pogge (1988: 230) has acknowledged that one of the reasons accounting for the relative neglect of justice analysis at the global level is that "comparative statistics are…harder to come by as there are no simultaneous alternative worlds to be observed." However, Pogge insists, and in my view rightly so, that it does not follow that many of our conclusions with regard to the workings of domestic institutions cannot safely be generalized onto the global plane. One example is the view that a more or less unrestrained market scheme, be it domestic or global, will over time generate certain centrifugal forces that lead to increasing inequalities in resources and bargaining power. Another example comes from Pogge's argument for a vertical dispersal of sovereignty on the basis of our ecological concerns. As in the domestic case, it is reasonable to expect that in the present states system the internalization of the negative environmental externalities generated by productive activities and global consumption will be incomplete due to the familiar isolation, assurance, and coordination problems. In view of the plausibility of these generalizations, I submit that the sweeping claim that we simply cannot assess with confidence the global distributive outcome that would tend to emerge upon the implementation of the reform proposals favored by Pogge or other global justice theorists should be treated with caution and be duly qualified.

References

Abizadeh, Arash (2008) "Democratic Theory and Border Coercion: No Right to Unilaterally Control Your Own Borders," *Political Theory* 36(1): 37–65.

Blake, Michael (2002) "Distributive Justice, State Coercion, and Autonomy," *Philosophy and Public Affairs* 30(3): 258–96.

Caney, Simon (2005) *Justice Beyond Borders*. Oxford: Oxford University Press.

Carens, Joseph (1987) "Aliens and Citizens," *Review of Politics* 49(2): 251–73.

Freeman, Samuel (2006a) "Distributive Justice and the Law of Peoples." In Rex Martin and David A. Reidy (eds.), *Rawls's Law of Peoples: A Realistic Utopia*. Malden, MA: Blackwell Publishing, 243–60.

Freeman, Samuel (2006b) "The Law of Peoples, Social Cooperation, Human Rights and Distributive Justice," *Social Philosophy and Policy* 23(1): 29–68.

Freeman, Samuel (2007) *Rawls*. New York: Routledge.

Miller, Richard (2010) *Globalizing Justice: The Ethics of Poverty and Power*. Oxford: Oxford University Press.

Pogge, Thomas (1988) "Rawls and Global Justice," *Canadian Journal of Philosophy* 18(2): 227–56.

Pogge, Thomas (1989) *Realizing Rawls*. Ithaca, NY: Cornell University Press.

Pogge, Thomas (1994) "An Egalitarian Law of Peoples," *Philosophy and Public affairs* 23(3): 195–224.

Pogge, Thomas (2002) "Responsibilities for Poverty-Related Ill Health," *Ethics and International Affairs* 16(2): 71–9.

Pogge, Thomas (2008) *World Poverty and Human Rights*. Cambridge: Polity Press.

Pogge, Thomas (2010) *Politics as Usual: What Lies behind the Pro-Poor Rhetoric*. Cambridge: Polity.

Rawls, John (1999a) *The Law of Peoples*. Cambridge, MA: Harvard University Press.

Rawls, John (1999b) *A Theory of Justice*, rev. edn. Cambridge, MA: Harvard University Press.

Risse, Mathias (2006) "What to Say about the State," *Social Theory and Practice* 32(4): 671–96.

Risse, Mathias (2012) *On Global Justice*. Princeton, NJ: Princeton University Press.

Spruyt, Hendrink (1994) *The Sovereign State and its Competitors*. Princeton, NJ: Princeton University Press.

FURTHER READING

Pogge, Thomas (2001) "Priorities of Global Justice," *Metaphilosophy* 32(1/2): 6–24.

Pogge, Thomas (2008a) "Cosmopolitanism and Sovereignty." In *World Poverty and Human Rights*. Cambridge: Polity Press, 174–201.

Pogge, Thomas (2008b) " Eradicating Systemic Poverty: Brief for a Global Resource Dividend." In *World Poverty and Human Rights*. Cambridge: Polity Press, 202–21.

CHAPTER 16

··

WHAT SECOND-BEST SCENARIOS REVEAL ABOUT IDEALS OF GLOBAL JUSTICE

··

CHRISTIAN BARRY AND DAVID WIENS

1 INTRODUCTION

IN this chapter we explore the options available to egalitarians confronting trade-offs between domestic and global equality, paying special attention to some of their respective benefits and costs. While there need be no conflict in theory between addressing global inequality (inequalities between people worldwide) and addressing domestic inequality (inequalities between people within a political community), there may be instances in which the feasible mechanisms for reducing global inequality risk aggravating domestic inequality. The burgeoning literature on global justice has tended to overlook the latter type of scenario. Consequently, theorists espousing global egalitarianism have not engaged with cases that are important for evaluating and clarifying the content of their theories.

Many who endorse policies to promote global equality are uncomfortable with the idea that such policies might undermine the living standards of disadvantaged people in their own societies. Thus, the trade-off we consider is likely to be a fraught one for them. We note that disregarding the evaluation of difficult trade-offs is not a sin unique to global egalitarians. Most justice theorists who endorse domestic egalitarianism but reject global egalitarianism posit a requirement—a duty of justice or of humanity—to promote the achievement of decent standards of living worldwide without considering how this requirement relates to their commitment to promote domestic equality.

2 Egalitarian Justice

Egalitarianism, broadly understood, has long been influential in theorizing about domestic justice. With some notable exceptions, justice theorists have repeatedly affirmed that the evaluation of domestic institutions should be sensitive to inequalities in distributive shares that they tend to generate over time.[1]

Egalitarians have, to put it mildly, often disagreed over precisely which conception of social justice is desirable. Egalitarian conceptions can be distinguished in terms of the subjects, goods, and distributive standards they consider when assessing distributive shares. The *subjects* of a conception of egalitarian justice indicate the subjects among whom equality is to be sought. Egalitarian conceptions may, for example, take individual persons as subjects, maintaining that there are limits to how steep inequalities in wealth, political influence, or other natural and social resources should be between them. Alternatively, they may focus on inequalities in the distribution of valued resources amongst social groups (e.g. as defined by gender, race, ethnicity, and so on).

The *goods* of a conception of egalitarian justice constitute the things to be distributed among subjects. Examples of such goods include capabilities and functionings, opportunities, income and wealth, economic power, civil and political rights—the last two putting the "liberal" in liberal egalitarianism.[2] Finally, egalitarian conceptions may differ in the *distributive standards* they employ. An egalitarian conception might defend strict equality as its preferred distributive criterion, but few do so.[3] Egalitarians need not be committed to viewing all inequalities in the relevant goods as wrong or regrettable. Which inequalities stand in need of redress, and to what extent, depends on the particular justification invoked in support of these standards. For instance, some such justifications might appeal to considerations of responsibility, holding that only inequalities due to circumstances, not to subjects' responsible choices, should be rectified.[4] Or they may insist on equality with respect to certain goods, but sufficiency or some reasonably high level of other goods.[5] Alternatively, egalitarians might follow Rawls and conclude that departures from equality are permissible so long as they can be justified to those who fare worst under them, thereby treating equality as a morally privileged benchmark, rather than a desired outcome.[6] And, of course, one can be an egalitarian while also embracing other values, such as giving some form of priority to concern for the less-advantaged.

We will refer loosely to all theories that express concern with equality in some way among some subjects with respect to some goods as "egalitarian justice." The literature on global justice has to this point focused largely on the *scope* of egalitarian justice, leaving aside questions pertaining to its content. This "question of scope" concerns whether conceptions of justice that are endorsed for the domestic sphere constitute appropriate standards on the global plane.

Two broad camps have emerged in this debate. Global egalitarians (we will call them "Extenders") support extending egalitarian justice to the global level.[7] Opponents of various stripes (we will call them "Restrictors") reject any such extension of scope.[8] Restrictors are not a cold-hearted lot. Many are egalitarians of some sort domestically, and nearly all of them advocate policies and institutional schemes that would likely mitigate inequalities worldwide to at least some degree.[9] Reforms with global-inequality-reducing effects may be adopted, for instance, in pursuit of the humanitarian goal—widely affirmed by Restrictors—of meeting people's basic needs so as to improve the absolute position of the globally disadvantaged. But Restrictors deny that inequalities per se are a reason for concern globally, even if they are so domestically.[10]

Many Restrictors advocate egalitarian justice domestically, so they need to provide good reasons why considerations that ground concern with equality within political communities do not also ground it globally. On the one hand, they must provide a plausible account of the grounds of egalitarian justice. On the other, they must show that these grounds are either not present at all or at least not in the requisite degree and form, on the global plane to justify concern with global equality per se.

The debate between Extenders and Restrictors has followed a fairly standard script. Restrictors assert that there is an empirical disanalogy between the global and the domestic spheres and argue that, in virtue of this disanalogy, restricting the scope of egalitarian principles of justice to the domestic sphere is justified. For Restrictors, everyone has certain "general duties," owed identically to everyone in the world. Over and above those, though, people also have "special duties" to particular others. Among those are often said to be "associative duties": people who are members of the same association (paradigmatically, family or country) owe things to one another that they do not owe to people who are not members of the association.[11] One of the things that members of some associations owe to each other but not to non-associates, Restrictors claim, is concern for equality.

What are the relevant features that associations must have for concern with equality to become a requirement of justice? Restrictors have focused mainly on two, cooperation and coercion. On the Cooperation Account, concern with distributive equality among some group of people is rooted in the fact that members of the group are cooperating in some joint venture. On the Coercion Account, concern with distributive equality among some group of people is rooted in the fact that members of the group are all subject to the same coercive authority. One can, of course, draw on *both* accounts in developing a conception of the scope of egalitarian justice, treating the existence of either or both Coercion and Cooperation as necessary or sufficient conditions for its application. Each of these accounts consists of a moral and an empirical claim.[12]

Take the Coercion Account. The moral claim here is that egalitarian justice *only* applies in the presence of some form of coercion.[13] The empirical claim is that coercion of the requisite sort is absent at the international level.[14] Extenders typically respond by trying to show either that this alleged empirical disanalogy between domestic and global with respect to the exercise of coercion does not obtain—pointing to the many ways in which coercion of the requisite sort is exercised on the global plane[15]—or that the empirical disanalogy is not morally relevant in the way that Restrictors suppose it to be, since coercion is not a necessary condition for the demands of egalitarian justice to apply.[16]

Two types of Extenders can be distinguished by the form of argument they emphasize in responding to Restrictors. The first group shares with Restrictors the view that the scope of egalitarian justice is limited to those who stand in some particular kind of social relation with one another (e.g. as set out in the Coercion or Cooperation Accounts, or in some other way). These "Associative Duty" Extenders, like Restrictors, treat duties to promote equality within some group as based on special duties that members of that group have to one another. However, they deny that the social relations that trigger these special associative duties are absent on the global plane. The second group of Extenders rejects this associationist picture entirely. These "General Duty" Extenders deny that the social relations emphasized by Restrictors and Associative Duty Extenders really are necessary for egalitarian justice requirements to apply. Extenders of this latter sort treat concern with equality as based on general duties held to all, rather than special associative duties held only to some.

3 THE IMPORTANCE OF TRADE-OFFS IN SECOND-BEST SCENARIOS

The debates between Extenders and Restrictors regarding the scope of egalitarian justice have been valuable; in particular, they have enriched thinking about the grounds for concern with equality more generally, and have led to deeper exploration of the nature of global institutions. Our aim here, however, is to draw attention to some of the important territory that they have left unexplored.

To provide a glimpse of that unexplored territory: Few Extenders have discussed whether *any* measure a state might adopt to bring about a decrease in global inequality would be justified were it to exacerbate inequality *within* that state.[17] One can surely argue that global inequality is an important normative concern in its own right, yet maintain that states wishing to participate in schemes to reduce global inequality should take special care to avoid measures that aggravate domestic inequality.[18] Such neglect arises in part from the fact that Extenders typically have in view the desirability of a specific kind of trade-off, namely that between the global rich and the global poor. Their advocacy of global egalitarianism typically begins by drawing attention to disturbing disparities in shares of global income among different quintiles or deciles before considering institutional reforms that would increase the life prospects of those in the bottom categories at the cost of decreasing (somewhat) the advantages of those in the top categories.[19] It is easy to see why Extenders take this route. It is very difficult to absorb these sorts of facts and not consider it to be a justice gain were the global rich to have less and the global poor more. Indeed, many Restrictors also view this distributive trade-off as a justice gain.[20] However, by concentrating on these ideal distributive trade-offs, Extenders have neglected ways in which the pursuit of egalitarian justice could lead to trade-offs that seem much more worrisome, morally speaking.

As initial motivation for attending to these trade-offs, notice that these worries are not merely academic; they concern many of the policy instruments that social scientists discuss when they consider such matters. For example, some economists claim that the best way to do something about poverty and inequality is not to engage in redistributive transfers from affluent countries to developing countries—this might be counterproductive (at least if provided in the form of intergovernmental aid[21]) and would probably be politically infeasible in any case—but to liberalize trade and immigration from poorer developing countries to affluent ones. Perhaps they are right. But trade and immigration liberalization are, as policy tools, too blunt to achieve with precision the distributive transfers desired by Extenders, namely from those with extremely high standards of living to those with very low standards of living. Such measures may instead engender aggregate transfers from the disadvantaged in affluent countries to the poor (and not so poor) in developing countries.

One might lodge two sorts of objections to excuse the aforementioned neglect: either that these policy prescriptions are misguided—immigration and trade liberalization might do little to address global inequality—or that the trade-offs we have suggested such policies might engender would not in fact obtain (e.g. liberalization of both sorts might both help address global inequality *and* promote the well-being of the disadvantaged in developed countries).[22] Suffice it to say that the empirical questions at issue here are hotly contested.[23] Yet it would be surprising if some of the general kinds of trade-offs we have raised—between protecting the interests of the domestic poor and promoting global equality—would *never* arise in considering the different policy instruments we might use to address global justice goals.[24] Indeed, there are good political economic reasons to think that they will arise.

The well-off in affluent societies typically wield preponderant political power. We can reasonably expect wealthy elites to use their power to resist policy reforms that could advance the interests of both the domestic and global poor at their expense. Even supposing wealthy elites are unable to prevent ostensibly pro-poor policy reforms, it seems reasonable to expect them to use their power to manage these reforms so as to capture a sizable portion of the aggregate gains, often at the expense of their less-advantaged compatriots. This is not to say that policies requiring the very affluent to bear most of the costs of improving the prospects of the global poor are altogether infeasible. We simply note that there are reasons to expect that attempts to close global inequality gaps will lead to trade-offs of the kind we raise here.

Even if one thinks that the risk of such trade-offs arising is slight, Extenders have more principled reasons to consider the kinds of trade-offs that would arise in second-best situations. We will show how Extenders address such scenarios reveals important aspects of their egalitarian *ideals*. (Extenders are not alone here; Restrictors, too, have overlooked the importance of considering the kinds of trade-offs that arise in second-best scenarios.)

Ideal theories are often said to illuminate the complexion of basic moral and social values (e.g. liberty, equality, community, efficiency, and so on) and the relationships among them, as well as providing guidance in our decidedly nonideal world.[25] Yet restricting our analysis to a narrow range of ideal scenarios—in which at best only a very limited set of trade-offs arise—leaves us with an impoverished understanding of basic values. To deeply understand the contours of a commitment to certain basic values, we must explore the implications of such a commitment across a broad range of scenarios, including those in which a host of desirable policy instruments for jointly realizing basic values will be unavailable. Political ideals remain indeterminate to the extent that we fail to consider the trade-offs that arise in such nonideal situations.

To sum up, both Extenders and Restrictors have typically specified their views in light of their implications for ideal contexts, have largely ignored the implications of their views in nonideal contexts, and have sidestepped what appears to be important test cases by focusing nearly exclusively on the question of scope. This is not just a problem in so far as it concerns the application of these conceptions of justice to the real world. It undermines a core objective of these conceptions, namely to offer a rich articulation of normative criteria for evaluating global distributive schemes.

4 COMPETING CLAIMS FOR EQUALITY

In what remains, we explore some of the trade-offs that arise when global equality can be achieved only through measures that diminish the position of less-advantaged people in affluent societies. Our aim is programmatic: to map certain types of trade-offs among moral and social values that might arise in this sort of scenario and the kinds of *ideal* moral considerations these types of trade-offs raise. We identify "choice points" for theorizing about broadly egalitarian approaches to global justice by revealing the normative commitments that are involved in saying one thing rather than another about how to address different types of trade-offs. The result will be a more detailed understanding of the range of views one might hold about global distributive justice that are egalitarian in spirit, not just for the nonideal case, but for the ideal case too. As we introduce these views, we will also note some of the justificatory challenges they face.

Consider a world that includes an affluent developed country (labeled D) and an underdeveloped country (labeled U). D is marked by nontrivial domestic inequality: the average income of D's elites (labeled Y_E) is notably higher than the average income of D's poorest residents (labeled Y_P). Let $G_D = Y_P/Y_E$ measure the degree of inequality within D (inequality increases as G_D diverges from 1). We assume that the institutional arrangements engendering inequality in D cannot be justified in ways that are congenial to egalitarians—e.g. they do not optimize the position of the least advantaged in society and are not necessary to sustain relatively high standards of living. This world is also marked by unjustifiable global inequality: even Y_P is higher than Y_U, the income of typical residents of U. Let $G_W = Y_U/Y_E$ measure the degree of global inequality.[26] Given our assumptions, $G_W < G_D$ (global inequality is greater than domestic inequality).

The status quo institutional scheme in this world, labeled Q, is such that D maintains some significant restrictions on cross-border economic interactions (trade, investment, etc.) with U.[27] In contrast, consider an alternative institutional scheme, labeled L, that liberalizes such cross-border interactions with U. We assume that, if implemented, L would greatly increase Y_U (by the familiar textbook mechanisms). We also assume that implementing L does not decrease D's aggregate income (so L is Pareto-efficient at the country level). However, L does increase domestic inequality (i.e., decrease G_D).[28] To ensure that shifting from Q to L decreases global inequality (i.e., increases G_W), we assume that Y_U increases at a greater rate than Y_E.

Given this scenario, should the egalitarian ideal imply that L is preferable to Q from the standpoint of justice?

5 BOUNDLESS AND BOUNDED GLOBAL EGALITARIANISM

Ideally, from an egalitarian standpoint, D would implement a tax and transfer policy T to offset the losses incurred by D's less-advantaged residents from establishing L. (Remember that L does not decrease D's aggregate income.) Any broadly egalitarian view affirms that D's less-advantaged residents have a reasonable complaint against those who stand in the way of implementing T if L is established. At a minimum, the package (L,T) would mitigate global inequality without increasing domestic inequality. Egalitarians agree in the ideal case: (L,T) is preferable to (L,not-T) from the standpoint of justice. But suppose (L,T) is not feasible (because, e.g., there is insufficient political will, D's elites use their political power to resist, or the technology required to implement the tax and transfer scheme is absent). According to the egalitarian ideal, is (L,not-T) preferable to Q = (not-L,not-T) from the standpoint of justice?

Global egalitarians encounter two broad options here. One response says that borders are simply irrelevant for settling the requirements of justice. Suppose justice requires us to mitigate inequality among a set of individuals, denoted N. Then, the fact that reducing inequality among the members of |N would lead to greater inequality among a proper subset of N is irrelevant: it does not provide a reason against reducing inequality among the members of N. Let us call this view "Boundless Egalitarianism." To provide some contrast, "Bounded Egalitarianism" (more precisely: "Boundary Weighted Egalitarianism") allows that borders may constitute a salient partition on N, such that justice requires us to (in some way) prioritize equality within parts before turning our attention to inequality within the superset N. According to Boundless Egalitarianism, (L,not-T) must be preferable to Q; Bounded Egalitarianism permits one to judge that Q is preferable to (L,not-T).

Boundless Egalitarianism has the advantage of neatly capturing one of the motivating intuitions of global egalitarianism: that all people everywhere are worthy of equal concern and respect and that people's life prospects should not be influenced—at least not unduly—by morally arbitrary factors such as race, gender, and place of birth. It is hard to see how General Duty Extenders can avoid this position. Boundless Egalitarianism must say that, under the specified circumstances, D's less-advantaged residents have no reasonable grounds to block the transition from Q to (L,not-T).[29] This implies that the Boundless Egalitarian ideal is ultimately undiscriminating when it comes to allocating the costs of increasing equality among the members of N. The magnitudes in losses to the disadvantaged in D would not matter, just so long as (L,not-T) yields a net gain toward global equality. This may be welcome news to General Duty Extenders, but it may also chase a fair few from the Boundless Egalitarian camp. No doubt, Boundless Egalitarians can agree that, as far as possible, it is preferable from the standpoint of justice to allocate these costs to those who are best positioned to bear them, namely the more advantaged members of N. But the scenario under consideration reveals an as yet neglected point: Extenders committed to Boundless Egalitarianism are committed to an egalitarian ideal that, in principle, places no limits on the subset of individuals who can be required to bear the costs of pursuing greater equality among the members of N.

Those who retreat from Boundless Egalitarianism at this point are left to consider Bounded Egalitarianism. Given a set of individuals N and a normatively salient partition on N, Bounded Egalitarians say that, all else being equal, inequalities within certain parts of N are more worrisome than inequalities within the superset N. Thus, Bounded Egalitarianism offers the prospect of reconciling a commitment to weighing domestic inequalities more heavily than global inequalities in the scales of justice with the view that (*pace* the Restrictors) global inequalities per se are, nonetheless, important.

This raises the question of how to weigh within-part inequalities relative to inequalities within the superset. Bounded Egalitarians have several options here. At one extreme, they might assert a lexical ordering of these requirements. In a weaker form, this lexical ordering could demand that policies addressing global inequality be adopted only in so far as they do not *exacerbate* domestic inequality. This would rule out the adoption of (L,not-T) over Q, but might permit global-equality-promoting policies that would leave the extent of domestic inequality unchanged, even if alternative (and incompatible) policies would increase domestic equality without commensurate gains in promoting global equality. In a stronger form, this lexical ordering demands that domestic egalitarian goals always take precedence over global egalitarian goals. This sort of view would not only rule out (L,not-T), but also any other set of policies that would fail to decrease domestic inequality, no matter how large the resultant decrease in global inequality. Alternatively, a Bounded Egalitarian view might eschew any form of lexical priority, yet still give extra weight to preventing or addressing domestic inequality gaps, all else being equal. Whether this sort of Bounded Egalitarian view would condemn or endorse (L,not-T) would depend on the magnitudes of gains and losses to the achievement of domestic and global egalitarian goals, and the weight that it attaches to each.[30]

Bounded Egalitarianism seems to capture a conviction, shared by many, that there is something objectionable about radically unequal distributive shares globally (in addition to the fact that those with less have so little), while at the same time permitting (or requiring) that agents regard unequal distributive shares within their societies as especially urgent concerns—to combine a kind of universal concern with associative duties. Perhaps more importantly here, in contrast with Boundless Egalitarianism, Bounded Egalitarian views can accommodate limits on the set of people who can be required to bear the costs of pursuing greater global equality, reserving the heaviest burden for the most affluent.

Bounded Egalitarians face two justificatory challenges: they must provide some rationale for treating a partition on N as normatively salient; and they must provide some rationale for treating within-part inequalities as normatively weightier than inequalities within the superset N. Associative Duty Extenders seem best positioned to address the latter.[31] It is hard to see what could motivate differential concern with domestic and global inequality, unless the conditions that fix the scope of egalitarian justice admit of degrees. For example, if the conditions of egalitarian justice are those set out in the Coercion or Cooperation Accounts, then Associative Duty Extenders might hold that the domestic sphere features more thoroughgoing coercion or cooperation than the global sphere, and that this provides us with a reason to give greater weight to domestic inequality.[32]

At the same time, however, attempts to meet the first challenge might leave Bounded Egalitarianism at risk of instability. Many of the reasons that theorists have invoked to justify concern with global equality may seem to steer us towards Boundless Egalitarianism in particular.[33] If concern with global inequality derives from the conviction that people's life prospects should not be influenced by morally arbitrary factors, then it is hard to see why we should not treat misfortunes due to one type of purportedly arbitrary factor (place of birth) to be of as much concern as other such factors (race, gender, etc.).[34] And if the conditions fixing the scope of egalitarian justice (coercion, cooperation, and so on) are thought of as thresholds, rather than a continuum, then this too would drive even Associative Duty Extenders toward Boundless Egalitarianism.

Putting the point differently, Bounded Egalitarians must provide reasons for departing from Boundless Egalitarianism that are consistent with their rationale for extending egalitarian justice from the domestic to the global plane in the first place. As noted, the most promising attempts to justify departures from Boundless Egalitarianism appeal to the kinds of factors that Restrictors have adduced in arguing against scope extension (coercion, cooperation, reciprocity, and so on). However, whereas Restrictors appeal to these factors to *restrict* the scope of egalitarian justice to the domestic sphere, Bounded Egalitarians must deploy them in a way that renders differential concern for domestic inequalities consistent with *extending* the scope of egalitarian justice to the global sphere. Bounded Egalitarians bear a different argumentative burden than Restrictors. The latter must show that the conditions that fix the scope of egalitarian justice are not present across the full set of individuals N, or not to a sufficient degree. Bounded Egalitarians must demonstrate something more subtle: that the conditions that fix the scope of egalitarian justice are satisfied across N, but that they are satisfied to a greater degree within certain subsets of N and that this differential degree of satisfaction warrants differential concern for the cause of equality. This is why the threat of instability looms for Bounded Egalitarians but not Restrictors. To avoid sliding toward a Restrictor position, the Bounded Egalitarian must prop up a concern for global equality. But the most promising attempts to do so threaten to push the Bounded Egalitarian toward Boundless Egalitarianism.

To conclude this section, we note that our discussion focuses on trade-offs between competing claims to equality "all else being equal." All else is unlikely to be equal, though—the less-advantaged residents of D might bear a normatively significant relationship to the poverty of U's residents. Here, we simply sketch two such relationships, only to set them aside. First, the less-advantaged residents of D might have contributed to the vulnerability of disadvantaged foreigners, for example by supporting policies that harm their environment or undermine their prospects for export-led growth.[35] Second, without themselves engaging in any wrongdoing, the less-advantaged residents of D might have been unjustly enriched from wrongs that had disadvantaged members of U, for example if D and U stood in a colonial relation of some sort or if D had engaged in unjust war against U in the past.[36] In either of these cases (although the second is perhaps more controversial), the relationship borne by the less-advantaged residents of D to the disadvantages to be addressed by L might serve to diminish the former's claim against implementing (L,not-T). Nonetheless, the issues we raise here remain important for elaborating and clarifying global egalitarian ideals.

6 EQUALITY VERSUS SUFFICIENCY

In the previous section, we considered various ways in which an Extender might handle trade-offs between competing concerns for distributive equality. We aimed not to advocate any particular resolution, but to expose the fact that any assessment of Extenders' egalitarian *ideals* turns on the resolution of these *nonideal* trade-offs, something that has been little noticed among global justice theorists. In this section, we show that our assessment of both Extenders' and Restrictors' ideals is sensitive to the ways in which they might handle nonideal trade-offs between distributive equality and distributive sufficiency.

To expose the relevant type of trade-off, we consider a modification of the base model introduced in Section 4. Recall that there is unjustifiable inequality both within D and between D and U. The policy choice continues to be between Q and (L,not-T), with L promising to raise Y_U, the income of the typical residents of U. Let H denote an income sufficiency threshold. We assume that the status quo is such that $Y_P > H$ and $Y_U < H$. The question of interest remains whether (L,not-T) is preferable to Q from the standpoint of justice.

> *Modification:* Suppose that implementing (L,not-T) holds D's aggregate income fixed and transfers income from D's poor to D's rich (again, so L is Pareto-efficient at the aggregate level). Hence, adopting (L,not-T) decreases $G_D = Y_P/Y_E$ (increases

domestic inequality). While adopting (L,not-T) increases Y_U, we assume that Y_E increases at a greater rate than Y_U, so $G_W = Y_U/Y_E$ decreases too (global inequality increases). We assume that the end result is such that (L,not-T) yields an outcome in which everyone achieves at least a sufficient share; hence, $H \leq Y_U \leq Y_P < Y_E$.

In other words, this case raises the following trade-off. On the one hand, (L,not-T) raises the global poor above sufficiency. On the other hand, these sufficiency gains come at the expense of both domestic and global equality; indeed, the less-advantaged residents of D bear the burden of bringing the global poor above sufficiency.

This case raises questions for Extenders and Restrictors alike. For Extenders: How important is global distributive equality relative to other values, distributive sufficiency in this case?[37] There is a rough consensus among Extenders that claims to sufficiency are more urgent than claims to equality. This judgment is typically meant to convey that a duty to realize global sufficiency is more *stringent* than a duty to realize global equality, where stringency is understood in terms of the costs one can be required to bear to satisfy the duty in question. This judgment is typically made in view of the ideal case, in which the global rich are (often tacitly) assumed to bear most of the costs of bringing the global poor to sufficiency. The implicit proposal, then, is that the global rich can be required, as a matter of justice, to bear quite heavy costs to realize global sufficiency, greater than the marginal costs they can be required to bear to move from global sufficiency to global equality.

Our nonideal case presses Extenders to refine their judgment that global sufficiency is more urgent than global equality, perhaps in ways that are surprisingly difficult to reconcile with their core theoretical commitments. Does the relative urgency of sufficiency imply that (L,not-T) is preferable to Q from the standpoint of justice? Extenders can go either way. Perhaps the more straightforward reply is to judge that (L,not-T) is preferable to Q—global sufficiency is, after all, more urgent than global equality. Notice that this reply is consistent with driving Y_P down to H; conditions might be such that, to raise Y_U to sufficiency, (L,not-T) yields $Y_U = Y_P = H$. We conjecture that any justification for judging (L,not-T) preferable to Q in view of this possibility is likely to be at odds with the egalitarian commitments at the core of the Extender position.

In *Modification*, (L,not-T) has a deeply inegalitarian implication: it accepts a *highly regressive* distribution of the costs required to realize sufficiency. The issue, then, is whether Extenders can square acceptance of a regressive distribution of costs with the extension of egalitarian justice to the global plane. It is no answer, at this point, to simply reiterate the moral urgency of relieving the global poor from their desperate plight. The question, after all, is whether Extenders' ideal of justice requires acceptance of a highly regressive distribution of costs *in exchange for* a state of affairs in which the global poor achieve distributive sufficiency.

Extenders might go the other way and judge that Q is preferable to (L,not-T) from the standpoint of justice, for at least a couple of reasons. Perhaps the costs borne by the domestic poor are more than justice requires in this case. Alternatively, perhaps there is some income threshold (between Y_P and Y_E), labeled Y^*, such that justice does not require individuals with incomes below Y^* to bear costs for the sake of realizing sufficiency. Notice, though, that both of these answers require Extenders to say something more nuanced about the relative urgency of realizing global sufficiency than they have said to this point.

Taking the second rationale first, what is the principle that picks out Y^* from among (infinitely) many options? We are skeptical that any particular Y^* can be given a principled rationale. But, setting that aside, we note that Y^* cannot be justified by appeal to the relative urgency of ensuring distributive sufficiency for the *domestic* poor—implementing (L,not-T) leaves $H \leq Y_p$ by assumption. Thus, any principle deployed to justify Y^* compels Extenders to identify conditions under which (domestic) equality takes precedence over (global) sufficiency or to introduce some additional consideration (reciprocity, liberty, and so on). Either way risks upsetting the Extender's rather simplistic normative landscape. (What if the most plausible justifications for imposing Y^* are in tension with extending the scope of egalitarian justice to the global plane?)

Regarding the first rationale, the domestic poor's income losses in our nonideal case are likely to be far less, in absolute terms, than the income losses Extenders seem prepared to impose on the rich in their ideal case. Given this, Extenders might reconcile a preference for Q over (L,not-T) with the judgment that justice can require the rich to bear quite heavy income losses for the sake of realizing global sufficiency in one of two ways. First, they might conceptualize costs in terms of some quantity that has diminishing marginal value in money—utility or well-being perhaps. Second, they might conceptualize the limit on the costs an individual can be required to bear in a way that is sensitive to her income—for instance, no more than a certain percentage of one's income. Both routes seem tenable to us, so our point is not to indicate that trouble awaits the Extender who seeks to impose a principled limit on the costs that the domestic poor can be required to bear for the sake of realizing global sufficiency. Rather, our point is that Extenders have yet to address the issues raised by our nonideal case and that neglecting to do so leaves us with an underspecified account of the relationship between basic distributive values.

For Restrictors, *Modification* raises questions, not about the relative importance of global sufficiency versus global equality, but about the relative importance of global sufficiency versus *domestic* equality.[38] Recall that Restrictors usually insist that, while we should not be concerned with distributive equality globally, we have a general duty to ensure that all people throughout the world achieve a decent standard of living. The question is how this goal fits with Restrictors' concern for domestic egalitarian justice. Restrictors have said little on the matter to this point.

Some Restrictors address this trade-off by saying that domestic equality is a requirement of justice, while helping people abroad achieve a decent standard of living is merely a humanitarian requirement.[39] For the purpose at hand, though, it is beside the point whether we treat global distributive sufficiency as a requirement of justice or a humanitarian requirement. If it is a requirement of justice, then the question is how these two justice requirements relate to one another. If it is a humanitarian requirement, then the question is how requirements of justice and humanity relate to one another. What matters is the importance attached to these different moral demands, rather than how they are categorized.

One possible way for Restrictors to address this trade-off claims that domestic equality has strict priority over global sufficiency; thus, Q is preferable to (L,not-T) from a moral standpoint. This view seems quite extreme. Imagine the feasible set includes two policy options: p_1 very slightly decreases domestic inequality, while leaving many people far below the sufficiency threshold, while p_2 leaves domestic equality untouched but raises everyone globally above the sufficiency threshold. We submit that the strict priority view bears a heavy burden in justifying a preference for p_1.

Restrictors might instead attach different weights to the achievement of these two requirements. Plausibly, a justifiable weighting scheme must be sensitive to at least the following two parameters. First, following from the last paragraph, the relative weighting of domestic equality gains versus global sufficiency gains should accommodate normative judgments that are sensitive to the relative size of the two kinds of gains (or losses). Second, our judgments are plausibly sensitive to the initial degree of domestic inequality and the initial extent of global deprivation. To wit, if G_D is quite close to 1 (so Y_P and Y_E are nearly equal) and the extent of global deprivation is high (many people are far below the sufficiency threshold), this would presumably count in favor of adopting a policy that would prioritize the achievement of global sufficiency gains rather than domestic equality gains. To be clear, our point here is not that Restrictors cannot plausibly address these issues in a way that can be reconciled with their core normative commitments (although doing so may be less straightforward than one might hope). Rather, our point is that Restrictors have yet to address these issues and, further, that they must do so if we are to gain an adequate understanding of their proposed ideals.

7 CONCLUSION

Philosophers often rely on considered judgments about particular scenarios when exploring the significance of more general normative principles. For example, if a normative theory you are considering implies that bonded or slave labor is permissible when it reduces economic inequality, but you find such a practice to be obviously objectionable, this is typically taken as a reason to reject the theory. Whether this reason is decisive depends on many other factors, including the availability of alternative theories that avoid this particular implication without having other implications that are more worrisome. Intuitive moral judgements of this sort—for example, that a society that permits bonded labor is seriously unjust—are often spontaneous, but they are also objects of reflection and thought. We are inclined to affirm certain general principles of global justice in large measure because, upon reflection, they cohere with these kinds of judgments about particular cases.

Of course, one *could* claim that moral principles do not need to be adjusted to our responses to particular cases. One could maintain that, although our judgments about some particular cases conflict with what would be the right thing to do according to certain principles, the latter are so obviously justified that we have no need to doubt them. But most philosophers working in this area have rejected this picture of justification and endorsed some version of John Rawls's method of reflective equilibrium (though often without the device of the original position). Roughly, a set of general principles is justified when they cohere with the moral judgments we endorse upon reflection.[40] The aim is to establish a theory but, at the same time, to retain considered judgments as far as possible. If this is the desired manner for developing a normative theory, it is important to consider as many cases as possible, since a theory that is consistent with firm intuitions in some instances may conflict with them in others. Our aim in this chapter has been to introduce a class of second-best scenarios that global justice theorists have neglected to this point and to demonstrate the importance of such scenarios as an aid to constructing and evaluating *ideals* of global justice.

ACKNOWLEDGMENTS

Many thanks to Glen Weyl, Michael Clemens, Robert Kirby, Laura Valentini, Richard Arneson, and participants in the Becker Friedman Institute's Conference on Normative Ethics and Welfare Economics at the University of Chicago and the seminar in Moral Social and Political Theory at the Australian National University for comments and suggestions on earlier presentations of these ideas.

NOTES

1. Exceptions include Nozick (1974); Raz (1986); Frankfurt (1988: ch. 11).
2. The literature on these topics is vast. Leading early discussions of such goods can be found in the essays in Nussbaum and Sen (1993).
3. For a good overview of some of the options, see Arneson (2002).
4. See, for example, Arneson (1989); Roemer (1993); and Cohen (2011). Notable critics include Anderson (1999) and Hurley (2003).
5. See, for example, Nussbaum (2006: esp., 292–5).
6. Rawls (1999).
7. Classic early defenses of the Extender position are Beitz (1979/1999) and Pogge (1989), both of whom adopted a broadly Rawlsian approach. More recent statements are offered by Moellendorf (2002); Tan (2004); and Caney (2005).
8. Armstrong (2012) makes a similar contrast between "egalitarian" and "minimalist" approaches.
9. D. Miller (2005).
10. Influential expressions of the Restrictor view are R. W. Miller (1998); Blake (2002); Nagel (2005); and D. Miller (2007).
11. Dworkin (1986: 195–206); Scheffler (2001).

12. One might appeal to something other than cooperation or coercion too. For example, D. Miller (1995) grounds a concern for distributive equality in shared national identity.

13. For example:

> We are required to accord equal status to anyone with whom we are joined in a strong and coercively imposed political community...There is a difference between voluntary association, however strongly motivated, and coercively imposed collective authority...Political institutions are different, because adherence to them is not voluntary...An institution that one has no choice about joining must offer terms of membership that meet a higher standard...once the state exists, we are in a new moral situation where the value of equality has purchase.   (Nagel 2005: 133; 140)

14. See, for example, Blake (2002); Nagel (2005); Risse (2006).

15. See, for example, Abizadeh (2007); Barry and Valentini (2009: 495–7); and Ypi, Goodin, and Barry (2009). Although his interest is not in justifying global egalitarianism, Pogge (2008: esp. ch. 4) has argued that the global economic order is coercively imposed by the world's wealthy and privileged on the world's poor.

16. See, for example, Arneson (2005: esp. 136–42), and Julius (2006: 179–80).

17. Two scenarios are worth considering. In the first, domestic inequality is increased *mechanically*, since the society has more poor people in it. A policy of immigration liberalization (IL) might mechanically increase the number of poorer people in some developed country (D). This could be consistent with it being the case that those who were less advantaged in D prior to the adoption of IL are not made worse off by the policy (or may even be made better off by it.) In this case, global inequality could be reduced and everyone made better off than they were prior to the adoption of IL. In the second, the increase in domestic inequality is not merely mechanical, but achieved by an increase in the wealth of the more advantaged or a decrease in wealth of the less advantaged in D. (The first type of case exposes some interesting fault lines in views on global justice, but we will set aside discussion of such cases here and return to it in our discussion of trade-offs faced by Restrictors in section 6).

18. This position is hard, if not impossible, to sustain if one is a General Duty Extender.

19. Pogge (2008); Brock (2009); Hassoun (2012).

20. R. W. Miller (1998); D. Miller (2005).

21. As argued, for example, in Easterly (2006).

22. See, for example, Pritchett (2006).

23. See for example, Borjas (1995), (2003), (2006); Card (2001); and González and Ortega (2011).

24. Many studies which argue that the effects of immigration liberalization on domestic wages are slight focus, reasonably enough, on immigration at historically observed levels. We note that when considering the potential effects of *very* large-scale immigration liberalization from affluent to developing countries at present, such studies do not necessarily provide a very trustworthy guide, and thus do not obviously support open-borders policies in the way that some of their advocates seem to suppose.

25. Robeyns (2008); Stemplowska (2008); Swift (2008); Simmons (2010); Gilabert (2012); Hamlin and Stemplowska (2012).

26. We will discuss the case in terms of income, but one could replace income by any favored metric (wealth, opportunities, capabilities, human rights, and so on).

27. We bracket cross-border migration so as to avoid the complications brought by dynamic population shifts. We also note that our specification of the status quo is consistent with the existence of a network of cross-border interactions that is sufficiently dense to trigger normative concern for the global inequality in our model among Associative Duty

Extenders. L does not represent a shift from no cross-border interaction to some interaction, but simply a shift to more intense or to different kinds of interaction than are present in the status quo. Hence, Associative Duty Extenders should assume that the relevant social or institutional features obtain. We wish to explore issues that are in some ways distinct from those that divide Associative and General Duty Extenders.

28. For now, we leave open which possibility consistent with this assumption obtains. As two examples, it could be that D's aggregate income is held fixed but some portion of it is transferred from the poor to elites; or it could be that the average income of D's less advantaged residents is held fixed and elites capture all the aggregate gains.

29. Moellendorf (2002: 63), an Associative Duty Extender, also seems to take this position. He argues (among other things) that if market competition for jobs is justified among compatriots, then "it is hard to find a reason" why it would not be justified between compatriots and non-compatriots, even if it is true that immigration negatively impacts domestic workers (though he expresses doubts about the veracity of the latter empirical claim).

30. The relative weight one gives to domestic equality might depend on the absolute levels of income of both the poorest domestic persons and the global poor. For example, one might treat income sufficiency as a more urgent concern than equality; hence, if (L,not-T) raises the global poor above sufficiency, that is a reason to favor (L,not-T) over Q, despite the fact that the former increases domestic inequality. We treat equality–sufficiency trade-offs in more detail in section 6.

31. Although we note that Bounded Egalitarianism neither entails nor is entailed by the views of Associative Duty Extenders.

32. Cf. Valentini (2012).

33. Cf. Caney (2005: ch. 5).

34. Gilabert (2011).

35. The notion of "contribution" is a relatively elastic one, extending from clear-cut cases of doing harm to more complex cases of enabling harm, and these different kinds of contributions might be relevant to such discounting to different extents. See, for example, the discussion in Barry and Øverland (2012).

36. See, for example, Thomson (1973); Butt (2007); Goodin (2013); and Barry and Wiens (2016).

37. For now, we set aside the complication—raised by our introduction of Bounded Egalitarianism—in which concerns for global and domestic equality are weighted differently. This possibility permits concerns for equality in different spheres to be traded off against global sufficiency in different ways. We take up trade-offs between domestic equality and global sufficiency in more detail in Section 6 below.

38. Notice that this question arises even if we relax our assumption that G_w, the degree of global equality, decreases. We continue to assume that G_D, the degree of domestic equality, decreases.

39. For example, Nagel (2005).

40. See Rawls (1971).

References

Abizadeh, Arash (2007) "Cooperation, Pervasive Impact, and Coercion: On the Scope (not Site) of Distributive Justice," *Philosophy & Public Affairs* 35(4): 318–58.

Anderson, Elizabeth (1999) "What Is the Point of Equality?" *Ethics* 109(2): 287–337.

Armstrong, Chris (2012) *Global Distributive Justice: An Introduction*. Cambridge: Cambridge University Press.

Arneson, Richard (1989) "Equality and Equal Opportunity for Welfare," *Philosophical Studies* 56(1): 77–93.

Arneson, Richard (2002) "Egalitarianism," Stanford Online Encyclopedia of Philosophy, http://plato.stanford.edu/entries/egalitarianism/, accessed August 20, 2019.

Arneson, Richard (2005) "Do Patriotic Ties Limit Global Justice Duties?" *Journal of Ethics* 9(1–2): 127–50.

Barry, Christian, and Gerhard Øverland (2012) "The Feasible Alternatives Thesis: Kicking Away the Livelihoods of the Global Poor," *Politics, Philosophy and Economics* 11(1): 97–119.

Barry, Christian, and Laura Valentini (2009) "Egalitarian Challenges to Global Egalitarianism: A Critique," *Review of International Studies* 35(3): 485–512.

Barry, Christian, and David Wiens (2016) "Benefiting from Wrongdoing and Sustaining Wrongful Harm," *Journal of Moral Philosophy* 13(5): 530–52.

Beitz, Charles R. (1979/1999) Political Theory and International Relations: With a New Afterword from the Author, rev. edn. Princeton, NJ: Princeton University Press.

Blake, Michael (2002) "Distributive Justice, State Coercion, and Autonomy," *Philosophy & Public Affairs* 30(3): 257–96.

Borjas, George J. (1995) "The Economic Benefits from Immigration," *Journal of Economic Perspectives* 9(2): 3–22.

Borjas, George J. (2003) "The Labor Demand Curve Is Downward Sloping: Reexamining the Impact of Immigration on the Labor Market," *Quarterly Journal of Economics* 118(4): 1335–74.

Borjas, George J. (2006) "Native Internal Migration and the Labor Market Impact of Immigration," *Journal of Human Resources* 41(2): 221–58.

Brock, Gillian (2009) *Global Justice: A Cosmopolitan Account*. Oxford: Oxford University Press.

Butt, Daniel (2007) "On Benefiting from Injustice," *Canadian Journal of Philosophy* 37(1): 129–52.

Caney, Simon (2005) Justice Beyond Borders: A Global Political Theory. Oxford: Oxford University Press.

Card, David (2001) "Immigrant Inflows, Native Outflows, and the Local Labor Market Impacts of Higher Immigration," *Journal of Labor Economics* 19(1): 22–64.

Cohen, Gerald A. (2011) *On the Currency of Egalitarian Justice and Other Essays in Political Philosophy*, ed. Michael Otsuka. Princeton, NJ: Princeton University Press.

Dworkin, Ronald (1986) *Law's Empire*. Cambridge, MA: Harvard University Press.

Easterly, William (2006) *The White Man's Burden: Why the West's Efforts to Aid the Rest Have Done So Much Ill and So Little Good*. Oxford: Oxford University Press.

Frankfurt, Harry G. (1988) "Equality as a Moral Ideal." In *The Importance of What We Care about*. Cambridge: Cambridge University Press, 134–58.

Gilabert, Pablo (2011) "Cosmopolitan Overflow," *The Monist* 94(4): 584–92.

Gilabert, Pablo (2012) "Comparative Assessments of Justice, Political Feasibility, and Ideal Theory," *Ethical Theory and Moral Practice* 15(1): 39–56.

González, Libertad, and Fransesc Ortega (2011) "How Do Very Open Economies Adjust to Large Immigration Flows? Evidence from Spanish Regions," *Labour Economics* 18(1): 57–70.

Goodin, Robert E. (2013) "Disgorging the Fruits of Historical Wrongdoing," *American Political Science Review* 107(3): 478–91.

Hamlin, Alan, and Zofia Stemplowska (2012) "Theory, Ideal Theory and the Theory of Ideals," *Political Studies Review* 10(1): 48–62.

Hassoun, Nicole (2012) *Globalization and Global Justice: Shrinking Distance, Expanding Obligations.* Cambridge: Cambridge University Press.

Hurley, Susan (2003) *Justice, Luck, and Knowledge.* Oxford: Oxford University Press.

Julius, Alexander J. (2006) "Nagel's Atlas," *Philosophy & Public Affairs* 34(2): 176–92.

Miller, David (1995) *On Nationality.* Oxford: Clarendon Press.

Miller, David (2005) "Against Global Egalitarianism," *Journal of Ethics* 9(1–2): 55–79.

Miller, David (2007) *National Responsibility and Global Justice.* Oxford: Oxford University Press.

Miller, Richard W. (1998) "Cosmopolitan Respect and Patriotic Concern," *Philosophy & Public Affairs* 27(3): 202–24.

Moellendorf, Darrell (2002) Cosmopolitan Justice. Boulder, CO: Westview Press.

Nagel, Thomas (2005) "The Problem of Global Justice," *Philosophy & Public Affairs* 33(2): 113–47.

Nozick, Robert (1974) *Anarchy, State, and Utopia.* Oxford: Blackwell.

Nussbaum, Martha (2006) *Frontiers of Justice: Disability, Nationality, Species Membership.* Cambridge, MA: Harvard University Press.

Nussbaum, Martha, and Amartya K. Sen (eds.) (1993) *The Quality of Life.* New York: Oxford University Press.

Pogge, Thomas W. (1989) Realizing Rawls. Ithaca, NY: Cornell University Press.

Pogge, Thomas W. (2008) *World Poverty and Human Rights: Cosmopolitan Responsibilities and Reforms,* 2nd edn. Cambridge: Polity Press.

Pritchett, Lant (2006) *Let Their People Come: Breaking the Gridlock on International Labor Mobility.* Washington DC: Center for Global Development; Baltimore, MD: Brookings Institution Press.

Rawls, John (1971) *A Theory of Justice.* Cambridge, MA: Belknap Press.

Rawls, John (1999) *A Theory of Justice,* rev. edn. Cambridge, MA: Belknap Press.

Raz, Joseph (1986) *The Morality of Freedom.* Oxford: Clarendon Press.

Risse, Mathias (2006) "What to Say about the State," *Social Theory and Practice* 32(4): 671–98.

Robeyns, Ingrid (2008) "Ideal Theory in Theory and Practice," *Social Theory and Practice* 34(3): 341–62.

Roemer, John E. (1993) "A Pragmatic Theory of Responsibility for the Egalitarian Planner," *Philosophy & Public Affairs* 22(2): 146–66.

Scheffler, Samuel (2001) *Boundaries and Allegiances.* Oxford: Oxford University Press.

Simmons, A. John (2010) "Ideal and Nonideal Theory," *Philosophy & Public Affairs* 38(1): 5–36.

Stemplowska, Zofia (2008) "What's Ideal about Ideal Theory?" *Social Theory and Practice* 34(3): 319–40.

Swift, Adam (2008) "The Value of Philosophy in Nonideal Circumstances," *Social Theory and Practice* 34(3): 363–87.

Tan, Kok-Chor (2004) Justice without Borders: Cosmopolitanism, Nationalism and Patriotism. Cambridge: Cambridge University Press.

Thomson, Judith Jarvis (1973) "Preferential Hiring," *Philosophy & Public Affairs* 2(4): 364–84.

Valentini, Laura (2012) *Justice in a Globalized World.* Oxford: Oxford University Press.

Ypi, Lea, Robert E. Goodin, and Christian Barry (2009) "Associative Duties, Global Justice, and the Colonies," *Philosophy & Public Affairs* 37(2): 103–35.

FURTHER READING

Armstrong, Chris (2009) "Global Egalitarianism," *Philosophy Compass* 4 (1):155–71.

Barry, Christian, and Pablo Gilabert (2008) "Does Global Egalitarianism Provide an Impractical and Unattractive Ideal of Justice?" *International Affairs* 84(5): 1025–39.

Estlund, David (2016a) "Just and Juster." In David Sobel, Peter Vallentyne, and Steven Wall (eds.), *Oxford Studies in Political Philosophy*, Vol. 2. New York: Oxford University Press, 9–32.

Estlund, David (2016b) "What is Circumstantial about Justice?" *Social Philosophy and Policy* 33(1–2): 292–311.

Farrelly, Colin (2007) "Justice in Ideal Theory: A Refutation," *Political Studies* 55(4): 844–64.

Gaus, Gerald (2016) *The Tyranny of the Ideal: Justice in a Diverse Society*. Princeton, NJ, and Oxford: Princeton University Press.

Gheaus, Anca (2013) "The Feasibility Constraint on the Concept of Justice," *The Philosophical Quarterly* 63(252): 445–64.

Gilabert, Pablo, and Holly Lawford-Smith (2012) "Political Feasibility: A Conceptual Exploration," *Political Studies* 60(4): 809–25.

Goodin, Robert E. (1995) "Political Ideals and Political Practice," *British Journal of Political Science* 25(1): 37–56.

Lawford-Smith, Holly (2013) "Understanding Political Feasibility," *The Journal of Political Philosophy* 21(3): 243–59.

Mills, Charles W. (2005) "'Ideal Theory' as Ideology," *Hypatia* 20(3): 165–84.

Räikkä, Juha (2000) "The Problem of the Second Best: Conceptual Issues," *Utilitas* 12(2): 204–18.

Schmidtz, David (2011) "Nonideal Theory: What It Is and What It Needs to Be," *Ethics* 121(4): 772–96.

Southwood, Nicholas (2018) "The Feasibility Issue," *Philosophy Compass* 13(8): e12509.

Stemplowska, Zofia, and Adam Swift (2012). "Ideal and Nonideal Theory." In David Estlund (ed.), *The Oxford Handbook of Political Philosophy*. New York: Oxford University Press, 373–92.

Valentini, Laura (2012) "Ideal vs. Non-Ideal Theory: A Conceptual Map," *Philosophy Compass* 7(9): 654–64.

Wiens, David (2015) "Political Ideals and the Feasibility Frontier," *Economics and Philosophy* 31(3): 447–77.

Wiens, David (2016) "Assessing Ideal Theories: Lessons from the Theory of Second Best," *Politics, Philosophy and Economics* 15(2):132–49.

CHAPTER 17

··

GLOBAL GENDER JUSTICE

··

ALISON M. JAGGAR

THIS chapter overviews some of the rapidly expanding philosophical work on global gender justice. In the space available, it is not possible to provide a comprehensive survey so I offer a sampling of issues and themes, none explored in depth. I aim to show that gender concerns are integral to many—perhaps all—aspects of global justice and that reflection on gender justice is encouraging fresh approaches to some important philosophical questions.

1 STARTING POINTS

··

1.1 What Is Justice?

Justice exists when social relationships are in moral balance. Plato thought of justice as a character trait, but this chapter takes it to be a desirable feature of the structures, institutions, and practices which provide the frameworks for systematic social relationships. Social relationships hold paradigmatically among human beings but may also hold among various kinds of collectivities and, arguably, even with animals. Philosophers concerned with justice ask how our collective life may best be arranged so as to produce a proper balance among the entitlements and obligations of all legitimate claimants. Philosophers perennially debate not only what should count as proper balance but also who/what are legitimate claimants of justice, what they may claim, and what are the spheres and circumstances in which these claims hold. For this reason, justice is called an "essentially contested" concept.

People's lives in every society are organized by structures, institutions, and practices which regulate divisions of labor, family relations, access to resources, and processes for dealing with conflict. Social structures create menus of available options for action and assign the respective benefits and costs of making various decisions. Unlike philosophers concerned with personal ethics, philosophers concerned with justice focus less on assessing specific decisions made by particular agents or entities and more on assessing the structure of the frameworks that open or close various options for those agents. When social structures are unjust, they provide systematically imbalanced sets of life options and prospects for the members of different social groups, enabling some to enjoy undeserved advantages and privileges while arbitrarily disadvantaging others and rendering them disproportionately vulnerable to ills such as violence, impoverishment, and political marginalization.

Gender is one dimension along which systematic injustice often occurs. Feminist social and political philosophy is dedicated to identifying injustices along this dimension and envisioning more gender-just social arrangements. Most feminist work has focused on relational and distributive justice, studying what would constitute just relationships among genders and fair distributions of social benefits and burdens, entitlements, responsibilities, and opportunities. However, feminist philosophers have also contributed to the literatures on retributive justice, which deals with how wrongdoing should be punished, reparative justice, which investigates how to compensate or repair past wrongs, and transitional justice, which considers how best to redress the legacies of massive human rights abuses.

1.2 What Is Gender?

Today, public discourse and official documents tend to use "sex" and "gender" interchangeably. However, sex is best understood as a biological classification, though not a simple one,[1] and gender as a complex set of social norms and expectations about the proper behavior of human individuals according to the biological sex they are assigned. People assigned to the male or female sexes are expected to behave in accordance with the respective gender norms prevailing in their societies. In most societies, more or less rigid gender norms shape most aspects of most peoples' lives, enabling and constraining their work opportunities and responsibilities and conditioning their access to resources. Gendered norms also regulate people's modes of self-presentation, dress, deportment, sexuality, and styles of speech.

Gender norms are often enforced coercively, so people who do not conform to prevailing standards of sex and/or gender may be subject to interventions intended to force compliance. Such interventions include involuntary sex assignment surgeries performed on intersex infants or children, and severe social sanctions for those whose behavior, including sexual behavior, violates gender norms. People who entirely reject their gender identities and even their initial sex assignments are often sanctioned with special severity, because transgender and transsexual people challenge widespread and deep-rooted beliefs that sex and even gender refer to natural kinds and that both are dichotomous.

Gender norms vary across societies, so different norms of masculinity and femininity characterize different social contexts. For example, farming, building, or trading may be regarded in one society as work for women and in another as work for men. Although multiple norms of masculinity and femininity prescribe different behavior for sexed individuals in various social contexts, transnational gender norms are also emerging, and some of these will be discussed in this chapter.

Gender everywhere is interwoven with other categories of difference and inequality, because people typically live within multiple systems of social power. In modern societies, no one is merely a man or a woman; in addition, we belong to specific nationalities, classes, religions, age cohorts, etc., and our gender identities are always shaped by these other social divisions.[2] The permeation of gender by other social categories and the consequent proliferation of gender identities are often called intersectionality. Both masculinities and femininities are intersectional.

Gender norms are not static but evolve in response to many factors, including direct efforts to change them. Feminist activists strive to transform institutions and practices that they believe embody unjust gender norms and produce systematically unjust relationships.

2 WHAT IS GLOBAL GENDER JUSTICE?

2.1 The Global as a Domain of Justice

If justice is a proper balance in social relationships, then questions about justice can arise only when entities are in some sort of social relation with each other. From the seventeenth to the mid-twentieth centuries, most Western philosophers agreed that the moral demands of justice held only among humans who shared a common way of life, and they typically identified the boundaries of this moral community with the frontiers of the sovereign state. Because no governance institutions existed to regulate relations among states, philosophers thought that the international sphere could not be a site of justice and instead regarded it as a potential battleground in which each state must be perpetually prepared for war against any or all of the others.

After WWII, several institutions of global governance were established and philosophers began revising their longstanding assumption about the spatial domain of justice. The 1945 establishment of the United Nations provided a framework for international cooperation and the 1948 Universal Declaration of Human Rights expressed a cosmopolitan concern for the rights of all human beings everywhere. The Nuremberg and Tokyo war crimes tribunals, as well as later tribunals, were designed to demonstrate that these rights must be respected universally. In 2002, the International Criminal Court was founded as a permanent international tribunal to prosecute individuals for genocide, crimes against humanity and war crimes. During the same period, the global economy became more tightly integrated and organized through the establishment of international financial institutions, notably the World Bank and the International Monetary Fund, and the World Trade Organization, designed to regulate global trade, was established in 1995. All these developments encouraged philosophers to begin recognizing the global arena as a domain of justice. However, philosophical controversy continues over which entities are properly considered claimants of justice in this domain, what type of claims may be negotiated, and what principles of justice are appropriate.

2.2 Women in Nonwestern Cultures

Scattered reflections on sex equality can be traced far back in the history of Western philosophy, but philosophical thinking about this topic increased dramatically in the early 1970s. Influenced by the second-wave feminist slogan "The personal is political," feminist philosophers challenged traditional understandings of the domain of justice, just as global justice theorists were beginning to do. However, whereas global justice theorists argued that the domain of justice extended beyond the frontiers of the state, feminist philosophers argued for recognizing claims of justice in the close quarters of so-called personal life, including sexual, procreative, and family relations. They pointed out that these areas of life were structured by gendered power imbalances and argued that justice questions should be raised about many issues hitherto neglected by academic philosophy, including domestic violence, unpaid domestic work, abortion, and many issues involving sexuality.

In the 1990s, a few philosophers began raising concerns about gender justice at the global level. Two prominent liberal feminists, Susan Okin and Martha Nussbaum, were troubled by various Nonwestern practices which they perceived as unjust to women. They sought philosophical justification for challenging those practices and were disturbed by what they saw as the relativism of postcolonial feminists who resisted simply condemning the practices. In Okin's and Nussbaum's view, the central philosophical issues of global gender justice were moral universalism versus cultural relativism and the possibility of "external" as opposed to "internal" social criticism (Okin 1994; Nussbaum 1992, 2000). Okin's and Nussbaum's work was extremely valuable in raising questions about some gendered aspects of global justice, but they framed some of the issues in ways that were unduly narrow and misleading.

2.3 Expanding Understandings of Global Gender Justice

Some of the limitations of Okin's and Nussbaum's work on global gender justice resulted from their using the term "culture" in a particular sense employed in the 1990s by many anglophone political philosophers. In this usage, culture was taken to refer primarily to religion, sexuality, and family life as opposed to politics and economics.[3] It was the same sphere of personal life that the feminist philosophers of the 1970s had emphasized. Okin wrote, "the sphere of personal, sexual, and reproductive life provides a central focus of most cultures" (Okin 1999: 12). When culture is interpreted in this sense, it has special significance for women, as Okin noted, because these are areas of life to which women are often relegated.

Okin's and Nussbaum's attention to matters of religion, family, and sexuality was certainly legitimate, but the heavy emphasis they gave to those areas tended to divert attention from the ways in which gender is also embedded in the basic political and economic structures of most societies. Not only are women a large and increasing proportion of the paid workforce in both the formal and informal economic sectors of most societies but even women's unpaid work at home produces crucial economic goods and services, such as food and healthcare. In addition, focusing on cultural issues, construed as somewhat distinct from economic and political structures, tends to suggest that achieving gender justice is more about changing beliefs and attitudes than it is about reforming basic structures. Thus, taking gender injustice to be primarily cultural, in the sense used by political philosophers of the 1990s, minimizes its extent and depth.

A further problem with Okin's and Nussbaum's conception of culture was its assumption that clear contrasts could be drawn among cultures. Uma Narayan argues that drawing such contrasts requires culturally essentialist generalizations, which offer totalizing characterizations of whole cultures treated as static, internally homogeneous, and externally sealed (Narayan 1998). More empirically adequate understandings recognize that cultures are internally contested and constantly evolving, often in response to external influences; for example, gender norms in many Asian, African, and Latin American societies were forcibly altered by colonization, and fading cultural traditions sometimes gained new life as symbols of resistance to colonialism.[4] In focusing on gender injustice in Nonwestern cultures, Okin and Nussbaum tended to treat those cultures as self-contained, rather than seeing them as interacting with larger global contexts.

Additional limitations of Okin's and Nussbaum's work included its implicit assumptions that West is Best for women and that they were personally able to assess "other" cultures impartially (Jaggar 2005). Okin and Nussbaum did not address the possibility that their own judgments might be biased by their specific global locations, partial perspectives, cultural values, and even adaptive preferences. Finally, by expressing concern only for women, they ignored gender injustice to men and boys.

Since the turn of the millennium, philosophical work on global gender justice has expanded and become more self-reflective. Through examining the gendered dimensions of issues such as war, global governance, political freedom, nationalism, migration, indebtedness, poverty, mental health, climate change, and more, feminist philosophers are revealing that gender is integral to virtually all aspects of global justice, not limited to a few marginal issues. As they study the ways in which local practices interact with global structures, they have recognized that many unjust practices are nore than self-contained local matters. Moreover, they are giving more attention to the gendered forces which shape and constrain men's as well as women's lives in the changing global order. Currently, philosophers working on global gender justice investigate how gendered norms and practices often cross across national borders and seek to identify emerging transnational gendered collectivities and identities. Finally, many philosophers working on global gender justice are reflecting on the ways in which their own philosophical perspectives might be shaped by their particular locations in the global order and exploring epistemological and methodological issues regarding situated assessments of global justice.

3 Some Normative Issues of Global Gender Justice

3.1 Some Structural Features of the Current Global Order

Although women's and men's situations vary widely among and within different regions of the world, many gender parallels exist. The *World Bank's 2012 World Development Report: Gender Equality and Development* provides a recent comprehensive overview (World Bank 2011). The report finds that advances toward gender equality have been made on several fronts. Gender gaps in primary education have closed in almost all countries, and in many countries girls now outnumber boys in secondary schools, and young women outnumber young men in universities. Nutrition and life expectancy have improved in general and for women in particular—though unevenly (World Bank 2011: xx). Women's labor force participation has risen, progress has been made towards women's formal rights, and in many countries fertility rates have declined rapidly (World Bank 2011: xi). Nevertheless, women worldwide tend to have less access to resources than men of the same ethnicity, class, and even family and to be more vulnerable to overwork, sexual violence, and political marginalization.

Philosophers concerned with the gender dimensions of global justice have identified several structural features of the current global order which are facially gender-neutral but profoundly influence gender relations worldwide. Below I list some of those features, whose relevance to issues of gender justice will emerge in subsequent sections.

1. The lingering effects of past colonization mean that countries becoming independent in the middle of the twentieth century were disadvantaged as they entered the new global order. Today, many of these countries still function in this order primarily as sources of raw materials and unskilled or semi-skilled labor. This radically affects the life prospects for women and men in those countries, though typically in different ways.

2. In order to meet their basic material needs, increasing numbers of people depend on an expanded and integrated global market. Dependence on this market has transformed the working lives of many women who continue to produce most of the world's food and clothing but do so now in context of global supply chains (Balakrishnan 2002). Expansion of the global market has not only transformed local economies; it has also rendered them more vulnerable to exogenous shocks.

3. Since 1970, when the period of formal colonization was ending, the economic gap has widened between what is now called global North and global South, giving the global North disproportionate influence in setting the rules of international trade.[5] These rules have often been criticized not only for general unfairness to poor countries but also specifically for placing disproportionately heavy burdens on the women of those countries.

4. Following the international debt crisis of 1970s, many nations in the global South were subjected to strict conditions for debt servicing and further borrowing. These conditions are often referred to as "structural adjustment" policies. They were guided by neoliberal political philosophy and characterized by reduction of trade tariffs, hostility to government regulation, private exploitation of hitherto public assets, and austerity in social services. Austerity weighed particularly heavily on women in countries subjected to structural adjustment, because their socially assigned responsibilities for family welfare made them especially dependent on social services (Jaggar 2002).

5. Shocks to the global economy, such as the oil crisis of the 1970s, which raised indebtedness among less-developed countries, and the 2008 financial crisis, which intensified structural unemployment, have increased inequality both within countries and among them. These inequalities have gender dimensions.

6. Global wealth inequality motivates millions of people to migrate internationally despite increasingly draconian restrictions on immigration into wealthy countries. Gender-structured labor markets and definitions of family mean that contemporary migration is deeply gendered.

7. Radically improved global communications, especially access to the Internet, have resulted in the transnational spread of ideas. Western ideas have disproportionate influence because much of the material is in English and produced in the West. They include gender ideologies characterized by distinctive conceptions of what it is for men and women to be successful, happy, and sexually desirable.

8. Conflicts over resources and proxy wars have drastic consequences for all affected populations, but these consequences differ systematically for groups differentiated by class, gender, and age (Jaggar 2014b). They include the breakdown of social order, forced conscription of boys and young men, and rape and sexual torture, whose victims include boys and men but are mostly girls and women.

These structural features of the current global order are reshaping gender relations and raising many questions of gender justice.

3.2 Feminization of the Global Labor Force

In many countries of the global South, women's traditional subsistence agriculture, local market food production, and small-scale textile and garment production have been undermined by the expansion of export agriculture and a flood of cheap mass-produced imports, often required by structural adjustment programs. Today, women not only produce much of the world's food and clothing in global supply chains; they also perform most jobs such as electronic assembly, often in the increasing numbers of export-processing zones scattered across the global South. These zones typically escape local taxation and local laws governing labor relations, equal pay, occupational safety, and health (United Nations 1999; Beneria 2003: 79). Women have been called the new global proletariat. In addition, women often do paid piecework at home, combining it with the care of children and/or older people. Home-based work is notoriously low-paid and lacking in labor protections, and children and older people are often enlisted to help (Khattak 2002).

Women's increased entry into the global paid labor force has occurred just as that labor force has become more "flexible." Over the past half century, much manufacturing industry has moved to the global South, and many formerly well-paying blue-collar jobs in the global North have been replaced by lower-paid, irregular jobs in service industries. There has been a worldwide increase in informal employment, which lacks social protection, and the distinction between formal and informal employment has blurred (Beneria 2003: 96, 110). Following the financial crisis of 2008, widespread unemployment spread to many countries in Western Europe and, to a lesser extent, the United States. Would-be workers confronting this dire situation have been named the "precariat." They are said to constitute a new class which is able to access only intermittent and casual work, enjoys no predictability or security, and is sometimes receptive to extremist ideologies (Standing 2011).

The global labor force is now feminized in several senses. Most obviously, women now comprise a larger proportion of the paid labor force than ever before (World Bank 2011). In addition, a larger proportion of the available jobs are regarded as "women's work." Finally, labor market conditions for many men have deteriorated, becoming more like the precarious labor market conditions that typically characterized many "women's jobs" (Standing 1999; Elson 2002: 94). The feminization of the global labor force raises many questions of global gender justice.

One extremely complicated cluster of questions concerns the justice of the emerging gendered divisions of global labor. It is well known that paid work provides women with new opportunities for economic independence and for escaping abusive family situations; yet these opportunities often come at the cost of economic insecurity, long hours, high pressure, and sexual harassment. Changing transnational arrangements bring gendered costs as well as benefits for many males too. In some ways, "boys and young men (are) at a relative disadvantage" (World Bank 2011: 9). In many countries girls now outnumber boys in secondary schools and young women outnumber young men in universities (World Bank 2011:ix, xx). Cultural definitions of masculinity in terms of underperformance in schooling and education may diminish men's future employment and earnings opportunities ,and boys may also use risk behavior and sexual experience to prove themselves "real" men (World Bank 2011: 173). Increased competition for historically male jobs and downward pressure on wages mean that many men find it difficult to marry and establish families, and the World Bank reports that "excess mortality" of men occurs in some countries. Worldwide, men tend to have higher suicide rates than women and also higher rates of premature death due to violence, accidents, coronary heart disease, and drug and alcohol abuse (Moeller-Leimkuhler 2003). It is hard to assess the justice of these gendered benefits and costs, including time costs (Jaggar 2013). Over the past thirty years, it is possible that the life prospects of the least-advantaged groups of both women and men have worsened relative to other groups because income inequality has risen and the relative share of income going to wages has decreased in comparison with the share going to profits (Razavi 2011: 9).

In studying the justice of the changing gender organization of the global economy, a crucial task is to develop categories capable of identifying which groups are legitimate claimants of justice. Much of the earlier philosophical discussion on global justice was framed as a dispute between the moral claims of nationalism and cosmopolitanism, but the ungendered categories of "citizen" and "foreigner," on the one hand, and "human being," on the other, obscure gendered divisions and collectivities that stretch across national boundaries. Gendered but otherwise universalistic terms like "women" and "men" are also too coarse-grained for many circumstances because they conceal multiple divisions of ethnicity, race, and nation. To capture whatever gendered groupings are morally significant in contemporary divisions of global labor, we need more finely tuned and empirically grounded categories (Kang 2014).

3.3 Migration for Gendered Employment

Today many people seek employment abroad. One out of every thirty-three persons in the world is a migrant, and an increasing proportion is composed of economic migrants rather than political refugees (International Organization for Migration 2012). Labor migration reflects transnationally continuous ideas about the gender division of labor. The International Organization for Migration says:

> Despite the fact that women increasingly migrate autonomously as the main income providers for the family, the labour markets in receiving countries remain sex-segregated. Thus, only certain sectors are open to the employment of women, including migrant women, including the so-called "traditional" female occupations such as domestic work, entertainment, nursing, care-giving, etc.   (IOM 2012)

In this section, I will sketch a few of the global justice issues associated with women's large-scale migration for domestic service and sex work.

The sex industry is said to be the largest and most profitable industry in the world, although reliable statistics are unavailable because much of the industry is illegal. The industry includes street prostitution, brothels, "massage parlors," stripping, erotic dancing, sex tourism, phone sex, and arguably "mail order brides." Much sex work remains local in scale but large-scale migration for work in the sex and entertainment industries also occurs and a multi-billion-dollar pornography industry exists. The domestic service industry also has global as well as local dimensions. Millions of women cross borders and oceans to seek employment in wealthy countries as maids and nannies in private homes (Parreñas 2001). Some of these migrants are legal, but many are undocumented. Both the sex and domestic service industries are highly gender-structured but in different ways. In both industries, the majority of the workers are women or girls, although many men and boys provide sexual services too. However, there is a gender difference between those who purchase the respective services: in the domestic service industry, most employers are relatively well-off women, but those who buy sexual services include all classes of men. Men also constitute most, though certainly not all, of those transporting sex-workers and establishing the infrastructure for the trade.

Both the supply of and the demand for feminized workers in the transnational sex and domestic service industries are influenced by global factors. On the supply side, women who need income have always been motivated to enter sex work or domestic service when employment options are limited, but usually they have performed these jobs in local contexts. However, several structural features of the current global order encourage them to migrate transnationally to do similar work. The most obviously motivating feature is wealth inequality among countries. Many families and less-developed countries rely heavily on the remittances from migrant domestic workers abroad. Some less-developed countries have official policies encouraging migration; for example, Philippine women are encouraged by government policy to migrate to the US, the Middle East, and Japan as "maids," which have been said to be the Philippines' most important export product (Lutz 2002: 92). Similarly, many families in less-developed countries depend on remittances from sex work, and increasing numbers of poor countries depend on the tourism industry, which is invariably accompanied by entertainment and sex work. Indeed, the IMF and the World Bank have encouraged many poor countries to view tourism as a development strategy, and they have received loans for this purpose. Sassen writes: "At some point it becomes clear that the sex trade itself can become a development strategy in areas with high unemployment and poverty and where governments are desperate for revenue and foreign currency" (Sassen 2002: 270). Women across the world have long used "marrying up" as a strategy for social mobility, but the privileging of heterosexual marriage in international immigration law enables the transnational mail-order bride industry to function.

Transnational factors influence not only the supply of women migrants but also the demand for their services. In wealthy countries, the demand for maids is fuelled by the gendered division of family labor, which throws the main burden of household work on women. This longstanding division of labor is slow to change: the 2012 World Development Report asserts that men worldwide resist assuming domestic responsibilities (World Bank 2011: 218). Another factor contributing to the demand for maids is the decline of real wages in wealthy countries, so that women as well as men must often work for pay. Moreover, inadequate public provision for children and elders in some wealthy countries means that private arrangements often have to be made for the care of those who cannot care for themselves. However, care work is widely regarded as a specifically feminine type of labor, so it is usually available only to women.

Gender ideology shapes the transnational sex trade as well as the transnational maid trade. It creates the social meanings of the services provided and determines how gendered individuals can participate. Gendered norms of sexual desirability are spread across the world by global media in entertainment, advertising, and pornography. They often eroticize gendered power inequalities, which are then further complicated by eroticizing inequalities of age, race, class, and nation. Exposure to these ubiquitous images molds the sexuality of both girls and boys, influencing their senses of their own and others' desirability and normalizing the idea of women servicing men. They prepare girls and boys to participate in the global sex-market as workers and as consumers respectively. Similarly, global media promote heterosexual marriage as an institution that will guarantee happiness, social status, sexual satisfaction, and economic security. Both women and men seek trophy spouses, but women seek husbands who are good providers, while men seek wives who are attractive and deferential (Hughes 2000, 2004).[6]

The global trade in sexual and domestic services brings up some of the same issues of gender justice raised by the general feminization of the global labor force. They include the balance of costs and benefits to various gendered groups as well as more general issues of decent work and fair wages. However, additional questions are raised by the facts that workers in these industries are migrants who often suffer exceptionally poor working conditions and that the work they do has more deeply gendered meanings.

Conditions for migrant sex-workers vary widely. Some are self-employed and mix occasional sex work with other paid occupations, while others find themselves trapped in situations of extreme abuse. In some countries, the vulnerability of migrant sex workers is increased by laws forbidding foreign women to engage in sex work, fostering their dependence on criminal gangs. Migrant domestic workers are also extremely vulnerable, especially those without work visas and/or living in their employers' homes. Male migrant workers are vulnerable too but they gain some protection by working in teams within a framework recognized by other employees, so that their relations with their employers are contractual (Altman and Pannell 2012: 299). By contrast, the relationship between women domestic workers and their employers is often based on trust and so involves a higher degree of personal vulnerability. Employers may take advantage of this vulnerability to force domestic servants to work long hours, to withhold pay, to subject them to violence and sexual abuse, and sometimes to hold them in conditions close to slavery (Anderson 2000, esp. ch. 8; Zarembka 2002). Mail-order brides are also often subjected to violence (Narayan 1995).

Despite frequently poor conditions for many who work in the global sex and domestic service trades, these industries would not flourish unless many people were benefiting. The global sex industry reportedly provides immense profits, though these accrue disproportionately to those (mainly men) who organize sex work rather than to those (mainly women) who perform the services directly. Nevertheless, sex work also provides some high-priced escorts and call girls with financial rewards that far surpass anything they could hope to earn in other fields, and for many ordinary women sex work creates welcome opportunities for extra income in a new country and (in the case of mail-order brides) for a new family. The global domestic work industry props up gender-structured marriage in receiving countries, but it can undermine oppressive forms of marriage in sending countries, since the savings accumulated by some migrant domestic workers may win them more respect in their communities of origin and enable them to renegotiate their family and work options (Huh 2008). The work may even contribute to "undoing gender" (Beneria 2007).

A different aspect of gender justice is raised by the specific character of sex and care work. Both of these provide services that are usually regarded as personal and intimate in the sense that much of their quality and meaning is thought to be lost when they are performed in an impersonal assembly-line manner. Although these services are not intrinsically dirty or degrading, it is often thought demeaning to perform them for pay. It may be particularly demeaning for men to provide such services which are widely regarded as women's work. A growing philosophical literature discusses the commodification of sexual and intimate care services and how this may be related to the subordination of feminized populations. Moral concern has also been raised about injustice to migrant care workers' family members who remain behind in sending countries, deprived of particular care relations (Parreñas 2002; Kittay 2014). Arlie Hochschild has spoken of a global "heart transplant" (Hochschild 2003).

Finally, the unfavorable work conditions experienced by many women migrants in the transnational sex and domestic service industries have brought into question the agency of these workers. Such questions become especially salient once it is realized that there is nothing natural about women providing sex and domestic services. Women are not naturally suited for domestic work; when they can, they often hire others to do it. Nor do women naturally "pleasure" men for money; indeed, they may buy sexual services when they are in a position to do so. Questions about the agency of service workers in these industries are often framed in terms of trafficking, which refers to the coerced movement of people across state borders.[7] The question of agency raises issues which are difficult to resolve both empirically and conceptually. Empirical information about how women enter these industries and why they stay is often unavailable and the notion of choice is conceptually contested. All choices are made in contexts of limited knowledge, rationality, and options, and it is a matter of judgment as to when these contexts become so constraining as to create offers that cannot be refused. Some women take up sex work as a way of earning a little extra money, while others are deceived, coerced, or seeking to satisfy addictions. Some women enter sex work voluntarily, as they move from rural to urban areas, while others are pressed into sex work by their parents or tricked by being told that a different job awaits them. In addition, exit from sex work is often extremely difficult so that participation in the sex industry creates long-term gendered vulnerabilities. The language of "trafficking," which conjures up passive victims, fits some cases better than others. Many migrant workers in the sex and domestic service industries may be said to have chosen their employment autonomously as the best options available within a global context of gender-structured constraints.[8]

3.4 Two More Examples Undeveloped Here

International travel for procreation. This involves individuals or couples from wealthy countries travelling to poorer countries to buy procreative goods (gametes) or gestational (often called "surrogacy") services. Since at least the 1980s, philosophers have been discussing whether or not the commercial exchange of body parts and reproductive services is intrinsically objectionable ,but increasing travel across borders to buy procreative goods and services has raised questions about whether, even if such market exchanges are not morally problematic in principle, they may be so in practice. One set of problems concerns the sellers' vulnerability or weak agency; the other concerns the desperation of the buyers (Anderson 1990; Satz 2010). Both of these have gendered aspects. The supply of procreative goods and services is generated by scarcity of alternative sources of income for women in many poor countries, by frequent lack of regulation, and even by national policies designed to make commercial gestational services a profitable export industry. India is a leader in commercial gestational services, because labor is cheap, doctors are highly qualified, English is spoken, adoptions are closed, and the government has worked aggressively to establish an infrastructure for medical tourism (Bailey 2011: 3). The demand for commercial procreative services is increased by the fact that many Western women postpone having children until their careers are well established, by which time conception is more difficult. However, assisted procreative services in the West are often difficult to obtain because of regulatory limitations, age restrictions, sexual preference, waiting times, and high cost. For these reasons, women from Western countries frequently travel abroad where they can purchase faster or cheaper services and/or undergo genetic or gender selection (Donchin 2010: 327).

Gender justice and the environment. A long-established philosophical literature addresses issues of environment and gender justice, and some of it takes a global perspective. Feminist philosophers have discussed supposed parallels between women and non-human nature and the disparately gendered consequences of toxins in weaponry, pesticides, and foods, and toxic dumping in poor communities (Plumwood 1993; Mies and Shiva 1993). A more recent focus has been the gendered implications of climate change (Terry 2009). For example, a new UN study explores how drought in India has gender-differentiated consequences for agricultural wages and work (UNDP 2014).

4 SOME CROSS-CUTTING THEORETICAL ISSUES

4.1 Measuring Well-Being and Gender Equity

In discussing global gender disparities, I have relied on readers' intuitive recognition that many of these are politically problematic. However, different societies may accept different standards. Many proposed metrics exist for assessing well-being and gender equity, and more are constantly being developed. This short discussion sketches three representative metrics, focusing less on their substantive content than on the methodology used in developing and applying them.

Human rights provide one important transnational standard of political morality. The 1948 Universal Declaration of Human Rights (UDHR) aspired to universal cosmopolitan ideals that provide the moral basis for much international law. The UDHR and related body of human rights law include commitments to both sex and race equality. However, feminist critics argued that early human rights documents utilized an understanding of rights which presupposed a fairly rigid public/private distinction (Okin 1998). On this model, rights protected individuals against abuses within the public realm of the state but also protected the so-called private realm of family, religion, and culture from external interference, even though this realm was the site of much gender discrimination and abuse of women. In the 1980s and 1990s, a global feminist movement rallied around the slogan, "Women's rights are human rights." One notable success of this movement was its influence on the 1993 *Vienna Declaration and Programme of Action,* which included a formal declaration of women's rights as human rights and violence against women as a human rights violation (United Nations 1993). In 1995, the Fourth World Conference on Women produced the *Beijing Declaration and Platform for Action,* which brought culture and religion under critical moral scrutiny and identified many gender-specific practices as rights violations (United Nations Women 1995).[9] The movement for women's rights as human rights has made vital contributions to exposing gender specific rights violations rationalized by appeals to religion and culture traditions, but some scholars and activists have argued that the Beijing documents utilize interpretations of women's rights that are culturally biased and lend themselves to being deployed in an oppressive and disrespectful way against some communities, particularly in Africa (Nnaemeka 2005). Critics argue that there is no culturally neutral interpretation of women's human rights; they must be interpreted in specific contexts rather than imposed from the top down (Tobin 2009).

The capabilities offer a second global standard proposed for assessing well-being and gender equity. The concept was developed originally by Amartya Sen, who defined capabilities as socially available opportunities for valuable functioning (Sen 1984).[10] Sen has resisted offering a substantive list of capabilities, but Nussbaum has developed an explicit list which purports to provide a universal standard for assessing local ways of life. Nussbaum's intention is to provide a concrete alternative to cultural relativism (Nussbaum 2000). She also asserts that the list contributes to a theory of justice by identifying the primary goods available for just distribution and setting a threshold that must be reached by all citizens before any society can be considered just (Nussbaum 2000: 12, 75, 86). The general idea of capabilities has been very influential, but so far there exists no generally accepted methodology for establishing a comprehensive list. Nussbaum's own justifications for her list face problems of authority and legitimacy (Robeyns 2005; Jaggar 2006).

Many other existing standards propose to measure human well-being and gender equity on a global scale. The last to be mentioned here is the Individual Deprivation

Measure (IDM) (Wisor et al. 2014). The team that produced the IDM aimed initially to develop a metric capable of revealing whether or in what ways global poverty might be gendered.[11] They also wanted their metric to minimize cultural narrowness by including values held by many poor people, women and men.[12] Finally, recognizing that human well-being, poverty, and gender equity are value-laden concepts, the team sought to make explicit the values and reasoning incorporated into the metric. The most striking feature of the IDM is the consciously feminist methodology used in developing it. The research was participatory and multidisciplinary, and gender analysis was central.[13] In addition, the team provided an explicit explanation of their reasoning in selecting the indicators they included. The IDM is certainly not an all-purpose metric, but its partici-patory and gender-sensitive methodology offers a model to be taken very seriously in developing future metrics of well-being and gender equity.

4.2 Causally Explaining Global Gender Disparities

Inequality is not necessarily unjust. Disparities may result from factors that are unpre-dictable or unavoidable or they may even be deserved. Systematic injustice occurs when groups are linked by structural relations of domination or when distributive disparities are morally arbitrary and produced by social structures whose outcomes are foreseeable and preventable. Investigating the nature and causes of gender disparities is important both for revealing global gender injustices and for assigning political responsibility for addressing them.

Because some patterns of gender inequality are extremely widespread, many Western philosophers have argued that women are invariably subordinated as a result of inherent sex differences. If this is true, then some gender disparities may not be unjust because they are natural or unalterable. Feminists have debunked many versions of the "natural-ness" claim, but new varieties constantly recur, often invoking evolution. Such causal claims typically rely on mistaken understandings of sex as contextually invariant, on speculative "just so" stories about evolution, and on simplistic views about biological determinism (Prinz 2012; Jordan-Young 2010). They all miss the more general philo-sophical point that it is social contexts which mainly determine whether, when, and how particular physical or other abilities are advantageous or disadvantageous. For philoso-phers concerned with gender justice, it is important to assess how social arrangements advantage some gendered groups while disadvantaging others and to explore how these arrangements could be redesigned to be more gender-just.

A second inadequate explanation of global gender disparities is that they result pri-marily from bad decisions made by poor women out of ignorance, false consciousness, or adaptive preferences. The emphasis placed by some Western philosophers on poor women's supposedly bad decisions has often been condescending and even victim-blaming, rationalizing Westerners' taking up the missionary role of "educating" or "raising the consciousness" of women in developing countries (Jaggar 2005; Khader 2013). It also directs philosophers' attention away from the proper focus of gender justice, which is less to evaluate individual choices and more to assess the social structures that construct relations of equality or domination and assign costs and benefits to various social options. Women's decisions to participate in painful, exhausting, or demeaning practices may be rational in so far as they represent the best bargains that those involved are able to strike in situations where their options are highly constrained or even no-win.

Systematic gender domination and disadvantage do not depend exclusively on singular causes, such as sexual biology, cultural norms, individual choices, or social structures; instead, they result from the ways in which these factors interact in particular contexts. I have proposed that structures and policies that are both national and transnational create interlocking cycles of gendered vulnerability which often place feminized populations in especially weak bargaining situations (Jaggar 2014a).[14] The idea of transnational cycles of gendered vulnerability is an explanatory schema or methodological approach. To explain particular gender disparities, the schema must be filled in by empirical descriptions of ways in which gendered norms and practices interact in specific contexts to enable and constrain people's possibilities for action. Interactions among national and transnational structures are further complicated by factors such as ethnicity, religion, and class, which may mitigate or multiply the disadvantages of particular gendered groups. The idea of transnational cycles of gendered vulnerability is a conceptual tool for use in figuring out which global gender disparities are unjust, who is causally responsible for those disparities, and how they might be addressed through structural changes.

The idea of transnational cycles of gendered vulnerability allows us to understand why gender disparities often resemble each other across the world without resorting to accounts that are either biologically determinist or victim-blaming. It acknowledges the causal relevance of sexed bodies but considers those bodies in various social contexts, conceptualizing them in a way that is not reductionist or deterministic. It also recognizes the causal influence of conditions that are both local and global without reducing one to the other. Finally, the idea of transnational cycles of gendered vulnerability does not "disappear" individual consciousness and choice but instead shows how women's and men's choices are shaped and limited by gendered ideologies and structural constraints.

4.3 Political Responsibility for Global Gender Injustice

Who or what is responsible for global gender injustice? Because global gender injustices come in many varieties and scales, no single account of responsibility can fit them all. This section outlines three feminist accounts of political responsibility in order to illustrate the wide range of possible approaches. The three accounts differ on several dimensions: they focus on different aspects of global gender inequities, explain them in different terms, and offer different accounts of the moral basis of political responsibility.

One view is global feminism, a perspective that descends from the radical feminism of the Western second wave. The radical feminists wished to establish that women were a group subjected to a distinct form of oppression and their earliest writings postulated a worldwide women's culture existing "beneath the surface" of all national, ethnic, and racial cultures and colonized by these "male" cultures (Burris 1973).[15] Global feminism emphasizes physical violence against women and forced sexual and reproductive labor. It attributed these abuses to "patriarchy," a broad concept covering most, if not all systems of male dominance. From this, it seems to follow that responsibility in the sense of culpability for these injustices belongs to male perpetrators and others complicit with patriarchy. This presumably includes most men and many women. However, global feminists exhort all women everywhere to combat patriarchy on the moral basis of global sisterhood (Morgan 1984). This call has something in common with the cosmopolitan/humanitarian spirit of Peter Singer's early work, in so far as it asks otherwise uninvolved individuals to help others on a moral basis of solidarity (Singer 1972). Gendered solidarity continues to be invoked by many women's NGOs which appeal to better-off women to help worse-off women everywhere.

Postcolonial feminism differs from global feminism on several counts. At the descriptive level, it resists assimilating diverse practices from many continents and time periods to universal misogyny or woman-hating. At the explanatory level, postcolonial feminists reject the idea of an ahistorical and universalistic patriarchy. They see gender injustices as caused by many factors, past as well as present, local as well as global, but they emphasize the causal preeminence of colonialism and neocolonialism (Volpp 2000). Accordingly, postcolonial feminists do not place responsibility exclusively on local perpetrators; they also blame functionaries and beneficiaries of colonialism, neocolonialism, and "development." They contend that even Western feminisms have often been implicated in imperial projects and charge that Western feminist criticisms of Nonwestern cultural traditions are often forms of "imperial feminism" or "feminist orientalism," patronizing continuations of the "colonialist stance" of former eras (Carby 1982; Amos and Parmar 1984; Mohanty 1991; Narayan 1998; Jaggar 2005). Although postcolonial feminism is distinct in its specific arguments, it has something in common with the work of philosophers like Thomas Pogge (2002/2008) or Richard Miller (2010), who argue that citizens of wealthy countries are culpably liable for suffering in the global South and therefore face moral obligations of justice as well humanity to redress this suffering.

Iris Young has proposed a third account of political responsibility which contrasts with both of the above approaches. She calls this the social connection model (Young 2007). Young is concerned primarily with injustices emerging from social processes that extend widely across regions of the world. Her paradigm example is garment sweatshops, which are links in complex transnational chains that produce, distribute, and market clothing. On Young's analysis, the sufferings of sweatshop workers are produced by densely interlocking social structures reinforced by the decisions of innumerable agents on multiple levels. Young explicitly rejects universalistic humanitarian models of political responsibility because she does not find it morally plausible that all moral agents have exactly the same duties as all other agents; presumably she would reject global sisterhood on similar grounds (Young 2007: 161). Young also argues that the model of individual liability or culpability is unsuitable for attributing political responsibility for these types of structural injustices because causal connections are hard to trace and many agents involved cannot be regarded as culpable because they lack *mens rea* or realistic alternatives. As an alternative to both the above accounts of responsibility for global injustice, Young locates the moral basis of her model in people's social connections with others who share participation in structures of cooperation and competition. Young offers several contrasts between hers and the liability model: the social connection model does not isolate perpetrators; it focuses less on individual actions than on the background conditions of their decisions; it is more forward-looking than backward-looking; its responsibility is essentially shared; and it can be discharged only through working together in collective action.

Critics of Young's social connection model of responsibility have suggested that it may let individual perpetrators too easily off the moral hook. I cannot consider here how far these various conceptions of responsibility should be regarded as alternatives or complements to each other.

4.4 Repairing Gender Injustices

In this space, it is not possible to trace the contributions made by feminist philosophers to the literatures on reparative and transitional justice. Many have given special attention to gendered violence, including genocidal rape and sexual torture in conflict zones. The causes of this violence are sometimes exclusively local but many conflicts result from interventions by larger players seeking access to resources in the global South (Pogge 2008; Jaggar 2014b). Feminist philosophers tend to advocate material restitution and compensation where these are appropriate, but they also recognize that much of the damage to lives and dignity is irreparable; people cannot be brought back to life nor their suffering and humiliation erased. Indeed, framing the issue exclusively in material terms can diminish the seriousness or gravity of the harm done (Walker 2015). In such circumstances, symbolic reparations such as properly worded apologies or reinventing traditional cleansing rituals may fulfill important restorative functions (Miller 2009).

5 How Can We Identify Global Gender Justice?

How to identify global gender justice is a matter of political epistemology. One time-honored methodological approach is ideal theory, which begins by imagining an ideal or "well-ordered" society (Rawls 1971). Ingrid Robeyns has referred to this as the "Paradise Island" method (Robeyns 2008). Several feminist philosophers have employed versions of ideal theory; for example, Susan Okin followed second-wave androgyny theorists in advocating the abolition of gender, and Martha Nussbaum has generated a universal list of capabilities (Okin 1989; Nussbaum 2000). In recent years, however, many feminist philosophers have become critical of ideal theory, because idealized models are likely to disregard aspects of the real world that are crucially relevant to assessing the justice of existing institutions and the practical feasibility of proposed alternatives (Anderson 2010).

A second approach to identifying global gender justice has been offered by the tradition of care ethics. Since the 1980s, this has been developed as a feminine or feminist approach to morality. Sometimes care ethics is presented as a contrast with the "justice" approach, but sometimes it is seen as complementary to justice or an alternative way of thinking about it. Different philosophers have used "care" to refer to different things, including a distinct emotional attitude, a type of personal caretaking labor, a moral methodology, and an epistemic virtue. Philosophers who advocate a care approach to global gender justice include Virginia Held (2006) and Fiona Robinson (2011).

Many feminist philosophers recommend a methodological approach to global justice that they call nonideal or "critical" theory. In nonideal theory, normative ideals do not function as unquestioned standards of assessment but rather as hypotheses to be tested in experience; for example, the British abolition of slavery is seen as initiating a worldwide experiment in free labor (Anderson 2014.) Nonideal theory starts "from a diagnosis of injustices in our actual world, rather than from a picture of an ideal world" (Anderson 2010: 3). However, even diagnosing injustices is far from simple in a world where the moral resources available are extremely diverse and where people are profoundly unequal in terms of epistemic credibility. Some feminist philosophers are seeking ways to address the global epistemic injustices that hamper cross-cultural expression and uptake of multiple points of view (Jaggar and Tobin 2013; Tobin and Jaggar 2013). Better understandings of global gender justice can emerge only from discussions that are epistemically more gender-just.

NOTES

1. Human sex is not dichotomous: Fausto-Sterling (2000) reports that individuals born as mixtures of male and female exist as one of five natural human variants, and she criticizes the arbitrariness and coercion that often characterize social processes of sex assignment. Humans' physical sex characteristics are shaped by social factors at both phenotypical and genotypical levels.

2. For example, masculine privilege is usually substantial but masculinity can also carry considerable costs for people who are disadvantaged on other dimensions. In the United States, men of African descent are far more likely than any other demographic group to be incarcerated and/or to die by violence. Making sense of the recently publicized, though longstanding phenomenon of unarmed young African American men being killed by police officers in the US requires understanding gender intersectionally. It is salient that the victims are black but also that they are masculine; it is equally salient that their killers are usually, though not always, both white and masculine. African American women also suffer gendered and racialized street harassment from the police but they are often taken to be sex workers and not killed by the police at such a high rate as African American men.

3. The word "culture" was mostly used in this way in the philosophical debate about "multiculturalism." For example, Nancy Fraser contrasts concerns about cultural recognition with concerns about economic redistribution (Fraser 1997).

4. In Kenya, "clitoridectomy became a political issue between the Kikuyu and Kenya's white settlers and missionaries, as well as a symbol of the struggle between African nationalists and British colonial power" (Brown 1991:262).

5. More recently, the economic rise of China and emergence of middle-income countries, such as Brazil and India, have blurred the sharp North/South division.

6.

> In both urban and rural settings around the world, in both poor and rich communities, the social norms for what makes a good wife are remarkably similar … Above all, the good wife adeptly handles her domestic responsibilities and is caring and understanding toward others … Being a good wife also systematically involves respecting one's husband—being faithful, supportive, respectful, and submissive.   (World Bank 2011:172 Box 4.5)

By contrast, "Across diverse contexts, what defines a good husband, over and above all, is the ability to provide" (ibid.).

7.

> Almost **21 million people are victims of forced labour**—11.4 million women and girls and 9.5 million men and boys. Forced labour takes different forms, including debt bondage, trafficking and other forms of modern slavery. The victims are the most vulnerable—women and girls forced into prostitution, migrants trapped in debt bondage, and sweatshop or farm workers kept there by clearly illegal tactics and paid little or nothing. Of those exploited by individuals or enterprises, **4.5 million are victims of forced sexual exploitation. Migrant workers and indigenous people** are particularly vulnerable to forced labour.   (ILO 2015)

8. For example, in the republics of the former Soviet Union, where the implementation of market policies led to unemployment rates as high as 70% and 80% among women (Sassen 2002: 268), many women enter sex work and dream of marriage to a foreign man who will provide protection and economic security.

9. This document was revised in 2005 and again in 2010 (UN 2010).

10. In the 1990s, the idea was adopted by numerous international agencies and nongovernmental organizations, including the United Nations Development Program, whose Human Development Index used a capability metric developed in collaboration with Amartya Sen.

11. Existing metrics were suspected of being gender-biased because they took households as their units of assessment, thereby obscuring intra-household disparities, and also because they used indicators of poverty that seemed to fit better with men's than women's lives.

12. The team was aware that people in some societies understand wealth and poverty not in terms of money but rather in terms of items such as land or cows or social relationships.

13. Researchers asked poor people in six poor countries what poverty meant to them. They worked with people situated differently, investigating how their social locations influenced their understandings of poverty. Although the research project used ethnographic methods, it was not anthropological in the sense of simply investigating what poor people in various societies believe poverty to be; instead, it drew on poor people's ideas to inform the metrics used by academics and experts. In an effort to determine whether and to what extent women and men might systematically disagree about the constituents of poverty, the researchers interviewed not ungendered "poor people," but rather poor women and poor men. They asked explicit questions about aspects of poverty found by other researchers to be especially important to women, such as free time, sexual autonomy, and family

planning. They employed female researchers to interview women and usually interviewed people in gender-separated groups, hoping this would encourage women participants to speak more freely. In addition, they took individuals rather than households as their units of assessment.

14. My work builds on Okin's idea that the division of labor in heterosexual Western marriage created a gendered cycle of vulnerability for women. She argued that "a cycle of power relations and decisions pervades both family and workplace, each reinforcing the inequalities between the sexes that already exist within the other" (Okin 1989: 4). Iris Marion Young utilized Okin's explanatory model to analyze the situation of women in some less-developed countries of Asia, Africa, Latin America, and the Middle East. She asserted that the division of family labor, which assigns women primary responsibility for care of the household, "operates as a strong and enforced norm among many newly urbanized women (and) produces and reproduces a (specifically gendered) vulnerability to domination and exploitation in wage employment" (Young 2009: 230).

15. For example, Mary Daly asserted that women worldwide were subjected to male violence, through such practices as witch burning, sati, foot-binding, and "female genital mutilation" (Daly 1978: 109–12).

REFERENCES

Altman, Meryl, and Kerry Pannell (2012) "Policy Gaps and Theory Gaps: Women and Migrant Domestic Labor," Feminist Economics 18(2): 291–315.

Amos, Valerie, and Pratibha Parmar (1984) "Challenging Imperial Feminism," Feminist Review 17: 3–19.

Anderson, Bridget (2000) Doing the Dirty Work? The Global Politics of Domestic Labour. London and New York: Zed Books.

Anderson, Elizabeth (1990) "Is Women's Labor a Commodity?" Philosophy and Public Affairs 19: 71–92.

Anderson, Elizabeth (2010) The Imperative of Integration. Princeton, NJ: Princeton University Press.

Anderson, Elizabeth (2014) Social Movements, Experiments in Living, and Moral Progress: Case Studies from Britain's Abolition of Slavery. Lawrence, KS: Department of Philosophy, University of Kansas.

Bailey, Alison (2011) "Reconceiving Surrogacy: Toward a Reproductive Justice Account of Indian Surrogacy," Hypatia 26(4): 715–41.

Balakrishnan, Radhika (2002) The Hidden Assembly Line: Gender Dynamics of Subcontracted Work in a Global Economy. Bloomfield, CT: Kumarian Press.

Beneria, Lourdes (2003) Gender, Development, and Globalization: Economics as if All People Mattered. New York and London: Routledge.

Beneria, Lourdes (2007) "Globalization, Gender and the Transformation of Women's Roles," Revista Catalana de Geografia 61: 305–24.

Brown, Dallas L. (1991) "Christian Missionaries, Western Feminists, and the Kikuyu Clitoridectomy Controversy." In Brett Williams (ed.), The Politics of Culture. Washington DC and London: Smithsonian Institution Press, 243–72.

Burris, Barbara (1973) "The Fourth World Manifesto." In Anne Koedt, Ellen Levine, and Anita Rapone (eds.), Radical Feminism. New York: Quadrangle/New York Times Book Co., 322–57.

Carby, Hazel (1982) "White Woman Listen! Black Feminism and the Boundaries of Sisterhood." In Centre for Contemporary Cultural Studies (eds), *The Empire Strikes Back: Race and Racism in Seventies Britain*. London: Hutchinson, 212–35.

Daly, Mary (1978) *Gyn/Ecology: the Metaethics of Radical Feminism*. Boston, MA: Beacon Press.

Donchin, Anne (2010) "Reproductive Tourism and the Quest for Global Gender Justice," *Bioethics* 24(7): 323–32.

Elson, Diane (2002) "Gender Justice, Human Rights, and Neo-Liberal Economic Policies." In Maxine Molyneux and Shahra Razavi (eds.), *Gender Justice, Development, and Rights*. Oxford, UK: Oxford University Press, 78–114.

Fausto-Sterling, Anne (2000) *Sexing the Body: Gender Politics and the Construction of Sexuality*, New York: Basic Books.

Fraser, Nancy (1997) "From Redistribution to Recognition? Dilemmas of Justice in a 'Postsocialist' Age." In *Justice Interruptus: Critical Reflections on the "Postsocialist" Condition*. New York and London: Routledge, 11–40.

Held, Virginia (2006) *The Ethics of Care*. New York: Oxford University Press.

Hochschild, Arlie Russell (2003) *The* Commercialization of Intimate Life: Notes from Home and Work. Berkeley, CA: University of California Press.

Hochschild, Arlie Russell (2002) "Love and Gold." In Barbara Ehrenreich and Arlie Russell Hochschild (eds.), *Global Woman: Nannies, Maids, and Sex Workers in the New Economy*. New York: Henry Holt, 15–30.

Hughes, Donna M. (2000) "The 'Natasha' Trade: The Transnational Shadow Market of Trafficking in Women," *Journal of International Affairs* 53(2): 625–51.

Hughes, Donna M. (2004) "The Role of 'Marriage Agencies' in the Sexual Exploitation and Trafficking of Women from the Former Soviet Union, *International Review of Victimology* 11: 49–71.

Huh, Ra-Keum (2008) "The Politics of Meaning: Care Work and Migrant Women," *Asian Journal of Women's Studies* 13(3): 37–60.

International Labour Organization (2015) "Forced Labour, Human Trafficking and Slavery," http://www.ilo.org/global/topics/forced-labour/lang—en/index.htm, accessed February 16, 2015.

International Organization for Migration (IOM) (2012) "Facts & Figures: Global Estimates and Trends," http://www.iom.int/cms/en/sites/iom/home/about-migration/facts—figures-1.html, accessed May 28, 2013.

Jaggar, Alison M. (2002) "A Feminist Critique of the Alleged Southern Debt," *Hypatia*, 17(4): 119–42.

Jaggar, Alison M. (2005) "'Saving Amina?' Global Justice for Women and Intercultural Dialogue," *Ethics and International Affairs* 19(3): 85–105.

Jaggar, Alison M. (2006) "Reasoning about Well-Being: Nussbaum's Methods of Justifying the Capabilities," *Journal of Political Philosophy* 14(4): 301–22.

Jaggar, Alison M. (2013) "We Fight for Roses Too: Time Use and Global Gender Justice," *Journal of Global Ethics* 9(2): 115–29.

Jaggar, Alison M. (2014a) "Transnational Cycles of Vulnerability: A Prologue to a Theory of Global Gender Justice." In Alison M. Jaggar (ed.), *Gender and Global Justice*. Cambridge: Polity Press, 18–39.

Jaggar, Alison M. (2014b) "'Are My Hands Clean?' Responsibility for Global Gender Disparities" in Diana Meyers (ed.), *Poverty, Agency, and Human Rights*. Oxford: Oxford University Press, 170–94.

Jaggar, Alison M., and Theresa Tobin (2013) "Situating Moral Justification: Rethinking the Mission of Moral Epistemology," *Metaphilosophy* 44(4): 383–408.

Jordan-Young, Rebecca (2010) *Brain Storm: The Flaws in the Science of Sex Differences.* Cambridge, MA: Harvard University Press.

Kang, Hye-Ryoung (2014) "Transnational Women's Collectivities and Global Justice." In Alison M. Jaggar (ed.), *Gender and Global Justice.* Cambridge: Polity Press, 40–61.

Khader, Serene J. (2013) "Identifying Adaptive Preferences in Practice: Lessons from Postcolonial Feminisms," *Journal of Global Ethics,* 9(3): 311–27.

Khattak, Saba Gul (2002) "Subcontracted Work and Gender Relations: The Case of Pakistan." In Radhika Balakrishnan (ed.), *The Hidden Assembly Line: Gender Dynamics of Subcontracted Work in a Global Economy.* Bloomfield, CT: Kumarian Press, 35–62.

Kittay, Eva Feder (2014) "The Moral Harm of Migrant Carework: Realizing a Global Right to Care." In Alison M. Jaggar (ed.), *Gender and Global Justice.* Cambridge: Polity Press, 62–84.

Lutz, Helma (2002) "At Your Service Madam! The Globalization of Domestic Service," *Feminist Review* 70: 89–103.

Mies, Maria, and Vandana Shiva (1993) *Ecofeminism.* London: Zed Books.

Miller, Richard (2010) *Globalizing Justice: The Ethics of Poverty and Power.* Oxford: Oxford University Press.

Miller, Sarah Clark (2009) "Atrocity, Harm, and Resistance: A Situated Understanding of Genocidal Rape." In Andrea Veltman and Kathryn J. Norlock (eds.), *Evil, Political Violence, and Forgiveness: Essays in Honor of Claudia Card.* Lanham, MD: Lexington Books, 53–76.

Moeller-Leimkuhler, Anna Maria (2003) "The Gender Gap in Suicide and Premature Death: Or, Why Are Men So Vulnerable? *European Archives of Psychiatry and Clinical Neuroscience* 252 (1): 1–8.

Mohanty, Chandra (1991) "Under Western Eyes: Feminist Scholarship and Colonial Discourse." In Chandra Talpade Mohanty, Ann Russo and Lourdes Torres (eds.), *Third World Women and the Politics of Feminism.* Bloomington, IN: Indiana University Press, 51–80.

Morgan, Robin (ed.) (1984) *Sisterhood is Global,* Garden City, NY:Anchor Press/Doubleday.

Narayan, Uma (1995) "'Male-Order' Brides: Immigrant Women, Domestic Violence, and Immigration Law," *Hypatia* 10(1): 101–19.

Narayan, Uma (1998) "Essence of Culture and a Sense of History: A Feminist Critique of Cultural Essentialism," *Hypatia* 13(2): 86–106.

Nnaemeka, Obioma (2005) "African Women, Colonial Discourses, and Imperialist Interventions: Female Circumcision as Impetus." In Obioma Nnaemeka (ed.), *Female Circumcision and the Politics of Knowledge: African Women in Imperialist Discourses.* Westport, CT: Praeger, 27–46.

Nussbaum, Martha C. (1992) Human Functioning and Social Justice: In Defense of Aristotelian Essentialism," *Political Theory* 20: 202–46.

Nussbaum, Martha C. (2000) *Women and Human Development: The Capabilities Approach.* Cambridge: Cambridge University Press.

Okin, Susan Moller (1989) *Justice, Gender and the Family.* New York: Basic Books.

Okin, Susan Moller (1994) "Gender Inequality and Cultural Differences," *Political Theory* 22(1): 5–24.

Okin, Susan Moller (1998) "Feminism, Women's Human Rights, and Cultural Differences," *Hypatia* 13(2): 32–52.

Okin, Susan Moller (with respondents) (1999) *Is Multiculturalism Bad for Women?*, ed. Joshua Cohen, Matthew Howard, and Martha C. Nussbaum. Princeton, NJ: Princeton University Press.

Parreñas, Rhacel Salazar (2001) *Servants of Globalization: Women, Migration, and Domestic Work*. Stanford: Stanford University Press.

Parreñas, Rhacel Salazar (2002) "The Care Crisis in the Philippines: Children and Transnational Families in the New Global Economy." In Barbara Ehrenreich and Arlie Russell Hochschild (eds.), *Global Woman: Nannies, Maids, and Sex Workers in the New Economy*, New York: Henry Holt, 39–54.

Plumwood, Val (1993) *Feminism and the Mastery of Nature*. New York: Routledge.

Pogge, Thomas (2002/2008) *World Poverty and Human Rights*. Cambridge: Polity Press.

Prinz, Jesse (2012) "Why Are Men So Violent?" Psychology Today, http://www.psychologyto-day.com, accessed February 10, 2012.

Rawls, John (1971) *A Theory of Justice*. Cambridge, MA: Harvard University Press.

Razavi, Shahra (2011) *World Development Report 2012: Gender Equality and Development, An Opportunity both Welcome and Missed (An Extended Commentary)*. New York: UNRISD.

Robeyns, Ingrid (2005) "Selecting Capabilities for Quality of Life Measurement," *Social Indicators Research* 74: 191–215.

Robeyns, Ingrid (2008) "Ideal Theory in Theory and Practice," *Social Theory and Practice* 34(3): 341–62.

Robinson, Fiona (2011) *The Ethics of Care: A Feminist Approach to Human Security*. Philadelphia, PA: Temple University Press.

Sassen, Saskia (2002) "Women's Burden: Counter-Geographies of Globalization and the Feminization of Survival," *Nordic Journal of International Law* 71: 255–74.

Satz, Debra (2010) *Why Some Things Should Not Be for Sale: The Moral Limits of Markets*. Oxford: Oxford University Press.

Sen, Amartya (1984) *Resources, Values and Development*. Oxford: Blackwell.

Singer, Peter (1972) "Famine, Affluence, and Morality," Philosophy and Public Affairs 1(1): 229–43.

Standing, Guy (1999) "Global Feminization through Flexible Labor: A Theme Revisited," *World Development* 27(3): 583–602.

Standing, Guy (2011) *The Precariat: The New Dangerous Class*. London and New York: Bloomsbury Publishing.

Terry, Geraldine (2009) *Climate Change and Gender Justice*. Rugby: Practical Action Publishing.

Tobin, Theresa W. (2009) "Using Rights to Counter 'Gender-Specific' Wrongs," *Human Rights Review* 10: 521–30.

Tobin, Theresa W., and Alison M. Jaggar (2013) "Naturalizing Moral Justification: Rethinking the Method of Moral Epistemology," *Metaphilosophy* 44(4): 409–39.

United Nations (1993) *Vienna Declaration and Programme of Action*, http://www.ohchr.org/EN/ProfessionalInterest/Pages/Vienna.aspx, accessed February 13, 2015.

United Nations (1999) *1999 World Survey on the Role of Women in Development: Globalization, Gender and Work*. New York: United Nations.

United Nations (2010) *Report on the Fifty-Fourth Session*, http://daccess-dds-ny.un.org/doc/UNDOC/GEN/N10/305/76/PDF/N1030576.pdf, accessed January 30, 2015.

United Nations Development Programme (UNDP) (2014) "Blame it on the Rain?: Gender Differentiated Impacts of Drought on Agricultural Wage and Work in India," http://www.asia-pacific.undp.org/content/dam/rbap/docs/Research%20&%20Publications/poverty/RBAP-PR-2014-Blame-It-on-the-Rain.pdf , accessed January 30, 2015.

United Nations Women (1995) "Report of the Fourth World Conference on Women: Beijing Declaration and Platform for Action," http://www.un.org/womenwatch/daw/beijing/plat-form/, accessed January 30, 2015.

Volpp, Leti (2000) "Blaming Culture for Bad Behavior, *Yale Journal of Law and Humanities* 12: 89–116.

Walker, Margaret Urban (2015) "Making Reparations Possible: Theorizing Reparative Justice." In Claudio Corradetti, Nir Eisikovits, and Jack Volpe Rotondi (eds.), *Theorizing Transitional Justice*. Farnham: Ashgate Press, 211–24.

Wisor, Scott, Sharon Bessell, Fatima Castillo, Joanne Crawford, Kieran Donaghue, Janet Hunt, Alison Jaggar, Amy Liu, and Thomas Pogge (2014) "The Individual Deprivation Measure: A Gender Sensitive Approach to Poverty Measurement," http://www.iwda.org.au/research/individual-deprivation-measure/, accessed February 1, 2015.

World Bank (2011) *World Development Report 2012: Gender Equality and Development*, Washington, DC: International Bank for Reconstruction and Development/ World Bank.

Young, Iris M. (2007) "Responsibility, Social Connection, and Global Labor Justice," In *Global Challenges: War, Self-Determination and Responsibility for Justice*, Cambridge: Polity Press, 159–86.

Young, Iris M. (2009) "The Gendered Cycle of Vulnerability in the Less Developed World." In Debra Satz and Rob Reich (eds.), *Toward a Humanist Justice: The Philosophy of Susan Moller Okin*. Oxford: Oxford University Press, 223–38.

Zarembka, Joy M. (2002) "America's Dirty Work: Migrant Maids and Modern Day Slavery." In Barbara Ehrenreich and Arlie Russell Hochschild (eds.), *Global Woman: Nannies, Maids, and Sex Workers in the New Economy*. New York: Holt, 142–53.

FURTHER READING

Aragon, Corwin, and Alison M. Jaggar (2018) "Agency, Complicity, and the Responsibility to Resist Structural Injustice," *Journal of Social Philosophy* 49(3): 439–46.

Farris, Sara R. (2017) *In the Name of Women's Rights: The Rise of Femonationalism*. Durham, NC: Duke University Press.

Higgins, Peter (2017) "A Feminist Approach to Immigrant Admissions," *Hypatia* 32(3): 506–22.

Khader, Serene J. (2019) *Decolonizing Universalism: A Transnational Feminist Ethic*. Oxford: Oxford University Press.

McLaren, Margaret A. (ed.) (2017) *Decolonizing Feminism: Transnational Feminism and Globalization*. London: Rowman and Littlefield International.

Scott, Joan (2017) *Sex and Secularism*. Princeton, NJ: Princeton University Press.

CHAPTER 18

....

INTERNATIONAL LAW

....

STEVEN R. RATNER

INTERNATIONAL law represents a system of norms and processes for resolving competing claims—moral, political, and otherwise—among international actors in a manner both authoritative to them and effective among them. It comprises legal rules with a range of normative valences; and international institutions, which can be seen as the conceptual building blocks of world order (for example, statehood, global commons, or human rights) or as formal regional and global organizations. Its breadth is enormous; among its rules and institutions are those regulating participation in the interstate system (rules on states, peoples, and territory), interstate cooperation (limits on extraterritorial jurisdiction, sovereign immunity, and technical subjects such as global health and aviation), common spaces (the law of the sea and international environmental law), economic welfare (trade, investment, finance, and intellectual property), human rights, and the use of armed force (both the *jus ad bellum* and the *jus in bello*).

International law is critical to global justice in three senses. *First*, international law transforms moral prescriptions into legally binding rules with implementation mechanisms and processes. Law and legal institutions both constrain and expand opportunities for carrying out visions to advance the cause of global justice. Without some sort of legal form, the ethics of global justice remains academic, or at least incompletely realized. As seen in the short list above, all of the key issues of global justice scholarship, and many more that have not yet engaged philosophers, are the subject of legal rules and institutions of a regional or global nature.

Second, international law tells us something about what morality and justice at the international level mean in the first place. The law is intrinsic to the normative universe of practices, institutions, and expectations that form our understandings about global justice. Law is where many of the key claims about what a just world should look like are contested and ultimately resolved through rules. We can thus learn a great deal about the current state, as well as future promise and limitations, of global justice by examining the legal regimes to which states have already agreed. And if we believe that "ought implies can," international law tells us much about the "can" and thus a great deal about the "ought." As Peter Cane writes:

> it is a philosophical mistake to think that morality can be properly and fully understood without reference to law.... [L]aw has institutional resources that enable it to make a distinctive contribution to answering practical questions about what one ought to do or what sort of person one should aim to be.   (Cane 2012: 83–4)

Third, because the rules of international law cover an enormous range of issues, and in many ways influence the way key actors like states behave regarding those issues, those rules are both a formalized instantiation, and in some cases even a causal factor, of the moral problems of global justice. All international legal regimes represent choices by states and other actors to regulate, or not regulate, international matters in ways that have winners and losers. As Nardin (2011: 2071) writes, "the global order that exists is substantially constituted by public international law."

Fourth, the rules and structures of international law turn out to have their own morality and represent a real-world, albeit far from ideal incarnation of a vision of global justice. One sense is that set out by Andrew Hurrell, who noted that "the ethical claims of international law rest on the contention that it is the *only* set of globally institutionalized processes by which norms can be negotiated on the basis of dialogue and consent, rather than being simply imposed by the powerful" (Hurrell 2003: 277; emphasis in original). A second sense, beyond the inclusive process by which international law emerges and evolves, concerns international law's content.[1] Even as some of its rules cover matters of convenience and coordination (e.g. what language international pilots should use), many reflect considered moral positions and have moral justifications based on values such as human dignity or welfare, preservation of peace, or protection of the planet.

Nonetheless, scholarship on global justice remains characterized by a high degree of mutual ignorance and suspicion between international law and philosophical ethics. Much philosophical work seems to assume the law irrelevant for the derivation of theory or has mischaracterized it to suggest fundamental incompatibilities between global justice and international law. International lawyers, for their part, especially academic ones, either ignore global justice as something belonging to morality and thus outside the law; construe it narrowly as international criminal justice or perhaps the decisions of international courts; or equate it, in an undertheorized way, with a greater concern for marginalized populations. Although law and philosophical ethics do and should ask different questions about global justice, the gaps between the two fields have resulted in shortcomings to theory on global justice.

1 THE CORE STRUCTURE OF
INTERNATIONAL LAW

1.1 Actors and Claims

To get a sense of international law's role in international justice, it is useful to identify the major actors that participate in the international legal process. By participation, I mean the process of making claims for advancement of various goals, where those claims lead to the creation and implementation of norms characterized by legal relationships (especially duties). Traditional legal scholars labeled certain participants as international "persons" based on the old concept of "legal personality," i.e. the capacity to be subject to legal rights and duties; but this notion is circular (participation flows from personality, and personality flows from participation) and unhelpful to understanding whether an entity has rights and duties.

1.1.1 *The State*

The state's fundamental claim in the international order is to its *sovereignty*, a mystical term best viewed as a shorthand for a series of claims. First among these is *territorial integrity*, the claim not to be invaded and conquered. Territorial integrity can include the idea of unity, a claim not to be broken up from within. Second is *political independence*, the claim not to be subservient to or controlled by another state. Governments generally insist upon the freedom to make certain essential choices and not have them made for them. This claim is fundamentally one of noninterference. Third is a claim to *participation*. This claim extends from negotiating and signing treaties as an equal partner to joining and contributing to international organizations. The sovereignty claim has extended to the claim to be left alone in a broad sense of opting out of emerging international norms or, more insidiously for international lawyers, of seeking to opt out of binding international norms.[2] These are claims that international law does not accept, though states continue to make them.

The state makes these sovereignty claims principally against other states—states seeking to dominate it through political or economic strong-arming, intervention, nonrecognition, or, rarely, aggression. But it can make the claim against other participants as well. Russia and China are making sovereignty claims against peoples—Chechen and Tibetans, respectively—and Israel against Palestinians. Those states are also making claims against NGOs that oppose their actions. Many poor states also make a sovereignty claim against the International Monetary Fund, an organization of states seen to be controlling the way a state can make fiscal and monetary policy. And the attempts by the developing world to regain control of their natural resources after decolonization were sovereignty claims in part against transnational businesses.[3]

A broad second category of state claims concern *economic security*. One group, which is an analogue of the political independence claim noted above, is the idea of *economic control*, in the sense of control over the exploitation of natural resources on its territory or adjoining seas, but also the freedom to choose its economic policy free from foreign pressure and to distribute the material benefits of commerce as its chooses. But a broader claim is to *access to economic benefits*, in the sense of participation in the international economic system to achieve material improvement of its residents. Poor states may seek global intellectual property rules that allow them to make products without compensating property owners; rich states may seek investment rules that protect their investors from local governments who want to renege on contracts.

1.1.2 *Peoples*

Although many groups within and across states call themselves a people, international law generally views peoples as having something beyond ethnic kinship—some sort of territorial claim, affiliation, or attachment (e.g. the Finnish, Corsican, or Sioux people).[4] Despite these definitional difficulties, the central claim of peoples is to *self-government*. This includes a claim to *recognition* as a distinct actor and not merely a loose group of individuals and, most significantly, claims to *control its future* through political arrangements ranging from self-administration within states up to creation of its own state. (Minority groups not usually regarded as peoples, such as territorially dispersed religious groups, typically make more modest claims, e.g. to assert and perpetuate their identity through linguistic, educational, cultural, and other practices.) This claim resonates with Iris Young's interpretation that self-determination concerns nondomination rather than simply noninterference (Young 2007). The primary target of these claims is the state or, in some cases (like secession) a community of states, as these entities generally have the power to act on these claims. Peoples also make claims against their members, in seeking to constrain their behavior, including by preventing exit.

1.1.3 *The Individual*

The individual's rise as a participant in the international legal process gained momentum in the nineteenth century in the anti-slavery movement; it stood on its own after World War I as states agreed to protect ethnic minorities in the new states created after the war and to protect some workers through international labor law. The era after World War II saw the rise of individual human rights and the codification of numerous treaties to advance them.[5] As David Held has noted, through these developments, "a bridge is created between morality and law where, at best, only stepping stones existed before" (Held 2002: 13). The individual's fundamental claims are of *personal freedom* and *governmental protection*. The claims of personal freedom (or autonomy) arise from an interest in being immune from governmental abuse, being left alone by those who have the power to interfere negatively with the person's welfare. The claim of governmental protection is, effectively, about not being left alone, in the sense of being left alone to suffer.

The individual principally makes these claims on the state, usually his or her own, for it generally has the readiest capacity to grant that which the claimant seeks. But at times an individual may make a claim on another state to protect him or her in some way.

An individual can assert a claim against a people, as when a member of an indigenous group seeks to opt out of a practice that the group mandates; or against business entities, as when an individual accuses such entities of not providing proper conditions of labor.

1.1.4 *International Organizations*

International organizations, consisting mostly of states, in many ways reflect the interests of their members. Yet international organizations also make claims generated by their own secretariat officials. While those claims can never be in opposition to the views of most of the members, they need not be in accordance with the views of all of them. Thus, for instance, the United Nations advances in many ways the claims of individuals and peoples. At a more general level, international organizations also make a claim for *relevance*. That is, even as states create international organizations, whether global or regional, they remain ambivalent as to how much authority to delegate to them. Leading states and the officials of these institutions want them to be key forums for decision-making.

1.1.5 *Nongovernmental Organizations*

NGOs share the same general claim as international organizations—*relevance*. With their resources confined to skilled staff, they must influence those who have the power or resources to advance their substantive agenda. In the two most significant areas for international NGOs, namely human rights and the environment, they must persuade, through the power of their research and argumentation, those with decision-making authority and influence of the rightness of their cause.

1.1.6 *Business Entities*

From the large multinational corporation to the small family enterprise, the preeminent claim of business is for *economic wealth*. Businesses may frame these claims in terms of consumer benefit, environmental protection, or even national security, and they may indeed donate some of their profits to charitable causes, but, in the end, they are making claims for a greater share of economic wealth.

1.2 The Fundamental Norms of International Law

When we say that international law (like all law) resolves claims, we mean that the law encompasses multiple rules and processes that assign to different entities, institutions, and persons various rights, duties, and powers, including the power to make the rules. In a pithy description of the 1982 United Nations Convention the Law of the Sea, Philip Allott wrote:

> It is comprehensive in dealing with the whole nonland area of the world.... It has a rule for everything. The rule may be a permissive rule. It may be an obligation. It

may confer an explicit freedom or leave a residual liberty by not specifying a right or a duty. But a Flying Dutchman wandering the sea areas of the world, carrying his copy of the Convention, would [find that] [t]he Convention would never fail him.

(Allott 1983: 8)

Most international law rules are in the form of duties, and the centrality of the state to the international order has meant that the most elaborate set of duties are those of *states* toward other *states*—although states also have important duties in the area of human rights and self-determination toward individuals and peoples, respectively. The other five actors may also have duties, though the law has not developed them in as much detail. Although earlier understandings of international law assumed that states were free to act as they chose unless the law specifically recognized a limitation on that freedom,[6] some norms are described in terms of permissions rather than duties. Moreover, some norms are described in other ways, e.g. the rights of self-determination, the principle of sovereign equality, and the special privileges of the permanent members of the UN Security Council.[7]

The legal form of these duties, rights, or privileges depends upon the process by which the norm is prescribed—processes that many international lawyers somewhat simplistically label as "sources" of law. As a general matter, norms derive from the consent of states. As a result, treaties are particularly authoritative as law because each state party to it has clearly consented to be bound. Customary international law is also based on consent—a consistent practice of states (usually) acting in accordance with the rule, with a sense that their actions are legally required (*opinio juris*). Consent may sometimes amount to non-objection, as when all states, even new ones, are bound to a new norm of custom as long as they did persistently not object to it earlier. Beyond these two forms, resolutions of international organizations can be binding if the states creating the organization delegate that power to it—as when the parties to the UN Charter agree that UN Security Council decisions are automatically binding. And judicial rulings are binding on states if they have agreed in advance to the jurisdiction of the tribunal, whether an interstate proceeding in the International Court of Justice, a suit by an individual against his or her own state in the European Court of Human Rights, a suit by an investor against a host state in international arbitration, or an arrest order of the International Criminal Court. Soft law emerges when states or other actors want to prescribe desired conduct and are prepared to act in accordance with it, but do not wish to face the same sorts of consequences for noncompliance that apply to legal rules (although the distinction may be slight). All of these processes of law formation raise enormous theoretical questions that are the topic of international law and jurisprudential scholarship.[8]

If we had to identify a group of norms as the most important, it might look something like this (with the legal source identified as well):

Norms Responding to Core State Claims:

1. States must not use military force against each other except in self-defense or pursuant to an authorization from the UN Security Council. (UN Charter)

2. States must not interfere in one another's internal affairs through coercive means. (Customary international law)

3. States can prescribe domestic law to address events on their territory and, under defined principles of jurisdiction, some conduct beyond their borders; but they must not enforce their law on another state's territory without the latter's consent. (Customary international law)

4. States are juridically equal, giving them an equal capacity to enter into treaties and equal duties to be bound by them. Each state must also respect the immunity of other states from the jurisdiction of its courts for their official sovereign acts. (Customary international law)

5. States must observe in good faith all treaties to which they are a party. (Vienna Convention on the Law of Treaties)

6. The obligations of states under the UN Charter, including their duty to carry out the decisions of the Security Council, prevail over any other inconsistent duties. (UN Charter)

7. States enjoy permanent sovereignty over their natural resources on their territory and, for the most part, on their continental shelf and in their exclusive economic zone. (Customary international law, UN Convention on the Law of the Sea)

Norms Responding to Claims of Peoples and Individuals[9]

8. The principle of self-determination grants the people of an existing state as a whole the right to maintain that status as a general matter. However, it grants peoples living in colonies the right to separate from the metropolitan state and form their own state. And it grants peoples within a state the right to participation within it, with secession as a possible remedy of last recourse. (UN Charter, customary international law)

9. States have duties to individuals under their jurisdiction to respect a large range of human rights as well as to protect them from human rights violations by private actors. State duties with respect to human rights entail both negative action—refraining from harm—and positive action—creating institutional mechanisms or providing various resources. (Global and regional treaties, as elaborated by jurisprudence)

10. States may not generally take coercive measures abroad to protect the human rights of those beyond their borders, but they may, and in some cases must, prosecute certain grave offenses against individuals that take place beyond their borders. (Customary international law and treaties on torture, war crimes, and other offenses)

11. During armed conflict, states must avoid causing unnecessary suffering to combatants, must not directly target civilians, and must use methods of attack that avoid disproportionate harm to civilians. (Geneva Conventions and Protocols and customary international law)

12. Some violations of international law, in particular serious harms to individuals in peacetime and wartime, incur individual criminal responsibility, allowing for the possibility of a trial for those crimes before an international criminal court or any domestic court. (Geneva Conventions, other treaties, customary international law)

Norms Responding to Claims of Business Entities

13. States must provide a minimal standard of treatment to foreign corporations operating on their territory. Where states are parties to international investment agreements, they must provide greater protections. (Customary international law and international investment treaties)

14. States must generally not discriminate among similar foreign products from different states with respect to tariffs, nor between domestic and foreign products in the implementation of domestic regulations. (World Trade Organization agreements)

15. Corporations are seen as having certain responsibilities in the area of human rights, notably a responsibility not to infringe on human rights in their business activities. (soft law)

Other Core Norms

16. State must avoid environmental harms that extend beyond their jurisdiction and must take precautions regarding measures whose environmental impact is uncertain (Various treaties and customary international law)

As noted, beyond this short list of core norms, the law has vast areas of specialized laws, including at levels of detail that rival domestic tax codes—e.g. concerning allocation of the radio spectrum, the length of airport runways, and the standards for vaccines. The result is, as Waldron has written:

> [a] dense thicket of rules that sustain our life together, a life shared by people and peoples, not just in any particular society [that] includes some of the most mundane things imaginable.... the ordinary as well as the extraordinary, the tedious as well as the exciting, the commercial as well as the ideological.   (Waldron 2006: 97)

1.3 Implementation and Enforcement

International law differs from domestic law in so far as it does not rely primarily on vertical enforcement, and courts in particular, to address violations. Rather, states respond to violations of many or even most norms through non-coercive means such as diplomatic protest as well as deployment of incentives and sanctions (carrots and sticks), on their own or in coordination with other states. States may also suspend performance of treaty provisions or rules of customary international law in response to violations, though the law puts some limits on these sorts of countermeasures. States' incentives to respond to violations by others depend on political factors, national interests, and power differentials. The law is also enforced through self-restraint. Each state generally has an incentive to refrain from unfounded interpretations of ambiguous rules lest another state rely on this interpretation as a precedent in the future in a way that could harm the first state or its friends.

Some regimes, such as global trade and the law of the sea, have standing tribunals in which states that cannot resolve their disputes through negotiation can sue one another with binding results. Regional human rights regimes in Europe, Latin America, and

Africa also have standing courts in which individuals can bring legal claims with binding results. And international investment treaties give foreign investors the right to take host states to binding international arbitration. But international law lacks a court of general jurisdiction, with the International Court of Justice able to hear cases between states and issue binding judgments only where both parties agree in advance to the court's jurisdiction through different processes. The only international body generally authorized to enforce international law on all states is the UN Security Council, through its special powers (principally under Chapter VII of the Charter) over matters of international peace and security, a term that has expanded to cover human rights as well.

In addition, many treaties, in particular concerning human rights and the environment, create governmental or expert bodies without binding powers that can subject states to mandatory reporting on their compliance with the treaty and allow states, individuals, or institutions to challenge a state's compliance or provide a forum for a negotiation of a solution. And numerous international organizations have standing procedures for overseeing state compliance with treaties and other rules. Those organizations can recommend centralized sanctions against violators as well as provide incentives for compliance. NGOs also play a large role with respect to implementation, whether in gathering information on state compliance, naming and shaming violators through public reports, or confidentially encouraging states to follow the rules (the modus operandi of the International Committee of the Red Cross).

Lastly, states may generally not use force to enforce international law. Only the Security Council may authorize states to use force. States may only use force in the absence of Council approval in self-defense, in response to an armed attack. All other uses of force are formally prohibited, although some (like some acts of humanitarian intervention) are at times tolerated.

2 International Law's Encounters with Global Justice

Even as international law is by its nature normative, most international law scholarship is empty or thin on questions of moral reasoning or ethical theory. It is descriptive or doctrinal, seeking to accurately portray the state of the law, advocate an interpretation of the law, or bring coherence to an area of law characterized by competing interpretations. This starting point is hardly surprising given the dominance of the positivist method within international law, but it nonetheless has so far limited possibilities of collaboration with ethics. To international lawyers, positivism is a two-pronged conception, to wit: (a) as with legal positivism generally, what we consider as law is a matter of social fact, making *lex lata* (the law as it is) and *lex ferenda* (the law as it should be) distinct issues; and (b) the fundamental formal criterion for law to be valid is the consent of states, particularly through the prescriptive processes of treaty and custom—though many scholars who call themselves positivists accept the importance of other sources, such as decisions of international organizations and courts. Positivism remains the lingua franca of international law and even its detractors know how to play the good positivist when the situation warrants it.[10]

As a consequence, many scholars write for an imagined audience, in particular a judicial one, that would consider moral arguments ultra vires.[11] They often move beyond description to prescribe and advocate legal norms and institutions that we should support, but they generally do the latter within a methodology that relies on accepted practices regarding sources and interpretation, with perhaps the occasional nod to political realities, or efficiency, to guide among competing choices.[12] As much as scholars may have strongly held views on morality or justice, many or even most seem to take it as a point of pride to divorce these concerns from their scholarship, or at least hide them well.[13] For many positivists, the emphasis on these formal sources is a way of accommodating the diversity of national systems across the planet (avoiding the one-size-fits-all approach of natural law), as a result of which they may well see discussions of global justice as simply beside the point. Jean d'Aspremont (2007) voices this strain in insisting that international law is about accommodating national interests, not furthering global values, a project he regards as antithetical to legal scholarship. Lawyers also see themselves as problem-solvers for clients, so issues of justice may seem too far from their everyday work.

Yet the lawyer's imperative to identify norms through formal sources should not make appraisal of those norms ethically beyond his or her writ, let alone threatening to it. And even if norms come about as a result of overlapping national interests, they can still correspond to global values. One can still endorse—or criticize—certain norms as reflecting certain values without conceding a degree of moral consciousness to states that they may well not deserve.

Indeed, even within the positivist tradition, issues of morality can never be completely avoided, as doctrine itself seems to find a place for it. In particular, scholarly treatment of *jus cogens* norms—peremptory norms that override even treaties—and some obligations *erga omnes*—duties extending to the community of states as a whole and not merely to individual states—generally assumes that part of the rationale for the distinctiveness of these norms is that states have recognized that some rules are, in a sense, more fundamental than others because they reflect important moral positions.[14] In determining the state of the law, the actual moral views of states become a relevant consideration.[15] Moreover, proposals for new norms could take into account moral views held by states and individuals.[16] And when states violate these norms, legal scholars should think more broadly about which states should take corrective measures and why.[17] Such an inquiry resonates with, but would also benefit from more engagement with, the work of philosophers regarding the division of global duties into national responsibilities.[18]

Looking beyond *jus cogens* and *erga omnes* duties, legal scholarship evinces three key encounters with ethics.

2.1 Mainstream Methodologies, European and American

Two prominent mainstream methodologies have found a place for ethics, even while skirting many key issues of global justice. A strand of positivist thinking that calls itself enlightened, highly influential in continental scholarship, seeks to soften positivism's formalistic light through subtle recourse to moral argumentation. Bruno Simma, one of its leading proponents, wants the positivist lawyer to engage with morality, as long as it does not threaten positivism's reliance upon formal sources to determine the validity of a claimed norm. International law should serve certain ends of justice, in particular advancement of human rights; and the lawyer has a responsibility to recognize which rules do or do not further those goals (Simma 1994). This position extends to the recognition that it may be morally required to disobey international law.[19]

Yet, as a good positivist, Simma emphasizes less the ideals of international law than the norms on which there is state consent. Indeed, he offers up a sociological observation in asserting that states and other actors are, in fact, acting as if they had some agreement on these moral ends and posits that international law has moved from a set of bilateral relations among states, each advancing its own interest, to one of community interest (Simma 1994; Peters 2009). The idea of community interests has become conventional wisdom among international lawyers, although the positivists' need to ground community interests in state consent represents the great limitation of their methodology, however enlightened.

In the United States, the policy-oriented New Haven School conceptualizes law as a process for advancing policy goals in an authoritative and controlling manner; so once lawyers and other participants can identify the goals of the community, we can prescribe legal norms to accomplish these goals.[20] Minimum and optimum public orders are the chief policy goals of the international legal process.[21] The basic content of these two concepts was grounded in sociology (Harold Lasswell's contribution to the endeavor) and instantiated in law. Minimum public order refers to the global state of affairs with limited recourse to unauthorized violence to solve disputes and authoritative procedures for deploying force in exceptional situations.[22] Optimum public order is a world in which human dignity is maximally protected. The result was a fountain of scholarship on a range of issues, including humanitarian intervention, secession, and human rights.

The identification of minimum and optimum public order was highly significant; yet the New Haven School's engagement with ethics has always been constrained. While never denying the role of morality in international law—certainly human dignity is a moral concept—it sees morality through an anthropological lens. International law reflects morality because it reflects the demands of the community as determined by their so-called "base values."[23] Any other theorizing was defective because it lacked social context. Thus, Myres McDougal and his associates attacked Rawls in particular for his lack of empiricism (see, e.g., McDougal, Lasswell, and Chen 1980). Yet the content of these base values is often contested by different communities and that moral argumentation is inherent in evaluating claims and ultimately identifying base values.[24]

As a result, the New Haven School's emphasis on context in gauging the expectations of international actors and projecting future policies leaves us wondering whether more general recommendations can be made. The inherently sociological approach of the New Haven School—one might call it "fact-based international law"—that is its great strength can be a shortcoming for finding generalized guidance on the trade-off between minimum and optimum public order.

2.2 Critical Approaches

For the past several decades, various critical methodologies have not merely engaged with morality, but in many ways put it at the center of their agenda. These approaches seek to identify hidden agendas and biases within international law—including its norms, institutions, practitioners, and methodologies—and reform it. Critical or "New Stream" legal scholars built their methodology of deconstruction from literary theory and linguistics to identify myriad tensions within international law. Where positivists saw consent and acceptance, critical legal scholars saw power and hegemony;[25] where positivists saw international law as a language of communication, critical scholars saw lawyers seeking to preserve their own relevance in a changing world.[26] Feminist scholars saw international law as dominated by male views of society and individuals. Looking to the building blocks of the international system, they found assumptions made by positivism to reflect the biases of male statesmen and scholars who developed and promoted them.[27] And Third World Approaches to International Law (TWAIL) took a similar path with regard to the lingering legacy of colonialism within international law.[28]

In one sense, ethics and global justice are *the* agenda of these methodologies. Each sees power as having both constituted and corrupted international law and argues for reform that takes into account voices marginalized for centuries. The solution for Martti Koskenniemi, the most influential voice among the critical scholars, is a return to formalism; for international legal scholarship that has incorporated approaches from other disciplines—whether sociology (the New Haven School) or international relations—has yielded descriptions and prescriptions that serve the interests of the most powerful voices (typically American). He fears that calls for global governance subject to a standard of legitimacy will simply erode the standards within law into mere interest-balancing that benefits the powerful (Koskenniemi 2000, 2004).

Yet the ethics seems to end with this agenda. Critical scholars generally do not make a significant effort to engage with contemporary ethical theory by philosophers. Some scholarship is based mainly on the fear that too much power in the hands of one state in the no longer bipolar world will be damaging to everyone. Critical legal studies, in particular, often vacillates between a skepticism, even cynicism, of ethical inquiry as somehow hegemonic at worst, or at least a subterfuge for advancing each side's power, on the one hand, and a generally unarticulated commitment to egalitarianism, on the other.[29] It is not that these works lack theory; it is just typically not theory about justice or ethics. They are all far better at identifying what is wrong with international law than providing a theoretical grounding for the way forward; and ethics offers such a foundation that would also make their criticisms far more powerful—as well as more nuanced.

2.3 Direct Engagement with Ethics

Some scholars have integrated philosophical ethics directly into their work. Thomas Franck's (1995) *Fairness in International Law and Institutions* offered an attempt to measure international law against a standard of justice, with "fairness" as encompassing the legitimacy of the process leading to the norm and the distributive justice within it in terms of compliance with Rawls's difference principle. Yet the ambition of Franck's reach was compromised by the narrowness of his criteria for substantive justice.[30] Recently, this author evaluated a range of norms of international law according to a standard of "thin justice"—asking whether the norms advance interstate or intrastate peace in a way that respects basic human rights (Ratner 2015).

Other legal scholars have offered less comprehensive and sometimes idiosyncratic visions of justice. In his book *Eunomia*, Philip Allott (1990) offered an original, but frustratingly abstract attack on international law for failing to take into account the interests of humanity as a whole. Yet the work remains mostly isolated from debates among philosophers as to the makeup of that new international society. Fernando Tesón (1992, 1998) offers a critique of the legal order grounded in Kantian justice, in which democratic legitimacy should be the lodestar of international legitimacy. Tesón deserves credit for bringing Kant back into the scholarship of international law, though his later work claimed that states that do not meet Kantian standards of legitimacy are proper targets of unilateral intervention, a view quite at odds with the law's core norms on the use of force (Tesón 2005). Partly in response to Tesón and other cosmopolitans, Brad Roth (2011) offers a robust defense of interstate diversity, arguing that, in a world of deep moral disagreement, law must remain tolerant of different moral visions, with accompanying skepticism about the project of global justice.

Lastly, certain topics of international law have been more open to ethical inquiry even in the absence of some general engagement with morality as seen in the works just mentioned. Human rights scholarship is replete with discussions of utilitarian vs. deontological justifications for international norms and the translation of rights into duties, although even much of that scholarship is still fairly divorced from contemporary ethical scholarship about global justice.[31] International environmental law has done a better job of reckoning with moral concepts such as intergenerational equity and the proper distribution of burdens to prevent and remediate environmental harm.[32]

Despite these brief encounters with global justice, international law scholarship has engaged fairly little with questions of distributive justice—a sharp contrast to political philosophy. Lawyers talk and write about some aspects of distributive justice, for example, the place of economic rights within the pantheon of human rights, or the balance between the rights of the foreign investor and those of the host state in international investment law. But for many years, discussion of redistribution did not extend far beyond scholars in international environmental law addressing North–South responsibilities for climate change and those associated with TWAIL focused on redistribution. In recent years, however, a number of scholars of international trade and investment law have offered justice-based critiques of those rules.[33]

Why this reluctance by legal scholarship? First, for positivists, even of the enlightened variety, distributive justice is a risky subject because the gap between the expectations of states as determined through recourse to formal sources and the demands of distributive justice is enormous. States have generally not recognized distributive justice in the sense of wealth transfer between North and South as a goal, let alone an obligation (even of conduct). The International Court of Justice has rejected it as a rationale for determining maritime boundaries.[34]

Second, international law is still dominated by Northern governments and scholars, who see wealth inequities as one of many global issues to be addressed, but not morally or politically more imperative than the others, such as improvement of basic human rights, resolution of festering conflicts, and nuclear nonproliferation. These other issues are, in my view, all morally compelling, and some more compelling than certain claims for distributive justice.

Third, international law and lawyers value solving problems through existing structures and institutions. During the heyday of international attention to distributive justice in the 1970s and 1980s, it seemed that such institutions were developing. But the end of the Cold War halted that process, as developing countries that had benefited from the largesse of the other superpower now vied for Northern investment. As they have sought to play in the institutions established by the North—in a word, to switch, rather than fight—the focus of attention has shifted to the WTO, the World Bank, and the IMF. As long as international law lacks a single mechanism or institution for addressing global economic inequities comprehensively, international lawyers will think about distributive justice only piecemeal.

3 Global Justice Scholarship's Approaches to International Law

3.1 The Range of Philosophical Engagement with International Law

The engagement of political and moral philosophy, as well as political theory, with international law has varied significantly, from some close scrutiny of legal rules to deep suspicion and misunderstanding.

3.1.1 *Philosophical Appraisal of Legal Rules*

One strand of moral and political philosophy makes its subject, or at least a central part of it, the morality of the rules of international law. That is, the inquiry itself, and any theory resulting from it, seems in significant part to be generated by a need to understand, justify, or challenge the existing law. Just war theory established a key foothold to this approach with Michael Walzer's (2006) *Just and Unjust Wars*, which saw as a significant part of its project the holding up of legal norms of *jus ad bellum* and *jus in bello* to ethical scrutiny. Others continue to appraise the rules of war.[35] And human rights norms have proved the subject of significant philosophical work to theorize their foundations.[36] The attention to these two topics and philosophy's longstanding attention to the criminal law theory may explain philosophical interest in international criminal law (ICL). The philosophy of ICL has been dominated by efforts to find a moral justification for states' decisions to make certain acts international crimes.[37] Lastly, philosophers have begun to appraise the morality of various international rules concerning title to territory, whether in the decolonization context or with respect to control over natural resources.[38] Thus, some within ethics regard these norms as mattering enough in international relations, or the ways that we think about international relations, to merit serious and direct scrutiny.

3.1.2 *General Theory First, Application to Law Second*

A more common practice within ethics is to present a general argument about some aspect of global justice and then to evaluate some relevant international legal rules. Charles Beitz's (1979) *Political Theory and International Relations* offered a normative account of the international order that called for a morality of states based on a link between state autonomy and just domestic institutions, as well as a deep form of distributive justice. After presenting his vision, he provided an ethical appraisal of certain international law norms, e.g. defending the right of colonial self-determination by conceptualizing it as a claim to rectify social injustice. From a very different standpoint, Mervyn Frost (1996) argued that the system of sovereign states itself helps constitute the individual and promote his or her flourishing, thereby justifying many of the basic rules of international law.

A great deal of the communitarian/cosmopolitan debates fall into this category, with theories that provide blueprints for key aspects of a just world order and then some testing of extant legal norms and institutions. David Held and others sharing his outlook present a comprehensive conception of a cosmopolitan world order, emphasizing its legal components, assessing, for example, the structure of the European Union and the United Nations (see, e.g., Held 1995, 2002; Archibugi, Held, and Köhler 1998). Jürgen Habermas (2006) has stepped into these debates by arguing that international law is now becoming a constitution for the Kantian-based international community, though certain improvements will need to be made. Though preferring constitutionalization to cosmopolitanism as the goal, he, like Held, sees positive trends from the trajectory of international law since 1945. In the course of this work, they propose radical reorganization of the UN's organs, based on a need to dilute the influence of powerful states, ensuring a greater role for individual voices and relying on judicial mechanisms for resolving disputes (including, for example, advocating for the compulsory jurisdiction of the ICJ).[39] While the project helps us see the big picture of the global order, it suffers from utopianism as well as skepticism about the morality of international law.[40]

Some of these theories give prominence to institutions whose centrality to the regulation of international order is taken for granted by international lawyers. Allen Buchanan (2004) persuasively argues that moral questions about the duties of individuals or states can be answered only with careful consideration of the institutions currently capable of allowing those duties to be carried out. Substantively, he argues that a state's legitimacy turns fundamentally on its observance of human rights and democratic participation, and institutional legitimacy turns on similar factors. For Thomas Pogge, the focus is on institutions that should mete out distributive justice. At first arguing for the globalization of Rawls' difference principle and later asserting a more robust view of equality, Pogge claims not only that the rules of international trade and intellectual property are unjust, but also that individuals in the North are violating duties not to harm those in the South by participating in that system (see, e.g., Pogge 1989, 2008). Institutions regarding international trade also figure prominently in the work of Mathias Risse (2012), who criticizes the World Trade Organization for failing to mete out distributive justice, and Leif Wenar (2016), who takes aim at the global rules giving dictators the right to profit from their states' mineral resources. On the other hand, Rawls (1999) derived his theory of global justice with virtually no consideration of the role of global or regional organizations.

3.1.3 *Integrating Law into Philosophical Arguments*

Ethical claims can incorporate the law in a further respect, by building an argument on international norms themselves. Terry Nardin (1998) took an early significant step with his call for a limited vision of interstate justice based on a traditional positivistic notion of international law. Held (1995) constructs his model of cosmopolitan democracy in part on the significant changes within the international legal order, notably the development of human rights, limitations on state immunity, the notion of common economic heritage, and the increased powers of international organizations. Peter Singer (2002) relies upon the UN Charter and actions of the Security Council to endorse limits on a state's domestic jurisdiction regarding human rights abuses. And Andreas Follesdal (2011) argues that the norms of international law and institutions create a global basic structure—regulated by principles of distributive justice—in so far as they have a direct impact on individuals and have evolved in part independently of states.

International law can also be used defensively in ethical reasoning. Goodin (1988), in his pioneering article justifying a state's special duties to its own nationals on consequentialist grounds, pointed out situations where, under international law, a state's duties to foreigners are actually greater than its duties to its citizens (e.g. with respect to protection of private property and the ability to draft people into an army). He uses these examples to rebut the strong nationalist claim that states should always owe greater duties to their own citizens than to foreigners, thereby assuming that these rules count as ethical arguments for rebutting the strong nationalist position. Kok-Chor Tan (2004) uses the presence of institutional coercion at the level of international law as one argument against the view that reciprocity limits duties of justice to the domestic level.[41] And arguing against much ethical theorizing about human rights, Beitz (2009) and Cohen (2004) effectively take human rights as they appear in legal instruments and generate arguments against a top-down derivation of such rights.[42]

3.1.4 *Missteps in Philosophical Approaches to International Law*

Despite these examples of integrating international law into philosophical work on global justice, philosophical work also falls prey to two sets of conceptual missteps. First, philosophers sometimes get the rules of international law wrong. Most notably, in *The Law of Peoples*, Rawls (1999) cites as support, or perhaps recognition, of his basic principles of mutual respect between peoples James L. Brierly's (1963) treatise *The Law of Nations*. On the one hand, Rawls seems to have accepted that international law already embodies certain ethical principles. For Rawls, those principles are defensible from a contractarian perspective, as he claims—though does not really prove—that they would be agreed to by democratic peoples in an original position and then supported by so-called decent peoples. On the other hand, Rawls cites and endorses an outdated restatement of international law that does not reflect the developments in human rights law that limit a state's freedom to govern itself however it chooses (as well as its immunity from external, non-military interference).[43]

From a different perspective, some philosophers challenge the notion of cosmopolitan justice in part by arguing that there is no global basic structure because no international power can assign rights and duties equally to all agents.[44] Setting aside whether a basic structure indeed requires such an authority, and whether that authority must be able to assign individual duties and rights as opposed to states' duties and rights, it is highly formalistic, if not simply wrong, to say that no international institution has such authority. In the most obvious cases, the Security Council may effectively assign duties to individuals (e.g. not to export certain items to a target state); and the International Criminal Court can throw (or order a state to throw) someone in jail.[45]

Second, many philosophical approaches treat international law merely as a vessel for delivering, institutionalizing, or enforcing a previously derived ethical position—or a second-best version of it (Ratner 2019b). Those who deploy this approach fail to consider whether the legal vessel can institutionally handle their theory; and the translation of moral principles into legal rules results in the philosophical equivalent of *faux amis*. For instance, some cosmopolitan scholars have suggested that the International Court of Justice serve as an arbiter for dealing with secessionist conflicts according to moral criteria of self-determination (Copp 1998: 237; Altman and Wellman 2009: 66–7). The ICJ is actually a highly conservative tribunal, whether in avoiding politically contentious cases, as it did concerning France's nuclear testing in the 1970s, NATO's bombing of Serbia in 1999, and Kosovo's 2008 declaration of independence, or in its overt disdain for distributive justice.[46]

3.2 Causes and Consequences of Philosophical Distance from International Law

Several factors seem to account for the disconnect between global justice scholarship and international law. First, philosophy will always be more abstract and foundational in some sense than law. A good philosophical argument about the morality of the international order is grounded in principles and intuitions; a good legal argument about the normative structure of that order is grounded in, and constrained by, precedent and practice. The two fields also treat the messiness of real life quite differently, with philosophers deriving necessary and sufficient conditions and legal scholars accepting that every law is in some way over- or underinclusive and thus a sort of rule of thumb. And lawyers are also more resigned to the role of power and politics—seeking to engage with those forces—while philosophers of global justice seek to blunt their influence.

Second, some theory in global justice addresses foundational questions where the state of international law seems beside the point. Thus, some scholarship is about interpersonal ethics, e.g. what each of us owes individually to those within and outside national borders. As Pogge (1992) has noted, this sort of interactional morality is quite distinct from institutional morality. Thus, a line of scholarship has focused on the identities, roles, and responsibilities of individuals, not institutions.[47] In this case, the lack of engagement with law can be justified on the ground that the content of norms that, at least in the first instance, regulate the activities of states is not relevant to the duties of individuals. But this reason cannot shield scholarship on global *institutional* ethics that shies away from international law and institutions. Much scholarship argues for duties states should have at the global level, yet with little regard to the rules that states *have in fact* derived and enforced.

Third, philosophical work on global justice is often concerned with the deep moral structure of the international order—why states have title to territory, whether individuals or states have any duties of redistribution beyond their borders, whether states should have open or closed borders, or the basic principles of justice for allocating responsibilities to combat climate change. That sort of work can offer insights into the moral fiber of the world order. Indeed, such work is important for international law development itself—to guide lawyers as they contemplate future lawmaking, to inform decision makers, including international judges, on the interpretation of existing rules; and to provide a template for evaluating the moral adequacy of existing rules on an issue as part of a project of reform of those rules.

Fourth, and of more concern, is a general suspicion of international law—namely that the practical arrangements that humans have derived for their global interactions—including legal norms—should not get in the way of good theorizing about ideal arrangements. As noted earlier, ideal theory surely has its place in ethics, and indeed there is nothing wrong with postponing the "ought implies can" questions until certain basic principles are derived. Yet the avoidance of international law by philosophers seems to go much deeper. Much of it seems based on the notion that (a) because much or most law emerges from a political process, it can neither ground nor undercut an ethical argument; and (b) because law inevitably involves compromises, either in its creation or enforcement, its content is marginal to principled ethical argumentation. Either way, as noted earlier, law becomes simply a vessel for delivering, institutionalizing, or enforcing a previously derived ethical position.[48] It is not that the law is morally wrong, but simply that it is irrelevant. But the first of these confuses the origin of a claim with its moral validity; and the second suggests that ethical reasoning does not involve compromise, whereas it typically includes weighing of competing considerations, maybe not at first but at some stage.

A further nuance is the possibility that philosophers see law and institutions as irrelevant to global justice because they see them as making no difference to how global actors will ultimately behave, a skepticism invented by some political realists.[49] Under this view, ethical theory should devise solutions, but those solutions will be realized through non-legal avenues. Yet if philosophers have this view, it is simply wrong descriptively. As a generation of international relations and legal scholarship and the lived experiences of international actors—from states, NGOs, corporations, international organizations, and even criminal syndicates—has demonstrated, international law and institutions both constrain the behavior of international actors and channel and frame discussions for international cooperation.[50] International law is a fundamental institution for the advancement of moral claims beyond borders.

Whatever its cause, avoidance of engagement with legal rules and institutions results in distinct gaps in scholarship on global justice. *First* is a general impoverishment of ethical theory for producing prescriptions that actually contribute to the project of a more just world order. As Buchanan writes, failure to understand global institutions means that philosophers derive "principles...not suitable for institutionalization because they are inconsistent with existing institutional arrangements whose abandonment would be morally prohibitive...or because institutionalizing them would generate incentives that undermine the realization of other important principles" (Buchanan and Golove 2002: 870).[51] As Habermas has said of cosmopolitanism, it "remains an empty, even deceptive, promise without a realistic assessment of the totality of accommodating trends in which it is embedded" (Habermas 2006: 144).

Put somewhat differently, the result is a failure to engage in *institutional moral reasoning*—reasoning that takes into account existing international institutions (including the lack thereof) in justifying, criticizing, or theorizing about the international political order. Because institutional moral reasoning is always considering—and, to a certain extent, accepting as somewhat fixed—the practices of global actors, including international law, the resulting theories have a groundedness that opens up possibilities for their ideas to be the basis for actual reforms of the system. The theories or conclusions from such reasoning need not be easily feasible, but they are more translatable into new practices and new norms than theories that ignore those practices.

Second is a dismissive attitude about the moral justification of key norms of international law. One might cite a particularly flagrant case. In a pioneering essay, Brian Barry found, with little argument, that the principle of national sovereignty over natural resources, a core norm of international law, "is without any rational foundation" (Barry 1981: 36). Such a position would strike a lawyer as astonishing, if only because of the notion of ownership to avoid the tragedy of the commons seems like such a basic idea, one easily justified on utilitarian grounds.[52] Ethical scrutiny of international law would allow for an exploration of a certain set of arguments not sufficiently discussed in philosophical circles. More generally, international law shows that these issues are not as simple as philosophers may conceive by highlighting contrary positions widely accepted by states that philosophers may have ignored.

Third, much philosophy zeroes in on issues and develops proposals that seem unconcerned with rather clear strictures of international law. For example, two remedies for oppressed people abroad—secession and humanitarian intervention—have elicited significant philosophical attention, particularly among cosmopolitan scholars, despite international law's overall stance against them.[53] If philosophers are concerned with responses to a state's abuse of its own people, then they should not leave out of the discussion the main methods that other states actually deploy in these situations—dialogue, capacity-building, diplomatic protest, naming and shaming, linkage of foreign assistance, and sanctions.[54] Granted, philosophy may simply be trying to focus on the hardest question—when has a state so lost its legitimacy that it can be dismembered or invaded?[55] But the other options, including diplomatic repercussions or sanctions, raise difficult moral issues as well, e.g. whether sanctions should be used, given uncertainties over their efficacy.

A *fourth* consequence is the derivation of prescriptions for aspects of global justice that are close to that recognized in international law, without any acknowledgment of the similarity. A number of philosophical proposals regarding self-determination resemble that of international law, though the connection goes unrecognized by their proponents.[56] Again, one might ask why this omission of the coincidence with law matters to the philosopher's task. Perhaps the question should be reversed: Is a philosopher deriving principles of justice ready to assert that it is *irrelevant* to his or her argument that his or her seemingly original vision is one that states have already accepted through international law? On the positive side, the existence of these rules suggests that the philosopher's position is indeed feasible, giving it support among those who believe that "ought implies can." On the other hand, it could also suggest that the philosopher's position may not be quite as original as he or she thought, as statesmen and women devising these rules indeed have been thinking along the same lines.

4 Toward a Deeper Engagement between Legal and Philosophical Approaches to Global Justice

Theoretical work on global justice should, then, incorporate the insights of both international law and philosophy, moral and political. On the one hand, international lawyers can gain from philosophy a carefully derived set of ideas for evaluating the existing state of the law, promoting changes in it, and developing institutions to implement it.

For instance, one of the most significant advances in our understanding of human rights law took place when the UN Committee on Economic, Social, and Cultural Rights endorsed the concept of a state's duties to respect, protect, and promote rights, first developed by Henry Shue (1996).[57]

More generally, legal scholars should move beyond any assumption that ethical inquiry is irrelevant or ultra vires. Lawyers must recognize that when they engage in normative and even descriptive scholarship, they often, if not inevitably, *are already taking an ethical and not just a pragmatic position* on issues of global justice. For all but the most mundane analysis, legal scholars are assuming something about key global values. Indeed, many of the disagreements among lawyers are about the relative value of peace compared to human rights. Moreover, as Martti Koskenniemi (2003) has pointed out, we cannot avoid issues of morality by focusing on the broader and more vague concept of legitimacy.

At the same time, philosophical approaches to global justice should recognize that the norms accepted by states through international law have become an important part of the moral universe that the philosopher considers. For global justice is, after all, about improving and changing the world—a project that must take account of certain realities and institutions of the international system. Beyond the engagement discussed in section 3.1 above, the philosopher could (or in some cases inevitably will) take account of the law in the following ways:

First, as an epistemological matter, scholars should recognize that in developing moral positions, it seems impossible to turn a blind eye to rules in fact accepted by states. Thus, for example, a philosopher of human rights seeking to come up with a list of basic human rights will inevitably have regard to those rights already protected by states. In theorizing about the rules of warfare, it seems impossible to ignore the *jus in bello*. While the legal status of certain positions does not imply moral acceptability, it is, nonetheless, an inevitable input.

Second, legal rules may assist philosophers in what Christopher McCrudden (2017: 73) has called "concept formation." To return to the human rights example, how can we know the meaning of the concept of freedom of expression—and whether it is a human right—without looking at the forms of expression that humans might attempt, which inevitably requires looking at those that governments have sought to regulate in some way? If we thought that expression meant only political expression and then discovered that some states require, permit, or forbid people to wear certain religious garb, our understanding of expression itself would change. This idea seems captured in Cane's observation above that aversion to law is a "philosophical mistake."

Third, philosophers can use international law as a sort of check as they develop their conceptions or theories of global justice. For the status of some norms as law could mean an acceptance by global actors of a moral and not merely a political position. If, for instance, the rules recognized by states deviate significantly from the moral position of the philosopher, they would seem to represent a set of counterexamples that argue for revisiting one's theory and asking whether there is a good reason for the deviation. Rather than dismissing the legal rules as the product of mere politics or history, the philosopher should give them serious consideration and be prepared to justify (1) why the rules agreed to by states do not advance global justice and (2) the systemic costs to changing the extant rule to one consistent with the theory.

Fourth, global justice theory can look to international law to define the ambit of its inquiry. As new norms develop, philosophers should be examining their ethical content. Philosophers have begun to recognize this in recent work on newer areas of international law, such as international criminal law and international environmental law, but the philosophical work lags behind the legal prescription. Global justice should cover *all* the areas where decision-makers have contemplated regulation through law, whether or not they have actually succeeded in doing so.

Beyond the academic realm, an understanding of international law and its moral content serves a deeper purpose for the project of global justice. If we accept international law's role in constructing a more just world order, then ethical scrutiny of those rules can give international actors—from presidents and prime ministers to ordinary citizens, from business tycoons to leaders of rebel movements—*good reasons* to respect it and develop it, or good reasons to change it or supplement it. If a set of legal norms turns out to be morally defensible under a considered moral viewpoint, we have provided those actors additional reasons for respecting it beyond just the fear of adverse consequences for ignoring the rules, or an appeal to some inner respect for the law as law, and a good reason to appreciate the consequences of altering the law and its institutions in one direction or another. Where, on the other hand, the law does not meet a moral standard, we have good reasons to change some rules, as well as guideposts for that change. With greater awareness of the values underlying a just international law, we can move to create new rules that will earn our respect as just. Such an evaluation of the justice of international law's norms does not overlook the possibility that there may be reasons for us to follow or tolerate even unjust rules—perhaps out of a respect for the rule of law generally or stability—but it gives us the ability to discern better what we are doing and why.

These connections between international law and philosophy can be synthesized in different manner, based on H. L. A. Hart's (2012) distinction between morality as a quality of certain societal norms of conduct as ethically good (so-called critical morality) and morality as simply the universe of those societal norms of conduct (so-called positive morality). First, the morality—in the first sense of its ethical defensibility—of legal rules can offer us a good (though not conclusive) reason for respecting those rules. International law is important for governing international affairs; the extent to which its norms are moral or just will affect our respect for these rules governing international affairs, and so it is important to explore that justice. And second, the legalized nature of some aspects of morality—in the second sense of the landscape of moral rules—can offer us a good (though not conclusive) reason for respecting that part of morality. International law's status as law and its institutionalized setting should influence, though hardly determine, our views as to what is moral or just in international affairs.

The two fields could go beyond integrating the insights of the other toward active collaboration. Two priorities seem to represent the most fertile ground for such joint consideration. First is the allocation of global responsibilities. Both disciplines ask about, in the most general sense, who is to blame or to praise, as well as be punished or rewarded, for a state of affairs; and who deserves in some sense, or is in the best position, to fix it.[58] What distinguishes a focus on responsibilities from one on duties is the idea of *multiplicity* and *allocation*: that in a world where numerous entities might well have duties, or indeed might have failed to carry out those duties, we must choose how to allocate among them in order to improve the state of affairs. It is about selecting who should do what when there are multiple plausible candidates.

The legal approaches to global responsibilities include forays into the meaning of obligations *erga omnes*, the environmental law concept of common but differentiated responsibilities among states, especially as it affects climate change; and the Responsibility to Protect. The law has also looked beyond states, by addressing the accountability of other actors. Philosophers have moved from basic questions such as whether artificial entities, such as states, even have responsibilities as compared to individuals, to flesh out ideas of group and institutional responsibility.[59] Many of the key philosophical contributions to global justice literature are ultimately about responsibility.

A second area for engagement is the challenge of nationalism and illiberalism in various corners of the world. On the one hand, cosmopolitan philosophical perspectives have tended to be dismissive of the legitimacy of non-democracies in the international order, a position that may seem validated by the threats of nationalist or illiberal regimes to their own populations and to global order. On the other hand, in the real world, most states, including one of the two most politically and economically influential in the world, are not liberal democracies, so the focus on democracy becomes a diversion to theorizing that connects to real-world problems. Because international law is based on cooperation between many different types of states, its practices may offer analogies or strategies for a moral account of diversity across governments and an approach to addressing the threats from some regimes.[60]

Breaching the barriers of inquiry of two major disciplines is not easy for the reasons discussed. But these differences also invite each to learn from the other. International law has shown itself generally open to the insights of other disciplines, whether political science, economics, or even literary theory. Ethics need not represent any greater a challenge. Philosophers have invoked domestic law in their arguments, and some have appraised international law or even used it as a building block in their arguments. Clearly, part of this process will involve a sort of division of labor—dare I say responsibilities—for the global justice project.

NOTES

1. See generally Ratner (2015).
2. See Henkin (1995); see also Krasner (1999).
3. See generally Ratner (2001).
4. See generally Musgrave (1997).

5. As stated by the UN's International Criminal Tribunal for the Former Yugoslavia, "A State-sovereignty-oriented approach has been gradually supplanted by a human-being-oriented approach.... [T]he maxim of Roman law *hominum causa omne jus constitutum est*...has gained a firm foothold in the international community." *Prosecutor v Tadic*, Case No. IT-94-1-T, Decision on the Defence Motion for Interlocutory Appeal on Jurisdiction (Oct. 2, 1995), para. 97, www.icty.org.

6. S. S. Lotus Case, PCIJ (1927).

7. While it is possible to describe most or all international law rules in terms of Hohfeldian correlatives, international lawyers do not typically do so.

8. See Besson and Aspremont (2017).

9. As a formal matter, these norms are also duties to other states, not merely to individuals.

10. Ratner and Slaughter (2004).

11. Cf. Bodansky (2011).

12. See Koskenniemi (2008).

13. See Koskenniemi (2008).

14. See, e.g., *Application of the Convention on the Prevention and Punishment of the Crime of Genocide*, ICJ Reports (2007) 43, paras. 161–62.

15. Cf. Hart (2012).

16. Goodin and Ratner (2011).

17. See, e.g., Nollkaemper and Jacobs (2015).

18. See, e.g., Miller (2001).

19. Simma (1999: 22).

20. McDougal Reisman (1981).

21. Wiessner and Willard (1999).

22. See UN Charter, arts. 2(4), 42, and 51.

23. These are respect, power, wealth, skill, enlightenment, rectitude, affection, and well-being.

24. See Gallie (1956).

25. See generally Koskenniemi (1989).

26. Kennedy (2000).

27. Charlesworth and Chinkin (2000).

28. See, e.g., Gathii (2011).

29. See, e.g., Koskenniemi (2001).

30. Tasioulas (2002).

31. See, e.g., Donnelly (2003); An-Na'im (2010).

32. See Stone (2007).

33. On TWAIL, see the works cited in Anghie and Chimni (2004); on recent approaches, see Carmody et al. (2012); Linarelli et al. (2018); and the discussion in Ratner (2019a).

34. *Continental Shelf*, Libya v. Malta, Judgment, ICJ Rep. 13, para. 46, 3 June 1985.

35. Luban, (2004); McMahan (2009); May (2008); Rodin (2002); Haque (2017).

36. See, e.g., Nickel (2006); Beitz (2009); Shue (1996); Talbot (2005); Buchanan (2013); Lafont (2016).

37. See, e.g., Luban (2004); Altman and Wellman (2004); Chehtman (2010); Song (2015).

38. See, e.g., Stilz (2015); Armstrong (2015).

39. Held (1995), (2002); Archibugi (1998).

40. For other applications of cosmopolitan thinking to international norms, see, e.g., Page (2011); Pierik and Werner (2010); Barry and Pogge (2005).

41. See also Cohen and Sabel (2006).

42. See also Raz (2010).
43. See, e.g., Buchanan (2000).
44. Saladin Meckled-Garcia, (2008); see also Blake (2001).
45. For a philosophical argument showing this effect, see Cohen and Sabel (2006).
46. See, e.g., *Legality of the Use of Force*, Serbia v. Belgium, ICJ Rep. 279, 15 Dec. 2004; *Accordance with International Law of the Unilateral Declaration of Independence in Respect of Kosovo*, Advisory Opinion, ICJ Rep. 409, 17 Oct. 2008; *Continental Shelf.*
47. See, e.g., Singer (1972); most of the essays in McKim and McMahan (1997); Scheffler (2001).
48. For one of many examples, see Copp (1998) ("[T]he question whether there is a moral right of secession is *morally prior* to the question about international law.").
49. See Buchanan and Golove (2002).
50. For a review of different perspectives on effectiveness, see Ratner (2013).
51. See also Hurrell (2002).
52. Permanent Sovereignty over Natural Resources, GA Res. 1803 (XVII), 14 Dec. 1962; UNCLOS, pts. V, VI (regimes on exclusive economic zone and continental shelf); Hardin (1968).
53. See, e.g., Altman and Wellman (2011); Caney (2005).
54. For a recognition of these options among philosophers, see Tan (2005).
55. See, e.g., Rawls (1999).
56. See, e.g., Stilz (2011); Philpott (1995).
57. Economic, Social, and Cultural Rights Committee, General Comment 12: The right to adequate food, 12 May 1999, para. 15, UN Doc. E/C.12/1999/5.
58. Compare, e.g., Cane (2002), with Miller (2007); Goodin (1985).
59. See, e.g., Erskine (2001); Goodin (1985); Shue (1998).
60. See, e.g., Buchanan and Keohane (2006); Pierik and Werner (2010).

References

Allott, Philip (1983) "Power Sharing in the Law of the Sea," *American Journal of International Law* 77(1): 1–30.

Allott, Philip (1990) *Eunomia: New Order for a New World*. Oxford: Oxford University Press.

Altman, Andrew, and Christopher Heath Wellman (2004) "A Defense of International Criminal Law," *Ethics* 115(1): 35–67.

Altman, Andrew, and Christopher Heath Wellman (2011) *A Liberal Theory of International Justice*. Oxford: Oxford University Press.

Anghie, Antony, and B. S. Chimni (2004) "Third World Approaches to International Law and Individual Responsibility in International Conflict." In Steven R. Ratner and Anne-Marie Slaughter (eds.), *The Methods of International Law*. Washington DC: American Society of International Law, 185–210.

An-Na'im, Abdullahi (2010) *Islam and Human Rights: Selected Essays of Abdullahi An-Na'im*. Mashood Baderin (ed.). Burlington, VT: Ashgate Publishing.

Archibugi, Daniele (1998) "Principles of Cosmopolitan Democracy." In Daniele Archibugi, David Held, and Martin Köhler (eds.), *Re-Imagining Political Community: Studies in Cosmopolitan Democracy*. Cambridge: Polity Press, 198–230.

Archibugi, Daniele, David Held, and Martin Köhler (eds.) (1998) *Re-Imagining Political Community: Studies in Cosmopolitan Democracy*. Cambridge: Polity Press.

Armstrong, Chris (2015) "Against 'Permanent Sovereignty' over Natural Resources," Politics, Philosophy & Economics 14(2): 129–51.

Aspremont, Jean d' (2007) "The Foundations of the International Legal Order," *Finnish Yearbook of International Law* 18: 219–55.

Barry, Brian (1981) "Do Countries Have Moral Obligations? The Case of World Poverty." In Sterling McMurrin (ed.), *The Tanner Lectures on Human Values*, Vol. 2 . Salt Lake City, UT: University of Utah Press, 25–44.

Barry, Christian, and Thomas W. Pogge (eds.) (2005) *Global Institutions and Responsibilities: Achieving Global Justice*. Malden, MA: Blackwell Publishing.

Beitz, Charles R. (1979) *Political Theory and International Relations*. Princeton, NJ: Princeton University Press.

Beitz, Charles R. (2009) *The Idea of Human Rights*. Oxford: Oxford University Press.

Besson, Samantha, and Jean d'Aspremont (eds.) (2018) *The Oxford Handbook of the Sources of International Law*. Oxford: Oxford University Press.

Blake, Michael (2001) "Distributive Justice, State Coercion, and Autonomy," *Philosophy & Public Affairs* 30(3): 257–96.

Bodansky, Daniel (2011) The Art and Craft of International Environmental Law. Cambridge, MA: Harvard University Press.

Brierly, J. L. (1963) *The Law of Nations: An Introduction to International Law of Peace*, 6th edn. Oxford: Oxford University Press.

Buchanan, Allen (2000) "Rawls's Law of Peoples: Rules for a Vanished Westphalian World," *Ethics* 110(4): 697–721.

Buchanan, Allen (2004) *Justice, Legitimacy, and Self-Determination: Moral Foundations for International Law*. Oxford: Oxford University Press.

Buchanan, Allen (2013) *The Heart of Human Rights*. Oxford: Oxford University Press.

Buchanan, Allen, and David Golove (2002) "Philosophy of International Law." In Jules Coleman and Scott Shapiro (eds.), *The Oxford Handbook of Jurisprudence and Philosophy of Law*. Oxford: Oxford University Press, 868–934.

Buchanan, Allen, and Robert O. Keohane (2006) "The Legitimacy of Global Governance Institutions," *Ethics & International Affairs* 20(4): 405–37.

Cane, Peter (2002) *Responsibility in Law and Morality*. Oxford: Hart Publishing.

Cane, Peter (2012) "Morality, Law and Conflicting Reasons for Action," *Cambridge Law Journal* 71(1): 59–85.

Caney, Simon (2005) *Justice Beyond Borders: A Global Political Theory*. Oxford: Oxford University Press.

Carmody, Chios, Frank J. Garcia, and John Linarelli (eds.) (2012) *Global Justice and International Economic Law: Opportunities and Prospects*. New York: Cambridge University Press.

Charlesworth, Hilary, and Christine Chinkin (2000) *The Boundaries of International Law: A Feminist Analysis*. Huntington, NY: Juris Publishing.

Chehtman, Alejandro (2010) The Philosophical Foundations of Extraterritorial Punishment. Oxford: Oxford University Press.

Cohen, Joshua (2004) "Minimalism About Human Rights: The Most We Can Hope For?," *Journal of Political Philosophy* 12(2): 190–213.

Cohen, Joshua, and Charles Sabel (2006) "Extra Rempublicam Nulla Justitia?," *Philosophy & Public Affairs* 34(2): 147–75.

Copp, David (1998) "International Law and Morality in the Theory of Secession," *Journal of Ethics* 2(3): 219–45.

Donnelly, Jack (2003) *Universal Human Rights in Theory and Practice*, 2nd edn. Ithaca, NY: Cornell University Press.

Erskine, Toni (2001) "Assigning Responsibilities to Institutional Moral Agents: The Case of States and Quasi-States," *Ethics & International Affairs* 15(2): 67–85.

Follesdal, Andreas (2011) "The Distributive Justice of a Global Basic Structure: A Category Mistake?," Politics, Philosophy & Economics 10(1): 46–65.

Franck, Thomas M. (1995) *Fairness in International Law and Institutions*. Oxford: Oxford University Press.

Frost, Mervyn (1996) *Ethics in International Relations: A Constitutive Theory*. Cambridge: Cambridge University Press.

Gallie, W. B. (1956) "Essentially Contested Concepts," *Proceedings of the Aristotelian Society* 56(1): 167–98.

Gathii, James Thuo (2011) "TWAIL: A Brief History of its Origins, its Decentralized Network, and a Tentative Bibliography," *Trade, Law, and Development* 3(1): 26–64.

Goodin, Robert E. (1985) *Protecting the Vulnerable: A Reanalysis of our Social Responsibilities*. Chicago, IL: University of Chicago Press.

Goodin, Robert E. (1988) "What is So Special About Our Fellow Countrymen?" *Ethics* 98(4): 663–86.

Goodin, Robert E., and Steven R. Ratner (2011) "Democratizing International Law," *Global Policy* 2(3): 241–7.

Habermas, Jürgen (2006) *The Divided West*. Frankfurt am Main: Suhrkamp Verlag.

Haque, Adil Ahmad (2017) *Law and Morality at War*. Oxford: Oxford University Press.

Hardin, Garrett (1968) "The Tragedy of the Commons," *Science* 162(3859): 1243–8.

Hart, H. L. A. (2012) *The Concept of Law*, 3rd edn. Oxford: Oxford University Press.

Held, David (1995) *Democracy and the Global Order: From the Modern State to Cosmopolitan Governance*. Stanford, CA: Stanford University Press.

Held, David (2002) "Law of States, Law of Peoples: Three Models of Sovereignty," *Legal Theory* 8(1): 1–44.

Henkin, Louis (1995) *International Law: Politics and Values*. Boston, MA: Martinus Nijhoff Publishers.

Hurrell, Andrew (2002) "Norms and Ethics in International Relations." In Walter Carlsnaes, Thomas Risse, and Beth A. Simmons (eds.), *Handbook of International Relations*. New York: Sage Publications, 137–54.

Hurrell, Andrew(2003) "International Law and the Making and Unmaking of Boundaries." In Allen Buchanan and Margaret Moore (eds.), *States, Nations, and Borders: The Ethics of Making Boundaries*. Cambridge: Cambridge University Press, 275–97.

Kennedy, David (2000) "When Renewal Repeats: Thinking against the Box," *New York University Journal of International Law and Policy* 32: 335–500.

Koskenniemi, Martti (1989) *From Apology to Utopia: The Structure of International Legal Argument*. Helsinki: Finnish Lawyers Publishing Company.

Koskenniemi, Martti (2000) "Carl Schmitt, Hans Morgenthau, and the Image of Law in International Relations." In Michael Byers (ed.), *The Role of Law in International Politics*. Oxford: Oxford University Press, 17–35.

Koskenniemi, Martti (2001) *The Gentle Civilizer of Nations: The Rise and Fall of International Law 1870–1960*. Cambridge: Cambridge University Press.

Koskenniemi, Martti (2002–) "Methodology of International Law." In. Rüdiger Wolfrum (ed.), *The Max Planck Encyclopedia of Public International Law*. Oxford: Oxford University Press, http://opil.ouplaw.com/home/EPIL, accessed August 21, 2019.

Koskenniemi, Martti (2003) "Legitimacy, Rights, and Ideology: Notes towards a Critique of the New Moral Internationalism," *Associations: Journal for Legal and Social Theory* 7(2): 349–74.

Koskenniemi, Martti (2004) "Global Governance and Public International Law," *Kritische Justiz* 37: 241–54.

Krasner, Stephen D. (1999) *Sovereignty: Organized Hypocrisy*. Princeton, NJ: Princeton University Press.

Lafont, Cristina (2016) "Sovereignty and the International Protection of Human Rights," *Journal of Political Philosophy* 24(4): 427–45.

Linarelli, John, Salomon, Margot E., and M. Sornorajah (2018) *The Misery of International Law: Confrontations with Injustice in the Global Economy*. Oxford: Oxford University Press.

Luban, David (2004) "A Theory of Crimes against Humanity," *Yale Journal of International Law* 29: 85–167.

McCrudden, Christopher (2017) "What Does it Mean to 'Compare', and What Should it Mean?." In Samantha Besson, Lukas Urscheler, and Samuel Jubé (eds.), *Comparing Comparative Law*. Geneva: Schulthess, 61–84.

McDougal, Myres S., Harold D. Lasswell, and Lung-chu Chen (1980) *Human Rights and World Public Order: The Basic Policies of an International Law of Human Dignity*. New Haven, CT: Yale University Press.

McDougal, Myres S., and W. Michael Reisman (1981) "The Prescribing Function in the World Consecutive Process: How International Law is Made." In Myres S. McDougal and W. Michael Reisman (eds.), *International Law Essays*. Mineola, NY: Foundation Press, 353–80.

McKim, Robert, and Jeff McMahan (eds.) (1997) *The Morality of Nationalism*. New York: Oxford University Press.

McMahan, Jeff (2009) *Killing in War*. Oxford: Clarendon Press.

May, Larry (2008) *Aggression and Crimes against Peace*. Cambridge: Cambridge University Press.

Meckled-Garcia, Saladin (2008) "On the Very Idea of Cosmopolitan Justice: Constructivism and International Agency," *Journal of Political Philosophy* 16(3): 245–71.

Miller, David (2001) "Distributing Responsibilities," *Journal of Political Philosophy* 9(4): 453–71.

Miller, David (2007) *National Responsibility and Global Justice*. Oxford: Oxford University Press.

Musgrave, Thomas D. (1997) *Self-Determination and National Minorities*. Oxford: Clarendon Press.

Nardin, Terry (1998) "Legal Positivism as a Theory of International Society." In David R. Mapel and Terry Nardin (eds.), *International Society: Diverse Ethical Perspectives*. Princeton, NJ: Princeton University Press, 17–35.

Nickel, James W. (2006) *Making Sense of Human Rights*, 2nd edn. Malden, MA: Blackwell Publishing.

Nollkaemper, André, and Dov Jacobs (2015) *Distribution of Responsibilities in International Law*. Cambridge. Cambridge University Press.

Page, Edward A. (2011) "Cosmopolitanism, Climate Change, and Greenhouse Emissions Trading," *International Theory* 3(1): 37–69.

Peters, Anne (2009) "Humanity as the A and Ω of Sovereignty," *EJIL* 20(3): 545–67.

Philpott, Daniel (1995) "In Defense of Self-Determination," *Ethics* 105(2): 352–85.

Pierik, Roland, and Wouter Werner (eds.) (2010) *Cosmopolitanism in Context: Perspectives from International Law and Political Theory*. Cambridge: Cambridge University Press.

Pogge, Thomas W. (1989) *Realizing Rawls*. Ithaca, NY: Cornell University Press.

Pogge, Thomas W. (1992) "Cosmopolitanism and Sovereignty," *Ethics* 103(1): 48–75.

Pogge, Thomas W. (2008) *World Poverty and Human Rights: Cosmopolitan Responsibilities and Reforms* 2nd edn. Cambridge: Polity Press.

Ratner, Steven R. (2001) "Corporations and Human Rights: A Theory of Legal Responsibility," *Yale Law Journal* 111(3): 443–545.

Ratner, Steven R. (2013) "Persuading to Comply: On the Deployment and Avoidance of Legal Argumentation." In Jeffrey L. Dunoff and Mark A. Pollack (eds.), *Interdisciplinary Perspectives on International Law and International Relations*. Cambridge: Cambridge University Press, 568–90.

Ratner, Steven R. (2015) *The Thin Justice of International Law: A Moral Reckoning of the Law of Nations*. Oxford: Oxford University Press.

Ratner, Steven R. (2019a) "Global Investment Rules as a Site for Moral Inquiry," *Journal of Political Philosophy* 27(1): 107–35.

Ratner, Steven R. (2019b) "International Law and Political Philosophy: Uncovering New Linkages," *Philosophy Compass* 14(2), https://doi.org/10.1111/phc3.12564.

Ratner, Steven R., and Anne-Marie Slaughter (2004) "Appraising the Methods of International Law: A Prospectus for Readers." In Steven R. Ratner and Anne-Marie Slaughter (eds.). *The Methods of International Law*. Washington DC: American Society of International Law, 1–21.

Rawls, John (1999) *The Law of Peoples*. Cambridge, MA: Harvard University Press.

Raz, Joseph (2010) "Human Rights Without Foundations." In Samantha Besson and John Tasioulas (eds.), *The Philosophy of International Law*. Oxford: Oxford University Press, 321–9.

Rodin, David (2002) *War and Self-Defense*. Oxford: Clarendon Press.

Roth, Brad R. (2011) *Sovereign Equality and Moral Disagreement: Premises of a Pluralist International Legal Order*. New York: Oxford University Press.

Scheffler, Samuel (2001) *Boundaries and Allegiances: Problems of Justice and Responsibility in Liberal Thought*. New York: Oxford University Press.

Shue, Henry (1996) *Basic Rights: Subsistence, Affluence, and U.S. Foreign Policy*, 2nd edn. Princeton, NJ: Princeton University Press.

Shue, Henry (1998) "Mediating Duties," *Ethics* 98(4): 687–7045.

Simma, Bruno (1994) "From Bilateralism to Community Interest in International Law," *Recueil des Cours de l'Académie de Droit International* 250: 217–384.

Simma, Bruno (1999) "NATO, the UN, and the Use of Force: Legal Aspects," *European Journal of International Law* 10(1): 1–22.

Singer, Peter (1972) "Famine, Affluence, and Morality," *Philosophy & Public Affairs* 1(3): 229–43.

Singer, Peter (2002) *One World: The Ethics of Globalization*. New Haven, CT: Yale University Press.

Song, Jiewuh (2015) "Pirates and Torturers: Universal Jurisdiction as Enforcement Gap-Filling," *Journal of Political Philosophy* 23(4): 471–90.

Stilz, Anna (2011) "Nations, States, and Territory," *Ethics* 121(3): 572–601.

Stilz, Anna (2015) "Decolonization and Self-Determination," *Social Philosophy and Policy* 32(1): 1–24.

Stone, Christopher (2007) "Ethics and International Environmental Law." In Daniel Bodansky, Jutta Brunnée, and Ellen Hey (eds.). *The Oxford Handbook of International Environmental Law*. Oxford: Oxford University Press, 291–312.

Talbot, William (2005) Which Rights Should be Universal? Oxford: Oxford University Press.

Tan, Kok-Chor (2004) *Justice without Borders: Cosmopolitanism, Nationalism, and Patriotism*. Cambridge: Cambridge University Press.

Tan, Kok-Chor (2005) "International Toleration: Rawlsian versus Cosmopolitan," *Leiden Journal of International Law* 18(4): 685–710.

Tasioulas, John (2002) "International Law and the Limits of Fairness," *European Journal of International Law* 13(4): 993–1023.

Tesón, Fernando R. (1992) "The Kantian Theory of International Law," *Columbia Law Review* 92(1): 53–102.

Tesón, Fernando R. (1998) *A Philosophy of International Law*. Boulder, CO: Westview Press.

Tesón, Fernando R. (2005) *Humanitarian Intervention: An Inquiry into Law and Morality*. Ardsley, NY: Transnational Publishers.

Waldron, Jeremy (2006) "Cosmopolitan Norms." In Seyla Benhabib (ed.), *Another Cosmopolitanism*. New York: Oxford University Press, 83–101.

Walzer, Michael (2006) *Just and Unjust Wars: A Moral Argument with Historical Illustrations*, 4th edn. New York: Basic Books.

Wenar, Leif (2016) *Blood Oil: Tyrants, Violence, and the Rules That Run the World*. Oxford: Oxford University Press.

Wiessner, Siegfried, and Andrew R. Willard (2004) "Policy-Oriented Jurisprudence and Human Rights Abuses in Internal Conflict: Toward a World Public Order of Human Dignity." In Steven R. Ratner and Anne-Marie Slaughter (eds.). *The Methods of International Law*. Washington DC: American Society of International Law, 47–79.

Young, Iris Marion (2007) *Global Challenges: War, Self-Determination and Responsibility for Justice*. Malden, MA: Polity Press.

FURTHER READING

Benvenisti, Eyal (2013) "Sovereigns as Trustees of Humanity: On the Accountability of States to Foreign Stakeholders," *American Journal of International Law* 107(2): 295–333.

Besson, Samantha (2009) "The Authority of International Law—Lifting the State Veil," *Sydney Law Review* 31(3): 343–80.

Besson, Samantha (2015) "The Bearers of Human Rights' Duties and Responsibilities for Human Rights: A Quiet (R)evolution?," *Social Philosophy and Policy* 32(1): 244–68.

Brunnée, Jutta, and Stephen J. Toope (2010) *Legitimacy and Legality in International Law: An Interactional Account*. Cambridge: Cambridge University Press.

Carlsnaes, Thomas Risse, and Beth A. Simmons (eds.) (2002) *Handbook of International Relations*. New York: Sage Publications.

Egede, Edwin, and Peter Sutch (2013) *The Politics of International Law and International Justice*. Edinburgh: Edinburgh University Press.

Erskine, Toni (2014) "Coalitions of the Willing and Responsibilities to Protect: Informal Associations, Enhanced Capabilities, and Shared Moral Burdens," *Ethics & International Affairs* 28(1): 115–45.

Goodin, Robert E. (2016) "Enfranchising All Subjected, Worldwide," *International Theory* 8(3): 365–89.

James, Aaron (2012) *Fairness in Practice: A Social Contract for a Global Economy*. Oxford: Oxford University Press.

McMahan, Jeff (2005) "Just Cause for War," *Ethics and International Affairs* 19(3): 1–21.

Margalit, Avishai, and Joseph Raz (1990) "National Self-Determination," *Journal of Philosophy* 87(9): 439–61.

Mégret, Frédéric (2019) "Justice." Pp. 585–606 In Jean d'Aspremont and Sahib Singh (eds.), *Concepts for International Law: Contributions to Disciplinary Thought*. Cheltenham: Edward Elgar, 585–606.

Mertens, Thomas (2005) "Defending the Rawlsian League of Peoples: A Critical Comment on Tan," *Leiden Journal of International Law* 18(4): 711–15.

Nagel, Thomas (2005) "The Problem of Global Justice," *Philosophy and Public Affairs* 33(2): 113–47.

Pavel, Carmen (2015) "Negative Duties, the WTO and the Harm Argument," *Political Studies* 63(2): 449–65.

Pavel, Carmen E., and Lefkowitz, David (2018) "Skeptical Challenges to International Law," *Philosophy Compass* 13(8), https://doi.org/10.1111/phc3.12511.

Pierik, Roland (2015) "Shared Responsibility in International Law: A Normative-Philosophical Analysis." In André Nollkaemper and Dov Jacobs (eds.), *Distribution of Responsibilities in International Law*. Cambridge: Cambridge University Press, 36–61.

Ratner, Steven R. (2013) "Ethics and International Law: Integrating the Global Justice Project(s)," *International Theory* 5(1): 1–34.

Simpson, Gerry (2004) *Great Powers and Outlaw States: Unequal Sovereigns in the International Legal Order*. Cambridge: Cambridge University Press.

Sornarajah, M. (2015) *Resistance and Change in the International Law on Foreign Investment*. Cambridge: Cambridge University Press.

Waldron, Jeremy (2011) "Are Sovereigns Entitled to the Benefit of the International Rule of Law?" *European Journal of International Law* 22(2): 315–43.

PART VI

BORDERS AND TERRITORIAL RIGHTS

CHAPTER 19

....

IMMIGRATION

....

DAVID MILLER

1 INTRODUCTION

IMMIGRATION is a hotly contested political topic at the present time. The number of people wishing to move between states, for many different reasons, is always on the rise. But this swelling tide has encountered increasing resistance from citizens of rich states, who fear the economic and social impact that immigrants from alien cultural backgrounds might make on their societies. Not surprisingly, therefore, the ethics and politics of immigration are subjects of increasing interest to academics. This chapter can only deal with a small fraction of the voluminous literature that has been produced. I focus here on the issues of *justice* that migration between states raises.

These issues are unfortunately quite complex. It may be helpful as a starting point to distinguish between three aspects of justice in migration. First, we can examine the claims that an individual migrant may make against the state she is leaving and the state she is trying to enter. Does she have an unrestricted right of exit, for example? Must the state she aspires to enter use only morally approved criteria when it decides whether or not to admit her? Second, we can ask about the effects that migration may have on social justice within either state. Might outmigration damage the prospects for social justice in the sending state by depriving it of its most productive members? What kinds of accommodation must the receiving state extend to incomers to ensure that they are fairly treated and become properly integrated? And third, we can approach migration from a global justice perspective and ask, for example, what effects it is likely to have on global inequality or on the protection of human rights worldwide. All of these appear to be relevant questions to raise, but there is, alas, no guarantee that the answers we give to them will all have the same implications for immigration policy. We are not likely to be able to say, unequivocally, that the movement of people between states is either "good" or "bad" for justice. Given the aims of this handbook, I shall in this chapter pay particular attention to the broader questions of justice that immigration poses, and leave to one side more specific questions about, for instance, selection policies or the rights of illegal migrants (see further Miller 2015, 2016a).

People who work on this topic tend to divide broadly into two camps: those who think that justice demands open borders, in other words the removal of all legal and physical restrictions on movement between states, and those who think that justice permits (or might even require) states to police their borders and decide who to let in and who to turn away. It is important not to caricature either of these positions. Open-borders advocates will stress that they are setting out what justice ideally requires, not what is immediately feasible in the world today, and they will usually concede that there are extreme circumstances in which justice may allow borders to be controlled. On the other side, few among those who defend the state's right to close its borders believe that this gives governments carte blanche to adopt any immigration policy that they like: there may, for example, be some categories of immigrants who must be admitted as a matter of justice. There seems, nonetheless, to be an underlying division of opinion over whether the onus is always on the state to explain why any given immigrant should *not* be admitted, or whether the onus is on the immigrant himself to explain why he *should* be admitted. Moreover the open borders/closed borders divide appears to correspond in some respects to the familiar division within debates on global justice between "cosmopolitans" and "communitarians" or "nationalists" (see Gibney 2004:chs. 1–2). Why this should be so will become apparent as we proceed. I will use this division to structure my analysis, beginning with cosmopolitan arguments in favor of open borders, and then afterwards considering some communitarian reasons that have been offered in support of border restrictions.

2 Arguments for Open Borders

The first argument for open borders I shall consider appeals to the idea that the earth belongs fundamentally to humankind as a whole, so that no subsection of the human race can claim exclusive rights over any part of the earth's surface. On this view, states may be able to establish rights of jurisdiction over particular territories by demonstrating that they are able to administer justice among the inhabitants, but they do not thereby gain the right to exclude potential immigrants. Someone living in the Côte d'Ivoire who wishes to move to France may do so by virtue of the fact that she, like everyone else, has common ownership rights that include the land that has now become French territory, and she exercises these rights when she immigrates.

This argument has a long pedigree that stretches back to early modern thinkers such as Grotius, according to whom "Almighty GOD at the Creation, and again after the Deluge, gave to Mankind in general a Dominion over Things of this inferior World" (Grotius 2005: Book II, 420). Although he immediately went on to explain how both individuals and collectives might acquire exclusive forms of ownership, Grotius argued that some common rights were retained, including rights of passage, rights to seek refuge in emergencies or in times of war, and the right to settle on land that is lying waste. Evidently, these do not add up to a right to cross state borders at will, even though they place some significant restrictions on the state's right to exclude foreigners from its territory. Could a more robust version of common world ownership be defended? Drawing inspiration from Grotius, Mathias Risse has recently argued in favor of what he calls the principle of proportionate use, which requires us to assign a use value to the resources that are present on any given territory, and then to divide this by the number of people who are resident there (Risse 2012: ch. 8). Territories in which the ratio is relatively high are described as underused, and subject to claims to enter by people living in states whose resources are relatively overused. In other words, immigration must be permitted until the ratio between resource value and population size is roughly the same everywhere. "Individuals would then populate the earth in proportion to the overall usefulness of its regions for human purposes" (Risse 2012:154). Although more demanding than Grotius's requirement that "if there be any waste or barren Land within our Dominions, that also is to be given to Strangers, at their Request, or may be lawfully possessed by them" (Grotius 2005: Book II, 448), it still entails much less than an unlimited right of free movement (for example, there would be no right to move between territories with similar resource/population ratios).

A rather different way of understanding the common ownership of the earth can be found in the writings of Kant, whose claim that "all nations stand *originally* in a community of land" entails that a state can only vindicate its right of jurisdiction over a particular territory if it complies with the principles of "cosmopolitan right" (Kant 1996:121). One such principle specified that "all men are entitled to present themselves in the society of others by virtue of their right to communal possession of the earth's surface," and those who arrived on the territory of a foreign state should be received without hostility (Kant 1971: 105–6). Kant called this "the natural right of hospitality," and some commentators have used this idea to develop a case for more open borders (see, for example, Benhabib 2004). For Kant himself, however, the right had a limited scope: it amounts essentially to the liberty to attempt to establish a relationship with the inhabitants of a country, especially for purposes of commerce, and, moreover, these inhabitants are entitled to turn the stranger away "if this can be done without causing his death" (Kant 1971: 105–6). It is explicitly *not* the right to settle, which according to Kant would require a specific contract with the natives. If we understand immigration as involving the right to reside permanently in the country one moves to (as opposed to merely the right to *visit*), Kant's version of common ownership no more entails fully open borders than does Grotius's or Risse's.

One might advance a still more radical understanding of common world ownership that granted people unlimited access to places anywhere on the globe.[1] It is hard to see, however, how this could be squared either with individual rights of property or with states' rights of territorial jurisdiction. One can imagine a borderless world, but one would then need to explain how more than minimal justice would be possible without the institutions that have provided it (albeit imperfectly) up to now.[2] If membership in geographical units is indeterminate, how will it be decided which authority has the responsibility to supply the wide range of goods and services demanded by social justice to any individual person?

A second cosmopolitan argument for open borders appeals to the principle of global equality of opportunity. In its domestic version, the principle is widely accepted: it holds that a person's opportunity to obtain jobs, educational places and other advantageous social positions should depend only on their own motivation and talent, and not on "arbitrary" factors such as race or the social class in which they are born (Rawls, 1971: ch. 2). The global version of this principle asserts that the society a person is born into is another such arbitrary feature. Thus, as one advocate puts it, "if equality of opportunity were realized, a child growing up in rural Mozambique would be statistically as likely as the child of a senior executive at a Swiss bank to reach the position of the latter's parent" (Moellendorf 2002: 49).[3] Now in theory global equality of opportunity might be achieved without migration if every society provided a similar range of opportunities internally, and adopted equal opportunity measures for its own citizens. Given the huge resource inequalities between states that currently exist, however, that is simply a pipe dream. Even if Mozambique were able to create as many senior banking positions as Switzerland relative to its population, it could not provide its rural youth with the education necessary to fill them. So allowing international migration is the only way forward, open-borders advocates will argue. As Carens puts it "you have to be able to move to where the opportunities are in order to take advantage of them. So, freedom of movement is an essential prerequisite for equality of opportunity." Moreover, "since the range of opportunities varies so greatly among states, this means that in our world, as in feudalism, the social circumstances of one's birth largely determine one's opportunities" (Carens 2013: 228).

At first sight this looks like a persuasive argument for open borders. But it needs to be examined carefully.[4] As the example of rural Mozambique suggests, its emotive force can be increased by starting with cases of severe deprivation, involving people who receive very little by way of education or healthcare, whose opportunities for employment of any kind are limited, and whose life expectancy is correspondingly low. These cases are real enough, but what moves us about them is the absolute lack of opportunity they reveal, not lack of opportunity relative to people living in other societies. We think that where people cannot be provided with the conditions for a minimally decent life in the places where they live, they should have the chance to migrate. But the equality of opportunity argument goes much further than this. It is about people's comparative prospects, no matter how absolutely rich or poor their society is. It should apply as much to people currently living in Slovenia as to people currently living in Bangladesh.

Having distinguished *equal* opportunity from *adequate* opportunity, we can ask why equality of opportunity should concern us at global level. In domestic contexts, equality of opportunity matters because opportunities will depend upon public policy decisions (concerning, for example, the provision of education) that the state makes for all of its citizens. If it allows opportunities to become significantly unequal despite having the resources to correct for this, it treats them unjustly. Internationally, however, in the absence of a world government there is no single agent responsible for creating opportunities, but instead a multiplicity of independent states. So, although a citizen of Slovenia might lack some opportunities that a citizen of Norway has, this is not because they are being treated unequally by any institution. It is hard, therefore, to see why the resulting state of affairs should be described as an injustice.

So it is far from clear that justice at global level requires that the opportunities open to people brought up in different states should always be identical. But even if it did, is opening borders the best way to achieve this? It will depend on who is able to take advantage of the additional opportunities that are created in this way. We can reasonably assume that far more people will try to move from poor countries to rich countries than in the opposite direction. But the ones who have the resources—the savings and the education—that enable them to do this will be the ones who are already relatively advantaged in their societies of origin (see Pogge 1997). Broadly speaking they will be the members of the local elite, or their offspring. So, although the opportunity gap that separates these migrants from people raised in the developed societies will be narrowed, the opportunity gap that separates them from their erstwhile compatriots will be widened. It may even turn out that the opportunities of those left behind are reduced in absolute terms, if those leaving are skilled professionals who would otherwise provide education, health services, or competent administration in their home country (for a careful discussion of the ethical implications of "brain drain," see Oberman 2013). It is a mistake, in other words, to judge equal opportunities by focusing attention simply on those who are able to migrate. One needs to consider the impact of migration in broader terms in order to judge whether opening borders would take us towards or away from this goal, either domestically or globally.

There is, however, a third way to defend open borders, which is probably more popular still, since it relies less heavily on cosmopolitan assumptions about distributive justice. This asserts simply that there is a human right to immigrate.[5] Since respect for human rights is now taken to be a *sine qua non* of legitimate government, a state that failed to open its borders would automatically cease to be legitimate unless it could show that some other human right was imperiled by allowing free movement. The argument, then, is straightforward, and at least at first glance independent of any considerations about the *consequences* of immigration, which, as we have just seen, may cause difficulties for other open-borders defenses.

This may depend, however, on how the human right to immigrate is interpreted. It can be understood as something that person can claim for its own sake, as one part of a wider right of free movement. Alternatively, it can be claimed as something that is necessary to protect *other* human rights, for example rights to subsistence or to bodily security. The claim in the latter case is that without a right to migrate to a place of greater safety, a person would be left vulnerable to various catastrophes that would prevent them from leading a minimally decent life, whether these were natural disasters such as flood or famine, or human transgressions such as religious persecution or genocide. Here, then, the right to immigrate is treated as instrumental to other human rights whose status is unchallengeable.

How could it be shown that the right to immigrate is simply one part of the right to freedom of movement—a human right that is already recognized in the international charters? According to its defenders such as Oberman (2016), the right is grounded on two human interests. One is the personal interest people have in being free to access the full range of existing life options when they make important decisions about their relationships, their religion, their employment, and so on. Any significant restriction on their freedom of movement will compromise this interest, by, for example, preventing them from getting together with the person they love, or taking the job they would most like to have. The second is the political interest people have in being able to associate with others for political debate, to gather information in different places, and to exercise their political rights. These activities too require freedom to move around in physical space. Once we understand why freedom of movement qualifies as a human right, however, we will also see that this must include the right to move freely across state borders. As Carens puts it:

> If it is so important for people to have the right to move freely within a state, isn't it equally important for them to have the right to move across state borders? Every reason why one might want to move within a state may also be a reason for moving between states. One might want a job; one might fall in love with someone from another country...The radical disjuncture that treats freedom of movement within the state as a human right while granting states discretionary control over freedom of movement across state borders makes no moral sense.   (Carens 2013: 239)[6]

To evaluate this argument, we should notice first that even within liberal states, our freedom of movement is severely restricted both by the institution of private property and by the rules that the state enacts to govern movement within public space, such as traffic laws. We take these restrictions for granted, even though they mean that we cannot move across most of the physical space within our own country without first obtaining permission either from private landowners or from state officials. Yet we do not regard our human right to freedom of movement as compromised by such constraints. Why not? First, there are good reasons for many of these restrictions, some of which protect other human rights, such as the right to privacy and the right to personal safety—and human rights need to be defined in such a way that they do not, under normal circumstances, conflict with one another. Second, despite these limitations, we are generally able to pursue the interests to which Oberman and others appeal; in other words we have *sufficient* freedom of movement to find jobs, meet partners, practice our faith, and so forth, and that is all that the human right requires (see Miller 2005, 2007: ch. 8; Pevnick 2011: ch. 4).

Why then should border controls be seen as a violation of the right to free movement? By denying entry to prospective immigrants, the state is certainly blocking certain specific opportunities that might otherwise have been available to the incomers, but it is not in normal circumstances damaging the general interests to which Oberman and others appeal in defense of the right. So long as they come from states in which a wide range of jobs, cultural opportunities, marriage partners, etc. are available to them, these interests are not set back by being denied entry to a foreign state. Of course, a person may have a specific aim that can only be realized by migrating, such as joining a particular religious cult, or studying a rare species of butterfly, but aims such as this are always liable to being thwarted by material costs, rules of property, or the unwillingness of other people to collaborate. There is no human right to carry out your ideal plan of life.

In some cases, however, the range of opportunities that is available in a person's home state is *not* adequate by human rights standards, and this introduces the second way in which a human right to immigrate might be defended, as instrumental to the protection of other human rights. If a person is starving, or unable to support her family, or is being persecuted for religious reasons, then escape to another society may be the only feasible option, at least in the short run. But this instrumental argument fails to justify a full-fledged human right to immigrate, understood as a right to enter and remain in any state of one's choice. First, it cannot apply to people wishing to move between states that are already rights-respecting—between Australia and Sweden, let us say. Second, even in the case of people who are fleeing disaster zones, their rights will be protected so long as they are allowed to enter at least one country that can offer them adequate security: they do not need to have a universal right of movement across borders. Third, their claim may also have a built-in temporal restriction: it holds so long as their society of origin remains a threatening place, either to them personally or in general. This is now widely recognized in international refugee law, where the refugee is regarded as somebody who has the right to sanctuary so long as they have a well-grounded fear of being persecuted in their own society, but who should be encouraged to return once that fear has subsided.[7]

These limitations reflect a general feature of human rights: that they are meant to protect basic human interests, or, in another formulation, provide the conditions for a minimally decent life. If they become stretched beyond this to encompass less essential claims and aspirations, they lose their normative force as claims that states are bound to meet if they are to remain in good standing both domestically and internationally. As an argument for open borders, the alleged human right to immigrate fails this test.

The final argument for open borders that I want to consider appeals to the principle of democracy: it claims that border-closing is undemocratic unless those who are being prevented from entering are given a say in the decision to exclude them. States, therefore, face a choice: either they must open their borders or they must submit their immigration policies for approval to a democratic forum that includes all those who might wish to immigrate. I will leave to one side the question of how the second alternative might be implemented in order to focus on the claim that border controls need to be democratically legitimated, and not only to existing citizens.

The main protagonist for this claim is Arash Abizadeh, who argues that when a state implements border controls it *coerces* all those who might have been admitted—not only those who are actually trying to enter, but even those who have no particular wish to do so (Abizadeh 2008). It is because border controls are coercive that they need to be justified democratically to those they exclude. The upshot is that no state is entitled to close its borders unilaterally. As Abizadeh puts it:

> the regime of control must ultimately be justified to foreigners as well as citizens. As a consequence, a state's regime of border control could only acquire legitimacy if there were cosmopolitan democratic institutions in which borders received actual justifications addressed to both citizens and foreigners.   (Abizadeh 2008: 48)

Abizadeh's argument raises two main questions: Why, exactly, are border controls coercive, even in the case of people who make no attempt to cross them? And why does the use of coercion always need to be justified in a democratic forum that includes the people being coerced? To take these questions in reverse order, it seems that coercion can often be justified simply in terms of the right that the person exercising it has to prevent harm or to protect something that she legitimately owns. Wellman imagines a case in which two strangers enter his house intent on eating his dinner and forcing him to have sex. When he repels their advances by coercive means, could they "rightfully object that, insofar as they were subject to coercion, they were entitled to an equal vote as to what my decision should have been? Presumably not" (Wellman and Cole 2011: 97). What this tells us is that the range of cases in which the use of coercion requires democratic ratification is much smaller than Abizadeh believes. It is only because states exercise coercive authority over their citizens in a systematic way and over matters where the justification for using it is less than self-evident that democratic control seems necessary. The coercion involved in excluding immigrants does not have this all-embracing character: it seems closer to Wellman's example of barring unwelcome strangers from his house.

This, however, takes us to the first question, which is whether border controls are inherently coercive. It is plain that coercive means, often unpleasant ones, are used to enforce them against immigrants who attempt to enter illegally. But in what sense is somebody who is refused an entry visa, and accepts that decision, or indeed someone who *would* be refused an entry permit but in fact has no wish to migrate, being coerced by the immigration rules? Coercion is problematic from an ethical standpoint because it involves one agent directing another to act in a certain way, infringing the latter's autonomy. But border controls as such, leaving aside particular methods of enforcement, are better described as preventative than as coercive: they rule out one course of action (entering the country) while leaving many others open (for the distinction between coercion and prevention, and its significance, see Miller 2010). They still require justification, but not the demanding form of justification that systematic coercion needs.

3 ARGUMENTS FOR THE STATE'S RIGHT TO CONTROL ITS BORDERS

Although none of the arguments for open borders found in the literature on global justice seems particularly robust, it remains true that the general human interest in *freedom* means that states that want to restrict immigration must provide some sound reason for doing so (see Kukathas 2005). Why deny people something they clearly want to have—the opportunity to join your society—unless there are grounds for the refusal? So we need now to explore the arguments that have been offered in defense of the state's right to control its borders. If none of these is successful, then open borders wins by default, for the reason just given.

In fact, it is widely recognized even by open-borders advocates that there are circumstances in which border-closing would be justified.[8] If so many immigrants try to enter that social order in the receiving society collapses, or it becomes unable to provide anyone with the conditions for a decent life, it would be permissible to prevent them.[9] The issue is whether other reasons for imposing restrictions, such as a desire to preserve an existing national culture, may also be sufficient.

One way to sidestep this dispute is to present the right to control borders as something that states possess simply as a result of being sovereigns in their own territory: having the right to legislate in a given area implies having the right to determine who falls under that jurisdiction and who does not. But although something like this principle seems to be assumed in international law, it is much less clear why it should be accepted. In federal unions, for instance, the provinces or states make and apply law internally without having any control over who enters and resides within their boundaries. Without further defense, an appeal to sovereignty cannot bear the weight that is being placed on it here.

An attempt to provide such a defense has been made by Christopher Wellman, who argues that the citizens of (legitimate) states enjoy a right of collective self-determination, and one essential component of this is freedom of association—the right to decide who does and who does not become a member of their collective (Wellman 2008; Wellman and Cole 2011: pt 1). Although Wellman suggests some plausible grounds that citizens might have for refusing association, his main point is that the right itself does not depend on these: a state that chooses to limit immigration for whatever reason is entitled to do so, since freedom of association always implies the right to refuse association.

Wellman builds his case by pointing first to the value of freedom of association in intimate relationships—being able to choose your life partner, for example—and in groups with a distinct expressive character, such as churches. But although the reasons for refusing unwanted association are strongest in such cases, he claims that the same general argument applies to other associations, such as golf clubs, and by extension to the state itself. We may have an interest, he argues, simply in limiting the numbers of people who join our association. We also have an interest, if the association is self-governing, in deciding on the composition of the future "self" who will do the governing: as he puts it, "a significant component of group self-determination is having control over the group which in turn gets to be self-determining" (Wellman 2008: 115). And he further argues that since being associated with someone may bring with it special responsibilities of distributive justice, we may have an interest in *not* acquiring potentially onerous obligations to those who are not presently members of the group (this argument is further developed in Blake 2013). Wellman's general point, however, is that although freedom of association can be supported by grounds such as those just given, it is fundamentally a *right* which we can exercise for good or bad reasons on any particular occasion. So, although it permits legitimate states to close their borders entirely—"to reject all potential immigrants, even those desperately seeking asylum from corrupt governments" (Wellman 2008: 141)—it does not follow that this would be the best policy for them to adopt, all things considered.

Wellman's powerful argument, nevertheless, has to confront a number of objections. One is that freedom of association is not a single overriding claim in the way that he assumes, but rather a complex right whose various components have to be traded off against one another, as is demonstrated, for example, by cases in which groups seek to discriminate by race or gender when deciding who to admit to membership (see the discussion in Blake 2012). Another problem is that when states close their borders to potential immigrants, they are also *denying* association to those of their citizens who might wish to associate for personal, economic, or cultural reasons with some of the people who are excluded. In other words a majority of citizens—assuming that the policy has a democratic mandate—may be exercising their right *not* to associate at the expense of the minority's right *to* associate freely: the same principle cuts both ways. So why should the majority have the deciding voice, since they are not being asked to enter into any close or intimate relationship with the newcomers, but simply to accept their presence on the same territory?[10] This connects to a third issue, which is that Wellman's argument about the self in self-determination implicitly assumes that immigration to a society automatically implies full citizen status and not simply residency (see Fine 2010). Wellman, in fact, accepts this assumption; nevertheless, it reveals an ambiguity about what is driving the argument from freedom of association. Is it about the mere physical presence of immigrants on the territory—the fact that we might encounter them in our daily lives— or is it about the composition of the demos that will decide upon the society's future direction?[11] Finally, Wellman seems not to pay enough attention to the possible costs, for the migrant, of being refused entry. If we are willing to allow golf clubs and other such associations wide latitude in deciding who to accept as members, this is partly because the burden of being turned away by a particular club is not so heavy, given that there will usually be other clubs willing to accept the applicant (and even if there are not, golf is still just golf). For immigrants, in contrast, the decision whether to admit may turn out to be literally a life-or-death decision.[12]

Taken together, these considerations suggest that freedom of association alone is not a sufficiently strong ground to justify the state's right to close its borders. We have to take the step that Wellman wants to avoid, and consider the weight of the substantive reasons that can be used to support controlling immigration. Perhaps the best-known of these is Michael Walzer's argument that such controls are essential if states are to be "*communities of character*, historically stable, ongoing associations of men and women with some special commitment to one another and some special sense of their common life" (Walzer 1983: 62). Behind this argument lies the assumption that human beings have a deep need to belong to distinct, cohesive cultures, and such cultures can only be upheld by allowing closure, that is the exclusion of those who are "strangers." Closure is best carried out at national level, by controlling immigration. If it is not, Walzer claims, it will be implemented locally, by turning neighborhoods into "closed or parochial communities" (Walzer 1983: 38). Thus, for freedom of movement between neighborhoods to be possible, the state must administer welfare on a national basis and control its borders. "Only if the state makes a selection among would-be members and guarantees the loyalty, security, and welfare of the individuals it selects, can local communities take shape as 'indifferent' associations, determined solely by personal preference or market capacity" (Walzer 1983: 38–9). Selection criteria should refer "to the conditions and character of the host country and to the shared understandings of those who are already members." This would not exclude selection by ethnicity or nationality in the case of a political community that was already homogeneous (Walzer, 1983: 40, 46–7).

Walzer's commitment to the right to close borders is not absolute. He grants that refugees have a strong claim to be admitted, based on the principle of mutual aid, but this can be accepted so long as the numbers involved remain small. But since justice "presupposes a bounded world within which distributions take place" (Walzer 1983: 31), and this bounded world is the political community, or in the modern world the state in particular, even refugees might have to be refused entry if so many arrive that the cohesion of the state is put at risk. Social justice, for Walzer, trumps the claims of the needy stranger if a choice has to be made.

Walzer's argument can be challenged at several points. Even accepting his premise that distributive justice presupposes a political community with rules to determine who belongs and who does not, one might question whether this needs to be a *cultural* community in Walzer's sense, or whether it is sufficient for the community be united around principles of justice that people with different cultural backgrounds can agree upon—the picture famously presented by Rawls (1971). Equally, it is possible to challenge the claim that cultural cohesion requires exclusion. This claim appears to overlook the extent to which immigrants, when they join the new society, are willing to integrate, in the sense of taking on board much of its public culture: Walzer's treatment of membership draws no line between public and private culture, but multicultural societies have shown that immigrant groups can retain much of their inherited private culture while simultaneously adopting not only the political principles but also the national narratives and symbols of their new home. This undermines any suggestion that social cohesion requires full cultural homogeneity. Finally, cosmopolitans will challenge the normative weight that Walzer attaches to the pursuit of social justice at the expense of the urgent claims of those outside of the political community, especially refugees and those who are seeking to escape from dire poverty. Carens (1987) argues that this weighting violates principles of equal treatment that liberal societies like Walzer's own have already included among their shared understandings.

I will discuss two other "communitarian" defenses of the state's right to control its borders more briefly. One appeals to the value of democracy, especially strong or "republican" democracy. Reversing the direction of Abizadeh's argument, it claims that democracy cannot flourish unless it is supported by a stable demos whose members share a common identity, and unrestricted immigration would threaten this (see Abizadeh 2002 for a critique of the first claim). Democracy requires at the very least that its subjects should be willing to accept the outcome of collective decisions even when they are in the minority, but stronger forms of democracy that rely on deliberation between the participants to arrive at consensual or near-consensual decisions demand higher levels of interpersonal trust. Since immigration tends to increase the extent of ethnic and religious diversity in a society, and this in turn is correlated with a reduction in the level of social trust, it needs to be kept below the level at which policies aimed at increasing social solidarity—such as nation-building policies—can operate effectively.[13]

This argument relies on some empirical claims—about the effect of diversity on social trust, and about the importance of trust for democracy—which may be challenged (for a discussion of both, see Lenard 2012); and it also relies on a normative claim about the weight that we should attach to a particular form of democracy as against the material interests of outsiders in joining the society. Nonetheless, since a further link can plausibly be drawn between democracy and the promotion of social justice, we see here how justice to immigrants and justice between citizens may be at odds with each other—and how a resolution may depend on what position we adopt on the spectrum between cosmopolitanism and communitarianism.

The second defense has been advanced by Ryan Pevnick, who argues that the members of a political community have collective rights over the community's assets that they and their forebears have built up over the course of history, and they are, therefore, entitled to deny access to immigrants, who have not contributed to this accumulation— he calls this "associative ownership" (Pevnick 2011: chs. 2–3; for a critical discussion, see Fine 2013). The community's right of self-determination, he claims, includes the right to decide who should share in the goods that it owns collectively. Since it is not usually possible to separate being present on the territory from having access to these public goods, states have a right to exclude incomers (though Pevnick concedes this does not apply to those who *only* seek access to the territory itself). This relies on the intuition that the right to inherit from one's predecessors is sufficiently strong to outweigh the claims of needy outsiders—who, it might be argued, will not actually diminish the supply of public goods available to the present owners. Pevnick himself goes on to argue that those who live in countries where income levels are extremely low should enjoy a legal right to move to wealthier societies (Pevnick 2011: ch. 4). So this argument, like the others considered in this section of the chapter, will not justify an unconditional right to exclude immigrants, but instead a more limited right to exercise discretion over who is admitted and who is refused entry.

4 Conclusion

I have framed the debate over immigration as occurring between open-borders advocates (whose background philosophy is usually cosmopolitan) and defenders of the state's right to close its borders (who usually rest their case on some form of communitarianism). Yet, as we examine the debate, we find a surprising degree of practical convergence between the two camps. Those who defend border-closing also recognize the state's obligation to admit a fair share of those who qualify as refugees—or at the very least to contribute financially to the support of refugees who are housed elsewhere. They also recognize that the state is morally constrained in its choice of which other immigrants to admit (see, for example, Blake 2002). On the other side, those who argue that in principle borders should always be open also concede that allowing immigration will rarely be the best way to promote global justice—that what is needed is a fundamental transformation of conditions of life in the world's poorest societies—and that fully open borders will only be politically feasible in a world in which current economic inequalities have been sharply reduced.

The debate has also been conducted on the shared assumption that immigrants who are admitted must be allowed after a short space of time to become full citizens of the society they are joining—this is common ground between Carens and Walzer, for instance. Breaking the link between immigration and citizenship would make it easier to reconcile freedom of movement and national self-determination, but at the cost of creating a new class of "denizens" who are denied access to citizen status. A question for the future is whether schemes that allow this, especially in the case of temporary migrants, might be rendered consistent with justice so long as the human rights of the migrants were sufficiently protected.

NOTES

1. Different conceptions of common ownership are helpfully distinguished in Risse (2012: ch. 6).
2. For further discussion of the relationship between borders and justice, see Miller (2012).
3. See also Moellendorf (2009). Another advocate of global equality of opportunity is Simon Caney: see Caney (2000), (2001).
4. One issue I shall not address is whether the principle of equal opportunity can meaningfully be applied at global level. In order to do this we would need to have a way of measuring opportunities such that we could say that the opportunities available to person A in country X were greater or smaller than the opportunities available to person B in country Y. Because of cultural differences in the way that opportunities are identified and valued this may be impossible: see Miller (2007: ch. 3) and Boxhill (1987). For present purposes I am setting this problem aside.
5. Defenders of a human right to immigrate include Carens (1992), (2013: ch. 11); and Oberman (2016). Michael Dummett (2001: ch. 3) draws back from claiming that there is a strong right to immigrate on the grounds that a genuine obligation-imposing right must be unconditional (whereas he acknowledges that there might be cases in which states could justifiably limit immigration), but he defends such a right in a "weaker, conditional sense."
6. I refer to this as the "cantilever" argument for the human right to immigrate, a label that Carens himself accepts. See my fuller discussion in Miller (2016b), on which I draw in what follows. See also Blake (2003) on the relevance of the state's exercise of coercive authority over its citizens to the case for freedom of movement.

7. "Voluntary repatriation" is the preferred policy, but states increasingly appeal to the principle of "safe return," which requires refugees to repatriate when the conditions on the ground that caused their flight have changed fundamentally. See Goodwin-Gill and McAdam (2007: 492–7).

8. See, for example, Dummett (2001: 14–20); Carens (2013: 277–79). Carens concedes the general point, but argues his open borders proposal should be taken in conjunction with his case for a radical reduction in global inequalities, which would imply a much-reduced demand for immigration.

9. For a bleak assessment of the likely consequences of unrestricted migration in the contemporary world, see Barry (1992).

10. See Fine (2010) and Miller (2007: ch. 8). For the libertarian argument from individual rights of association to the conclusion that only the unanimous agreement of its citizens would give the right to exclude an outsider, see Steiner (2001).

11. Wellman does partially recognize this ambiguity when he concedes that his argument "would leave much more room for freedom of movement than the status quo," because it would permit free travel for tourists, students, and others so long as they did not stay indefinitely without permission: see Wellman (2008: 137).

12. Wellman responds to the case of refugees by arguing that the state's duty towards them can normally be discharged by providing them with a safe haven in their country of origin or elsewhere, if the state so chooses. See Wellman and Cole (2011: ch. 6).

13. For discussion of the impact of immigration on social trust in the receiving society, see Putnam (2007); Collier (2013: ch. 3).

References

Abizadeh, Arash (2002) "Does Liberal Democracy Presuppose a Cultural Nation? Four Arguments," *American Political Science Review* 96(3): 495–509.

Abizadeh, Arash (2008) "Democratic Theory and Border Coercion: No Right to Unilaterally Control Your Own Borders," *Political Theory* 36(1): 37–65.

Barry, Brian (1992) "The Quest for Consistency: A Sceptical View." In Brian Barry and Robert E. Goodin (eds.), *Free Movement: Ethical Issues in the Transnational Migration of People and of Money*. Hemel Hempstead: Harvester Wheatsheaf, 279–87.

Benhabib, Seyla (2004) *The Rights of Others: Aliens, Residents and Citizens*. Cambridge: Cambridge University Press.

Blake, Michael (2002) "Discretionary Immigration," *Philosophical Topics* 30(2): 273–89.

Blake, Michael (2003) "Immigration." In R. G. Frey and Christopher Heath Wellman (eds.), *A Companion to Applied Ethics*. Oxford: Blackwell, 224–37.

Blake, Michael (2012) "Immigration, Association and Anti-Discrimination," *Ethics* 122(4): 748–62.

Blake, Michael (2013) "Immigration, Jurisdiction and Exclusion," *Philosophy and Public Affairs* 41(2): 103–30.

Boxhill, Bernard (1987) "Global Equality of Opportunity and National Integrity," *Social Philosophy and Policy* 5: 143–68.

Caney, Simon (2000) "Global Equality of Opportunity and the Sovereignty of States." In Anthony Coates (ed.), *International Justice*. Aldershot: Ashgate, 130–49.

Caney, Simon (2001) "Cosmopolitan Justice and Equalizing Opportunities." In Thomas W. Pogge (ed.), *Global Justice*. Oxford: Blackwell, 123–44.

Carens, Joseph H. (1987) "Aliens and Citizens: The Case for Open Borders," *Review of Politics* 49(2): 251–73.

Carens, Joseph H. (1992) "Migration and Morality: A Liberal Egalitarian Perspective." In Brian Barry and Robert E. Goodin (eds.), *Free Movement: Ethical Issues in the Transnational Migration of People and of Money*. Hemel Hempstead: Harvester Wheatsheaf, 258–47.

Carens, Joseph H. (2013) *The Ethics of Immigration*. New York: Oxford University Press.

Collier, Paul (2013) *Exodus: Immigration and Multiculturalism in the 21st Century*. London: Allen Lane.

Dummett, Michael. (2001) *On Immigration and Refugees*. London: Routledge.

Fine, Sarah (2010) "Freedom of Association Is Not the Answer," *Ethics*, 120(2): 338–56.

Fine, Sarah (2013) "The Ethics of Immigration: Self-Determination and the Right to Exclude," *Philosophy Compass* 8(3): 254–68.

Gibney, Matthew J. (2004) *The Ethics and Politics of Asylum*. Cambridge: Cambridge University Press.

Goodwin-Gill, Guy S., and Jane McAdam (2007) *The Refugee in International Law*, 3rd edn. Oxford: Oxford University Press.

Grotius, Hugo (2005) *The Rights of War and Peace*, ed. R. Tuck. Indianapolis, IN: Liberty Fund.

Kant, Immanuel (1971) "Perpetual Peace: A Philosophical Sketch." In H. S. Reiss (ed.) *Kant's Political Writings*. Cambridge: Cambridge University Press, 93–130.

Kant, Immanuel (1996) *The Metaphysics of Morals*, ed. Mary J. Gregor. Cambridge: Cambridge University Press.

Kukathas, Chandran (2005) "The Case for Open Immigration." In Andrew L. Cohen and Christopher Heath Wellman (eds.), *Contemporary Debates in Applied Ethics*. Oxford: Blackwell, 207–220.

Lenard, Patti Tamara (2012) *Trust, Democracy, and Multicultural Challenges*. University Park, PA: Pennsylvania State University Press.

Miller, David (2005) "Immigration: The Case for Limits." In Andrew L. Cohen and Christopher Heath Wellman (eds.), *Contemporary Debates in Applied Ethics*. Oxford: Blackwell, 193–206.

Miller, David (2007) *National Responsibility and Global Justice*. Oxford: Oxford University Press.

Miller, David (2010) "Why Immigration Controls Are Not Coercive: A Reply to Arash Abizadeh," *Political Theory* 38(1): 111–20.

Miller, David (2012) "Justice and Borders." In Gerald F. Gaus and Fred D'Agostino (eds.), *The Routledge Companion to Political and Social Philosophy*. London: Routledge, 526–36.

Miller, David (2015) "Justice in Immigration," *European Journal of Political Theory* 14(4): 391–408.

Miller, David (2016a) *Strangers in Our Midst: The Political Philosophy of Immigration*. Cambridge, MA: Harvard University Press.

Miller, David (2016b) "Is there a Human Right to Immigrate?" In Sarah Fine and Lea Ypi (eds.), *Migration in Political Theory: The Ethics of Movement and Membership*. Oxford: Oxford University Press, 11–31.

Moellendorf, Darrel (2002) *Cosmopolitan Justice*. Boulder, CO: Westview Press.

Moellendorf, Darrel (2009) *Global Inequality Matters*. Basingstoke: Palgrave Macmillan.

Oberman, Kieran (2013) "Can Brian Drain Justify Immigration Restrictions?" *Ethics* 123(3): 427–55.

Oberman, Kieran (2016) "Immigration as a Human Right." In Sarah Fine and Lea Ypi (eds.), *Migration in Political Theory: The Ethics of Movement and Membership*. Oxford: Oxford University Press, 32–56.

Pevnick, Ryan (2011) *Immigration and the Constraints of Justice*. Cambridge: Cambridge University Press.

Pogge, Thomas (1997) "Migration and Poverty." In Veit Bader (ed.), *Citizenship and Exclusion*. Basingstoke: Macmillan, 12–27.

Putnam, R. 2007. "*E Pluribus Unum*: Diversity and Community in the Twenty-first Century," *Scandinavian Political Studies* 30(2): 137–74.

Rawls, John (1971) *A Theory of Justice*. Cambridge, MA: Harvard University Press.

Risse, Mathias (2012) *On Global Justice*. Princeton, NJ: Princeton University Press.

Steiner, Hillel (2001) "Hard Borders, Compensation and Classical Liberalism." In David Miller and Sohail H. Hashmi (eds.), *Boundaries and Justice: Diverse Ethical Perspectives*. Princeton, NJ: Princeton University Press, 137–74.

Walzer, Michael (1983) *Spheres of Justice: A Defence of Pluralism and Equality*. Oxford: Martin Robertson.

Wellman, Christopher Heath (2008) "Immigration and Freedom of Association," *Ethics* 119(1): 109–41.

Wellman, Christopher Heath, and Phillip Cole (2011) *Debating the Ethics of Immigration*. New York: Oxford University Press.

FURTHER READING

Cole, Phillip (2000) *Philosophies of Exclusion: Liberal Political theory and Immigration*. Edinburgh: Edinburgh University Press.

Fine, Sarah, and Lea Ypi (eds.) (2016) *Migration in Political Theory: The Ethics of Movement and Membership*. Oxford: Oxford University Press.

Hidalgo, Javier (2019) *Unjust Borders: Individuals and the Ethics of Immigration*. New York: Routledge.

Hosein, Adam (2019) *The Ethics of Migration: An Introduction*. Abingdon: Routledge.

Song, Sarah (2019) *Immigration and Democracy*. New York: Oxford University Press.

Swain, Carol M. (ed.) (2007) *Debating Immigration*. Cambridge: Cambridge University Press.

CHAPTER 20

POLITICAL LEGITIMACY AND TERRITORIAL RIGHTS

CHRISTOPHER HEATH WELLMAN

THE most promising accounts of political legitimacy are functional; they explain that states are legitimate just in case they perform the requisite political functions. Functional theories of political legitimacy have recently come under attack, however, for their inability to satisfactorily account for territorial rights. In particular, critics contend that we must at least supplement, if not replace, functional approaches with nationalist and/or transactional theories if we are to accommodate our pre-theoretic intuitions about a state's rights to jurisdiction, border control and natural resources.[1] It is tempting to respond by criticizing these alternative theories, but I shall not do so here.[2] Instead, I want to challenge the supposition that functional theorists cannot adequately explain these territorial rights. I will argue that functional theorists are much better equipped than one might suspect to explain a legitimate state's rights to jurisdiction and border control. It is less clear that advocates of this approach can vindicate resource rights, but I conclude by suggesting that this may give us more reason to doubt the existence of these particular rights than to abandon functional theories of political legitimacy.

1 THE PROBLEM

There are three core territorial rights commonly ascribed to states: (1) a state has the right of *jurisdiction* when it enjoys the exclusive right to make and enforce laws governing everyone within its territory; (2) a state's right of *border control* entitles it to unilaterally decide who may enter its territory; and (3) a state enjoys *resource* rights when it alone owns all of the natural resources within its territory. To appreciate why these three rights are thought to be so problematic for functional theorists, it may help to begin by comparing this approach to other types of theories. Historically, transactional theories of political legitimacy have dominated. According to transactional theorists, a state is legitimate just in case it has emerged from the appropriate transactional history. The most popular of these accounts, of course, is social contract theory, which contends that a state is legitimate only when it has garnered the morally valid consent of all of its citizens. On the Lockean version of this story, for instance, individual landowners get together and unanimously agree to form a state which thereby acquires authority over each of them and their property.[3] A state's territorial rights pose no problem for theorists of this stripe, then, because consent theorists simply allege that a state acquires its rights to jurisdiction, border control, and resources when they are voluntarily transferred from the initial property owners.

But while transactional theories have no problem explaining territorial rights, they are widely rejected for other reasons. In particular, even if there is nothing normatively suspicious about a property owner's consensually alienating her rights over her land, it is historically inaccurate to suppose that existing states have in fact garnered the morally valid consent of all of their constituents. And because other transactional theories require their own descriptively inaccurate premises, they too must be rejected on the same grounds.

Given the demise of transactional theory, one must either accept anarchism or develop an alternative account of political legitimacy. Most are unwilling to embrace anarchism, however, because of the horrible conditions that they imagine would inevitably obtain in the absence of a functioning state. This aversion to anarchism is instructive, though, because if we are horrified by what we believe would necessarily happen in a stateless environment, then perhaps states are justified in coercively imposing themselves on us even in the absence of our consent because this imposition is necessary to help us avoid these perilous circumstances. Or put in functional terms, perhaps states are non-consensually justified because of the vital functions which they alone are capable of performing.

Which functions? Here there is room for disagreement, but the prevailing answer is securing justice. And while justice can be cashed out in any number of currencies, the most popular is human rights, where human rights are understood as the protections we all need against the standard threats to living a minimally decent human life.[4] Putting all of this together, one particularly prominent functional account of political legitimacy contends that a state is legitimate just in case it satisfactorily protects the human rights of all of its constituents.[5]

I think there is a great deal to like about this particular brand of functional theory, but now that we have moved away from our initial transactional account, it is no longer clear how we can explain a state's territorial rights. We would be in good shape on this score if states could not perform their requisite political functions unless they enjoyed perfectly general and absolute rights to jurisdiction, border control, and natural resources, but this claim seems just as descriptively implausible as social contract theory's allegation that citizens have uniformly consented to their state's presence. With this in mind, let us now look more closely at how a functional theorist might try to justify each of the territorial claims.

2 THE RIGHT OF JURISDICTION

At first glance, the functional theorist appears to have a perfectly straightforward explanation for why legitimate states enjoy exclusive rights of jurisdiction over their territory, namely states could not satisfactorily perform their requisite political functions unless they were territorially delineated. On this view, it is not merely an accident that states are currently defined in territorial terms; rather, as Kant famously emphasized, we need the same set of rules to bind all of those who regularly interact. We cannot sort citizens into states according to hair color, religion, or individual preference, then, as long as people of different hair colors, religions, and political preferences all live amongst and thus interact with one another. And if states must be territorial in order to perform their requisite political functions, functional theorists would seem to have a compelling justification for the territorial right of jurisdiction.

But this is too quick. Even if we assume that (1) certain crucial functions such as protecting human rights could not be performed in the absence of states, (2) states cannot do this unless they are territorially delineated, and (3) a state like Norway, for example, does a good job performing these requisite political functions, it still would not follow that Norway has a valid claim to all of its territory. Why not create a single world state, for instance? After all, if the rationale for territorially defined states is that we need a uniform set of rules for those who regularly interact with one another, then the contemporary fact of international interaction would seem to recommend instituting a single state that governs everyone on earth. And if Norway's claim to its territory is justified solely in virtue of its performance of the requisite political functions, then it is hard to see how it would have a claim to remain independent of a global state if this larger arrangement could better perform these very functions that are thought to ground Norway's right of jurisdiction. To emphasize: if the only thing that justifies Norway's right to create and enforce laws over the Norwegian territory is that its doing so enables it to perform the vital chore of protecting human rights, then Norway's claim would not prevail in the face of a prospective global state that could do a better job protecting these human rights.

For a variety of reasons, however, most who work in this area recoil from the idea of a world state. Most notably, many worry either that such a large state will suffer from diseconomies of scale or that having only one global power will leave us utterly defenseless if this lone state were ever to tyrannically turn on (some of) its subjects. But even if we abandon the idea of a world state and insist that earth must be governed by a plurality of territorially districted sovereign countries, this still would not necessarily vindicate each legitimate state's claim to jurisdiction. Imagine, for instance, that Sweden or perhaps the European Union could do a better job performing the requisite political functions in the Norwegian territory than Norway does. If this were the case, why may Sweden or the EU not forcibly annex Norway? Again, if Norway's right of jurisdiction is grounded solely in its performing the requisite political functions, then it is hard to see what moral standing it would have to resist merging with a larger body that would subsequently be better able to perform these same justifying functions.

Here we come to a crossroads. If we endorse a purely functional theory of political legitimacy, then we appear unable to resist the conclusion that Sweden and/or the EU has the right to unilaterally annex Norway. If we think that Norway has a territorial right to jurisdiction which entitles it to resist non-consensual mergers, however, then we must somehow supplement the functional theory of political legitimacy. As I will argue later in this section, functional theories can be buttressed in ways that ultimately vindicate a legitimate state's right to jurisdiction, but it is worth noting that reasonable people can disagree about whether or not functional theories should be endorsed in their pure form. Albert Einstein, for instance, famously alleged that "The state to which I belong does not play the least role in my spiritual life; I regard allegiance to a government as a business matter, somewhat like the relationship with a life insurance company" (quoted in Snyder 1977: ix). And for people of this orientation, any change in their country's territorial boundaries that does not negatively affect the state's capacity to perform its functions is of no real consequence. In my own case, when I was notified that my life insurance company had been bought by a larger company, this scarcely registered with me because it did not affect the terms of my policy. If my annual premiums had increased or the amount my beneficiaries were guaranteed to receive had been reduced, then I certainly would have cared, but since neither the benefits nor the costs of the insurance were altered, I really did not mind that the company to which I was contractually related had changed. If we take Einstein at his word, then he felt similarly about his political state; as long as the political reconfigurations would not negatively affect the taxes he was required to pay or the functions his state performed, any changes in his country's territorial boundaries would have been mere "noise" that he would prefer to ignore.

There are no doubt many ways in which we should strive to be more like Einstein, but the plain truth is that most of us care a great deal more about our relationship to our states than we do about our relationship with our insurance companies. After all, while we may admire Einstein for his claim that "I want to know God's thoughts; the rest are details," for most of us, the contours, constitution and complexion of our state do not strike us as mere "details." It may not matter to whom we send our insurance check, but we care a great deal about those with whom we cooperate politically, because changes in a state's territorial boundaries and constituency alter the way it operates, and states pervasively influence our lives. It is not difficult to see, then, why most of us would be uncomfortable with a theory of political legitimacy which implied that a state like Norway would have no right to reject an unsolicited annexation by a neighboring country or regional association as long as the post-merger arrangement was no less able and willing to perform the requisite functions for the (former) Norwegians. In sum, straightforward functional accounts of political legitimacy appear unable to vindicate Norway's territorial right of jurisdiction because they have no means of justifying a legitimate state's right of self-determination. Thus, those of us who do not share Einstein's orientation must somehow supplement the functional account so as to vindicate this first territorial right.

In my view, the key to understanding a legitimate state's self-determination is to appreciate that thresholds of competence are compatible with functional analysis, and perhaps the best way to see this is by examining analogous relations, like a parent's dominion over her children. To see why parental authority is particularly illustrative, notice that we emphatically reject the idea that children should be raised by whoever could do the best job. Instead, we think that parents retain authority over their biological children as long as they are adequate parents. Take Donna and me, for instance. We are far from perfect parents, but presumably we do a satisfactory job carrying out our parental responsibilities and, as a consequence, we enjoy exclusive parental authority over our two boys, Alexander and Jackson. This parental dominion obviously has limits (we may not torture our children when they are disobedient, for instance), but our privileged position over their lives entitles us to make various choices about their upbringing, such as whether they will attend public or private school. Most importantly, decisions such as these are ours to make even if others are better equipped to make them. Even if some neighbor who knows vastly more about early education understands that our boys would be better off attending the local private school, for instance, she has no right to unilaterally remove them from the public school we have chosen. And if our neighbor did interfere in this way, she would wrong Donna and me by disrespecting our parental authority, authority to which we are entitled in virtue of our adequately fulfilling our parental responsibilities.

I think we should conceive of political self-determination in analogous terms. Just as Donna and I enjoy our parental dominion in virtue of our ability and willingness to satisfactorily perform the requisite parental functions, Norwegians are entitled to political dominion because of their collective ability and willingness to adequately perform the requisite political functions. Even if Sweden could do a better job governing those on Norway's territory than Norway currently does, the Swedes have no right to unilaterally assign themselves this task. And if they did interfere in this way, the Swedes would wrong the Norwegians by failing to respect their political authority, authority to which they are entitled in virtue of adequately securing the human rights of everyone within Norway.[6] And if it seems perfectly natural to invoke a threshold of adequacy for a functionally justified right like parental dominion, then there is nothing ad hoc or otherwise suspicious about adding a similar component to our functional analysis of political legitimacy. And once we do, we appear capable of explaining a legitimate state's territorial right to jurisdiction.

Not everyone will accept this story, though, and here I would like to focus on two particularly salient worries. First, even if one accepts the analogy between parental and political authority, it generates striking conclusions regarding state-breaking. And second, one might worry that the core analogy is inapt. Let us consider these two objections in turn.

On my account of sovereignty, Sweden must respect Norway's jurisdiction over its territory because Norway is currently doing a satisfactory job carrying out its political responsibilities. But if external parties must respect Norway's political self-determination because of its ability and willingness to perform the requisite political functions, then why must not Norway also respect the political self-determination of internal parties? Imagine, for instance, that a portion of Norway sought to secede from Norway, just as Norway seceded from Sweden in 1905. If this separatist region were clearly able and willing to satisfactorily protect the human rights of its constituents, then it is hard to see how my theory can justify Norway's denying this internal region's request for a political divorce.[7] Many will bristle at this conclusion. One might be prepared to concede that Norway could *forfeit* its right to a portion of its territory if it treated the separatists sufficiently unjustly, but the case under consideration is quite different from that. Here we are imagining a political scenario analogous to no-fault divorce, where a group of separatists seeks independence from what they acknowledge is a perfectly just state. And because my theory of political self-determination implies that even legitimate states like Norway have no right to contest these no-fault secessions, many will reject it outright.

For two reasons, however, I embrace these implications as a virtue, rather than a vice, of my theory. First, it is important to remember that political states are so hard to justify precisely because they are non-consensually imposed. If social contract theorists were right that we had all given our morally valid consent to our state's coercive presence, then there would be nothing problematic about states fortifying their commands with the punitive force of criminal law. But the plain truth is that many of us have not consented, and thus political theorists have reluctantly but decidedly turned their backs on the elegant transactional approaches to political legitimacy. Those of us who remain statists, though, are convinced that political order is necessary to avoid the perils that would inevitably accompany anarchy. Here I want to stress that the key word in the previous sentence is *necessary*: it is only because political coercion is the only way to ensure that everyone's human rights are satisfactorily protected that we are willing to allow states to non-consensually coerce folks. But notice: in the case we are imagining, it is *not* necessary for Norway to impose itself upon those people in the separatist region because, by hypothesis, the separatists are able and willing to adequately protect human rights on their own. Thus, once one recognizes the role that necessity must play in any plausible account of political legitimacy, it seems clear that political coercion is justified only where it is in fact necessary. And if so, it seems perfectly natural that we should allow separatist groups to secede even in the absence of injustice, as long as neither the act of breaking up nor the resulting political reconfiguration will leave the secessionist or the rump state unable or unwilling to satisfactorily perform the requisite political functions.[8]

Secondly, notice that this analysis is reinforced by the parental analogy, because parental dominion is also justified only to the extent that it is necessary. Donna and I have the right to decide where our young sons go to school, for instance, only because our boys are not mature enough to make this type of decision on their own. If and when they mature, however, our parental guidance will no longer be necessary, and thus we will not have the same authority to determine whether and where they go to college, for example. So, for these reasons, I think we need not retreat from an account of political legitimacy that vindicates Norway's right to jurisdiction against all outsiders but leaves Norway potentially vulnerable to territorial claims made by politically viable groups within its own borders. Still, despite my comfort with these implications, I should acknowledge that this stance diverges from the common assumption that legitimate states have a right to retain their territorial integrity in full, against both external and internal competing claims.

The second objection stems from a worry that, even if my analysis of parental dominion is entirely correct, it does not support my account of political legitimacy, because there are morally significant disanalogies between these two realms. Specifically, one might counter that whatever authority Donna and I have over our children is not due merely to the fact that we are satisfactorily performing the requisite parental functions; it is also because *we made our children*. This observation is thought to be telling, of course, because citizens do not have a similar claim to their land. It would be one thing if all and only Norwegians somehow deserved to have been born on Norwegian soil, for instance, but they do not; they just happened to have been born there. And in the absence of some factor that grounds the Norwegians' claim to "their" territory, we should dismiss my attempted analogy between parental and political dominion as inapt.

This is a powerful objection, and it certainly highlights the appeal of nationalist and/ or transactional approaches to this question. After all, if one can tell a story about how the Norwegians as a people have mixed their culture with the territory or for some other reason come to identify with it has their "homeland," then we appear much better positioned to say why they have a function-independent claim to it, just as Donna and I have a function-independent connection to our natural children which explains our right to retain our children even in the presence of prospective adoptive parents who are better equipped to perform the requisite parental functions.[9] But while I certainly understand the temptation to invoke a cultural or political group's connection to the land, I am inclined instead to emphasize an individual's right of occupation. In my view, whether she is in a political state or not, each individual has a right of occupancy, a preinstitutional right not to be displaced from the land she not unjustly occupies.[10]

The basic idea here is that, even in the absence of the institutional structure afforded by political society, each of us has a right to reside on the territory we occupy. And as a preinstitutional right, the right of occupancy serves as a side-constraint which limits the property regimes and political institutions we might like to create. In other words, whatever advantages there might be to designing property rights or political states in a way which disrespected each individual's right to occupancy, these arrangements would be ruled out on principled grounds. Thus, just as we are not free to create our preferred state if doing so required us to violate some people's right to life, we may not construct any state or property regime which conflicted with the right of occupancy.[11]

For a state to be legitimate, it must perform the requisite political functions without imposing unreasonable burdens upon those who (not unjustly) occupy the territory over which it presides.[12] And because displacing inhabitants would clearly be requiring too much of those ushered off of *their* land, one of the conditions of political legitimacy is that the state not displace any of the territory's rightful occupants.[13] On my view, then, the Norwegians do not necessarily have some special group claim to the territory. Rather, Norwegians as individuals have a natural (that is, non-institutional) right to reside on and live off of the land that they occupy. And because this natural connection to the land is individual rather than collective, there is neither an individual right possessed by each particular Norwegian nor a group right enjoyed by the Norwegians as a collective to the entire territory of Norway. This is why no party's rights would necessarily be violated if a region of Norway seceded (just as no individual or group rights were violated by Norway's secession from Sweden in 1905). In sum, individuals have a right to stay where they are and (as long as it is not too costly for others) a right to the protection of a government that satisfactorily protects their human rights, but they do not have a right that their existing state retains its current boundaries. Put in terms of a slogan: Individuals may have a right to a legitimate state, but they do not have a right to the statist quo. This explains why no German who was against reunification had her rights violated when East and West Germany reunited, and it implies that no individual German would have her rights violated if East and West Germany decided tomorrow to part ways again.

Before concluding this section, it might be helpful to compare my position to those of Allen Buchanan, David Miller, and Anna Stilz in light of an example that Stilz (2011 : 590) discusses in her article, "Nations, States and Territories."[14] Stilz asks us to imagine that the occupying forces had remained in Germany after World War II. Intuitively, it seems to her that if Germans were able and willing to perform the requisite political functions, then they should be able to reclaim their independence and evict the occupying forces. The question is: which theory is best able to capture this intuition? According to nationalists like Miller (2012), a necessary component of the story must be that the Germans as a cultural group have a special claim to their territory. In contrast, Stilz argues that the Germans qualify as a people because of their collective performance of the requisite political functions (my words, not exactly hers). Stilz feels the need to talk of the German people to explain why Germans can reclaim their territory after they regain their ability and willingness to perform the requisite political functions. I worry that this story is so similar to the one Miller (2012) tells, that it is vulnerable on the same grounds.[15] I will not explore this concern here, though, because on my account, establishing such a group claim to territory is unnecessary. Germans need establish neither that they are some kind of "people" nor that they, qua people, have a special claim to German territory, because they are antecedently entitled to secede by virtue of their ability and willingness to perform the requisite political functions. But while my view can easily handle the particular problem Stilz raises, it also opens the door to no-fault secession, something that some may find intuitively unattractive. So while I worry that Stilz's account can be undermined on the same grounds that she uses to reject Miller's view, others might eschew my approach in order to avoid its implications regarding the primary right to secede from perfectly just states.

Finally, as a straightforward functional theorist who is skeptical of group rights to political self-determination, Allen Buchanan (2004) avoids the questionable premises that Miller and Stilz invoke without having to endorse a primary right to secede. On the other hand, because he leaves no room for political self-determination, Buchanan appears unable to explain why contemporary Germans would have any principled grounds on which to object if they were still occupied. Indeed, Buchanan's position seems to align with the "Einsteinian" view discussed earlier. And if this is right, Buchanan could not explain why a foreign country like Sweden would necessarily do anything wrong in forcibly annexing Norway, as long as this hostile takeover neither violated any individual rights nor resulted in a country which was less able and willing to perform the requisite political functions in (what used to be) Norway.[16]

As this comparison among various authors working on these topics shows, depending on how they are supplemented, the functional theories of political legitimacy can at least come close, if not perfectly match, our pretheoretic understanding of the territorial right of jurisdiction.

3 BORDER CONTROL

Turning now to a state's right to border control, functional accounts of political legitimacy could readily supply a clear case for the right to exclude prospective immigrants if it were true that states could not perform their requisite political functions unless they were able to design and enforce their own immigration policies. The obvious problem, however, is that it is simply not true that states could not function unless they had complete discretion to exclude all outsiders. It may well be that a select few particularly popular states would not be able to sustain anything like their current levels of political functioning if they were not allowed to restrict immigration, but this more limited claim would not suffice for two reasons. It would not justify a right of exclusion for those states not in high demand, and even high-demand states would not have complete discretion; they would be permitted to begin excluding outsiders only at levels that were necessary to sustain political legitimacy. Thus, as in the case of the right of jurisdiction, we appear to be at a fork in the road: If we stick with a purely functional account of political legitimacy, then we cannot justify anything like our pretheoretic notion of a state's right to control its borders; if we once again invoke the right to political self-determination, however, then perhaps we can explain a state's right to exclude outsiders.

In my view, the most promising argument for a legitimate state's right to design and enforce its own immigration policy requires three core premises: (1) legitimate states are entitled to political self-determination, (2) freedom of association is an integral component of self-determination, and (3) freedom of association includes the right to refuse to associate with others.[17]

My claim that legitimate states enjoy the right to political self-determination should be clear from our discussion of the right of jurisdiction, so let me now focus more specifically on freedom of association. The second premise is merely that one is not fully self-determining unless one is free to choose with whom one associates. Imagine that your father gets to select your spouse, for instance. If he chooses well, then you might lead a happy life, but there is a clearly an important sense in which you lack self-determination. And this same example illustrates well why freedom of association necessarily includes the right to refuse to associate. It is not enough that one be allowed to marry; one is in a position to be the author of one's own life only if one has the option to refuse to marry any and all suitors whom one would prefer not to accept as a spouse.

Of course, most associations are neither as intimate nor as important as marriage, but this observation does not undermine the more general lesson that self-determination is compromised when freedom of association is not respected. It matters a great deal less whether one's golf club can exclude prospective members than it does whether you can reject suitors who seek your hand in marriage, for example, but it nonetheless remains true that a golf club's self-determination would be restricted if it were not allowed to design and enforce its own membership rules. The central idea here is that, just as an individual is not self-determining when she may not reject a prospective spouse, a group is not self-determining when it may not select among potential new members as it sees fit, because in the case of groups, an essential component of self-determination is having effective control over who the group is. This logic applies no less to political collectives, of course, so even if states need not have complete control over their borders in order to perform the requisite political functions, any country which lacked the right to screen potential immigrants would not be self-determining. Thus, for the same reasons that Norway has the right to either accept or decline an invitation to merge with Sweden, say, it has the right to either permit or prohibit a prospective Swedish immigrant from joining the Norwegian political community. In sum, then, just as an individual has the right to determine whom (if anyone) she would like to marry, a group of fellow-citizens has a right to determine whom (if anyone) it would like to invite into its political community. And just as an individual's freedom of association entitles him or her to remain single, a corporate political entity's freedom of association entitles it to exclude all foreigners.

One might worry that territorial rights cause problems for this analysis as well because, unlike in the case of marriage, Norwegians do not merely assert a right to exclude prospective immigrants from their political community; they claim a right to keep them off Norwegian territory. As Sarah Fine puts it, "Wellman's position begs the question whether citizens and/or their states have the relevant rights over the territory from which they wish to exclude others and thus whether they are within their rights not just to control the rules of membership but also to control settlement within that territory" (Fine 2010: 354). This is an important point, but I think the necessity of states presiding over territorially defined districts can help us respond to this potential objection, at least if one believes that a condition of a state's imposing itself upon its constituents is that it treats all citizens as free and equal. In particular, the egalitarian prong of this requirement mandates that a state not admit anyone into its political community unless it welcomes them as equal members. And because a state imposes its coercive authority over everyone who resides on its territory, this requires that a state not admit anyone to enter and stay indefinitely on its territory unless it grants her equal citizenship.

Invoking relational egalitarianism in this way is necessary, but it may not be sufficient. As the quotation from Sarah Fine reminds us, this move presupposes that citizens of a country not only have a special claim to control the membership in their political community; they also have a right to the territory over which this community presides. If Norway wanted to exclude a prospective Swedish immigrant, for instance, it would not be enough for the Norwegians to explain why they should have freedom of association over their political community; they must also explain why Norwegians rather than Swedes (or anyone else, for that matter) are entitled to preside over the territory on which Norway currently exercises jurisdiction. (And remember, merely invoking the fact that Norway performs the requisite political functions for everyone within this territory will not necessarily rebut Sweden's competing claim if the Swedes could do a better job performing these functions on this territory than Norway currently does.)

If my explanation of the right of jurisdiction outlined in the previous section is on target, then presumably this objection can be rebutted in similar terms. More specifically, if the right of occupancy helps explain why Norwegians have a claim to Norway's territory which outsiders lack, then this privileged position is relevant to immigration as well. As emphasized in the discussion of jurisdiction in Section 2 above, the right of occupancy is held by Norwegians as individuals, not by the Norwegian "people" as a group or the Norwegian state as a single corporate political entity. Still, I think that when one combines the Norwegians' individual rights of occupancy with the Norwegians' group right to political self-determination, one can satisfactorily explain why Norwegians as a group have at least a presumptive right to decide who among the prospective immigrants may enter the political community and who may not, and that this right entitles Norway not only to deny citizenship to outsiders; it entitles Norwegians to forcibly prohibit outsiders from entering their territory.

For the sake of argument, let us suppose that this line of reasoning is sound. Even so, its implications would have at least two considerable limitations. First, this right is only presumptive and thus is potentially vulnerable to being overridden by competing claims of outsiders. My contention has been that a country like Norway is entitled to exclude prospective immigrants as it sees fit based on freedom of association, which is a component of self-determination. In essence, then, my suggestion is that a legitimate state's right to border control is an element of its self-determination. I think a country's political autonomy is important, but clearly there are other values with which it must compete, so we cannot infer an absolute right to control borders. Many who write on border control allege that even if states enjoy a presumptive claim to limit immigration, this right is clearly overridden in the case of refugees, for instance. I agree that those of us in affluent liberal democracies have stringent duties to come to the rescue of imperiled foreigners, but because I think it would often be permissible to help these refugees in their homelands, I am less inclined than others to assume that refugees necessarily have a decisive claim to immigrate.[18] Others, however, like those who seek to reunite with family members, appear incapable of being accommodated in any fashion other than immigration, so the more general point stands: We should not presume that a legitimate state's presumptive right to freedom of association necessarily gives it a decisive claim to accept or reject all prospective immigrants as it sees fit.

The second potential drawback to my arguments in this section is that, even if they show why a state has a right to limit immigration, they do not necessarily vindicate a state's right to restrict other types of traffic across its borders. To see why, recall that a crucial step in the argument is the relational egalitarian claim that all immigrants must be welcomed as free and equal citizens. Importantly, though, this requirement presumably applies only to those who come and stay indefinitely; there is nothing morally problematic about denying equal citizenship to tourists, visiting students, and business travelers who visit for only a short time. If I travel to Norway for a semester as a visiting professor, for instance, then there seems nothing objectionable about Norway's denying me the right to vote in local elections during my stay. Thus, while one may be able to construct a parallel argument which explains why legitimate states may restrict the entry of tourists and other short-term visitors (one might worry that massive visitation could interfere with the inhabitants' rights of occupancy or self-determination, for instance), it is important to recognize that the arguments featured in this chapter are not on their own sufficient for this task.

Acknowledging these two limitations is important, then, because, while I think the arguments outlined here explain why legitimate states have a presumptive right to limit immigration, the pretheoretic understanding of the right to border control may well be thought to involve an *absolute* right to restrict *all* travel into one's territory. And to the extent that one insists upon clinging to this pretheoretic conception, one may at the very least think my account needs to be supplemented.

4 NATURAL RESOURCES

The territorial right to natural resources is a property right. The basic idea here is that gold, diamonds, oil, and other natural resources within the territorial boundaries of Norway are owned exclusively by Norwegians, so Norwegians are free to unilaterally consume, sell, or otherwise dispose of these resources as they see fit. Once again, the most straightforward way for a functional theorist to defend this right would be to argue that states could not perform their requisite political functions unless they enjoyed exclusive dominion over any and all natural resources within their territories. The obvious problem, though, is that this claim appears patently false. If individual foreigners can own property in Norway without this interfering with Norway's capacity to secure political order, for instance, why cannot everyone in the world own a share of the North Sea oil? So, if we want to explain why citizens necessarily own the natural resources located within their country's territory, we will need a supplemental argument. Others with more imagination may be able to furnish this argument, but I must confess that I cannot.

Given that it is simply a matter of brute luck whether one is born in Norway rather than Sweden, it is hard to fathom why Norwegians have a sufficient moral connection to the North Sea oil which would entitle them, and only them, to conserve or consume it as they see fit.[19] To appreciate this point, consider our intuitions about a very different type of relationship between people and natural resources. Imagine that a volcano in Norway erupts and then steady winds blow the smoke toward Sweden, where it interrupts airline travel for weeks, causing billions of dollars of damage to the economy.[20] Do the

Norwegians owe compensation to the Swedes because "their" volcano caused so much damage to the Swedish economy? Few would think so. It might be different if these same conditions were caused by Norwegian industrial pollution, but it seems far-fetched to say that Norwegians are morally liable to foreigners for expenses caused by the entirely natural eruption of a volcano in Norwegian territory. But if Norwegians are not morally liable for costs imposed on foreigners by natural events which merely happen to occur in Norway, then why think that Norwegians are morally entitled to exclude foreigners from the benefits of natural resources which just happen to be located on or beneath Norwegian soil?[21]

In the absence of the required moral connection between citizens and the natural resources that lie within their country's jurisdictional borders, perhaps a better strategy would be to emphasize the practical difficulties which would result if we failed to treat countries *as if* they owned "their" natural resources. Even if Norway's self-determination would not be significantly undermined if it had no standing to exclude foreigners from attempting to extract the North Sea oil, we could certainly imagine other circumstances in which the domestic populations would be left unacceptably vulnerable. Suppose that vast oil reserves were discovered under Mecca, for instance.[22] Surely Saudi Arabia would be entitled to prohibit foreign companies from buying land in Mecca in order to access these resources. Or consider developing countries that are rich in natural resources but saddled with fragile political institutions. If ever it made sense to say that a domestic population should have the right to exclude foreigners from accessing "its" natural resources, this would seem to be a promising case. Indeed, the movement to enshrine resource rights in international law was motivated precisely by the concern to institutionally protect the constituents of developing countries who were vulnerable to the predatory practices of wealthy states and their business interests.

It is admittedly problematic to say that countries have no claim to exclude outsiders from accessing natural resources within their territorial boundaries when this excavation would undermine the host state's effective capacity to exercise political self-determination, but acknowledging this does not imply that all citizens collectively own the natural resources within their state's territory. More minimally, it indicates only that *some* political communities have the right to *control* the conditions under which these resources are accessed. The first thing to emphasize here is that owning property involves enjoying an extensive constellation of Hohfeldian advantages against others, only one portion of which is control over access.[23] As Chris Armstrong emphasizes:

> we can easily imagine regimes of mixed individual (including foreign), common and state ownership where the state reserved for itself key jurisdictional rights, regulated the extraction, exchange and expatriation of resources, and perhaps taxed owners at each stage, without claiming for itself the status of owner. It would be much too strong to suggest that such a state would not enjoy self-determination.
> (Armstrong 2015: 140)

Thus, even if we agree that Chadians, say, should have the right to exclude foreign companies from accessing natural resources located in Chad, this does not amount to saying that Chadians have a property right to these resources, because (among other things) our conclusion about limited foreign access says nothing about the Chadians' claim to exclusively consume these resources. And secondly, even if we insist that developing countries like Chad are entitled to limit the access of powerful international companies, it does not necessarily follow that an institutionally secure country like Norway has the right to exclude all foreigners from accessing the North Sea oil, especially if foreign countries could effectively operate in this region without undermining Norway's capacity to autonomously govern itself.

Since it is such an interesting scenario, it is worth pausing to comment specifically on the hypothetical case of oil under Mecca. To begin, let me say that I certainly believe that Saudi Arabia is entitled to ensure that foreign companies motivated solely by profit do not destroy this religiously significant city. For several reasons, though, I do not think this example is enough to vindicate citizens' property rights to natural resources. First and most obviously, while I do believe Saudi Arabia has the moral standing to limit the operations of foreign companies, I think it has a *duty*, not merely a *liberty*, to do so. In my view, Saudi Arabia's standing in this case stems from the importance of preserving such a culturally significant environment, rather than any special claim to the resources in question. Consider, for instance, what we would say if there were no Muslims in Saudi Arabia and an entirely Saudi-owned firm wanted to destroy Mecca in order to retrieve the oil. If we believed that the question turned on whether Saudi Arabia has an exclusive claim to this oil, then we would have no objection to the Saudis allowing domestic firms to destroy Mecca. But this does not seem acceptable. It strikes me that, even if Saudi Arabia did not have a single Muslim citizen, it would still have a duty of stewardship, owed to Muslims around the world, to preserve the physical integrity of this holy city.[24]

Thus, while it seems plausible to insist that countries will in many cases have a presumptive right to control the ways in which foreign firms access the natural resources on their territory, I know of no way to supplement the functional approach to political legitimacy which shows why the citizens of these states enjoy exclusive moral dominion over these resources. So, even if Norway should have a decisive say in the manner and rate at which the North Sea oil is extracted, for instance, it is not clear why the Norwegians should not have to share this oil (or the proceeds of its sale) with others. As Margaret Moore, one of the most sophisticated defenders of the link between self-determination and resource rights acknowledges: "At best, the idea of collective self-determination offers a limited and defeasible right to *control* the rules governing the acquisition, transfer and use of natural resources but does not justify a right to the full stream of benefits from the resources" (Moore 2012: 85). As a consequence, even if the citizens of a country should in some cases enjoy the discretion to decide whether, how, and at what rate the local resources are used, it does not follow that these citizens have any grounds on which to object to international taxes or redistributive measures such as Thomas Pogge's Global Resource Dividend (Pogge 2008: 202–21).

Critics may object that these conclusions are radically at odds with common-sense thinking. Leif Wenar, for instance, states that "The idea that the natural resources of a country belong to the people of that country is so intuitive that most will need no more proof than its statement" (Wenar 2008: 10).[25] I must confess, however, that it seems at least as plausible to me to say that natural resources belong to everyone in the world. For the sake of argument, however, let us assume that I am wrong. That is, suppose that Wenar is correct to suggest that virtually everyone is happy to assume without argument that natural resources belong wholly and exclusively to the citizens of the country in which they are found. Even in this case, the issue of resource rights would give us no cause to abandon the functional accounts of political legitimacy, because we would no longer ask accounts of political legitimacy to provide a justification for this particular type of territorial rights, since, by hypothesis, we are happy to simply assume that these rights exist.

In the end, then, while functional accounts of political legitimacy can come reasonably close to justifying the rights of jurisdiction and border control, they appear unable to vindicate resource rights. Does this mean that we should abandon functional accounts of political legitimacy? Some will no doubt think so, but I am more inclined to question whether citizens necessarily enjoy exclusive property rights over the natural resources located within their state's territorial boundaries.

5 Conclusion

Is the functional approach to political legitimacy without supplement from nationalist or transactional considerations ultimately acceptable? It depends. As I have argued in this chapter, functional theory can approximate our pretheoretic convictions regarding a state's territorial rights. Whether one is satisfied with these results will depend on how firmly and closely one wants to cling to the prevailing understanding of these rights. I am comfortable with the functional approach's implications for territorial rights, but I appreciate that others will not be. For them, it will be interesting to see what kinds of competing accounts can be constructed by those more sympathetic to nationalist and/ or transactional theories of political legitimacy.

Acknowledgments

I am grateful to Chris Armstrong, Avery Kolers, David Lefkowitz, Alejandra Mancilla, David Miller, Margaret Moore, Cara Nine, John Simmons, Anna Stilz, and Leif Wenar for very helpful feedback on earlier drafts of this chapter.

Notes

1. See Miller (2012) and Simmons (2013).
2. For a critical assessment of David Miller's nationalist approach, see Stilz (2011).
3. See Simmons (2001).

4. A number of prominent theorists understand human rights more or less in these terms, but a particularly clear explanation and defense of this conception can be found in Buchanan (2004: 118–90).

5. Most theorists insist that a legitimate state must also *respect* the rights of others. One theorist who denies that states can forfeit their legitimacy by disrespecting the rights of outsiders is Arthur Applbaum, but it is important to appreciate that he understands legitimacy narrowly. For Applbaum, legitimacy is solely the right to rule insiders; it does not include a right against outside interference. See Applbaum (2010).

6. This account is developed and defended at greater length in Altman and Wellman (2009).

7. Norway might rightly resist this political divorce if it would not be politically viable after the breakup, so let us assume that both the separatists and the remainder state will be left able and willing to satisfactorily protect human rights.

8. For a full explanation and defense of this account, see Wellman (2005).

9. Meisels (2005) and Miller (2007) press the former, more Lockean line of argument, while Gans (2003) explores the latter.

10. For an excellent analysis and defense of occupancy rights, see Stilz (2013).

11. As a preinstitutional right related to land, the right of occupancy is obviously reminiscent of Locke's understanding of property rights. It is not clear to me, though, to what extent one must establish a morally relevant connection with a given piece of territory before one enjoys this right of occupancy. Does one acquire this right only after one has become sufficiently attached to one's place of residence? Consider, for instance, how we might adjudicate conflicting claims of occupancy. Imagine, for example, that Anna, Betty, and Carol all reside on a small island that can sustain only three people. If Denise then comes to this island, it seems clear that Anna, Betty, and Carol each have a claim to occupy this island which Denise lacks. If the island could sustain more than three people, then none of the three occupants would have a claim to exclude Denise from the territory. But now imagine that the territory could sustain four people, and that Denise arrives by boat just as Anna is giving birth to her child Ellen. Does Ellen have priority over Denise? There are three possible answers. If we think the right of occupancy must parallel Locke's understanding of property, then it appears that Denise has just as much right to stay on the island as Ellen, since Ellen has not done anything to establish a morally significant connection to the land before Denise's arrival. I am not convinced that the right of occupancy must parallel Locke's understanding of property in every respect, though, so I am open to claiming either that Ellen has a stronger claim to occupy the island simply because she was born there or that, even if Ellen's claim is no stronger than Denise's, perhaps Anna has a claim that her child be given priority over Denise. Reasonable people might disagree over these matters, but the purposes of this essay do not require us to settle these disputes here.

12. On political legitimacy, see Wellman (1996).

13. I do not necessarily rule out forcible exile as a criminal punishment.

14. For a similar analysis involving Iraq, see Wellman (2005: 173–4).

15. Notice, for instance, how similar to the nationalist Stilz (2011: 597) appears when she stresses that "Over time, we shape our institutions together with our fellow citizens in accordance with our shared values and principles of justice, even though we did not choose these institutions or these compatriots."

16. As a consent theorist, John Simmons (2001) would also deny Germany's right to evict the occupying forces, but he would do so for very different reasons. On his view, even though both the occupying regime and the Germans are able and willing to perform the relevant

political functions, neither is legitimate because neither has garnered the consent of those who are coerced. For Simmons (2001), a country which has been usurped by an external party has no more of a claim to have "its" territory returned than a slave-owner has a right to reclaim "her" slave from someone who "stole" this slave from her.

17. For a more thorough articulation and defense of this view, see Wellman (2008).
18. For an explanation of our moral responsibilities to refugees, see Wellman and Cole (2011:117–24).
19. As Beitz (1999: 138) puts it: "the fact that someone happens to be located advantageously with respect to natural resources does not provide a reason why he or she should be entitled to exclude others from the benefits that might be derived from them."
20. I owe this example to Alejandra Mancilla (p.c.).
21. Someone like David Miller might object to this analogy on the grounds that, whereas the volcano's smoke is a purely natural occurrence, the revenue from resources does not just naturally appear in citizens' bank accounts; work must be done to transform these natural resources into valuable assets. (These issues raise difficult questions about how we should even conceive of resources. On this topic, see Kolers (2012). Miller (2012) is certainly right to remind us that not all of the economic value of what is produced from natural resources should be attributed to the natural resources themselves, but I still believe that the natural resources retain some value, and I think the volcano example helps motivate the concern that citizens do not necessarily have an exclusive claim to this value.
22. I owe this example to Chris Armstrong (p.c.).
23. On this point, see Honoré (1987).
24. Or imagine that technology enabled foreign countries to extract the oil from 500 miles away. If we stipulated that this extraction would have no discernible impact on Mecca or those who live there, it is no longer so clear why Saudi Arabia should be entitled to prohibit foreigners from accessing the oil.
25. Wenar (p.c.) has emphasized that he does not necessarily believe citizens have exclusive ownership over the natural resources within their states' territory; more modestly, he seems to think only that citizens have some type of claim to control these resources. And for his purposes, he need establish only that illegitimate rulers do not necessarily own these natural resources.

References

Altman, Andrew, and Christopher Heath Wellman (2009) *A Liberal Theory of International Justice*. Oxford: Oxford University Press.

Applbaum, Arthur Isak (2010) "Legitimacy without the Duty to Obey," *Philosophy & Public Affairs* 38(3): 215–39.

Armstrong, Chris (2015) "Against 'Permanent Sovereignty' over Natural Resources," *Politics, Philosophy & Economics* 14: 129–51.

Beitz, Charles (1999) *Political Theory and International Relations*. Princeton, NJ: Princeton University Press.

Buchanan, Allen (2004) *Justice, Legitimacy and Self-Determination*. Oxford: Oxford University Press.

Fine, Sarah (2010) "Freedom of Association Is Not the Answer," *Ethics* 120: 338–56.

Gans, Chaim (2003) *The Limits of Nationalism*. Cambridge: Cambridge University Press.

Honoré, Tony (1987) "Ownership," in *Making Law Bind: Essays Legal and Philosophical*. Oxford: Oxford University Press, 161–92.

Kolers, Avery (2012) "Justice, Territory and Natural Resources," *Political Studies* 60: 269–86.

Meisel,Tamar (2005) *Territorial Rights*. Dordrecht: Springer.

Miller, David (2007) *National Responsibility and Global Justice*. Oxford: Oxford University Press.

Miller, David (2012) "Territorial Rights: Concept and Justification," *Political Studies* 60: 252–68.

Moore, Margaret (2012) "Natural Resources, Territorial Right, and Global Distributive Justice," *Political Theory* 40: 84–107.

Pogge, Thomas (2008) *World Poverty and Human Rights*. 2nd edn. Malden, MA: Polity.

Simmons, John (2001) "On the Territorial Rights of States," *Nous* 35: 300–26.

Simmons, John (2013) "Democratic Authority and the Boundary Problem," *Ratio Juris* 26: 326–57.

Snyder, Louis (1977) *Encyclopedia of Nationalism*. New York: Paragon House.

Stilz, Anna (2011) "Nations, States, and Territory," *Ethics* 121: 572–601.

Stilz, Anna (2013) "Occupancy Rights and the Wrong of Removal," *Philosophy & Public Affairs* 41: 324–56.

Wellman, Christopher Heath (1996) "Liberalism, Samaritanism, and Political Legitimacy," *Philosophy & Public Affairs* 25: 211–37.

Wellman, Christopher Heath (2005) *A Theory of Secession*. New York: Cambridge University Press.

Wellman, Christopher Heath (2008) "Immigration and Freedom of Association," *Ethics* 119: 109–41.

Wellman, Christopher Heath, and Phillip Cole (2011) *Debating the Ethics of Immigration: Is There a Right to Exclude?* New York: Oxford University Press.

Wenar, Leif (2008) "Property Rights and the Resource Curse," *Philosophy & Public Affairs* 36: 2–32.

Further Reading

Armstrong, Chris (2017) *Justice and Natural Resources*. Oxford: Oxford University Press.

Kolers, Avery (2009) *Land, Conflict, and Justice: A Political Theory of Territory*. Cambridge: Cambridge University Press.

Moore, Margaret (2015) *A Political Theory of Territory*. Oxford: Oxford University Press.

Nine, Cara. (2012) *Global Justice and Territory*. Oxford: Oxford University Press.

Simmons, John (2016) *Boundaries of Authority*. Oxford: Oxford University Press.

Stilz, Anna (2019) *Territory Sovereignty: A Philosophical Exploration*. Oxford: Oxford University Press.

Wenar, Leif (2017) *Blood Oil*. Oxford: Oxford University Press.

CHAPTER 21

....

SETTLEMENT AND THE
RIGHT TO EXCLUDE

....

ANNA STILZ

A number of theorists have recently argued for a right to global free movement on moral grounds. One view justifies free movement contingently, as an appropriate remedy for global deprivation or inequality. But a different view suggests that global freedom of movement is an important liberty in itself. This argument usually begins from the importance of freedom of movement domestically.[1] Most theories of human rights hold that it would be unacceptable for the US, say, to deny a citizen who lives in Buffalo the right to move to Boston.[2] Domestic freedom of movement is important in part because it protects access to opportunities: by moving to Boston, the citizen of Buffalo may take a job that did not exist back home, find a more congenial culture or range of activities, or meet like-minded people. But Joseph Carens emphasizes that many of the reasons why the citizen of Buffalo ought to be able to move to Boston could equally ground a reason why the citizen of Buffalo ought to be able to move to Tokyo:

> Every reason why one might want to move within a state may also be a reason for moving between states. One might want a job; one might fall in love with someone from another country; one might want to belong to a religion that has few adherents in one's native state and many in another; one might want to pursue cultural opportunities that are only available in another land.   (Carens 2013: 239)

Kieran Oberman (2014) has argued on similar grounds for a human right to immigrate, which he sees as rooted in a basic human interest in being free to access the full range of existing "life options," including associations, religions, jobs, and marriage partners, some of which may be found in other states. If it is truly to guarantee access to the full range of life options, these theorists argue that the right to free movement must be global in scope.

Let us call this the *freedom-based* argument for cross-border movement, to distinguish it from positions that justify free movement as a response to inequality or poverty.

While freedom-based theorists often reference the case of poor migrants seeking to move to wealthy countries, technically, their view implies a much broader thesis: everyone—including the highly advantaged—should have a right to move wherever they wish. If inequalities between states were greatly reduced or even eliminated, there would remain a right to move on freedom-based grounds.[3] Further, the freedom-based view implies not just a right to travel to other countries, but also a right to settle there permanently: "in principle, borders should generally be open and people should normally be free to leave their country of origin and settle in another" (Carens 2013: 225). On this view, a person's freedom to access opportunities in other countries ought to be unrestricted, unless very good reasons can be given for restricting it.

Though one could raise doubts about the freedom-based view, I largely adopt the account's assumptions for the purposes of this chapter. The idea is worth exploring: it has sophisticated defenders, and it is garnering increasing support. Here, I ask an applied, institutional question about it: can a right to global free movement be reconciled with other people's rights of *territorial occupancy*? By a right of territorial occupancy, I refer to the right of people who not unjustly reside in in a country to stay there, and to continue leading the lives they have built in that particular place.[4] This includes residents' claim to participate in the social, cultural, and economic practices ongoing in their area, and to be immune from interference with their residence on and use of that space. Acts like expulsion, removal, and dispossession are wrong because they violate territorial occupancy rights.

Historically, we can cite many examples of migration flows that involved similarly devastating effects on native inhabitants' ability to maintain their social, cultural, and economic practices, and sometimes even to continue residing on their territory. An example is the population flows associated with *settler colonialism*. Settler colonialism involves the transfer of migrants onto a territory with the aim of acquiring control of an area.[5] It is tendentious to suggest that proponents of global free movement are advocating anything like settler colonialism, and I am not trying to suggest this. As Joseph Carens stresses, his argument for open borders is "an argument about the moral claims of ordinary, peaceful people seeking to build decent, secure lives for themselves and their families" (Carens 2013: 276). Indeed, in recent work, Carens (2013: 229–31, 297–313) has redescribed his open borders position as an ideal for a fully just world, and has restricted his prescriptions to North America and Europe.[6] Still, settler colonialism is an interesting case. Unlike Carens, other theorists wish to apply the freedom-based argument to our own world, and to all states.[7] Against this background, settlement raises intriguing questions about how we ought to conceptualize the scope and limits of a possible right to free movement. How broadly or narrowly should our global freedoms extend?

It seems doubtful that receiving countries have even a non-enforceable moral duty to admit people who are likely to be settler colonists. Yet if they do not, this would considerably narrow the scope of a possible right to global free movement. Both Carens and Oberman accept that social costs can sometimes justify restricting freedom of movement, though they see the range of costs that are weighty enough to justify restrictions as quite limited.[8] This chapter argues for an important expansion to this range: if global free movement is not simply to recreate the domination and exploitation that have tragically characterized the population flows of the past, it must allow for the permissible exclusion of potential colonists. Yet who counts as a potential colonist turns out to be a tricky question to answer. Rather than rejecting the case for global free movement, then, my strategy here is to define a "colonial" exception to it, in a way that protects foreigners' legitimate interests in crossing borders while avoiding tragic costs for indigenous populations. I should stress at the outset that nothing I say here touches the poverty-based case for freer migration. Instead, I focus only on the freedom-based account, and—for the most part—on the neglected case of relatively well-off people seeking to migrate to less powerful communities.

The chapter is structured as follows. In Section 1, I describe two historical cases of colonial settlement, in the US and Israel/Palestine. My aim here is not to provide a full treatment—beyond the scope of the chapter in any case—but rather to sketch enough detail to illustrate the moral complexity of these processes. In Section 2, I say more about the nature of the occupancy rights that I attribute to indigenous inhabitants. In particular, I stress that occupancy rights are not necessarily exclusive, though they may generate a contingent right to exclude under certain conditions. The key question is: what are the relevant conditions? At what point, if at all, does a flow of migrants begin to undermine current occupants' claims on the land? In Section 3, I consider three possibilities: (1) when newcomers fail to assimilate to the local language and culture, (2) when newcomers migrate as part of a *project* of political domination, and (3) when newcomers severely damage the life-plans of current inhabitants. (These hypotheses are not mutually exclusive: occupants' claims may be undermined by some combination of these three effects).

1 Two Cases

I begin with a brief description of the history of settlement in the US and Israel/Palestine. Including this history is important because it helps us to see that colonial settlement is not as easy to distinguish from "normal" immigration as one might think. Often settlement projects start slowly, with a scattered flow of individuals seeking to migrate and stay in another land. If there is indeed a right to global free movement, it is hard to see why these unstructured processes are objectionable (and, indeed, perhaps they are not). Moreover, there are many similarities between immigrants and settler colonists. Like immigrants, colonists are often culturally distinct from the population of the receiving society. They may come from countries with different levels of socioeconomic development, or different religions, mores, or traditions. Both colonists and immigrants often settle together in distinctive enclaves that are relatively enclosed from the majority population. Finally, both immigration and settlement can induce significant social, political, and economic changes in the host society. It is worth appreciating this moral complexity.

In both the US and Israel/Palestine, the earliest phases of colonial settlement were characterized by a flow of migrants who engaged in mostly contractual exchanges with indigenous inhabitants to obtain land. In the early US, as Stuart Banner (2005: 26) puts it, "from Maine to Georgia, the ordinary way to acquire Native American land was to buy it."[9] This was not the only method—some areas were conquered, and sometimes settlements were founded on what colonists took to be "waste" ground. Still, most land acquisitions in the pre-revolutionary period proceeded via written contract, and many transactions were reasonably free and fair. A good example is William Penn's purchase of land for the colony of Pennsylvania. Penn acknowledged the Lenape tribe as legitimate owners, and permitted settlement only where he had previously bought land from them. He also paid reasonable prices, and since they had more land than they could use, the Lenape were eager to sell for coveted European trade goods.[10] Some early transactions were only quasi-voluntary. Initially, Native Americans did not understand European property concepts, and thought that they were offering to share territory rather than alienating it, though they appear to have quickly caught on. Later, some transactions were marred by fraud: Native Americans were made drunk in order to sell land, deeds misdescribed the parcel sold, or land was purchased from individuals who lacked clearly defined authority to alienate it. Still, the initial settlement of the eastern US for the most part occurred in a piecemeal fashion through contractual land sales.

The first waves of Jewish settlement in Palestine unfolded similarly. Small groups of Jews left Eastern Europe following pogroms in the 1880s, and bought land from the native Arabs in order to establish agricultural settlements. From 1881 to 1903 about 20,000–30,000 people came to Palestine in this fashion.[11] In 1897, the World Zionist Organization was founded in Basle with the program of creating "a home for the Jewish people in Palestine to be secured by public law" (Smith 2010: 31). At this point, Zionism became an organized movement with the goal of establishing a territorial base for the Jewish people in Palestine, though it was not clear until 1942 that the movement aimed at independent statehood.[12] A second wave of immigrants—also precipitated by a wave of pogroms—came between 1904 and 1914. These people generally entered the Ottoman Empire as tourists or pilgrims and, once there, bought land in order to settle permanently. In 1901 the Jewish National Fund was established to coordinate these land purchases and to ensure that land, once bought, would remain in Jewish hands. Often land was acquired from wealthy Arabs who were non-resident landowners. Tenant farmers who had traditionally cultivated the land were usually expelled when it was turned over. The first two waves of Jewish settlers lived interspersed with the Arab inhabitants and in regular contact with them.[13]

In both these cases, the initial outcome of colonization was the establishment of scattered settlements of newcomers intermixed with the native population. Yet the settlers—who were wealthier, more technologically advanced, and better politically organized—quickly became the dominant political, social, and economic force in the new land. Native Americans became dependent on English colonists for access to trade goods that that were central to their new lifestyles but that they were unable to manufacture themselves, leading to a vicious cycle of land-selling that impoverished them.[14]

After the American Revolution, many tribes were treated as defeated enemies who had fought on the side of the British, and whose land could be confiscated by force. In a series of "treaties" dictated in the mid-1780s, large areas east of the Mississippi were confiscated from them without compensation. A similar dynamic characterized mandatory Palestine. Jewish settlers were much better off than Arabs, so they tended to be their employers and landlords. They were also much better politically organized, and in 1917 were able to gain Great Power backing for their project with Britain's Balfour Declaration, which stated its support for "the establishment in Palestine of a national home for the Jewish people." Britain continued to support Jewish immigration to the region until the late 1930s. In both cases, once initial settlement had occurred, the newcomers quickly began to behave in a superior manner toward the natives. An integrated, relatively equal society proved very difficult to establish.

Later, both settlement projects turned to more forceful methods. By 1815, the US had effectively destroyed most of the Native American communities east of the Mississippi, though native peoples remained a powerful force in the West. In 1825, the US designated the area west of the Mississippi as "permanent Indian Country," reserving it for the sole occupation of Native Americans, and removed all remaining Eastern tribes to this region. Though removal treaties were negotiated with the Cherokee, Creek, and Chickasaw, and some compensation paid for their lands, in practice these treaties were dictated, and the relocation process was brutal. In 1838, around 15,000 Cherokees were forced from their homes, gathered into detention forts, and marched to Indian Territory. Traveling in inadequate clothing through a harsh winter, they encountered freezing temperatures, impassable roads, famine, and sickness. An estimated 4,000 people died on the journey.[15]

A similar expulsion phase occurred in Israel/Palestine. After the Holocaust, the Jewish community demanded a sovereign state in Palestine to which European refugees could be relocated. Britain handed over the issue to the United Nations, which recommended that Palestine be partitioned. When Israel declared independence in 1948, the surrounding Arab states invaded. In the course of the war, 750,000 Palestinians fled or were expelled from the new state. Some left voluntarily, fearing Arab-Jewish civil conflict, but many were deliberately pushed out by the Israeli army, which cleared certain areas of their Arab residents.[16] Very few were allowed back after hostilities ceased. About half of the Palestinian Arab community became refugees, scattered through the West Bank, the Gaza Strip, Jordan, Syria, and Lebanon. They were dispossessed of their property and left with little control over many aspects of their lives.[17] Many Palestinians still live in refugee camps today, and some face host-country restrictions barring them from many occupations, from owning property, or petitioning for citizenship.[18]

Finally, both cases saw a third phase of renewed post-expulsion settlement. In the 1840s, American pioneers began to cross "permanent Indian Country" in ever greater numbers, travelling to Oregon and California in the gold rush. Destroying the buffalo, these emigrants quickly jeopardized the Plain Indians' way of life, which led to skirmishes between the two groups. In reaction, the US federal government abandoned any concept of a territorial line dividing areas of white settlement from independent Indian

Country, and instead developed a reservation policy. Reservations were small parcels of land "reserved" out of the original holdings of the Native Americans (or sometimes not even part of their original home territories), where Native Americans were resettled, usually following brutal wars of conquest and subjugation. Initially conceived as a temporary expedient to assimilate Native Americans into mainstream society, reservations quickly became a permanent feature of Native American life.

Once on reservations, Native Americans were subjected to various paternalizing interventions at the hands of the US federal government. Children were taken from their parents and sent to off-reservation boarding schools, where they were forced to cut their hair, to wear suits and dresses, to learn English, and given Christian names. All affairs on the reservation were administered by federal agents from the US Bureau of Indian Affairs. Native Americans economic practices were also transformed: they were forced to lead a sedentary life, not to roam; and required to farm rather than hunt. And in 1887, tribally owned land was converted to fee simple property under the Dawes Act, and tribal political structures were banned.[19] As a result of these interventions, many Native Americans became dispirited and lost all sense of a meaningful life. They saw their culture, economy, and political system destroyed in a very short period of time. By the 1920s, the Native American population was decimated. Those who remained largely lived in poverty, ill health, and despair.

Settlement in Israel has similarly involved an initial dividing line (the Green Line) that was later politically abandoned. In 1967, Israel occupied the West Bank, Sinai, and Golan Heights in the Six Day War. Initially it seemed that these lands would be restored to Palestinians in exchange for a permanent peace. But beginning in the mid-1970s, a mass religious movement (Gush Emunim) began to call for Jewish settlement throughout the biblical land of Israel. They had in part a strategic rationale, intending to lessen the amount of territory that might be designated for future Palestinian rule. This settler movement was largely successful in pressuring the Israeli government to grant them permits to stay in the occupied territories, or to legitimize the illegal settlements that they de facto created.[20] The construction of these new settlements has greatly changed the landscape of the occupied West Bank. Jewish apartment buildings and highways built to serve the settlements now run throughout the country, and these settlements have been integrated into the legal and government structure of Israel proper. Jews and Palestinians live intermixed on the territory of the West Bank, though in largely separate enclaves.[21] Currently, there are 400,000 Jewish settlers in the West Bank, about 17% of the population.[22] It remains to be seen what the final outcome of this Israeli occupation will be, and whether the settlements will be dismantled in a final status agreement, or whether they will form the basis for a renewed politics of dispossession and imperial rule.

The narrative I have offered is a highly compressed outline of these events. Many books have been written about the episodes sketched here, and one could add a great deal more nuance and complexity. Still, I think this basic summary adds welcome concreteness to our theorizing about cross-border movement. While the proponents of global free movement would, of course, condemn most of these events, these cases raise complicated questions for their view. For if there is a human right to free movement, then at least the first elements in this story—the initial migration and establishment of settler enclaves—would seem to be morally unobjectionable. Indeed, on the freedom-based view, Native Americans and Palestinians may have had a *moral duty* to allow British and Jewish settlers to come and stay in their lands. At what point in the narrative might it have become permissible for the natives to have excluded new migrants? And would this point have come too late, in terms of forestalling the dynamics of domination and exploitation that later unfolded between these communities?

2 TERRITORIAL OCCUPANCY RIGHTS

Many people would say that in both these cases lands rightfully belonging to the indigenous inhabitants were stolen from them by the settlers. This way of speaking is popular among the colonized themselves, as an interview with an Israeli Arab politician attests:

> At the end of the day, the ones with the superior right to the land are the natives, not the immigrants—the ones who have lived here for hundreds of years and have become part of the land just as the land has become a part of them.
> (Interview with Mohammed Dahla, quoted in Shavit 2013: 315)

But in what sense, if any, did the land of Palestine or North America "belong" to its prior inhabitants?

I believe that these lands did "belong" to their inhabitants, though in a rather weak sense. In my view, inhabitants do not *own* their country; rather, they have rights of *occupancy* in it.[23] While less robust than a property right, occupancy does have some "property-like" qualities. An occupancy right comprises two main elements:

> *First*, a liberty to reside permanently in a particular geographical space, and to make use of that space for social, cultural, and economic practices. This extends to the liberty to travel freely through the area in order to access the places in civil society where those practices occur. (An occupancy right does not confer liberty of access to others' private property, but it does entitle one to access public spaces, e.g. parks, roads, byways, as well as businesses or buildings that offer services to the general public, whether publicly or privately owned).
>
> *Second*, a claim-right against others not to remove one from that area, and not to interfere with one's use of the space in ways that undermine the shared social practices in which one is engaged.

While occupancy does confer some "property-like" incidents—namely, claims to secure access, use, and possession of a particular geographical area—it is distinct from an ownership right.[24] Occupancy rights are not exclusive: many people can share occupancy of the same area, and occupancy does not confer rights to alienate, to derive income, and so on. Still, the fact that inhabitants have occupancy rights in their territory is important: though they do not fully "own" their country, local inhabitants have special claims to live there, and that is why actions like removal, ethnic cleansing, and exile are wrong.

What grounds occupancy rights, and makes them important? I believe that the claim to territorial occupancy is rooted in the role that geographical space plays in individuals' most important projects and relationships. Many of our comprehensive goals require us to form expectations about the use of, and secure access to, a permanent place of residence. Geography and climate may affect the economic and subsistence practices we take up, making it difficult for us to reconstitute those in some very different place. Our religious, cultural, and recreational activities also often have territorial components. Finally, people form personal bonds and enter work, religious, and friendship relations in part because they expect to remain spatially arranged in certain ways. We structure our daily activities and associate together under the assumption that current patterns of residence will not be massively disrupted. I call these situated goals, relationships, and pursuits our *located life-plans*.

We can separate out several significant categories of located life-plans:

(1) *Economic practices.* Many economic practices can only be carried on in a territory with certain geological, ecological, or infrastructural characteristics. The Sioux economy was based on hunting wild buffalo, so they had an interest in living somewhere that could sustain these animals. Many modern Americans work in white-collar professional jobs, so they have an interest in living where there is office space, Internet access, etc.

(2) *Membership in religious, social, cultural, educational organizations.* Many located life- plans require individuals to have access to spaces that are shared with other people. For a person to have the option to pursue a religious, recreational, educational, or work activity means being able to access the physical spaces and infrastructure—churches, mosques, schools, meeting houses, and so on—where these activities occur.

(3) *Personal Relationships.* People are engaged in networks of relationships—with colleagues, family, and friends—that are fundamental to their well-being. They have an interest in continuing these relationships with the particular people who matter to them, and that requires living near enough to do so. Since individuals are tied to differing networks, it is difficult to draw bounds around communities such that we could move all and only these people without breaking any personal ties. Sustaining people's important personal relationships requires maintaining their current spatial arrangements to a significant degree.

(4) *Attachment to locality*: Some, though not all people have fundamental projects based on a special identification with a unique locality. The Taos Pueblo's religious rituals center on Blue Lake, the Sioux attribute spiritual significance to the Black Hills, and the Highland culture of Switzerland is focused specifically on the Alps.

Because people have an interest in pursuing the projects and relationships central to their lives, they also have an interest in the background conditions necessary to carry them out, one of which is stable territorial occupancy. If occupancy of a particular place is fundamental to a person's located life-plans, and if he has established these plans without wrongdoing—including not expelling prior inhabitants, undermining their social, cultural, and economic practices, or infringing foreigners' claims to an equitable distribution of space, as in Section 3.3—then I believe he has a right to occupy that place. I understand this as a *preinstitutional* moral right: occupancy is not the product of positive law, or of a society's conventional practices.

I should stress that on my view the bearers of occupancy rights are individuals, not national groups. People living in close proximity to one another may have interests in different spaces and participate in different practices, yet share occupancy rights in roughly the same area. A Cuban immigrant may have a claim to live in Miami because it contains his family, his workplace, his Catholic church, and his fellow Spanish speakers, while a Jewish Miamian may have an occupancy claim in the same area because it contains his soccer club, his synagogue, and his school. Though there is little overlap between the social practices in which these two people participate, each has a right to live *in Miami* because it contains shared spaces that are fundamental to him. Nor does length of time in the territory matter: as long as his located life- plans were not unjustly formed, a recent immigrant's occupancy right is just as valid as a descendant of long-standing natives. Unlike nationalist theorists, then, I do not attribute the right to occupy territory to a transgenerational, culturally unified group.[25] Instead, on my view, it is the individual inhabitants of a place who are the ultimate possessors of it, and people with diverse cultural attachments may share occupancy rights in the same space.

Finally, it is important for our purposes to note that the occupancy rights of local inhabitants do not necessarily extend to a right to exclude outsiders from access to their territory. If outsiders' entry is not disruptive to the prior occupants' residence and their ability to participate in valued social practices, then it does not infringe their occupancy rights. Because occupancy is not an *exclusive* right, outsiders may even settle on previously occupied territory, as long as the area can accommodate additional persons, and as long as their settlement does not harm current occupants' legitimate interests. This is another sense in which an occupancy right is less robust than an ownership right: instead, it is more like a right to a library carrel. One has a right to securely occupy one's carrel, free from interference, for as long as one is using it. This is not just a right to occupy the carrel while one's body is in the chair, but also, for example, a right to get up and find a book and return to the carrel one has claimed. But a use-right over one's carrel does not extend to the power to exclude other people from legitimate uses of the library. They may occupy other unclaimed carrels, or travel past one's desk in search of a book. Similarly, foreigners' claims to global free movement may often be consistent with the native inhabitants' rights to land. But the key question is: under what conditions? Certain forms of access—population flows that disrupt inhabitants' residence or destroy their social practices—do infringe local occupancy rights. Removal or expulsion are obvious examples. Here I am primarily interested in less striking ways one can subvert people's located life-plans. For example, one can interfere with their use of geographical space in ways that undermine the located social practices in which they are involved. Do these acts constitute violations of occupancy rights? And at what point precisely does such an infringement occur?

Before taking up this question, I offer a clarificatory remark. For the purposes of this chapter, I am interested in whether territorial occupancy *alone* can justify excluding would-be migrants. I make no appeal to sovereignty-based claims to exercise discretionary control over immigration. Thinkers such as Michael Walzer (1983: 31–63) and Christopher Wellman (2008) have argued that sovereign communities have claims of political self-determination to control the character of their membership, which entitles them to exclude migrants. If their view is correct, this may provide an additional justification for exclusion rights. Still, an occupancy-based justification is worth investigating separately. As I conceptualize occupancy, it is a moral right held even by people who lack sovereign institutions—e.g. nonstate tribes, or populations subject to military occupation or imperial rule. Since neither of the groups in our historical examples had an independent state at the time of settlement, this case seems worth exploring. Making the moral right to exclude settlers dependent on Westphalian sovereignty would unduly disadvantage nonstate groups. So, for now, I focus on the occupancy-based case, remaining agnostic about whether sovereignty might ground an additional reason to exclude.

3 WRONGFUL VIOLATIONS

Consider a continuum of possible interactions a newcomer might have with current territorial occupants, starting with a request to travel through their region and extending all the way to forced removal. Does simple entry into someone else's territory violate occupancy? No: again, occupancy rights are not exclusive. I believe that current occupants have a standing obligation to accept outsiders whose entry would be harmless to their practices, just as the carrel user has a standing obligation to allow other uses of the library. Much contemporary movement *is* harmless, so this standing obligation is not trivial. Rightful occupants have prima facie duties to allow outsiders to enter for travel, study abroad, business trips, visits to friends, relatives, and associates, and so on. Still, this position is compatible with holding that the occupants of a territory have rights to exclude *in certain circumstances*, namely when outsiders' entry would be harmful to their legitimate interests.

What about migrants who intend to permanently settle in the territory? On the located life-plans account, *modulo* qualifications about numbers and consequences, some permanent settlement also seems innocuous. Suppose the United States government admits some new immigrants to American territory. Does this undermine my ability to reside where I do, or to participate in the social practices that are important to me? No. It may bring new people into my immediate environment, with different practices or cultural heritage from those I am used to. But this fact does not undermine *my* ability to live in my hometown, speak my language, attend my church, work in my job, or associate with my friends and family.

One might object that I am assuming (perhaps unjustifiably) that increases in population density and heterogeneity alone do not threaten our occupancy rights. Yet in a community of cattle ranchers, adding additional residents would quickly threaten the community's viability. I concede this. But I believe that density and heterogeneity become important only in so far as they threaten harms to valuable social practices; they are not significant in themselves. Moreover, the threshold at which density and heterogeneity begin to matter depends heavily on the character of a community's practices. In a community of urbanites, one might be able to increase the population density without undermining anyone's located life-plans. Since I discuss harms to located practices in Section 3.3, I set aside this point for now.

One might also hold that a duty to allow migrants to settle permanently seems most plausible in cases where those migrants come as individuals, not as an organized group, where they disperse throughout the receiving territory, and where they assimilate into the dominant language and culture. Our intuition is that such "normal" immigration is permissible, while colonial settlement is morally problematic. But how do we draw the line? Let me explore three hypotheses: (1) unlike immigrants, colonial settlers refuse to assimilate to the natives' language and culture; (2) unlike immigrants, colonial settlers come with a *project* of political domination; or (3) unlike immigrants, colonial settlers severely damage the prior inhabitants' located life- plans. Again, these hypotheses are not mutually exclusive: it could be that the wrong of colonial settlement rests on some combination of these facts.

3.1 Culture

Does the intention to culturally assimilate explain the distinction between legitimate immigrants and wrongful settlers? Will Kymlicka (1995: 15) has argued that colonial settlers "have no expectation of integrating into another culture, but rather aim to reproduce their original society in a new land."[26] He holds that that migrants can reasonably be expected to waive their linguistic and cultural rights as a condition of entry into a new territory. Similarly, Philippe Van Parijs sees a "colonial" attitude where newcomers fail to adapt to the local language. For him, the newcomer should adjust to the locals, "rather than the other way round" (Van Parijs 2011: 133). Both thinkers hold that the locals' claims to territory extend to a claim to make others' assimilation into their language and culture a condition of entry.

I doubt that the intention to culturally assimilate draws the line between immigration and settler colonialism in the right place. Intuitively, there seem to be many cases where newcomers settle together in linguistically or culturally distinct enclaves, yet without violating the occupancy rights of prior inhabitants. Consider Cuban refugees in Miami, who have substantially recreated Spanish-speaking institutions; Amish or Mennonite communities; Orthodox Jewish communities on Long Island; or Indian and Lebanese diaspora trading communities in Africa and South America. Do these people violate the occupancy rights of other residents by significantly preserving their distinctive culture? It is hard to see how: the previous residents could live where they always had, and continue their cultural, social, and economic practices unscathed.

One might object that there is a difference between maintaining one's language and culture in the private sphere, and using state institutions—like public schools—to reproduce and disseminate it. Perhaps what distinguishes settlers from immigrants is their desire to use institutions in this way. But—controversially—I believe it is often permissible to use public institutions to reproduce one's language or culture, so long as this project is compatible with the state's pursuit of its legitimate public purposes. I concede that the state has reasons of democratic participation and equality of opportunity to ensure that its citizens enjoy sufficient proficiency in a common language, for example. But I doubt these reasons suffice to ground a requirement of linguistic homogeneity throughout the state's territory. So, if new migrants use public institutions to preserve their language alongside the common language—say, by settling together in migrant neighborhoods, where they establish bilingual signage and bilingual schooling—it is hard to see how they infringe other people's rights to land in doing so. Unlike Kymlicka and Van Parijs, then, I deny that the local inhabitants' claims to territory extend to the right to ensure that their culture indefinitely enjoys paramount status within that region. As long as migrants are willing to acquire the competences necessary for the government to carry out its essential legitimating functions, locals are not wronged if migrants fail to assimilate more fully.

What is distinctive about the enclaves mentioned above (Miami Cubans, Amish and Mennonites, Orthodox Jews, and so on) is that their located life-plans—while different from the life-plans of the locals—are more or less compatible with them. For that reason, the enclave's establishment did not jeopardize prior inhabitants' ability to use the area for their valued social, cultural, and economic practices. In this case, different sets of social, cultural, and economic practices are *corealizable* in a roughly shared space. Surely the existence of a Mexican neighborhood across town—with its different prevailing language, cuisine, and cultural traditions—does not undermine my ability to sustain the social, cultural, and economic practices that are fundamental to me.

3.2 Political Domination

Next, I consider our second hypothesis, which suggests that unlike immigrants, colonial settlers characteristically come with a *project* of establishing political domination. Certainly this explains much of what seems troubling about our historical cases, and it is likely to strike most people as the primary wrong. Settlement projects usually transfer migrants onto a territory with a specific aim: eventually establishing political control of the area.

Lea Ypi has attempted to theorize the injustice of colonialism, in this vein, as a form of political domination, without postulating the existence of any local rights to territory. Instead, she argues that what is wrong with colonialism is its imposition of a form of political association that "denies its members equal and reciprocal terms of cooperation" (Ypi 2013: 158). Equality and reciprocity, as she understands these values, require a fair process of interaction in establishing political institutions, which necessitates the consent of those who are prospective parties to the new arrangement (Ypi 2013: 179). It is unjust to politically incorporate groups who are unwilling to associate with us. If newcomers are party to a colonizing project of this kind, then it seems permissible to exclude them even where their reasons for entry would otherwise be compelling.

It is important to note that a colonizing project need not be undertaken by a foreign power. Consider the ongoing settlement of Han Chinese in Tibet. Like the US settlement of the West, this is a case of "internal colonialism": the government is supporting the massive influx of majority nationals into an area largely inhabited by a cultural minority, by paying them to relocate there. The main goal of this project is to create a local Chinese majority to forestall Tibetan political autonomy. As a result, Tibetans find it difficult to continue living in their native towns, because they are priced out, to continue their economic practices, because Han Chinese are preferentially hired, and to speak their language and sustain their cultural practices.

I agree that one reason why settler colonialism is wrong is that it usually aims at political domination. Whether or not one's migration has harmful effects on the local inhabitants, it is wrong to come to a place with the intent to control the area against the will of its inhabitants. Since most "normal" immigrants do not aim at political domination, this might seem sufficient to distinguish them from wrongful settlers. Yet it also is characteristic of settler colonialism—as opposed to other forms of empire—to engage in widespread dispossession of native inhabitants and interference with their use of land. It is possible to interfere with people's *use of land*, however, without *politically ruling* them: for example, one can simply appropriate their territory and force them to move elsewhere. Indeed, this is what settlers in America and Israel actually did: Native Americans and Palestinians were not subjected to alien political control until relatively late in our narrative. Until then, they remained politically autonomous, but saw their use of land undermined by settlers. So is interference with the local inhabitants' use of land an additional wrong? To answer this question, we must investigate the harm that settler colonialism often causes to inhabitants' territorially based practices.

3.3 Damage to Territorially Based Practices

To investigate this issue I turn to our third hypothesis, which holds that unlike "normal" immigrants, colonial settlers severely damage the prior inhabitants' located life-plans. Recall that located life-plans are territorially based goals and projects that usually depend on collective practices, and play an important role in structuring individual well-being. When large numbers of newcomers enter at once, it can become difficult for local inhabitants to maintain their located life-plans. Consider once again the case of white settlers moving west across the Plains. By driving away the buffalo, they destroyed the hunting patterns of the Plains tribes, causing them to face starvation and economic collapse. Are occupancy rights violated here, when inhabitants' economic and social practices are significantly impaired by newcomers' arrival? According to our third hypothesis, the answer is yes. Yet in the Plains Indians case, these harms were not inflicted as part of a project of political domination. The settlers aimed to make it to Oregon or California; they were not explicitly setting out to exercise political control over the Native Americans. As Avery Kolers (2009: 61) puts it, "antagonists in territorial disputes are often fighting not just for a piece of land, but for their ability to be who they are and live as they 'always' have." On our third view, occupancy rights are infringed when a flow of newcomers significantly impairs local inhabitants' way of life.

Our third hypothesis can be articulated in more and less plausible ways, and it is important to consider its most compelling formulation. "Normal" immigration changes local practices too: just consider how Mexican food has increasingly become incorporated into the American diet. Other people affect us all the time, and it would be implausible to suggest that rights are violated whenever our plans change as a result of contact with them. Some of these effects are innocuous: if more people begin to use my neighborhood, and I can no longer park in front of my house, I may have to change my plans, but I cannot complain that my rights have been violated. A plausible formulation of the second hypothesis will limit it to *significant* harms to *comprehensive* plans that are *fundamental* to our lives. Not all located life-plans are equally important in grounding a claim to territorial occupancy. Some plans are *comprehensive*, in the sense that they organize many choices, and are integral to our sense of our lives as our own. Careers or economic pursuits, family, friendships, and other personal relationships, religious or cultural activities, and political and educational endeavors are good examples of comprehensive projects. Other life-plans are *peripheral*: they do not structure many choices and do not contribute to our sense of our lives as our own. What color to paint my house, what to have for dinner, and which supermarket to shop in are good examples of peripheral plans. Our well-being is not particularly threatened by changes in our peripheral plans, since they are normally of little weight. But migration can be highly threatening to the well-being of local inhabitants when it significantly damages their comprehensive life-plans, by causing them to lose their jobs, destroying their culture or religion, or revolutionizing their political system.

When formulated in terms of significant harms to comprehensive life-plans, I believe our third hypothesis has considerable force. After all, the key reason we recognize occupancy rights in the first place is to guarantee inhabitants territorially stable access to the collective practices on which their comprehensive goals—and thus their well-being—significantly depend. It therefore seems plausible that an occupancy right would underwrite a pro tanto case for excluding outsiders when those outsiders' entry threatens severe harms to locals' located life-plans.

One might object here, however, that the life-plans argument cuts both ways: perhaps the project of relocation plays as important a role in the life of a migrant as located life-plans play in the lives of the locals. As the lives of American pioneers show, relocation can be a very important goal. In balancing their own located life-plans against the projects of prospective migrants, must local inhabitants grant the migrants' plans equal weight? I doubt it, for two reasons. First, while the endeavors of current inhabitants are *attachments* that *already* figure centrally in their lives, the projects of migrants are mere *possibilities* that they desire to see realized in the *future*.[27] Other things equal, it seems reasonable to prioritize avoiding the destruction of people's existing attachments over disappointing their future desires, since attachments play a far greater role in people's well-being than possibilities do. It is far easier to adjust to the news that I did not receive a new job for which I had applied than it is to adjust to the news that I have just been fired. It is far harder to cope with the loss of my best friend than to cope with the loss of someone with whom I hoped to become friends in the future. Even viewed impartially, then, there are compelling reasons to grant existing located life-plans greater weight than the project of establishing such plans somewhere in the future. Second, I doubt that the locals are obliged to view their own projects completely impartially with the projects of everyone else around the world. People have a moral prerogative to show some partiality to their projects. That prerogative is not infinite, of course, but faced with two projects of equal importance—the first in one's own life and the second in the life of a prospective migrant—it is not unreasonable, all else being equal, for the local to grant her own project greater weight in her practical deliberations. For example, it is permissible for her to devote more time and energy to her project. By parity of reasoning, local inhabitants may prioritize, to some extent, their located life-plans over the life-plans of would-be newcomers.[28]

Still, there may be times when, all things considered, locals are obliged to accept even significant harms to their located life-plans in order to accommodate newcomers. If would-be migrants are economic or political refugees, for example, or have some other very urgent reason for coming, might that not outweigh the prior occupants' interests in maintaining their social, cultural, and economic practices?

If occupancy rights are to be generally justifiable, locals must acknowledge that geographical space is a scarce resource, and other people have claims to a fair share of it. Just like locals, then, outsiders have parallel rights to an adequate share of space in which to lead flourishing lives. So if would-be migrants currently lack a space in which to form and carry out located life-plans, then locals cannot cite damage to their collective practices as a reason for excluding them. What makes a territory sufficient for a flourishing life is a complex question, which I cannot hope to fully answer here. Let me simply highlight two types of means—*material* and *social*—that an adequate territory must possess. First, if would-be migrants are to be permissibly excluded, locals must show that they possess sufficient material resources where they come from. Each person must live in a space where his subsistence needs are guaranteed, i.e. he disposes of adequate food, shelter, basic health, and a livable environment. If outsiders lack these basic material resources, then locals are obliged to share their territory with them, or to provide these resources in some other manner. Second, if would-be migrants are to be permissibly excluded, locals must also show that their current territorial base guarantees them sufficient *social resources*.[29] This includes political institutions that ensure (1) their personal security is protected, i.e. they are free from torture, arbitrary imprisonment, or threats to basic liberty and safety; and (2) their most basic interests in life-plans are guaranteed—they can practice their religion and culture, and associate together with others, including being free to establish long-term family relationships. If outsiders lack these minimal social resources, then again, locals will be obliged to share their territory with them, or provide these resources in some other way. The main idea is that where prospective migrants lack a territorial base on earth that provides them with the resources necessary to lead flourishing lives, current inhabitants cannot appeal to their occupancy rights to refuse them entry, since these other people have equally valid conflicting claims to a share of space. Responding to others' conflicting claims may require accepting even severe harms to local practices. Chaim Gans (2008: 37–47 applies this justification to Jews fleeing pogroms and Nazi persecution: if he is right, then at least some Jewish settlers did not count as colonists—instead, they were refugees that Palestine was obliged to accept.

So there is an important distribution constraint on occupancy rights, which limits current occupants' ability to appeal to harms to their collective practices as a justification for excluding would-be migrants. Still, there is a significant range of cases where the distribution constraint is not in play. Think again of US pioneers crossing the Great Plains, or of present-day settlement in Israel's occupied territories. These are cases where prospective migrants have a perfectly adequate "territorial base" somewhere else, and they lack any particularly urgent interest in moving. They are not economic or political refugees; instead, they move in pursuit of greater wealth, low-cost housing, the achievement of nationalist goals, or simply a sense of adventure. Where their entry would threaten significant harms to the locals' social practices, I believe that the locals have a good justification for excluding them. Local inhabitants have special claims to live in this region, and to use the area for the social, cultural, and economic practices that they value, and the entry of these migrants would undermine their ability to do that. Appeal to the prior inhabitants' rights to occupy the area, in my view, is a sufficient justification for exclusion here.

On our third hypothesis, then, it is wrong to settle in another country in cases where (1) one has an adequate territorial base in another part of the world and (2) one's migration to another region would severely harm the collective practices of people with occupancy rights there. But migrants whose entry would not cause significant damage, or who have very urgent reasons to come despite the damage they may cause, should be allowed entry.

4 CONCLUSION

To sum up, then, recall that the aim of this chapter is not to reject the case for global free movement, but to define a "colonial" qualification to it, based on the importance of protecting native inhabitants' ability to permanently reside on their territory, and to use it for the social, cultural, and economic practices they value. How extensive is this qualification?

I have argued that—no matter how needy they are and regardless of whether they have an adequate territorial base somewhere else—it is impermissible for migrants to come with a *colonizing project*. It is wrong to subject people to political control against their will, and it is equally wrong to migrate to another land with this aim in mind. It is always permissible, in my view, to exclude newcomers who aim at political domination.

But what about people who do not come with a colonizing project, people we are likely to think of as "normal" immigrants? I believe it is sometimes permissible to exclude these people too, namely where (1) they have a territorial base in another part of the world that provides them with sufficient resources to lead flourishing lives, and (2) their entry threatens severe harms to the social, cultural, and economic practices of local inhabitants. What is objectionable about *settler* colonialism—as opposed to other forms of imperial rule—is, at least in part, the severe harms it does to territorially based indigenous practices. Yet "normal" immigrants sometimes threaten the same kinds of harms. Where that is the case, and they have no urgent reason for coming, I believe the locals can restrict the migrants' entry. Their occupancy rights give them a special claim to live in this area, and to use it for the social, cultural, and economic practices they care about.

Still, occupancy rights ground only a limited case for exclusion. Where migrants' entry threatens no harm, the locals are obliged to allow it—in cases such as travel, study abroad, business trips, and visits to friends and family. Occupants are also obliged to allow a degree of permanent settlement by outsiders who desire to move to their land, even if those outsiders are linguistically and culturally distinct, so long as settlement does not interfere with their ability to use the area for the practices they value. Finally, locals are almost always obliged to admit foreigners who lack an adequate territorial base elsewhere (unless they come with colonizing intent). These people have extraordinarily urgent reasons to enter, despite the harms they pose to local practices, and locals are obliged to accommodate them.

What emerges, then, from our effort to reconcile global free movement with the right of territorial occupancy is a qualified claim: we have a right to move freely around the world, so long as we come with good intentions and our entry does not threaten significant harm to current residents. That, I think, is a plausible interpretation of the limits of our global freedom.

NOTES

1. See Carens (1987), (1992), and, most recently, (2013).
2. Blake (2003).
3. Carens (2013: 278).
4. I have developed this account of occupancy rights at greater length in Stilz (2013).
5. Theorists of colonialism typically distinguish between "colonies of settlement," involving colonists who become permanent residents, and "colonies of exploitation," involving colonial bureaucrats who stay temporarily. See Osterhammel (2005: 1–22). See also Elkins and Pedersen (2005: 1–19).

6. I proceed in this chapter on the assumption that the freedom-based argument is intended to provide at least some guidance for the world as we know it, and investigate the qualifications we might want to place on it in that context.

7. See Oberman (2014), and also Cole (2009). Many libertarian theorists defend the current applicability of freedom-based views of immigration.

8. Oberman (2014: 23) holds that social costs can justify restricting immigration only where "the costs are particularly severe" and "there is no acceptable alternative means to address them." Carens suggests the following considerations might be compelling enough to warrant limiting free movement: maintaining public order, protecting liberal institutions, or preserving a distinct culture. Since in a just world the material inequalities between states would be reduced or eliminated, Carens (2013: 285) thinks "it would very rarely be necessary to restrict immigration to protect the public culture".

9. See also Taylor (2001: 192–3) and Calloway (2008: 166).

10. Taylor (2001: 268–9).

11. Morris(1999: 19).

12. This aim was declared at the 1942 Biltmore Conference in New York. See Smith (2010: 171–2) for an overview.

13. Morris (1999: 46).

14. Richter (2003: 50–2).

15. Perdue and Green (2007: 124–5).

16. See Morris (1987: 588–603). For a Palestinian account, see Khalidi (2006).

17. Hanafi (2005: 63–5).

18. Khalili (2005: 21–4).

19. For a good overview of this history, see Lazarus (1999). For Native American policy generally, see Prucha (1984).

20. For useful discussions of the settler movement, see Gorenberg (2007); Shavit (2013); Zertal and Eldar(2005).

21. Gorenberg (2007: 264–5).

22. Statistics from Central Intelligence Agency (2014).

23. Section 2 adapts and extends some remarks in Stilz (2013).

24. The *locus classicus* for this view of property rights as containing a bundle of separate "incidents" that can be configured in different ways is Honoré (1987: 161–92).

25. For a contrasting nationalist view, see Meisels (2005); Miller (2012: 259); and (2007: 214–24). I criticize nationalist accounts in Stilz (2011).

26. See also Patten (2014: ch. 8) for a discussion of this issue.

27. I take this distinction between attachments and possibilities from Oberman (2014: 14).

28. See Patten (2014: ch. 8) for a similar argument.

29. My argument here is similar to arguments made by David Miller and Christopher Wellman about states' rights to exclude migrants in urgent need. See Miller (2007: 220–30); Wellman (2008: 127–9).

References

Banner, Stuart (2005) *How the Indians Lost their Land*. Cambridge, MA: Belknap Press.

Blake, Michael (2003) "Immigration." In R. G. Frey and Christopher Heath Wellman (eds.), *A Companion to Applied Ethics*. Malden, MA: Blackwell, 224–37.

Calloway, Colin (2008) *First Peoples: A Documentary Survey of American Indian History*. Boston, MA: Bedford/Saint Martin's.

Carens, Joseph H. (1987) "Aliens and Citizens: The Case for Open Borders," *Review of Politics* 49: 250–73.

Carens, Joseph H. (1992) "Migration and Morality: A Liberal Egalitarian Perspective." In Brian Barry and Robert Goodin (eds.), *Free Movement: Ethical Issues in the Transnational Migration of People and of Money*. University Park, PA: Pennsylvania State University Press, 25–47.

Carens, Joseph H. (2013) *The Ethics of Immigration*. Oxford: Oxford University Press.

Central Intelligence Agency (2014) "The World Factbook", https://www.cia.gov/library/publications/the-world-factbook/geos/we.html, accessed July 12, 2014.

Cole, Philip (2009) *Philosophies of Exclusion*. Edinburgh: Edinburgh University Press.

Elkins, Caroline, and Pedersen, Susan (eds.) (2005) *Settler Colonialism in the Twentieth Century*. New York: Routledge.

Gans, Chaim (2008) *A Just Zionism: On the Morality of the Jewish State*. Oxford: Oxford University Press.

Gorenberg, Gershom (2007) *The Accidental Empire: Israel and the Birth of the Settlements, 1967–1977*. New York: Times Macmillan.

Hanafi, Sari (2005) "Social Capital and Refugee Repatriation; A Study of Economic and Social Transnational Kinship Networks in Palestine/Israel." In Ann M. Lesch and Ian S. Lustick (eds.), *Exile and Return: Predicaments of Palestinians and Jews*. Philadelphia, PA: University of Pennsylvania Press, 57–84.

Honoré, Tony (1987) *Making Law Bind: Essays Legal and Philosophical*. Oxford: Clarendon Press.

Khalidi, Rashid (2006) *The Iron Cage*. Boston, MA: Beacon Press.

Khalili, Laleh (2005) "Commemorating Contested Lands." In Ann M. Lesch and Ian S. Lustick (eds.), *Exile and Return: Predicaments of Palestinians and Jews*. Philadelphia, PA University of Pennsylvania Press, 19–40.

Kolers, Avery (2009) *Land, Conflict, and Justice: A Political Theory of Territory*. Cambridge: Cambridge University Press.

Kymlicka, Will (1995) *Multicultural Citizenship*. Oxford: Oxford University Press.

Lazarus, Edward (1999) *Black Hills/White Justice*. Lincoln, NE: University of Nebraska Press.

Meisels, Tamar (2005) *Territorial Rights*. Dordrecht: Springer.

Miller, David (2007) *National Responsibility and Global Justice*. Oxford: Oxford University Press.

Miller, David (2012) "Territorial Rights: Concept and Justification," *Political Studies* 60(2): 252–68.

Morris, Benny (1987) *The Birth of the Palestinian Refugee Problem*. Cambridge: Cambridge University Press.

Morris, Benny (1999) *Righteous Victims*. New York: Random House.

Oberman, Kieran (2014) "Immigration as a Human Right." In Sarah Fine and Lea Ypi (eds.), *Migration in Political Theory: The Ethics of Movement and Membership*. Oxford: Oxford University Press, 32–56.

Osterhammel, Jürgen (2005) *Colonialism: A Theoretical Overview*. Princeton, NJ: Markus Wiener.

Patten, Alan (2014) *Equal Recognition*. Princeton, NJ: Princeton University Press.

Perdue, Theda, and Green, Michael D. (2007) *The Cherokee Nation and the Trail of Tears*. New York: Viking Penguin.

Prucha, Francis (1984) *The Great Father: The United States Government and the American Indians*. Lincoln, NE: University of Nebraska Press.

Richter, Daniel (2003) *Facing East from Indian Country*. Cambridge, MA: Harvard University Press.

Shavit, Ari (2013) *My Promised Land: The Triumph and Tragedy of Israel*. New York: Random House.

Smith, Charles D. (2010) *Palestine and the Arab-Israeli Conflict*. Boston, MA: Bedford/St. Martin's.

Stilz, Anna (2011) "Nations, States, and Territory," *Ethics* 121(3): 572–601.

Stilz, Anna (2013) "Occupancy Rights and the Wrong of Removal," *Philosophy and Public Affairs* (41(4): 324–56.

Taylor, Alan (2001) *American Colonies*. New York: Penguin.

Van Parijs, Philippe (2011) *Linguistic Justice for Europe and for the World*. Oxford: Oxford University Press.

Walzer, Michael (1983) *Spheres of Justice*. New York: Basic Books.

Wellman, Christopher Heath (2008) "Immigration and Freedom of Association," *Ethics* 119(1): 109–41.

Ypi, Lea (2013) "What's Wrong with Colonialism," *Philosophy and Public Affairs* 41(2): 158–91.

Zertal, Idith, and Eldar, Akiva (2005) *Lords of the Land: The War over Israel's Settlements in the Occupied Territories, 1967–2007*. New York: Nation Books.

FURTHER READING

Gans, Chaim (2015) *A Political Theory for the Jewish People*. Oxford: Oxford University Press.

Miller, David (2016) *Strangers in our Midst*. Oxford: Oxford University Press.

Moore, Margaret (2015) *A Political Theory of Territory*. Oxford: Oxford University Press.

Simmons, A. John (2016) *Boundaries of Authority*. Oxford: Oxford University Press.

Stilz, Anna (2019) *Territorial Sovereignty: A Philosophical Exploration*. Oxford: Oxford University Press.

PART VII

GLOBAL INJUSTICE

CHAPTER 22

A CRITICAL THEORY OF TRANSNATIONAL (IN-)JUSTICE

Realistic in the Right Way

RAINER FORST

1 CRITICAL REALISM

RECENT discussions about justice beyond borders are not just about the scope or the content of justice; in addition, they also concern how the very concept of justice should be understood in the first place, how the injustice existing in the world we live in should be thought of, and what function justice ought to have in this world. In what follows, I will try to shed light on the conceptual, normative, and empirical issues at stake in this debate. In doing so, I want to develop further what I call a "critical theory of transnational justice" (Forst 2012: chs. 11 and 12, 2017a: chs. 9 and 10). By this I understand a theory of justice as justification grounded in a constructivist conception of reason which is at the same time "realistic" when it comes to assessing the current world order as one of multiple forms of domination. There is no contradiction in combining abstract reflection in moral philosophy with sociological empirical realism in a single theory; on the contrary, that should be our aim. If we lack a clear picture of the reality of the injustices surrounding us, our normative thinking is situated in a void or will lead us astray; at the same time, if we do not have a context-transcending normative idea of justice to orient us and enable us achieve distance from the status quo, realism becomes a form of thinking that affirms this status quo.

2 Avoiding Parochialism and Cultural Positivism

It is a truism that any notion of justice that applies to transnational contexts needs to be properly universalizable, a requirement which raises the Rawlsian bar for theories based on ethically and culturally particular "comprehensive doctrines" to a higher level than that envisaged by Rawls (1993) himself in his reflections on liberal social pluralism in *Political Liberalism*. But we should also aim at more than what Rawls (1999b) suggests in *The Law of Peoples*, namely at more than a conception of international justice from a liberal standpoint that "tolerates" non-liberal but "decent" peoples and essentially provides the "ideals and principles of the *foreign policy* of a reasonably just *liberal* people" (Rawls 1999b: 10). Rather, we should come to develop a non-parochial approach, that is, one which avoids liberal as well as non-liberal one-sidedness and reified culturalist conceptions of "peoples." To be fair to Rawls, it might be better to be aware of one's parochialism than to hide or ignore it; and it is surprising how many tracts on global or international justice leave the question of universalizability and cultural pluralism out of account or marginalize it.[1]

However, criticism of liberal theories often presents the mirror image of that mistake by embracing a certain form of positivism concerning culture, as if the world consisted of separate, identifiable ethical-cultural units—some "Western," some "non-Western"— that need to engage in a conversation about the values they share in order to achieve an overlapping consensus on minimal notions of justice or human rights (see, e.g., Taylor 1999). In their most problematic versions, such approaches fall prey to the inverse form of thought that Edward Said (2003) once called "Orientalism," that is a reification of "non-Western" cultural wholes that do not understand or share "Western" values, just adding a positive rather than a negative demeaning evaluation of these cultures.[2] The irony of this is that the justified attempt to "provincialize" the West (Chakrabarty 2000) and criticize false assumptions of the universal validity of its values and institutions ends up by provincializing the "non-West" in a non-dialectical way. Yet if we want to develop a proper notion of transnational justice, we must avoid such cultural positivisms, that is, forms of thought which reify societies and regions into unified and separate systems of order and value, while disregarding the dynamics and tensions within and between different societies. In doing so they position themselves outside of such dynamics and try to provide an "objective" account of normative cultural differences.[3]

3 Avoiding Practice Positivism

Avoiding such forms of cultural positivism calls for a turn toward practice and the development of a critical notion of justice that participants in social struggles in Western or non-Western societies can and do make use of. What is required is reflection on the *practical* meaning of justice when used in different political and social contexts, within and beyond particular normative orders, that is, orders of rule that determine the basic standing of persons and groups (or organized collectives) within a social structural framework. But the practical turn I have in mind differs from many current "practice-dependent" theories that regard legitimate justice claims as claims immanent in already established institutional contexts of social cooperation that are fixed in legal-political terms.[4] Such theories are forms of what I call *practice positivism* in a fourfold sense: first, they refer to complex social relations as forms of "cooperation"—say, within the EU or the WTO—and thus run the risk of neglecting the power structures and forms of domination that characterize such institutional settings; second, they aim to reconstruct the animating "idea" or "ideal" of justice immanent in such institutional contexts, as if any such idea or ideal free from social contestation or normative ambivalence could be hermeneutically unearthed;[5] third, they lack a justifying reason why such an immanent notion of justice, even if it could be reconstructed, would have a claim to validity, and thus potentially call might right—or, in other words, lend normative credibility to a status quo that is taken for granted;[6] and finally, fourth, the focus on already established legal-political frameworks obscures the many informal, non-institutionalized modes of power and domination, especially of an economic or cultural nature, that may be part of or exist alongside such institutional forms.

These four aspects are part of what I call practice positivism: giving a positive account of a social setting that should raise our hermeneutic suspicion; assuming that there could be an objective account of its normative idea, neglecting its contestedness from the perspective of social participants—including oneself, who is not an objective observer; granting the status quo a certain normative standing it may not merit; and, finally, providing a one-dimensional account of such a normative order of power relations. To avoid such forms of positivism, we should regard normative orders as contested and contestable orders of justification—where the term "justification" is used both descriptively and normatively, that is both analyzing the justifications that determine the social space of reasons (and may be bad or ideological) and asking for reciprocally and generally non-rejectable justifications and for an order of justification that could produce such justifications (or at least could be conducive to that aim).[7]

Hence in our initial analysis of the proper location of the concept of justice we need to focus on two forms of practice different from those highlighted by practice-dependent theories, namely, firstly, on the *practice of resisting injustice* and on the meaning of justice in such struggles and, secondly, on the *practices of rule and domination* in which such struggles are located and against which they are directed. If we follow Wittgenstein in trying to determine the meaning and "grammar" of a term by its practical use (Wittgenstein 2001), we should be aware that the question of justice is not an innocent, purely theoretical question. On the contrary, it is motivated by reflection on the relations and structures of domination characteristic of our time that people in concrete social conflicts and emancipatory struggles strive to overcome. So a genuine practice-guided view focuses on these practical contexts. Assuming that such a theoretical goal can be achieved, it makes possible a critical theory in the sense in which Marx once spoke of critical philosophy as the "self-clarification of the struggles and wishes of the age" (Marx 1975: 209).

At the same time, since we do not have a general materialist theory to guide us, we must abstract from these contexts and struggles and reflect on which struggles for justice are emancipatory and which are not. We cannot simply read off from social facts of protest and resistance whether they express *justified* forms of struggle against injustice; that would amount to another form of positivism, namely "resistance positivism." For a critical conception of justice, the question of justification as an independent, albeit contextual, normative question is indispensable. As Habermas argued, understanding the need for reflexive justification of social claims, including one's own, is what distinguishes critical from positivist theory (see Habermas 1976: 218–19).

4 A REFLEXIVE AND DISCURSIVE CONCEPTION OF JUSTICE

Let us start from a reflection on the grammar of justice, taking our lead from Rawls, who defined the core concept at the center of different conceptions of justice as implying that institutions are just when "no arbitrary distinctions are made between persons in the assigning of basic rights and duties and when the rules determine a proper balance between competing claims to the advantages of social life" (Rawls 1999a: 5). The most important qualifiers here are "no arbitrary distinctions" and "proper balance," and Rawls's theory makes a detailed proposal as to how to spell these out. Remaining at the basic conceptual level, I think that the meaning of "proper balance" is that no arbitrary, but only reciprocally and generally justifiable criteria for weighing claims should be used. As a result, the avoidance of arbitrariness and the idea of justifiability come to the fore in our search for a core concept of justice.

According to that concept, justice as a human virtue in a general moral sense implies that humans do not subject others to arbitrary actions and decisions, where "arbitrary" here means "not justifiable with good reasons between the subject and object of action." Hence *political and social justice* refers to the legitimate claim—or the basic right—of each person not to be subjected to a set of institutions, formal or informal, to rules and structures of action in an arbitrary way, such as by the powerful imposing an order on the less powerful, as in Thrasymachus' famous definition of what justice means, realistically speaking (Plato 2001: book 1). Again, the meaning of arbitrariness is "without good reasons." But, as I said before, what counts as a good reason here is a highly contested matter: Does one accord priority to the most talented, those who are ethically deserving, the needy, the industrious, or to all equally?

At this point, we must take a *reflexive* turn and work our way up from the core concept of justice to a conception of justice as containing a *practice* of public justification, while taking care to avoid arbitrariness. If we want to overcome arbitrary social and political relations and institutions and also exclude arbitrary justifications for such relations and institutions, and if we have no "natural" or objective candidate for what "non-arbitrary" means, then we must take the principle of justification, as a principle of reason (defined as the faculty of justification),[8] as the core of the conception of justice—call it a conception of *justice as justification*. According to the principle of reasonable justification, those justifications for social relations and institutions are free from arbitrariness that can withstand the discursive test of reciprocal and general justification among free and equal persons (as members of a justification community defined in a non-arbitrary way—a problem to which I will return). We arrive at the principle of reciprocal and general justification by a reflexive and recursive[9] consideration of the validity claim[10] of social and political justice norms that claim to be reciprocally and generally binding on all those who are part of a normative order, that is, an order that determines the basic standing within a social structural framework and is the proper context of claims to justification. Hence a conception of justice as justification relies on just those principles that are implicit in the very claim to justifiability which characterizes justice norms. We can call this reflection a transcendental one, because it reconstructs the conditions of the validity of claims and norms of justice. If we aim at non-arbitrariness as a conceptual core of our notion of justice, such a reflection is what we need to hold onto.

The criteria of reciprocity and generality mean that one may not make a claim on others within a context of justice that one is not willing to grant all others (reciprocity of claims); and they mean, furthermore, that the justification of such claims has to be conducted in a normative language that is open to all and is not determined by just one party (for example, by a religious majority) and that no party may impose its own contestable notion of justified needs or interests on others who could reasonably reject it (reciprocity of reasons). Generality means that no one subject to a normative order must be excluded from participation in the justificatory discourse.

The move from reflection on the core concept of justice to a conception of social and political justice is not yet complete because more needs to be said (and will be said in Section 8 below) about the principles of a "basic structure of justification" entailed by this conception. But here I need to say a few more words about the issue of grounding. For my last remarks led us onto Kantian terrain, and it may seem that we have lost touch not only with the social struggles of various actors and groups but also with our earlier discussion of cultural pluralism.

However, this is not the case. Just as the outworn distinction between "ideal" and "nonideal" (or "realist") theory should not irritate us, so too we should not let ourselves be irritated by the dichotomy between a transcendental and a context-immanent mode of theorizing. To begin with the latter: as I argued above, we need to focus on the right practice rather than taking pregiven institutional contexts for granted; and the focus on resistance to injustice is essential in this regard. In a discursive conception of justice, the proper authority for determining what justice means is the subjects who participate in a normative order *themselves*—while empirically speaking, these are not generally equals but find themselves in very different situations of subjection. Thus, struggles for justice within such a scheme aim first and foremost to achieve a higher level of justificatory quality and equality, that is, to secure a better legal, political, and social standing for groups who have been marginalized and who struggle to become well-respected subjects of justification.

Given such a context of social and political justice, the question whether the principle of reciprocal and general justification is a transcendental one—as a principle of practical reason—or is immanent in such contexts does not really constitute an alternative, for it is both simultaneously. And that is how it should be. For how could a principle of *practical* reason not be implicit in practice, at least as a principle to which social agents adhere in their struggles for justification, and how could a principle of practical *reason* not transcend social practice in which the right to justification is all too often violated?

The topic of ideal-based versus realist approaches has attracted a lot of attention in recent debates.[11] But it is a false opposition that haunts philosophical thinking. A critical conception of justice cannot get off the ground without principled argument, although it neither needs to nor ought to design an "ideal" model of the well-ordered society that would only have to be "realized" by intelligent and well-meaning politicians, which is at best a naive and at worst a technocratic conception.[12] A discursive conception of justice as justification is not compatible with such ideas. But, at the same time, as much as we need critical realism in order to understand and assess our social reality as one involving multiple forms of domination (though also as one that hopefully harbors the potential for critique and emancipation), there is nothing "realistic" about looking at the world as an endless Nietzschean game of Thrasymachean actors, such that every struggle for justice becomes just another struggle for the power to determine social structures your way. From the perspective of a critical theory of justice, there either is what Marx called *Unrecht schlechthin* (Marx 1976: 390)—injustice as such—or there is not;[13] but if you believe the latter, then normative reflection on justice or emancipation lacks any point. Still, it is important to keep in mind that a conception of political and social justice is not a form of ethical thought that needs to be "applied,"[14] because it is an imperative of political autonomy and justice that those who are subject to a normative order should become its collective authors. The authority of justice is *theirs*—but in the form of a collective project of emancipation bound to principles of justification and equal respect.

The question of authority is important here, since on a truly emancipatory conception of justice the definition of justice is a matter for the participants themselves—but, of course, in a fashion that excludes justificatory arbitrariness, according to the critical theory principle that Williams, following Habermas, expresses adequately when he says that "the acceptance of a justification does not count if the acceptance itself is produced by the coercive power which is supposedly being justified" (Williams 2005: 6). Hence the need for a basic structure of justification that overcomes the danger that social forces and privileges are merely reproducing themselves within asymmetrical and dominating discursive relations. The authority to define justice rests with those subjected to a normative order; but they need to be, and to respect each other as, equal justificatory authorities if such justification is to be authoritative. Otherwise, it might just be another form of majoritarian domination.

The Kantian groundwork I have been laying down is based on a fundamental moral claim of free and equal persons to be respected as autonomous normative authorities when it comes to the normative orders to which they are subject. This is my version of the Kantian idea of respecting others as "ends in themselves." Their "dignity" means that they *are* such justificatory authorities (see Forst 2014a: ch. 4), and it implies a basic moral *right to justification*. It is a right to justification with respect to all morally relevant actions in moral contexts of interaction, and in contexts of social and political justice it is a right to participate fully in justificatory discourses about the normative order to which you are subject, so that in such contexts it becomes a legal and political right (see Forst 2016).

5 Struggles for Justice and the Problem of Universality

Struggles for justice aim at social changes that ensure that those who are subject to a normative order become the social and political authorities who codetermine the essential aspects of that order. As Barrington Moore argued in his historical and cross-cultural study of social resistance, the sense of injustice that motivates people to revolt against a social order always focuses on particular social injustices; but its essential core is what he calls a "pan-human sense of injustice" (Moore 1978: 46) that leads to moral outrage and anger when persons have the impression that an implicit social contract has been broken by the authorities or powerful groups in society. To affirm their moral and social self-respect, people resist forms of rule that lack proper justification; and, as Moore stresses, what makes people stop complying within a normative order is not so much a certain level of pain or suffering but the moral sense of being dominated or ignored by others. The "iron in the soul" (p. 90) that makes them feel insulted and leads them to resist requires a certain form of moral courage and a sense of self-respect; the language of injustice is directed against man-made situations of domination as violations of basic expectations of reciprocity and social cooperation that individuals "need not, cannot and ought not to endure" (p. 459) as human beings and members of a particular society.

It is important to maintain a firm grasp of the connection between the sense of justice and the sense of self-respect as an autonomous, non-dominated being (see Forst 2017b). For the essential impulse of resistance based on demands of justice is not the particularist desire to have more of certain social goods but instead the general desire to be a subject of justification, that is, a normative authority and not a justificatory "nullity" in the order of which one is part. If that sense of being "someone" and of being a justificatory subject in the first place is violated, the result is often rebellion—as an act of self-defense, that is, of the defense of a basic moral and political sense of self. To call this the claim to have one's basic right to justification fulfilled is indeed to use an abstract language; but it is an abstraction that captures the structure of emancipatory demands of justice. They are demands not to be governed "like that," as Foucault (2007: 44) famously put it, i.e. the demand—in negative terms—not to be subject to normative imposition or—in positive terms—to be a justificatory agent on an equal footing with others when it comes to determining the social structures to which one is subject, be they of a national or transnational nature. The demand in question is one of autonomy, where autonomy is not understood in liberal terms as the freedom and capacity to pursue one's conception of the good, but in a republican, Rousseauean-Kantian fashion as the autonomy to be the co-author of the norms that bind you. It is here that we find the difference from a neo-republican notion of non-domination (on this difference, see Forst 2013; Gädeke 2017). So, to put it in a nutshell, if we understand the normative grammar of resistance properly as a struggle for emancipation, then we discover the normative core and grammar of a critical theory of justice.

Again, one might object that it is questionable how a reflection that started from cultural pluralism and deep disagreement about conceptions of justice could have ended up within a discourse-theoretical, Kantian framework.[15] But the worry that hereby controversial normative assumptions about subjective freedom or collective self-determination are being slipped in by the back door is unfounded, because what I am suggesting is in no way an imposition of a selective and partial normative framework but is instead a matter of *countering* normative imposition. It is not based on any values or principles other than that of critique among free and equal persons who are themselves justificatory authorities; therefore, it contains the core of any valid—justifiable—critique of the imposition of norms or values, be it within a state or beyond it. In fact, the normative core of the critique of colonial[16] or neocolonial (see Dübgen 2014; Gädeke 2017) impositions as a critique of domination rests on the right to justification, that is, the right not to be subject to a normative order that has not been and cannot be justified to all as equal autonomous subjects. Whether this is expressed in the language of a right or not is not essential here; what is important is the position of not being willing to accept a normative language and order being imposed on you that you cannot share as a justificatory authority.

As I argued in section 2 above, non-Western normative perspectives should neither be "Westernized" nor "Orientalized" in an essentialist way. Liberal parochialism must be avoided as much as other forms of cultural positivism—for example, the unquestioned assumption that certain societies are unified cultural wholes that can be determined by, say, their dominant religious traditions, ignoring the dissent of possibly marginalized groups within such contexts. As Uma Narayan forcefully argues with respect to the rejection of gender as well as cultural essentialism, one needs to avoid both forms of identity and norm imposition:

> Postcolonial feminists have good reason to oppose many of the legacies of colonialism, as well as ongoing forms of economic exploitation and political domination by

Western nations at the international level. However, I do not think that such an agenda is well served either by uncritically denigrating values and practices that appear to be in some sense "Western" or by indiscriminately valorizing values and practices that appear "Non-Western." Political rhetoric that polarizes "Western" and "Non-Western" values risks obscuring the degree to which economic and political agendas, carried out in collaboration between particular Western and Third World elites, work to erode the rights and quality of life for many citizens in both Western and Third World Contexts.   (Narayan 1998: 99)

Narayan not only points to the realities of multiple domination that need to be captured in ways that avoid one-sided social analyses; she also shows why false universalisms that impose a notion of "sameness" on others, and thus lead to the imposition of Western normative orders on other societies in order to dominate them, have to be rejected. The same applies to false notions of "difference" that essentialize and unify other societies and thus silence critical voices within them, as if to call for respect for women's rights were an "alien" and alienating claim in a non-Western society, "leaving feminists suscep-tible to attacks as 'Westernized cultural traitors' who suffer from a lack of appreciation for 'their traditions' and respect for 'their culture'" (Narayan 1998: 102). Narayan argues against both what Foucault (1984: 39) once called "Enlightenment blackmail" and the reverse, orientalist form of blackmail: either to be uncritically for "enlightened" forms of modern political and social life while ignoring their dominating aspects or to be against them and thus ignore the dominating effects of traditional forms of life.

Reflexive universalism, as I call it, avoids such one-dimensional reductions and essentialist forms of cultural positivism by providing a normative yardstick that consists in the very idea and structure of questioning *any* form of domination or normative imposition. The principle of critique, of challenging normative orders, is at the core of such questioning, and thus any concrete narrative or structure of justification can be made the subject of radical questioning that asks whether the structure in question is truly reciprocally and generally justifiable. The principle of asking for better justifica-tions and of asking for structures of justification in the first place is as immanent to nor-mative orders, as it transcends their historical and social forms if they are repressive, narrow, exclusionary, or in other ways deficient. Since the principle leaves the authority to determine justice with those who participate in discourses among free and equal per-sons and thus aim to establish such discursive structures in the first place, it never speaks a language of justice that is alien to them. Rather, it locates the power to define that language with the participants and their discursive constructions. Keeping in mind the critical theory principle that Habermas and Williams remind us of, such discourses can only claim to construct justice if they do not structurally reproduce the social asymme-tries and forms of power that define a given normative order. Social critique can never do without a counterfactual standard of reciprocal and general justifiability; in other words, the principle of critique that grounds critical theory is never exhausted by the existing social forms of justifiability. Thus, the first task of justice is to establish a basic structure of justification that facilitates a reflexive practice of critique and construction by according roughly equal justificatory power to all those subjected to it.

6 Contexts of (In-)Justice

The focus on a grammar of justice as expressed by the resistance to injustice provides us with orientation with regard to a number of further distinctions that need to be questioned: relational versus non-relational approaches to justice; the question of the "all affected" versus the "all subjected" principle; and the difference between internationalist and cosmopolitan approaches to the question of the duties and institutions of justice.

If we follow Sangiovanni's view that relational conceptions of distributive justice consider certain social relations—relations of cooperation or institutions of coercion, for example—as the proper "ground" (Sangiovanni 2007: 8) of justice duties, while non-relational conceptions locate the grounds of justice claims in general considerations of human dignity or human needs, the position laid out so far does not clearly fall on either side. The basic right to justification is an unconditional moral claim of respect based on the dignity of human beings as equal normative authorities. In moral, interactional contexts, this means that each person is owed reciprocal and general justifications for any actions that affect him or her in a relevant way, while, in social and political contexts, this means that no one should be subjected to a normative order in which he or she has no standing as a justificatory equal. Thus, the moral grounds of this right are both relational, since moral persons are always regarded as co-authorities of valid norms, and non-relational, since the right to justification does not depend on a particular social context in order to constitute a valid moral claim. Still, only when situated in contexts of justice (i.e. concrete contexts of rule and/or domination) does this general "ground" of justice claims "ground" particular claims to justice, depending on the nature of the rule or domination to which one is subjected.

Normatively speaking, a context of social or political justice is one in which one's *moral* status of being an equal normative authority needs to be transformed into a *social and political* status of being a justificatory agent because one is subjected to a normative order of rule and/or domination in need of reciprocal and general justification. This is a relational view, but not of the positivistic sort criticized earlier that focuses on (what it sees as) relations of cooperation or positive institutions of (intrastate or superstate) coercion. If we develop a critical theory of justice from the situated perspective of social agents struggling against injustice, we should avoid positivistic restrictions on the kinds of context we focus on, and we should especially avoid calling a context of asymmetrical social relations a context of "cooperation." A social and political status of normative co-authorship and non-domination (understood in that way) is not only required where one is part of a social (economic) and political scheme of reciprocity and cooperation or where one is subject to state power and coercion, but also more generally where power is exercised over persons as a kind of rule within a certain framework of justification or as a kind of domination lacking a proper scheme of justification. These forms of rule or domination can be formal and legally constituted, but they can also be of a rather informal nature, like economic forms of power and domination where persons or groups are subjected to a general normative order of production and exchange on a global scale which is not as tightly legally regulated and institutionalized as the market within a state. A normative order is any order of social norms and rules that governs persons and collectives with regard to their social and political status and determines their options as members of a social framework. We live in multiple orders of such a kind, and a theory of transnational justice requires a nuanced view of these different orders of subjection (a point to which I will return).

From a critical perspective, the argument by Nagel, for example, that "justice is something we owe through our shared institutions only to those with whom we stand in a strong political relation" (Nagel 2005: 121; see also Blake 2001) of state power mistakes a conclusion for a premise, because such strong political relations should not be seen as an a priori condition, but instead as an a posteriori, conclusion of justice duties—that is, such political relations are required to overcome certain forms of unregulated and arbitrary rule, whether it be formal or informal.[17] State-like forms of regulation, viewed from a normative point of view, can be demanded by justice when arbitrary rule violates the—in a moral perspective prepolitical, in a political perspective contextual—rights to justification of persons not to be subjected to domination (defined as arbitrary rule in its two forms: rule without proper structures of justification being in place and rule that is not properly, i.e. reciprocally and generally, justified). In this way, the right to justification precedes institutional contexts but only gains specific traction and form in being directed against certain forms of domination calling for the establishment of structures of justification necessary to ban arbitrary rule. Such a right to justice has its place in political relations, but the right to have such relations, as a right to non-domination, is prior to them. And whether the political relations demanded by justice are to be strong or weak depends on the nature of the arbitrariness to be overcome.

Similarly, Sangiovanni's claim that "we owe obligations of egalitarian reciprocity to fellow citizens and residents in the state, who provide us with the basic conditions and guarantees necessary to develop and act on a plan of life, but not to noncitizens, who do not" (Sangiovanni 2007: 20) is too restrictive. It does not sufficiently take into account the many ways in which the welfare of one society (or of parts of one society) often thrives by benefiting from a system of unequal exchange and dominated markets that make it impossible for certain societies to reach a level of cooperation and productivity that Sangiovanni regards as essential for a context of justice to exist. Furthermore, it is true that "the global order does not have the financial, legal, administrative, or sociological means to provide and guarantee the goods and services necessary to sustain and reproduce a stable market and legal system" (Sangiovanni 2007: 21); but there is no reason not to regard this as a failure rather than as a normatively relevant fact that constrains duties of justice. Such duties cannot be restricted to the existing frameworks of political life; rather, they call for the establishment of new ones.

A critical theory of (in-)justice needs to avoid such restrictive, positivistic views and locate contexts of injustice wherever forms of rule within a normative order exist or wherever forms of domination within such an order exist, be it an order of the state or of economic exchange. Thus, we need a nuanced view of such normative orders that avoids a non-dialectical opposition between the state, on the one side, and a system of voluntary international cooperation, on the other, such as we also find in Rawls (1999b). Relational views should focus exclusively neither on positive relations of cooperation nor on relations of coercion within a state; rather, they must also focus on the negative and structural forms of domination that characterize global and national realities.[18] What we need is a negative version of relationism that can then provide the starting point for a theory of a basic structure of justification to address and overcome relations of domination.

A proper conception of transnational justice tracks forms of rule and domination where they exist. It need not reduce contexts of (in-)justice to contexts of legal coercion, for that criterion tends to be too rigid. To overcome the state-centeredness of such views, Valentini, for example, argues for a notion of systemic coercion designed to capture structural justice-relevant relations beyond the state. According to her definition, "a system of rules S is coercive if it foreseeably and avoidably places non-trivial constraints on some agents' freedom, compared to their freedom in the absence of that system" (Valentini 2011: 137). But take the case of a country that is dependent upon the global market in order to exchange its resources for other goods but is too poor and dependent to alter the rules of that exchange and has to accept its asymmetries which disproportionately benefit other partners in the exchange. Thus, the country is forced to accept the arrangement in question if it wants to exchange its resources; yet by doing so it acquires essential goods and market recognition and thus also achieves greater freedom as compared to the absence of the exchange and its possibility. Thus, the system is one of domination, but not of coercion in Valentini's sense. It is a system of domination that imposes a set of norms that cannot be justified among equals. So, rather than freedom in the absence of a coercive system of rules, the proper baseline for a system of domination is justifiability among equals.

7 THE NATURE OF INJUSTICE

However, the critique of positivistic or coercion-based forms of relationism that do not use a proper conception of domination does not vindicate non-relational accounts of justice. For their basic notion of justice is incompatible with the grammar of justice as shown through the lens of the practice of resistance and the ideas of justice as justifiability and discursive non-domination. According to non-relational views, we ought to focus on the well-being of persons in a cosmopolitan perspective, disregarding more specific contexts of cooperation or domination. These theories start from a normative theory of basic global entitlements of every human being, since, as Caney argues, persons "throughout the world have some common needs, common capacities, and common ends" (Caney 2005: 37). According to such considerations, persons should be seen on a global scale as "rightful recipients of goods" (p. 103) of a certain kind, and in arguing for a level of entitlement to certain goods, "it is hard to see why economic inter-action has any moral relevance from the point of view of distributive justice" (p. 111). To be sure, Caney is right to criticize the priority that some relational accounts of distribu-tive justice give to members of a state or context of cooperation, but his non-contextual view of what justice demands is problematic in a number of ways.[19] First, by denying the positive relevance of particular social relations, Caney also disregards the negative rele-vance of relations of domination, say, of economic exploitation and political oppression. Thus, the victim of a natural disaster appears to be similar to the victim of exploitation if they lack the same material means. But the difference in question is important from the perspective of justice, and especially from that of struggles for justice. For the social movements Moore and others analyze do not protest against natural or cosmic forces that distributed the "luck" of being born here or there, with these or other resources and talents, in an arbitrary and unequal way and call for compensation for bad luck. Rather, they oppose man-made injustice, that is, particular relations and structures of domina-tion within and/or beyond their society. So for them, and for the grammar of justice generally, relations and contexts matter: in a structural view, one cannot easily pinpoint concrete responsibilities for generating and reproducing injustice (Young 2011), but one can reconstruct the development of social asymmetries, how they function and who benefits from them in what ways. Otherwise, what is a human structural context of domination gets anonymized and naturalized as something that simply happened as a matter of contingent luck or, in an older language, divine whim. Luck-egalitarian accounts of injustice, in particular, which argue that ambition and desert count as criteria of distribution, but brute luck, whether positive or negative, does not, are out of tune with a practical and emancipatory account of injustice in so far as they reconstruct justice claims as claims for compensation for anonymous bad luck. Such a view turns a narrative of injustice into a narrative of fate, albeit a fate that grounds claims for com-pensation. The result is a distorted picture of injustice. The struggle against injustice is a struggle against concrete forms of domination, not a struggle against the forces of contingency. Injustice is one thing, fate and fortune another.

Consequentialist accounts of justice thus understood not only provide a misleading picture of injustice but also, secondly, a one-dimensional account of responsibilities for justice. As difficult as an account of structural responsibility is in a postcolonial age (see Lu 2017), a proper understanding of the history and current system of social and trans-national forms of economic, legal, or cultural domination (e.g. with respect to race and gender) matters from the perspective of justice. Otherwise, political action lacks orien-tation. Furthermore, in a dialectic of morality, richer states could offer generous "aid" to poor countries as an act of benevolence, while in reality they owe the latter major struc-tural changes in a global asymmetrical economic system from which they derive unjust benefits. As Kant (1991: 248) and, following him, Pogge (2002) have argued, one must not mistake duties of justice for duties of benevolence.[20]

This does not mean that there are no general duties of moral solidarity with people in need apart from existing contexts of relational (in-)justice, and it does not mean that duties of justice always take priority over duties of solidarity and assistance, especially in times of grave need and misery, when urgent help is called for. The conceptual distinction between such duties does not accord priority to the one or the other; it just helps us to understand the world we live in and the particular reasons for moral and political action. One owes it to victims of domination not to treat them as "weak" and miserable human beings in need of "help."

The view defended here also does not deny that there is a "natural duty of justice" with respect to victims of domination elsewhere to which, on a counterfactual assumption, one's society has no relevant relation. Every human being has a right to justification and must not be subjected to domination, and every other human being in a position to help has a natural duty to do so—in addition to the more concrete relational duties of those who benefit from or uphold a system of domination—though in complex political structures the conclusion about the right course of action is very difficult to draw and any intervention needs to observe strict criteria of justifiability. Although I cannot go into this here, this natural duty of justice highlights a kind of solidarity based on justice, while the solidarity mentioned above with people in need and misery, even though not victims of domination, also rests on respect for the right to justification, but in a larger moral sense, since nobody has good reasons to deny others in severe need necessary and possible help. The right to justification grounds many moral duties, not just duties of justice, but it is important to sort these duties out, because they all respond to moral evils of different kinds, and it is required to respond in the right way.

Thirdly, we should also regard those who suffer from injustice as persons whose political agency is being denied; but viewing them primarily as subjects who should receive certain goods does not adequately take this into account. Those who suffer from economic exploitation suffer as much from political exclusion and powerlessness as do those who are oppressed politically, because the key to improving economic conditions of production and distribution is the opportunity to change an economic system by political means. So the question of social and political power is the first question of justice, whether we are speaking about political *or* distributive justice. There is no distribution machine that would only need to be reprogrammed; there only are normative orders in need of political transformation. Justice is a political construction by way of procedures and practices of justification—a construction by those who are subject to a normative order themselves. Theories which disregard this constructive aspect and leap to conclusions about the right patterns of the distribution of goods ignore this essentially political character of justice. The struggle for effective political agency and for sufficient justification power within a normative order is the first and major struggle for justice. That is also the right way to contextualize claims for justice and not to predetermine what people in societies very different from Western ones "really" want or can justifiably claim.

In sum, a critical theory of justice avoids positivistic and reductive forms of relationism as well as non-contextual non-relationism. It starts from an account of existing structures of rule and/or domination in various normative orders, ranging from the national to the international and the global, and thus develops a critical form of relationism based on a general moral right to justification. In concrete social contexts, this translates into the right to be an equal justificatory authority within the normative orders to which one is subject—either as a subject of justified rule or of domination. Thus, there is a single normative ground of justice but a range of different contexts of justice according to the nature of the subjection in question.[21]

In this section, I highlighted the notion of subjection rather than that of being "affected" by certain norms and structures. In contexts of justice, subjection is the proper term, whereas the notion of being affected is too broad (see also Fraser 2009: ch. 2). Still, just as different people are differently affected by certain normative structures, so too people are subjected in different ways to certain normative orders—if one compares, for example, the level of subjection to a state with that of subjection to the rules of a global market. So what we require is a nuanced view of relations of subjection; but at the same time we must resist the tendency to say that tighter, state-like normative orders have priority as contexts of justice over looser, transnational contexts. For the domination exercised, say, in a neocolonial international relation may be so severe that overcoming it should have priority as a matter of justice. The strength of duties of justice depends on the nature of the domination to be overcome; the more extreme it is, the more stringent are the relevant duties of justice. As I will show in the next section, a critical analysis of contexts of subjection will also take us beyond another overworked distinction, namely that between a cosmopolitan and an international normative order of justice as an alternative. A theory of transnational justice must combine aspects of both.

8 Constructing Transnational Justice

A critical analysis of contexts of subjection shows how intertwined several normative orders are, and how much different dimensions of power intersect. Subnational, national, regional, international, supranational, and global contexts of rule and domination overlap, as do economic, racial, gender-based, citizenship-based, religious, and other dimensions of domination. I call this the fact of *multiple domination*; as an illustration, think of all the forms of domination to which a low-paid woman from a low social rank in a poor country with authoritarian rule and gendered structures of the division of labor is subjected. We will only find an answer to the question of transnational justice if we address the situation of such persons in the right way.

For that, a critical theory of justice does not start with an internationalist or cosmopolitan thought experiment, but with a realistic view tracking the relevant structures of domination and/or rule and how they interrelate and reinforce each other.[22] The aim of justice is to overcome relations of domination where they exist and to establish structures of justification for that purpose; in contexts of justified rule and government its aim is to prevent structures of rule from degenerating into contexts of domination by strengthening and equalizing relations of justification.

In reconstructing these different contexts as contexts of domination and rule, we have to follow a principle of proportionality which states that the required structures of justification have to be sufficiently strong to overcome or avoid the kind arbitrary rule (i.e. domination) that exists or threatens to appear. This must be combined with the main principle of justice as justifiability, namely that the construction of norms of justice has to be a common, autonomous practice of reciprocal and general justification. This means that the first task of justice is to establish basic structures of justification in which the "force toward the better argument" can be generated and exercised by those subject to a normative order—especially those who are in danger of marginalization. I call the establishment of basic structures of justification the achievement of "fundamental justice," while on that basis constructions of "full justice" can be achieved by way of discursive, democratic practice.

I cannot lay out such a theory at this point. Instead I will sketch a few major lines of argument concerning an account of *fundamental transnational justice*.[23] It aims to create structures of participation and justification that can perform the tasks of opening and critique in various contexts of justice, pointing to structures of asymmetrical rule and exchange, culminating in the justification and adoption of binding national, transnational, and international norms. The guiding principle is that of political autonomy and equality, within, between, and beyond states, which point to the three main dynamics of domination to be addressed and overcome: domination within states, domination between states, and domination beyond states, such as in a global economic order characterized by an unjustifiable distribution of opportunities and benefits with lots of powerful nonstate actors involved.

Realistically and politically speaking, the most important agents in this process are in the first instance democratic states, since these constitute the main normative order capable of generating democratic power both within their borders and beyond, in international and supranational contexts (see also Ypi 2012; Culp 2014). A transnational basic structure of justification with sufficient critical force to address current relations of domination will not arise if it is not supported by a relevant number of democratic states. But being aware of the many forms of domination of which states are part, internally and externally, reflexive forms of participation must be found that prevent governments from continuing to dominate parts of their own population or other states or transnational normative orders. Principles of fundamental transnational justice give every political community the right to participate in cross-border normative discourses on an equal footing, and affected parties below the state level simultaneously have the right to demand participation in such discourses—think, again, of issues of class, gender, or racial injustice. This means that corresponding forums must be opened up to opposition parties from states, though also to civil society actors as organized, for example, in the World Social Forum (see Zürn and Ecker-Ehrhardt 2013). To start with states as the main—but not the only—political units of agency for a politics of transnational justice is not to conserve or strengthen the existing state-centered international system; rather, it is to overcome the latter by generating political power within, between, and beyond political communities which understand that globalized forms of politics represent the only way to address and overcome global injustice. But there is a paradox here, in so far as the more powerful states often use their position to prevent the construction of more emancipatory political structures. That is why internal and transnational social movements are essential when it comes to generating the public power required to motivate structural change.[24]

Democracy as the main practice of justice acquires special importance in this context. In the first place, it must be liberated from the narrow choice between a "world state or world of states." It is best understood as a normative order in which those who are subject to rule or norms should also be the normative authority, and should exercise it in an active sense within a practice of justification. Thus, the question of the relevant demoi is answered in a non-arbitrary way in terms of the existing structures of rule and/or domination, and the requisite institutional form depends on the degree of subjection. This idea of "demoi of subjection" extends the question of democratic rule conceptually beyond national borders according to the relations of rule or domination in which a state is actively or passively embedded (see also Bohman 2010). The principle of political proportionality asserts that structures of justification must be sufficiently open to participation and sufficiently effective to react to a given situation of domination. However, this principle does not predetermine which model of order—ranging from federalist internationalism to global supranationalism—follows. That must be decided with a view to the situation that is supposed to be transformed from an unregulated form of domination into a regulated form of justification or rule; sometimes this can only be done through supranational institutions, sometimes through international contracts.[25] With respect to the global economic order, proportionality calls for relatively strong supranational institutions for regulating production, exchange, and distribution. The point of this regulation is not only, as an internationalist neo-republican theory would assert (see Pettit 2014; Laborde and Ronzoni 2016), to protect and enable particular political self-determination within states, important as that is; rather, the main point is to establish distributive justice on a transnational level by political means, because nation-states have lost the capacity to do so in a fundamental, system-transforming way. The same holds for the questions of regulating migration or responding to climate change.

In so far as democratic justice is understood in processual terms as a practice of justification, it expresses the collective aspiration to subsume the exercise of rule under relations of effective justification and authorization of norms by those who are subjected to them. Justice and democracy are primarily recuperative and processual in nature, because they aim to transform existing forms of rule or domination into structures of justification. Habermas once coined the image of "besiegement" for the exercise of communicative, democratic power: public discourses generate justifying reasons that the political system cannot ignore (Habermas 1996: 486–7). The concept of "justificatory power"[26] that takes up these reflections is open when it comes to the question of whether the mode of producing and exercising communicative power is an institutionalized one or not. Democratic justice as a practice is always a matter of *democratization*, of expanding and equalizing justificatory power. However, the construction of justice is eventually to become reality within binding institutions of justification in which those who are subject to rule become the authors of their normative orders—and the first struggle for justice is the struggle for the establishment of such basic structures of justification. Thus, to be theoretically agnostic with respect to the institutional forms that transnational justice should take is not just a reflection of sociological realism; rather, it follows from an understanding of the autonomous and constructive character of a politics of discursive non-domination.

ACKNOWLEDGMENTS

Versions of this chapter were presented at the Association for Social and Political Philosophy Annual Conference at the London School of Economics, a workshop at Durham University, the Frankfurt Global Justice Summer School, the Wissenschaftszentrum Berlin, King's College London, McGill University in Montreal, the Free University in Berlin, the University of Toronto, the University of Manchester, Princeton University, the Society for Applied Philosophy Conference in Cardiff, the University of Michigan, and the University of Chicago. I owe particular thanks to Thom Brooks, Julian Culp, Dorothea Gädeke, Stefan Gosepath, David Held, Tamara Jugov, Mattias Kumm, Catherine Lu, Steve Ratner, Arthur Ripstein, Andrea Sangiovanni, John Tasioulas, Melissa Williams, Lea Ypi, and Michael Zürn for their detailed comments. Thanks also to Ciaran Cronin for correcting my English and to Felix Kämper for his help in preparing the manuscript.

NOTES

1. There are exceptions to this, such as Caney (2005); Nussbaum (2006); and Sen (2011).
2. In a powerful afterword to his *Orientalism*, Edward Said (2003: 329–54) criticizes romanticizing and essentializing readings of his argument. They celebrate the "other" of the West and wrongly combine postmodern and postcolonial thought in such a way that they no longer criticize the perversions of the "grand narratives of emancipation and enlightenment" and renounce the general imperative of emancipation. I expand on this in Forst (2019).
3. Here I rely on and modify the notion of positivism developed by Jürgen Habermas (1976).
4. See Sangiovanni (2008), and the contributions in Banai, Ronzoni, and Schemmel (2011). Sangiovanni has reconsidered his approach in Sangiovanni (2016).
5. In this, the approach shares a lot with Michael Walzer (1983). For a critique, see Forst (2002: ch. IV.1.).
6. On this third point, see also Darrel Moellendorf's critique of "justice positivism" in Moellendorf (2002: 38–9). Sangiovanni (2016) addresses this critique of his view and responds in a way that a theory based on the right to justification would also suggest, namely that for "a conception of justice to get off the ground, there must be some sense in which the terms of the institution are at least capable of being justified to all persons" (p. 163). Still, Sangiovanni (2017) criticizes the Kantian account of the right to justification and does not follow the path toward a critical theory of justice.
7. For an account of orders of justification, see Forst (2017a).
8. I develop this view in Forst (2012: chs. 1 and 2) and Forst (2017a: ch. 1).
9. On the notion of recursive justification, see O'Neill (1989).
10. The notion of validity claims was developed by Jürgen Habermas and Karl-Otto Apel in their discourse ethics. See Habermas (1990).

11. See, for example, the discussions in Geuss (2008); Larmore (2013: 276–306); Rossi and Sleat (2014: 689–701); and Erman and Möller (2018).
12. An example of an approach that calls for an "egalitarian distributor" to realize justice is G. A. Cohen's (2011: 61).
13. On Marx's notion of justice, see Forst (2017a: ch. 7).
14. This is a point of agreement with Geuss (2008); Allen (2017: ch. 4) criticizes my view as one of applied ethics, which I think is a misinterpretation.
15. For this worry, see Allen (2017) and my reply in Forst (2019).
16. See the classic by Frantz Fanon (2004), and, recently, Ypi (2013).
17. I develop this argument more fully in Forst (2017a: ch. 10). See also Cohen and Sabel (2006).
18. A number of approaches that differ from mine also stress the importance of existing relations of power and domination, for example, Miller (2010); Ypi (2012); Nardin (2013); and Wenar (2015). Wenar in particular follows the groundbreaking work of Thomas Pogge (2002).
19. For the following, see my debate with Caney (2014); Forst (2014b).
20. This is the problem of consequentialist approaches like that of Peter Singer (2002).
21. This is the essential difference from Mathias Risse (2012), who distinguishes various "grounds" of justice which have distributive relevance, some relational, some non-relational. I think there is only one ground of justice but various contexts of justice marked by different forms of domination. I used that notion of "context" for the first time in Forst (2001), and it differs from the use I make of it in Forst (2002).
22. See, for example, the complex analyses to be found in Avant, Finnemore, and Sell (2010), as well as Hale, Held, and Young (2013).
23. For the following, see also Forst (2017a: ch. 10).
24. On this, see the analysis of transnational politicization in Zürn (2016).
25. See, for example, the suggestions by Jürgen Habermas (2006, 2012: 56–7).
26. See my concept of "noumenal power" in Forst (2017a: ch. 2).

References

Allen, Amy (2017) *The End of Progress*. New York: Columbia University Press.
Avant, Deborah D., Martha Finnemore, and Susan K. Sell (eds.) (2010) *Who Governs the Globe?* Cambridge: Cambridge University Press.
Banai, Ayelet, Miriam Ronzoni, and Christian Schemmel (eds.) (2011) *Social Justice, Global Dynamics*. Abingdon: Routledge.
Blake, Michael (2001) "Distributive Justice, State Coercion, and Autonomy," *Philosophy and Public Affairs* 30: 257–96.
Bohman, James (2010) *Democracy across Borders*. Cambridge, MA: MIT Press.
Caney, Simon (2005) *Justice Beyond Borders*. Oxford: Oxford University Press.
Caney, Simon (2014) "Justice and the Basic Right to Justification." In Rainer Forst, *Justice, Democracy, and the Right to Justification*. London and Oxford: Bloomsbury, 147–66.
Chakrabarty, Dipesh (2000) *Provincializing Europe*. Princeton, NJ: Princeton University Press.
Cohen, G. A. (2011) *On the Currency of Egalitarian Justice, and Other Essays in Political Philosophy*. Princeton, NJ: Princeton University Press.

Cohen, Joshua, and Charles Sabel (2006) "Extra Rempublicam Nulla Iustitia," *Philosophy and Public Affairs* 34: 147–75.

Culp, Julian (2014) *Global Justice and Development*. New York: Palgrave.

Dübgen, Franziska (2014) *Was ist gerecht?* Frankfurt and New York: Campus.

Erman, Eva, and Niklas Möller (2018) *The Practical Turn in Political Theory*. Edinburgh: Edinburgh University Press.

Fanon, Frantz (2004) *The Wretched of the Earth*. New York: Grove.

Forst, Rainer (2001) "Towards a Critical Theory of Transnational Justice," *Metaphilosophy* 32: 160–79.

Forst, Rainer (2002) *Contexts of Justice*. Berkeley, CA: University of California Press.

Forst, Rainer (2012) *The Right to Justification*. New York: Columbia University Press.

Forst, Rainer (2013) "A Kantian Republican Conception of Justice as Non-Domination." In Andreas Niederberger and Philipp Schink (eds.), *Republican Democracy: Liberty, Law and Politics*. Edinburgh: Edinburgh University Press, 154–68.

Forst, Rainer (2014a) *Justification and Critique*. Cambridge, MA: Polity Press.

Forst, Rainer (2014b) "Justifying Justification. Reply to my Critics." In *Justice, Democracy, and the Right to Justification*. London and Oxford: Bloomsbury, 169–216.

Forst, Rainer (2016) "The Justification of Basic Rights: A Discourse-Theoretical Approach," *Netherlands Journal of Legal Philosophy* 45: 7–28.

Forst, Rainer (2017a) *Normativity and Power*. Oxford: Oxford University Press.

Forst, Rainer (2017b) "Noumenal Alienation: Rousseau, Kant and Marx on the Dialectics of Self-Determination," *Kantian Review* 22: 523–51.

Forst, Rainer (2019) "The Justification of Progress and the Progress of Justification." In Amy Allen and Eduardo Mendieta (eds.), *Justice and Emancipation: The Critical Theory of Rainer Forst*. University Park, PA: Penn State University Press, 17–37.

Foucault, Michel (1984) "What is Enlightenment?." In Paul Rabinow (ed.), *The Foucault Reader*. New York: Pantheon, 32–50.

Foucault, Michel (2007) "What is Critique?." In *The Politics of Truth*. Los Angeles: Semiotexte, 41–82.

Fraser, Nancy (2009) *Scales of Justice*. New York: Columbia University Press.

Gädeke, Dorothea (2017) *Politik der Beherrschung*. Berlin: Suhrkamp.

Geuss, Raymond (2008) *Philosophy and Real Politics*. Princeton, NJ: Princeton University Press.

Habermas, Jürgen (1976) "A Positivistically Bisected Rationalism." In Theodor W. Adorno et al. (eds.), *The Positivist Dispute in German Sociology*, tr. Glynn Adey and David Frisby. London: Heinemann, 198–225.

Habermas, Jürgen (1990) *Moral Consciousness and Communicative Action*. Cambridge, MA: MIT Press.

Habermas, Jürgen (1996) "Popular Sovereignty as Procedure." In *Between Facts and Norms*. Cambridge, MA: MIT Press, 463–90.

Habermas, Jürgen (2006) "Does the Constitutionalization of International Law Still Have a Chance?." In *The Divided West*. Cambridge, MA: Polity Press, 115–93.

Habermas, Jürgen (2012) *The Crisis of the European Union: A Response*. Cambridge, MA: Polity Press.

Hale, Thomas, David Held, and Kevin Young (2013) *Gridlock: Why Global Cooperation is Failing When We Need it Most*. Cambridge, MA: Polity Press.

Kant, Immanuel (1991) The Metaphysics of Morals, ed. Mary Gregor. Cambridge, MA: MIT Press.

Laborde, Cécile, and Miriam Ronzoni (2016) "What is a Free State? Republican Internationalism and Globalization," Political Studies 64: 279–96.

Larmore, Charles (2013) "What is Political Philosophy?" Journal of Moral Philosophy 10: 276–306.

Lu, Catherine (2017) Justice and Reconciliation in World Politics. Cambridge: Cambridge University Press.

Marx, Karl (1975) "Letter to Ruge, September 1843." In Marx, Early Writings, ed. Quintin Hoare. New York: Vintage Books, 206–9.

Marx, Karl (1976) "Zur Kritik der Hegelschen Rechtsphilosophie. Einleitung." In Karl Marx and Friedrich Engels, Marx-Engels-Werke I. Berlin: Dietz, 201–13.

Miller, Richard W. (2010) Globalizing Justice. Oxford: Oxford University Press.

Moellendorf, Darrel (2002) Cosmopolitan Justice. Boulder, CO: Westview Press.

Moore Jr., Barrington (1978) Injustice: The Social Bases of Obedience and Revolt. White Plains, NY: Sharpe.

Nagel, Thomas (2005) "The Problem of Global Justice," Philosophy and Public Affairs 33: 113–47.

Narayan, Uma (1998) "Essence of Culture and a Sense of History: A Feminist Critique of Cultural Essentialism," Hypatia 13: 86–106.

Nardin, Terry (2013) "Realism and Right: Sketch for a Theory of Global Justice." In Cornelia Navari (ed.), Ethical Reasoning in International Affairs: Arguments from the Middle Ground. London: Palgrave, 43–63.

Nussbaum, Martha (2006) Frontiers of Justice. Cambridge, MA: Harvard University Press.

O'Neill, Onora (1989) Constructions of Reason. Cambridge: Cambridge University Press.

Pettit, Philip (2014) Just Freedom. New York: Norton.

Plato (2001) The Republic, ed. G.R.F. Ferrari, tr. Tom Griffith. Cambridge: Cambridge University Press.

Pogge, Thomas (2002) World Poverty and Human Rights. Cambridge, MA: Polity Press.

Rawls, John (1993) Political Liberalism. New York: Columbia University Press.

Rawls, John (1999a) A Theory of Justice, rev. edn. Cambridge, MA: Harvard University Press.

Rawls, John (1999b) The Law of Peoples. Cambridge, MA: Harvard University Press.

Risse, Mathias (2012) On Global Justice. Princeton, NJ: Princeton University Press.

Rossi, Enzo, and Matt Sleat (2014) "Realism in Normative Political Theory," Philosophy Compass 9: 689–701.

Said, Edward (2003) Orientalism. repr. with a new afterword and preface. London: Penguin.

Sangiovanni, Andrea (2007) "Global Justice, Reciprocity, and the State," Philosophy and Public Affairs 35: 3–39.

Sangiovanni, Andrea (2008) "Justice and the Priority of Politics to Morality," The Journal of Political Philosophy 16: 137–64.

Sangiovanni, Andrea (2016) "How Practices Matter," The Journal of Political Philosophy 24: 3–23.

Sangiovanni, Andrea (2017) Humanity without Dignity. Cambridge, MA: Harvard University Press.

Sen, Amartya (2011) The Idea of Justice. Cambridge, MA: Harvard University Press.

Singer, Peter (2002) One World Now. New Haven, CT: Yale University Press.

Taylor, Charles (1999) "Conditions of an Unforced Consensus on Human Rights." In Joanne R. Bauer and Daniel A. Bell (eds.), *The East Asian Challenge for Human Rights*. Cambridge: Cambridge University Press, 124–44.

Valentini, Laura (2011) *Justice in a Globalized World*. Oxford: Oxford University Press.

Walzer, Michael (1983) *Spheres of Justice* New York: Basic Books.

Wenar, Leif (2015) *Blood Oil*. Oxford: Oxford University Press.

Williams, Bernard (2005) *In the Beginning Was the Deed*, ed. G. Hawthorn. Princeton, NJ: Princeton University Press.

Wittgenstein, Ludwig (2001) *Philosophical Investigations*, ed. and tr. G. E. M. Anscombe. Oxford: Blackwell.

Young, Iris M. (2011) *Responsibility for Justice*. Oxford: Oxford University Press.

Ypi, Lea (2012) *Global Justice and Avant-Garde Political Agency*. Oxford: Oxford University Press.

Ypi, Lea (2013) "What's Wrong with Colonialism?" *Philosophy and Public Affairs* 41: 158–91.

Zürn, Michael (2016) "Four Models of a Global Order with Cosmopolitan Intent: An Empirical Assessment," *The Journal of Political Philosophy* 24: 88–119.

Zürn, Michael, and Matthias Ecker-Ehrhardt (eds.) (2013) *Die Politisierung der Weltpolitik*. Berlin: Suhrkamp.

FURTHER READING

Pogge, Thomas, and Darrel Moellendorf (eds.) (2008) *Global Justice: Seminal Essays*. St. Paul, MN: Paragon.

CHAPTER 23

....

PERSONAL RESPONSIBILITY AND GLOBAL INJUSTICE

....

KOK-CHOR TAN

1 INTRODUCTION

....

ON what we may call the "institutional approach" to global justice, persons may pursue nationalistic, patriotic, and other personal and associational goods and ends so long as these pursuits are within, and do not upset, the rules of just global institutions. The institutional approach to justice thus provides a way of reconciling the demands of justice on the one hand and the demands and concerns of personal life and special memberships on the other. It provides a way of conceptualizing justice that allows for but also limits the various collective and personal commitments people reasonably value and act on.

But, on this approach, the reconciliation of global justice and patriotic and nationalistic commitments presumes the presence of a just global institutional order or a just global "basic structure" (to invoke Rawls's term). Under ideal conditions, when there is a just global basic structure in the background, we take it that persons, individually or in association with others, may do as they wish within the just terms of this global order, including pursuing particular (and narrow) nationalistic and patriotic ends.[1] There can be societies or persons who are less well off than others even under this ideal global condition, but any further redistribution to them will not be a requirement of justice. On the institutional approach, *from the standpoint of distributive justice*, richer countries do not owe poorer countries distributive obligations in the presence of existing just institutions. Their duty of justice is primarily to support and maintain just institutions, and to interact with others in accordance with institutional rules.

If the institutional approach appears objectionably lax as an understanding of justice to some critics,[2] especially in the context of global justice, it is perhaps because they are evaluating an ideal against existing reality. One can reasonably expect that if, counterfactually, a reasonably just global institutional order exists, there will not be the degree of global economic inequality, let alone the abject poverty, that we see in the present world. Assuming that a just global order can admit some economic inequalities, these inequalities need not necessarily be of the sort and scale that intuitively present a moral problem.

At any rate, granting the institutional approach as an ideal, my main focus here is with its application and implication for a particular nonideal situation. Assuming the institutional approach, what duties of justice do persons have, either individually or in association with others, when just institutions *do not exist*, or when the background order is clearly unjust?[3] If the global order is clearly unjust (as many of us would agree), what obligations do the global rich have towards the poor?

To start, let us bracket one institutional-type response. One might think that if there is an existing unjust institutional arrangement, then one duty, perhaps the most immediate one, is to exit from that arrangement. The duty in this case is the duty to avoid complicity in injustice. We might call this *the duty to disengage* from unjust institutions. But disengaging from an unjust arrangement is a viable moral response to the injustice only if two conditions are presumed: (a) that exit is realistically possible, and (b) that one's duty of justice is merely to avoid complicity in an injustice. Yet, regarding the first condition, there are some arrangements that one cannot effectively exit from, the global order being one possible example. As for the second condition, it is disputable that one's duty of justice is limited to just that of avoiding injustice. If we hold that we have the duty to prevent and correct certain injustices whether or not we are causally implicated in them, then exiting from an unjust situation, even if feasible, is not morally permissible if there is the alternative of remaining engaged and correcting the injustice. Indeed, there are social relationships that one is free not to form, but which, *once formed*, create obligations and responsibilities that preclude voluntary unilateral exit.

So, putting aside moral disengagement as a general solution to our problem, what responsibilities of justice do agents have in an unjust world, meaning by this a world *lacking just institutions* and where present *institutions are mostly unjust*? I am more interested in the form rather than the substance of the responsibility in the following sense.

In an unjust world, persons can take two kinds of actions in response. First, they can directly attend to and assist the victims of global injustice, through direct interagential aid for example. This is something persons can do individually, or something they can deliver in association with others, for example, through NGOs or through their respective states. Although these are actions done either individually or through associations and organizations, I will call them as a class *interpersonal* in that they are acts directed at other agents. Second, they can, again either individually or in association, agitate for global institutional changes, the creation of just global arrangements where they do not exist, and the correction of existing ones that are unjust. Here the individual response to injustice is not directed at the victims of injustice but at institutions or the lack thereof that are causing the injustice. Instead of attempting to provide relief for others directly, this kind of response aims at restructuring or creating new institutional arrangements. Of course, an institutional duty ultimately aims at improving the life prospects of individuals. But it does this, and indeed defines improvement in life prospects as required by justice, via institutions. We can call this form of response an *institutional duty*.[4]

What does the institutional approach say about these two forms of duties? I do not think the institutionalist is necessarily committed to the institutional response in the above sense. After all, an institutionalist could say that the institutional approach is meant only as an ideal theory, and that its proposed division between interpersonal action and the demands of institutions holds only under the perfect condition where *just institutions are in place*. Under the nonideal condition where just arrangements are lacking, she can say this neat division does not apply. This is certainly a plausible and non-ad hoc institutional response. But this way of responding to the problem seems to surrender the institutional approach at the point where it is most needed. To construct an ideal theory of justice, only to quickly rescind it the moment real-world problems threaten and put the theory under stress (on the excuse that the theory is meant only as an ideal) seems to take the force and purpose out of constructing any ideal theory in the first place. We identify ideal theories of justice not for the sake of theorizing, but for the purpose of illuminating and addressing real-world problems. If this is right, then the more interesting and challenging institutionalist response to the above nonideal case is one that privileges the institutional duty: when just arrangements are absent, the most important duty of justice is the institutional duty, that is, the duty to create just institutions. This way of responding maintains the key features of the institutional approach even in nonideal situations, thus sustaining the relevance of the institutional approach as an ideal. The challenge, of course, is that this special focus on institutions, when there are alternative ways of responding to injustices, including through direct interpersonal action, seems rather "fetishistic" to some.[5] My general aim in this chapter is to show that privileging the institutional duty is not as implausible as it might sound.

The institutional duty—that we have the duty to create just institutions when they are absent—will recall (the italicized part) of John Rawls's famous statement: "The [natural duty of justice] requires us to support and to comply with just institutions that exist and apply to us. *It also constrains us to further just arrangements not yet established, at least when this can be done without too much cost to ourselves*" (Rawls 1971: 115, italics added). But my purpose is not to engage in Rawls exegesis and interpretation. That is, I do not make the claim that the account of natural duty I will examine is that which Rawls is committed to. Rather, I will use Rawls's statement mainly as a springboard for exploring two questions. First, what is the significance of the duty to create just arrangements, and why might we think that this duty has a certain primacy in relation to other moral duties (such as directly assisting another)? Second, how are we to understand the limit of this duty to create just arrangements?

2 THE DUTY TO CREATE JUST INSTITUTIONS

The question we are exploring concerns the application of the institutional approach to justice to the nonideal case where just institutions are absent. Thus, it will help to clarify the motivation behind the institutional approach as an ideal. Recollecting the distinctive features of the institutional approach as an ideal, of course, is not equal to a defense of that ideal. But my goal, to reiterate, is not to defend the institutional approach in its ideal formulation, but to clarify and suggest its plausible extension and application to a nonideal situation.

There are several reasons behind the institutional approach.[6] First, given the profound and pervasive impact of institutions on persons' life prospects—institutions determine people's fundamental entitlements and responsibilities—justice cannot be realized without the appropriate institutions. Given this fundamental role of institutions with respect to people's life prospects, justice is considered the first virtue of institutions.

Second, just institutions help secure and maintain conditions of background justice. The endurance of background justice cannot be left to the vagaries of the cumulative effects of personal decisions and actions, but will require that special societal and collective effort be directed towards its creation and maintenance.

Third, related to the second point, the implementation of justice requires social coordination, and common and publicly acknowledged institutional rules help regulate and direct individual conduct in ways conducive to and consistent with justice.

Fourth, justice is a collective project. It is a collective project in two ways. The first is that the enforcement and maintenance of justice are a collective power exercised through the state. Just institutions ensure this collective enforcement and maintenance of justice. That is, justice presumes the rule of law, and the ideal of the rule of law is an institutional one. The second and more important way is that justice is not collective only in its enforcement but in its determination. What justice demands of persons cannot be understood individually, by agents in isolation from each other, but collectively by society as a whole.

For instance, what an individual owes to others on grounds of distributive justice is not something she can decide on her own. Now, she may be able to reason that Rawls's difference principle is the right distributive principle for her society, but what the difference principle in fact demands of her is not something she knows in isolation from others. The detailed implementation of the difference principle is a collective enterprise, involving shared agreement and understanding of the appropriate terms of ownership, contracts, right of transfers, tax schemes, wage laws, and so on. No single person can determine by herself what exactly she owes to others (or what she is entitled to) in her society even if she is able to conclude that the difference principle is the right distributive principle for her society. Accordingly, on this view, justice is a collective project and this collective character of justice necessitates an institutional focus for justice.

The basic idea here, then, is that, on the institutional view, justice is institutionally constituted in the sense that it is only under an institutional order, under a "public system of rules," that agents are able to know more specifically their duties of justice. For example, what the respect for another's property rights will require of me, and what rightly belongs to whom depend on the institutional scheme of property rights that is in force in my society. On the institutional approach, there is no preinstitutional response to this question.[7]

Fifth, and finally, justice in the background conditions of society provides the parameters for individuals' personal and associational pursuits. Put another way, justice sets the bounds of ethical personal life: the kinds of ends people may pursue, how they can go about pursuing them, the kinds of relationships and special commitments they can form and exercise, the range of responsibilities they owe to each other interpersonally are constrained by background justice. For instance, background justice determines the point at which ethical concerns of kinship or friendship degrade into nepotism or cronyism. Institutional justice, by helping define and secure background justice, is necessary for personal ethical life, one might say.[8] The idea is not that the principles of justice "justify" personal pursuits, but that justice has a certain regulative authority over these pursuits. It establishes their bounds even as it allows that there are independent justificatory grounds for persons' ideas of the good life. An institutional focus allows a feasible method of demarcating the boundary between justice and personal and associational life under this assumption of the plurality and independence of ends.

The above familiar points about institutional justice help to explain why there is the primary duty to create just global institutions when they do not exist. Absent just institutions, we risk unjust pervasive and profound effects on persons' lives, effects that non-institutionally focused responses can at most mitigate but not preempt.

Second, without just institutions, we are unable to coordinate individual activity in ways consistent with and conducive to the requirements of justice; without just institutions, not only are we without the means of enforcing justice, but we are unable to each determine what justice requires of us.

And finally, without just institutions, we are unable to pursue personal ends and remain confident that background justice is maintained. Thus, given the primacy of justice, and the significance of institutions for justice, the first duty is to create just institutions when they do not exist.

3 THE PRIMACY OF INSTITUTIONAL DUTY

The above considerations attest to the significance of an institutional target for personal responsibility when just institutions are absent. It is worth noting that to "create just institutions" has wide scope. It can include (i), as stated literally, the creation of new institutions to fill an institutional gap or vacuum (e.g. creation of human rights institutions and laws as in the post-WWII period); (ii) the replacement of existing unjust ones with just institutions (GATT with WTO; reforming existing trade rules); (iii) the reforming of existing unjust institutions without getting rid of them; and (iv) the creation of new specific institutional mechanisms to offset the unjust effects of existing institutions that are impossible or difficult to demolish.[9]

But why should the institutional duty have *primacy* over interpersonal duties? To home in on this question, let us ask the following: is the institutional duty *morally substitutable*? By this, I mean the following. Can agents, instead of striving to create just institutions, opt to provide direct personal assistance and aid to the unjustly disadvantaged, without any loss to the cause of justice? For example, instead of working towards a more just global institutional order, perhaps expending time and resources to help produce structural changes in order to facilitate a more equitable global economic order, may persons (individually, in associations, or as members of a state) use their time and resources to contribute to humanitarian assistance directly to the global disadvantaged?[10]

The institutional approach holds that justice is better served if we create better institutions than if we simply engage in direct interpersonal assistance. In fact, it is necessary that we do so. Accordingly, an institutional duty cannot be wholly substituted with an interpersonal one. Now this might seem to be a case of "institutional fundamentalism," as Amartya Sen (2009: 413) points out. After all, there are situations in which direct interpersonal assistance (e.g. providing direct food aid, foreign aid) seems more urgent than correcting unjust institutional conditions (correcting unjust political institutions that have caused the food shortage). So why should it not be allowed, at least in some instances, that an interpersonal duty can supplant the institutional duty? Moreover, institutions matter because persons matter; thus, prioritizing institutions at the cost of personal suffering seems to be a case of confusing means with end. The institutional view that we may not replace an institutional duty with an interpersonal one without loss in all cases seems to some commentators to be a *reductio* of the approach.

But the non-substitutability claim need not be as glaring a *reductio* as it might seem at first glance. Let me consider some reasons that might temper this charge. First, on the presumption of the pervasive and profound impact of background institutions on persons' life prospects (as mentioned in Section 2 above), taking on "interpersonal duties" without also attending to institutional matters can at best only deal with the *symptoms of injustice*. An interpersonal response will be, at most, palliative rather than curative, we might say. Moreover, interpersonal responses will not secure the background conditions of justice, and might even, since they are uncoordinated, risk canceling each other out. Most significantly, these responses, in the absence of just background institutions, can be blind to what justice requires. Given that the determination of justice is collective in nature, as mentioned above, whether an ethical response is commensurate or responsive to what justice demands cannot be fully ascertained in the absence of just institutions.

Thus, without adequate background institutions in place, individuals not only are unable to coordinate their joint objective of promoting justice. They will be left in the dark as to what it is that they owe to one another. What is rightly mine that I may rightly redistribute in the name of economic justice? Which of the many needy individuals should I redistribute resources to? And to which particular problem of social injustice—abject poverty, inequality in education, or lack of access to healthcare—do I devote my attention?

These three questions—*what* is rightly mine and *what* I owe to others, *to whom* I owe, and to *which* aspect of injustice I should devote attention—highlight the necessity of social institutions. Without social arrangements in the background, individuals cannot know precisely what they rightly own and what they owe to others. Without just distributive institutions that are publicly affirmed, there is the danger of partiality regarding the recipients of redistribution, as when a philanthropist decides on her own which subset of individuals to assist. And social agendas and causes that are identified and pursued privately rather than publicly through shared institutions are prone to a certain arbitrariness and lack of accountability.

It is true that an advantaged country like the United States can go it alone and increase its direct assistance to poorer countries severalfold, and still be fairly confident that this will be in the direction of justice without any danger of exceeding or otherwise transgressing its limits. But what exactly, what more, does global justice require of the United States? What is the minimum that its government should do? Moreover, while the demands of justice remain unspecified and unarticulated, direct personal assistance risks getting misclassified as charitable or supererogatory acts rather than as requirements of justice. One implication of this is that, in the absence of specified duties of justice, personal responses tend to fall far short of what justice should require.[11]

The above does not deny that the treatment of symptoms of injustice can be hugely important and, in some cases, the more important thing to do. But it has to be recognized that such responses have very different goals. They deal with the symptoms of injustice rather than with its causes. To be sure, certain situations may demand a trade-off in favor of providing immediate treatment of symptoms versus addressing the cause (background institutions). But the cost with respect to institution creation has to be acknowledged. An interpersonal duty cannot be substituted for an institutional duty without some loss from the standpoint of justice.

The apparent implausibility of the non-substitution claim is further mitigated if we recall the collective character of promoting justice (see Section 2 above). If justice is a collective enterprise, a shared task of members of a social order, then the requirement that just institutions be created is a requirement of that social order. The non-substitution claim thus applies to the social order as a whole, to wit, that a society's duty to establish just institutions cannot be replaced by some other moral action. That is, within a given social order, there has to be a collective effort directed at creating the necessary just institutions. This means, however, that at the level of the individual agent, when there are sufficient others in society already engaged in institution-building, there will be space for some individuals to trade in the institutional duty for some interpersonal duty to mitigate the effects of prevailing injustice. Considered as a collective enterprise, the primary duty to create just institutions need not be a duty that has to fall on all persons equally. It is a collective duty belonging to the relevant social order (e.g. the global order as a whole), and how that collective duty is divided up among specific agents is a further matter. It is not necessarily the case that the collective duty must be divided up in exactly the same way for all individuals.

There is the possibility, then, on this collective reading of the natural duty to create just institutions, for a division of moral labor among individuals that can make room for some individuals to take on direct interpersonal duties. Where there is sufficient societal effort aimed at creating just institutions, the fact that some persons are opting to engage in direct interpersonal duties (to alleviate suffering) does not by itself compromise the (collective) cause of realizing justice. Seen as a collective responsibility, what is most important is that the duty to create institutions is discharged by the group, and not how that collective duty is parceled out among individuals of the group. The institutional approach, therefore, does not absurdly renounce the individual who is choosing to do good non-institutionally. Perhaps there can be the worry that these individuals are free-riding in that they are able to attend fully to promoting the good only because others (but not they) are doing their share of the collective duty of justice. But if this is free-riding, it is a very innocuous case of free-riding—they are after all performing a needed moral service here by taking on other duties in response to the effects of injustice (even though responding to the cause is still more fundamental).

Here one might wonder if the exclusive focus on institution creation looks too much to the long term and forgets that injustice can have immediate and urgent implications that call for short-term remedial responses as well. Against this point, three points can be reiterated. First, the duty to create just institutions, as noted above, includes a range of different institutionally directed activities, and these in fact can have various more immediate mitigating effects against injustice. The duty to remove unjust institutions can require the cessation of personal support for and participation in the tainted institution, and this can have near-term direct implications for persons affected by the injustice. For example, the act of subverting racist legal arrangements is an institutional response that can have immediate remedial effects for the discriminated. Second, as noted above, the duty to create just institutions is a collective one, and a division of labor among persons in society allows space for certain individuals to personally perform acts of mitigation. This opens up the possibility that when a society as a whole is furthering the cause of justice (by promoting the right institutions), certain individuals are available and prepared to undertake interpersonal mitigating duties towards victims of injustice. Thirdly, justice does not exhaust the whole of morality; so even when our work of justice is done or is being done, there can be additional moral demands on us. Just as we can have duties of beneficence to the unfortunate victim of an accident *even in an ideally just society*, so too we have duties of beneficence to persons in an unjust society. Indeed we have these duties a fortiori when the needy person's condition is due to background injustice. In short, prioritizing institutional duty does not mean that in practice actions aimed at more immediately mitigating human suffering will be ignored.

Finally, a key function of the institutional focus is that of establishing stable and publicly known background conditions against which persons form their legitimate expectations and claims against each other. Background institutions secure a state of affairs that is not at the mercy of the happenstance goodwill of private individuals. Imagine a society whose economic institutions are unjust, but whose advantaged members happen to have an enlarged sense of *noblesse oblige*. So they privately redistribute their (unjust) gains to their least-advantaged compatriots, and in doing so achieve a distributional state of affairs not different from that which a just set of institutions would obtain (assuming that this is possible without public institutions to impartially carry out the distribution). So we have an end state that would be preferable to that of a similar society with the same kind of unjust institutions but whose inhabitants lack the same degree of personal generosity. Still we would not say that justice is realized in that first society. The unjust effects of its institutions are happily offset by the goodwill of its inhabitants, but this is hardly a stable situation or one that the disadvantaged can confidently count on and build expectations around. The happy distributional outcome is wholly contingent on the whim and fancy of the privileged. Just institutional arrangements, on the other hand, ensure that a just distributional outcome does not rest on the "arbitrary will" of others.[12] While, interpersonally, the inhabitants of a society with bad institutions but very good people can appear to be on equal terms with each other, its unjust background institutions in fact betray a hierarchical society in which domination of some by others remains in place even if not at the moment in play.

Indeed, we would prefer a society where persons grumpily (but out of a sense of justice) comply with the requirements of just institutions to one with unjust institutions but very nice, big-hearted persons. There is a certain stability and reliability of legitimate expectations in the former that will be absent in the latter.

The arguments in this section might appear to be question-begging to some readers. If I assume the institutional approach as an ideal, then my recommendations with regard to the nonideal case follow (the readers might grant). But how can this be a defense of the institutional approach, one might object?

This objection, however, misunderstands the challenge I am confronting. The challenge I have in mind, to reiterate, insists that the institutional approach is bunk because its recommendation, that we attend to institution creation even when more good could be done through direct personal action, is patently counterintuitive. That is, even if we accept the approach in its ideal formulation, we should ultimately reject it because of this absurdity of application, so the objection charges. For example, how could it be right, Liam Murphy (1999: 281) asks rhetorically, that our duty of justice requires us to focus on institution building even when we "could do more to reduce inequality, alleviate suffering or whatever by direct action [interpersonal duty]." My arguments in this chapter are directed at this particular challenge. I have tried to show that the proposal of the institutional approach that we attend to and prioritize institutions is hardly implausible on the face of it. To the contrary, it rather makes sense, so I have tried to argue, on one plausible understanding of the nature of justice. One might find other problems with the institutional duty, and one would if one rejects the institutional approach from the start. But this is not because it is starkly counterintuitive. In this regard, my claim that the institutional duty is not counterintuitive is not any more question-begging than the objection (as raised by Murphy, for example) that it is.

4 THE LIMITS OF DUTY

On the institutional approach, in the ideal situation where there are just institutional rules in the background, persons are free to pursue their various ends on the condition that they meet the demands of justice. As noted at the start of this chapter, in the ideal case, persons' duty of justice is limited to supporting, maintaining, and complying with just institutions, and to ensuring that the cumulative effects of their decisions do not undermine these institutions. The institutional approach thus provides a way of specifying the limits of our duty of justice and demarcating the space for legitimate personal pursuits.

It does not follow, however, that the duty of justice in the ideal case is thus undemanding: supporting and complying with just institutions require individual attentiveness and action. What the institutional approach offers is not the relaxation of the demands of justice but a means by which the limits of our responsibility for justice can, in principle, be identified. We have the non-trivial duty to comply with and support just institutions, but we are also free within the terms of just institutions to set and pursue their own personal or associational ends.

But the limitation specified by the institutional approach under ideal theory is not straightforwardly applicable in the nonideal case where just institutions are lacking. In this situation, there are no just institutional terms for individuals to support and to comply with, which can then define the limits of their duty and correspondingly define the space for their permissible personal pursuits. As an example, if the global institutional order is not sufficiently just, how can we determine the limits of our duties of global justice and accordingly the acceptable scope of our personal and national projects?

A possible response to this problem is that all personal and associational pursuits are to be put on hold until just arrangements are brought about and all capable agents are to devote their energy towards the creation of these just arrangements in the meantime. The argument here might be that since it is just arrangements that define the permissible bounds of personal and associational ends and pursuits, there can be no admissible personal and associational ends and pursuits until just institutions are in place (to do the defining). Thus, any personal pursuit will be morally questionable, and if agents have an interest in setting and realizing personal goals, they must acknowledge that it is necessary for them to first direct all their efforts towards the creating of just institutions.

The obvious problem with this solution is that it will radically impoverish human morality as we know it. If we think that the attainment of fully just institutions is only aspirational, that a fully just state of affairs is an ideal that we can try to aim at and be closer to or further from, but it is not a condition that we should expect to realize on earth, then no personal and associational projects can ever be morally legitimate as part of the human condition. But this, for some, will be a rather bleak conclusion. We will have to either resign ourselves to, and lament, the fact that none of our valuable personal and associational goals and projects can be fully morally legitimate or renounce the setting and pursuit of such goals. The latter will of course radically alter human relations and our moral conceptions beyond recognition. As Ronald Dworkin notes:

> When injustice is substantial and pervasive in a political community, any private citizen who accepts *a personal responsibility to do whatever he possibly can* to repair it will end by denying himself the personal projects and attachments, as well as the pleasures and frivolities, that are essential to a decent and rewarding life.
>
> (Dworkin 1989: 502–4; see also Dworkin 2000: 266, 278–80)

Even if we do not sign up to the aspirational view of justice, but hold instead that the attainment of ideal justice among humans is possible, it still is the case that pro tem, while just institutions are lacking, there is no permissible scope for personal pursuits on this solution. Such a moral worldview, even if it is not taken to be descriptive of our permanent state, will still be rather impoverishing. Even if we accept that justice is attainable within human existence, it need not be attainment necessarily within particular persons' lifetimes. It will mean that, for some people, a "decent and rewarding life" is not available to them.

The institutional approach, I believe, can offer a more appealing understanding of the limits of individuals' duty of justice to create just institutions. It can say the following: "Persons have the duty of justice to do their share as part of *a collective effort* to bring about *just arrangements*. If individuals are doing their part to create just arrangements, they are then free to set and pursue personal and associational projects."

The italicized phrases ("just arrangements" and "collective effort") of this proposal highlight two ways the institutional approach can help identify the limits of one's duty. One is its specification, and thus the delimitation, of one's moral target. Instead of attending to all possible moral situations, including attending to the needs of persons whom she can directly affect, the agent is asked to direct her attention primarily to institutions. The field of her moral concern, in other words, is significantly situated or circumscribed on this institutional account. Instead of thinking that she should be responsive to all the problems of injustice around her that she can effectively do something about, the agent need only concentrate her efforts on the background institutions of her society.

This target specification limits the site of an agent's concern of justice, and so goes some way towards making her duty of justice more manageable. It identifies the arena where justice matters. Still, it should be pointed out that a target specification alone does not ensure that a duty of justice cannot be excessively burdensome. It is consistent with an institutional target to hold that while individuals' concern for justice is limited to institutions, they should, nonetheless, do all they can, give their all, to bring about just arrangements, and that until they achieve this end, they should drop everything else they are doing.

Thus, it is still necessary to state a personal cost limitation here: that agents are required to try to bring about just arrangements "where this can be done without too much cost" to the agent. Unlike in the ideal case, where just institutional rules specify the limits of one's duty of justice, there is no built-in limitation in the nonideal case where just institutional rules are absent. Thus, there is a need to specify a personal cost limitation that does not presume just institutional rules.

How is this cost limitation to be defined? The ambiguity of "without too much cost" might appear to some readers to count against the institutional view. So it is worth noting that a personal cost limitation to one's moral duty is not a problem for the institutional view alone. Any plausible moral theory needs to acknowledge and specify certain limits to personal responsibility, and it is not the case that these limits are always easy to clearly define. So, even if the limitation can only be rough and ready, such as "persons ought to do their part to create just arrangements up to the point where further action will undermine their morally significant personal and association goals and projects," the lack of exactitude is not a problem afflicting the institutional view of justice alone.

To the contrary, I think the institutional approach can in fact go some way towards specifying a personal cost limitation. Here, the "collective" character of the institutional duty comes into play. Recall that one of the motivating reasons for its institutional focus is the belief that justice is a collective enterprise. The duty to bring about justice is a collective project rather than a personal one. But a collective duty needs to be assigned *fairly* amongst members of the collective.

The question of how a collective duty is to be assigned fairly among the constituents of the collective is one that is well trodden in the philosophical literature. Here I will sketch the form of an answer that I hope is plausible and promising. The main thing is to notice the way in which this solution draws on a key feature of the institutional approach, namely the centrality of a collectively and mutually supported background arrangement for justice. The basic idea is that a fair assignment of a collective duty among individual agents will depend on what each agent is reasonably expected to do on the ground of mutuality. Thus, a necessary condition of any fair assignment of a collective duty (to create just institutions) among the constituents is that the assignment satisfies the criterion of mutuality, that is, that it is an assignment that all having a share in the responsibility can reasonably accept. This condition of mutuality will place some limits on the demandingness of the duty on any individual. For if the share of each has to be collectively determined, subject to the criterion of mutuality to be fair, no one will impose an unreasonably strong demand on another that she herself, when similarly situated, cannot reasonably accept.[13] Now, it is in principle possible that, on this collective determination of each person's duty, the duty turns out to be implausibly overly demanding. But what makes this an unlikely outcome is that an implausibly demanding share for each is unlikely to be mutually acceptable.

This understanding of the limits of one's institutional duty accommodates the common-sense belief that it is possible, if not all the more likely, that our duties of justice will be more demanding under unjust conditions than under conditions of ideal justice. We normally expect that, in times of war, in situations where there is pervasive injustice, and so on, we each, as agents of justice, will have more work to do, more sacrifices to make, than in conditions of peace and justice. And we normally think that the burden each agent has in response to injustice can be heavier the more severe the degree of injustice being confronted. The mutuality condition allows a flexible upper limit to duties under nonideal conditions. The limit it specifies is sensitive to the degree of injustice that is being confronted. In the case of extreme injustice, where we are facing a tyrannical order, for instance, we can imagine a mutual acceptance of a high level of personal sacrifice (in terms of personal projects and special commitments) in the pursuit of justice. Facing less severe injustices, we can expect mutual acceptance of a lower level of personal sacrifice of personal and associational ends.

In sum, the institutional approach as an ideal can provide guidance in the nonideal case with respect to the question of the limits of one's duty of justice. The limit to an agent's duty to create just institutions is defined by its circumscribed target (institutions) and the requirement of a mutually acceptable distribution of the collective burden of establishing just institutions.

Applying the above discussion to global justice, we can say the following: In the absence of just global background institutions, individuals—either personally or as members of associations like states—have the duty of justice to do their part to bring about just global arrangements. Their more partial projects and pursuits—including personal and national ones—are morally questionable if they pursue these ends without also doing their part to bring about just global arrangements. But it also means that a country's national pursuits are morally acceptable only if that country is also doing its part to create just institutions. Because each country's share of this (global) collective duty to create just global arrangements is subject to mutual acceptance, we can expect that there will be some reasonable limits on this duty, thus preserving space still for valuable national pursuits at the same time.

In my quest to show how the institutional approach can help identify the reasonable limits on our duty of justice even under conditions of injustice, an objection might be raised that I have proved too much. That is, a critic might complain from the other direction that the institutional approach is objectionably lax. But in response to this complaint, it is worth reiterating that an institutional focus by itself does not make a duty lax. As I have said, it is compatible with an institutional target specification to place a very unrestrictive personal cost limitation to one's duty, such that, although a person's duty is limited to the creation of just institutions, she must not cease in this quest, may not sleep the sleep of the just, till that very goal is achieved. The target specification given by the institutional view clarifies the agent's moral site, in this sense making her responsibilities more organized and to this extent less unmanageably burdensome. But, in this case, her duty is in fact very (and unreasonably) demanding. Thus, there is nothing inherently slack about an institutional duty.

Neither does the mutual acceptance of one's personal share of a collective duty to create just institutions weaken her individual responsibility to promote justice. If it cannot be mutually acceptable to require agents of justice to give up their personal life for the sake of justice, neither is it mutually acceptable to the victims of injustice in the same society to not expect potential agents to take on significant obligations to realize justice. The mutual acceptability condition, therefore, cuts both ways: it both limits and requires personal action.

5 CONCLUSION

The aim of this reflection is to see if the institutional approach to global justice can provide some guidance for nonideal theory: that is, what responsibilities do persons have in the context of global injustice, where just institutions are lacking?

I suggest that the institutional approach, in this nonideal case, specifies that our concern is primarily to create just global arrangements, and that it can also provide reasonable guidance concerning the limits of our personal responsibility in this regard.

The institutional approach acknowledges that the demands of global justice have to allow space for legitimate patriotic, nationalist, and other individual and associational pursuits. Limiting the demands of justice to institutions provides a way of feasibly demarcating the demands of justice from other associational and personal demands. But personal and associational values are not *wholly* annulled or morally delegitimized necessarily under conditions of injustice. Under this nonideal condition, the institutional approach would require that agents do their part to create and promote just institutions. And their fair share will not typically require that persons drop all their associational and personal projects while justice is not yet realized. While it is the case that sacrifices will have to be made, unless the injustice at hand is extraordinary, the pursuit of justice will not require the denial of all personal or associational ends. The institutional view recognizes the limit of our duty of justice and can offer a way of identifying this limit that is sensitive to the level of injustice being confronted.

Rather than being overly lax about justice, the institutional approach, in fact, reaffirms the normative priority of justice. Global justice has regulative primacy over nationalist and patriotic pursuits. Nationalistic and patriotic pursuits are morally tainted when people engage in these without also doing their bit to bring about a more just global institutional order. Thus, far from trivializing our duties of justice, the institutional view gives them moral importance and urgency: the legitimacy of our personal and national lives is in doubt if we do not do our part to bring about more justice in our world order.

ACKNOWLEDGMENTS

I had the opportunity to discuss this paper at the Georgia State/Biefeld Conference on Global Justice (Fall 2012), and at Villanova University (Fall 2013). I am grateful to participants and audiences at these venues, with very special acknowledgement to Rüdiger Bittner for his critical commentary at the Georgia State conference. Thanks also to Chris Melenovsky, Collin Anthony and Eric Boot for several helpful discussions. Most especially, I thank Thom Brooks for his helpful comments and suggestions. Finally, this paper draws on some arguments outlined in my "Injustice and Personal Pursuits" (unpublished ms.), and I am indebted to many individuals for comments, including Daniele Botti, Michael Kates, Rainer Forst, Darrel Moellendorf, Eszter Kollar and Pietro Maffetone.

NOTES

1. Consider John Rawls's remark that "within the framework of background justice set up by the basic structure, individuals and their associations may do as they wish insofar as the rules of institutions permit" (Rawls 2001: 50).
2. See, e.g., the challenge by Cohen (2008). I survey the debate inspired by Cohen's challenge in Tan (2012: pt I).

3. In the case of global justice, it is typically the case that much of individuals' responsibility for justice will be discharged via their respective states. In this case, their efforts in bringing about global justice are associational in their performance rather than personal.

4. There are, of course, actions that blur the distinction between these two forms of duties. For example, when an individual contributes to an NGO that is both in the business of providing humanitarian relief where needed and in the business of campaigning for global structural changes, her action can be described as both institutional and interpersonal, since her contribution will go towards institutional building as well as humanitarian relief. But there are cases where one course of action falls more clearly under one category than the other. For instance, it reasonable to say that a country providing assistance directly to another country (e.g. direct food aid) within an existing global framework is responding in a different way from another country that is attempting to restructure the global order (e.g. supporting reform in trade laws). The first response is aimed directly at assisting another agent, so is interpersonal in form, whereas the second is aimed at reforming and creating institutions, and is institutional in form.

5. For instance, see Murphy (1999: 281).

6. The following paragraphs draw on Tan (2012).

7. The last comment aligns with Kant's position on duties of right and institutions. For one account of this Kantian idea, see Christiano (2008, esp. ch. 2). The idea of the basic structure as a "public system of rules" is in Rawls (1971: 55).

8. e.g. Rawls (1971: 110).

9. For relevant and related discussions on institutional responses to global injustice, see especially Pogge, (2001) and Miller (2010).

10. Imagine, on the one hand, providing funding and advocating for organizations like the UN to create better global institutions and laws, and means of law enforcement and reporting of violations, and, on the other hand, unilaterally providing food aid directly to impoverished persons and societies.

11. Sen is right to worry that we have a problem if a fixation on what justice is or is not distracts us from the prospect and urgency of mitigating injustice. But mitigating injustice without understanding what justice is is blind, so I would argue, even as understanding what justice is without acknowledging that we need to mitigate injustice along the way is empty.

12. See Pettit (1997). I thank Eric Boot (p.c.) for reminding me of the connection between a just institutional arrangement and non-arbitrariness.

13. There is some resemblance here with Liam Murphy's view that one's personal share of the collective duty to promote well-being is to be determined relationally under presumption of full compliance, and one's actual responsibility does not increase just because others fail to comply (Murphy 2000: 76–8). But this resemblance in our accounts should not obscure the difference between our positions concerning the relationship between institutions and justice that is central to the present discussion.

References

Christiano, Thomas (2008) *The Constitution of Equality: Democratic Authority and its Limits.* Oxford: Oxford University Press.

Cohen, G. A. (2008) *Rescuing Justice and Equality.* Cambridge, MA: Harvard University Press.

Dworkin, Ronald (1989) "Liberal Community," *California Law Review* 77: 471–504.

Dworkin, Ronald (2000) *Sovereign Virtue: The Theory and Practice of Equality*. Cambridge, MA: Harvard University Press.

Miller, Richard W. (2010) *Globalizing Justice: The Ethics of Poverty and Power*. Oxford: Oxford University Press.

Murphy, Liam B. (1999) "Institutions and the Demands of Justice," *Philosophy and Public Affairs* 27: 251–91.

Murphy, Liam B. (2000) *Moral Demands in Nonideal Theory*. New York: Oxford University Press.

Pettit, Philip (1997) *Republicanism: A Theory of Freedom and Government*. Oxford: Oxford University Press.

Pogge, Thomas (2001) *World Poverty and Human Rights*. Oxford: Polity Press.

Rawls, John (1971) *A Theory of Justice*. Cambridge, MA: Harvard University Press.

Rawls, John (2001) *Justice as Fairness*. Cambridge, MA: Harvard University Press.

Sen, Amartya (2009) *The Idea of Justice*. Cambridge, MA: Harvard University Press.

Tan, Kok-Chor (2012) *Justice, Institutions, and Luck*. Oxford: Oxford University Press.

FURTHER READING

Berkey, Brian (2016) "Against Rawlsian Institutionalism about Justice," *Social Theory and Practice* 42(4): 706–32.

Cohen, G. A. (2001) *If You're an Egalitarian, How Come You're So Rich?* Cambridge, MA: Harvard University Press.

Freeman, Samuel (2011) "The Basic Structure of Society as the Primary Subject of Justice." In Jon Mandle and David A. Reidy (eds.), *A Companion to Rawls*. Malden, MA: Wiley Blackwell, 88–111.

Hodgson, Louis-Philippe (2012) "Why the Basic Structure?" *Canadian Journal of Philosophy* 42(3/4): 303–34.

Young, Iris Marion (2011) *Responsibility for Justice*. Oxford: Oxford University Press.

CHAPTER 24

THINKING NORMATIVELY ABOUT GLOBAL JUSTICE WITHOUT SYSTEMATIC REFLECTION ON GLOBAL CAPITALISM

The Paradigmatic Case of Rawls

JIWEI CI

1 INTRODUCTION

ON the back cover of *Justice as Fairness*, we find what amounts to a candid admission by Rawls (2001) that "since the publication of *A Theory of Justice* in 1971, American society has moved farther away from the idea of justice as fairness."[1] One might add, in the same vein, that since the publication of *The Law of Peoples* in 1999, international society has moved away just as much from Rawls's vision of a just Society of Peoples, despite the fact that this vision is less demanding (and hence widely considered less attractive) than Rawls's conception of domestic justice. In both cases, what is true of Rawls may be said to be true of the fate of liberal egalitarianism in general.

The blurb for *Justice as Fairness* gives no hint of the causal story of these unhappy trends. Nor, more significantly, is such a causal story anywhere to be found in the book itself or, to the best of my knowledge, in Rawls's other writings. More generally, one could be forgiven for the impression that liberal normative political philosophy as a whole does not seem too keen to get to the bottom of what has caused the ever-widening gap between what liberal egalitarianism prescribes, domestically and globally, and where the world is heading.

Even in the absence of a causal account that might serve as a basis for rational hope (and fear), the blurb insists, in a spirit it would not be unreasonable to attribute to Rawls himself, that Rawls's "ideas retain their power and relevance" and serve as proof that "moral clarity can be achieved even when a collective commitment to justice is uncertain." The same, one surmises, might be said by Rawls in the face of the widening gap between his vision of a just Society of Peoples and the reality of the world as a whole.

Now is not the time to subject Rawls's *normative* vision of global justice to yet another, perhaps more severe critique. As the prospect of this vision coming true is receding ever farther, one would not be amiss to perceive the vision itself as more attractive from a purely normative point of view. I for one often cannot help warming to this vision much more than I was able to when it was first proposed. What is troubling about it, rather, and calls for further, and a different kind of, scrutiny lies elsewhere—in a certain lack of relevance and clarity that is reflected in the inability of Rawls's conception of global justice to come to grips with a real world it is designed to understand and shape. This is a problem of understanding—above all, of democracy's relation to capitalism, and hence of democracy itself, in the real world—rather than one of purely normative appeal as such.

2 A Realistic Utopia with No Reference to Capitalism

The relevance and moral clarity claimed by or on behalf of Rawls are to be understood in the context of what Rawls calls "realistic utopia":

> I begin and end with the idea of a realistic utopia. Political philosophy is realistically utopian when it extends what are ordinarily thought of as the limits of practical political possibility. Our hope for the future of our society rests on the belief that the nature of the social world allows reasonably just constitutional democratic societies existing as members of the Society of Peoples. In such a social world peace and justice would be achieved between liberal and decent peoples both at home and abroad. The idea of this society is realistically utopian in that it depicts an achievable social world that combines political right and justice for all liberal and decent peoples in a Society of Peoples.   (Rawls 1999: 6)

What Rawls means by *realistic* utopia is less straightforward than may appear at first sight. The obvious part of his meaning is that human nature and the nature of the social world as we know them—to be more precise, the nature of human social existence in abstraction from the actual constitution, however stable and enduring, of any particular society such as contemporary American society or the societies that make up the world today—do not make the utopia impossible. But Rawls seems also to have in mind something considerably more realistic than this. For he speaks routinely of liberal democracies and gives us to understand that actual liberal democracies, as exemplified by the Unites States (Rawls 1999: 101), imperfect as they may be, are close enough to the ideal to count as the real thing. If liberal democracies alone made up the Society of Peoples, it would seem, Rawls's utopia would be realistic not only in the first sense but even in the stronger sense of being close at hand. Indeed, this much is quite readily infer-able from what Rawls has to say about "democratic peace" (more of this later). If we are actually farther removed from Rawls's utopia, the main reason must be that what Rawls calls decent peoples are few and far between. Such peoples are perhaps as yet more ficti-tious than real in Rawls's estimation, with Rawls finding it necessary to invent an imagi-nary example of a decent hierarchical people in the shape of "Kazanistan."[2] But for this unfortunate circumstance, for which liberal democracies are not to blame, a just Society of Peoples as prescribed by Rawls's ideal theory would already be more real than uto-pian, with the occasional cases of so-called outlaw states and burdened societies to be handled in accordance with nonideal theory. As far as the liberal democratic members of the Society of Peoples are concerned, Rawls would thus have every reason, given his line of argument, to describe his conception of global justice in terms of realistic utopia; if anything, to call this conception realistic is an understatement.

But is it really true that what chiefly stands in the way of realizing Rawls's ideal theory—of making total what would otherwise only be a partial democratic peace—is the lack of decent peoples, which leaves the world populated with far too many outlaw states or burdened societies? Even if this were true to one degree or another, such a scenario would not explain the fact with which we began, namely, that the United States, among other liberal democracies, is itself departing ever more sharply from the ideal of justice as fairness. Nor would it help quell the suspicion that the worsening of injustice in the domestic setting of liberal democracies, by Rawls's standard, has not merely coincided with growing injustice in the global setting, also by Rawls's standard, but is actually part of a larger dynamic in which the two trends are intimately connected.[3] However one may be inclined to account for these trends, it is undeniable that both trends have devel-oped at a time when, with the ending of the Cold War, liberal democracies led by the United States have increasingly become the truly hegemonic power bloc in the world, defining the only game in town and setting its rules as never before. Now, if actual liberal democracies remain close enough to the democratic ideal to be spoken of as such, as Rawls clearly seems to think, and if they are dominant in the world, as is manifestly the case, it would be hard to resist the hypothesis that liberal democracy is not the solution to global injustice that Rawls takes it to be but rather the problem in its present form. That part of Rawls's realistic utopia which involves liberal democracies is simply too good to be true. And Rawls's illusions to the contrary make his intended realistic utopia completely unrealistic and thoroughly utopian.

Not that Rawls treats liberal democracies as they exist today as already perfect or even nearly so. In advancing his ideal theory, however, Rawls is clearly presupposing actually existing liberal democracies such as the United States to be imperfect in ways that do not make them incapable, in principle, of progressing toward the requirements of ideal the-ory. This is a crucial presupposition, one that underpins Rawls's entire realistic utopia. For if this presupposition turns out to be mistaken, then Rawls's utopia of a just Society of Peoples would be doomed from the start—not on account of the irredeemable immorality hypothetically feared by Rawls, as by Kant before him (Rawls 1999: 128) but because Rawls's utopia is insufficiently realistic in its understanding and appraisal of liberal democracy and its moral potential.

What may well be insufficiently realistic in this regard is Rawls's separation—one is tempted to say utopian separation—of liberal democracy from capitalism, and, in more general terms, of the political system from the mode of production. This separation is not incidental to Rawls's theory but fundamental to it, both normatively and method-ologically. I am not implying the blanket suggestion that any contemporary normative political philosophy that does not take account of capitalism in some way is open to the charge of being out of touch with reality. The problem with Rawls is rather more specific: if one is thinking normatively about global justice and is assigning an important and positive role to liberal democracies in this context, as Rawls is doing, one would be missing a structurally and dynamically essential part of our world and of liberal democracy by leaving capitalism normatively and causally out of account. This is all the more true if, as is also the case with Rawls, one requires one's normative vision to have a realistic grip on the world.

Where could things have gone wrong with a thinker as informed and scrupulous in his knowledge of the world as Rawls was? Some such question is unavoidable in view of Rawls's systematic attention to relevant facts about the world. Rawls mentions, for example, four such facts (reasonable pluralism, democratic unity in diversity, public reason, and liberal democratic peace) which in his view support his realistic utopia, facts that are supposedly "confirmed by reflecting on history and political experience" (Rawls 1999: 124). What is striking is that none of these facts concerns capitalism in general or global capitalism in particular, and yet these facts, if such they indeed are, are not generic properties of human nature or human society but rather specific, empirical features of the modern world. Implicit in Rawls's exclusion of capitalism from consideration is the belief that the fact of capitalism in general and of global capitalism in particular is not relevant to his project at hand. Why? Because, as one might reasonably surmise, Rawls sees himself as continuing the tradition of liberal political philosophy, and, given this, nothing should have come more naturally to him than a certain sepa-ration between the political and the economic that has been so central to liberal political philosophy.[4]

Some such separation is clearly at work in Rawls's description of the two main ideas that motive his Law of Peoples:

> One is that the great evils of human history—unjust war and oppression, religious persecution and the denial of liberty of conscience, starvation and poverty, not to mention genocide and mass murder—follow from political injustice, with its own cruelties and callousness.... The other main idea...is that, once the gravest forms of political injustice are eliminated by following just (or at least decent) social policies and establishing just (or at least decent) basic institutions, these great evils will eventually disappear.   (Rawls 1999: 6–7)

Both of these ideas, as we can readily see, rest on the separation of the political and the economic. This is not to say that the political and the economic in general, and liberal democracy and capitalism in particular, may not be related in various ways, even very closely, according to the liberal tradition or to Rawls as its most influential contemporary exponent. Yet it remains importantly true that it is only as two distinct categories of human activity, each with its relatively independent logic and dynamic, that they are viewed as thus related. Nor is it to imply that the economic structure cannot be more or less guided or regulated by considerations of justice as determined, say, through the use of public reason. Yet it remains equally importantly true that, whatever the degree of guidance or regulation, what happens in the economic domain is largely left to the distinctive motivations of economic agents, even though such motivations have profound spillover effects on the same agents in their capacity as citizens and on society as a whole.[5] It follows that political philosophy, whether pursued in a domestic or global setting, has every reason to address liberal democracy without conjoining it with capitalism. Indeed, the integrity of political philosophy may be taken to demand no less.

Matters may seem somewhat complicated by an important feature of Rawls's theory. Rawls distinguishes between principles of justice on the one hand and the realization of these principles in an appropriate regime type on the other. As far as the latter is concerned, Rawls favors a property-owning democracy, along with liberal (democratic) socialism, over a capitalist welfare state and sees such a democracy as an alternative to capitalism.[6] Here we see the conscience and daring of Rawls's liberalism at its best. Unfortunately, however, this applies only to Rawls's account of domestic justice, and there is no trace of it in his conception of the Law of Peoples. The result is that the liberal democracies that figure in Rawls's Society of Peoples are not specified as, or required to be, property-owning democracies. This seems to imply that in this context liberal democracies are to be understood by default as capitalist welfare states (at best) and that, as such, they are good enough for Rawls's Law of Peoples. In any case, the very insistence on *realistic* utopia rules out construing liberal peoples in terms of property-owning democracies for now and the foreseeable future. It is only reasonable, therefore, that we approach Rawls's global realistic utopia on this understanding of liberal democracy.

"What would a reasonably just constitutional democracy be like under reasonably favorable *historical* conditions that are possible given the laws and tendencies of society?," asks Rawls, "And how do these conditions relate to laws and tendencies bearing on the relations between peoples?" (Rawls 1999: 11, emphasis added). His answer: "These *historical* conditions include, in a reasonably just domestic society, the fact of reasonable pluralism. In the Society of Peoples, the parallel to reasonable pluralism is the diversity among reasonable peoples with their different cultures and traditions of thought, both religious and nonreligious" (Rawls 1999: 11, emphasis added). Since Rawls makes no reference here to capitalism as being among the relevant historical conditions, the question naturally arises as to whether these historical conditions, as Rawls understands them, strictly exclude the facts of capitalism in general and of global capitalism in particular. Rawls does not say, but the supposed realism of his realistic utopia clearly depends on assuming the independence of what he calls political life, on the belief that political life as narrowly conceived by him can take place in a way or in a setting that is largely independent of (to use Rawls's terms) the "laws and tendencies" of the capitalist mode of production. That is why Rawls is able to speak of "the *political* Society of well-ordered Peoples" (Rawls 1999: 123, emphasis added) as if it were an independently functioning entity.

The above assumption is as precarious as it is indispensable. For any serious recognition of capitalism as constituting part of the logic and dynamic of the relevant historical conditions would introduce a determinant with the distinct possibility of overwhelming what one might otherwise comfortably treat as more or less independent considerations of political justice. In particular, once capitalism is deemed to belong among the relevant historical conditions, one important factor bearing on the relations between peoples, even perhaps the most important such factor, will be whether they all live in societies that are capitalist or whether some of them, say, the decent hierarchical societies, are not capitalist or not fully so. If the first scenario is true, all societies will have capitalism as their common denominator, and this fact must then be weighed against the fact that only some societies are liberal democratic, while others are not, without assuming in advance that their shared capitalism will determine international relations less strongly than differences in their political regime do. If the second scenario is true, we must once again entertain the possibility that the nature of a society's economy may be as powerful a determinant of its relations with other societies as its political structure is. In either case, our world will look very different from the way it does when it is accepted, as an article of faith, that the political is able to operate with "laws and tendencies" of its own or that liberal democracy is able to promote the cause of justice, domestic and global, with a high measure of independence from the powerful workings of capitalism. This altered perspective will allow us to resist the comfortable expectation that those societies that are both capitalist and liberal democratic will, thanks to their liberal democratic political structure, be able to restrain the infinitely expansionist tendencies intrinsic to capitalism and to place considerations of justice, domestic and global, above the desire for markets and profits—or, put another way, social justice above so-called market justice.

This change in perspective will also help save us from two important distortions in Rawls's nonideal theory. One such distortion occurs when Rawls claims, against a great deal of historical evidence, especially concerning the age of global capitalism, that the only cause of war lies with outlaw states, whereas liberal democracies (along with the fictitious decent peoples) "go to war only when they sincerely and reasonably believe that their safety and security are seriously endangered by the expansionist tendencies of outlaw states" (Rawls 1999: 90–1).[7] The other has to do with the empirical factors responsible for the plight of burdened societies; on this subject, Rawls passes over the historical and current role of capitalism in creating inequality both within and between economies and takes as a "guideline for thinking about how to carry out the duty of assistance" the presumption that "the political culture of a burdened society is *all-important*" (Rawls 1999: 108, emphasis added).

Distortions such as these miss what is arguably the single most important determinant of what happens in our world, including relations among societies. When Rawls writes, "Political liberalism, with its ideas of realistic utopia and public reason, denies what so much of political life suggests—that stability among peoples can never be more than a *modus vivendi*" (Rawls 1999: 19), it seems plausible to suggest that in our predominantly capitalist world the difficulty of rising above a modus vivendi in relations between societies is due chiefly to the interests and motivations inherent in the capitalist, now largely global-capitalist economy. If this is so, Rawls's negation of pessimism on behalf of political liberalism amounts to the denial that the capitalist economy has a powerful impact on the prospect of achieving liberalism's global political agenda. This denial, therefore, is one that Rawls must first make plausible. It is thus a major failing of Rawls's entire conception of Law of Peoples that, instead of taking up this essential challenge, he has rendered it largely invisible by proceeding on the implicit assumption of the independence of the political from the economic.

3 The Purity of Liberal Democracy even in Nonideal Theory

This is a move with profound implications. To begin with, it serves to keep liberal democracy clean and pure from potential moral contamination by the more unsavory features of capitalism and hence to keep it immune to critical scrutiny and potential rejection on account of its connection to capitalism. At the same time, it has the significant side effect of rendering capitalism in turn unfit as an object of examination and critique within political philosophy strictly conceived. If we put these consequences together, it becomes obvious why there is little conceptual space within liberal normative political philosophy in which liberal democracy and capitalism can be examined together and, if necessary, critiqued and rejected together. This is tantamount to shielding *liberal democratic capitalism* from systematic critical examination by implicitly denying its very existence, or the importance of its existence, thanks to the entrenched separation of the political and the economic. None of this is substantially changed, for purposes of Rawls's realistic utopia, by the somewhat speculative and intuitive remarks Rawls elsewhere makes in favor of the as yet entirely hypothetical regime of property-owning democracy.

Once liberal democracy is granted its own independence and integrity and miraculously purified, one might even say beautified, through its separation from capitalism, it is easy to believe its essential benignity and thus to blame anything but liberal democracy for domestic or global injustice. Whatever the actual record of liberal democratic *states*, not least of the United States, it is always possible to point the finger elsewhere, if only because liberal democracy is only *part* of such states, and who could reasonably fault it for not always being able to get the better of other, more venal aspects of any society?

Outlaw states, burdened societies, and even decent hierarchical peoples do not enjoy the same degree of separation between the political system and the rest of society and certainly do not derive anything like the same radical facelift of their political system from any such separation. It is easier to blame them in a wholesale fashion, and liberal political philosophy such as Rawls's helps make them fair game for such blame. The moment one puts capitalism into the equation, however, it becomes as clear as daylight that non-capitalist or barely capitalist societies are not the arenas in today's world where the action is and thus not the places where the principal causes of injustice between states could possibly have originated. But this is precisely why some powerful states may have a vested interest in keeping the connection between liberal democracy and capitalism—and thereby between liberal democratic capitalism and war—in the dark. The appearance of moral superiority that liberal democratic states gain in this way is as incalculable as it is morally cowardly.

In this light, it turns out to be not quite true, as I may seem to have suggested at the beginning, that Rawls has no causal story to tell about global justice. His work is actually full of hints regarding the main culprits of global injustice. But it is almost invariably societies other than liberal democratic ones that are deemed responsible for significant departures from a just international order, and it is the existence of these societies alone that seems to make Rawls's nonideal theory necessary. What is particularly striking is that in his nonideal theory Rawls is concerned exclusively with how liberal democracies are to respond to so-called outlaw states and burdened societies, all the while implying that liberal democracies by their very nature seldom, if ever, cause problems that are serious enough to come under nonideal theory and, of course, conveniently forgetting that liberal democracies are by far the most powerful subset of societies in the world today. There is an almost total absence of self-directed critical causal understanding of global injustice.

There is one consequence of liberalism's separation of the political and the economic, however, that is, at least on the face of it, self-undermining. For this separation prevents the utopian promise of liberal democracy from coming anywhere near realization and does so by keeping even the most sincere and committed liberals in the dark about the real causes of the unconquerable distance of their egalitarian ideals from a reality shaped by capitalism more than by anything else. Oblivious of the real causal story and shorn of professional or civic interest in figuring it out by the artificially narrowed focus on the political, much of normative political philosophy today knows only how to hurl yet more moral ideas at a reality that follows a capitalist logic utterly indifferent to such ideas.

It should thus come as no surprise that there is an intractable lack of motivation in liberal democracies to realize egalitarian ideals not only domestically but also, even more conspicuously, in the global setting.[8] It is a fundamental fact of citizens of liberal democracies that most of them are also employees in the capitalist—now increasingly global-capitalist—economy. It is in their latter, far more personally consequential capacity (given the preeminence of the so-called liberties of the moderns) that they acquire their most effective interests, values, and motivations. And in so far as the moral self gravitates toward unity rather than compartmentalization, it is the competitive and acquisitive culture of corporations that will prevail over the more fraternal and egalitarian culture of democratic citizenship. It follows that if the desire for justice is in short supply in corporate culture, and the desire for global justice in even shorter supply in global corporate culture, then there must be an overall lack of motivation to promote domestic and global justice in any liberal democracy as a whole.

Despite this, the message that cumulatively emerges from the pages of Rawls's *Law of Peoples* seems to be that capitalism is not part of the problem of global injustice, while liberal democracy is a big part of the solution. Global injustice is duly noted, of course, but it is chiefly attributed to outlaw states and burdened societies and to the fact that the category of decent hierarchical peoples, though greatly to be welcomed as at least worthy of toleration in theory, is pretty much an empty set in practice. In this context, the challenges of promoting global justice come down to three: containing and, if necessary, going to war with outlaw states; seeing to it that burdened societies get the minimal assistance they need to become well-ordered; and converting outlaw and otherwise morally unacceptable states into decent and, better still, liberal democratic ones. And who better to take care of these challenges—challenges that require both moral rectitude and political and military power—than the most admirable protagonists of the just Society of Peoples and the only ones that actually and abundantly exist? The mission of promoting global justice thus falls fairly and squarely on the liberal democracies, with the United States as the natural leader, given its power and influence. This is actually pretty much what the more active and self-righteous liberal democracies of the world, led by the United States, have been doing since before the publication of Rawls's *Law of Peoples*, promoting human rights, democracy, open markets, and mobility of capital, and, especially since 2001, fighting terrorism and going after weapons of mass destruction, all in one unified agenda. Is it too far-fetched to suspect that this is precisely why the world has moved ever farther away from Rawls's "realistic utopia" of a just Society of Peoples—that is, on our familiar view of what this utopia is meant to bring about? Or would it perhaps be more advisable to suspend this view and entertain the possibility that despite Rawls's best intentions the kind of theory developed in *The Law of Peoples* may actually be complicit with the status quo?

4 "Democratic Peace" as an Ideological Construction

To pursue the latter line of questioning, especially in view of Rawls's description of his own project as realistic *utopia*, is unavoidably to bring up the distinction between ideology and utopia, as formulated, say, by Karl Mannheim, and to determine, *in terms of this distinction*, whether Rawls's vision of a just Society of Peoples, is utopian or ideological. At issue here is what function a normative theory apparently far removed from reality is meant to perform in relation to that reality, or, for those allergic to any functionalist-sounding formulation, how such a normative theory tends to intervene in that reality. Mannheim draws our attention to two very different possibilities called utopia and ideology respectively. By utopia Mannheim means those reality-transcending orientations which, "when they pass over into conduct, tend to shatter, either partially or wholly, the order of things prevailing at the time" (Mannheim 1936: 192). By contrast, ideological are those seemingly reality-transcending orientations which actually help maintain the existing order.

In speaking of his normative vision as (realistically) utopian, Rawls assumes that it is situated at a very considerable distance from reality as we find it, or, in Mannheim's terminology, is reality-transcending. It is doubtful, as I have argued earlier, that Rawls's vision is as far removed from reality as he seems to think, and this is especially the case with that part of the Society of Peoples which is made up of liberal peoples, those closest to Rawls's heart. If this is true, there is reason to ask whether Rawls does not identify with the (liberal democratic) status quo much more closely—or, put another way, whether the (liberal democratic) status quo is not already much nearer to Rawls's normative vision—than his utopian-sounding discourse gives one to understand. Admittedly, some gap remains between Rawls's vision and the reality of the social world even in the case of liberal democracies as Rawls sees them. With regard to this gap, it is necessary to ask the further question whether Rawls has provided a reasonably accurate understanding of how it has come about and how effectively this understanding can contribute to narrowing or removing it. At stake in the two questions just raised is what kind of relation Rawls's normative theory bears to reality and thus, in Mannheim's terms, whether it is utopian or ideological. There is perhaps no better way to approach these questions than through careful scrutiny of what Rawls has to say about the idea of so-called democratic peace, this idea being the nearest Rawls ever got to relating liberal democracies as conceived in his normative theory to actual liberal democracies as he saw them in reality.

Now, central to Rawls's reasoning about democratic peace is the idea of liberal *peoples* as distinct from liberal states:

> A difference between liberal peoples and states is that just liberal peoples limit their basic interests as required by the reasonable [i.e. the criterion of reciprocity]. In contrast, the content of the interests of states does not allow them to be stable for the right reasons: that is, from firmly accepting and acting upon a just Law of Peoples.
> (Rawls 1999: 29)

With this subtle, yet radical substitution of liberal peoples for liberal states, Rawls is able to redefine democratic peace as holding among liberal peoples rather than states:

> The interests which move peoples (and which distinguish them from states) are reasonable interests guided by and congruent with a fair equality and a due respect for all peoples.... [I]t is these reasonable interests that make democratic peace

> possible, and the lack thereof causes peace between states to be at best a *modus vivendi*, a stable balance of forces only for the time being.   (Rawls 1999: 44–5)

The idea of a liberal democratic people may sound normatively appealing, but any attempt to identify its embodiment in the real world will soon show it to be a fiction. If this fiction, nevertheless, seems to have a measure of plausibility, it is only because it rests on the tacitly accepted assumption of the independence of the political from the economic and of the consequent separation of liberal democracy from capitalism.

I have already argued at some length against this assumption. In the case at hand, even Rawls himself finds it necessary to reinstate some connection between a liberal people and capitalism when he puts forward the idea of "democratic peoples engaged in commerce" as a recipe for democratic peace. It is the idea of "the *moeurs douces* of Montesquieu, the idea that a commercial society tends to fashion in its citizens certain virtues such as assiduity, industriousness, punctuality, and probity; and that commerce tends to lead to peace." Thus:

> we might surmise that democratic peoples engaged in commerce would tend not to have occasion to go to war with one another. Among other reasons, this is because what they lacked in commodities they could acquire more easily and cheaply by trade; and because, being liberal constitutional democracies, they would not be moved to try to convert other peoples to a state religion or other ruling comprehensive doctrine.   (Rawls 1999: 46)

If this is granted, there seems little use left for the distinction between a democratic people and a democratic state. For if commerce is a cheaper and more peaceful substitute for war in the case of a democratic people, why should the same not equally hold for a democratic *state*? What is it about a democratic state that would give it the incentive to go to war when a "democratic people engaged in commerce" have no such incentive? Surely, a *democratic* state, in so far as it is democratic (and liberal constitutional), may be supposed to be no less free than a democratic people are of what Rawls calls the familiar motives for war such as religious conversion, political domination, and territorial expansion (Rawls 1999: 19). If this supposition does not stand even for a fully (liberal constitutional) democratic state, one may reasonably conclude that there is something bad about states as such, whether democratic or not, that is detrimental to peace. One may also reasonably conclude that a political regime being democratic does not divest it of the familiar motives for war. But if this is the case, why should a *people* being democratic have the miraculous effect of curing such motives? Surely it cannot be the mere fact of their being a people that does the trick; if that were the case, one would need to speak no longer of democratic peace, since democracy no longer makes any or much difference, but of peace among peoples, and this is clearly not what Rawls has in mind.

The distinction between liberal democratic peoples and states, it turns out, is a distraction. The real question is whether those engaged in commerce, the kind of commerce that is embedded in the capitalist mode of production in the modern world, have any significant, even powerful motive for war, regardless of whether they are thought of as a people or a state, and regardless of whether they are liberal democratic or not (although it is no mere accident that most developed capitalist societies today are also liberal democratic). As far as this question is concerned, conspicuously absent from Rawls's list of the familiar motives for war is the distinctively capitalistic motive for war in the interest of continuously expanding markets and profits whenever such expansion encounters stubborn resistance from societies not yet incorporated into the global capitalist order. This motive has been an extremely consistent and powerful cause of wars and conquests since the advent of capitalism, and, even with the supersession of colonial empire by "informal" empire in our time, it has by no means been laid to rest, as evidenced by the frequent involvement of powerful liberal democratic states in wars conducive in ways both subtle and blatant to capitalist expansion.[9]

It is, therefore, quite striking that when Rawls allows capitalism to make an unobtrusive and entirely benign appearance in his argument, he sees fit to take over from Montesquieu the cozy picture of capitalism in terms of "a commercial society." This borrowing across well over two centuries allows one to turn a blind eye to the much more complex and violent trajectory of capitalism in between, with its dynamic, expansionist tendencies, its need and willingness to use force where necessary, and its ability to use other, less violent, yet almost equally coercive means where possible, and in the many forms it has gone through which the bland description "commercial society" cannot even begin to capture.[10] Thus, we find on the part of Rawls an entirely unrealistic picture of the nature and dynamic of capitalism, and even more symptomatic in this regard is the way Rawls invokes Raymond Aron and extends the latter's line of thought to liberal democracy. According to Aron, Rawls writes, politic units "must not seek to extend themselves, either to increase their material or human resources, to disseminate their institutions, or to enjoy the intoxicating pride of ruling" (Rawls 1999: 47). And Rawls goes on: "I agree with Aron that these conditions are necessary to a lasting peace, and I argue that they would be fulfilled by peoples living under liberal constitutional democracies.... All being satisfied in this way, liberal peoples have nothing to go to war about" (Rawls 1999: 47). Here Rawls is inviting us to believe that liberal peoples, even as they are engaged in a capitalist mode of production, will not seek to extend themselves and hence will have nothing to wage war about.[11]

This is a manifestly unrealistic view of the purity of "democratic peoples engaged in commerce." But lest we attribute such a view to flights of normative fancy, we have a reminder from Rawls himself that his idea of democratic peace has its basis in historical experience. "The absence of war between major established democracies is as close as anything we know to a simple empirical regularity in relations among societies. From this fact, I should like to think the historical record shows that a society of democratic peoples... is stable for the right reasons" (Rawls 1999: 52–3). Do we really have a fact here? Even if we suppose so, for the sake of argument, it is by no means clear what the fact exactly is or signifies. For the fact—if it be such—that "democratic peoples engaged in commerce" are not motivated to go to war *with one another*, all being participants in a capitalist regime of more or less open markets and more or less free trade, does not entail that when one or more of them go to war with a state that is not a "democratic people engaged in commerce," the motive for war must come from the latter. It is at least equally plausible to explain this scenario by locating the motive for war in the incentive of capitalist societies, even if democratic, to expand markets and profits and to go to war to this end, if necessary (while opting for more peaceful and efficient means, if possible).

As Rawls is well aware, "An enumeration of favorable historical cases is hardly sufficient, since the idea of democratic peace sometimes fails." For such cases, however, Rawls has a ready answer: "In these cases, my guiding hypothesis leads me to expect to find various failures in a democracy's essential supporting institutions and practices" (Rawls 1999: 53). Self-critical as it may sound, this "guiding hypothesis" is actually a typical instance of ideological interpretation. Such an interpretation works by refusing in principle seriously to entertain the possibility that liberal democratic capitalist societies—"democratic peoples engaged in commerce"—may have a *built-in* motive for war from which no actual liberal democracy can be free, especially if it happens to be an empire and is determined to remain one. Instead, it insists, no matter what the evidence, that the motive for war found in a liberal democracy must be an anomaly attributable only to departures from what a liberal democracy ideally is supposed to be. But such an ideal picture is a figment of the liberal normative imagination to begin with, making possible an ideological explanation of the inevitable gap between fictitious theory and disproving reality. If taken on board, this renders the idea of democratic peace unfalsifiable.[12]

As it turns out, then, Rawls's reasoning behind the idea of democratic peace leaves one in little doubt that, as far as the Law of Peoples is concerned, he is not deeply bothered by the gap between his liberal democratic ideals and actual liberal democracies. Rawls clearly regards actual liberal democracies, despite all their flaws, as good enough approximations to his liberal democratic ideals to count as the genuine article, while he takes his ideal conception of liberal democratic peoples to require no fundamental modification in the light of the historical record of liberal democracies. If the idea of democratic peace is true, as it manifestly is in Rawls's view, it may be inferred that actual liberal democracies are already quite close to Rawls's conception of them in a just Society of Peoples, at least as far as peace is concerned, and that, if all societies were liberal democratic, the world as a whole would be just as close to Rawls's realistic utopia in its entirety. In other words, the status quo—the *liberal democratic* status quo—is already one that we should be reasonably happy with and there is definitely nothing in it that calls for fundamental change.

It is in this context that the role of political philosophy in reconciling us to the social world takes on the meaning and importance it has for Rawls. When Rawls speaks of this function of political philosophy, he sees it as fulfilled by the demonstration that a just Society of Peoples is a realistic prospect toward which people here and now may work with reasonable hope. As far as that prospect is concerned, Rawls is careful to couch it in the rather weak terms of possibility—"not a mere logical possibility," to be sure, "but one that connects with the deep tendencies and inclinations of the social world" (Rawls 1999: 128). But such possibility is good enough for the purpose of reconciliation.[13] We are given to understand that, as far as the liberal democratic status quo is concerned, this possibility is already amply, if not fully, realized, and thus we have extra reason to be reconciled to it. The effect of such reconciliation, as Rawls puts it in another context with more overtly Hegelian overtones, is that of "calm[ing] our frustration and rage against our society and its history by showing us the way in which its institutions, when properly understood from a philosophical point of view, are rational, and developed over time as they did to attain their present, rational form" (Rawls 2001: 3). If we recall Mannheim's distinction between utopia and ideology, then, Rawls's realistic utopia is utterly ideological in relation to the status quo of the liberal democratic social world: though moderately reality-transcending, it serves to maintain the existing liberal democratic order by reconciling us to it even in its present form, with hardly any need for normative projection onto a distant future, and calls for change and progress largely within it. This is true in Mannheim's technical sense even if, like Rawls, one is reasonably content with the liberal democratic status quo. To the degree that one regards the liberal democratic status quo as part of the root cause of global injustice, however, Rawls's realistic utopia will come across as ideological in a deeper, less innocuous sense: it will be seen to perform, regardless of Rawls's authorial intentions, a function that is central to the concept of ideology in the negative or pejorative sense, namely, that of shielding an unjust social order from proper understanding, critique, and truly utopian transformation.[14]

Apparently oblivious of the ideological trap for normative political philosophy, Rawls provides the simplest of explanations for the gap between his normative vision and the reality of the social world. With regard to liberal democracies, the gap is just a matter of actual exemplars departing understandably, if regrettably, from the ideal, presumably as exemplars of any ideal will. With regard to relations between liberal democracies and the rest of the social world, liberal democracies are presumed not to be at fault when things go wrong, or else the first explanation applies. In neither case does Rawls see liberal democracy as standing in a close—let alone symbiotic—relationship with capitalism, and therefore the idea that liberal democracy's moral agenda, however sincerely pursued, will inevitably be thwarted or compromised by capitalism does not occur to Rawls as a possible explanation of the stubborn gap between his vision of a just Society of Peoples and the reality of the social world. If capitalism is indeed what stands in the way of realizing Rawls's vision, or any reasonably stringent conception of global justice, as I have argued, then the fact that Rawls's approach is informed by the separation of the political and the economic has the effect of diverting diagnostic and critical attention away from the real cause of the status quo, even of preempting such attention. This effect, just like that of the reconciliation to the status quo, is a perfect instance of a normative theory being ideological in Mannheim's sense of serving to maintain the status quo. The presence of these two ideological effects undermines the credentials of Rawls's normative theory as a realistic utopia: it is both too positive about the status quo and too incapable of showing a realistic way to bridge the gap between theory and practice that is part and parcel of the status quo.

5 Lessons for Normative Political Philosophy

The case of Rawls as a philosopher who thinks normatively about global justice without systematic reference to global capitalism is a paradigmatic one, in that a number of important lessons can be drawn from it that are worth considering for normative political philosophy of global justice as a whole. The first such lesson is the need to think about the political with close reference to the economic, to think about global justice with close reference to global capitalism. The respect for the unity of the political and the economic that informs this approach is not a matter of method, still less an article of faith, but is based on the *fact* that in the capitalist order as we find it in both a domestic and the global setting the political and the economic work together as one integral system of class relations, and yet they do so, and could only do so in their unique way, through their formal separation. Liberal normative political philosophy is understandably predicated on this formal separation but makes the serious mistake of proceeding as if this is more than a formal separation—as if the causalities of the social world are largely compartmentalized so that one could usefully think normatively about global justice (or about domestic justice, for that matter) in isolation from the operation of global capitalism. This is an illusion that dooms the liberal project of achieving global justice from the start, for the implicit picture of our social world as involving more than the formal separation of the political and the economic bears no resemblance to the real world.

Rawls's theory, as we have seen, is marked by the structural absence of capitalism from his understanding of the nature and dynamic of modern society, domestic and international, and by the implicit understanding of liberal democracy as distinct and indeed separate from capitalism and as free in principle from determination by capitalism. As a result, while Rawls sees himself as thinking about global justice for our world, his main concepts, even "democracy" and "liberal peoples," have no exact or even approximate referents in our world, because the essential link to capitalism is missing, and his normative vision for a just Society of Peoples, for all its apparent realism and moderation, has no chance of coming true in our world. The world being what it is, with its "laws and tendencies," Rawls's exclusion of the logic and dynamic of global capitalism from systematic consideration in his theory cannot but weaken the moral clarity of his otherwise trailblazing and monumental intellectual efforts. It is symptomatic of this flaw in his approach that, in the face of the widening gap between his normative theory and the reality of the social world, Rawls, instead of searching for an adequate causal explanation of it in order to better live up to his idea of *realistic* utopia, prefers to retreat into an assumed relevance of pure normativity.[15]

The way Rawls separates the political from the economic not only renders him unable to offer the right kind of causal explanation but also seems to suggest a lack of more than cursory interest in seeking one in the first place. Had Rawls shown more interest, he might well have been led to call into question his separation of the political and the economic and his thinking about global justice without serious reference to capitalism. Why did he not? One might suggest, in the spirit of ideology critique, that there is a sense in which Rawls did not seek the cause because he was not deeply motivated to know the cause, and the latter in turn because, despite occasional statements to the contrary, he was on the whole reasonably well disposed toward the capitalist world-system (in contrast with his more critical stance in the domestic context), and his political philosophy was essentially aimed at, and confined to, making the moral best of it. As far as global justice was concerned, capitalism was for him not the main problem or the main cause of the problem, so he could pursue his normative reflections in comfortable disregard of the causal potency of global capitalism, which would otherwise have been all too oppressively obvious.[16]

If this oblivion of the causal potency of capitalism has its origin in a certain disposition toward capitalism, it is no doubt made easier still, and more plausible, by what appears to be an independent factor, and that is the deeply ingrained tendency on the part of a certain kind of political philosopher to see normative projects as sufficient onto themselves and requiring no correlative empirical understanding of our social world in the form, say, of social theory and history.[17] To the degree that the latter is taken to be relevant, it does not figure as an integral part of the former but serves only as a contingently useful supplement, especially at the stage of application, to a normative undertaking that is pursued independently and is supposed to have its own, distinctively normative cogency and integrity subject only to the broadest limits of human nature. There is no *integration* of normative philosophy and causal understanding of the social world, only an ad hoc division of labor between them. Thus, what is responsible for the conspicuous absence of capitalism as part of the causal nexus of the social world from liberal normative political philosophy is the implicit understanding not only of the political as largely independent from the economic but also of the normative as independent from the causal and hence of normative political philosophy as a doubly independent inquiry with its own integrity.

This is a luxury that Rawls's kind of normative theory can ill afford. For every normative theory with the objective, if only implicit, of intervening in the social world is subject to the familiar constraint known as "'ought' implies 'can,'" and for the "can" to be "realistic" rather than merely possible, as Rawls insists for his realistic utopia, there is no avoiding the need to spell out how a normative theory is realistic in the social world as we now find it and will in all probability continue to do so in the foreseeable future, and, in the event that a normative theory with this pretension to realism has failed to change reality in its image given a sufficiently long passage of time, to explain why this has happened. As a matter of fact, every normative theory of this kind implies its own understanding of what the social world is like and what is realistic within it. There is no generally applicable account of what is realistic in the social world and no master explanation of normative failure that can work for all normative theories, and this is for the simple reason that there is no definitive, comprehensive understanding of what the social world is like in the relevant respects. So our second lesson is that every normative theory must do its own work in this regard, or else it cannot seriously claim to be realistic rather than merely possible.

If it, nevertheless, does make such a claim, however, it will fairly invite the charge of being ideological, in that it serves to maintain the existing social world by encouraging people to believe the feasibility of a normative conception within it without first doing the necessary homework to understand what the social world is really like and how the normative conception may succeed or fail within it. Thus, the problem with both the separation of the political from the economic and the separation of the normative from the causal (or explanatory or diagnostic) boils down to the ideological function of the separation. Accordingly, the call for the integral consideration of the political and the economic, and of the normative and the causal, is also a call against the ideological use of normative philosophy. Herein lies our third lesson and one that encompasses the first two.

There need, of course, be nothing ideological about normative political philosophy per se. Any normative political theory at all, just in virtue of being a normative theory, exhibits a counterfactual character and, if conceived as more or less feasible, a practical intent—directing values at what is bound to be, to some extent, a recalcitrant social world. Hence we routinely speak, in both theoretical and pre-theoretical discourse, of political ideals and reality and of the gap between them. All this is easily attributable to the very normativity of normative theories, and thus the problem is not with normativity but its use.

In this connection, the exceptional case of the kind of normative political philosophy pursued by G. A. Cohen in, say, *Rescuing Justice and Equality* is instructive. In this work Cohen (2008) takes the radical step of treating reflection on justice as no longer strictly subject to the constraint of potential realizability and hence in effect as no longer strictly part of practical philosophy. This gives the political philosopher the freedom to theorize about justice with little regard for contingent facts about society and even human nature. Such theory is different from utopia (in Mannheim's sense), in that even (Mannheim's) utopia respects the constraint of potential realizability. It is also different from ideology, in that it does not serve to maintain the existing order, which it manifestly wants to see radically changed, if possible, although it does not say that it is possible. Given these differences, Cohen's way of thinking about justice may be said to constitute a distinct species of normative political philosophy. It is distinguished by the fact that it is not meant to shape in its image the social world as we find it.[18]

Unlike this rare species in the field, Rawls's brand of normative political philosophy conceived as realistic utopia may be called *normal* normative theory. Such theory is meant to be so situated vis-à-vis the social world as simultaneously to shape it and overreach it, to a greater or lesser extent, to be a source of both immediate guidance and long-term aspiration. The relation of such theory to reality is one of gradual, incremental, and non-revolutionary improvement. Rawls's theory of justice, both domestic and international, is an instance of normal normative theory, concerned with what Cohen calls rules of regulation. Now in so far as normal normative theory is meant to bring about change, especially major change, it has something in common with utopian thinking and can, upon prolonged frustration, escalate into utopia in Mannheim's sense (as distinct from Rawls's). And in so far as normal normative theory abhors revolutionary ruptures in the existing order, it has a certain affinity with ideology and can easily itself become ideology. This risk is amply realized for normal normative theories about global justice whenever, for reasons I have explained, such theories attend to the political in isolation from the economic and pursue the normative with scant interest in the causal, that is, when such theories engage in normative reflection about global justice without systematic reference to global capitalism. Rawls's theory is paradigmatic in this regard and, for this reason, despite its many great virtues and the undoubted sincerity and good intentions of its distinguished author, is an object lesson in how not to think normatively about global justice.

ACKNOWLEDGMENTS

An earlier version of this chapter was discussed at a workshop at the University of Hong Kong in 2014. Thanks to all the participants in the workshop, especially Hon-Lam Li, who not only organized the event but also provided very helpful written comments.

NOTES

1. Rawls (2001).
2. If one were to identify actual societies that most resemble Rawls's idea of decent peoples, in spirit if not in literal detail, one would perhaps most naturally think of those countries that do not yet belong among the advanced democracies but are approvingly, yet condescendingly called "emerging markets."
3. See, e.g., Wolin (2008).
4. On the nature and implications of this separation, see Wood (1995: ch. 1).
5. As G. A. Cohen puts it, comparing Marx's conception of the relationship between state and society in "On the Jewish Question" with Rawls's, "There is not, then, on the one hand, as there is in Rawlsian perception, an economic structure that is organized to achieve a certain form of justice, and, on the other, a set of economic choices that need show no respect for that justice" (Cohen 2008: 2). See also Cohen (2000: chs. 8–9).
6. See Rawls (2001: pt IV).
7. For views contrary to this presumption, see Wolin (2008: 87); Wood (2003: 134–5); and, from a scholar whose political values are otherwise not far from Rawls's, Mann (2013: esp. ch. 10).
8. As powerfully deplored and analyzed by Thomas Pogge in, for example, Pogge (2010). See also Ci (2010: 84–102).
9. On "informal empire," see Mann (2013: 86–7) and Panitch and Gindin (2012: 5–6). On the distinctively capitalist motive for war, especially as manifested in the age of globalization, see Wood (2003: ch. 7).
10. For a brief, more plausible account, see Wallerstein (1983).
11. Thus, Rawls is forced to conclude, against a great deal of historical evidence, especially in the age of global capitalism, that the only cause of war lies with outlaw states, whereas

liberal democracies (along with the fictitious decent peoples) "go to war only when they sincerely and reasonably believe that their safety and security are seriously endangered by the expansionist tendencies of outlaw states" (Rawls 1999: 90–1), with no higher authority to judge what counts as "sincere" and "reasonable" belief in this regard. For the actual record, accounts such as the following deserve to be reckoned with: Johnson (2000), (2005); Bacevich (2002); and Gowan (1999: ch. 8), (2010: 19–46).

12. A variation on this theme runs: "Of course, so-called liberal societies sometimes do this [i.e. wage war], but that only shows they may act wrongly" (Rawls 1999: 91). On the face of it, this is a candid admission of liberal democracy's fallibility. What is lightly passed over is the question whether in thus "acting wrongly" a liberal democracy, say, the United States, is acting in character or out of character. Rawls assumes the latter without even entertaining the other possibility. In the same vein, Rawls writes, "A liberal society cannot justly require its citizens to fight in order to gain economic wealth or to acquire natural resources, much less to win power and empire" (p. 91). Read normatively, this is entirely unrealistic, with no "can" supporting the "ought." Read empirically, this is something that happens all the time, especially with the United States, notwithstanding the fact that the means adopted are often more subtle, though not always so.

13.   While realization is, course, not unimportant, I believe that the very possibility of such a social order can itself reconcile us to the social world.... For so long as we believe for good reasons that a self-sustaining and reasonably just political and social order both at home and abroad is possible, we can reasonably hope that we or others will someday, somewhere, achieve it; and we can then do something toward this achievement. This alone, quite apart from our success or failure, suffices to banish the dangers of resignation and cynicism. By showing how the social world may realize the features of a realistic utopia, political philosophy provides a long-term goal of political endeavor, and in working toward it gives meaning to what we do today.   (Rawls 1999: 128)

14. For ideology in this sense, see Geuss (1981: 13, 21).

15. An explanation that would be devastating to liberalism, if largely true—and therefore is worth reckoning with by liberal political philosophers—comes from Immanuel Wallerstein. As is well known, Wallerstein sees liberalism as the "geoculture" (or ideology) of the modern capitalist world-system and argues that, as such, liberalism (along with socialism) has completely exhausted its moral and political potential since the late 1960s and especially since the late 1980s, thus giving way to the reign of conservatism in the shape of neoliberalism. See, e.g., Wallerstein (1995), (1999: ch. 4). For a fuller and more scholarly account of how liberalism came to serve as the geoculture of modern capitalism, see Wallerstein (2011).

16. As it is, for example, to Panitch and Gindin:

> Just as the liberal democratic project of reconciling formal equality of citizenship with the inherently unequal social relations of capitalism obscured the realities of class, so did the attempt to reconcile national self-determination and the formal equality of states with the inherently asymmetric inter-state relations in a capitalist world economy likewise obscure the realities of empire.   (Panitch and Gindin 2012: 9)

Whereas Rawls laments the widening gap between egalitarian ideals and the reality of the social world and pins his hopes on moral clarity and long-term effort, critics like Panitch and Gindin (2012) find the causal story all too plain with regard to the main culprit: global capitalism, especially in the shape of American empire, is responsible for growing inequalities both in the United States, among others, and in the world as a whole. This is not to say that these authors must be correct but only to suggest that their claims are of a kind to which it is intellectually incumbent on Rawls's kind of normative political philosophy to respond.

17. For an argument against such normative theory in favor of "diagnostic practice," see Sluga (2014: ch. 1).

18. Here are two representative statements by Cohen: "The question for political philosophy is not what we should do but what we should think, even when what we should think makes no practical difference" (Cohen 2008: 268); and:

> The Rawlsians, who believe that the constraints of human nature and human practice affect the content of justice, are inclined to regard me as unrealistic and/or utopian in that I believe that justice is unaffected by those mundanities. But it is worth pointing out that they are in one way more Utopian than I. For in believing that justice must be so crafted as to be bottom-line feasible, they believe that it is possible to achieve justice, and I am not so sanguine. It follows from my position that justice is an unachievable (although a nevertheless governing) ideal.   (Cohen 2008: 254)

For Cohen's reasoning, see Cohen (2008: ch. 6).

REFERENCES

Bacevich, Andrew (2002) *American Empire: The Realities and Consequences of U. S. Diplomacy.* Cambridge, MA: Harvard University Press.

Ci, Jiwei (2010) "What Negative Duties? Which Moral Universalism?." In Alison M. Jaggar (ed.), *Thomas Pogge and his Critics.* Cambridge: Polity Press, 84–102.

Cohen, G. A. (2000) *If You're an Egalitarian, How Come You're So Rich?* Cambridge, MA: Harvard University Press.

Cohen, G. A. (2008) *Rescuing Justice and Equality.* Cambridge, MA: Harvard University Press.

Geuss, Raymond (1981) *The Idea of a Critical Theory: Habermas and the Frankfurt School.* Cambridge: Cambridge University Press.

Gowan, Peter (1999) *The Global Gamble: Washington's Faustian Bid for World Dominance.* London: Verso.

Gowan, Peter (2010) *A Calculus of Power: Grand Strategy in the Twenty-First Century.* London: Verso.

Johnson, Chalmers (2000) *Blowback: The Costs and Consequences of American Empire.* New York: Henry Holt.

Johnson, Chalmers (2005) *The Sorrows of Empire: Militarism, Secrecy, and the End of the Republic.* New York: Henry Holt.

Mann, Michael (2013) *The Sources of Social Power, vol. 4: Globalizations, 1945–2011.* Cambridge: Cambridge University Press.

Mannheim, Karl (1936) *Ideology and Utopia,* tr. Louis Wirth and Edward Shils. New York: Harcourt, Brace and World.

Panitch, Leo, and Sam Gindin (2012) *The Making of Global Capitalism: The Political Economy of American Empire.* London: Verso.

Pogge, Thomas (2010) *Politics as Usual: What Lies behind the Pro-Poor Rhetoric.* Cambridge: Polity Press.

Rawls, John (1999) *The Law of Peoples with "The Idea of Public Reason Revisited".* Cambridge, MA: Harvard University Press.

Rawls, John (2001) *Justice as Fairness: A Restatement*, ed. Erin Kelly. Cambridge, MA: Harvard University Press.

Sluga, Hans (2014) *Politics and the Search for the Common Good*. Cambridge: Cambridge University Press.

Wallerstein, Immanuel (1983) *Historical Capitalism*. London: Verso.

Wallerstein, Immanuel (1995) *After Liberalism*. New York: New Press.

Wallerstein, Immanuel (1999) *The End of the World as We Know It: Social Sciences for the Twenty-First Century*. Minneapolis, MN: University of Minnesota Press.

Wallerstein, Immanuel (2011) *The Modern World-System, vol. 4, Centrist Liberalism Triumphant, 1789–1914*. Berkeley, CA: University of California Press.

Wolin, Sheldon S. (2008) *Democracy Incorporated: Managed Democracy and the Specter of Inverted Totalitarianism*. Princeton, NJ: Princeton University Press.

Wood, Ellen Meiksins (1995) *Democracy against Capitalism: Renewing Historical Materialism*. Cambridge: Cambridge University Press.

Wood, Ellen Meiksins (2003) *Empire of Capital*. London: Verso.

FURTHER READING

Anderson, Perry (2015) *American Foreign Policy and its Thinkers*. London: Verso.

Kinzer, Stephen (2006) *Overthrow: America's Century of Regime Change from Hawaii to Iraq*. New York: Henry Holt.

McNeill, William H. (1982) *The Pursuit of Power: Technology, Armed Force, and Society since A.D. 1000*. Chicago: University of Chicago Press.

Martin, Rex, and David A. Reidy (eds.) (2006) *Rawls's Law of Peoples: A Realistic Utopia?* Malden, MA: Blackwell.

Mearsheimer, John J. (2018) *The Great Delusion: Liberal Dreams and International Realities*. New Haven, CT: Yale University Press.

Risse, Mathias (2012) *On Global Justice*. Princeton, NJ: Princeton University Press.

Stone, Oliver, and Peter Kuznick (2012) *The Untold History of the United States*. New York: Gallery Books.

....

CHAPTER 25

THE RIGHT TO RESIST
GLOBAL INJUSTICE

....

SIMON CANEY

1 INTRODUCTION

....

THE world we live in is marked by severe and extensive poverty, inequality, and dangerous climate change. According to many accounts of global distributive justice, the world is characterized by very great injustice. In the light of this, accounts of global justice very often ascribe responsibilities to the rich and powerful. Thus, Henry Shue (1996), for example, affirms positive duties to aid the poor and disadvantaged so that they may enjoy their basic rights. He is followed in this by David Miller (2007: ch. 7, esp. 164) and John Rawls (1999b: 65). Others, such as Thomas Pogge (2008), eschew positive duties but affirm negative duties not to impose unjust orders on others, arguing that global poverty arises because the rich and powerful have violated this negative duty.

Political thinkers like Pogge and Shue are right to insist on the responsibilities of the wealthy and those with power. But what about those who have been treated unjustly and who lack what they are just entitled to? What are they entitled to do to realize their own rights and the rights of others?

This topic has not, so far, received very much systematic analysis by scholars participating in the recent debates in anglophone political philosophy about the nature of global justice.[1] It is, though, an important question, and answering it requires addressing several complex normative issues.

In what follows I shall try to motivate support for what I term the *Right of Resistance against Global Injustice*, where this should be understood as a right to bring about greater global justice. More specifically, I shall defend two conceptions of this core idea. Roughly stated, the first maintains that persons have the right to take direct action that will immediately and directly secure their rights or the rights of others (what I shall refer to as the *Right of Resistance against Global Injustice$_i$*—hereafter *RRGI$_i$*). The second holds that persons have the right to engage in action that transforms the underlying social, economic, and political structures that perpetuate injustice in order to bring about greater justice in the future (what I shall refer to as the *Right of Resistance against Global Injustice*$_{ii}$—hereafter *RRGI*$_{ii}$). These formulations are approximate and need to be explicated more fully, but they express the key ideas. In what follows I seek to specify these more fully, and to address various questions about the meaning, content, grounding, and limits of these rights.

Before we turn to those questions, two further points bear noting. First, we should recall that whilst there is a well-established body of works discussing civil disobedience (for example, Rawls 1999a: ch. VI, especially sections 55, 57, and 59), the questions we are considering here go beyond the "nearly just society" that Rawls (1999a: 319) posits. Second, there are, of course, long-standing debates about the rights of individuals to rebellion and revolution. Aquinas, Calvin, Locke, Kant, Burke, and many others have grappled with some aspects of these questions. However, one distinctive aspect of the questions I am posing concerns their focus on *global* injustice. This raises some new questions. For example, if a state oppresses its own citizens, then it is reasonably clear against whom they should target their activities. However, given that there is no global state, it is less obvious whom those seeking to combat global injustice should target.

The *Right of Resistance against Global Injustice*, thus, raises many interesting and complex questions. In this chapter I aim to do four things. First, I shall outline the two rights and illustrate what they would mean in practice (Sections 2–3). Second, I shall then set out two lines of argument that might be adduced in defense of rights to resist global injustice (Sections 4–5). The chapter then, third, examines two kinds of limits—some arise from a commitment to justice, and some arise from a commitment to political legitimacy (Sections 6–7). Fourth, and finally, I conclude with reflections on the moral significance of these rights and their limits (Section 8).

2 THE RIGHT OF RESISTANCE AGAINST GLOBAL INJUSTICE$_I$

As I noted briefly in Section 1 above, I shall argue here that those denied what they are entitled to as a matter of justice have two rights. The first is for the right-holder to take action that directly secures the enjoyment of the right that is violated (or, reduces the extent to which they and others are denied that right). We might define this right as follows.

The Right of Resistance against Global Injustice$_i$ *(RRGI*$_i$): Persons have a right to act in ways
(1)   that are contrary either to (a) existing domestic law or (b) to international law; and that;
(2)   have the immediate effect that the agents in question, or others, are better able to enjoy what they are entitled to as a matter of global justice.[2]

To elaborate its content more fully: one might relate it to what has traditionally been referred to as "the right of necessity." The core idea of the right of necessity is that, in extreme circumstances, persons may (subject to certain moral conditions) engage in actions that would otherwise not be permitted in order to protect their most vital interests. It is a view defended by many political philosophers from Cicero and Aquinas to Grotius and Paley.[3] Most recently, it has been defended by Alejandra Mancilla (2016). As noted above, one striking feature of these thinkers is that the right is limited to covering basic needs (e.g. Paley 2002 [1785], Book II, ch. 11, section 3, 61; Mancilla 2016: esp. ch. 4). I shall argue, however, that we should not adopt such a constrained view, and I hold that persons have a right to resist injustice even if their basic needs are in fact met. Drawing on an egalitarian conception of global justice, I believe that persons are entitled to resist in order to better realize global egalitarian justice (Caney 2005).

But what would the *Right of Resistance against Global Injustice*$_i$ entail in practice? I now outline its practical implications:

(a) *Migration and Violating Border Controls*: Consider, for example, those who are persecuted in their country of origin and are unable to live there without serious threats to their life—or, more moderately, without facing severe discrimination and victimization. Many of these cross borders in an attempt to be free from such persecution and violence.

Or consider those from poor countries who illegally cross borders in order to try to avoid poverty and destitution. Many face no prospect of finding employment—those in war-torn states or those where the economy has collapsed or those afflicted by famine—and they frequently seek to cross borders in order to try to attain a reasonable standard of living. Others face only exploitation and dangerous working conditions. May they thus illegally cross borders in order to secure their prospects of living a decent life?

(b) *Stealing Food, Medicines, and Water*: A second kind of activity is stealing food and vital medicines. The poor often lack access to essential medicines because they are overpriced. They are also often unable to feed themselves and their family. As Amartya Sen (1981) has exhaustively shown, famines often occur in countries with plenty of food: it is just that the food is hoarded by some, and others lack the relevant entitlements. In other cases there may be food, but a spike in food prices leaves some unable to afford to feed themselves. May those deprived of necessary foodstuffs and medicines steal what they need?

Or consider communities deprived of access to water. Consider for example, energy companies that use enormous amounts of water in developing countries to grow crops for fuel.[4] May indigenous people divert water to their crops?

(c) *Intellectual Property Rights*: Some may be unable to use certain technologies because of the existing intellectual property system. Much research finds that intellectual property regimes can, in some cases, harm development, leaving some unable to afford healthcare and medicines, and restricting the kinds of plant genetic resources that members of developing countries can use for agriculture (Commission on Intellectual Property Rights 2002). Given this, can the poor violate intellectual property rights—for example, illegally copy scientific knowledge or use seeds that have been patented by Western companies?

(d) *Stealing Energy*: The International Energy Authority reported in 2016 that "[a]n estimated 1.2 billion people—16% of the global population—did not have access to electricity" (International Energy Authority (2016). Without electricity they are often unable to meet their core needs (warmth, cooking, protection from the elements, health). They are forced to use energy sources that endanger their own health (Wilkinson et al. 2007: esp. 967). Given this, many steal electricity by diverting it from power lines for their own personal use. It is estimated, for example, that in India there are over one million illegal electricity pumpsets (Tongia 2007: 125). Other research finds that theft of electricity by the poor is extensive in Pakistan, South Africa, and Mexico (Smith 2004: 2069).

In short, then, many of the disadvantaged can take direct action (through illegal migration and theft) that will immediately improve their standard of living. The question then arises as to whether this is justified and, if so, in what circumstances. Before we consider those, I turn now to the second conception of the *Right of Resistance against Global Injustice*.

3 THE RIGHT OF RESISTANCE AGAINST GLOBAL INJUSTICE$_{\mathrm{II}}$

This second conception is defined as follows:

The Right of Resistance against Global Injustice$_{ii}$ (*RRGI$_{ii}$*): Persons have a right to act in ways
(1)   that are contrary either to (a) existing domestic law or (b) international law
(2)   in order in order to attempt to change certain practices, policies, or political systems
(3)   so that the agents in question, or others, are better able to enjoy what they are entitled to as a matter of global justice.[5]

The key difference between *RRGI$_i$* and *RRGI$_{ii}$* is that *RRGI$_i$* does not seek to change the underlying laws or policies or institutions. *RRGI$_i$* is not aimed at effecting long-term change. Rather it is short-term and reactive in nature. Its focus is on coping within the existing system. In the case of *RRGI$_{ii}$*, however, the focus is on changing the underlying practices, politics, or political institutions. It is, in this sense, less reactive and more pro-active. It does not take the status quo as a given and seek to adjust within it. It is also more long-term in character.

Again, though, we might ask: What does this mean in practice? One can distinguish different kinds of activities. Some are negative in character and involve disobeying rules imposed on them. This conforms to a long-standing tradition—articulated by Étienne de La Boétie, Mohandas Gandhi, Václav Havel, and more recently James Scott—which argues that existing political regimes depend for their survival on the compliance of their subjects, and hence that their subjects can undermine them by engaging in non-cooperation.[6] This can take the form of refusing to comply with rules on borders, or respecting property rights (in land, food, or medicine), or rules prohibiting forming unions. Consider the following examples:

- *Land Occupations*: For example, many peasant communities respond to their dispossession by engaging in reoccupying land. La Via Campesina, a powerful transnational peasant movement, has, for instance, called for peasants to occupy lands that they claim have been illegitimately taken from them and the offices of companies that have invested in the land grabs (La Via Campesina 2013: 25). In Brazil the Movimento dos Trabalhadores Rurais Sem Terra (MST), engages in similar action (Bello 2009: 129). Another example of this strategy is provided by Peter Klein in his analysis of resistance against the construction of the Belo Monte dam in Brazil. He describes how fishermen whose livelihood was threatened by the dam occupied the building site (Klein 2015: 1150).[7]
- *Blockades and Obstruction*: Some others engage in obstruction and blockades. In Uttarakhand in the North of India, villagers faced by logging companies responded by preventing them from cutting down the trees. For example, villagers in the forest of Mandal, near Gopeshwar, obstructed a commercial enterprise from taking ash trees by hugging the trees. Since the Hindi for "to hug" is "chipko," this became known as the Chipko movement, and it (and its strategy) spread throughout Uttarakhand (Guha 2000: 157ff.).[8] To give another example, Dayak communities in Sarawak have also used barricades to prevent logging companies from engaging in deforestation (Keck and Sikkink 1998: 151–2: see also 150–60).
- *Sabotage*: Some engage in sabotage. The Movimento dos Trabalhadores Rurais Sem Terra, for example, has destroyed crops using GM technology (Bello 2009: 129). Sidney Tarrow (2005: 65) also records cases where people have protested against international institutions, such as the IMF, by targeting their offices. Peasants who have been forcibly displaced from their lands also resorted to sabotage. For example, Karen McAllister (2015: 833) reports that when they were removed from their lands in Northern Laos (because of a Chinese rubber tree plantation) "Khmu villagers combined various tactics of resistance to undermine the concession, including anonymous acts of sabotage." And Borras and Franco (2013: 1734) record that when 1,000 villagers in Kampon Speu, Cambodia, were displaced from their land by biofuels companies, the villagers resisted, employing "covert and overt forms of resistance, including sabotage, arson, and stoning of bulldozers." They further note that when the government in Mozambique sold land to a foreign company seeking to grow trees, resulting in some villagers being forcibly displaced, the villagers responded by occupying some land, and also destroying 60,000 trees as a protest (Borras and Franco 2013: 1737).

- *Noncompliance with Debt*: In other cases, governments take steps to combat global injustice. For example, in December 2008 the president of Ecuador, Rafael Correa, refused to pay back Ecuador's debt to the IMF, arguing that it was unjust (Lienau 2014: 215–22).[9]
- *Riots*: On many occasions people have resorted to riots. Now, some instances of rioting might be closer to the first kind of right (that is, people simply taking food to meet their needs). It would, however, be a mistake to leave it at this, for, as historians and social scientists have made clear, it is often part of the political process. Indeed, there is a long tradition of this. Eric Hobsbawm, for example, wrote of the "machine breakers" of the seventeenth to nineteenth centuries in Britain that they engaged in "collective bargaining by riot" (Hobsbawm 1952: 59). He tells of weavers in the West Country in England in the first half of the eighteenth century threatening to riot to get clothiers to agree reasonable terms, and miners in Northumberland in the 1740s whose rioting earned them a considerable pay increase (Hobsbawm 1952: 59).[10] More recently, as Walton and Seddon (1994) chronicle in their *Free Markets & Food Riots*, there have been food riots throughout the 1980s in Latin America, the Middle East, Africa, Asia, and Central and Eastern Europe as a response to poverty and the austerity policies adopted by governments in the context of Structural Adjustment Programs.
- *Rebellion*: Of course, in some cases people have resisted global injustice by overthrowing foreign rule. A good example of this is the slave revolt that took place in the French colony of Saint-Domingue between 1791 and 1804. The rebellion, which is memorably described in C. L. R. James's (1980 [1938]) *The Black Jacobins*, was led by Toussaint L'Ouverture, among others, and ultimately culminated in the formation of the independent state of Haiti. More recently, of course, we have seen the decolonization of the British Empire, as former colonies have sought and achieved independent statehood.

4 THE CORE ARGUMENT FOR THE RIGHT OF RESISTANCE AGAINST GLOBAL INJUSTICE

Having delineated the nature of the *Right of Resistance against Global Injustice* and illustrated what it might entail, I now turn to consider its underlying normative rationale. The two conceptions of the *Right of Resistance against Global Injustice* outlined in Sections 2 and 3 above seem intuitively plausible to me, but can we say anything more in their defense? I think that we can, and will seek to motivate support for these rights.

To do so, it is useful to begin with an analysis of the concept of a right and the normative foundations of rights. In particular I shall begin with the concept of a "claim right" as that is defined by Wesley Hohfeld (1919) in his seminal *Fundamental Legal Conceptions*. On Hohfeld's view, if A has a "claim right" to enjoy X, then others, singly or jointly, are obligated to act in such a way that A enjoys X (Hohfeld 1919: 36, 38). Claim rights thus impose correlative obligations on others.

Consider, then, a claim right, say, to a good X. Now suppose that the duty-bearers do not comply with their obligations. Then, we may say that a second set of agents have what Henry Shue terms "default" duty-bearers to act in such a way that A enjoys X (Shue 1996: 171–3). But suppose that they too fail to do so. Then, we might say that a third set of agents is required to act in such a way that A enjoys X. And so on. However, suppose that others do not act in this way. Does anything else follow?

My proposal here is that *if* other agents are *morally required* to act in such a way that A enjoys a right X (honoring, of course, some moral constraints) then that gives us good reason to think that, other things being equal, A (him or herself) is *morally permitted* to act in such a way that A enjoys right X (again, subject to honoring certain moral constraints). A does not have a duty not to act in ways that will secure his or her rights. For how could it be the case that A has a duty *not* to secure this right for him- or herself when others have a duty to provide the very same right? Would it not be implausible to say that A has a right to X and yet that A is not allowed to act in such a way that her or she enjoys X even though others are required to ensure that? Furthermore, would it not be especially implausible to say this when the interests at stake are so vital?

This argument is strengthened further if we consider two auxiliary points.

First, consider the normative foundations underlying rights. Suppose that, following Raz (1986: ch. 7), one adopts an interest theory of rights. Then, my proposal is that the interest that grounds the duty on the part of others is also sufficient to ground a permission on the part of A. If it is sufficient to impose duties on others, it would seem very unlikely that it is not weighty enough to create a permission on the right-holder (Caney 2015: 60).

Second, some further support for my claim can be found in the following observation. Suppose that A has a right that entails an obligation on the part of B. If B fails to comply with this duty (he assaults A, say), then we think that A is entitled to pursue B (e.g. through the courts) in order to gain compensation. But if we allow A to act in ways to restore his own rights after they have been violated, should we not also allow A to act in ways to secure his own rights so that they do not become violated in the first place?

To sum up, then, my claim is that reflecting on the normative bases of rights and the reasoning underlying the ascription of responsibilities to others, and, furthermore, bearing in mind our recognition of the legitimacy of the retrospective pursuit of justice by right-holders all suggest that right-holders are entitled to secure their own rights. Put otherwise, my claim is that when the duty-bearers fail in their responsibilities to right-holders, the right-holders are entitled (in certain yet to be fully specified conditions) to *enforce* their own rights. To affirm a set of claim rights but to deny this is—I think—to betray the thought that they are entitled—as right-holders—to these resources or the enjoyment of these vital interests.

Five further points should be made. First, it is important to note that I am *not*, of course, saying that the rights-bearer has carte blanche here. As I noted earlier in this section and in Section 1, my aim is first to present the general case for thinking that there is a *Right of Resistance against Global Injustice* before introducing moral limits to this right later. Furthermore, just as there are moral constraints which limit how *A* discharges his duty to *B* to ensure that *B* enjoys X, so there will also be—for similar reasons—moral constraints which limit how *B* can exercise his right to ensure that he enjoys X. Duty-bearers are hedged in by other rights that constrain how they may fulfill their responsibilities to others. By the same token, so too are rights-bearers. Both the *Right of Resistance against Global Injustice* and the duty to uphold others' rights are thus constrained by certain moral parameters. (Note that this does not entail that they are *identical* constraints.) In what follows, rather than repeat each time that the *Right of Resistance against Global Injustice* that I am defending is a right that is hedged in by several moral constraints that will be explicated later on, I shall simply take it as read that it is a morally constrained right.

Second, it is important to be clear that I am not making the general claim that if *A* has a duty to *B* to do X, then *B* is entitled to take X from *A*. That claim is false. For example, I have a duty to send my father a birthday gift, but it does not entail that he has a permission to take something of the equivalent value if I fail to do my duty. My argument is about certain *rights* and their correlative obligations. My claim is that if *A* has a *duty of justice* to respect/uphold *B*'s *right* to enjoy X (where X is some good), then *B* is entitled (in a morally constrained way) to secure the right to enjoy X him- or herself. The point about rights is that the right-holder is *entitled* to certain goods; and this entitlement grounds both the duty on the part of others and the permission on the part of the right-holder. Note, in addition to this, that my focus is on rights to goods that people can themselves secure (e.g. food, water, medicines, safety from physical violence). There are some rights which require a certain attitude and kind of behavior on the part of the duty-bearer to the right-holder. For example, one might say that persons have a right that public officials treat them with respect and not engage in patronizing or disrespectful behavior towards them. Since this type of right demands a certain kind of *attitude* on the part of the duty-bearer (rather than some external goods or the enjoyment of some physical state of affairs), then it may not be possible for the right-holder to secure this right for him- or herself. They cannot directly ensure—on their own—that they enjoy the right, whereas they can with rights to *goods*) (though they can act in ways that might jolt someone into seeing that the other is a person worthy of recognition and bring about a change in attitude).[11]

Third, we should record that on the argument I have just made, the right of resistance is a *remedial* right. That is to say, it comes into operation when others—the duty-bearers in question—have not properly discharged their responsibilities (or perhaps when it is overwhelmingly clear that they will not discharge their responsibilities). Fourthly, it is worth observing that nothing in the line of reasoning presented above supports the view that resistance should be restricted to basic necessities. As such, as was noted earlier, my argument goes beyond the notion of a right to necessity as advanced by Grotius (2005 [1625]): Book II, ch. II, sections VI–X), Pufendorf (1717: Book II, ch. VI, 202–12), and more recent advocates like Mancilla (2016: esp. ch. 4). For the argument shows that persons have rights to secure their entitlements, and so if, as global egalitarians argue, persons have rights to an equal standard of living, then they are entitled to take action to secure that objective. To deny this and to endorse only a restricted set of rights as grounds for resistance is tantamount to denying that persons are *entitled* to those egalitarian standards.

A fifth and final comment. My defense of resistance against global injustice has not so far distinguished between $RRGI_i$ and the $RRGI_{ii}$. One might reasonably ask: Why do we need both? My answer is as follows: Consider $RRGI_i$. If someone is denied their rights, then—barring some countervailing considerations (to be considered in Sections 6 and 7 below)—there would seem to be a strong case for them to have a moral permission to secure their own rights. In such circumstances $RRGI_i$ seems hard to deny. However, on its own $RRGI_i$ will almost certainly be insufficient to bring about the fairest world possible. It permits people to take action in ways that do not bring about any deep change: it is, as I mentioned above in Section 3, a reactive measure and a short-term one. It is about coping in an unjust world, and not changing it. To say this is not to belittle it, but to recognize its limitations and to note that on its own it is incomplete. Given this, we are led to $RRGI_{ii}$. This remedies the limitations in $RRGI_i$, for it permits people to engage in action that brings about sustained long-term change. So we need to accept the $RRGI_{ii}$ too. To this it is worth adding that just as it would be wrong to defend only $RRGI_i$, so it would also be wrong to defend only $RRGI_{ii}$, for many might be unable to engage in the kind of long-term structural change that $RRGI_{ii}$ celebrates, but they *are* able to engage in the kinds of activities defended by $RRGI_i$. Consider, for example, a marginalized woman who lacks political power and influence, but who can smuggle herself across a border or steal vital foodstuffs for herself and her family. The two conceptions of the *Right of Resistance against Global Injustice*, thus, address each other's limitations (though, as we shall see, this does not entail that the two are never in conflict).

5 A Second Argument for the Right of Resistance against Global Injustice

At this point it is necessary to introduce a complication. My argument for the two versions of the *Right of Resistance against Global Injustice* rested on a commitment to some "claim rights." Some, however, deny the normative assumption that all persons have claim rights to socioeconomic goods. Some dispute the egalitarian conception I was invoking, and others deny the sufficientarian version affirmed by Shue. Given this, it is worth noting that there are arguments for *a version* of the *Right of Resistance against Global Injustice* that do not rely on claim rights to socioeconomic goods (either to the provision of basic needs or to equal shares). I say a *version* of the *Right of Resistance against Global Injustice*, because, as we shall see, the conclusion differs in one morally relevant sense from that defended in Section 4.

My argument invokes Hohfeld's notion of a "liberty right," and so I need to begin by defining that. Hohfeld defines "liberty rights" as follows: *A* possesses a liberty right to do

X when *A* is not under a duty not to do X.[12] Note that unlike a claim right, a liberty right does not, in itself, impose duties on others toward the bearer of the (liberty) right.

To illustrate, and motivate support for my second argument (what might be termed the "Liberty Rights Argument"), consider a conception of the *Right of Resistance against Global Injustice* that appeals either to some basic needs (Shue 1996) or to some more egalitarian criterion (Caney 2005). Now, one very common objection to these claims is that they are unduly demanding.[13] Such critics invoke what we might term the "Demandingness Constraint": this maintains that persons do not have a duty to X where X is "unreasonably" demanding. Of course, specifying what constitutes unreasonably demanding is both important and hard to do, but the argument that I wish to advance does not require us to take a stand on quite how to understand this.

Now suppose that someone rejects the sufficientarian or egalitarian ideals of socio-economic justice *solely* for this reason. Consider, for example, someone who accepts that persons have an important interest in meeting a certain standard of living, but, because they think that it would impose excessive demands on the affluent, concludes that the affluent do not have a duty of justice to distribute to them. The crucial point that I want to make here is that it does not follow from the Demandingness Constraint that the poor in this situation do not have *any* right *in any sense* to the meeting of their subsistence needs. For an advocate for the very poor may point out that a system in which the severely disadvantaged lack any access to meet their vital needs is also very demanding for them. Indeed, it is almost certain to be very much more demanding on them than a distributive scheme would be on the affluent. Now, if the affluent are not under a positive duty of justice to distribute, because (and only because) it is too demanding for them, then it follows that, other things being equal, the disadvantaged cannot be under a duty not to take the necessary resources (because abstaining from taking such resources would be just as demanding, if not more demanding, for them). If this is right and they lack a duty not to take, then, by definition, they have a Hohfeldian "liberty right" to take steps needed to meet their rights (where this does not entail carte blanche on their part but does some imply a kind of liberty right where the precise details of its content need to be specified).[14]

We can go further. Recall that the view under consideration maintains that the *only* reason the poor do not have a "claim right" to a certain standard of living is that the correlative duties are too demanding. It holds that if the duties were less onerous, it would not dispute them. This view thus does *not* deny that the poor have morally urgent interests (and it need not deny that—setting aside demandingness—there is a case for equality). But given that it accepts this and given the severe threats to these interests, it is not clear how one could resist the conclusion that the poor are entitled to meet these urgent needs. One cannot argue against this on the grounds that this imposes unreasonable burdens on the rich, for it is just as demanding—indeed, almost certainly much more demanding—for the poor not to take. So if their *only* reason for denying claim rights is an appeal to demanding burdens, then, whilst that might release the rich from a duty to give, that alone cannot generate on the poor a duty not to take.

Given this, we reach the conclusion that those who deny global principles of justice that affirm claim rights to the provision of basic needs (or to something even stronger) can still endorse a version of the *Right of Resistance against Global Injustice* and indeed that they should do so. Informed by the argument above, someone might then hold both that individuals can act in ways that directly realize their rights and the rights of others (in line with what $RRGI_i$ claims) and that persons can act in ways designed to bring about more far-reaching reform in the underlying structures (in line with what $RRGI_{ii}$ claims). However, there is one potential difference in the conclusion reached in the last section and that reached in this section.

It is this. The argument given in Section 4 is grounded in persons' claim rights, and so it seems reasonable to think that when those denied their (claim) rights take steps to secure those rights, then others have, at the very least, a negative duty not to interfere with others when they are securing their own rights in ways that respect others' rights. I think that, given that persons have positive duties to further the cause of justice, it is also the case that others are under a positive duty to assist them to better secure a just world if doing so does not come at unreasonable cost (Shue 1996; Caney 2005, 2007).[15] So, I think that the position discussed in Section 4 would ground negative and positive duties. The argument given in this section, however, does not generate this conclusion. It entails a moral permission on the part of those denied their rights, but that does not necessarily entail that others have duties not to interfere (let alone duties to aid).

As promised then, I have outlined a second argument for a kind of *Right of Resistance against Global Injustice*—an argument that is available to some who deny my starting point. Before considering the potential limits on this right, it may be instructive at this point to consider a discussion of a related point by Thomas Nagel (1991) in *Equality and Partiality*. Drawing on T. M. Scanlon's (1982) seminal work, Nagel holds that principles of justice are those principles that no one can reasonably reject, taking into account both the demands of others and persons' agent-relative values.[16]

In Chapter 15 of Equality *and Partiality* Nagel (1991) maintains that his approach entails that sometimes legitimacy is impossible because there is no outcome which no one can reasonably reject. And he argues that the vast inequalities that exist at the global level are a case in point. The poor can reasonably reject the status quo and any merely modest revisions to it. The affluent can, however, Nagel says, reasonably reject dramatic losses in their condition of the kind that would be required to enable the poor to reach a standard of living high enough for it to be the case that they could not reasonably reject it.[17] We thus have a situation in which no position commands legitimacy. For any outcome, some could reasonably reject it (Nagel 1991: 170–4).[18]

It is worth quoting Nagel at length. Nagel puts the point as follows:

> In cases of extreme inequality the poor can refuse to accept a policy of gradual change and the rich can refuse to accept a policy of revolutionary change, and neither of them is being unreasonable in this. The difference for each of the parties between the two alternatives is just too great.... The degree of sacrifice by the rich that it would be reasonable for the poor countries to insist on in some

hypothetical collective arrangement is one which it would not be unreasonable for the rich to refuse.   (Nagel 1991: 171–2)

What follows from this? Nagel draws the following conclusion:

If there is no solution that no one could reasonably reject, neither party to the conflict can be reproached for trying to impose a solution acceptable to him but unacceptable to his opponent. Both the status quo and a revolutionary alternative may meet this condition. The fact that the status quo *is* the status quo usually means that those whom it favors have the power to impose it; but if in such circumstances others acquire the power to overthrow it, they cannot be reproached for using it.

(Nagel 1991: 173)

This is similar in spirit to the argument I presented earlier in this section on behalf of sceptics of my starting point. Two points should, however, be noted. The first is that it is unclear precisely what Nagel is claiming. For instance, the statement that the poor "cannot be reproached" if they use power to reduce inequalities (to such an extent that the rich may reasonably reject such reductions) appears to be saying that the actions of the poor are *excusable*. But to say that a person's actions can be excused is not to say that they acted rightly or that they did not fail to comply with a duty. It just means that there are mitigating factors that entail that we should not condemn them (or, at the least, we should condemn less than we otherwise would). So, it is not clear from the passage from Nagel whether he is saying that the poor are not under a duty not to impose radical reductions in global inequality, that is, that they have a Hohfeldian liberty right to impose such radical reductions.

That said, Nagel's argument—that the poor can reasonably reject the status quo and any merely slight modifications of it—would seem to me to give ample support for the claim that they lack a duty to abstain from radical changes to the status quo. If they can reasonably reject the status quo, how could it be the case that they are required to comply with it?[19] I conclude, then, that Nagel's framework points to the same conclusion as the Liberty Rights Argument presented above.

6 MORAL LIMITS: JUSTICE

Thus far I have made clear that the *Right of Resistance against Global Injustice*$_i$ and *Right of Resistance against Global Injustice*$_{ii}$ are morally constrained, but I have not said what those moral limits are. I do so in the next two sections.

One set of constraints concerns people's obligations of justice to others. The case for *RRGI* appeals to a respect for people's rights. It is animated by a commitment to ensure that people enjoy what they are entitled to as a matter of global justice. Now, given this rationale for the *RRGI*, it follows that people's exercise of the *RRGI* should be compatible with the underlying values. The *justification* of RRGI should, we might say, inform the *moral parameters* of the exercise of RRGI. In light of this, our starting point should be the following:

> *The Justice Constraint*: a person may engage in resistance (either $RRGI_i$ or $RRGI_{ii}$) only if doing so does not set back the *cause of justice*.

This, though, needs to be fleshed out. What does it mean?

In reply: it has, at least, two implications:

(1) First, acts of resistance should be judged in terms of whether they better advance people's rights. If resistance—either short-term ($RRGI_i$) or long-term ($RRGI_{ii}$)—results in greater injustice, then it is impermissible.

(2) Second, those engaged in resistance should, other things being equal, employ the least harmful means available.

Note that although (1) and (2) have a common foundation—a commitment to securing rights in ways that do not set back the cause of justice—they do differ. For example, a course of action may satisfy Principle (2) (stealing some food, say, may be less bad than any other means of redress available) but might fail (1). Suppose it would result in such severe repercussions for others, including the very poor, that this outweighs the benefit to the person engaging in the theft.

Principle (2) needs little further elaboration, but (1) requires further clarification. There are at least three other points that need to be borne in mind when determining what it means to "set back the cause of justice" (there may be more), and it is worth making them explicit.

First, we should not interpret this phrase to entail that agents may *never* act in ways that reduce the entitlements of others. Let us suppose that someone can act in a way that secures their own entitlements. Suppose, though, that it would lead others to act in ways that result in even more injustice for others. Are they prohibited from so acting? Those deprived from enjoying their entitlements might make the following point: our actions will have these malign effects, but they do so only because others have failed in their responsibilities. Why should we have to bear the whole weight of the responsibility to ensure that there is not a net reduction in justice? To give an example: suppose that some lack access to vital medicines because others who could and should provide them choose not to do so. Suppose, then, that stealing leads to an even worse outcome for some third parties because the owners increase the price even more. Those who are tempted to steal might say, "Our actions, on their own, do not cause this bad outcome. The latter could have been averted if only others had complied with their responsibility. So, why should we sacrifice our core interests and pick up the whole of the duty not to cause more injustice?" The thought might then be that in cases of noncompliance those who lack their own entitlements are not required to bear the *whole* burden of the duty not to set back the cause of injustice.

Second, and independently of this point about the implications of noncompliance, it is commonly accepted that an agent has a moral permission to give extra weight to his or her own interests in any such decision. In light of this, we might reword the above principle to recognize what Scheffler (1982) terms an "agent-centred prerogative": persons are entitled to give extra weight to their own interests.

Thirdly, we might also reword the principle so that it includes a proviso stating that anyone who exercises the *Right of Resistance against Global Injustice$_i$* has a duty to share the benefits they acquire equitably. Without such a clause, a right of resistance would seem to reward the strongest among the least advantaged and to penalize the very weakest. If we just say that the disadvantaged can secure their own rights, then that might mean in practice that the most able-bodied and skillful can do so, but that the most frail, the sickest, and the most vulnerable and marginalized would fare disproportionately badly. To counteract this undesirable outcome, we should, I think, add a clause about sharing the benefits fairly and with a concern for all the disadvantaged. For example, those crossing borders illegally would have an obligation to send remittances to those they left behind who were too sick or poor or young or elderly to undertake the dangerous journey.

Given these points, we should reword the *Justice Constraint* as follows:

The Revised Justice Constraint: A person may exercise the right of resistance only if it does not set back the cause of justice, where this:
(a)   includes a particular emphasis on the impacts of their action on the least advantaged;
(b)   does not require agents to bear the whole of the duty not to create injustice for others;
(c)   allows the possibility of an agent-centered prerogative;
(d)   requires those exercising the right of resistance to share the benefits equitably and with a concern for all; and
(e)   requires using the least harmful means available.

One final comment: when considering the implications of the *Revised Justice Constraint,* it is worth noting that the *RRGI$_i$* and *RRGI$_{ii}$* can, in some circumstances, stand in tension with each other. That is, short-term acts of resistance in which some flout rules in order to survive and make ends meet can, in some cases, help perpetuate an unjust system and thus make it hard to realize long-term structural change. This is not just a theoretical possibility but has been borne out by studies of repressive regimes. In his illuminating discussion of China under Mao, Frank Dikötter (2010: esp. pt IV) makes a compelling case that small acts of resistance helped perpetuate the regime. As he puts it, "[s]urvival depended on disobedience, but the many strategies of survival devised by people at all levels, from farmers hiding the grain to local cadres cooking the account books, also tended to prolong the life of the regime" (Dikötter 2010: xvi).

Of course, sometimes the two rights can complement each other. Where this is possible, resistors have reason to choose forms of $RRGI_i$ that further $RRGI_{ii}$. (To use the terminology coined by the social and political thinker and ecologist André Gorz (1967 [1964]: 7–8), one might seek what he termed "non-reformist reforms" (where these are defined as reforms which do not accept the prevailing system but seek to change it)[20] over what he termed "reformist reforms" (where these accept the status quo and seek to do the best possible within it). But this may not always be possible, and here we face a choice—a choice that must, though, be made in line with the underlying rationale for the right of resistance, and so the ultimate touchstone here has to be "whatever best fulfills the ideals of justice."

Note that the dilemma facing those considering how best to resist global injustice is similar to one that faces affluent individuals considering what obligations they have to help the global poor. I am thinking here of the ethical debates surrounding "effective altruism" and the emphasis made by some on making charitable donations (including by taking highly paid jobs in order to maximize the possible size of the charitable donation). Some are critical of this emphasis on giving money and the concentration on immediate relief; for they argue that our focus should instead be on trying to effect structural change. Some critics also argue that aid (and the means used to generate the income to fund the aid) actually helps maintain the status quo. *To the extent that this is true* (I do not take a stand on this here, since the issues seem to me complex), then we see a similar tension between short-term coping and long-term change. The difference concerns the agents in question.[21]

7 Moral Limits: Political Legitimacy

Suppose that resistance helps bring about a more just society. It does not straightforwardly follow from this that it is justified. One reason it does not is because *RRGI* (as I have defined it) involves unlawful conduct.[22] Given this, it follows that for the *RRGI* to be justified it must be the case that agents do not have a binding (that is, "all things considered") obligation to obey the law. Wherever they do, *RRGI* would be impermissible.

Now, obviously, to determine when this holds and what this implies requires us (a) to identify what kinds of law are at stake and then (b) to determine if there are binding obligations to obey these laws even when they may be unjust.

(1) Let us start with (a). Political philosophers have discussed extensively what citizens may do when their state treats them unjustly. However, the cases we are considering are not so straightforward, for those resisting global injustice might conceivably break three different kinds of laws. These can be described as follows:

(a) *domestic law cases*: An agent's acts of resistance violate the law of the state to which they belong;

(b) *foreign law cases*: An agent's acts of resistance violate the law of a foreign state; and

(c) *international law cases*: An agent's acts of resistance violate international law.

Of course, some actions may violate more than one of the above. Some examples help illustrate the possibilities. To start with an example of the first kind: Consider a situation in which a corrupt government passes a law that prevents people from using resources to which they have a moral right. Suppose, for example, that it seizes control over access to minerals and authorizes a foreign company to mine there, and shares the profits with the company and corrupt government officials. This is, on my account, a violation of global justice.

Consider now the second kind: a state may implement an immigration law that unjustly excludes others and unjustly expels those seeking to immigrate. What is unjust here is the law of that state and its impacts on the rights of non-citizens. In such a situation, some may flout the law to secure their own rights ($RRGI_i$) or seek to change it ($RRGI_{ii}$) through violating it. Other examples also illustrate the phenomenon: some might try to import goods illegally—seeking to avoid unjust tariffs. Similarly members of several states might engage in cyberattacks on firms located in another state. In all these cases persons are defying the law of another state.

Let us turn finally now to (c): governments may act in violation of international law. They might, for example, defy WTO laws on protectionism or subsidies. Or they might default on their debts. Consider, for instance, the example mentioned earlier, of when the government of Ecuador led by President Rafael Correa refused in December 2008 to comply with its debt (Lienau 2014: 215–22). Or consider the interesting proposal made by Fritz Scharpf, a leading scholar of the European Union. He discusses the possibility of a government of an EU member state defying a ruling of the European Court of Justice (ECJ). His idea is this: a government can permissibly engage in "open noncompliance" with a decision of the ECJ if it does so in order to appeal to the shared values held by the members of the European Council of Ministers and it pledges that it will comply with the ECJ's decision if a majority of the Council of Ministers endorse the ECJ's decision (Scharpf 2009: 200). We could see this as a principled act of civil disobedience.

Now which kind of law an agent breaks can make a moral difference. For example, an individual may have political obligations to obey his or her own state, but no such obligation to other states. We need, thus, to consider the sources of political obligation and consider whether, and if so when, they entail political obligations in these distinct situations.

(2) Having distinguished between the three kinds of laws, we can turn now to normative evaluation (part (b)). A great deal has been written on the question of political obligation, and it is not my aim to analyze the strengths of each of the different accounts. Rather, what I seek to do is to consider the central theories of political obligation and to examine whether *any* of them establish that agents have a binding political obligation to obey laws that perpetuate global injustice (whether they are of type (a),(b), or (c)) and, if so, in what circumstances.

If we do this, I argue, we reach two conclusions. The first is that where there is great injustice then—according to each of the main theories—there is no binding obligation to obey the state. The second is that where there is a relatively minor injustice, then it is possible that, where certain conditions obtain, there could be a content-independent reason to obey, but, so I submit, those conditions are unlikely to obtain (though not impossible) in the cases we are discussing.

To see the reasoning for my first conclusion, consider some standard theories of political obligation.

1. *Fair Play.* John Rawls (1999a: 96–8) and H. L. A. Hart (1955: 185–6) are famous for having argued that when a just cooperative scheme is in place then those who receive benefits have a duty to reciprocate and obey the rules of the scheme.

Now some have raised forceful questions about whether this can show that citizens have a political obligation to their own state. Many thinkers have argued that benefiting from a scheme of social cooperation does not necessarily entail obligations to obey the state. Nozick (1974: 93–5) and Simmons (1979: ch. V, esp. 118–42) are well-known examples.

Suppose, however, that we can show that the fair-play account is not vulnerable to Nozick–Simmons-type objections or that it can be revised to accommodate them. We then have to confront the question: What implications does this theory have when the political institution(s) governing individuals are unjust? Hart (1955: 186) maintains that the principle of fair play does generate obligations even in unjust arrangements, but he says that these are overridable. And they surely would be in conditions of great injustice. Rawls (1999a: 96) takes a similar position, holding that the principle of fairness does not generate any obligations in institutions that are not "reasonably just." This suggests that it could generate political obligations where an institution is not perfectly just; and Rawls (1999a: section 53) explicitly holds that there can be duties to obey unjust laws. Now, given this formulation, then, it follows that for Rawls—as for Hart –where there is major injustice, there can be no political obligation to obey.[23] So, in cases where some face severe deprivation or exploitation, or where some are exposed to avoidable and unnecessary environmental hazards, there can be no political obligation grounded in fair play to obey unjust laws of the kind covered by (a), (b), or (c).

2. *Natural Duty of Justice.* Consider then a second well-known theory. Rawls (1999a: 99–100) argues that persons are under a natural duty of justice to support just institutions. If we consider its implications for our questions, it is clear that this too cannot support political obligations to obey severely unjust laws. Given its commitment to realizing justice, this view would simply rely on the conclusions given in Section 6. And in all three scenarios described above (that is, (a)–(c)) it would sanction illegal action in the face of severely unjust laws if that would serve the cause of justice. (This can generate reasons to comply. For example, a government facing an unjust demand for the repayment of debt might have a reason to comply if by not doing so it leads to even more unjust retaliation.) The central point, however, is that this argument cannot justify content-independent obligations to obey laws that perpetuate great injustice.

Now, as noted above, Rawls does think that there can, nonetheless, be an obligation to obey unjust laws in some circumstances. I come to that below. The salient point here is that his argument entails (and he concurs) that it would not justify obligation when there is unreasonable injustice.

3. *Consent.* Consider now a third theory of political obligation. As above, let us start with (a)-like cases. Two points can be made here. First, as the literature on political obligation generally attests, very few people consent to the government of the state to which they belong. This will be the case to an even greater extent in the situations we are considering. So those who engage in acts of resistance against their own state are highly unlikely to have engaged in the relevant consent-implying acts. Similarly, in cases where they defy the law of another state, it is also extremely unlikely that they will have consented.

Secondly, even if people had consented, the conditions necessary for it to generate moral obligations are highly likely to be absent. For consent to generate binding obliga- tions it is, for example, necessary for agents to have a reasonable degree of choice (so that they are free not to consent) and, furthermore, that they can refuse to dissent without incurring unreasonable burdens (for example, they will not suffer from persecution or the imposition of severe harms (such as economic sanctions or force or social exclusion) (Simmons 1979: 81–2).

The upshot of this short survey, then, is that:

[1] On all plausible accounts of political obligation, agents lack any such obligation to institutions that are severely unjust

(3) But what about laws that are unjust but not severely unjust (however we define that)? Might there be a content-independent reason for political obligation? I think that the most promising way to justify such a claim is to be found in Rawls's (1999a: section 53) discussion in *A Theory of Justice.* There Rawls writes that "[w]hen the basic structure of society is reasonably just, as estimated by what the current state of things allows, we are to recognize unjust laws as binding provided that they do not exceed certain limits of injustice" (Rawls 1999a: 308). He reasons that in a reasonably just political system deci- sions are taken by majority rule, and in democratic political systems it is unreasonable for citizens to expect the political process to deliver the right outcomes as they see it in every single case. We should expect human fallibility, and recognize all realistic political procedures will sometimes result in error. Given this, we would choose to have one of these procedures rather than have no system at all. Since majority rule is part of a fair constitutional structure, then, bearing in mind the point made above, we should accept its outcomes (Rawls (1999a: section 53, esp. 311–12).

However, Rawls then adds, persons can have a content-independent reason to obey an unjust law only if certain conditions obtain. In particular, as he argues, for persons to have an obligation to obey an unjust law "the burden of injustice should be more or less evenly distributed over different groups in society" (Rawls 1999a: 312). If it is the case that unjust decisions are taken which sometimes burden one group, sometimes another, sometimes a third group, then, so Rawls claims, there can be a duty to obey. However, if one group systematically suffers, then they are not obligated (Rawls 1999a: 312).

Such an account seems plausible to me. However, it would seem to have little force in the global context. For it to apply we would have to find a case where some suffer from global injustice; this injustice stems from the actions of a given political system to which they belong; and, moreover, this political system is a reasonably just democratic political system run according to majority rule. Second, it is very rarely the case that the burden of injustice is shared around equitably. Given this we should accept the following:

[2] Whilst in principle agents might have content-independent reasons to obey political institutions that engage in minor injustice, these apply only in certain conditions which rarely exist.

My conclusion here, then, is that if the injustices are great, then there is no obligation to obey; and if the injustices are reasonably minor, then there could, in principle, be an obligation to obey if the injustice issues from a democratic process within which they are included and they are not systematically penalized, but I think it unlikely that there will be situations that meet these conditions. In practice, then, those facing global injustice may generally engage in acts of resistance that are illegal and, to all intents and purposes, they lack an obligation to obey laws that perpetuate global injustice.

This concludes my analysis of the moral parameters that should constrain the rights to resist global injustice. The main limits on the right to resist are those that stem from the duties of *justice* that resistors owe to others (Section 6). However, a complete account should also acknowledge the possibility of duties to obey *legitimate* political authorities (Section 7).

8 CONCLUDING REMARKS

Having defined the right of resistance against global justice, identified its foundations, and explored its limits, I conclude with four reflections.

The first is that it is important to recognize the agency of those treated unjustly. To a disturbing extent they have been treated as "objects" of moral concern and not as subjects. To do this is not only factually inaccurate (since very many struggle against injustice and oppression), but also betrays a lack of respect.

Second, it can lead to principles being rejected without reason. It is common to encounter people rejecting a principle on the basis that the powerful and advantaged will not act on that. But that is not the end of the story.

Third, it is important to note, self-emancipation has a value that is absent from cases where some liberate others. Many who have experienced injustice and struggled against it make the same point. They argue that when people emancipate themselves, they thereby enjoy certain important goods. For example, resistance engenders a sense of self-respect and self-worth. Consider, in this context, the words of Frederick Douglass (2014 [1845]) in his *Narrative of the Life of Frederick Douglass, an American Slave*. Douglass discusses when he fought back against a white farmer, Mr Covey, who regularly beat him; and he gives a compelling description of how his fighting back so successfully restored his sense of self-worth (Douglass (2014 [1845]: ch. X).[24] He writes:

> This battle with Mr. Covey was the turning-point in my career as a slave. It rekindled the few expiring embers of freedom, and revived within me a sense of my own manhood. It recalled the departed self-confidence, and inspired me again with a determination to be free. The gratification afforded by the triumph was a full compensation for whatever else might follow, even death itself. He only can understand the deep satisfaction which I experienced, who has himself repelled by force the bloody arm of slavery. I felt as I never felt before. It was a glorious resurrection, from the tomb of slavery, to the heaven of freedom. My long-crushed spirit rose, cowardice departed, bold defiance took its place; and I now resolved that, however long I might remain a slave in form, the day had passed forever when I could be a slave in fact. I did not hesitate to let it be known of me, that the white man who expected to succeed in whipping, must also succeed in killing me.   (Douglass (2014 [1845]: 73)

The Trinidadian writer C. L. R. James (1980 [1938]) makes a similar observation in *The Black Jacobins: Toussaint L'Ouverture and the San Domingo Revolution*. This is an account of the slave revolt that took place in what was the French colony of Saint-Domingue that began in 1791 and culminated in the creation in 1804 of Haiti as a separate state. James writes:

> At bottom the popular movement had acquired an immense self-confidence. The former slaves had defeated white colonists, Spaniards and British, and now they were free.... Black men who had been slaves were deputies in the French Parliament, black men who had been slaves negotiated with the French and foreign governments. Black men who had been slaves filled the highest positions in the colony. There was Toussaint, the former slave, incredibly grand and powerful and incomparably the greatest man in San Domingo. There was no need to be ashamed of being a black. The revolution had awakened them, had given them the possibility of achievement, confidence and pride. That psychological weakness, that feeling of inferiority with which the imperialists poison colonial peoples everywhere, these were gone.   (James 1980 [1938]: 244)

James's account—with its emphasis on the acquisition of "immense self-confidence," the lack of any "need to be ashamed of being a black," the "possibility of achievement, confidence and pride" and the banishment of a "feeling of inferiority"—accurately capture some of the beneficial effects that result from self-liberation, but which would not result from other-liberation.

I end, though, on a fourth, more somber note. I have drawn attention to the agency of the marginalized and disadvantaged. We should, however, recognize that those suffering from global injustice are often particularly vulnerable. As many thinkers (ranging from La Boétie to Gandhi to Havel) have recognized, unjust rulers have often depended on those whom they oppress: it is this that enables resistance to get a footing. However, when those who are unjustly disadvantaged are geographically remote from those responsible for their plight, or when they are temporally remote (for they live in the future but those responsible precede them), then their capacity to initiate change is reduced, sometimes drastically.[25] The more, then, that global injustice involves these geographical and temporal barriers between those responsible for these injustices and those suffering from them, the more bleak the prospects for success.

ACKNOWLEDGMENTS

I presented an earlier version of this at the EUI and I am very grateful to the audience, especially Richard Bellamy, Claus Offe, Philippe Van Parijs, Jennifer Welsh and Lea Ypi for their comments.

NOTES

1. There are exceptions. See, for example, Blunt's (2011) exploration of whether Pogge's account of global injustice justifies a right to (potentially violent) resistance; Cabrera's (2010: ch. 5, esp. 132–50) discussion of migration and civil disobedience as well as his discussion of the role that some who are disadvantaged can and do play in assisting those immigrating to the USA (Cabrera 2010: 154 & 157–64); Deveaux's (2015) discussion of the capacity of members of developing countries to combat global poverty; Hidalgo's (2015) analysis of immigration and the legitimacy of violating border controls; Pogge (2008: 152–73) on what democratic governments in developing countries can, and should, do to promote the continued existence of democracy; and Ypi (2012: ch. 7) on the cosmopolitan avant-garde. See also the literature on the rights of the global poor to wage war to rectify that situation (eg Fabre 2012: ch. 3). In addition, I have argued elsewhere that "the unjustly treated" can be "primary agents of justice (Caney 2013: 143–4) and have defended a "right of resistance against global injustice" (Caney 2015) and a right of necessity (Caney n.d.).

    Note: my comment in the text refers to the interest taken in this topic by *scholars who are participating on the recent anglophone debates about global justice*. If we look more widely—as we should—then we will find an extensive discussion of colonialism, the challenges facing postcolonial societies, and philosophical reflections on them. Many from countries that were colonized wrote about the phenomenon and responses to it. Important examples include Fanon (2001 [1961]) and Gandhi (2010 [1909]). See also C. L. R. James's (1980 [1938]) account of the Haitian revolution, *The Black Jacobins*, and Cugoano (1999 [1787]).

2. This formulation builds on, but crucially differs from, my earlier formulation of the right to resist global injustice in Caney (2015: 52–3).

3. In an earlier unpublished paper I have argued that we find a version of this claim in many previous thinkers, including Cicero, Aquinas, Grotius, Hobbes, Locke, Pufendorf, Wolff, and Paley (Caney n.d.).

4. For an analysis of the ethical issues raised by biofuels, see Nuffield Council on Bioethics (2011).

5. This formulation is identical to that which I gave in (Caney 2015: 52–3).

6. See La Boétie (2012 [1576]: esp pp.5–8); Gandhi (2010 [1909]: ch. VII, 39, 2001a [1920]: 157); Havel (1991 [1978]: 133–4, 136, 148ff.); and, more generally, the work of James Scott (1985, 1990).

7. See also Tarrow (1998: 35). Eric Hobsbawm also distinguishes between two kinds of land occupation: one as a measure to persuade people to change their behavior and the other as the goal in and of itself (Hobsbawm 1974: 128–9). This is a good point at which to note (a) that some of the actions covered by $RRGI_{ii}$ might also be deployed as part of the $RRGI_i$ and (b) that the distinction between the two should not, in practice, be drawn too sharply.

8. See, more generally, Ramachandra Guha's (2008: esp. ch. 7) discussion of peasant resistance.

9. For discussions of the ethical issues surrounding if and when governments may break international law, see Buchanan (2004: ch. 11); Goodin (2005); and Scharpf (2009: 200).

10. See also Charles Tilly's (1975: 380–455) seminal treatment of how peasants and others have frequently employed riots as a way of changing practices and policies. Writing in a similar vein E. P. Thompson chronicles the ways in which those denied their rights used riots—what he terms "the logic of crowd pressure" (Thompson 1971: 125)—to deter those who held food from imposing high prices (Thompson 1971: 76–136).

11. For example, Gandhi (2001b [1925]: 191)argued that his particular conception of resistance (*satyagraha*) should involve self-sacrifice, in part, because this might induce sympathy on the part of the oppressors, and bring about a change of heart.

12. Hohfeld (1919: 38–9, 40–50) often refers to what I am terming liberty rights as "privileges." He writes that "a privilege is the opposite of a duty, and the correlative of a 'no-right'" (Hohfeld 1919: 38–9).

13. Thomas Pogge (2009: 125–8), for example, resists Shue's account on these grounds. Note Pogge's concerns are specifically about positive duties of justice. Others, however, might think that the negative duties of justice posed by global sufficientarians or egalitarians are too demanding.

14. This point could be put another way: consider Samuel Scheffler's (1982) concept of an "agent-centred prerogative." This is often invoked to justify limits on how much "we," advantaged members of the world, are required to give. It is said to give the wealthy, agent-relative reasons to forgo giving more. However, even if it gives an advantaged person a reason not to give, it clearly does not mean that it gives others (the destitute, the poor, the malnourished of the world) a reason not to take.

15. See Mancilla (2016: 85) who defines the right of necessity with respect to a negative duty of non-interference, and does not affirm an analogous positive duty to assist (though Mancilla 2016: 5, 86–7 does not eschew positive duties altogether). However, if we accept the existence of positive duties of justice, as I think we should (Caney 2007; Shue 1996), then others have positive duties to aid those engaged in justified resistance.

16. I am setting aside Nagel's (2005) paper, for unlike Nagel (1991), it does not discuss the issues under consideration.

17. For the record, I deny this claim by Nagel. However, I grant it here for the sake of argument to bring out that even those who dissent from my starting point have (as Nagel notes) good reason to endorse *RRGI*.

18. David Miller (2007: 274: cf. 274–6) makes a similar point, discussing what he terms "a justice gap". Miller does not then explore whether the disadvantaged may engage in the kinds of activities described in this chapter.

19. I discuss reasons why they might be in Sections 6 and 7.

20. Gorz (1967 [1964]: 6) also termed these "revolutionary reforms".

21. For a recent statement and defense of "effective altruism," see MacAskill (2016). For a discussion of criticisms, including the concern that effective altruism is too concerned with giving money and insufficiently committed to structural reform, see Gabriel (2017).

22. I stress that this is "one reason." There are other relevant considerations. For example, in addition to asking if, and when, unlawful conduct is justified, we also need to inquire whether those acting have the legitimate authority to act. When some—say, social movements or NGOs—act on behalf of others and when they impose involuntary burdens on others, we need an account of political authority that can explain why they have (or do not have) the right to engage in such action. I address this in Caney (forthcoming: ch. 8, section VI, ch. 9, sections VIII–IX).

23. One might reasonably ask "What constitutes a 'major injustice'?" Rawls (1999a: 96) refers to institutions being "reasonably just", so one could ask: What does it mean for an institution to be "reasonably just" or "unreasonably unjust"? I hope to bypass these questions. These are questions that Rawls and Rawlsians need to be able to answer. However, my conclusion, recall, is that, in the kinds of cases I am discussing, agents are in practice permitted to disobey both moderately unjust or severely unjust laws (since the conditions needed for us to have a duty obey moderately unjust laws do not obtain). Given this, my conclusion does not require me to be able to identify where injustice counts as being "reasonable" or "moderate" and when it is no longer reasonably just.

24. For an interesting discussion which analyses Douglass's resistance in terms of an exercise of freedom see Julius (forthcoming). My emphasis here by contrast is on "self-confidence" and self-respect.

25. In the case of temporal remoteness, their capacity to prevent injustice or even constrain it may be non-existent. In the case of geographical remoteness, it may be possible (for example, through the use of cyberactivism) to limit the capacity of those physically far removed from them to inflict injustice.

References

Bello, Walden (2009) *The Food Wars*. London and New York: Verso.

Blunt, Gwilym David (2011) "Transnational Socio-Economic Justice and the Right of Resistance," *Politics* 31(1): 1–8.

Borras Jr, Saturnino M., and Jennifer C. Franco (2013) "Global Land Grabbing and Political Reactions 'From Below'," *Third World Quarterly* 34(9): 1723–47.

Buchanan, Allen (2004) *Justice, Legitimacy, and Self-Determination: Moral Foundations for International Law*. Oxford: Oxford University Press.

Cabrera, Luis (2010) *The Practice of Global Citizenship*. New York: Cambridge University Press.

Caney, Simon (2005) *Justice beyond Borders: A Global Political Theory*. Oxford: Oxford University Press.

Caney, Simon (2007) "Global Poverty and Human Rights: The Case for Positive Duties." In Thomas Pogge (ed.), *Freedom from Poverty as a Human Rights: Who Owes What to the Very Poor?* Oxford: Oxford University Press, 275–302.

Caney, Simon (2013) "Agents of Global Justice." In David Archard, Monique Deveaux, Neil Manson, and Daniel Weinstock (eds.), *Reading Onora O'Neill*. London and New York: Routledge, 133–56.

Caney, Simon (2015) "Responding to Global Injustice: On the Right of Resistance," *Social Philosophy and Policy* 32(1): 51–73.

Caney, Simon (forthcoming) *On Cosmopolitanism*. Oxford: Oxford University Press.

Caney, Simon (n.d.) "Global Injustice and the Right of Necessity." MS.

Commission on Intellectual Property Rights (2002) *Integrating Intellectual Property Rights and Development Policy*. London: Report of the Commission on Intellectual Property Rights, http://www.iprcommission.org/papers/pdfs/final_report/CIPRfullfinal.pdf, accessed August 24, 2019.

Cugoano, Quobna Ottobah (1999 [1787]) "Thoughts and Sentiments on the Evil and Wicked Traffic of the Slavery and Commerce of the Human Species, Humbly Submitted to the Inhabitants of Great-Britain, by Ottobah Cugoano, a Native of Africa." In *Thoughts and Sentiments on the Evil of Slavery and Other Writings*, ed. with an introduction and notes by Vincent Carretta. New York: Penguin, 1–111.

Deveaux, Monique (2015) "The Global Poor as Agents of Justice," *Journal of Moral Philosophy* 12(2): 125–50.

Dikötter, Frank (2010) *Mao's Great Famine: The History of China's Most Devastating Catastrophe, 1958–62*. London: Bloomsbury.

Douglass, Frederick (2014 [1845]) *Narrative of the Life of Frederick Douglass, an American Slave*. New York: Penguin Books, ed. with an introduction by Ira Dworkin.

Fabre, Cécile (2012) *Cosmopolitan War*. Oxford: Oxford University Press.

Fanon, Frantz (2001 [1961]) *The Wretched of the Earth*. London: Penguin.

Gabriel, Iason (2017) "Effective Altruism and its Critics," Journal of Applied Philosophy 34(4): 457–73.

Gandhi, M. K. (2001a [1920]) "Non Cooperation Explained." In *Non-Violent Resistance (Satyagraha)*. Mineola, NY: Dover), 156–61, originally published in *Young India*, August 18, 1920.

Gandhi, M. K. (2001b [1925]) "Vykom Satyagraha." In *Non-Violent Resistance (Satyagraha)*. Mineola, NY: Dover, 191, originally published in *Young India*, March 19, 1925.

Gandhi, M. K. (2010 [1909]) "Indian Home Rule [or *Hind Swaraj*]." *In "Hind Swaraj" and Other Writings*, ed. Anthony J. Parel. Cambridge: Cambridge University Press, 1–123.

Goodin, Robert E. (2005) "Toward an International Rule of Law: Distinguishing International Law-Breakers from Would-Be Law-Makers," *Journal of Ethics* 9(1–2): 225–46.

Gorz, André (1967 [1964]) *Strategy for Labor: A Radical Proposal*. Boston, MA: Beacon Press.

Grotius, Hugo (2005 [1625]) *The Rights of War and Peace*, ed. with an introduction by Richard Tuck, from the edn by Jean Barbeyrac. Indianapolis, IN: Liberty Fund.

Guha, Ramachandra (2000) *The Unquiet Woods: Ecological Change and Peasant Resistance in the Himalaya*, expanded edn. Berkeley and Los Angeles: University of California Press.

Hart, H. L. A. (1955) "Are There Any Natural Rights?" *The Philosophical Review* 64(2): 175–91.

Havel, Václav (1991 [1978]) "The Power of the Powerless." In *Open Letters: Selected Prose 1965–1900*, selected and edited by Paul Wilson. London: Faber and Faber, 125–214.

Hidalgo, Javier (2015) "Resistance to Unjust Immigration Restrictions," *Journal of Political Philosophy* 23(4): 450–70.

Hobsbawm, E. J. (1952) "The Machine Breakers," *Past & Present* 1(1): 57–70.

Hobsbawm, E. J. (1974) "Peasant Land Occupations," *Past & Present* 62(1): 120–52.

Hohfeld, Wesley N. (1919) *Fundamental Legal Conceptions, as Applied in Judicial Reasoning and Other Legal Essays*. New Haven, CT: Yale University Press.

International Energy Authority (2016) *World Energy Outlook: The Gold Standard of Energy Analysis*, http://www.worldenergyoutlook.org/resources/energydevelopment/energyaccessdatabase/, accessed February 28, 2017.

James, C. L. R. (1980 [1938]) *The Black Jacobins: Toussaint L'Ouverture and the San Domingo Revolution*. London: Allison and Busby.

Julius, A. J. (forthcoming) *Reconstruction*. Princeton, NJ: Princeton University Press.

Keck, Margaret E., and Kathryn Sikkink (1998) *Activists beyond Borders: Advocacy Networks in International Politics*. Ithaca, NY, and London: Cornell University Press.

Klein, Peter Taylor (2015) "Engaging the Brazilian State: The Belo Monte Dam and the Struggle for Political Voice," *Journal of Peasant Studies* 42(6): 1137–56.

La Boétie, Étienne de (2012 [1576]) *Discourse on Voluntary Servitude*, tr. James B. Atkinson and David Sices, with an Introduction and Notes by James B. Atkinson. Indianapolis, IN, and Cambridge: Hackett Publishing Company.

Lienau, Odette (2014) *Rethinking Sovereign Debt: Politics, Reputation, and Legitimacy in Modern Finance*. Cambridge, MA, and London: Harvard University Press.

McAllister, Karen E. (2015) "Rubber, Rights and Resistance: the Evolution of Local Struggles against a Chinese Rubber Concession in Northern Laos," *Journal of Peasant Studies* 42(3–4): 817–37.

MacAskill, William (2016) *Doing Good Better: Effective Altruism and a Radical New Way to Make a Difference*. London: Guardian Books and Faber & Faber.

Mancilla, Alejandra (2016) *The Right of Necessity: Moral Cosmopolitanism and Global Poverty*. London and New York: Rowman and Littlefield.

Miller, David (2007) *National Responsibility and Global Justice*. Oxford: Oxford University Press.

Nagel, Thomas (1991) *Equality and Partiality*. New York: Oxford University Press.

Nagel, Thomas (2005) "The Problem of Global Justice," *Philosophy and Public Affairs* 33(2): 113–47.

Nozick, Robert (1974) *Anarchy, State, and Utopia*. Oxford: Blackwell.

Nuffield Council on Bioethics (2011) *Biofuels: Ethical Issues*. London: Nuffield Council on Bioethics.

Paley, William (2002 [1785]) *The Principles of Moral and Political Philosophy*, with a foreword by D. L. Le Mahieu. Indianapolis: Liberty Fund.

Pogge, Thomas (2008) *World Poverty and Human Rights: Cosmopolitan Responsibilities and Reforms*, 2nd edn. Cambridge: Polity.

Pogge, Thomas (2009) "Shue on Rights and Duties." In Charles R. Beitz and Robert E. Goodin (eds.), *Global Basic Rights*. Oxford: Oxford University Press, 113–30.

Pufendorf, Samuel (1717) *Of the Law of Nature and Nations. Eight Books*, 3rd edn, tr. Basil Kennet. London: printed for R. Sare, R. Bonwicke, T. Goodwyn, J. Walthoe, M. Wotton, S. Manship, R. Wilkin, B. Tooke, R. Smith, T. Ward, and W. Churchill.

Rawls, John (1999a) *A Theory of Justice*, rev. edn. Oxford: Oxford University Press.

Rawls, John (1999b) *The Law of Peoples with "The Idea of Public Reason Revisited"*. Cambridge MA: Harvard University Press.

Raz, Joseph (1986) *The Morality of Freedom*. Oxford: Clarendon Press.

Scanlon, Thomas M. (1982) "Contractualism and Utilitarianism." In Amartya Sen and Bernard Williams (eds.), *Utilitarianism and Beyond*. Cambridge: Cambridge University Press, 103–28.

Scharpf, Fritz W. (2009) "Legitimacy in the Multilevel European Polity," *European Political Science Review* 1(2): 173–204.

Scheffler, Samuel (1982) *The Rejection of Consequentialism: A Philosophical Investigation of the Considerations Underlying Rival Moral Conceptions*. Oxford: Clarendon Press.

Scott, James C. (1985) *Weapons of the Weak: Everyday Forms of Peasant Resistance*. New Haven, CT, and London: Yale University Press.

Scott, James C. (1990) *Domination and the Arts of Resistance: Hidden Transcripts*. New Haven, CT, and London: Yale University Press.

Sen, Amartya (1981) *Poverty and Famines: An Essay on Entitlement and Deprivation*. Oxford: Clarendon Press.

Shue, Henry (1996) *Basic Rights: Subsistence, Affluence, and U.S. Foreign Policy*, 2nd edn with a new afterword. Princeton, NJ: Princeton University Press.

Simmons, A. John (1979) *Moral Principles and Political Obligations*. Princeton, NJ: Princeton University Press.

Smith, Thomas B. (2004) "Electricity Theft: A Comparative Analysis," *Energy Policy* 32(18): 2067–76.

Tarrow, Sidney (1998) *Power in Movement: Social Movements and Contentious Politics*, 2nd edn. New York: Cambridge University Press.

Tarrow, Sidney (2005) *The New Transnational Activism*. New York: Cambridge University Press.

Tilly, Charles (1975) "Food Supply and Public Order in Modern Europe." In Charles Tilly (ed.), *The Formation of National States in Western Europe*. Princeton, NJ: Princeton University Press, 380–455.

Thompson, E. P. (1971) "The Moral Economy of the English Crowd in the Eighteenth Century," *Past & Present* 50(1): 76–136.

Tongia, Rahul (2007) "The Political Economy of Indian Power Sector Reforms." In by David G. Victor and Thomas C. Heller (eds.), *The Political Economy of Power Sector Reform: The Experiences of Five Major Developing Countries*. Cambridge: Cambridge University Press, 109–74.

Via Campesina, La (2013) *Land is Life! La Via Campesina and the Struggle for Land*. Jakarta: La Via Campesina.

Walton, John, and David Seddon (1994) *Free Markets & Food Riots: The Politics of Global Adjustment*. Oxford and Cambridge, MA: Blackwell.

Wilkinson, Paul, Kirk R Smith, Michael Joffe, and Andrew Haines (2007) "A Global Perspective on Energy: Health Effects and Injustices," *Lancet* 370(9591): 965–78.

Ypi, Lea (2012) *Global Justice and Avant-Garde Political Agency*. Oxford: Oxford University Press.

INDEX